# Energy Conversion Systems

# Energy Conversion Systems

**Rakosh Das Begamudre**

Consultant, Power Transmission and Energy
Vancouver, British Columbia, Canada
*(Formerly, Visiting Professor in
Electrical Engineering
Indian Institute of Technology, Kanpur, India)*

PUBLISHING FOR ONE WORLD

**NEW AGE INTERNATIONAL (P) LIMITED, PUBLISHERS**
New Delhi • Bangalore • Chennai •Cochin • Guwahati • Hyderabad
Jalandhar • Kolkata • Lucknow • Mumbai • Ranchi

Visit us at **www.newagepublishers.com**

Published by New Age International (P) Ltd., Publishers
First Edition: 2000
**Reprint:** 2015



**BRANCHES**

- **Bangalore** 37/10, 8th Cross (Near Hanuman Temple), Azad Nagar, Chamarajpet, Bangalore-560 018, Tel.: (080) 26756823, Telefax: 26756820 **E-mail: bangalore@newagepublishers.com**
- **Chennai** 26, Damodaran Street, T. Nagar, Chennai-600 017 Tel.: (044) 24353401, Telefax: 24351463, **E-mail: chennai@newagepublishers.com**
- **Cochin** CC-39/1016, Carrier Station Road, Ernakulam South, Cochin-682 016 Tel.: (0484) 2377303, Telefax: 4051303, **E-mail: cochin@newagepublishers.com**
- **Guwahati** Hemsen Complex, Mohd. Shah Road, Paltan Bazar, Near Starline Hotel, Guwahati-781 008 Tel.: (0361) 2513881, Telefax: 2543669, **E-mail: guwahati@newagepublishers.com**
- **Hyderabad** 105, 1st Floor, Madhiray Kaveri Tower, 3-2-19, Azam Jahi Road, Near Kumar Theater Nimboliadda, Kachiguda, Hyderabad-500 027, Tel.: (040) 24652456, Telefax: 24652457 **E-mail: hyderabad@newagepublishers.com**
- **Kolkata** RDB Chambers (Formerly Lotus Cinema) 106A, 1st Floor, S N Banerjee Road, Kolkata-700 014 Tel.: (033) 22273773, Telefax: 22275247 **E-mail: kolkata@newagepublishers.com**
- **Lucknow** 16-A, Jopling Road, Lucknow-226 001, Tel.: (0522) 2209578, 4045297 Telefax: 2204098, **E-mail:lucknow@newagepublishers.com**
- **Mumbai** 142C, Victor House, Ground Floor, N.M. Joshi Marg, Lower Parel Mumbai-400 013, Tel.: (022) 24927869, Telefax: 24915415 **E-mail: mumbai@newagepublishers.com**
- **New Delhi** 22, Golden House, Daryaganj, New Delhi-110 002 Tel.: (011) 23262368, 23262370, Telefax: 43551305 **E-mail: sales@newagepublishers.com**

**ISBN: 978-81-224-1266-6**

**₹ 295.00**

**C-15-02-8319**

Printed in India at Ajit Printing Press, Delhi.

**PUBLISHING GLOBALLY**
**NEW AGE INTERNATIONAL (P) LIMITED, PUBLISHERS**
7/30 A, Daryaganj, New Delhi - 110002
Visit us at **www.newagepublishers.com**

To

A Distinguished Couple

Rama C. and T. Kochu Menon

# Preface

The field of Energy Conversion is undoubtedly the single most important area of human endeavour and ingenuity whose impact on life on this planet in the future can be both constructive and destructive. An understanding of the harmful effects helps to concentrate the attention of physicists and engineers on beneficial effects, and a balance must be struck between the two opposite aspects. Progress in energy development in the past 50 years has revealed that the initial over-optimism has now levelled to a stable situation, in which many of the exciting developments have not seen practical applications to the extent which were envisaged. Examples are: Magnetohydrodynamics, Fuel Cells, Ocean Energy (Tidal, Waves, Thermal Gradient), Nuclear Fusion, and several others. The main reason is the non-availability of finances for their full and rapid development. The energy industry has suffered this drawback because the cost of new energy systems is compared to conventional well-proven systems and nuclear fission. Nevertheless, it is true that fossil fuels (coal, oil, natural gas) have only a finite life and eventually alternative sources of energy must replace conventional ones. These new systems could be Wind Energy, Ocean Energy, Solar Voltaic or direct heat, Breeder Reactors, Hydrogen on large scale and several others on a small scale such as Biomass Energy.

The beginning of large-scale interest in energy development could be considered to have commenced from 1945 after the cessation of World War II, and the commencement of Space and Nuclear programmes of the 1950's. Problems of physics, both pure and applied, the engineering difficulties and environmental aspects have taken on immense dimensions. The developments have been so rapid that the information, justly so, was available in conference proceedings mainly. Initially, in the 1960's new books on Energy Conversion were published in large numbers for students and research scholars. The author has been involved in teaching energy problems for general undergraduates and advanced undergraduates during this period of development. In the early years, most engineering institutions were at a loss on how to implement "energy" as a part of the curricula and at the same time include Electro-Mechanical Energy Conversion (EMEC) involving electrical machines, which formed the bulk of an undergraduate programme prior to the invention of the transistor which was the beginning of the emphasis on electronics. A period of soul-searching began and a compromise was to combine both EMEC and Energy problems into a one-semester course designated Energy Conversion. This provided the instructor with a lot of freedom to emphasize the one or the other topic; but this naturally diluted the coverage since the physics of energy conversion became very vast.

In recent years, it has become increasingly evident that EMEC cannot remain as part of a course combined with energy, not only because of the inclusion of physics but also because of the inclusion of rapid developments in energy in contrast to established theory and practice of electrical machines which are now based on an application of solid-state devices for control of machines. Thus the two subjects parted company for good. In the past decade and a half, the author has been involved in giving lectures on these two topics as separate entities, after having given a combined course to undergraduates. The result is the present book.*

This book recognizes three types of learners to whom the contents are addressed: the undergraduate student, the advanced undergraduate student offering this subject as an elective, and finally the general reader interested in energy and the environment. The physics portion of the book is limited to its application to energy conversion. Four chapters on Atomic, Nuclear, Solid State and Plasma physics are provided along with their immediate application. These are followed by seven chapters on engineering aspects of several energy conversion systems. With environmental problems assuming such prominence in recent years, it is but appropriate that a concerned person should be exposed to the harmful effects (knowledgewise) and ways to improve pollution conditions such as acid rain, $CO_2$-greenhouse effect, and nuclear wastes and accidents, as well as to global aspects of energy. Thus, a complete chaptr, Chap. 12, has been included to emphasize these aspects.

Data pertaining to atomic and nuclear properties have been abstracted from the following two sources: (1) K.S. Krane: *Introduction to Nuclear Physics, and* (2) Sybil P. Parker: *Nuclear and Particle Physics Sourcebook.* The author is indebted to these two books, their authors and to their publishers. They have been listed in the Bibliography.

Every chapter is provided with figures, tables where necessary, Objective Type Questions, and problems for self-test. These are directed towards practical exam-

---

* See also the author's book *Electromechanical Energy Conversion with Dynamics of Machines*, New Age International, 1988 and 1997 (2nd ed.).

ples occuring in this field. A bibliography giving a list of books, technical reports and conference papers is provided, arranged by chapters and topics. The vast number of periodicals published and available in this field is a boon to any reader wanting to keep abreast of exciting developments occuring every month. In this regard, the author has benefitted from the *Annual Review of Energy* for some aspects of the developments of energy problems.

A final note is in order regarding the arrangement and use of the material of this book. General readers interested in energy and environmental problems can use all the material sequentially (or in parts) to achieve their ends. Undergraduate students as well as graduate students and their instructors possessing a background of relevant physics and electrical subjects can omit the whole of Chapter 1 on Atomic Physics, Sections 2.2 to 2.8 in Chapter 2 on Nuclear Physics, Sections 3.3 to 3.8 in Chapter 3 on Solid State Physics, Sections 4.2 to 4.4 in Chapter 4 on Plasma Physics, and the entire chapter on Electrical Equipment for Energy Conversion. It is, however, recommended that all readers should work through the Worked Examples, Objective Type Questions and Review Questions and Problems in all chapters, since they are based on practical applications. Omission of the suggested material in class lectures will enable the instructor to cover the rest of the material in one semester.

The author is indebted to the New Brunswick Electric Power Corporation in Canada for providing excellent photographs of their various power development plants, and to the staff of the libraries of the University of New Brunswick for their courteous help at all times.

**Vancouver, B.C., Canada** **RAKOSH DAS BEGAMUDRE**
**2000**

# Contents

# CHAPTER 1

# Atomic Physics

Atomic physics shows two clearly-marked divisions which are easily visualized: (1) Pre Wave-Mechanics Physics; and (2) Post Wave-Mechanics Physics. The former is usually known as early or old quantum mechanics and the latter as the new quantum mechanics. Many properties of the atomic particles, excluding those inside the nucleus, and of radiation including relativistic properties had been established firmly by the old quantum mechanics. The new quantum mechanics interpreted properties of all atomic phenomena as being the probabilistic viewpoint and opened the doors for such basic new phenomena as tunnelling, high-energy physics and existence of anti-particles. We will first describe and discuss the enormous amount of information provided by the old quantum mechanics using as little mathematical derivations as possible, laying stress on physical aspects and atomic properties useful for energy-conversion problems. Nuclear physics will be dealt with in the next chapter. Once the salient behaviour of atomic particles and radiation are understood, the new quantum mechanics will be discussed for spin-0 particles at non-relativistic energies using the de Broglie and Schrodinger equations.

## I. PRE WAVE-MECHANICS ATOMIC PHYSICS

### 1.1 The Rutherford Atom

The year 1911 marks the birth of the Rutherford atomic model, which states that the atom consists of a heavy nucleus of radius in the order of $10^{-15}$ m (1 Fermi or femtometre, fm). The radius of nucleus of any atom is given well by $R = R_0A^{1/3}$, where $R_0 \approx 1.4$ fm and A = atomic mass number = number of atomic protons + neutrons inside the nucleus. The nuclear volume is $4\pi R^3/3 \propto A$. Therefore, the density for all nucleii is nearly constant and is approximately $10^{17}$ kg/m$^3$ (water: $10^3$ kg/m$^3$).

The electric charge of the nucleus is $+Ze$, where $Z$ = number of protons and $e = 1.6022 \times 10^{-19}$ Coulomb. This nucleus is surrounded by $Z$ high-velocity electrons each with charge $-1.6022 \times 10^{-19}$ C. Thus the atom is electrically neutral on the whole. This "planetary model" of the atom was the result of very painstaking scattering experiments using α-particles (helium nucleus) emitted by a radio-active source which Rutherford and his co-workers used.

The first electron orbit in hydrogen ($A = Z = 1$) was postulated by Bohr to be $a_0 = 0.52858$ Å, so that the diameter is about 1 A, which is nearly $10^5$ times the nuclear diameter. Thus the atom is almost empty space like our sun and planetary system. We will describe the all-important consequences of Bohr's work in the following sections.

Since the nucleus consists of only positively-charged protons and electrically neutral neutrons, there must exist only repulsive electrostatic force between the protons. However, since the nucleus is held very firmly together inside such a minute space, there must exist very strong binding force to counteract the electrostatic force of repulsion. This is called the strong interaction, which is entirely different in nature from electrostatic and is a new kind of force present in nature. We will describe this nuclear force in the next chapter and the exchange-particle model for all forces present in nature.

## 1.2 Bohr's Model for Orbiting Electrons

In the year 1900, Planck put forward the world-shattering hypothesis that energy in all forms consists of quanta of discrete amount. The product of energy and time is known as 'action' and the basic quantum of action is $h = 6.6262 \times 10^{-34}$ Joule-second with $\hbar = h/2\pi = 1.054589 \times 10^{-34}$ J-s $= 6.58217 \times 10^{-16}$ eV-s, since 1 electron-volt (eV) $= 1.602189 \times 10^{-19}$ J, which is numerically equal to the charge of an electron in Coulomb.

This property was utilized by Einstein five years later in 1905 to explain the properties of the photo-electric effect according to which a photon of frequency ν has the energy $E_{ph} = h\nu$, Joules. Since frequency is attributed to wave and $h$ to particle, this resulted in a revolution in physical thought. It compromised in one equation the two different aspects of photon radiation, namely, a wave and a particle, which had been handled separately in pre-quantum physics. We note first of all that there have been long time gaps involved in realizing the importance of a new discovery such as Planck's quantum hypothesis.

As soon as Rutherford's planetary model of the atom was accepted, Niels Bohr from Denmark crossed the channel to work in the Cavendish Laboratory and in two years, by 1913, established his quantum model for electron orbits using Planck's quantum of action. His (Bohr's) postulates and the consequences of the theory resulting from it established the beginning of the quantum atomic model. The theories of Bohr are set forth now as follows:

(a) An electron with charge (–e) revolves in a circular orbit of radius $r$ around a nucleus of charge (+Ze). The attractive electrostatic force between them is central and of magnitude $F = Ze^2/4\pi\,\varepsilon_0 r^2$, with $\varepsilon_0$ = permittivity of free space = $10^{-9}/36\pi$ Farad/m = 8.84194 μμF/m

(b) This attractive force is balanced by the centrifugal force $m\,a = m\,v^2/r$, where $v$ = velocity of electron, $a$ = centrifugal acceleration, and $m$ = mass of electron = $9.10954 \times 10^{-31}$ kg. This is shown in Fig. 1.1

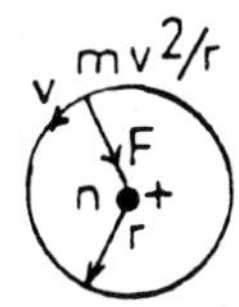


**Fig. 1.1** Bohr's model for hydrogen atom

(c) The electron orbit settles down to a radius $r$ and velocity $v$ given by the equality of the two forces.

Therefore $$mv^2/r = Ze^2/4\pi\,\varepsilon_0\,r^2 \tag{1.1}$$

giving $$v^2 = Ze^2/4\pi\,\varepsilon_0\,m\,r \tag{1.2}$$

and $$r = Ze^2/4\pi\,\varepsilon_0\,m\,v^2 \tag{1.3}$$

The angular momentum of the electron is: $m\,v\,r = m\omega r^2$ (1.4)

where $\omega$ = angular velocity of electron in rad/sec = $v/r$.

(d) Bohr's originality was in hypothesizing that only those orbits are permissible for which the angular momentum is an integral multiple of $\hbar = h/2\pi$. Thus

$$m\,v\,r = n\,\hbar,\ n = 1, 2, 3, \ldots \tag{1.5}$$

or $$m^2 v^2 r^2 = n^2 \hbar^2 \quad \text{giving} \quad mv^2 r = n^2\hbar^2/mr \tag{1.6}$$

But from Eq.(1.1), $m\,v^2\,r = Z\,e^2/4\pi\,\varepsilon_0$ (1.7)

or $$r = n^2\,\hbar^2\,4\pi\,\varepsilon_0/Z\,e^2\,m \tag{1.8}$$

For hydrogen, which Bohr concentrated upon, $Z = 1$. Therefore

$$r_n = [\hbar^2\,4\pi\,\varepsilon_0/e^2\,m]\,n^2 = 0.52858 \times 10^{-10}\,n^2, \text{ metre} \tag{1.9}$$

For the first orbit, $n = 1$, and the first Bohr radius for the electron in a hydrogen atom is denoted by $a_0$ = 0.52858 Å.

(e) Considering the total energy of the rotating electron in a central-force field, we obtain the potential energy of the negatively-charged electron to be

$$E_{pn} = -Ze^2/4\pi\,\varepsilon_0\,r_n \tag{1.10}$$

The kinetic energy at velocity $v_n$ is

$$E_{kn} = \tfrac{1}{2}\,m\,v_n^2 = Ze^2/8\pi\,\varepsilon_0\,r_n \tag{1.11}$$

Therefore, the total energy in the n-th orbit is

$$E_n = E_{pn} + E_{kn} = -Z e^2 / 8\pi \varepsilon_0 r_n = -(Z^2 e^4 m / 32\pi^2 \varepsilon_0^2 \hbar^2) \cdot (1/n^2)$$
$$= -2.186182 \times 10^{-18} Z^2 / n^2, \text{J}$$
$$= -13.645 Z^2 / n^2, \text{eV} \quad (1.12)$$

In particular for hydrogen ($Z = 1$) the energy of an electron in any orbit number $n$ is

$$E_n = -13.645 / n^2, \text{eV} \quad (1.13)$$

We observe that as $n$ increases, the energy decreases negatively, or, increases positively, as shown in Fig. 1.2. The lowest energy state is in the orbit closest to the nucleus and is –13.645 eV, where the radius is $a_0 \approx 0.5$ Å. For the next orbit $n = 2$, the energy is –3.411 eV and radius $r_2 = 4 \times 0.52858$ Å $\approx 2$ Å. The difference in energy between these two orbits is $\approx 10.2$ eV. This property will be used later on in describing maser and laser action.

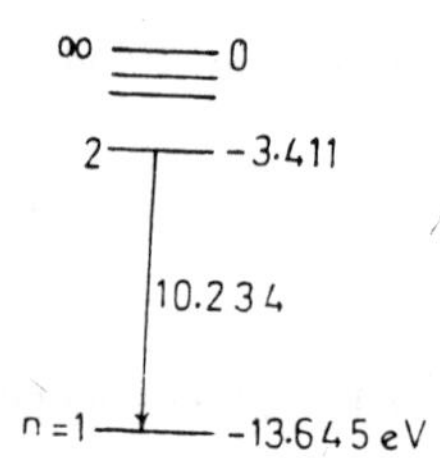

**Fig. 1.2** Energy levels for hydrogen atom

For $n = \infty$, the energy is 0. The energy value 13.645 eV is known as the ionization potential of hydrogen, whereby by giving this amount of energy to the electron at the "lowest" energy state ($n = 1$), the electron can be removed from the attractive force of the positively-charged nucleus (one proton). The resulting atom will be positively charged and becomes an ion.

(f) The energy $|E_n| = h\nu_n$, so that the frequency is

$$\nu_n = |E_n| / h = |E_n| / 2\pi\hbar = [e^4 m / 64\pi^3 \varepsilon_0^2 \hbar^3] Z^2 / n^2$$
$$= 3.299 \times 10^{15} Z^2 / n^2, \text{Hz} \quad (1.14)$$

[$1\ eV = 1.602189 \times 10^{-19} / 6.6262 \times 10^{-34} = 0.241796 \times 10^{15}$ Hz.

Therefore, 13.645 eV = $3.299 \times 10^{15}$ Hz]

For hydrogen, the energy difference between the orbit for $n = 1$ and $n = 2$ is about 10.2 eV = $2.4664 \times 10^{15}$ Hz. For $NH_3$, the energy difference is $10^{-4}$ eV, which corresponds to a frequency of $2.418 \times 10^{10}$ Hz = 24,180 MHz. This property was used in the first ammonia maser for microwave frequency ranges. For a solid such as ruby which contains chromium, the transition frequency falls in the optical range and the stimulated emission is called the laser.

(g) The velocity of electron in any orbit is given by Eq. (1.5) as

$$v_n = n\hbar / m\,r = (Z\,e^2 / 4\pi\,\varepsilon_0\,\hbar)\,(1/n) \tag{1.15}$$

The Bohr theory of the atom and explanation of energy levels and transition between them opened up the entire field of atomic physics like floodgates in a dam. However, the physics community had to wait another 11 years before wave mechanics based on wave-particle duality was extended to matter by Louis de Broglie in 1924, and the mathematical background was developed by Schrodinger and Heisenberg in 1926, and followed by others.

In this one decade, properties pertaining to the electron were discovered before wave mechanics discovered many more.

### 1.3 X-Ray Production

X-Rays are high-energy photons with wave length of 1 Å = $10^{-10}$ m and less. Visible light has wavelength in the range from 6562.8 Å (red) to 4340.5 Å (violet) with frequencies between $0.4568 \times 10^{15}$ Hz and $0.6907 \times 10^{15}$ Hz. Gamma Rays given out by radioactive nucleii are more penetrating than even X-rays and have wavelengths in the range from 0.5 to 0.005 Å. (1 Å = 12,400 eV).

We found that the energy level of electrons in any orbit is $E_n = -13.645\ Z^2/n^2$, eV. Taking $n_1 = 1$ and $n_2 = 2$, an electron falling from the higher to the lower level emits a photon with an energy of $13.645\ Z^2\ (1/1^2 - 1/2^2) = 10.234\ Z^2$ eV, which corresponds to a frequency of $2.4664 \times 10^{15}\ Z^2$ Hz. A wavelength of 1 Å corresponds to a frequency of $\nu = c/\lambda = 2.9979246 \times 10^8/10^{-10} \approx 3 \times 10^{18}$ Hz. Therefore, in an atom with $Z^2 = 3000/2.4664$ or $Z = 35$, X-Ray production is possible. The usual metal used as target is Molybdenum with $Z = 42$. At a difference of 10.234 eV, the wavelength of generated X-ray is $\lambda = 12400/(10.234 \times 42^2) = 0.69$ Å.

When an electron is accelerated over a potential of V volts, it acquires an energy of $E = V\,e = h\,\nu$ electron volts. The corresponding wavelength is

$$\lambda = c/\nu = ch/Ve = (2.9979246 \times 10^8 \times 6.6262 \times 10^{-34}) / (1.6022 \times 10^{-19}\ V)$$

$$= 1.24 / V,\ \mu\, m = 12400 / V,\ \text{Å} \tag{1.16}$$

Therefore, a wavelength of 1 Å requires an energy of 12400 eV = 12.4 keV. Thus, if an electron which is accelerated by at least 12.4 keV hits a target atom, X-Rays are generated. In addition to a direct hit or collision with a target atom, a high-energy electron also makes glancing collision, which yields a wide range of frequencies called a continuous or band spectrum. The electron in any case is retarded or braked, and the resulting radiation is called braking radiation or bremsstrahlung.

## 1.4 Compton Scattering (Fig. 1.3)

When once the wave-particle model of the photon was established, the interaction of a photon with matter became an important aspect of atomic physics. The Compton scattering gave a beautiful proof of this dual aspect of the photon by using X-ray frequencies.

Figure 1.3 shows a photon of wavelength $\lambda_i$ incident on a particle with rest mass $m_0$ with energy $m_0c^2$. (For an electron, $m_e = m_0 = 9.109538 \times 10^{-31}$ kg = 0.511 MeV). The photon is then scattered after imparting some of its energy to the particle, so that the scattered photon has lower energy and longer wavelength $\lambda_s$. Compton showed that the change in wavelength is

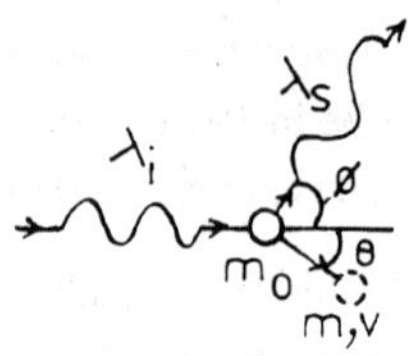


**Fig. 1.3** Compton scattering of photon

$$\Delta \lambda = \lambda_s - \lambda_i = h(1 - \cos \phi) / m_0 c \tag{1.17}$$

For an electron, the factor $(h/m_0c)$ = 0.0242631 Å and is known as Compton Wavelength. We discuss the derivation of this result.

The energy of the photon is $E = m_{ph} c^2 = h\nu = hc/\lambda$,

so that
$$m_{ph} = h\nu / c^2 = h / c\lambda \tag{1.18}$$

Since a photon has zero rest mass and can travel only at the speed of light $c$, it can only have an equivalent mass corresponding to its energy $E$. Its momentum then is

$$p = m_{ph}\, c = h / \lambda \tag{1.19}$$

We also define
$$k = \text{wave number} = 2\pi / \lambda \tag{1.20}$$

which is equal to the number of wavelengths in unit length × 2π.

Therefore
$$p = h/\lambda = \hbar/k \tag{1.21}$$

Also, the relativistic mass of a particle is

$$m = m_0 / \sqrt{1 - v^2/c^2} \tag{1.22}$$

where $v$ = velocity of electron or any other target particle used.

Referring to Fig. 1.3, the following three equations hold:

(1) Conservation of energy requires initial energy in the system = final energy. Assuming that the target mass is at rest initially when the photon collides with it, we have

$$m_0 c^2 + hc/\lambda_i = mc^2 + hc/\lambda_s \tag{1.23}$$

(2) Conservation of momentum requires equality of *x*- and *y*-components.

(a) *x-components*: $h/\lambda_i = (h/\lambda_s)\cos\phi + m\,v\cos\theta$ (1.24)

(b) *y-components*: $0 = (h/\lambda_s)\sin\phi - m\,v\sin\theta$ (1.25)

We now eliminate the properties of the target particle ($m$, $v$, $\theta$) after collision, and concentrate only on the properties of the incident and scattered wavelengths of the photon and the rest mass $m_0$ of the particle.

From Eq. (1.22) $m^2 v^2 = c^2(m^2 - m_0^2)$, or, $m_0^2 c^2 = m^2(c^2 - v^2)$ (1.26)

$$\left.\begin{aligned} &\text{From Eq. (1.24)} \quad m\,v\cos\theta = h/\lambda_i - (h/\lambda_s)\cos\phi \\ &\text{and from Eq. (1.25)} \quad m\,v\sin\theta = (h/\lambda_s)\sin\phi \end{aligned}\right\} \qquad (1.27)$$

Squaring and adding,

$$m^2 v^2 = h^2[1/\lambda_i^2 + 1/\lambda_s^2 - (2/\lambda_i\lambda_s)\cos\phi] \qquad (1.28)$$

Using Eq. (1.26) for $m^2 v^2$, there results

$$c^2 m^2 = c^2 m_0^2 + h^2[1/\lambda_i^2 + 1/\lambda_s^2 - (2/\lambda_i\lambda_s)\cos\phi] \qquad (1.29)$$

From Eq. (1.23), $c\,m = c\,m_0 + h\,(1/\lambda_i - 1/\lambda_s)$ (1.30)

Squaring both sides of Eq. (1.30) and equating to Eq. (1.29), we obtain

$$2h^2(1 - \cos\phi)/(\lambda_i\lambda_s) = 2\,m_0\,c\,h\,(\lambda_s - \lambda_i)/(\lambda_i\lambda_s) \qquad (1.31)$$

Therefore the change in wavelength is

$$\Delta\lambda = \lambda_s - \lambda_i = (h/m_0 c)(1 - \cos\phi) \qquad (1.32)$$

Since $(1 - \cos\phi)$ is positive (for $0 < \phi \le \pi$), the scattered photon has longer wavelength than that of the incident photon. Using $\lambda = c/\nu$ and $E = h\nu$, we obtain the changes in frequency and energy of the incident photon as compared to the scattered as:

$$1/\nu_s - 1/\nu_i = (1 - \cos\phi)\,h/(m_0 c^2) \qquad (1.33)$$

and $$1/E_s - 1/E_i = (1 - \cos\phi)/(m_0 c^2) \qquad (1.34)$$

The Compton Wavelength for a particle is $\lambda_c = h/m_0 c$ (1.35)

For an electron, $\lambda_c = 0.0242631$ Å $= 2.42631$ μμm.

From Eq. (1.34), the energy in the scattered photon is

$$E_s = E_i/[1 + (E_i/m_0 c^2)(1 - \cos\phi)] \qquad (1.36)$$

## 1.5 Quantum Numbers

Principal ($n$), Orbital ($l$), Orbital Magnetic Moment ($m_l$), and Spin ($m_s$)

In hydrogen, the one electron moves at the radius

$$r = (\varepsilon_0 h^2 n^2 / \pi m_e Z e^2) = 4\pi \varepsilon_0 \hbar^2 n^2 / m_e Z e^2 \tag{1.8}$$

with $Z$ = atomic number = 1. But when more electrons are added in heavier elements, the orbits are not circular; they are elliptic, the extreme forms of the ellipse being a straight line and a circle. Thus, the radius $r$ represents the average distance between the proton and the electron in a hydrogen atom. The quantum number $n$ is called the Principal Quantum Number.

The motion of many electrons in an atom is governed by certain rules and the orbits are not randomly distributed. Any electron can move in an orbit such that the axial vector representing the normal to the plane of motion has to be multiples of $h/2\pi = \hbar$. This orbital quantum number is denoted by $l$ and is restricted to 0, 1, 2, 3, ..., n−1.

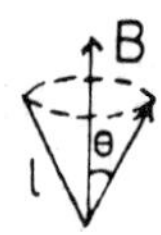

**Fig. 1.4** Larmour precession

An electron carries a negative electric charge, so that it can be imparted energy through an electric field or a magnetic field. The resulting responses are called the Stark Effect and Zeeman Effect, respectively. Furthermore, in an applied magnetic field, the orbit of the electron can precess about the direction of the magnetic field as shown in Fig. 1.4. This is known as Larmour Precession. Under the influence of an applied magnetic field or B-field, the axial vector for a given value of orbital momentum $l$ is restricted to occupy discrete directions such that ($l \cos \theta$) = an integer, that is, $l \cos \theta = m_l$. The quantum number $m_l$ is known as the magnetic quantum number and its value can be from ($-l$) to ($+l$) through 0, i.e., $m_l = -l, -(l-1), ..., 0, ..., (l-1), l$. This gives $(2l + 1)$ values for $m_l$, as shown in Fig. 1.5.

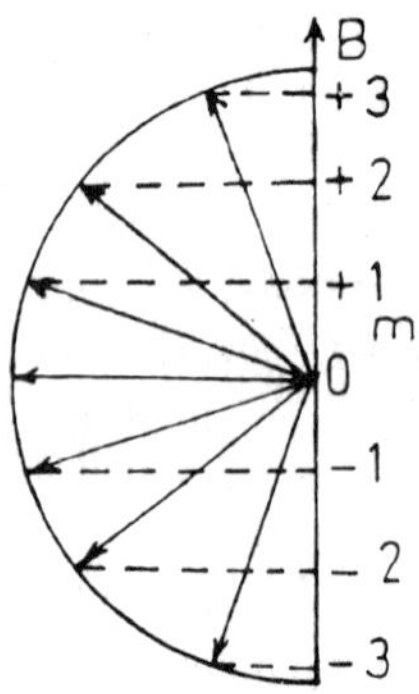

**Fig. 1.5** Magnetic quantum numbers, $m_l$, for $l = 3$

As an example, for n = 3, $l$ can be 0, 1, 2. Electrons can exist with the following quantum states:

For $l = 0$, $m_l = 0$

For $l = 1$, $m_l = -1, 0, +1$

For $l = 2$, $m_l = -2, -1, 0, +1, +2$

This quantized behaviour for the orbital magnetic moment was first observed by Stern and Gerlach, who also observed that for any given value of $m_l$, the electron occupied two different states, i.e., the radiation line was split. This was interpreted by Uhlenbeck and Goudsmit that in addition to an orbital angular momentum and precession of the plane of rotation, the electron possessed spin about its own axis, much like the earth. But this spin axis orientation can be in only two directions, one along the direction of the applied magnetic field and the other antiparallel to it. These two states are described by spin quantum numbers $m_s = +½, -½$, and the spin angular momentum has the values $½\hbar$ and $-½\hbar$.

Consequently, for a given principal quantum number $n$, the following states are possible for an electron:

Principal Quantum Number: $n$,

Orbital Quantum Number: $l = 0, 1, 2, 3, ..., (n - 1)$,

Orbital Magnetic Quantum Number: $m_l = -l, -(l - 1), ..., 0, ..., (l - 1), l$,

Spin Quantum Number: $m_s = +½, -½$.

These lead to the presence or electron arrangement in shells and subshells as will be discussed in Sec. 1.7. This behaviour is governed by the Pauli Exclusion Principle.

### 1.6 Pauli Exclusion Principle

In many-electron atoms, each electron is identified with a set of quantum numbers $(n, l, m_l, m_s)$. This is known as the state of the electron. In each state the electron energy can be computed, but we will not go into details as this involves wave-mechanical considerations. Even for $Z = 2$ a diagram like Fig. 1.2 gets very complicated but essential. Pauli hypothesized that in an atom, no two electrons can be in the same state simultaneously, i.e., have the same set of quantum numbers. At least one quantum number has to be different. This applies to spin-½ particles only, which is the electron. In nuclear physics in the next chapter, we consider other spin-½ particles such as the proton and the neutron. Pauli's Exclusion Principle does not apply to particles with 0 or integer spins such as the photon. In wave-mechanical theory, which describes the state of a particle by probabilistic considerations, spin-½ particles obey Fermi-Dirac statistics. But spin-0 or spin-integer particles obey the Bose - Einstein statistics. Every statistical description involves a suitable probability distribution function. Solid-state physics depends on the Fermi-Dirac statistical distribution function as will be discussed in Chap. 3.

### 1.7 Shell Structure of Electrons in an Atom

In many-electron atoms, the electrons arrange themselves in sub-shells and shells, either completely filled or partially filled as described below.

Consider an atom of helium which has $Z = 2$ and two orbiting electrons. The principal quantum number is $n = 1$. Therefore, $l = 0$ and $m_l = 0$. However, $m_s = \pm ½$ so that one electron can be in state (1, 0, 0, ½) and the other in state (1, 0, 0, −½). These two states form a closed first shell. No more electrons can occupy this shell even for atoms with $Z > 2$. Since there is no free electron outside this shell for helium, the element is chemically very stable and does not react with other elements. The spectroscopic description is denoted by $1s^2$. This means that $n = 1$, and the first shell (designated $s = 1$) has 2 electrons. Other numbers used are $p = 2$, $d = 3$, $f = 4$, and so on alphabetically.

Next consider the element neon with $Z = 10$.

For $n = 1$, there are 2 electrons with the first shell closed.

For $n = 2$, the possible values of $l$ are 0 and 1.

For $l = 0$, $m_l = 0$, $m_s = \pm½$. Therefore, 2 electrons can fit in. The first subshell in the second shell is complete.

For $l = 1$, $m_l = -1, 0, +1$ and $m_s = \pm½$. This gives a total of 6 states and 6 electrons can exist in the second subshell in the second shell. No more electrons can be present in this subshell and consequently in the second shell. All possible 10 states are now filled (2, 2, 6).

Therefore, the first and second shells are completely filled and the total number of electrons is $2 + (2 + 6) = 10$. Note that $2 = 2 \times 1^2$ for a closed first shell and $8 = 2 \times 2^2$ for the closed second shell. But in the second shell, we have $2 + 6 = 2 \times 1 + 2 \times 3$. We will observe that such rules hold for shells and subshells for atoms with more electrons. The spectroscopic designation for neon is $2p^6$, which denotes that $n = 2$ and in the second subshell ($p = 2$) there exist 6 electrons. Once again, because of closed subshells and shells, the element is chemically stable and is described as a rare gas like helium. They are inert gases.

The next rare gas is argon with $Z = 18$. There are 18 protons inside the nucleus and the 18 orbiting electrons can arrange themselves as follows:

*For n = 1*: 1st shell has 2 electrons and is closed.

*For n = 2*: 2nd shell has 8 electrons. This is also closed.

*For n = 3*: $l = 0$, $m_l = 0$, $m_s = \pm ½$. 2 electrons in 1st subshell.

$l = 1$, $m_l = -1, 0, +1$, $m_s = \pm ½$. 6 in 2nd closed subshell.

The total number of electrons is now 18. The last value of $l = 2$ possible with $n = 3$ is not necessary. The spectroscopic description or designation for argon is thus $3p^6$, denoting that in the 3rd shell ($n = 3$), the second subshell ($p = 2$) has 6 electrons with all lower levels also filled. This state of affairs is shown in Fig. 1.6.

*Ex. 1.1*: Continue the above steps for krypton, $Z = 36$, and give its spectroscopic designation.

***Solution***: For $n = 1$, 2 electrons. 1st shell is closed.

For $n = 2$, 8 electrons. 2nd shell is completely filled.

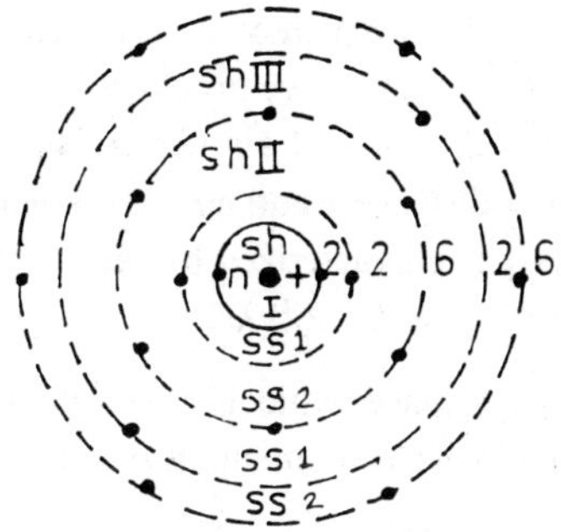


**Fig. 1.6** Shell model of electrons

For $n = 3$, the three possible subshells for $l = 0, 1, 2$ are closed with 2, 6, 10 electrons. This makes 18 ($= 2 \times 3^2$) electrons in the 3rd closed shell.

For $n = 4$: $l = 0$: 2 electrons exist in the 1st closed subshell in the 4th shell.

$l = 1$: 6 possible electron states are occupied and the second subshell is closed.

This brings the total number of electrons to ($2 + 8 + 18 + 8 = 36$). Since the second ($p = 2$) subshell in the 4th shell ($n = 4$) has 6 electrons the designation is $4p^6$. Krypton is also a rare gas.

*Ex. 1.2*: Show that the spectroscopic notation for xenon gas with $Z = 54$ is $5p^6$.

***Solution***: The first three complete shells ($n = 3$) have electron numbers 2, 8, 18 making a total of 28. If the 4th shell is to be complete there would be 32 states with subshells containing 2, 6, 10, 14 which are ($2 \times 1, 2 \times 3, 2 \times 5, 2 \times 7$) electrons. But then the total will amount to $28 + 32 = 60$ electrons. Therefore, the 4th shell is not complete. This is one instance where electrons can occupy states in the 5th or a higher-numbered state before the previous shell is not yet completed.

Therefore, the 4th shell has 3 subshells complete with $2 + 6 + 10 = 18$ electrons leaving $54 - 28 - 18 = 8$ electrons to occupy the 1st and 2nd subshells in the 5th shell. In this shell therefore the remaining 8 electrons arrange themselves in completed 1st and 2nd subshells. This brings the final tally to ($2 + 8 + 18 + 18 + 8$) $= 54$ electrons.

The spectroscopic notation for $n = 5$, $p = 2$ with 6 electrons is $5p^6$.

A periodic table of elements gives details of electron numbers for all elements and their spectroscopic designations or notations.

### 1.8 Waves, Particles and de Broglie's Hypothesis

Electromagnetic radiation has revealed that it behaves both as waves and a stream of particles. This is evidenced from interference, black-body radiation, photo-electric effect and X-ray absorption. As a wave it propagates in space and time, while as a particle it interacts with matter as evidenced by Compton scattering.

A wave is characterized by frequency $\nu$, wavelength $\lambda$, phase velocity $u$, amplitude $A$ and intensity $I$. A plane wave propagating in the $x$-direction only has the equation $A \sin (2\pi x/\lambda - 2\pi \nu t) = A \sin (kx - \omega t)$, where $kx = 2\pi$ times the number of wavelengths in a distance $x$ and $\omega t = 2\pi \times$ number of cycles in a time interval $t$. A constant phase is characterized by $(kx - \omega t) =$ constant. Therefore, the phase velocity is $u = dx/dt = \omega/k = 2\pi\nu\lambda/2\pi = \nu\lambda$.

A wave also spreads out in space while as a particle it occupies a point, and is characterized by mass $m$, velocity $v$, momentum $p$ and energy $E$.

In describing the effects of electromagnetic radiation, both concepts have to be accepted. One does not occur to the exclusion of the other, although in some experiments because of the type of instrument used it acts as one or the other. The interrelation occurs through two basic relations, as follows:

(a) Energy of particle is $E = h\nu$ of the wave (1.37)

(b) Momentum of particle is $p = h/\lambda$ of the wave.

Therefore $$\lambda = h/p = h/mv \tag{1.38}$$

If electromagnetic radiation or photons can exhibit such dual properties, Louis de Broglie hypothesized (as a student) that all matter must exhibit such wave-particle properties also. For matter, de Broglie assumed that the wavelength is also given by Eq. (1.38). This wave is known as a pilot which guides the particle.

The energy of a particle of mass $m$ is $E = mc^2$. Therefore, the frequency of the matter wave is

$$\nu = E/h = mc^2/h \tag{1.39}$$

The phase velocity of the wave is consequently

$$u = \nu\lambda = (mc^2/h) \times (h/mv) = c^2/v \tag{1.40}$$

If the particle is other than a massless photon, then $v < c$, so that $u > c$. This is on the face of it strange, but Einstein's postulate that no velocity can exceed light velocity (the signal used in relativity) in free space applies only for mass-energy relation, and therefore it does not apply to de Broglie waves.

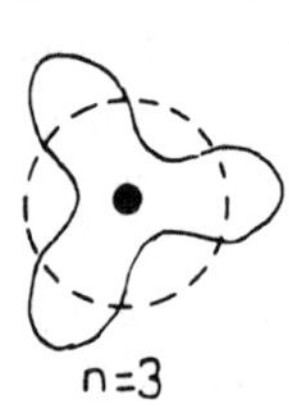

**Fig. 1.7** De Broglie's electron wave in an orbit ($n = 3$)

The second of de Broglie's hypotheses is that, when an electron moves in an orbit around the nucleus for an assigned value of $n$, then the matter wave accompanying it subtends an integral multiple of wavelengths on the circumference of the circle of radius $r$ applicable to that particular value of n, as shown in Fig. 1.7. Thus

$$n\lambda = 2\pi r, \text{ or, } \lambda = h/p = 2\pi r/n \tag{1.41}$$

With $p = mv$, there results

$$h/mv = 2\pi r/n, \text{ or, } mvr = nh/2\pi = n\hbar \quad (1.42)$$

But this is precisely the first of Bohr's postulates of a dozen years ago. De Broglie's matter-wave hypothesis explains most of the results derived from Bohr's work earlier. Thus, an electron moves only in discrete orbits with quantified energy levels, which can support integral numbers of matter wavelengths accompanying the electron, or looking at it in another way as Schrodinger did, the frequency of the electron wave is quantized.

Another relation is by Davisson and Germer for the wavelength of an electron when accelerated through a voltage $V$. The energy is

$$E = \tfrac{1}{2} m v^2 = V e, \text{ or, } v = \sqrt{2Ve/m} \quad (1.43)$$

But by de Broglie's hypothesis,

$$\lambda = h / mv = h / \sqrt{2mVe}$$

For an electron, $m = 9.10958 \times 10^{-31}$ kg, $e = 1.6022 \times 10^{-19}$ C, and with $h = 6.6262 \times 10^{-34}$ J-s, if $V$ is in volts, then

$$\lambda_e = 1.22643 \times 10^{-9} / \sqrt{V}, \quad \text{metre} = 12.2643 / \sqrt{V}, \text{ Å}$$

## 1.9 Heisenberg's Uncertainty Principle

Because of the wave-particle duality, it is also established that in any one single experiment, a particle cannot show both wave-like and particle-like properties. Thus, both properties cannot be exhibited or measured simultaneously. This is known as Bohr's complimentary principle.

However, if we wish to consider one or other of the wave-particle properties in an experiment, then they can be carried out only to a certain degree of uncertainty. This is Heisenberg's Uncertainty Principle which has far-reaching implications, consequences and applications. We will observe that the exchange-particle hypothesis for all forces existing in nature is the consequence of this uncertainty principle (see Chap. 2).

A basic property of a group of waves, called a wave-packet, is that the product of their extent $\Delta x$ and the number of wavelengths in that distance is nearly equal to unity, i.e.

$$\Delta x \cdot \Delta k \approx 1 \quad (1.44)$$

Now, by de Broglie's hypothesis

$$k_x = 2\pi / \lambda = 2\pi p_x / h = p_x / \hbar \quad (1.45)$$

Taking $\Delta k_x = \Delta p_x / \hbar$, Eq. (1.44) becomes $\Delta x \cdot \Delta p_x \approx \hbar$ (1.46)

Similarly for the position and momentum variations or uncertainties in the other two directions

$$\Delta y \cdot \Delta p_y \approx \hbar, \text{ and } \Delta z \cdot \Delta p_z \approx \hbar \tag{1.47}$$

Similarly in the 4th coordinate $t$, we obtain

$$\Delta t \cdot \Delta E \approx \hbar \tag{1.48}$$

where $\Delta E$ = uncertainty in measured value of energy in the experiment. Thus, longer a measurement takes the more certain is the measured energy of the particle, because of lowering of uncertainty $\Delta E$. Equation (1.48) is a consequence of Eq. (1.44), since

$$\Delta x = v_g \cdot \Delta t, \text{ and } \Delta p = h / \Delta\lambda = h \cdot \Delta\nu / v_g = \Delta E / v_g$$

where $v_g$ is known as the group velocity of a packet of waves consisting of the sum of a large number of plane waves as given by the Fourier analysis of the wave phenomenon. We omit the details for now. Therefore

$$\Delta x \cdot \Delta p = v_g \cdot \Delta t.\ \Delta E / v_g = \Delta t \cdot \Delta E \approx \hbar.$$

We now have most of the properties of an atom up to the advent of wave mechanics proper, which is the consequence of de Broglie's hypothesis of wave-particle duality.

## 1.10 Wave Packet and Particle Location

In physical reality a particle or a set of particles have matter waves which are not all of the same frequency, i.e. non-monochromatic. However, since particles of one type are nearly identical, the frequencies of the accompanying waves are very close to each other. Addition of sinusoidal waves of several frequencies close to each other yields the wave with an average frequency whose amplitude is modulated by another wave of low frequency, as shown below.

Let there be two waves of equal amplitudes A but with frequencies ($\nu$ and $\nu+\Delta\nu$), and wave numbers ($k$ and $k + \Delta k$). When added, the resultant is

$$A \sin(\omega t - kx) + A \sin[(\omega + \Delta\omega)t - (k + \Delta k)x] \tag{1.49}$$

Now, using $\sin\theta + \sin\phi = 2\sin(\theta+\phi)/2 \,.\, \cos(\theta-\phi)/2$, Eq. (1.49) becomes

$$2A \sin[(\omega + \Delta\omega/2)t - (k + \Delta k/2)x] \cdot \cos(\Delta\omega \cdot t/2 - \Delta k \cdot x/2)$$

By using $\omega + \Delta\omega/2 \approx \omega$, and $k + \Delta k/2 \approx k$, this simplifies to

$$2A(\omega t - kx) \cdot \cos(\Delta\omega \cdot t/2 - \Delta k \cdot x/2) \tag{1.50}$$

The amplitude of the original wave is doubled and modulated by another gliding wave, whose frequency is $\nu_g = \Delta\omega/4\pi$, which is very low compared to $\omega/2\pi$ of the original wave. The velocity of the modulating wave is known as the group velocity, $v_g$. This is

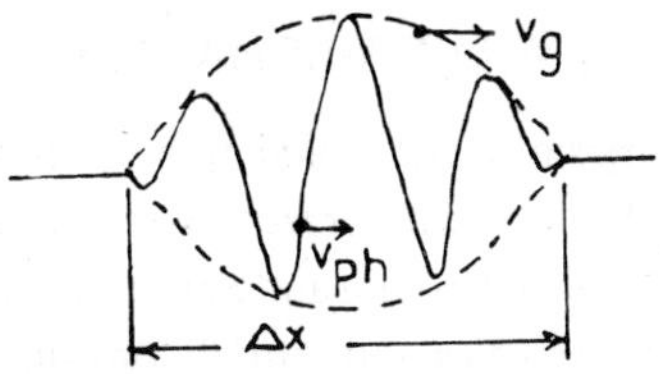


**Fig. 1.8** Group and phase velocities of wave packet

$$v_g = dx/dt = \Delta\omega/\Delta k = d\omega/dk \tag{1.51}$$

Figure 1.8 shows the result. For the high-frequency wave, the phase velocity from Eq. (1.50) is

$$u = dx/dt = \omega/k \tag{1.52}$$

Let us now consider the de Broglie relationships.

$$E = h\nu = \hbar\omega, \text{ and } p = mv = \hbar k \tag{1.53}$$

We also use Einstein's equivalence of mass and energy according to relativity theory: (*)

$$E^2 = p^2c^2 + m_0^2c^4 \tag{1.54}$$

Then $d\omega = dE/\hbar$, and $dk = dp/\hbar$, giving $v_g = d\omega/dk = dE/dp$.

From Eq. (1.54), $2E\,dE = 2c^2 p\,dp$, or, $dE/dp = pc^2/E$.

Considering the particle velocity, $v = p/m$, from Eq. (1.53).

But the energy of the particle is $E = mc^2$, or, $m = E/c^2$. Using this in Eq. (1.53), there results

particle velocity $$v = p/m = pc^2/E \tag{1.55}$$

We observe at once that the particle velocity equals the group velocity i.e. the velocity of the modulating wave. Therefore the particle rides the wave packet and is located on it. In general, by adding more waves with close frequencies the modulating wave becomes narrower and the particle location is more accurate. Its position is at the peak of the modulating wave. It is one of the properties of Fourier analysis that the sharper a pulse, the more frequency components it contains.

In later wave mechanics, using probabilistic concepts, these wave functions become probability functions of finding the particle at a certain location at a given time, governed by Heisenberg's Uncertainty Principle.

---

(*) $E = mc^2$, $p = mv$, $m = m_0/\sqrt{1 - v^2/c^2}$, $m^2 = m_0^2c^2/(c^2 - v^2)$.

Therefore $E^2 = m^2c^4$; $p^2 = m^2v^2$. Therefore, $E^2 - p^2c^2 = m^2(c^2 - v^2)c^2 = m_0^2c^4$. Consequently, $E^2 = p^2c^2 + m_0^2c^4$.

## II. WAVE MECHANICS

Just as the classical mechanics of Newton and others was modified, enlarged upon and replaced in most areas by Einstein's relativity mechanics and theories, so also wave mechanics introduced by de Broglie and Schrodinger brought about a radical change in thought in atomic physics and particle physics. We will discuss only certain elementary but basic ideas of this new quantum mechanics since the mathematical rigour of the new wave mechanics is beyond the scope of this book, which is primarily devoted to energy conversion principles. Atomic and nuclear particles and other elementary particles in general are divided into four categories, in so far as developing wave-mechanical (quantum mechanical) ideas:

(i) Particles with zero spin moving at non-relativistic velocities. This was developed by Schrodinger.

(ii) Particles with spin-½ moving at non-relativistic velocities. This is known as Pauli's electron or particle.

(iii) Particles with spin-0 moving at relativistic velocities. These are described by the Klein - Gordon - Fock equation.

(iv) Particles with spin-½ moving at relativistic velocities. These are described by the Dirac equation. This work is a complete description of the behaviour of most of atomic and nuclear particles. It is considered one of the most advanced and complete theories in human thought of this century, paralleling those of Maxwell of the 19th century.

Dirac's theory also predicted the existence of the positron, anti-particles for every existing particle in nature (even though some particles like the photon are their own anti-particles), and holes which are essential for the description of solid-state physics and materials. The entire field of solid-state electronics depends on this concept.

In the remaining portions of this Chapter we will describe and discuss Schrodinger's wave mechanics, confined to non-relativistic particles without spin. Several new properties that were not explained by the old quantum mechanics will be indicated, which are caused by the dual wave-particle properties of matter. When electron behaviour is described, magnetic field will not be taken into account, so that its spin will not enter into the discussion.

### 1.11 The Schrodinger Equation

For matter waves, the momentum and energy as a particle are related to the wavelength and frequency of the accompanying or guiding or pilot wave according to the following relations:

$$p = h/\lambda = \hbar k, \text{ and } E = h\nu = \hbar\omega \qquad (1.56)$$

An equation $\Psi = A \sin (kx - \omega t)$ describes a wave with a phase velocity $u = \omega/k$, as discussed earlier. Therefore the wave-function $\Psi$ is a function of $(kx - \omega t) = 2\pi x/\lambda - 2\pi \nu t = px/\hbar - Et/\hbar$. We write this as an exponential function which is easier to handle:

$$\Psi = A\, e^{i(px - Et)/\hbar} = A\, e^{ipx/\hbar} \cdot e^{-iEt/\hbar} \tag{1.57}$$

This immediately brings in the concept that the wave-function can be written as the product of two terms: one a function of $x$ only and the other a function of $t$ only. This is characteristic of the solution of most partial differential equations of physics involving two variables, $x$ and $t$ in this case. In four dimensions there will be found four product terms. But we restrict ourselves to a plane wave involving only one dimension in space for the present.

Now(*) $$\delta\Psi/\delta x = (ip/\hbar)\, A\, e^{i\,(px - Et)/\hbar} = i\, p\Psi/\hbar$$

giving $$(\hbar / i)\, \delta\, \Psi / \delta\, x = p\, \Psi \tag{1.58}$$

Thus the momentum $p$ can be expressed as the complex operation

Also $$\left.\begin{aligned} p &= (\hbar / i)\, \delta / \delta\, x = -\, i\hbar \cdot \delta / \delta\, x \\ p^2 &= -\, \hbar^2\, \delta^2 / \delta\, x^2 \end{aligned}\right\} \tag{1.59}$$

Similarly $$\delta\, \Psi / \delta\, t = -\,(i\, E / \hbar)\, A\, e^{i\,(px - Et)/\hbar} = -\,(iE / \hbar)\, \Psi \tag{1.60}$$

Therefore $$i\hbar \cdot \delta\, \Psi / \delta\, t = E\, \Psi \tag{1.61}$$

Thus the total energy $E$ of the particle can in turn be expressed as the complex operation

$$E = i\hbar \cdot \delta / \delta\, t \tag{1.62}$$

Since $\hbar$ has unit of Joule-sec and $\delta / \delta\, t$ is $\sec^{-1}$, the product gives Joules, the energy. The relation between energy $E$ and momentum $p$ is

$$E = \tfrac{1}{2} m\, v^2 = m^2\, v^2 / 2m = p^2 / 2m \tag{1.63}$$

Using the differentiation operators of Eqs. (1.60) and (1.62), we obtain the differential equation for the wave function in the absence of potential energy:

$$i\hbar\, \delta\, \Psi / \delta\, t = -\,(\hbar^2 / 2m)\, \delta^2\, \Psi / \delta\, x^2 \tag{1.64}$$

In case the particle is moving in a field of potential energy $V$, the total energy is $E = V + p^2/2m$. Then the governing differential equation for $\Psi$ is

$$-\frac{\hbar^2}{2\,m} \frac{\delta^2\, \Psi}{\delta\, x^2} + V\Psi = i\hbar\, \frac{\delta\, \Psi}{\delta\, t} \tag{1.65}$$

This most famous equation is Schrodinger's equation in one space dimension. The potential energy in its turn can be a constant, a function of $x$, or a function of

(*) The symbol $\delta/\delta x$ is to be read as the partial derivative with respect to $x$, etc.

both $x$ and $t$. If $V$ is independent of time, the resulting equation is called the time-independent Schrodinger's equation. This is much easier to handle than the time-dependent Schrodinger's equation. We will obtain solutions to the former equation for several types of $V$ which represent the motion of a particle such as the electron in an atom, i.e. in the presence of the potential energy of the nucleus. In this case, the solution for $\Psi$ contains a product of a term in $x$ only and a term in $t$ only, i.e. the two are separable.

## 1.12 The Hamiltonian

The total energy $E$ of a system is the sum of the kinetic energy and potential energy, which we wrote as $H = (p^2/2m + V)$. This is known as the Hamiltonian of the system. According to this, Schrodinger's equation is written as

$$H\Psi = E\Psi \tag{1.66}$$

For a given potential energy function, we can set up the Hamiltonian and write the governing equation for the wave function. The Hamiltonian in its turn becomes the complex differential operator

$$H = -(\hbar^2/2m)\ \delta^2/\delta x^2 + V \tag{1.67}$$

Some typical cases are illustrated below for using the Hamiltonian.

*Case 1*: For a mass $m$ moving with a velocity $v$ and possessing momentum $p = mv$, when placed in a potential $V$, the Hamiltonian is $H = p^2/2m + V$. The resulting Schrodinger's equation is

$$-\frac{\hbar^2}{2m}\frac{\delta^2\Psi}{\delta x^2} + V\Psi = i\hbar\frac{\delta\Psi}{\delta t} \tag{1.68}$$

*Case 2*: For an electron moving in a central-force field of charge (Ze)

$$V = -Ze^2/4\pi\varepsilon_0 r^2 \tag{1.69}$$

This does not readily apply to the 1-dimensional Schrodinger equation but to its 3-dimensional version. The resulting problem is known as the simple-harmonic oscillator. For this case

$$H = p^2/2m - Ze^2/4\pi\varepsilon_0 r^2 \tag{1.70}$$

*Case 3*: When an electron encounters the nucleus which is represented as a barrier $V_0$, as shown in Fig. 1.9 (a) for the case when the energy $E$ of the electron exceeds the potential barrier height ($E > V_0$), then

$$H = V_0 + p^2/2m$$

The resulting Schrodinger equation is

$$-\frac{\hbar^2}{2m}\frac{\delta^2\Psi}{\delta x^2} + V_0\Psi = i\hbar\frac{\delta\Psi}{\delta t} = E\Psi$$

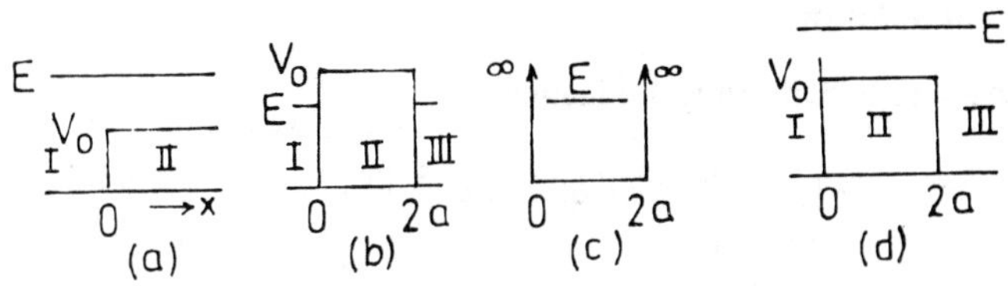


**Fig. 1.9** Potential barriers $V_0$ and electron energies $E$

or
$$\frac{\delta^2 \Psi}{\delta x^2} - \frac{2m}{\hbar^2} V_0 \Psi = -\frac{2mi}{\hbar}\frac{\delta \Psi}{\delta t} \tag{1.71}$$

*Case 4*: If a nucleus can be represented as a potential barrier $V_0$ of width $2a$ ($a$ = radius of the nucleus in general but half-width in 1 dimension), and the barrier height is greater than the total energy $E$ of the particle, Schrodinger's equation takes on three forms:

*Region I*: $-\infty < x < 0.\ V = 0$

$$\frac{\delta^2 \Psi}{\delta x^2} = -\frac{i2m}{\hbar}\frac{\delta \Psi}{\delta t} \tag{1.72}$$

*Region II*: $0 < x < 2a.\ V = V_0$

$$\frac{\delta^2 \Psi}{\delta x^2} = \frac{2m}{\hbar^2}(V_0 - E)\Psi = \frac{2m}{\hbar^2} V_0 \Psi - \frac{i2m}{\hbar}\frac{\delta \Psi}{\delta t} \tag{1.73}$$

*Region III*: $2a < x < \infty.\ V = 0$

$$\frac{\delta^2 \Psi}{\delta x^2} = -\frac{i2m}{\hbar}\frac{\delta \Psi}{\delta t} \tag{1.74}$$

One of the most dramatic or new result of this problem is that even though an electron encounters a potential barrier higher than its total energy $E$, the electron moving from $-\infty$ towards the barrier has the probability of being found in Region III, surmounting or tunnelling through the barrier. This is not possible according to classical physics. We will observe this after solving the differential equation in the next sections.

*Case 5*: The infinite potential well, Fig. 1.9(c). When an electron is trapped inside a potential well of height $V_0$ and width $2a$, the Schrodinger equation becomes

$$\frac{\delta^2 \Psi}{\delta x^2} = -\frac{2mi}{\hbar}\frac{\delta \Psi}{\delta t} = -\frac{2m}{\hbar} E,\ 0 < x < 2a \tag{1.75}$$

The rest of the discussion in this chapter will be devoted to observing how the wave-functions turn out for several simple cases, restricting to the time-independent Schrodinger equation.

## 1.13 General Solution

Consider the simple Schrodinger equation

$$-\frac{\hbar^2}{2m}\frac{\delta^2 \Psi}{\delta x^2} + V\Psi = i\hbar\frac{\delta \Psi}{\delta t} \tag{1.67}$$

If $V$ is independent of time $t$ but could be a function of $x$ only, the solution for $\Psi$ resulting from Eq. (1.67) can be written as the product of two functions, one of them a function of $x$ only and the other a function of $t$ only, as follows:

$$\Psi = X(x) \cdot T(t) \tag{1.76}$$

Substituting these in Eq. (1.67) above, we obtain

$$-\frac{\hbar^2}{2m}\frac{\delta^2 X}{\delta x^2}T + V \cdot X \cdot T = i\hbar X\frac{\delta T}{\delta t} \tag{1.77}$$

Dividing all terms by $(X.T)$, the result is

$$-\frac{\hbar^2}{2m}\frac{1}{X}\frac{\delta^2 X}{\delta x^2} + V = i\hbar\frac{1}{T}\frac{\delta T}{\delta t} \tag{1.78}$$

Since the left side is a function of $x$ only and the right side is a function of $t$ only, they must be equal individually to a constant, $K$. Therefore the equation in $x$ only becomes

$$-(\hbar^2/2m)\,\delta^2 X/\delta x^2 + VX = KX \tag{1.79}$$

But $$-(\hbar^2/2m)\,\delta^2/\delta x^2 + V = E \text{ ,the total energy} \tag{1.80}$$

Consequently, the separation constant $K$ equals $E$.

Therefore $-(\hbar^2/2m)\,\delta^2 X/\delta x^2 + VX = EX$ (1.81)

while the equation in $t$ only becomes from Eq. (1.78)

$$i\hbar\,\delta T/\delta t = ET \tag{1.82}$$

The solution to this is

$$T = e^{-iEt/\hbar} \tag{1.83}$$

Since the total solution is $\Psi = X.T$, we will pick up any constant in Eq. (1.83) after solving for $X$, so that there is no need for including it in $T$. Since $E = h\nu = \hbar\omega$, $T = e^{-i\omega t}$ as assumed in Eq. (1.57).

The $x$-part of $\Psi$ can be obtained in any given situation only when the functional relationship of $V$ and $x$ is known. We now proceed to do this by referring to Fig. 1.9.

### 1.14 Potential Barrier $V_0 < E$ from $x = 0$ to $+\infty$

Referring to Fig. 1.9(a) we can divide space into two regions:

*Region I*: $-\infty < x < 0$, with $V = 0$

Therefore

$$-(\hbar^2/2m)\,\delta^2 X_1/\delta x^2 = E X_1\,,\ \text{or}\,,\ \delta^2 X_1/\delta x^2 + (2m/\hbar^2)\,E X_1 = 0 \quad (1.84)$$

Let $$\alpha^2 = 2mE/\hbar^2 \quad (1.85)$$

Then $$X_1 = A\,e^{i\alpha x} + B\,e^{-i\alpha x} \quad (1.86)$$

*Region II*: $0 < x < \infty$, $V = V_0$, constant

Therefore $$-(\hbar^2/2m)\,\delta^2 X_2/\delta x^2 + (2m/\hbar^2)(E - V_0)\,X_2 = 0 \quad (1.87)$$

Let $$\beta^2 = 2m(E - V_0)/\hbar^2 \quad (1.88)$$

Then $$X_2 = C\,e^{i\beta x} + D\,e^{-i\beta x} \quad (1.89)$$

$A, B, C, D$ are independent of $x$ and are constants. They can be determined from given boundary conditions. The wave-function is well behaved and its properties are as follows:

(a) The function $\Psi$ is continuous at any discontinuity in potential.

(b) The first derivative is also continuous at a discontinuity.

Therefore at $x = 0$, $X_1 = X_2$ and $\delta X_1/\delta x = \delta X_2/\delta x$ (1.90)

Now, $A\,e^{i\alpha x}$ is a wave travelling in the positive $x$ direction (when combined with the time part of the complete solution) in Region I while $B\,e^{-i\alpha x}$ is travelling in the same region from right to left. This is caused by the forward-travelling wave being reflected at the barrier discontinuity. The total wave-function in Region I is the sum of the incident wave and the reflected wave. Therefore, both are retained here. However, the component $D\,e^{-i\beta x}$ is a wave travelling from $+\infty$ to 0 due to any possible discontinuity at $x = \infty$. Since such an eventuality does not exist, this component is absent. Therefore, $D = 0$.

Or $$X_1 = A\,e^{i\alpha x} + B\,e^{-i\alpha x}\ \text{and}\ X_2 = C\,e^{i\beta x} \quad (1.91)$$

Applying the boundary conditions of Eqs. (1.90) to (1.91), there result the following relations:

$$A + B = C,\ i\alpha(A - B) = i\beta C,\ \text{or},\ A - B = (\beta/\alpha)\,C \quad (1.92)$$

Then $$A = \tfrac{1}{2}(1 + \beta/\alpha)\,C\,,\ \text{and}\ B = \tfrac{1}{2}(1 - \beta/\alpha)\,C$$

or $$C/A = 2\alpha/(\alpha + \beta)\,,\ \text{and}\ B/A = (\alpha - \beta)/(\alpha + \beta) \quad (1.93)$$

The factor $(B/A)$ is the reflection coefficient in Region I and $(C/A)$ is the transmission coefficient into Region II. The sum of the incident and reflected waves is $(1 + B/A) = 1 + (\alpha - \beta)/(\alpha + \beta) = 2\alpha/(\alpha + \beta)$ = the transmission coefficient.

### 1.15 Potential Barrier of Finite Width, 2a. $E > V_0$ (Fig. 1.9(d))

Here, $a$ = possible radius of a nucleus. The energy of the particle (electron) is taken to be higher than the potential-barrier height $V_0$, so that it pertains to a high-energy particle, but is still non-relativistic. There are now three regions to consider.

*Region I*: $-\infty < x < 0, \quad V = 0$

$$\delta^2 X_1 / \delta x^2 + (2m/\hbar^2) E X_1 = 0$$

Therefore $$X_1 = A e^{i\alpha x} + B e^{-i\alpha x} \tag{1.94}$$

*Region II*: $0 < x < 2a, \quad V = V_0$

$$\delta^2 X_2 / \delta x^2 + (2m/\hbar^2)(E - V_0) X_2 = 0$$

Therefore $$X_2 = C e^{i\beta x} + D e^{-i\beta x} \tag{1.95}$$

*Region III*: $2a < x < \infty, V = 0$

$$\delta^2 X_3 / \delta x^2 + (2m/\hbar^2) E X_3 = 0$$

Therefore $$X_3 = F e^{i\alpha x} + G e^{-i\alpha x} \tag{1.96}$$

As discussed earlier, in Region III the term $G e^{-i\alpha x}$ does not exist and so $G = 0$. We now have five constants, $A, B, C, D, F$ to evaluate. We note that $(F/A)$ is the transmission coefficient beyond the barrier and we will determine this only. The relevant boundary conditions are:

(a) At $x = 0$, $X_1 = X_2$, and $\delta X_1 / \delta x = \delta X_2 / \delta x$

Therefore $$A + B = C + D, \text{ and } A - B = (\beta/\alpha)(C - D) \tag{1.97}$$

(b) At $x = 2a$, $X_2 = X_3$, and $\delta X_2 / \delta x = \delta X_3 / \delta x$

$$\left.\begin{aligned} &\text{Therefore } C e^{i2a\beta} + D e^{-i2a\beta} = F e^{i2a\alpha} \\ &\text{and } C e^{i2a\beta} - D e^{-i2a\beta} = (\alpha/\beta) F e^{i2a\alpha} \end{aligned}\right\} \tag{1.98}$$

$$\left.\begin{aligned} &\text{Therefore } C = F[(\beta + \alpha)/2\beta]\, e^{i2a(\alpha - \beta)} \\ &\text{and } D = F[(\beta - \alpha)/2\beta]\, e^{i2a(\alpha + \beta)} \end{aligned}\right\} \tag{1.99}$$

Then from Eq. (1.97) there result

$$A + B = F[(\beta + \alpha)/2\beta]\, e^{i2a(\alpha - \beta)} + F[(\beta - \alpha)/2\beta]\, e^{i2a(\alpha + \beta)}$$

and $$A - B = F[(\beta + \alpha)/2\alpha]\, e^{i2a(\alpha - \beta)} - F[(\beta - \alpha)/2\alpha]\, e^{i2a(\alpha + \beta)}$$

Thus $$\frac{A}{F} = \frac{1}{4}\left[\frac{(\alpha+\beta)^2}{\alpha\beta}\, e^{i\,2a\,(\alpha-\beta)} - \frac{(\alpha-\beta)^2}{\alpha\beta}\, e^{i\,2a\,(\alpha+\beta)}\right] \tag{1.100}$$

This is a complex number. In order to find the amplitude we have to find $|A/F|^2 = (A/F)\cdot(A/F)*$, where * indicates the complex conjugate. Thus

$$(A/F)* = \frac{1}{4}\left[\frac{(\alpha+\beta)^2}{\alpha\beta}\, e^{-i\,2a\,(\alpha-\beta)} - \frac{(\alpha-\beta)^2}{\alpha\beta}\, e^{-i\,2a\,(\alpha+\beta)}\right] \tag{1.101}$$

Therefore $$|(A/F)|^2 = 1 + [(\alpha^2-\beta^2)^2/8\alpha^2\beta^2]\,(1-\cos 4a\beta) \tag{1.102}$$

where use has been made that $$e^{i\,4a\beta} + e^{-i\,4a\beta} = 2\cos 4a\beta \tag{1.103}$$

Consequently, $$|(F/A)|^2 = [1 + (\alpha^2-\beta^2)^2\;(1-\cos 4a\beta)/8\alpha^2\beta^2]^{-1} \tag{1.104}$$

Using $\alpha^2 = 2mE/\hbar^2$ and $\beta^2 = 2m(E-V_0)/\hbar^2$, there is

$$(\alpha^2-\beta^2)^2/8\alpha^2\beta^2 = V_0^2/E(E-V_0) \tag{1.105}$$

Finally $$|(F/A)|^2 = [1 + (V_0^2/E(E-V_0)\cdot(1-\cos 4a\beta)]^{-1}$$

$$= \frac{E(E-V_0)}{E(E-V_0) + V_0^2(1-\cos 4a\beta)} \tag{1.106}$$

Note that when $V_0 = 0$, then $|(F/A)|^2 = 1$. The incoming wave from $-\infty$ goes undisturbed. The same holds when $\cos 4a\beta = 1$. This is true when $4a\beta = 0$, or $2n\pi$, with $n = 1, 2, \ldots$. But both $a$ and $\beta$ are not zero unless $V_0 = E$. Therefore, even when the energy of the particle equals the height of the potential barrier, there is the probability that the incoming wave will go past the potential barrier.

The other case is $4a\beta = 2n\pi$, or, $\beta = n\pi/2a$. This gives

$\beta^2 = 2\,m\,(E-V_0)/\hbar^2 = n^2\pi^2/4\,a^2$. Therefore $E - V_0 = \pi^2\hbar^2 n^2/8\,a^2\,m$.

This gives $$V_0 - E - \pi^2\hbar^2 n^2/8\,a^2\,m \tag{1.107}$$

We observe that for this to happen, the quantity $(n^2/4\,a^2)$ is the governing factor, i.e. the barrier width $2a$ and the frequency $\nu$ of the particle-wave must satisfy this relation. We also observe that $\alpha^2\beta^2 = 2\,m\,a^2\,(E-V_0)/\hbar^2$ is a dimensionless number, since the numerator is kg-m$^2$-J = N-m-J-s$^2$ = J$^2$-s$^2$, which is the dimension of the denominator $\hbar^2$

## 1.16 Potential Barrier of Width 2a. $E < V_0$.

Referring to Fig. 1.9(b) and following the steps in the previous section, we obtain the following expressions for $X_1, X_2, X_3$ in the three regions, with $\alpha^2 = 2mE/\hbar^2$ and $\beta^2 = 2m(V_0-E)/\hbar^2$.

*Region I*: $-\infty < x < 0. \quad X_1 = A e^{i \alpha x} + B e^{-i \alpha x}$ (1.108)

*Region II*: $0 < x < 2a. \quad X_2 = C e^{\beta x} + D e^{-\beta x}$ (1.109)

*Region III*: $2a < x < \infty. \quad X_3 = F e^{i \alpha x}$ (1.110)

The boundary conditions are the same as before. As discussed in the previous section, the term $e^{-i \alpha x}$ is not permissible in Region III.

At $x = 0, X_1 = X_2$ and $\delta X_1 / \delta x = \delta X_2 / \delta x$

Therefore $A + B = C + D$, and $A - B = -i (\beta/\alpha) (C - D)$ (1.111)

At $x = 2a, X_2 = X_3$, and $\delta X_2 / \delta x = \delta X_3 / \delta x$

Therefore $C e^{2 a \beta} + D e^{-2 a \beta} = F e^{i 2 a \alpha}$

and $C e^{2 a \beta} - D e^{-2 a \beta} = i (\alpha / \beta) F e^{i 2 a \alpha}$ (1.112)

Solving for $(A/F)$, there results

$$\frac{A}{F} = \frac{1}{4}\left[\left\{2 + i\left(\frac{\alpha}{\beta} - \frac{\beta}{\alpha}\right)\right\} e^{-2 a (\beta - i \alpha)} + \left\{2 + i\left(\frac{\beta}{\alpha} - \frac{\alpha}{\beta}\right)\right\} e^{2 a (\beta + i \alpha)}\right] \quad (1.113)$$

$$\left(\frac{A}{F}\right)^* = \frac{1}{4}\left[\left\{2 - i\left(\frac{\alpha}{\beta} - \frac{\beta}{\alpha}\right)\right\} e^{-2 a (\beta + i \alpha)} + \left\{2 - i\left(\frac{\beta}{\alpha} - \frac{\alpha}{\beta}\right)\right\} e^{2 a (\beta - i \alpha)}\right] \quad (1.114)$$

Multiplying the two, the amplitude ratio is

$$|(A / F)|^2 = (1 / 16 \alpha^2 \beta^2) [16 \alpha^2 \beta^2 + (\alpha^2 + \beta^2)^2 (e^{2 a \beta} - e^{-2 a \beta})^2] \quad (1.115)$$

With $16 \alpha^2 \beta^2 = 64 m^2 E (V_0 - E) / \hbar^4$, $(\alpha^2 + \beta^2)^2 = 4 m^2 V_0^2 / \hbar^4$ and $(e^{2 a \beta} - e^{-2 a \beta})^2 = 4 \sinh^2 2 a \beta = 2 (\cosh 4 a \beta - 1)$, Eq. (1.115) can be re-written as

$$|(F / A)|^2 = E (V_0 - E) / [E (V_0 - E) + V_0^2 (\cosh 4 a \beta - 1) / 8] \quad (1.116)$$

The reader can show that another equivalent expression is

$$|(A / F)|^2 = (e^{2 a \beta} + e^{-2 a \beta})^2 / 4 + [ (\alpha^2 + \beta^2)^2 / 16 \alpha^2 \beta^2] (e^{2 a \beta} - e^{-2 a \beta})^2$$

$$= \cosh^2 2 a \beta + [V_0^2 / 4 E (V_0 - E) ] \sinh^2 2 a \beta \quad (1.117)$$

From Eq. (1.116), note that even though the electron energy $E$ is lower than the barrier potential $V_0$, there is a probability of finding it in Region III beyond the barrier. This is due to the wave property of the particle by which it can go over the "hill" or potential barrier. This case corresponds to the earlier theorizing of Sommerfeld, soon after Bohr's circular-orbit theory was put forward, that electron orbits are elliptical, around which a particle moves past the nucleus, one extreme form being a straight line which passes right through the nucleus. This result has been beautifully taken care of by wave mechanics of de Broglie and Schrodinger, but led to its own conceptual difficulties until Born and Jordan offered the probabilistic interpretation of the wave-function $\Psi$.

At this juncture it is to be remembered that the wave-function is

$$\Psi = X \cdot T = X \cdot e^{-iEt/\hbar} \tag{1.118}$$

## 1.17 Electron Inside a Potential Well $V_0$

As a last example, consider a potential well of height $V_0$ in which a particle with energy $E$ is trapped. Because of repeated reflections from the walls of the well, the wave-function becomes a standing wave exhibiting its own amplitude pattern in space. The potential $V$ is zero inside the well while outside it, it is $V = V_0$. The particle will end up subtending loops in its standing-wave pattern, so as to have nodes at the walls, i.e. the wave-function $X = 0$ at $x = 0$ and $x = L$, since the incident wave is completely reflected. [Fig. 1.10(a) and (b)].

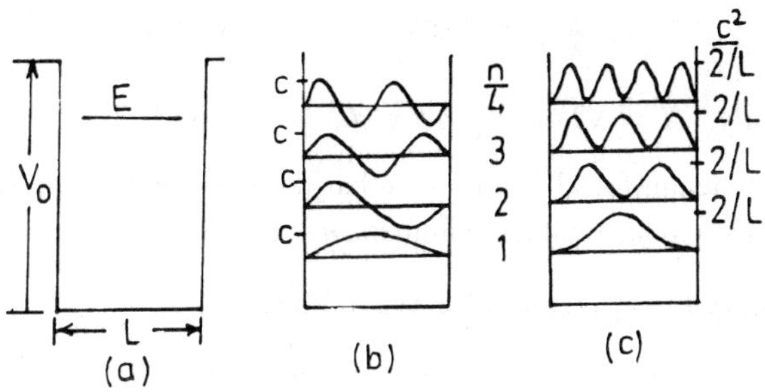


**Fig. 1.10** Electron in a potential well

Inside the potential well, $0 < x < L$, Schrodinger's equation is

$$-(\hbar^2/2m)\,\delta^2 X/\delta x^2 = EX, \text{ or, } \delta^2 X/\delta x^2 + \alpha^2 X = 0 \tag{1.119}$$

where again $\alpha^2 = 2mE/\hbar^2$.

Therefore $X = A e^{i\alpha x} + B e^{-i\alpha x} = C \sin \alpha x + D \cos \alpha x$ (1.120)

At $x = 0$, $X = 0$. Therefore $D = 0$.

At $x = L, X = 0$. Therefore $C \sin \alpha L = 0$, giving $\alpha L = n\pi, n =$ integer. We note that the value of $\alpha$ is $\alpha = n\pi/L$, so that only those energy levels that are satisfied by this condition can exist. These are:

$$E_n = \hbar^2 \alpha_n^2/2m = \hbar^2 \pi^2 n^2/2mL^2 \tag{1.121}$$

Therefore $X = C \sin \alpha x = C \sin n\pi x/L$ (1.122)

This is a sine wave with 0 at $x = 0$ and $x = L$, and the number of half-cycles or loops subtended equals the value of $n$, as shown in Fig. 1.10(b). As will be described later, the wave-function represents the probability of finding the particle at any given location at a given time. The probability is the amplitude of the wave-function (its square) and the sine wave represents the fact that the probability is greatest at the peaks [Fig. 1.10(c)].

The square of the amplitude of $\Psi$ is always real for physically realizable or observable systems. Now, the probability of finding the particle over all space is unity. Therefore

$$\int_{-\infty}^{\infty} \Psi^* \cdot \Psi \cdot dx = 1 \tag{1.123}$$

Using this property, the square of amplitude $C$ of $\Psi$ is found from

$$\int_0^L C^2 \sin^2 \alpha x \cdot dx = 1 , \text{ since } e^{-iEt/\hbar} \cdot e^{iEt/\hbar} = 1$$

$$\text{Therefore } \tfrac{1}{2} C^2 \left( x - \frac{1}{2\alpha} \sin 2\alpha x \right) \Bigg|_0^L = 1 , \text{ giving } C^2 = 2/L \tag{1.124}$$

$$\text{Consequently, } X = \sqrt{2/L} \, \sin n\pi x/L, \quad n = 1, 2, 3, \ldots \tag{1.125}$$

The wave-function for all values of n has the same amplitude $\sqrt{2/L}$ but the number of loops will have integer numbers, $n = 1, 2, 3, \ldots$

## 1.18 Probability Interpretation for Wave Function

From the wave-particle duality of matter, we observed that the particle is located on the accompanying wave. When we consider that a guiding wave incident upon a discontinuity in potential can show reflection and transmission properties, naturally the question arises whether the concept of the particle splitting into several components has any physical meaning. This posed a grave shortcoming to the concept of the wave-function as a wave, since by usage from previous thought this term was attributed to matter waves. This difficulty was satisfactorily solved by invoking the probability interpretation, namely, that the square of the amplitude of a complex wave-function obtained by solving Schrodinger's equation which is always a real quantity, denotes this probability. The constants of integration ($A$, $B$, $C$, $D$, ...) which we have used by solving Schrodinger's equation with given boundary conditions must have values restricted to only those values which give a unit probability when the square of amplitude of the wave-function is integrated over all space, since the particle must exist somewhere in space. This is called normalization of the wave-function.

$$\int_{-\infty}^{\infty} \Psi^* \cdot \Psi \cdot dx = 1 \tag{1.126}$$

We used this property in Eq. (1.124) in anticipation to evaluate the constant $C^2$, which was the square of amplitude of the wave-function in the previous section.

## 1.19 Energy Level Transitions, Masers and Lasers

The presence of discrete energy levels for electrons in an atom and the transitions from one level to another in response to energy changes has far-reaching consequences, both for the theory of atomic phenomena and practical applications. Bohr's theory successfully explained the photon radiation wavelengths in spectroscopy of a hydrogen atom, which can be divided into several series known as the Lyman, Balmer, Paschen, Brackett and Pfund, after their original discoverers. The energy level of electron in the nth orbit was found to be given by Eq. (1.12), $E_n = -13.645\ Z^2/n^2$. For hydrogen, the difference in energy between two levels $n = n_1$ and $n = n_2$ is

$$E = E_{21} = 13.645\,(1/n_1^2 - 1/n_2^2)\,,\ \text{eV}\,,\ n_2 > n_1 \tag{1.127}$$

The corresponding frequencies and wavelengths are

$$\Delta\nu = \nu_{21} = E/4.1357\times 10^{-15}\ \text{Hz} = c/\lambda_{21} \tag{1.128}$$

and

$$\Delta\lambda = \lambda_{21} = 12400/E\,,\ \text{Å} \tag{1.16}$$

The following table gives: (a) the name of the series, (b) the value of $n_1$, the lower energy level to which the transition occurs, (c) energy level differences between various values of $n_2$ holding $n_1$ constant, (d) corresponding wavelength of photon radiation, and (e) frequency of radiation, all for a hydrogen atom.

| | Series | $n_1$ | $n_2$ | = | 2 | 3 | 4 | 5 | $\infty$ | |
|---|---|---|---|---|---|---|---|---|---|---|
| 1) | Lyman | 1 | $\Delta E$ | = | 10.234 | 12.129 | 12.792 | 13.1 | 13.645 | eV |
| | | | $\Delta\lambda$ | = | 1211.7 | 1022.35 | 969.34 | 946.56 | 908.76 | Å |
| | | | $\Delta\nu$ | = | 2.475 | 2.932 | 3.093 | 3.1675 | $3.3\times10^{15}$ | Hz |
| 2) | Balmer | 2 | $\Delta E$ | = | | 1.895 | 2.5584 | 2.8655 | 3.411 | eV |
| 3) | Paschen | 3 | $\Delta E$ | = | | | 0.6633 | 0.871 | 1.516 | eV |
| 4) | Brackett | 4 | $\Delta E$ | = | | | | 0.3 | 0.853 | eV |
| 5) | Pfund | 5 | $\Delta E$ | = | | | | | 0.545 | eV |

For $n_2 = 2, 3, 4, 5$ and $\infty$, the reader should fill in the values of $\Delta\lambda$ and $\Delta\nu$ in the above table. This is left as an exercise. The wavelengths and frequencies of visible light are 6562.8 Å/$0.4568\times10^{15}$ Hz (red) to 4340.5 Å/$0.6907\times10^{15}$ Hz (violet). The corresponding energy transitions will be from (12400/6562.8 = 1.89 eV) to (12400/4340.5 = 2.857 eV). Note that these are pre-eminently shown in the Balmer series with $n_1 = 2$. The Lyman series produces very short wavelength radiation in the ultraviolet region, while the others are in the infra-red region.

If an external agency can impart sufficient energy to an electron in any orbit to raise it beyond the level $n = \infty$, then the electron is freed from the nuclear force of attraction and in turn acquires a kinetic energy equal to this excess energy. Very early the question arose, where the photon released in the radiation due to an electron transition from one energy level to another came from, since the electron is still present in one state or the other without having undergone any change to itself. It was this problem that worried physicists until Einstein came up with one of his brilliant ''mental experiments'' that the energy imparted to the photon in a spontaneous transition could only have come from a reduction in mass of the electron, which satisfies the equation $\Delta E = \Delta m.c^2$. For example, for the highest transition in the hydrogen atom equal to 10.234 eV, the electron mass reduction is $\Delta m = 10.234 \times 1.602189 \times 10^{-19}/2.99792458^2 \times 10^{16}$ kg $= 1.822 \times 10^{-35}$ kg $= 2 \times 10^{-5}$ electron mass. This is also equal to 10.234 eV/0.511 MeV. Such a mass reduction cannot be noticed, but is present nevertheless. This mental experiment was the forerunner for Einstein's further thoughts about mass-energy equivalence.

Another useful property of the energy-level transition has already been given in X-Ray production in Sec. 1.3. Fluorescence is another visible indication of energy-level transition. In recent years the advent of masers and lasers with extraordinarily high energy densities has led to far-reaching applications in human endeavours. We will briefly outline their principles.

Consider for present purposes, although hydrogen is not used in masers and lasers, the transition energy of 10.234 eV when an electron jumps from orbit $n = 2$ to $n = 1$. Three possibilities exist for the following mechanisms:

(1) An electron can absorb an external photon (light) and raise itself from $n = 1$ to an excited state, for example, $n = 2$.

(2) This excited electron fall back to the orbit $n = 1$ (the ground state) and emit a photon of 10.234 eV energy.

(3) If an electron is already in an excited state ($n = 2$) and a photon of 10.234 eV impinges on the atom, then if at the same instant the excited electron also falls to the ground state, it can also emit a photon so that there are two photons of the same frequency and energy. In coherent emission, the two photons are made to be in the same phase.

The principle in masers (molecular or microwave amplification by stimulated emission of radiation) and lasers (l = light) is to excite or pump the orbiting electrons to higher energy states, then to pump in photons from an external source with proper energy or wavelength, and obtain coherent emission by making the orbiting electron release its photon in phase with the incoming photon. This provides amplification and high energy densities. The first is called induced absorption, the second is spontaneous emission, and the third is stimulated emission.

A ruby laser beam can be concentrated to as small as $10^{-6}$ metre in diameter. Among its other uses as cutting tool, a laser beam is used in nuclear fusion power generation to yield about $10^7$ K by irradiating the fuel consisting of D (deuterium) and T (tritium) with very high energy densities available in the laser.

## OBJECTIVE TYPE QUESTIONS

1. A photon in red wavelength region $\lambda = 0.8\ \mu m = 8000$ Å collides with an electron at rest. The energy of the incident photon in Joules is
(a) $24.83 \times 10^{-20}$ J, (b) $1.9865 \times 10^{-25}$ J, (c) $8 \times 10^{-7}$ J, (d) none.

2. The energy of the above photon in eV is
(a) 12.8 eV, (b) 1.55 eV, (c) 1 MeV, (d) none are true.

3. The frequency of the above photon is
(a) $8 \times 10^{7}$ Hz, (b) $1.25 \times 10^{6}$ Hz. (c) $3.75 \times 10^{14}$ Hz, (d) $4.8 \times 10^{15}$ Hz.

4. In the above problems, the scattered photon has a maximum wave length of
(a) 8000 + 0.048526 Å, (b) 8000 – 0.048526 Å, (c) 8000 Å, (d) none of the three.

5. In a colour TV set, electrons with kinetic energy of 20 keV are involved. Its de Broglie wavelength is
(a) $0.62 \times 10^{-10}$ m = 0.62 Å, (b) $5 \times 10^{-5}$ m, (c) 1 μm, (d) none of the three.

6. In the above problem, the frequency of the electron wave is
(a) $4.836 \times 10^{18}$ Hz, (b) $3 \times 10^{15}$ Hz, (c) $0.2418 \times 10^{15}$ Hz. (d) none.

7. Molybdenum has $Z = 42$. Its spectral notation is
(a) $3p^4$, (b) $4d^6$, (c) $4s^1$, (d) none of the three.

8. An element has a principal quantum number $n = 4$. The total of magnetic quantum numbers $l$ *and* $m_l$ can be
(a) 15, (b) 18, (c) 9, (d) 7.

[*Answers*: 1. (a); 2. (b); 3. (b); 4. (a); 5. (a); 6. (a); 7. (b); 8. (b).]

## REVIEW QUESTIONS AND PROBLEMS

1. For a hydrogen atom, based on Bohr's theory of electron orbits, derive Eqs. (1.9) and (1.13).

2. (a) For X-rays or any other radiation, show that the wavelength is $12400/V$, Å where $V$ = electron acceleration potential in volts. (b) Calculate the frequency corresponding to a wavelength of 1 Å. Using Bohr's hypothesis show that X-ray production is possible for elements with $Z \geq 35$. Use results based on Eq. (1.12).

3. Derive the relation (1.32) for change in wavelength of a photon when scattered by an electron at rest. Then show that the Compton wavelength for a particle is $\lambda_c = h/m_0c$, and for an electron, $\lambda_{ce} = 2.42631$ μμm.

4. (a) Explain the meaning of the terms: (a) principal quantum number, (b) magnetic quantum numbers, (c) orbital quantum number, (d) orbital magnetic quantum number, (e) spin quantum number. Give their usual symbols.
(b) For $n = 4$, give all possible quantum states.

5. The atomic number of copper is 29. Give the shell structure of its orbiting electrons and the spectroscopic notation.
6. Give the de Broglie wavelength for a proton with $m_p$ = 1.0072765 $u$ at a potential of $10^6$ Volts. ($u$ = 931.502 MeV = 1.660566 × $10^{-27}$ kg).
7. Derive Eq. (1.53). State all assumptions involved.
8. Derive Schrodinger's equation (1.65) in one-dimensional space. Explain all quantities involved and the assumptions.
9. Check all equations from (1.108) through (1.117). Explain the phenomenon of tunnelling from these equations.

*CHAPTER 2*

# Nuclear Physics and Nuclear Reactors

## 2.1 General

The following topics will be described and discussed in this chapter, which are applied to nuclear power generation by fission and nuclear-reactor operation:

(i) Nuclear properties; (ii) Nuclear binding energy; (iii) Force between nucleons; (iv) Exchange force model; (v) Nuclear models; (vi) Nuclear reactions and cross-sections; (vii) Nuclear decay processes; (viii) Radiation measures; (ix) Data and units.

## 2.2 Nuclear Properties

*Isotopes* have the same atomic numbers Z or number of protons in the nucleus, but have different atomic masses A = N + Z caused by different numbers of neutrons N. They refer to the nucleii of the same element.

*Isotones* have same number of neutrons N but different numbers of protons Z. They refer to nucleii of different elements.

*Isobars* have same mass number A. They refer to nucleii of different elements.

Some examples of isotopes of elements important for nuclear power are:

| | | | | | | | | |
|---|---|---|---|---|---|---|---|---|
| *Thorium*: | *Z = 90* A-M | A | 227 | 228 | 229 | 230 | | |
| | | N | 137 | 138 | 139 | 140 | | |
| *Uranium*: | *Z = 92* | A | 231 | 232 | 233 | 234 | 235 | 238 |
| | | N | 139 | 140 | 141 | 142 | 143 | 146 |
| *Plutonium*: | *Z = 94* | A | 238 | 239 | 240 | 241 | 242 | |
| | | N | 144 | 145 | 146 | 147 | 148 | |

**Table 2.5 Periodic Table**

| | | | | | | | | |
|---|---|---|---|---|---|---|---|---|
| $^{1}_{1}$H<br>Hydrogen | | | | | | | | |
| $^{7}_{3}$Li<br>Lithium | $^{9}_{4}$Be<br>Beryllium | | | | | | | |
| $^{23}_{11}$Na<br>Sodium | $^{24}_{12}$Mg<br>Magnesium | | | | | | | |
| $^{39}_{19}$K<br>Potassium | $^{40}_{20}$Ca<br>Calcium | $^{45}_{21}$Sc<br>Scandium | $^{48}_{22}$Ti<br>Titanium | $^{51}_{23}$V<br>Vanadium | $^{52}_{24}$Cr<br>Chromium | $^{55}_{25}$Mn<br>Manganese | $^{56}_{26}$Fe<br>Iron | $^{59}_{27}$Co<br>Cobalt |
| $^{85}_{37}$Rb<br>Rubidium | $^{88}_{38}$Sr<br>Strontium | $^{89}_{39}$Y<br>Yitrium | $^{90}_{40}$Zr<br>Zirconium | $^{93}_{41}$Nb<br>Niobium | $^{98}_{42}$Mo<br>Molyb-<br>denum | $^{97}_{43}$Tc<br>Technitium | $^{102}_{44}$Ru<br>Ruthenium | $^{103}_{45}$Rh<br>Rhodium |
| $^{133}_{55}$Cs<br>Cesium | $^{138}_{56}$Ba<br>Barium | $^{139}_{57}$La<br>Lanthanum | $^{180}_{72}$Hf<br>Hafnium | $^{181}_{73}$Ta<br>Tantalum | $^{184}_{74}$W<br>Tungsten | $^{187}_{75}$Re<br>Rhenium | $^{192}_{76}$Os<br>Osmium | $^{193}_{77}$Ir<br>Iridium |
| $^{233}_{87}$Fr<br>Francium | $^{226}_{88}$Ra<br>Radium | $^{227}_{89}$Ac<br>Actinium | | | | | | |
| | | Rare Earths<br>Lanthanides<br>57-71 | | $^{140}_{58}$Ce<br>Cerium | $^{141}_{59}$Pr<br>Praseo-<br>dymium | $^{142}_{60}$Nd<br>Neo-<br>dymium | $^{145}_{61}$Pm<br>Pro-<br>methium | $^{152}_{62}$Sm<br>Samarium |
| | | Actinides<br>89-103 | | $^{232}_{90}$Th<br>Thorium | $^{231}_{91}$Pa<br>Proto-<br>actinium | $^{238}_{92}$U<br>Uranium | $^{237}_{93}$Np<br>Neptunium | $^{244}_{94}$Pu<br>Plutonium |

Trans-

**of the Elements**

| | | | | | | | | ${}^{4}_{2}He$ Helium |
|---|---|---|---|---|---|---|---|---|
| | | | ${}^{11}_{5}B$ Boron | ${}^{12}_{6}C$ Carbon | ${}^{14}_{7}N$ Nitrogen | ${}^{16}_{8}O$ Oxygen | ${}^{19}_{9}F$ Fluorine | ${}^{20}_{10}Ne$ Neon |
| | | | ${}^{27}_{13}Al$ Aluminium | ${}^{28}_{14}Si$ Silicon | ${}^{31}_{15}P$ Phosphorus | ${}^{32}_{16}S$ Sulphur | ${}^{35}_{17}Cl$ Chlorine | ${}^{40}_{18}Ar$ Argon |
| ${}^{58}_{28}Ni$ Nickel | ${}^{63}_{29}Cu$ Copper | ${}^{64}_{30}Zn$ Zinc | ${}^{69}_{31}Ga$ Gallium | ${}^{74}_{32}Ge$ Germanium | ${}^{75}_{33}As$ Arsenic | ${}^{80}_{34}Se$ Selenium | ${}^{79}_{35}Br$ Bromine | ${}^{84}_{36}Kr$ Krypton |
| ${}^{106}_{46}Pd$ Palla-dium | ${}^{107}_{47}Ag$ Silver | ${}^{114}_{48}Cd$ Cadmium | ${}^{115}_{49}In$ Indium | ${}^{120}_{50}Sn$ Tin | ${}^{121}_{51}Sb$ Antimony | ${}^{130}_{52}Te$ Tellu rium | ${}^{127}_{53}I$ Iodine | ${}^{132}_{54}Xe$ Xenon |
| ${}^{195}_{78}Pt$ Platinum | ${}^{197}_{79}Au$ Gold | ${}^{202}_{80}Hg$ Mercury | ${}^{205}_{81}Tl$ Thallium | ${}^{208}_{82}Pb$ Lead | ${}^{209}_{83}Bi$ Bismuth | ${}^{209}_{84}Po$ Polonium | ${}^{210}_{85}At$ Astatine | ${}^{222}_{86}Rn$ Radon |

| ${}^{153}_{63}Eu$ Europium | ${}^{158}_{64}Gd$ Gadolinium | ${}^{159}_{65}Tb$ Terbium | ${}^{164}_{66}Dy$ Dyspro-sium | ${}^{165}_{67}Ho$ Holmium | ${}^{166}_{68}Er$ Erbium | ${}^{169}_{69}Tm$ Thulium | ${}^{174}_{70}Yb$ Ytterbium | ${}^{175}_{71}Lu$ Lutetium |
|---|---|---|---|---|---|---|---|---|
| ${}^{243}_{95}Am$ Americum | ${}^{247}_{96}Cm$ Curium | ${}^{247}_{97}Bk$ Berkele-yium | ${}^{251}_{98}Cf$ Californi um | ${}^{254}_{99}Es$ Einsteini um | ${}^{257}_{100}Fm$ Fermium | ${}^{258}_{101}Md$ Mende-levium | ${}^{259}_{102}No$ Nobelium | ${}^{260}_{103}Lr$ Lawren-cium |

Uranium Elements

Properties of many nucleii involved in nuclear power are given in Table 2.1.

**Table 2.1 Properties of Nucleii Involved in Nuclear Power**

| | | Atomic Mass (u) | Half-Life/Abundance | Fission x-section (b) (for thermal neutrons) |
|---|---|---|---|---|
| *Thorium* | *Z = 90* | | | |
| | A = 227 | — | — | 200 ± 10% |
| | 228 | 228.028715 | 1.91 yr | < 0.3 |
| | 229 | 229.031755 | 7300 yr | 30 ± 10 % |
| | 230 | 230.033128 | 75400 yr | < 0.001 |
| | 231 | 231.036299 | 25.52 hr | |
| | 232 | 232.038051 | Abund. 100% | |
| | 233 | 233.041577 | 22.3 min | |
| *Uranium* | *Z = 92* | | | |
| | A = 231 | | | 300 ± 10% |
| | 232 | | | 76 ± 4 |
| | 233 | 233.039628 | $15.92 \times 10^4$ yr | 530 ± 5 |
| | 234 | 234.040947 | $24.5 \times 10^4$ yr | < 0.005 |
| | 235 | 235.043924 | Abund. 0.72% | 584 ± 1 |
| | 236 | 236.045563 | $23.42 \times 10^6$ yrs | |
| | 237 | 237.048725 | 6.75 days | |
| | 238 | 238.050785 | Abund. 99.275% | $(2.7 \pm 0.3) \times 10^{-6}$ |
| | 239 | 239.054290 | 23.5 min | |
| *Plutonium* | *Z = 94* | | | |
| | A = 237 | 237.048401 | 45.3 days | |
| | 238 | 238.049555 | 87.74 yr | 17 ± 6% |
| | 239 | 239.052158 | 24,100 yr | 742 ± 3 |
| | 240 | 240.053808 | 6,570 yr | < 0.08 |
| | 241 | 241.056846 | 14.4 yr | 1010 ± 1% |
| | 242 | 242.058737 | $37.6 \times 10^4$ yr | < 0.2 |
| | 243 | 243.061998 | 4.96 hr | |

Nuclear properties important for present purposes can be classified as follows:

(a) Mass; (b) Radius; (c) Abundance of stable nucleii; (d) Decay modes and half-lives for radioactive nucleii; (e) Electric charge; (f) Reaction modes. Other properties discussed by nuclear physicists may include: (g) Spin; (h) Magnetic dipole moment; (i) Electric quadrupole moment; (j) Excited states; (k) Parity.

Counting all isotopes, physicists have discovered over 1000 nuclides with atomic numbers ranging to 107. But the heaviest naturally-occurring element is uranium with $Z = 92$. The trans-uranium nucleii exhibit strong decay properties and short half-lives, so that they are produced only in high-energy particle accelerators. Nucleii of elements heavier than helium are generally the products of exploding stars prior to the time of formation of the earth, so that elements or isotopes with short half-lives have become rare. The instability of trans-uranic elements is caused by the binding energy between nucleons and the need for nucleons to occupy positions of lowest potential energy in the nucleus. This will be elaborated later on.

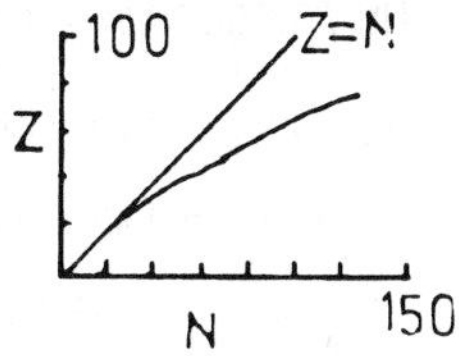

**Fig. 2.1** Relations between protons and neutrons in elements

Figure 2.1 shows a graph of relation between $Z$ and $N$. We observe that $N \geq Z$. This is necessary if the strong nuclear force between nucleons is to exceed the coulomb repulsive force between protons. This will be discussed later on.

## Nuclear Mass and Mass Defect

Nucleii consist of $Z$ protons and N neutrons which are strongly bound, so that energy has been necessary to bring them together. Thus the $A = Z + N$ nucleons are bound by the work done by an external agency to bind them. This results in the mass of the nucleus thus formed to be less than the combined masses of the $Z$ protons and $N$ neutrons. A mass defect exists which is equal to the energy of binding. For a nucleus $X$ let

$m\left({}^{A}_{Z}X_N\right)$ = mass of nucleus (measured from mass spectroscopic or other suitable methods)

$\Delta m$ = mass defect

$m_p, m_n$ = masses of individual proton and neutron, respectively.

Then, $$\Delta m = Z \cdot m_p + N \cdot m_n - m\left({}^{A}_{Z}X_N\right) \tag{2.1}$$

Masses in nuclear physics are presented in atomic mass units, $u$, which is defined as 1/12th of the mass of a stable carbon nucleus, ${}^{12}_{6}C$. Thus

$$u = 1.660566 \times 10^{-27}\ \text{kg} = 931.502\ \text{MeV}$$

$$m_p = 1.00727647\ u = 938.28\ \text{MeV}$$

$$m_n = 1.00866501\ u = 939.573\ \text{MeV}$$

The mass defect in $u$ is expressed in energy units by multiplying by 931.502 MeV.

***Example 2.1***: The mass of ${}^{235}_{92}U$ = 235.043924 $u$. Calculate: (a) the ratio $N/Z$; (b) mass of $U$-235 nucleus in kg; (c) the mass defect $\Delta m$ in $u$, kg and MeV; (d) number of atoms in 1 gram of the element.

Avagadro's number $N_A = 6.022045 \times 10^{23}$ atom/mole. Mass of electron $= 5.485803 \times 10^{-4}\ u$.

***Solutions***: (a) $N/Z = 143/92 = 1.5543478$.

(b) $235.043924 \times 1.660566 \times 10^{-27} = 390.30594 \times 10^{-27}$ kg

(c) $92\ m_p = 92 \times 1.00727647\ u = 92.669392\ u = 153.88364 \times 10^{-27}$ kg

$143\ m_n = 143 \times 1.00866501\ u = \underline{144.2391\ u} = 239.51854 \times 10^{-27}$ kg

$$Z\,m_p + N\,m_n = 236.9085u$$

$$\Delta m = (236.9085 - 235.043924)\ u = 1.864576\ u = 3.0962515 \times 10^{-27}\text{kg}$$

$$= 1.864576 \times 931.502 \text{ MeV} = 1736.8563 \text{ MeV}.$$

Note that $3.0962515 \times 10^{-27} \times (2.99792458 \times 10^8)^2/1.602189 \times 10^{-19}$

$$= 1736.8444 \times 10^6 \text{ eV} = 1736.8444 \text{ MeV}.$$

$$(\text{Also}, \ B/A = 7.39 \text{ MeV / nucleon}).$$

(d) 235 grams of *U*-235 contain $N_A$ atoms. Therefore, in 1 gram, number of atoms $= N_A/A = 6.022045 \times 10^{23}/235 = 2.5625723 \times 10^{21}$.

**Nuclear Radius**

The radius of an atom $\approx 10^{-10}$ m (1 Å) which approximately gives the radius to the farthest orbiting electron. For hydrogen, we calculated the first Bohr orbit to have the radius $a_0 = 0.52845$ Å. On the other hand, the nuclear radius is measured in femtometre or fermi. 1 fermi $= 10^{-15}$ *m*. The radius is not a precisely defined quantity, but is taken to be that value at which the density of nucleus falls to 50% of that in the centre. This is

$$R = R_0 A^{1/3} \tag{2.2}$$

where
$$R_0 = 1.2 \sim 1.35\,fm \tag{2.3}$$

Such dimensions are ascertained from scattering experiments. With $R_0 = 1.2\,fm$, we obtain for $A = 1$, $R = 1.2\,fm$, which is the radius of a proton. For $A = 242$, $R = 1.2 \times 242^{1/3} = 7.48\,fm$ for the heaviest isotope of ${}^{242}_{94}Pu$. Note also that $(A/R^3)$ is a constant which denotes that the average density of nucleon packing is the same for all nucleii.

**Nuclear Charge Distribution**

From scattering experiments with high-energy electrons and photons, it has been established that (a) the charge density in the nucleus is nearly constant up to a certain radius, then (b) the charge drops gradually to zero. Figure 2.2 shows an example for two nucleii. (c) The distance over

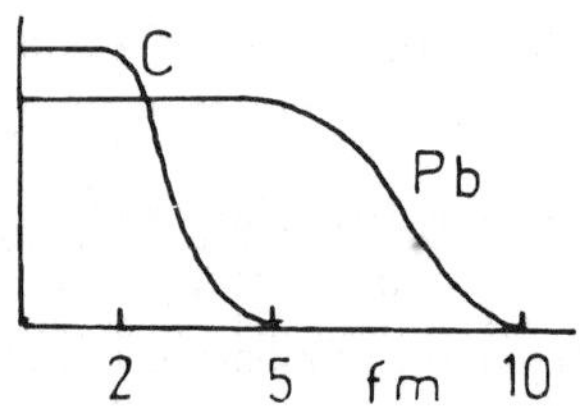

Fig. 2.2 Nuclear charge distribution

which this drop occurs is nearly the same for all nucleii and does not depend either on the proton number $Z$ or the atomic mass number $A$, i.e. it is independent of the size of the nucleus.

A parameter used for describing the fall is "skin thickness" defined as skin thickness $t$ = distance over which the charge falls from 90% to 10% of maximum value. For all nucleii, $t \approx 2.3\, fm$.

***Example 2.2***: For ${}^{12}_{6}C$, calculate $R$ from Eq. (2.2) taking $R_0 = 1.2\, fm$. Then find the radius to which the charge is constant, by assuming that the value of $R$ is where the charge is 50% of maximum value.

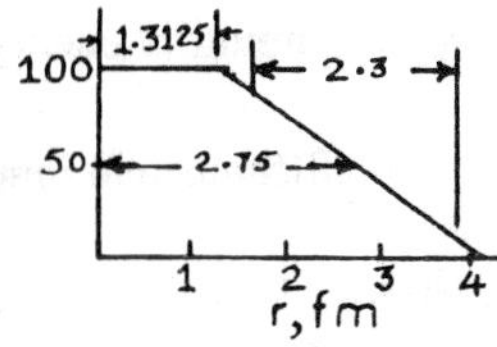

**Fig. 2.3** Charge distribution for Example 2.2

***Solution***: By linearizing the charge-radius graph, we obtain the following from Fig. 2.3:

$$R = 1.2 \times 12^{1/3} = 2.75\, fm; \; t = 2.3\, fm.$$

Therefore $\quad R_C = 2.75 - \frac{1}{2} \times 2.3 \times 100/80 = 2.75 - 1.4375 = 1.3125\, fm$

### 2.3 Nuclear Binding Energy

The release of binding energy $B$ is responsible for the kinetic energies of the fission products in a nuclear reactor. Experimental results show that the binding energy per nucleon $(B/A)$ follows a curve as shown in Fig. 2.4. It has a maximum of 8.79 MeV/nucleon for ${}^{56}$Fe and falls off on both sides. From previous discussion

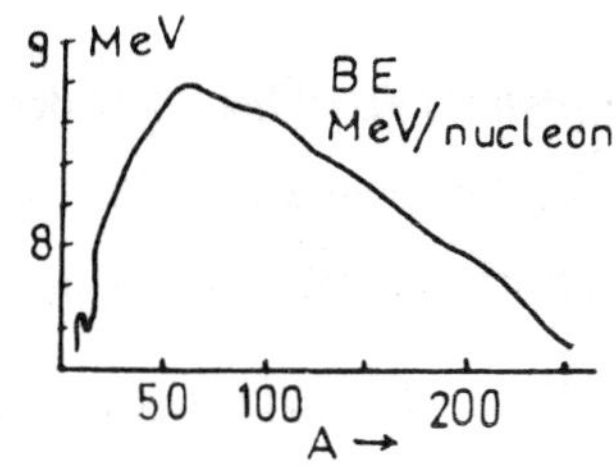

**Fig. 2.4** Binding energy, MeV/nucleon. Variation with mass number A

$$BE = \text{mass defect} \times 931.502 \text{ Mev}$$

$$= \left\{Z\, m_p + N\, m_n - m\left({}^{A}_{Z}X_N\right)\right\} \times 931.502 \text{ Mev} \qquad (2.4)$$

For $U$-235 of Example 2.1, this is 1736.8563 MeV giving $(B/A)$ = 7.39 MeV/nucleon. The main fact of interest is that $(B/A)$ is nearly constant for $A > 50$.

***Example 2.3***: Calculate the value of $B/A$ for ${}^{238}_{92}U$, whose mass is $m\left({}^{238}_{92}U\right) = 238.050785\, u$.

***Solution***: The binding energy of the nucleus is

$$B = 931.501\, [92 \times 1.007825 + 146 \times 1.008665 - 238.050785]$$

$$= 1801.5024 \text{ MeV}$$

Therefore $B/A = 7.569338$ MeV per nucleon.

This is less than the maximum by $8.79 - 7.57 = 1.22$ MeV/nucleon.

In addition to the binding energy, there are two other energies of interest and importance. These are:

(1) *Neutron Separation Energy*

$S_n$ = amount of energy required to remove a neutron from a nucleus

= difference in binding energies between two nucleii, ${}^{A}_{Z}X_N$ and ${}^{A-1}_{Z}X_{N-1}$.

Now $$B\left({}^{A}_{Z}X_N\right) = Z\,m_p + N\,m_n - m\left({}^{A}_{Z}X_N\right)$$

and $$B\left({}^{A-1}_{Z}X_{N-1}\right) = Z\,m_p + (N-1)\,m_n - m\left({}^{A-1}_{Z}X_{N-1}\right)$$

Therefore $$S_n = m\left({}^{A-1}_{Z}X_{N-1}\right) + m_n - m\left({}^{A}_{Z}X_N\right) \tag{2.5}$$

(2) *Proton Separation Energy*

$$S_p = B\left({}^{A}_{Z}X_N\right) - B\left({}^{A-1}_{Z-1}X_N\right) \tag{2.6}$$

***Example 2.4***: When ${}^{235}_{92}U$ decays spontaneously into ${}^{231}_{90}Th$ and an α-particle $\left({}^{4}_{2}He\right)$ along with γ-ray of 0.204 MeV, calculate the release of kinetic energy of the α-particle and the recoiling nucleus of ${}^{231}_{90}Th$. Atomic masses are:

$${}^{235}U = 234.99345586\,u,\quad {}^{231}Th = 230.98692634\,u,\ {}^{4}_{2}\alpha = 4.00150609\,u.$$

***Solution***: $m\,({}^{235}U) - m\,({}^{231}Th) - m\,({}^{4}\alpha) = 0.00502344\,u = 4.6793344$ MeV. [Note that taking $m\,({}^{235}U) = 235\,u$, $m\,({}^{231}Th) = 231\,u$, and $m\,({}^{4}\alpha) = 4\,u$ gives 0 MeV release !]

Therefore release of k.e. = 4.4753344 MeV.

% k.e. acquired by the α-particle = $100 \times 230.99/(230.99 + 4)$

= 98.3% of k.e. released = 4.4 MeV

The remaining 1.7% is carried by the recoiling ${}^{231}$Th nucleus.

*Semi-Empirical Formula for Binding Energy*

In a later section 2.6 under nuclear models, a formula is derived for the binding energy $B$ based on the liquid-drop model of the nucleus by Bohr. This is

$$B = a_v\,A - a_s\,A^{2/3} - a_c\,(Z-1)\,Z\,A^{-1/3} - a_{sym}\,(A - 2Z)^2\,A^{-1} + \delta \tag{2.7}$$

where $a_v$ = a volume effect constant (B/A ≈ constant)

**Plate 1:** Nuclear Power Station at Point Lepreau, New Brunswick Power Corporation, Canada. Reactor house on left, thermal power station on right.

**Plate 2:** Reactor at Point Lepreau showing fuel and control rods and loading machine. Lower left corner - Bolometer for measuring temperature.

**Plate 3:** Interior of Point Lepreau turbine-generator hall. One 650 MW alternator coupled to 3-stage steam turbine (H.P., I.P., L.P. stages).

**Plate 4:** Hydro-electric power station on River St. John at Mactaquac, New Brunswick Power Corporation.

**Plate 5:** Thermal power station of New Brunswick Power Corporation at the city of St. John.

**Plate 6:** Interior of turbine-generator hall at Mactaquac showing pilot exciter, main exciter and alternator with vertical shaft. Thrust bearing and turbine are below floor level.

**Plate 7:** Transmission lines of N.B. Power Corporation. Far left : 500-kV 2-bundle conductor S/C line. Middle : 230-kV S/C horizontal line. Far right : 132-kV S/C line.

$a_s$ = a surface effect constant for nucleon on the surface of the liquid drop with no neighbours

$a_c$ = a coulomb repulsion term ($A^{1/3} \propto R$)

$a_{sym}$ = a constant that takes into account the result of making the nucleus stable by symmetry

and $\delta$ = an energy term denoting the coupling or pairing of like nucleons into a stable configuration

$= +a_p A^{-3/4}$ for $Z$ and $N$ even

$= -a_p A^{-3/4}$ for $Z$ and $N$ odd

$= 0$ for $A$ odd.

The best values for the constants in MeV obtained through experiments are as follows:

$$a_v = 15.5;\ a_s = 16.8;\ a_c = 0.72;\ a_{sym} = 23;\ \text{and } a_p = 34.$$

***Example 2.5***: In Example 2.1, the value of ($B/A$) was obtained as 7.39 MeV/nucleon. Compare this with value obtained from Eq. (2.7).

***Solution***: $A = 235,\ Z = 92,\ \delta = 0.$

$$B = 15.5 \times 235 - 16.8 \times 235^{2/3} - 0.72 \times 92 \times 91 \times 235^{-1/3}$$

$$- 23\,(235 - 2 \times 92)^2 / 235 + 0$$

$$= 1780.351 \text{ MeV}.$$

Therefore $B/A = 1780.351/235 = 7.576$ MeV/nucleon as compared to 7.39 MeV.

For nucleii with $N/Z > 1$, the $BE$ per nucleon is lower than when $N/Z = 1$.

## 2.4 Force Between Nucleons

***Example 2.6***: Calculate the coulomb repulsive force between two protons separated by 2 *fm* according to the inverse square law of electrostatic repulsion.

***Solution***: Charge of proton $q_p = 1.602 \times 10^{-19}$ $C$, separation $r = 2 \times 10^{-15}$ $m$, $4\pi\varepsilon_0 = 10^{-9}/9$, Farad/m.

Therefore $F_{p-p} = 1.602^2 \times 10^{-38} \times 9/(10^{-9} \times 2^2 \times 10^{-30})$

$$= 57.75 \text{ Newtons}$$

Notice that at long distances of the order of atomic dimensions of $10^{-10}$ m, the electrostatic force is extremely small. Prior to the detailed discovery of meson forces, it was theorized that nuclear forces inside the nucleus followed the relation

$F \propto 1/r^5$. According to this law the force of repulsion between two protons would be ($8 \times 10^{45}$) times the above-calculated value of 57.75 Newtons. But now the presence of a strong interaction through meson interaction explains nuclear forces. The following are few properties of nucleon-nucleon forces:

(1) At short distances inside the nuclear size (about 5 fm), the nuclear force is stronger than the coulomb force by a factor of $10^4$.

(2) At long distances of atomic size (about $10^{-10}$ m) nuclear forces are extremely weak.

(3) Electrons and neutrinos (leptons) do not experience nuclear forces. They take part in weak interactions which are $10^{-15}$ times the strong nuclear forces and $10^{-11}$ times the coulomb force or the electromagnetic forces.

(4) The strong nuclear force is nearly independent of the electric charge of the nucleon. This means that it is the same between *P* - *N*, *P* - *P*, and *N* - *N*. This is explained by the exchange-force model.

(5) The nucleon - nucleon force depends on spin orientation of the two particles. The pair with spins having the same direction experience a larger force than those whose spins are opposite.

(6) The nuclear force is attractive between nucleons, but in order to preserve the identity of particles in the same nucleus, there is a repulsive force which keeps the nucleons at a certain average distance apart.

## 2.5 Exchange Force Model

Forces in nature are now explained in terms of exchange of virtual particles. This idea has its origin in explaining the strong nuclear forces based on Heisenberg's Uncertainty Principle. The evidence for exchange force between nucleons comes from two observed facts: (1) the saturation in binding energy per nucleon or the nearly constant value of ($B/A$); and (2) nearly constant nuclear density or nearly constant value of ($A/R^3$), i.e $R \propto A^{1/3}$

The development of concept of force itself has undergone the following changes:

(a) In early development of classical physics prior to the introduction of the field concept, objects were said to interact by ''action at a distance''.

(b) Maxwell explained this as being through fields and showed that these fields themselves are transmitted through space with a finite velocity.

(c) When quantum mechanics took over the field of atomic and nuclear forces, it was postulated that all interactions must occur in discrete multiples of *h*, Planck's constant. In order to describe the quantized action, the field must also be quantized. Instead of the first object setting up a continuous field with which the second particle interacts, in quantum mechanics the field quanta were postulated to be emitted from the first particle which was absorbed by the second. Then the second particle re-emitted back to the first object.

For the nucleon-nucleon interaction, the exchanged particles are the pi-mesons or pions with masses of 135 MeV for $\pi^0$ and 140 MeV for $\pm\pi$. These are involved in the following reactions:

$$n \rightarrow n + \pi^0, p \rightarrow p + \pi^0, n \rightarrow p + \pi^-, p \rightarrow n + \pi^+.$$

In these reactions, charge conservation demands that there exist three types of exchange particles with electric charges +1, –1, and 0. However, on the surface it appears that energy is not conserved, since the difference in energy between neutron and proton is only 1.3 MeV and 0 between nucleons of the same type. But the exchange particle has much more energy. This is explained by the Uncertainty Principle and its consequences.

The energy that is thought to be conserved must be capable of being measured. But if the time taken for measurement $\Delta t$ is finite, then the uncertainty in measurement of energy is $\Delta E \approx \hbar / \Delta t$. If the exchange particle moves from one nucleon to another over a distance of 1 fm = $10^{-15}$m at light velocity, then $\Delta t = 10^{-15} / 3 \times 10^8 = 0.333 \times 10^{-23}\, s$. Therefore, the uncertainty in energy amounts to nearly $\Delta E = 1.0546 \times 10^{-34} / 0.333 \times 10^{-23} = 3.16 \times 10^{-11}\, J = 200$ MeV. The pi-mesons have energies of this order. The exchange particles exist for such a short instant of time that there is no way of measuring and verifying that the energy-conservation law is violated. During the exchange, the particles exist as virtual particles and have no real existence, although they have all the properties of real-life particles.

## 2.6 Nuclear Models

From known measured properties of nucleons, models have been developed from time to time not only to explain these properties but also to predict further behaviour in order to guide future experiments. Thus it is that there developed several models which are: (1) Liquid drop model of Bohr; (2) Fermi gas model; (3) Shell model; (4) Collective model for even-even nucleii; and (5) Unified nuclear model.

We will only describe the shell model, although it may be mentioned that the liquid drop model explains binding energy equation (2.7) and nuclear fission of a heavy nucleus into lighter nucleii. Nuclear shell model follows atomic shell model in principle, differing in the size of dimensions involved by a factor of $10^5$. Electron orbits in an atom are of the order of $10^{-10}$ m (= 1 Å), while nucleons exist in spaces of the order of $10^{-15}$ m (1 fm).

Neutrons and protons are spin-½ particles and are fermions. Therefore they obey the Pauli Exclusion Principle like electrons. Also, at the neutron number N = 126, a very sudden increase in energy of emitted α-particle was observed in the α-decay of the nucleus, which indicated that there exists a mechanism by which sudden transitions could occur in the nucleus. Figure 2.5 shows the arrangement of nucleons in subshells and filled shells. Completed shells have the following nucleon numbers (Z or N) which are known as Magic Numbers:

2, 8, 20, (28), 50, 82, 126, 184.

**Fig. 2.5** Nucleon arrangement in subshells and shells, showing magic numbers

The last two refer to neutrons only. Some nucleii have double magic numbers: e.g. ${}^{4}_{2}He_2$, ${}^{16}_{8}O_8$, ${}^{40}_{20}Ca_{20}$, ${}^{56}_{28}Ni_{28}$.

Proton shells are filled by totals of 2, 8, 20, 50, 82. Neutron shells have totals of 2, 8, 20, 50, 82, 126. The number 28 is known as semi-magic.

Nucleii with these numbers of protons or neutrons exhibit exceptionally high nuclear stabilty having high binding energy per nucleon (B/A value). Abundance of elements also shows that these have magic-numbered nucleii, as for example:

$${}^{90}_{40}Zr_{50}, {}^{112-124}_{50}Sn, {}^{138}_{56}Ba_{82}, {}^{204-208}_{82}Pb.$$

Magic-numbered nucleii exhibit a large number of isotopes. These nucleii have very low probability of capturing extra neutron and reacting with it, which is very essential for nuclear power. For heavier nucleii, $N/Z > 1$ in order for nucleons to overcome the force of electrostatic repulsion between protons. Nucleii with $Z > 92$ have high instability and are radioactive.

In analogy with an atom with valence electrons, isotopes possessing extra nucleons beyond the magic numbers in unfilled subshells also exhibit properties which are governed by the valence nucleons. For example ${}^{17}_{8}O_9$ which is an excited state of stable ${}^{16}_{8}O_8$. An isotope such as ${}^{43}_{20}Ca_{23}$ consists of a magic number in protons, a filled shell of 20 neutrons, a filled subshell of 2 nucleons plus an additional nucleon. Most of its properties are due to this valence nucleon.

## 2.7 Nuclear Reactions and Cross-Sections

In nuclear reactors and nuclear power generation, we shall be mostly concerned with interaction of neutrons with the nucleus. In the theory called the compound-nucleus theory, the neutron is first captured by the target nucleus forming an excited state, which exhibits a lifetime of about $10^{-14}$ s. This is $10^7$ times greater than the time taken for a neutron with 1 MeV energy to travel a nuclear diameter of about 10 fm. The excitation energy is equal to the binding energy BE of the compound nucleus. The maximum probability of capture corresponds to one of the allowed energy levels in the nucleus and is known as resonance. The probability of capture and chain reaction is described through the cross section for the phenomenon, called the reaction cross-section.

There are several types of reactions which can be described by the following general equations:

(1) *Elastic Scattering*: ${}_{Z}^{A}X_{N} + n \rightarrow {}_{Z}^{A}X_{N} + n$

There is no change in either the identity of the target nucleus or its internal energy. This takes place only if the neutron produces resonance with one of the intrinsic energy levels present in the target nucleus.

(2) *Excitation*: ${}_{Z}^{A}X_{N} + n \rightarrow {}_{Z}^{A}X_{N}^{*} + n$; ${}_{Z}^{A}X_{N}^{*} \rightarrow {}_{Z}^{A}X_{N} + \gamma$-emission

Here, the neutron energy is equal to the threshold energy for excitation and is a case of inelastic scattering. In elastic scattering, the neutron can have any energy.

(3) *Neutron Capture Reactions*

(a) *γ-radiation*: ${}_{Z}^{A}X_{N} + n \rightarrow {}_{Z}^{A+1}X_{N+1} + \gamma$

The nucleus produced is due to radiative capture and is frequently radioactive.

(b) *Proton-Release*: ${}_{Z}^{A}X_{N} + n \rightarrow {}_{Z-1}^{A}X_{N} + p + \beta^{-}$

Here, the neutron releases a proton accompanied by $\beta^{-}$ (or electron) emission.

(c) *α-emission*: ${}_{Z}^{A}X_{N} + n \rightarrow {}_{Z-2}^{A-3}X_{N-1} + {}_{2}^{4}\alpha$

(d) *Neutron Production* (for Chain Reaction):

$$ {}_{Z}^{A}X_{N} + n \rightarrow {}_{Z}^{A-1}X_{N-1} + 2n $$

This is the most important process of neutron capture and release for nuclear fission leading to a chain reaction which can be sustained under favourable conditions. However, the above is not a fission reaction, since the nucleii on both sides belong to the same element. A typical reaction of the type depicted above is

${}^{9}_{4}Be_5 + n \rightarrow {}^{8}_{4}Be_4 + 2n$. The presence of beryllium in a reactor can generate many neutrons.

*Reaction Cross-Section*

It will be shown that larger the cross-section the greater is the probabilty that such a reaction will occur. We will derive this relation. The reaction cross-section is defined as follows, when neutrons strike a target nucleus:

$$\sigma = \frac{\text{reaction rate per second per unit area of target}}{\begin{pmatrix}\text{nucleii per unit}\\ \text{area of target}\end{pmatrix} \times \begin{pmatrix}\text{number of neutrons striking}\\ \text{unit area of target per second}\end{pmatrix}} \tag{2.8}$$

The unit for cross-section is the barn, b: 1 barn = $10^{-24}$ $cm^2$. $\sigma$ is called the microscopic cross-section. The relation (2.8) is derived as follows:

Figure 2.6 shows a neutron beam of velocity $v$ striking a target of thickness $t$. We consider unit area of the beam, and a density of $n$ neutrons per unit volume of the beam. Then, number of neutrons striking unit area of the target per second, also called the neutron flux, is $(nv)$.

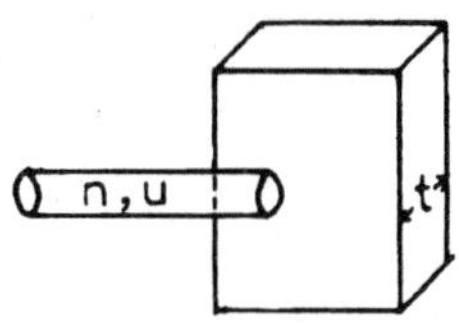


**Fig. 2.6** Reaction cross-section calculation

If $N$ = number of nucleii in target material per unit area, then the number of nucleii per unit area of target = $N.t$, because the volume of unit area of the target material is $t \times 1$.

We define the reaction cross-section for any type of nuclear reaction listed before through the number of reactions taking place per second or the reaction rate per unit area of the target, thus:

$$R = \sigma \cdot (N\,t) \cdot (n\,v) \tag{2.9}$$

From this follows Eq. (2.8). We observe that

$(R/nv)$ = probability that the incident neutrons will react with one nucleus of the target material, and

$\sigma\,(Nt)$ = $\sigma \times$ total number of nucleii per unit area of target.

Thus the cross-section $\sigma$ may be visualized as the target area presented by each nucleus to the incoming neutron beam. Its dimension is

$$[1/\text{sec-cm}^2]/[(1/\text{cm}^2) \times (1/\text{sec-cm}^2)] = \text{cm}^2 \text{ (or m}^2) \tag{2.10}$$

Note the absence of neutron-beam velocity.

The value of $(N\sigma)$ is known as the macroscopic cross-section and denoted by $\Sigma$.

Now, if $\rho$ = density of target material in gm/cc

$A$ = atomic mass

and $N_A$ = Avagadro's number = $0.6022 \times 10^{24}$ atom/mole

then A grams of target material contains $N_A$ nucleii. Therefore number of nucleii per $cm^3$,

$$N = \rho N_A / A \tag{2 11}$$

Therefore $$\Sigma = \sigma \cdot \rho N_A / A, \text{ cm}^{-1} \tag{2.12}$$

Figure 2.7 shows cross-section for absorption for $^{235}U$ and $^{238}U$ as a function of neutron energy. This is of primary interest in fission mechanism.

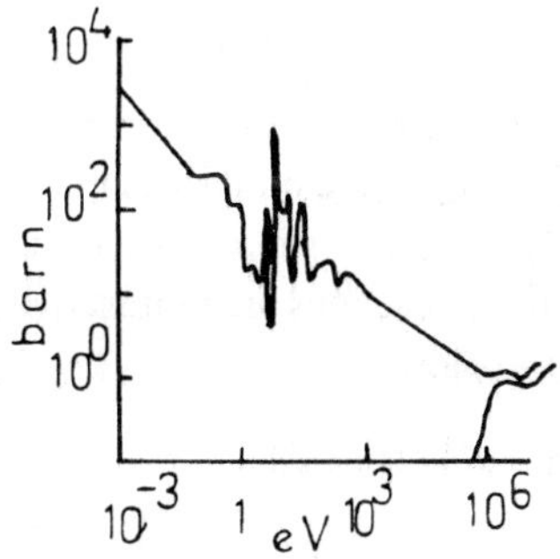


**Fig. 2.7** Fission cross-sections in U-235 and U-238 as a function of neutron energy showing resonance region

***Example 2.7***: In a nuclear reactor using graphite as moderator, there exists a uniform mixture of $^{12}C$ and $^{235}U$ with a ratio of 1000/1. The microscopic absorption cross-sections for neutrons of a certain energy are $\sigma_C = 0.003$ and $\sigma_U = 680$ barns. Calculate the macroscopic absorption cross-section of this mixture. The densities of the two materials are $\rho_C = 1.6$ gm/cc and $\rho_U = 19$ gm/cc.

***Solution***: We first calculate the number of nuclides per cc.

$$N_C = \rho_C N_A / A_C = 1.6 \times 0.6022 \times 10^{24} / 12 = 0.08 \times 10^{24}.$$

$$N_U = 10^{-3} N_C = 0.08 \times 10^{21}. \text{ (Note that } \rho_U / \rho_C = A_U / A_C).$$

Therefore $$\Sigma_C = \rho_C N_C = 0.003 \times 10^{-24} \times 0.08 \times 10^{24} = 24 \times 10^{-5} \text{ cm}^{-1}$$

$$\Sigma_U = 680 \times 10^{-24} \times 0.08 \times 10^{21} = 5.44 \times 10^{-2} \text{ cm}^{-1}.$$

Therefore total $\Sigma_a = \Sigma_C + \Sigma_U = 5.464 \times 10^{-2}$ cm$^{-1}$

Note that in spite of the large number of carbon atoms, the reaction takes place almost entirely with uranium atoms.

*Mean Free Path*

The mean free path $\lambda$ is defined as the average distance travelled by neutron between two successive interactions and is the reciprocal of the macroscopic cross section $\Sigma$. Thus

$$\lambda = 1/\Sigma, \text{ cm (or m)} \tag{2.13}$$

Thus, larger the cross-section the shorter the neutron has to travel between reactions and greater the probability of reaction in unit time.

## 2.8 Nuclear Decay Processes $\alpha$, $\beta$, $\gamma$

Nuclear decay processes are alpha ($\alpha$), beta ($\beta^{\pm}$) and gamma ($\gamma$). $\alpha$ ($^4_2He$) and $\beta^{\pm}$(positron + or electron –) particles are emitted from unstable nucleii and become other stable nucleii, while $\gamma$-rays are emitted when a nucleus in an excited state reaches the ground state. $\gamma$-rays have shorter wavelengths than visible light and X-rays (see sec. 1.3). All these reactions are radioactive. An example of decay in a nuclear reactor is depicted below:

$$^{235}_{92}U + n \rightarrow\ ^{140}_{56}Ba + ^{96}_{36}Kr$$

$$^{140}_{56}Ba \xrightarrow{\beta^-}\ ^{140}_{57}La \xrightarrow{\beta^-}\ ^{140}_{58}Ce\ ;\ ^{96}_{36}Kr \rightarrow\ ^{94}_{36}Kr + 2n$$

$$^{94}_{36}Kr \xrightarrow{\beta^-}\ ^{94}_{37}Rb \xrightarrow{\beta^-}\ ^{94}_{38}Sr \xrightarrow{\beta^-}\ ^{94}_{39}Y \xrightarrow{\beta^-}\ ^{94}_{40}Zr$$

The daughter elements stabilize to $^{140}_{58}Ce$ and $^{94}_{40}Zr$ (cerium and zirconium). Other examples are:

$$^{27}_{13}Al + n \rightarrow\ ^{24}_{11}Na + ^{4}_{2}\alpha\ ;\ ^{235}_{92}U \rightarrow\ ^{231}_{90}Th + ^{4}_{2}\alpha$$

$$^{131}_{53}I \xrightarrow{\beta^-}\ ^{131}_{54}Xe$$

Emission of $\alpha$ or $\beta$ particle is frequently (but not always) followed by the emission of high-energy photon radiation $\gamma$-ray.

***Example 2.8:*** Calculate the energy release in the reaction for $^{235}_{92}U + n \rightarrow\ ^{140}_{58}Ce + ^{94}_{40}Zr + 2n + 6\,\beta^-$ emissions, given the following masses (in atomic mass units u = 931.5 MeV):

$^{235}U = 234.993454$, $^{140}Ce = 139.873623$, $^{94}Zr = 93.884375$, $m_n = 1.008665$, and $m_e = 0.00054856$.

***Solution:*** $^{235}U + n = 236.002119$

$$^{140}Ce + ^{94}Zr + 2\,n + 6\,\beta^- = 235.77862$$

Therefore mass reduction = 0.2235 u = 0.2235 × 931.5 MeV = 208 MeV.

The decay of nucleii and emission of $\alpha$, $\beta$, $\gamma$ radiations affect the metabolic condition of all living cells and tissues causing harm or benefit (as in cancer therapy).

All these decay processes take some time called decay times, bringing in the concepts of mean decay time and half-lives. We consider these now. The actual mechanisms involved in $\alpha$, $\beta$, $\gamma$ decays are not discussed but form an extensive portion of nuclear physics.

*Radioactive Decay Law*

When we have a number N of radioactive nucleii and these decay, two points are involved: (a) it is impossible to predict which nucleus decays at what particular instant of time; (b) the number of decays in unit time is proportional to the number of nucleii present at time *t*. The first is known as the principle of absence of causality, which forms the very basis of quantum phenomena with each individual particle behaving in its own individual manner. But we are interested in their collective behaviour in so far as nuclear reactions are concerned.

If $N$ = number of radioactive nucleii present at time $t$, they decay according to the law

$$-dN/dt = \lambda \dot{N} \tag{2.14}$$

where $\lambda$ = disintegration or decay constant. This gives $dN/N = -\lambda t$, or, $\log N = -\lambda t + K$, giving $N = K_2 e^{-\lambda t}$. Consequently, if $N_0$ = number of nucleii at time t = 0 to begin with, then the number remaining at time t will be

$$N(t) = N_0 e^{-\lambda t} \tag{2.15}$$

*Activity, A*: This is the rate at which decays occur in a sample of nucleii.

Thus $\quad A = |dN/dt| = \lambda N e^{\lambda t} \quad$ (2.16)

Initially $\quad A_0 = |dN/dt|_{t=0} = \lambda N_0 \quad$ (2.17)

From Eq. (2.15), $\quad dN/dt = -\lambda N_0 e^{-\lambda t}$

Therefore $\quad A = |dN/dt| = \lambda N_0 e^{-\lambda t} = A_0 e^{-\lambda t} \quad$ (2.18)

Activity is measured in decays/second. Its SI unit is the Becquerel. The older unit was 1 Curie = $3.7 \times 10^{10}$ decays/sec or Becquerel, (Bq).

*Mean Lifetime (or Lifetime)* $\tau$

This is defined as the average time that a nucleus is likely to remain before it decays. This is an ensemble phenomenon and as mentioned earlier it is not possible to determine which nucleus decays at what particular instant $t$. Now, the number of nucleii decaying between $t$ and $(t + dt)$ in the interval $dt$ is $(dN/dt) \cdot dt$. The mean lifetime in seconds is

$$\tau = \frac{\int_0^\infty t \mid dN/dt \mid dt}{\int_0^\infty \mid dN/dt \mid dt} = \frac{\int_0^\infty \lambda N_0 \; t \; e^{-\lambda t} \; dt}{\int_0^\infty \lambda N_0 e^{-\lambda t} \; dt} \tag{2.19}$$

Now $$\int_0^\infty \lambda t e^{-\lambda t} \; dt = -(1/\lambda) e^{-\lambda t}(1+\lambda t)\Big|_0^\infty = 1/\lambda$$

and $$\int_0^\infty \lambda e^{-\lambda t} \; dt = -e^{-\lambda t}\Big|_0^\infty = 1$$

Therefore $\tau = 1/\lambda$ = reciprocal of decay constant (2.20)

*Half-Life,* $t_{0.5}$

If $N(½) = ½ N_0$, then $e^{-\lambda t_{0.5}} = 0.5$ ,then $\lambda \, t_{0.5} = \ln 2 = 0.693$

Therefore $t_{0.5} = 0.693/\lambda = 0.693 \, \tau$ (2.21)

Typical examples of half-lives are given below:

$^{226}_{88}Ra \xrightarrow{1600 \text{ yr}} {}^{222}_{86}Rn + {}^{4}_{2}\alpha$ of 4.8 MeV energy (Natural radioactivity).

$^{131}_{53}I \xrightarrow{6 \text{ days}} {}^{131}_{54}Xe + \beta^-$ (These are called poisons in a nuclear reactor).

$n \xrightarrow{10 \text{ min}} p + e^- + \bar{\nu}$ (Decay of free neutron into proton, electron and electron neutrino).

Some other decay times (half-lives) are:

$$^{212}Po \rightarrow 3 \times 10^{-7} \text{ s}; \; ^{232}Th \rightarrow 1.4 \times 10^{10} \text{ yr}$$

$$^{238}U \rightarrow 4.5 \times 10^{9} \text{ yr}; \; ^{60}Co \rightarrow 5.2 \text{ yr}$$

Because of very long lifetimes, radioactive materials pose grave danger. On the other hand, it is because of the long life of $^{60}Co$ that it has therapeutical value in cancer treatment.

***Example 2.9***: A mass of $^{60}Co$ has an activity $A = 5.55 \times 10^7 \; Bq$ = 1.5 mCi (milli Curie); $t_{0.5}$ of Co = 5.2 yr. Calculate the mass of the sample. Take $N_A = 0.6 \times 10^{24}$ atom/mole.

***Solution***: 60 g of $^{60}C$ contain $0.6 \times 10^{24}$ atoms.

Now, $t_{0.5} = 0.693/\lambda$ and $A_0 = \lambda N_0$, or, $1/\lambda = N_0/A_0$

Therefore $t_{0.5} = 0.693 \, N_0/A_0$ giving $N_0 = A_0 \, t_{0.5}/0.693$

or $N_0 = 5.55 \times 10^7 \times (5.2 \times 365 \times 24 \times 60 \times 60)/0.693$

$= 1.3133 \times 10^{16}$ nucleii.

And therefore mass $= 1.3133 \times 10^{16} \times 60/0.6 \times 10^{24} = 1.3133 \times 10^{-6}$ g.

## 2.9 Radiation Measures

Since radiation effects are extremely important, quantitative aspects will be discussed now. Damaging or beneficial effects of radiation depend on the type of nucleus radiating and not entirely on the radiation rate in Bq or Ci. Damage to tissue depends on the electric charge per unit mass deposited in coulomb/kg.

Consider 1 cc of air at 0°C and 760 mm-Hg, whose mass is $1.293 \times 10^{-3}$ g. Therefore, volume of 1 kg of air = $10^6/1.293 = 0.7734 \times 10^6$ cc = $0.7734$ m$^3$.

The exposure is defined as X = Q/m, coulomb/kg. The unit of exposure is the Roentgen, which is defined as a charge of $0.333 \times 10^{-9}$ c in 1 cc of air. ($0.333 \times 10^{-9}$ c = 1 e.s.u. of charge).

Therefore $\quad 1 \text{ R} = 0.333 \times 10^{-9} \times 0.7734 \times 10^6$ c/kg

$\quad = 2.578 \times 10^{-4}$ c/kg of air.

We can calculate the number of ions (having a charge equal to an electronic charge) involved in 1 R. This is $2.578 \times 10^{-4}/1.602 \times 10^{-19} = 1.6086 \times 10^{15}$ ion/kg of air = $2.08 \times 10^9$ ion/cc.

***Example 2.10***: If it requires 30 eV to form an ion in air, calculate the energy in Joules per cc and per gram absorbed when the exposure is 1 R. (1 eV = $1.602 \times 10^{-19}$ J).

***Solution***: 1 R = $2.08 \times 10^9$ ion/cc.

Therefore energy $= 2.08 \times 10^9 \times 30$ eV/cc $= 62.4 \times 10^9$ eV/cc

$= 62.4 \times 1.602 \times 10^{-10}$ J/cc $= 10^{-8}$ J/cc $= 0.1$ erg/cc.

Since 1 g of air $= 0.7734 \times 10^3$ cc,

energy $= 77.34$ erg/g $= 7.734 \times 10^{-6}$ J/g.

Since the exposure is a function of the number of ions or nucleii, its rate is related to the activity $A$, the decay of the radioactive sample per second. The danger from exposure is also very much dependent on the distance between radioactive source and the ionization spot. The specific γ-ray exposure constant is defined as

$$\Gamma = (\Delta x / \Delta t) \cdot d^2/A \tag{2.22}$$

or, the rate of exposure is $\Delta x / \Delta t = \Gamma \cdot A/d^2$ (2.23)

Thus, larger the activity (rate of decay of nucleii) larger is the rate of exposure of the affected tissue. The unit for Γ is found as follows: Activity $A$ is in Ci, exposure X is in Roentgen. Therefore the unit of specific exposure constant Γ is (R/hr) · (m$^2$/Ci). As an example, for medical use of $^{60}$Co, with $t_{0.5}$ = 5.2 yr, for γ-ray energy of 1.3 MeV, Γ has the value of 1.28 at d = 1 m. Higher the energy of γ-ray emitted larger is the Γ value as measured in experiments.

*Roentgen Equivalent Man, REM*

Tissue damage is measured in terms of energy deposited by ionizing source per unit mass of the material. The radiation absorbed dose is the RAD.

1 RAD = energy absorption of 100 erg/g of material. The SI unit of RAD is the GRAY = 1 J/kg, (Gy).

Therefore 1 RAD = 100 erg/g = $10^{-5}$ J/$10^{-3}$ kg = $10^{-2}$ Gray, or 1 Gy = 100 RAD.

Different types of radiation ($\alpha$, $\beta$, $\gamma$) behave differently in causing damage. So a quality factor QF is introduced based on experiments, which is measured in Joule/metre distance. Average values of QF for absorbed radiation are as follows:

| | |
|---|---|
| X-, $\beta^-$, and $\gamma$ rays | — 1 |
| Low energy (~ keV) p, n | — 2 to 5 |
| High energy (~ MeV) p, n | — 5 to 10 |
| $\alpha$-particle | — 20 |

The REM is the dose equivalent which is the actual dose in Gray times the quality factor QF. The SI unit of REM is the SIEVERT (Sv). Thus 1 Sv = 100 REM, where 1 REM = 1 RAD × QF.

A typical chest X-ray gives a value of 0.05 REM. Nuclear bombs give in excess of 100 REM and results in sure death. Cosmic-ray radiation amounts to 0.1 to 0.2 REM/year. For radiation levels in public, a dose up to 0.5 REM/year is allowed to be absorbed while the limit for those who handle radioactive materials it is 5 REM/year.

## 2.10 Nuclear Data and Units

Some important and useful data for nuclear power production are given here. Table 2.3 gives characteristics of some important nucleii.

**Table 2.2: Particle Rest Masses and Constants**

| | Mass Equivalent (u) | Energy Equivalent (MeV) |
|---|---|---|
| Electron | $5.485803 \times 10^{-4}$ | 0.511003 |
| Proton | 1.00727647 | 938.28 |
| Neutron | 1.00866501 | 939.573 |
| Deuteron | 2.01355321 | 1875.628 |
| Alpha | 4.00150618 | 3727.409 |
| ± Pion | 0.14983 | 139.5669 |
| 0 Pion | 0.1449 | 134.9745 |
| μ-Meson | 0.1134292 | 105.6595 |

*Constants and Conversion Factors*

$1\ eV = 1.602189 \times 10^{-19}$ J, $1\ MeV = 1.602189 \times 10^{-13}$ J

$e = 1.602189 \times 10^{-19}$ c (coulomb)

$1\ u = 1.660566 \times 10^{-27}$ kg = 931.502 MeV/$c^2$ (c = velocity of light)

$c = 2.99792458 \times 10^8$ m/s. $c^2 = 8.98755 \times 10^{16}\ m^2/s^2$

$h = 6.62618 \times 10^{-34}$ J-s $= 4.1357 \times 10^{-15}$ eV-s

$\hbar = h/2\pi = 1.054589 \times 10^{-34}$ J-s $= 6.58217 \times 10^{-16}$ eV-s

$N_A = 6.022045 \times 10^{23}$ atom/mole

1 barn $= 10^{-28}\ m^2 = 10^{-24}\ cm^2$

1 Curie = 1 Ci = $3.7 \times 10^{10}$ decays/sec = $3.7 \times 10^{10}$ Bequerel (Bq)

1 Bq = 1 decay/s

1 fm $= 10^{-15}$ m $= 10^{-5}$ Å

1 fm/c $= 0.333 \times 10^{-24}$ s (nucleon transit time at light velocity)

1 cal = 4.2 J = 4.2 W-s; 1 k-cal = 4.2 kW-s.

## 2.11 Miscellaneous Worked Examples

*(1)* Calculate the density of $^{238}U$ nucleus in kg/m$^3$.

***Solution***: Radius $R = R_0 A^{1/3} = 1.2 \times 238^{1/3} = 7.436572$ fm.

Therefore volume $= 4\pi R^3/3 = 4\pi \times 1.2^3 \times 238/3 = 1722.6986\ fm^3$

Mass = 238 u $= 238 \times 1.660556 \times 10^{-27}$ kg $= 395.21471 \times 10^{-27}$ kg

Therefore density $= 395.21471 \times 10^{-27}/1722.6986 \times 10^{-45}$

$= 0.229416 \times 10^{18}\ kg/m^3$

(Density of water = 1 g/cc = 1000 kg/m$^3$ = 1 tonne/m$^3$)

*(2)* Calculate the number of nucleii in 1 gram of $^{235}U$.

***Solution***: 235 g contain $6.022045 \times 10^{23}$ atoms.

Therefore 1 g contains $2.5625723 \times 10^{21}$ atoms

*(3)* The energy release when 1 nucleus of $^{235}U$ fissions is 200 MeV. Calculate the energy released per gram of $^{235}U$.

***Solution***: Number of atoms/g $= 2.5625723 \times 10^{21}$

Therefore energy release $= 2.5625723 \times 10^{21} \times 200$ MeV

$= 8.2114503 \times 10^{10}\ J = 8.2114503 \times 10^4$ MW-s.

(1 MW-h = 60 × 60 MW-s = $3.6 \times 10^9$ J. 1 MW-d
= 24 MW-h = $8.64 \times 10^4$ MW-s)

Therefore energy release by 1 g of $^{235}$U in MW-d = 8.2114503/8.64
= 0.95 MW-d ≈ 1 MW-d.

*(4)* If coal fired in a thermal station has a calorific value of 6000 k-cal/kg, calculate the weight of coal required to generate the same energy as 1 g of $^{235}$U. (1 k-cal = $4.2 \times 10^3$ J).

***Solution***: Energy release from 1 kg of coal = $4.2 \times 10^3 \times 6000$ J
= $25.2 \times 10^6/8.64 \times 10^{10}$ MW-d = $2.91667 \times 10^{-4}$ MW-d

Therefore weight of coal = $0.95 \times 10^4/2.91667$ = 3257 kg = 3.257 tonne.

*(5)* A sample of $^{226}$Th has activity of A = $10^8$ Bq. Its half-life is $t_{0.5}$ = 30 min. Calculate the mass of sample, and the decay constant λ.

***Solution***: $\lambda = 0.693/t_{0.5} = 0.693/30 \times 60 = 0.385 \times 10^{-3}\ s^{-1}$

Now, A = λ N, or, N = A/λ = $10^8/0.385 \times 10^{-3} = 2.5974 \times 10^{11}$

226 g of $^{226}$Th contain $6.022045 \times 10^{23}$ atoms.

Therefore mass of sample = $2.5974 \times 10^{11} \times 226/6.022045 \times 10^{23}$
= $97.47735 \times 10^{-12}$ g.

(Note that N = A/λ = A $t_{0.5}$/0.693, so that for the same activity A (number of decays per sec), if the half-life is longer, it requires a larger mass of sample. Compare with Example 2.9).

*(6)* The mass of neutral atom of $^{27}_{13}$Al = 26.9815413u. Calculate the value of (B/A) = binding energy per nucleon.

***Solution***: Mass of 13 electrons = $13 \times 5.485803 \times 10^{-4}$ u
= 0.007131544 u.

Therefore mass of nucleus = 26.9744126 u, which is equal to the mass of atom – the mass of 13 orbiting electrons.

Now $13\ m_p + 14\ m_n$ = 27.21626 u. (13 × 1.00727647 + 14 × 1.00866501)

Therefore Δm = 0.241848 u = 225.28 MeV.

Consequently, B/A = 225.28/27 = 8.343756 MeV/nucleon.

*(7)* A beam of neutrons strikes a target of thickness of 0.1 mm. The atomic mass of sample is 10.8. If the cross-section is $\sigma_a$ = 200 b, calculate the fraction of the beam absorbed. Density of target material is 0.6 g/cc.

***Solution***: By definition

$$\sigma = \frac{\text{reaction rate per second per unit area of target}}{\begin{pmatrix}\text{nucleii per unit}\\ \text{area of target}\end{pmatrix} \times \begin{pmatrix}\text{number of neutrons striking}\\ \text{unit area of target/ sec}\end{pmatrix}}$$

Therefore $\sigma = R/[(Nt) \cdot (nv)]$

The fraction of beam absorbed = $R/nv = \sigma \cdot N\,t$

N = number of nucleii per cm$^3$ of target when $\sigma$ is in cm$^2$ and $t$ in cm.

Now, 1 cc of target material = 0.6 g, and 10.8 g contain $6.022045 \times 10^{23}$ nucleii.

Therefore 1 cc contains $N = 0.6\ N_A/10.8 = 3.34558 \times 10^{22}$ nucleii.

And $R/nv = 200 \times 10^{-24} \times 3.34558 \times 10^{22} \times 0.01 = 0.0669$.

Fraction of beam absorbed = 6.69%.

*(8)* Using Eq. (2.7), calculate (B/A) for $^{238}$U and compare with worked example 2.3. (7.569338 MeV/nucleon).

***Solution***: $B/A = 15.5 - 16.8 \times 238^{-1/3} - 0.72 \times 91 \times 92 \times 238^{-4/3} - 23\,(238 - 2 \times 92)^2 \times 238^{-2} + 34 \times 238^{-7/4}$

$= 15.5 - 2.71097 - 4.0869 - 1.184026 + 0.002$

$= 7.52046$ MeV/nucleon as compared to 7.569338 MeV/nucleon

**Table 2.3: Some Nuclear Data (Other than Th, U, Pu)**

| | A Mass, u | Half-Life | Abundance |
|---|---|---|---|
| *Hydrogen* | | | |
| Z = 1 | 1 1.007825 | | 99.985% |
| | 2 2.014102 | | 0.015% |
| | 3 3.016049 | 12.3 yr | |
| *Helium* | 3 3.016029 | | $1.34 \times 10^{-4}$% |
| Z = 2 | 4 4.002603 | | 99.99986% |
| *Beryllium* | A = 7 to 11 | | $^9$Be — 100% |
| Z = 3 | 7.016928 to 11.021658 | $0.07 \times 10^{-15}$ s to $1.6 \times 10^6$ yr | |
| *Boron* | A = 8 to 13 | | |
| Z = 5 | 8.024606 to 13.017780 | $0.85 \times 10^{-6}$ s to 17.4 ms | $^{10}$B — 19.8%<br>$^{11}$B — 80.2% |
| *Carbon* | A = 9 to 15 | | |
| Z = 6 | 9.031039 to 15.010599 | 0.13 sec to 5730 yr | $^{12}$C — 98.89%<br>$^{13}$C — 1.11% |
| *Strontium* | A = 81 to 93 | | |
| Z = 38 | 80.923270 to 92.913987 | 22 min to 28.8 yr | $^{84}$Sr — 0.56%<br>$^{86}$Sr — 9.8%<br>$^{87}$Sr — 7%<br>$^{88}$Sr — 82.6% |

| | A Mass, u | Half-Life | Abundance |
|---|---|---|---|
| *Zirconium* | A = 87 to 98 | | |
| Z = 40 | 86.914817 to 97.912735 | 31 sec to $1.5 \times 10^6$ yr | $^{90}Zr$ — 51.5%<br>$^{91}Zr$ — 11.2%<br>$^{92}Zr$ — 17.1%<br>$^{94}Zr$ — 17.4%<br>$^{96}Zr$ — 2.8% |
| *Iodine* | A = 123 to 132 | | |
| Z = 53 | 122.905594 to 131.907987 | 25 min to $16 \times 10^6$ yr | $^{127}I$ — 100% |
| *Xenon* | A = 121 to 137 | | |
| Z = 54 | 120.911450 to 136.911557 | 3.82 min to 36.4 days | $^{124}Xe$ — 0.096%<br>$^{126}Xe$ — 0.09%<br>$^{128}Xe$ — 1.92%<br>$^{130}Xe$ — 4.1%<br>$^{131}Xe$ — 21.2%<br>$^{132}Xe$ — 26.9%<br>$^{134}Xe$ — 10.4%<br>$^{136}Xe$ — 8.9% |

## OBJECTIVE TYPE QUESTIONS

1. Isotopes have (a) same atomic numbers, (b) same number of protons, (c) same atomic masses, (d) both (a) and (b) are true.

2. Isotones have (a) same number of protons, (b) same number of neutrons, (c) same atomic masses, (d) none are true.

3. Isobars have (a) same number of protons, (b) same number of neutrons, (c) same atomic masses, (d) none are true.

4. Radioactivity is due to (a) odd number of neutrons in the nucleus, (b) even number of protons in the nucleus, (c) unpaired nucleons of the same type, (d) none of them are necessary.

5. The number of atoms in 235 g of $^{235}U$ is (a) same as in 233 g of $^{233}U$, (b) 239 g of $^{239}Pu$, (c) Avogadro's number, (d) all are true.

6. Using dimensional analysis, check which expression is valid for the radius of the first Bohr orbit. (a) $4 \pi \varepsilon_0 m / \hbar^2 e^2$, (b) $\hbar^2 e^2 / 4 \pi \varepsilon_0 m$, (c) $4 \pi \varepsilon_0 \hbar^2 / m e^2$, (d) none are true.

7. For $^{238}_{92}U$ the radius of nucleus is approximately (a) 5.4 fm, (b) 7.5 fm, (c) 7.5 Å, (d) 6.3 fm.

8. Which of the reaction(s) given is(are) valid? (a) $n \rightarrow n + \pi^-$, (b) $p \rightarrow n + \pi^\circ$, (c) $p \rightarrow n + \pi^+$, (d) $n \rightarrow n + \pi^\circ$.

9. Which of the sets or subsets given are magic numbers? (a) 2, 8, 18, 32; (b) 50, 82, 126; (c) 2, 8, 20, 50 ; (d) 2, 8, 20, 50, 82, 126.

10. Which reactions given are valid? (a) ${}^{A}_{Z}X_N + n \to {}^{A+1}_{Z}X_{N+1} + \gamma$, (b) ${}^{A}_{Z}X_N + n \to {}^{A}_{Z-1}X_N + p + \beta^-$, (c) ${}^{A}_{Z}X_N + n \to {}^{A-4}_{Z-2}X + {}^{4}_{2}\alpha$, (d) all are valid.

11. When a neutron hits an aluminium target (${}^{27}_{13}Al$), one product is ${}^{24}_{11}Na$. Which other product is given out first? (a) β-particle, (b) γ-radiation, (c) alpha particle, (d) none of the three.

12. Exposure to radioactivity is measured in (a) coulomb/kg of air, (b) ion/kg of air, (c) ion/cc of air, (d) Roentgen, (e) all four.

13. Tissue damage is measured in (a) energy per unit mass, (b) radiation absorbed dose RAD, (c) Gray, (d) all three.

14. Activity is measured in (a) decays per second, (b) Bequerel, (c) Curie, (d) all three.

**Answers:** 1. (b); 2. (b); 3. (c); 4. (c); 5. (d); 6. (c); 7. (b); 8. (c),(d); 9. (b),(c),(d); 10. (d); 11. (c); 12. (e); 13. (d); 14. (d).

## REVIEW QUESTIONS AND PROBLEMS

1. From the atomic masses given in Table 2.1, calculate the mass defects for the following in MeV/nucleon:
(a) Thorium - 231, 233; (b) Uranium - 233, 238, 239; (c) Plutonium 239, 243.
${}^{231}Th$ : 1.84035 $u$, 1714 MeV, 7.42117 MeV/nucleon;
${}^{233}Th$ : 1.852405 $u$, 1725.519 MeV, 7.405661 MeV/nucleon;
${}^{233}U$ : 1.85153 $u$, 1724.7039 MeV, 7.4021627 MeV/nucleon;
${}^{238}U$ : 1.883697 $u$, 1754.6675 MeV, 7.3725526 MeV/nucleon;
${}^{239}U$ : 1.88886 $u$, 1759.4769 MeV, 7.361828 MeV/nucleon;
${}^{239}Pu$ : 1.888272 $u$, 1758.89 MeV, 7.35937 MeV/nucleon;
${}^{243}Pu$ : 1.913092 $u$, 1782.049 MeV, 7.333535 MeV/nucleon.

[From the above figures, note that for the same element, (a) m and MeV increase with A, (b) MeV/nucleon decrease with A].

2. (a) Show that the density of nucleus is $(Z\,m_p + N\,m_n)/4\,\pi\,R_0^3\,A/3$

$$= \frac{10^{-27}}{4.1888\,R_0^3}\left(1.6726491 + \frac{N}{A} \times 0.002306\right),\ \text{kg}/\text{m}^3$$

(b) Calculate the approximate nuclear radii R, density in kg/m$^3$, and specific gravity, taking $R_0 = 1.2$ fm.
(a) ${}^{1}_{1}H$; (b) ${}^{4}_{2}He$; (c) ${}^{27}_{13}Al$; (d) ${}^{140}_{58}Ce$; (e) ${}^{243}_{94}Pu$ .

[$\rho = 0.2311 \times 10^{18}$; $0.2312 \times 10^{18}$; $0.23125 \times 10^{18}$; $0.231272 \times 10^{18}$; $0.23128 \times 10^{18}$.

Sp. Gr. = $0.2311 \times 10^{15}$; $0.2312 \times 10^{15}$; $0.23125 \times 10^{15}$; $0.231272 \times 10^{15}$; $0.23128 \times 10^{15}$.

Note that the densities differ from that of hydrogen ($^1_1H$) by the small factor $N\,(m_n - m_p) \times 10^{27} / (4\,\pi\,R_0^3\,A/3)$, $kg/m^3$]

3. (a) Show that the average charge density of a nucleus is
$\delta = 0.3825 \times 10^{-19}\ Z/A\,R_0^3$.

(b) For the above 5 isotopes in Problem 2, calculate the charge density in coulomb/fm$^3$.

[$^1_1H$ : $0.22135 \times 10^{-19}$; $^4_2He$ : $0.110675 \times 10^{-19}$; $^{27}_{13}Al$ : $0.106576 \times 10^{-19}$; $^{140}_{58}Ce$ : $0.0917 \times 10^{-19}$; $^{243}_{94}Pu$ : $0.0856255 \times 10^{-19}$ coul/fm$^3$]

4. Using the empirical relation, Eq. (2.7), for the binding energy B, calculate (B/A) for the isotopes given in Problem 1. Compare the two values.

[$^{231}_{90}Th$ : 7.5719 against 7.42117; $^{233}_{90}Th$ : 7.55749 – 7.405661;

$^{233}_{92}U$ : 7.548552 – 7.402163; $^{238}_{92}U$ : 7.5198 – 7.3726;

$^{239}_{92}U$ : 7.51 – 7.362; $^{239}_{94}Pu$ :7.5–7.36; $^{243}_{94}Pu$:7.4384–7.333.]

5. Describe the exchange force model for nucleons and the discovery of $\pi$-mesons.

6. Referring to tables of isotopes and the Periodic Table, give 4 elements possessing magic numbers, and 2 elements with double magic numbers. Specify their numbers of protons, neutrons and atomic masses.

[Proton numbers: 2, 8, 20, 50, 82.
Neutron numbers: 2, 8, 20, (28), 50, 82, 126, 184.

Magic: He, O, Ca, Sn, Pb. Double: He, O, Ca, Ni. Also, $^{48}_{20}Ca_{28}$, and $^{208}_{82}Pb_{126}$]

7. Two radioactive sources have an initial activity of 5 μCi at $t = 0$, with half-lives of 1 day and 1 year.

(a) Calculate the number of radioactive nucleii present at $t = 0$.

(b) How many nucleii decay between 6 hr and 12 hr for the first and between 3 month and 6 month for the second from their initial values? Give in %.

[(a) $N_1(0) = 18.5 \times 10^4 \times 24 \times 3600/0.693 = 2.3065 \times 10^{10}$;
$N_2(0) = 8.4187 \times 10^{12}$.

(b) At 6 hr : $N_1 = 1.94 \times 10^{10}$; at 12 hr : $N_1 = 1.631 \times 10^{10} \cdot 13.4\%$.
At 3 months: $N_2 = 7.0793 \times 10^{12}$, at 6 m: $N_2 = 5.953 \times 10^{12} \cdot 13.4\%$.]

8. (a) Prove that $N = N_0 \cdot 2^{-n}$, and $N_0 = A_0 \cdot t_{0.5}/0.693$ for the decay of radioactive nucleii, where $N_0$ = initial number of nucleii present, and $N$ = number present after $n$ half-lives ($t_{0.5}$ = half-life).

(b) The activity of radioactive Carbon-14 in a sample is 15,000 Bq, when the amount of $^{14}C$ measured in a sample of bone is 25% of that in a similar bone specimen just removed from an animal. Determine:

(i) The age of the bone if half-life $t_{0.5}$ of $^{14}C$ is 5,730 years.

(ii) The initial number of nucleii in the sample.

[11,460 years. $N_0 = 1.5645 \times 10^{16}$; $N = 0.3911 \times 10^{16}$ nucleii.]

## II. NUCLEAR FISSION AND NUCLEAR REACTORS

Conversion of energy from nuclear sources can be achieved through fission of heavy nucleii into light ones, or by fusing very light nucleii into heavy ones. We will discuss here the fission mechanism only which has been achieved in a very big way in the past five decades. The latter mechanism, namely, nuclear fusion power, will be discussed in chapter 4.

The following topics will be discussed here: (a) Nuclear fission mechanism; (b) Neutron energy; (c) Types of nuclear reactors and their description; (d) Fast reactors and breeding.

### 2.12 Introduction

Generation and control of nuclear energy through fission depends upon: (a) Nuclear fission; (b) Chain reaction; (c) Moderation (in thermal reactors utilizing slow neutrons); (d) Control of reaction rate and heat produced by neutron-absorbing materials; (e) Exchange of kinetic energy of daughter nucleii and other energetic fission products into heat in a coolant; (f) Breeding of fuel in breeder reactors or converters; (g) Conventional turbine-generator (steam turbine or gas turbine); (h) Radiation shielding; and (i) Safety and emergency procedures in the event of accidents.

The last item has become the governing factor in installation and operation of a nuclear reactor. Although this is an engineering subject, it has become more of a socio-economic and environmental topic involving regional, national and international interest and concerned organizations. A brief review of environmental aspects and accidents will be discussed in the last chapter of this book. Many nuclear power stations which had already been constructed have been unable to commence operation and have been moth-balled and become museum pieces. In many cases, licences for locating nuclear power stations have either not been sanctioned or withdrawn by pressure brought to bear upon regulating bodies by environmental groups.

However, even with all these constraints and objections, nuclear power is still depended upon to supply a minor or major fraction of a country's electric power or total energy consumption. France's nuclear power programme, especially with the development of breeder reactors, amounts to 40% of the total national power consumption. In contrast, all nuclear power stations in southern Sweden never got off the ground, as also several in the USA.

### 2.13 Nuclear Fission

Because of nuclear instability, heavy nuclei with odd number of nucleons readily split into fragments when bombarded by neutrons with the required energy. The neutron is selected because certain nuclear fission mechanisms or reactions give rise to more neutrons as a result of the fission, which in turn cause fission of the fuel nucleii. This sets up a chain reaction which is sustained until stopped by inserting materials with high neutron-capturing property. Typical of such neutron-induced fission processes important for nuclear power generation is the following:

$$^{235}U + n\ (0.025\ eV) \rightarrow\ ^{93}Rb +\ ^{141}Cs + 2n\ (1\ MeV) + (\approx)\ 200\ MeV \quad (2.24)$$

The neutrons released in this fission reaction are called prompt or instantaneous neutrons. One of the released neutrons is capable of inducing a further fission process, even if the other is absorbed by components other than the fuel in the reactor, such as the moderator, shield, etc. Normally, more than 1 neutron is absorbed, so that it requires more than 2 neutrons to sustain a chain reaction. The neutron emission in this process is from the nucleii of fission fragments or daughter nucleii which have odd number of nucleons. Note that the fission fragments have a mass unit ratio of 141/93 = 1.516. This is characteristic of fission by slow neutrons. But in fast-neutron-induced fission, the product nucleii have nearly equal masses.

In becoming more stable nucleii, $^{93}Rb$ sheds 5 neutrons to have a Z/A ratio of 0.41, $^{141}Cs$ sheds 3 neutrons. Therefore, in general, more than 2 neutrons are available. The following are typical examples of average number of neutrons available in fission reactions involving fissile isotopes:

$$^{233}U \rightarrow 2.48;\ ^{235}U \rightarrow 2\ 42;\ ^{239}Pu \rightarrow 2.86$$

In Eq. (2.24), the daughter nucleii $^{93}Rb$ and $^{141}Cs$ are radioactive and the further decay process leads to $^{93}Zr$ and $^{141}Ce$ which accumulate in the core of the reactor, thereby slowing down nuclear fission rate with time. A nuclear reactor is fuelled with fertile materials ($^{238}U$, $^{232}Th$) and fissile materials ($^{239}Pu$, $^{233}U$, $^{235}U$, etc.) once in 3-4 years, after removing the radioactive wastes. These decay processes are as follows, involving $\beta^-$ decay in all cases:

$$^{93}_{37}Rb \xrightarrow{6\,s}\ ^{93}_{38}Sr \xrightarrow{7\,m}\ ^{93}_{39}Y \xrightarrow{10\,h}\ ^{93}_{40}Zr \xrightarrow{10^6\,y}\ ^{93}_{41}Nb \quad (2.25)$$

$$^{141}_{53}Cs \xrightarrow{25\,s}\ ^{141}_{54}Ba \xrightarrow{18\,m}\ ^{141}_{55}La \xrightarrow{4\,h}\ ^{141}_{56}Ce \xrightarrow{33\,d}\ ^{141}_{57}Pr \quad (2.26)$$

The decay products form the nuclear wastes and are radioactive. Many of these decay rapidly in the reactor itself, but other long-lived isotopes have to be removed and stored in safe places (such as the proposed dumping grounds on the moon!).

***Example 2.11***: In the fission reaction of Eq. (2.24), calculate the energy release.

***Solution***: $^{235}U + n\ (\rightarrow\ ^{236}U^*) \rightarrow\ ^{93}Rb +\ ^{141}Cs + 2\ n$

*Atomic masses* $m(^{235}U + n) = 236.052589\ u$

$$m(^{93}Rb +\ ^{141}Cs + 2\ n) = (92.9211172 + 140.91949 + 2 \times 1.008665)\ u$$

$$= 235.85851\ u$$

Therefore $\Delta m = 0.194079$ u and energy $= \Delta m \times 931.502 = 181$ MeV.

Note that the binding energy of $^{235}U$ nucleus is about 1762 MeV or 7.5 MeV/ nucleon. This is released in the products as kinetic energy and energy in neutron. We consider this later.

Experiments show that the products carry the following % energies:

| | |
|---|---|
| Kinetic energy of fragment nucleii | 82.5%; |
| β-decays from radioactive nucleii | 9%; |
| γ-rays | 7.5%; |
| Prompt-neutron energy | 1%. |

Furthermore, neutrinos released from β-decays carry 65% of the β-decay energy, which is lost from the reactor. The rest is available for power production as useful heat in coolants and heat exchangers to raise steam.

In addition to prompt neutrons released in $10^{-14}$ sec, some neutrons from the daughter nucleii are also released after about 1 second. These are called ''delayed neutrons'', which increases the neutron yield to preserve the chain reaction. They are also useful for generating heat.

Reactions occurring in breeders or converters involve fertile $^{238}U$ transformed into fissile $^{239}Pu$, and $^{232}Th$ into $^{233}U$, according to the following sequences:

$$^{238}U + n \longrightarrow {}^{239}U \xrightarrow{23\,m} {}^{239}Np + \beta^- + \nu^- \xrightarrow{2.3\,d} {}^{239}Pu + \beta^- + \nu^- \tag{2.27}$$

$$^{232}Th + n \longrightarrow {}^{233}Th \xrightarrow{22\,m} {}^{233}Pa + \beta^- + \nu^- \xrightarrow{27\,d} {}^{233}U + \beta^- + \nu^- \tag{2.28}$$

Uranium-235 occurs in nature along with Uranium-238 in the ratio of 0.72% to 99.28%. Also see Table 2.1.

## 2.14 Neutron Energy and Fission Cross-Section

Figure 2.7 shows the fission cross-sections of $^{235}U$ and $^{238}U$ as a function of neutron energy. Typically for $^{235}U$, in the thermal region (< 1 eV) the cross-section shows (1/energy)-relation. In the energy range 1 to 100 eV, there are numerous resonances, these being the energy levels in the shell structure of the uranium nucleus. The thermal cross-section is nearly $10^3$ times the fast-neutron cross-section. Therefore, MeV-energy neutrons must be slowed down by a moderator. The lightest element is hydrogen, but because of its large absorption of neutrons, it is not used in reactors. Heavy water (deuterium) with a proton and a neutron in its nucleus is one of the best moderators. It occurs in sea water and can also be manufactured from light water.

For $^{238}$U fission occurs only with neutron energies of 1 MeV range. The difference between these two isotopes of uranium to fission lies in the pairing energy term δ in the binding-energy equation (2.5). For $^{238}$U, $\delta = a_p A^{-3/4}$ while $\delta = 0$ for $^{235}$U. Because of this, extra energy is required to fission $^{238}$U. Odd-N nucleii such as $^{235}_{92}U_{143}$ and $^{239}_{94}Pu_{145}$ have larger fission cross-sections than even-N nucleii, such as $^{238}_{92}U_{146}$ and $^{232}_{92}U_{140}$.

Some examples of cross-sections are given below with 1 b = 1 barn = $10^{-24}$ cm$^2$:

$^{229}_{90}Th_{139}$ — 1500 b; $^{230}_{90}Th_{140}$ — < 0.001 b;

$^{231}_{92}U_{139}$ — 300 to 600 b; $^{232}_{92}U_{140}$ — 75 b; $^{233}_{92}U_{141}$ — 530 b;

$^{234}_{92}U_{142}$ — < 0.005 b; $^{235}_{92}U_{143}$ — 584 b; $^{238}_{92}U_{146}$ — $3 \times 10^{-6}$ b;

$^{238}_{94}Pu_{144}$ — 17 b; $^{239}_{94}Pu_{145}$ — 742 b; $^{240}_{94}Pu_{146}$ — < 0.008 b;

$^{241}_{94}Pu_{147}$ — 1010 b; $^{242}_{94}Pu_{148}$ — < 0.2 b.

Energy of neutrons released in fission ranges from 0.1 to 10 MeV with an average of about 2 MeV. Table 2.4 shows some representative data for fissile and fertile nuclides.

**Table 2.4**

| Nuclide | Neutron energy | Fission cross-section $\sigma_f$, barns | Av. no. of neutrons released per neutron absorbed |
|---|---|---|---|
| $^{233}$U | 0.253 eV | 527 | 2.51 |
| | 1 MeV | 2 | 2.94 |
| $^{235}$U | 0.025 eV | 582 | 2.05 |
| | 1 MeV | 1.25 | 2.6 |
| $^{238}$U | 0.025 eV | N.A. | N.A. (doesn't fission) |
| | 2 MeV | 0.58 | N.A. |
| $^{232}$Th | 0.025 eV | N.A. | N.A. |
| | 2 MeV | 0.01 | N.A. |
| $^{239}$Pu | 0.025 eV | 746 | 2.08 |
| | 1 MeV | 1.8 | 3.04 |
| | 0.3 eV | 3300 | 1.64 |

*Fertile materials* used in nuclear reactors are:

$^{238}$U with $t_{0.5} = 4.5 \times 10^6$ yr, and $^{232}$Th with $t_{0.5} = 1.4 \times 10^{10}$ yr.

*Fissile materials* are: $^{233}$U ($t_{0.5} = 1.6 \times 10^5$ yr);

$^{235}$U ($t_{0.5} = 3.26 \times 10^4$ yr); $^{239}$Pu ($t_{0.5} = 2.4 \times 10^4$ yr).

Properties of some useful *moderators* are as follows:

$H_2O$ — $3.3 \times 10^{22}$ moderating atoms/cm$^3$;

$D_2O$ — 3.3 atoms/cm$^3$;

Beryllium — 1.24 atom/cm$^3$;

BeO — 7.5 atoms/cm$^3$.

***Example 2.12***: Natural uranium is composed of 0.72% $^{235}U$ and 99.28% $^{238}U$. At thermal neutron energies, the fission cross-sections are 584 b and 0. The absorption cross-sections are $\sigma_a = 97$ and 2.75 b, respectively. A reaction generates $\nu = 2.5$ neutrons. Calculate the effective number of neutrons, $\eta$, available for the next fission reaction.

***Solution***: Because of absorption in the fuel itself, some of the generated neutrons are lost and unavailable for the next fission reaction. This ratio is $\eta = (\sigma_f/(\sigma_f + \sigma_a))\ \nu$.

Now, the effective fission cross-section is

$$\sigma_f = (0.72 \times 584 + 99.28 \times 0)/100 = 4.2 \text{ b}$$

The absorption cross-section for the mixture is

$$\sigma_a = (0.72 \times 97 + 99.28 \times 2.75)/100 = 3.43 \text{ b}$$

Therefore $\qquad \eta = 2.5 \times 4.2/(4.2 + 3.43) = 1.33$

[Out of these, some are absorbed in the moderator, shield, container vessel, etc.].

***Example 2.13***: If enriched fuel containing 3% $^{235}U$ and 97% $^{238}U$ is used, calculate the value of $\eta$, the effective number of neutrons available for the next reaction.

***Solution***: $\qquad \sigma_f = 3 \times 584/100 = 17.52$

$$\sigma_a = (3 \times 97 + 97 \times 2.75)/100 = 2.91 + 2.6675 = 5.5775$$

Therefore $\qquad \eta = 17.52 \times 5.5775/(17.52 + 5.5775) = 1.8963.$

This is an improvement of 42.6% over the $\eta$ without enrichment.

In Example 3, it was shown that 1 gram of $^{235}U$ can generate an energy of about 1 MW-d. If 3% enriched $^{235}U$ is used instead of naturally-occuring uranium ore with 0.72% $^{235}U$ content, it is easy to visualize that the reactor for generating the same amount of energy will need only 24% of the amount of fuel and so its size is correspondingly smaller. Enrichment is an expensive process, but it will more than compensate for reduction in cost of reactor core, shield, containment vessel and reactor structure with buildings, etc. The process of separation of the two isotopes of uranium (235 and 238) involves centrifugal or gaseous diffusion, since they have unequal masses. With the unfortunate manufacture of nuclear warheads and submarines, enrichment plants are very necessary. The by-products are used for nuclear reactors, for electrical power generation in enriched form, so that each reactor need not have its own enrichment plant.

## 2.15 Nuclear Reactor Types and Description

The essential parts of a nuclear reactor, whether thermal or fast, are the following:

1. *Fuel* : Combination of fertile and fissile materials.
   Fertile : $^{238}$U and $^{232}$Th
   Fissile: $^{233}$U, $^{235}$U, and $^{239}$Pu
2. *Moderator* : In thermal reactors (using slow neutrons after moderation of MeV neutrons to eV neutrons), fast neutrons are converted to slow or thermal neutrons.
3. *Core* : Contains fuel, moderator if any, and control rods.
4. *Reflector* : Surrounds the core and reduces neutron leakage.
5. *Containment vessel* : Prevents escape of radioactive fission products. Usually made of stainless steel.
6. *Shielding* : Prevents neutrons and $\gamma$-rays from escaping into the environment, thereby causing harm to operating staff.
7. *Coolant* : Removes heat from the core and transfers it to water to generate steam. In some types of reactors, the coolant passes directly to the turbine, such as in boiling-water and gas-cooled reactors.
8. *Control system* : Made from highly neutron-absorbing material such as boron or cadmium. These rods are inserted into the core to lower the reaction rate and withdrawn to increase power output.
9. *Emergency system* : Also includes evacuation means of personnel and citizens affected in the area of the power station. Many nuclear plants have been unable to operate because of lack of proper ways to evacuation of people, even though technically sound otherwise and licence was granted, but later withdrawn after completion of the power plant.

There are essentially three types of reactors depending on their intended purpose:

(1) Power generation; (2) Research; (3) Conversion of $^{238}$U into $^{239}$Pu, and $^{232}$Th into $^{233}$U. This is essentially a breeder reactor.

Figures 2.8 and 2.9 show schematic sketches of five important reactor types used in the world for power generation. A brief description of these reactors are as follows:

(1) *BWR and PWR*: Boiling Water and Pressurized Water Reactors

In the BWR, steam is raised in the core and flows directly to the turbine, as shown in Fig. 2.8. In the PWR the heated water flows to a heat exchanger,

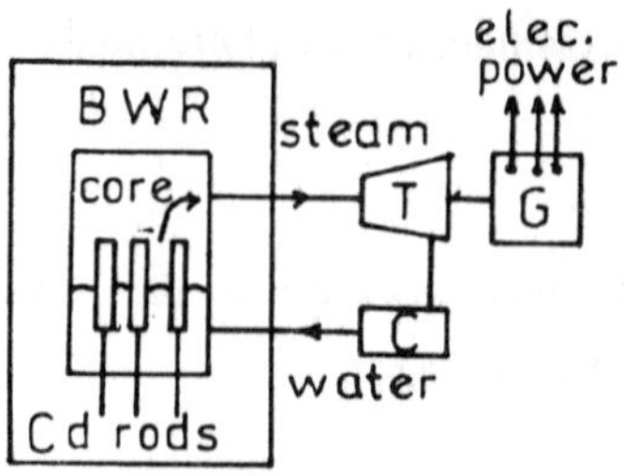


**Fig. 2.8** Schematic of boiling water reactor (BWR)

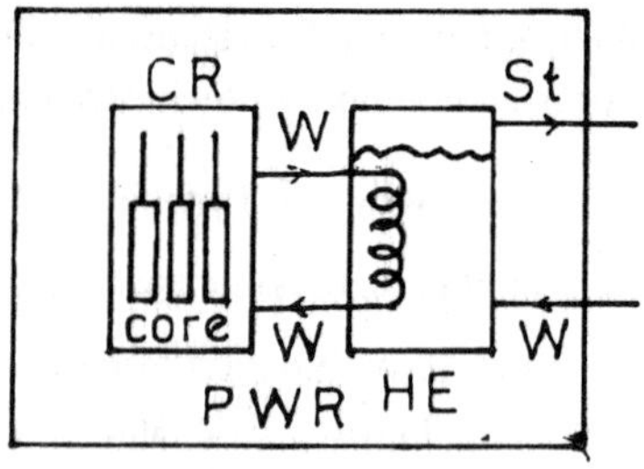


**Fig. 2.9** Schematic of pressure water reactor (PWR)

Fig. 2.9, where water is converted into steam and then to the turbine. The pressure used is > 100 atm (1470 lb/in$^2$) in order that the water may not become steam in the pipes. (1 atm = 0.101 MPa). Ordinary water used in both BWR and PWR acts as moderator and coolant, and does not become radioactive, except for some atoms of oxygen, $^{18}O$, present. The fuel in both types is enriched uranium containing 2-3% $^{235}U$. Such reactors form the majority in the USA.

(2) *CANDU*: Canadian Deuterium Uranium

Deuterium ($D_2O$) or heavy water is used both as moderator and coolant in a closed circuit, as shown in Fig. 2.10. In the heat exchanger, ordinary $H_2O$ is used and the steam flows into the turbine from the heat exchanger. $D_2O$ is under pressure to keep it in the liquid state. Fuel used is natural uranium and is not enriched, saving on its cost.

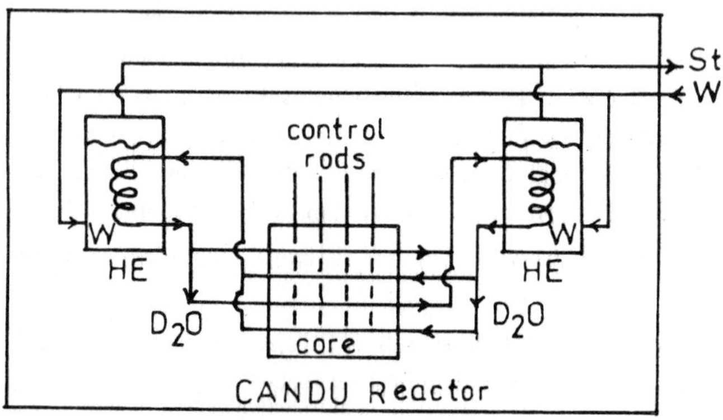


**Fig. 2.10** Schematic of CANDU reactor

(3) *GCR* : Gas-Cooled Reactor (Fig. 2.11)

Graphite is used as moderator and helium gas as the coolant. The heat exchanger heats either water into steam running a steam turbine, or the He gas is used directly to run a gas turbine. Fuel used is either natural or enriched uranium. These reactors are used mostly in the UK and Europe.

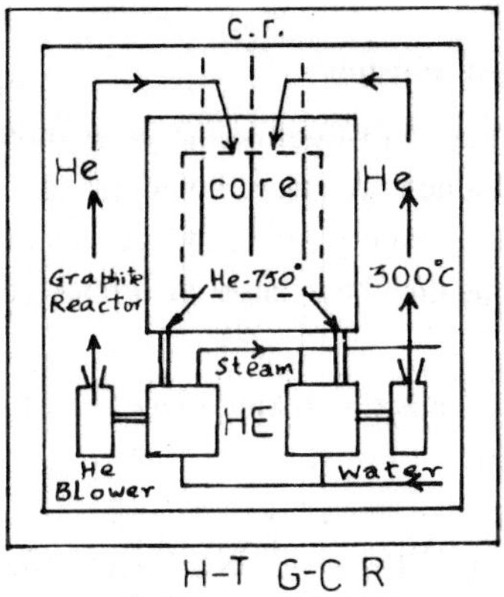


**Fig. 2.11** Schematic of high temperature gas cooled reactor (H-T G-C-R)

(4) *LMFBR* : Liquid Metal Fast Breeder Reactor (Fig. 2.12)

The core containing either fissile $^{235}U$ or $^{239}Pu$ is surrounded by a blanket of fertile $^{238}U$. There are two liquid-sodium loops. The primary loop has the liquid metal as coolant, flowing in the core and blanket, while the secondary-loop Na takes the heat from the primary-Na in a first heat exchanger. It then transfers its heat in a second heat exchanger using ordinary $H_2O$, raising steam at about 550°C. Since $H_2O$ and Na form an explosive mixture, $H_2O$ is kept clear of the core and the primary Na loop. Normally, the $^{239}Pu$ (as also $^{233}U$) are converted in thermal reactors for initial fuelling in the breeder reactor. The transportation of these fissile materials causes grave concern and several accidents have been reported causing radioactive spills from the railcars carrying these materials from converters to breeder reactor sites. Once the reactor is in operation it

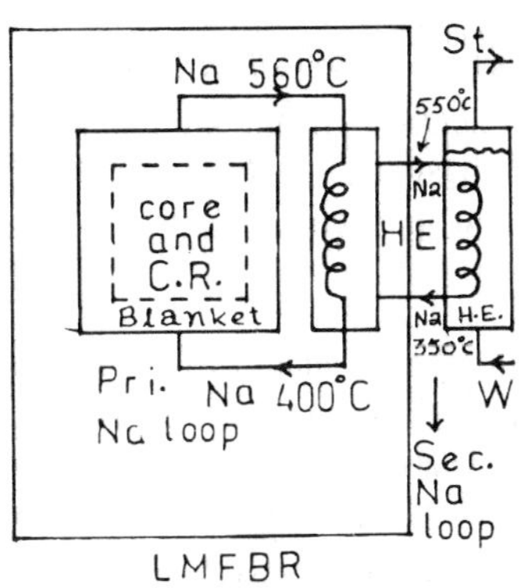


**Fig. 2.12** Schematic of liquid metal fast breeder reactor (LMFBR)

breeds more fuel inside the core and blanket. Most countries in the world, especially France, use LMFBRs. We discuss this in more detail in Sec. 2.17.

### 2.16 Fission Products and Poisons

Residues that have very long half-lives (some years) are radioactive and present grave danger. Some residues are used, however, for such beneficial uses as research and cancer cure. Certain fission products accumulate in the fuel rods to slow down reaction rates as they have large absorption cross-sections for thermal neutrons.

Another sequence of $\beta^-$-reaction taking place is as follows, which forms $^{135}I$ and $^{135}Xe$ which are harmful:

$$^{135}Sb \xrightarrow{1.7\,s} {}^{135}Te \xrightarrow{19\,s} {}^{135}I \xrightarrow{6.6\,h} {}^{135}Xe \xrightarrow{9.1\,h} {}^{135}Cs \xrightarrow{3.6 \times 10^6\,y} {}^{135}Ba \quad (2.29)$$

There is an accumulation of $^{135}Xe$ in a matter of hours, which has a cross-section for capture of thermal neutrons of $2.7 \times 10^6$ barn. This reduces the number of thermal neutrons available for fission. Because of this the control system will operate by neutron counters to increase the reaction rate. Such isotopes are called poisons.

The iodine isotope $^{135}I$ has beneficial medical applications in studying and controlling the functioning of the thyroid gland, as well as curing cancer of this gland. Other isotopes used are $^{132}I$ and $^{131}I$. Xenon gas is given to patients with lung infection problems.

### 2.17 Breeding

It was shown earlier that 1 gram of fissile $^{235}U$ yields as much energy as 3 tonne of coal (3 million gram), with average calorific value of 6000 kcal/kg. However, natural uranium contains only 0.72% of $^{235}U$, so that 1 g of this fissile material requires uranium ore of weight ($1/72 \times 10^{-4}$) = 139 g = 0.139 kg. Furthermore, only less than 1% natural uranium ore contains $^{235}U$, which is known as yellow pitch blend, as it comes out of the mine. Furthermore, since only $^{235}U$ is utilized in thermal reactors using neutrons in the eV-range, all the $^{238}U$ which forms 99.28% of the reactor fuel goes to waste. Therefore, breeding of new fuel is necessary out of the $^{238}U$, if nuclear reactors are to supply safe energy for centuries to come.

By using neutrons in the MeV range or fast neutrons, $^{238}U$ can be converted to fissile $^{239}Pu$. Similarly, fertile $^{232}Th$ can be converted to fissile $^{233}U$. Thorium is not available as plentifully as uranium in wealthy countries, who originally developed the process of power generation from nuclear energy. But less affluent countries like India produce 50% of the world's thorium, and require converter or breeder reactors to suit their economy. $^{232}Th$ and $^{238}U$ are called fertile isotopes while $^{233}$U, $^{235}$U and $^{239}$Pu are known as fissile isotopes. When conversion and power generation take place simultaneously in a reactor, it is a breeder nuclear reactor or simply a breeder. However, the two processes can take place in different reactors, in which case the reactors are known as a converter and a power reactor, respectively. The converted fissile isotope has to be physically transferred into the power reactor involving the danger of handling and transportation.

The basic physics of conversion or breeding sequence of the fertile isotopes into fissile isotopes is as follows:

*Uranium Chain* : The required cycle is $^{238}U \rightarrow {}^{239}Pu$, which takes 2.75 days as follows:

$$^{238}_{92}U \xrightarrow{n,\gamma} {}^{239}_{92}U \xrightarrow[\beta^-]{23.5\,m} {}^{239}_{93}Np \xrightarrow[\beta^-]{2.35\,d} {}^{239}_{94}Pu \xrightarrow{n,\gamma} {}^{240}_{94}Pu \text{ ——}$$

$$\xrightarrow{n,\gamma} {}^{241}_{94}Pu \xrightarrow{n,\gamma} {}^{242}_{94}Pu$$

$$^{241}_{94}Pu \xrightarrow[\beta^-]{14.3\,y} {}^{241}_{95}Am$$

*Thorium Chain* : The required cycle is $^{232}Th \rightarrow {}^{233}U$, which takes 27.4 days as follows, and is a slower process than the uranium - plutonium chain by being ten times longer:

$$^{232}_{90}Th \xrightarrow{n,\gamma} {}^{233}_{90}Th \xrightarrow[\beta^-]{23.4\,m} {}^{233}_{91}Pa \xrightarrow[\beta^-]{27\,d} {}^{233}_{92}U \xrightarrow{n,\gamma} {}^{234}_{92}Pu \xrightarrow{n,\gamma} {}^{235}_{92}U \xrightarrow{n,\gamma} {}^{236}_{92}U$$

**Breeding Ratio**

Let $\eta$ = number of neutrons produced in a reaction when one neutron is absorbed by the nucleus of the fertile material. Out of these neutrons, some are lost by absorption and leakage. Let this number be L. For the next reaction in the chain, 1 neutron is necessary. In the fissile material, one more neutron is lost. Therefore

$\eta - (1 + L)$ = number of neutrons captured by the fertile material, which has to convert to the fissile material.

In order to therefore replace the 1 neutron destroyed in the fissile nucleus, we must have

$$\eta - (1 + L) \geq 1 \tag{2.30}$$

Therefore, the minimum value of $\eta$, the number of neutrons released from the fission reaction of the fissile material, must be

$$\eta \geq 2 + L \tag{2.31}$$

Now, $\eta - (1 + L)$ is the number of fissile nucleii produced when 1 fissile nucleus is destroyed, and is called the ''breeding ratio'', BR.

Thus $$\text{BR} = \eta - (1 + \text{L}) \tag{2.32}$$

Over a long time of 1 year, the breeding gain is

$$\text{BG} = \frac{\text{net fuel buildup per year}}{\text{fuel destroyed per year}} = \text{BR} - 1 \tag{2.33}$$

For a typical LMFBR using Na as coolant, the breeding ratio BR achieved to date is 1.2 to 1.3, so that breeding gain BG is 20 to 30%.

When the fuel consists of oxides of uranium and plutonium ($UO_2 - PuO_2$), the values of $\eta$ are 2 to 2.26 for 0.025 eV neutrons and 2.1 to 2.45 in LMFBR. Higher breeding ratios are anticipated in carbide fuels such as (UC - PuC). Both oxides and carbides release gases ($O_2$, CO and $CO_2$) inside the reactor, which tend to clog the fuel rods. Sulphides are being tried to improve performance.

**Doubling Time**

The efficiency of a breeder reactor is measured in its ability to generate an amount of fissile material (Pu-239 or U-233) equal to the initial charge or amount of fissile material. It is indicated by a "doubling time" defined as

$$T_d = \frac{\text{Initial mass of fissile material}}{\text{Rate of production of fissile material}}$$

The period is measured in days or years depending on the rate. Since both the fissile and fertile materials U-235 and U-238 are loaded in the core and there is a blanket of U-238 for conversion to Pu-239, this external amount should also be included in the mass of the initial charge as well as any other source of neutrons.

If $M_i$ = initial mass of fissile material inside the core, kg,

and $\varepsilon$ = fraction external to the core, the total load is $M_i\ (1 + \varepsilon)$, kg.

If $q$ = amount consumed per day in kg, then $(q \cdot BG)$ = mass of fissile material gained per day. Not all this undergoes fission, since a portion is absorbed. This ratio is

$$\eta / \nu = \sigma_f / (\sigma_f + \sigma_c) = 1 / (1 + \sigma_c / \sigma_f) = 1 / (1 + \alpha)$$

where $\nu$ = number of neutrons released per fission. Then, actual amount undergoing fission is $q / (1 + \alpha)$.

It has already been mentioned earlier that 1 g of U-235 generates an energy of 1 MW-d. Therefore, if $P$ = thermal rating of the reactor in MW, the amount of fuel required in 1 day for generating a MW-d of $P$ will be $q = P(1 + \alpha)$ for U-235. Therefore the doubling time is

$T_d = M_i\,(1 + \varepsilon) / q \cdot BG = M_i\,(1 + \varepsilon) / (BG) \cdot P \cdot (1 + \alpha)$, days where $M_i$ is in grams and $P$ in MW.

For Pu-239, 1 g generates roughly 0.5 MW-d. Therefore, $q/(1 + \alpha)$ will generate $0.5q/(1 + \alpha)$ MW-d giving $q = 2\,P(1 + \alpha)$, which is the quantity required per day. The slower rate of consumption for U-235 yields a larger doubling time than for Pu-239 in the ratio 2/1. Also, doubling time is reduced if the breeding gain BG and the value of $\alpha = \sigma_c / \sigma_f$ are increased.

***Example 2.14***: A breeder reactor has a rating of 1200 $MW_e$ at an efficiency of 33.3% and annual load factor of 0.75. The initial fuel load (Pu-239) is 3 tonne. Take $\alpha = 0.25$ ($\nu = 3$, $\eta = 2.4$) and the breeding ratio BR = 1.3. Calculate the doubling time in years if 1 g of Pu-239 generates 0.5 MW-d ($\varepsilon = 0.5$ for external sources).

***Solution***: $P = 1200 \times 0.75/0.333 = 3000\ MW_{th}$. 3 tonne = $3 \times 10^6$ g.

$$\text{Therefore } T_d = \frac{M_i (1 + \varepsilon)}{BG \cdot P \cdot 2\,(1 + \alpha)} = \frac{3 \times 10^6 \times 1.5}{(1.3 - 1) \times 3 \times 10^3 \times 2 \times (1 + 0.25)}$$

$$= 2 \times 10^3 \text{ day} = 5.48\text{yr}.$$

Pu-239 is loaded in a reactor initially, if it is brought from a converter in which U-235 has been used as fissile material, or if U-235 has been initially loaded in this breeder reactor. For U-235 as initial load, the doubling time for the above reactor will be 10.96 yr ≈ 11 yr. The doubling time has been described in a simplified manner. There are a number of other details for which the reader is directed to consult highly specialized works on fast breeder reactors.

## 2.18 Nuclear Fuel and Power Control

The fuels used for several types of power reactors, moderators, shield and type of control are given below:

| | Reactor Type | Fuel | Moderator and Reflector | Control | Shield |
|---|---|---|---|---|---|
| 1. | BWR (USA) | 1-4% $^{235}U$, and $^{238}U$ | $H_2O$ (67 atm) | $B_4C$ in steel | $H_2O$ and steel |
| 2. | PWR (USA) | Same | $H_2O$ (100 atm) | $B_4C$ or Ag-In-Cd | Same |
| 3. | CANDU (Canada and India) | 0.72% $^{235}U$, and $^{238}U$ | $D_2O$ | Boron-steel | Concrete |
| 4. | GCFR (USA and Germany) Also used for breeding $^{233}U$ and $^{239}Pu$ | Pu (10-30%), $^{232}Th$ and $^{238}U$ | None | $B_4C$ | Steel and Graphite |
| 5. | LMFBR (USA) Phenix (France) PFR (UK) | Pu (10-30%), $^{238}U$ | None | $B_4C$ in AISI-316 steel | Steel Concrete |

${}^{10}_{5}B$ has a very large cross-section of about 4000 barn for thermal neutrons and follows 1/energy law. Detectors of neutrons based on conversion of n → p and n → α-particles are used in ionization chambers or proportional counters which are filled with boron-fluoride gas, or boron metal compounds. Other detectors use ${}^{6}_{3}Li$ which has a cross-section of about 950 b for thermal neutrons of 0.026 eV energy. Time-of-flight measurement of neutrons generate pulses which operate on the control system, which consists of computerized automatic circuits.

**Fuel Assembly**

The fuel is made in rod form of 1 cm diameter × 2-4 m in length introduced into hollow zirconium alloy with 0.5 mm thick wall and containing 2-4% Sn with a trace of Nb (< 0.1%) to control corrosion. These rods are formed in a grid-like honeycomb having hundreds of holes. A representative figure is 250. 80% of these holes carry the fuel rods clad in Zr tubes with about 100 tonne of fuel necessary for 3 years of power generation before re-fuelling. Another set of holes, about 20%, carry control rods and a few instrument sensors. The fission products absorb neutrons and reduce power level after a few years.

***Example 2.15***: A nuclear reactor for generating 1200 MWe has an overall efficiency of 30% and a load factor of 70%. Calculate: (a) thermal capacity of reactor; (b) energy delivered per year in MW-h and MW-d; (c) amount of fuel consumed in 3 yr if 1 g of 0.72% $^{235}U$ generates 1 MW-d; (d) repeat (c) for 3% enriched uranium.

***Solution***: Efficiency = $MW_e/MW_{th}$

(a) MW-thermal = $MW_{th}$ = 1200/0.3 = 4000 MW

(b) Average generated power over the period = $MW_e \times LF$ = 1200 × 0.7 = 840 MW at the terminals of generator.

Therefore, energy output per year = 840 × 365 MW-d = $0.3066 \times 10^6$ MW-d = $0.3066 \times 10^6 \times 24$ MW-h = $7.3584 \times 10^6$ MW-h

(c) Energy produced in reactor core = $0.3066 \times 10^6/0.3 = 1.022 \times 10^6$ MW-d at 30% efficiency. Therefore, amount of $^{235}U$ required per year = $1.022 \times 10^6$ g = 1.022 tonne.

Since this forms only 0.72% of the natural uranium fuel in the reactor, total fuel necessary = 1.022 × 100/0.72 = 142 tonne/yr

= 426 tonne for 3 years.

(d) If 3% enriched uranium is used, fuel necessary for 3 yr

= 426 × 0.72/3 = 24% of 426 = 102.24 tonne.

In a fast-breeder reactor, for a typical output of 1200 $MW_e$, about 5 tonne of $^{239}Pu$ and 20 tonne of $^{238}U$ will be used in the core, and 30 tonne of $^{238}U$ in the blanket, which will breed into $^{239}Pu$. The fuel is clad in stainless steel tubes.

**Power Control**

Control of reactor power-generation rate is of the utmost concern and poses some dangers too. This power can vary from zero output to maximum rated value, and in emergencies the power level has to be quenched instantaneously to zero. To shut down a reactor in its normal course, the neutron-absorbing control rods are inserted into the core to the maximum extent, while during accidents they are made to fall rapidly into the core all the way. To control the power level from instant to instant during normal operation to suit the load demand at the generator terminals, neutron sensors pick up signals and through a computerized automatic logic-decision circuit, control the position of the control rods. As indicated before, these are generally stainless-steel tubes filled with boron carbide ($B_4C$) or alloys of Ag-In-Cd. These are good neutron-absorbing materials.

**The Four-Factor Formula**

When a fission reaction releases $N$ neutrons, only those in the MeV range or fast neutrons can enter into reaction with $^{238}U$. Let $(fN)$ be the number of fast neutrons after the reaction. Not all of these $fN$ neutrons have a chance of colliding with the nucleii of $^{238}U$ present. Let the fraction that take part in fission be $\varepsilon$. Then $(\varepsilon fN)$ = number of fissions in $^{238}U$ out of the total number $N$ neutrons released from a fission reaction earlier. Some of these will be absorbed by the moderator and slowed down. If $p$ = fraction surviving after passing through the moderator, the number of neutrons finally surviving will be

$$n = p\varepsilon fN \tag{2.34}$$

This is known as the four-factor-formula. The number $n$ denotes the number of neutrons which are available for the next collision with a $^{238}U$ nucleus. The number $n$ is known as the reproduction factor. It usually takes about 100 collisions with moderator atoms before a fast neutron can lose enough energy from 1 MeV to become a thermal neutron of 0.025 eV energy. From Fig. 2.7 it is clear that the neutron has to pass through many resonance peaks in the range 10-100 eV. Performance of neutrons in this process can be improved by ingenuous designs in graphite moderators, since these can have powdered to block forms in shape. But with liquid moderators these resonant conditions and time delays are unavoidable.

**2.19 Miscellaneous Worked Examples**

*(1)* Consider the fission reaction $^{235}U + n \rightarrow {}^{93}Rb + {}^{141}Cs + 2n + Q$.
$[m(^{235}U) = 235.043924$ u, $m(^{93}Rb) = 92.92172$ u, $m(^{141}Cs) = 140.9195$ u,

$m(n) = 1.008665$ u, 1 u = 931.5 MeV = $1.660566 \times 10^{-27}$ kg, 1 MeV = $1.6022 \times 10^{-13}$ J]

(a) Compute the energy released or $Q$-value;

(b) The velocities of Rb and Cs nucleii assuming equality of their momenta and the neutron to carry away very little momentum;

(c) The kinetic energy of the Rb and Cs nucleii.

***Solution***: Left side = 236.05259 u; Right side = 235.85844 u.

Therefore $Q = \Delta m = 0.19415$ u = 180.85 MeV.

(b) We have the following relations: $m_1 v_1 = m_2 v_2$, and $\frac{1}{2} m_1 v_1^2 + \frac{1}{2} m_2 v_2^2 = Q$.

Therefore $\frac{1}{2} m_1 v_1^2 (1 + m_1/m_2) = Q = 181$ with $m_1/m_2 = 92.9217/140.9195 = 0.6594$.

This gives for Rb:

$$v_1^2 = (181/1.6594) \times 1.6022 \times 10^{-13} \times 2/[92.92172 \times 1.660566 \times 10^{-27}]$$

$$= 2.035162 \times 10^{14}.$$

Thus $v_1 = 1.4266 \times 10^7$ m/s = 4.7553% of light velocity.

Then, velocity of Cs nucleus, $v_2 = 14266 \times 10^7 \times 92.92172/140.9195$

$= 0.9407 \times 10^7$ m/s = 3.136% c.

(c) Kinetic energy of Rb nucleus = 181/1.6594 = 109 MeV.
Kinetic energy of Cs nucleus = 181 – 109 = 72 MeV.

*(2)* A fission reaction with $^{235}U$ and $^{238}U$ produces on the average $\nu = 3$ neutrons. The cross-sections for fission are $\sigma_f = 600$ b and 0 for the two nucleii while the absorption cross-sections are $\sigma_a = 100$ b and 3 b, respectively. Find the mean value of number of fission-neutrons produced for the next event for the following two cases:

(a) 0.72% $^{235}U$; and (b) 4% $^{235}U$.

***Solution***: $\eta = \nu \sigma_f / (\sigma_f + \sigma_a)$

(a) $\sigma_f = 0.72 \times 600/100 + 0 = 4.32$ b
$\sigma_a = 0.72 \times 100/100 + 99.28 \times 3/100 = 3.6984$ b

Therefore $\eta = 3 \times 4.32/(4.32 + 3.6984) = 1.6163$ neutrons

(b) $\sigma_f = 4 \times 600/100 + 0 = 24$ b. $\sigma_a = 4 \times 100/100 + 96 \times 3/100 = 6.88$ b

Therefore $\eta = 3 \times 24/(24 + 6.88) = 2.3316$ neutrons

*(3)* Consider the reaction $^{239}_{94}\text{Pu} + \gamma \longrightarrow {}^{92}_{38}\text{Sr} + {}^{144}_{56}\text{Ba} + 3\,n + Q$

Atomic masses: Pu-239 = 239.052158 u, Sr-92 = 91.910944 u
Ba-144 = 143.986014 u

(a) Compute the energy released Q

(b) Energy released by 1 gram of $^{239}$Pu in MW-d

***Solution***: $m$(left side) = 239.052158 u, $m$(right side) = 238.922958 u

Therefore $\Delta m = 0.1292$ u = 120.35 MeV = Q.

(b) 1 gram of $^{239}$Pu has $10^{-3}/(239.052158 \times 1.660566 \times 10^{-27})$

$= 2.519 \times 10^{21}$ nucleii.

Therefore energy released = $303.18 \times 10^{21}$ MeV = $485.76 \times 10^{8}$ J

Since 1 MW-d = $10^6 \times 24 \times 60 \times 60 = 86.4 \times 10^9$ J, 1 g of $^{239}$Pu releases 485.76/864 = 0.5622 MW-d.

*(4)* Note that for the reaction $^{239}\text{Pu} + n \longrightarrow {}^{92}\text{Sr} + {}^{144}\text{Ba} + 4n$ the energy release is the same as above.

*(5)* The number of fast neutrons released in a fission reaction with $^{238}$U is 2.8, when 1 neutron is absorbed. The leakage amounts to 2 neutrons by being absorbed by shield and other structures.

(a) Will this arrangement breed fissile $^{239}$Pu ?

(b) What is the maximum number of neutrons that can be permitted to leak for breeding to commence?

***Solution***: (a) For breeding, $\eta \geq 2 + \text{L}$. But $2 + \text{L} = 4$ and $\eta = 2.8$. The arrangement will not breed.

(b) Maximum number of permissible leakage neutrons = 2.8 – 2 = 0.8 on the average per fission.

*(6)* The breeding gain for 1 year is 25% for a reactor and leakage L = 1 neutron/fission reaction. Calculate:

(a) The breeding ratio;

(b) The number of neutrons that should be released per fission reaction with this breeding ratio.

***Solution***: (a) BG = BR - 1. Therefore BR = BG + 1 = 1.25.

(b) BR = $\eta - (1 + \text{L})$, or, $1.25 = \eta - (1 + 1)$. Therefore $\eta = 3.25$.

## OBJECTIVE TYPE QUESTIONS

1. Examples of fissile materials are: (a) U-233; (b) Pu-239; (c) U-235; (d) all three.
2. Examples of fertile materials are: (a) U-233; (b) Pu-239; (c) U-235; (d) none of the three.
3. U-233 occurs in nature along with U-238 in the ratio (a) 0.72%; (b) 3%; (c) 99.28%; (d) none of the three.
4. A chain reaction uses (a) prompt neutrons; (b) delayed neutrons; (c) both; (d) none.
5. Prompt neutrons are released from: (a) fissile material; (b) daughter nuclei; (c) moderator; (d) all three.
6. Delayed neutrons are used for (a) sustaining chain reaction; (b) control of generated heat; (c) both.
7. In a breeder reactor: (a) U-238 is converted to Pu-239; (b) Th-232 is converted to U-233; (c) U-233 is converted to Th-232; (d) both (a) and (b) can take place but in different reactors.
8. The fission cross-section is large in U-238 at neutron energy of (a) 1 MeV; (b) 1 eV; (c) 0.025 eV; (d) none of the three.
9. The fission cross-section is large in U-235 at neutron energy of (a) 1 MeV; (b) 1 eV; (c) 0.025 eV; (d) none of the three.
10. The fission cross-section is large in Pu-239 at neutron energy of (a) 1 MeV; (b) 0.025 eV; (c) 0.3 eV; (d) 1 eV.
11. Moderators used in fission reactors are: (a) $H_2O$; (b) $D_2O$; (c) C; (d) any or all three.
12. Boron is an example of (a) poison; (b) absorber; (c) fissile material; (d) fertile material.
13. Xenon is an example of (a) poison; (b) absorber; (c) fissile material; (d) fertile material.
14. North American reactors are mostly (a) PWR; (b) BWR; (c) CANDU; (d) all three.
15. LMFBR's are used until now in (a) USA; (b) Canada; (c) France; (d) all three countries.
16. The moderator used in LMFBR is (a) light water; (b) heavy water; (c) liquid sodium; (d) none of the three.
17. In the CANDU reactor, the fuel used is (a) 3% enriched U-235; (b) 0.72% U-235; (c) Pu-239; (d) all three.

18. Isotopes recovered from spent fuel in a reactor for medical purposes can be (a) Xe; (b) I; (c) Pu-239; (d) Co-60; (e) both (a) and (b).

19. When power (heat) developed is to be reduced in a reactor, the control rods are (a) inserted deeper in the core; (b) withdrawn more; (c) none.

20. 1 g of U-235 generates an energy of roughly (a) 1 MW-d; (b) $86.4 \times 10^3$ M Joule ; (c) 20.64 G Cal; (d) all three. (M = Mega = $10^6$).

21. 1 g of Pu-239 generates roughly (a) 0.5 MW-d; (b) 1 MW-d; (c) 2 MW-d; (d) none of the three.

***Answers*:** 1. (d); 2. (d); 3. (d); 4. (c); 5. (a); 6. (c); 7. (d); 8. (a); 9. (c); 10. (c); 11. (d); 12. (b); 13. (a); 14. (d); 15. (c); 16. (d); 17. (b); 18. (e); 19. (a); 20. (d); 21. (a).

## REVIEW QUESTIONS AND PROBLEMS

1. A nuclear reactor using U-235 has a thermal rating of 2500 MW. Assume 200 MeV of energy released per fission reaction. Calculate the amount of U-235 used in 1 yr. (100 kg)

2. A nuclear power station is rated 650 MW electrical and has an efficiency of 30%. The annual load factor is 0.8. Calculate the amount of 3% enriched uranium ore fuel required for 5 yr. (105.44 tonne).

3. For the same output, estimate the tonnes of coal consumed with heating value of 6000 kcal/kg. (10.88 M tonne).

4. Draw the schematics of a PWR, BWR and CANDU reactor showing all coolant and steam-generating loops.

5. The Chernobyl nuclear reactor in the Ukraine is called a uranium-fuelled water-cooled, carbon-moderated (graphite) type. Draw the schematic of this type of reactor. Discuss possible weak spots of this reactor, which brought a run-away thermal condition severe enough to cause the worst disaster to date in nuclear-reactor experience. (Use the fact that for any reason whatsoever the temperature of the graphite moderator increases, the reaction rate increases and that steam impinging on the graphite (carbon) generates CO, $CO_2$ and $O_2$).

6. A neutron in a fission reaction with fuel consisting of a mixture of U-235 and U-238 generates on the average $\nu = 2.8$ neutrons. The fission cross-sections are $\sigma_f = 500$ barn and 0 for the fissile and fertile materials, while the absorption cross-sections are $\sigma_a = 100$ and 5 b, respectively. Calculate the mean value of number of fission neutrons produced for the next event when (a) 0.72% U-235 is used, and (b) 3% enriched U-235 is used. [(a) 1.08574; (b) 1.838].

7. Compute the energy released in 1 g of Pu-239 in MW-d in the reaction $^{239}_{94}\text{Pu} + n \longrightarrow {}^{92}_{38}\text{Sr} + {}^{144}_{56}\text{Ba} + 4\,n$. Atomic masses are:
Pu-239: 239.052 u; Sr-92: 91.911 u; Ba-144: 143.986 u; $n$ = 1.0086 u;
$N_A = 6.022 \times 10^{23}$. (0.565 MW-d)

8. Define the terms: (a) Breeding ratio; (b) Breeding gain for breeder reactors.

9. A LMFBR with a breeding ratio of 1.5 produces $\eta$ = 2.45 neutrons per fission. Assume a leakage of 1 neutron and $\nu = 3$.

   (a) Will this arrangement breed new fuel?

   (b) What is the maximum amount of leakage permitted per fission reaction, if breeding is to take place?

   (c) If the ratio $\sigma_a/\sigma_f$ is denoted by $\alpha$, what is its value?

   (d) If the neutron leakage is brought down which allows the reactor to just start breeding, find the breeding gain.
   [(a) No; (b) 0.45; (c) $\alpha$ = 0.2245; (d) 0.5]

10. The initial load of Pu-239 in an LMFBR is 6 tonne. $\varepsilon = 0$. The rating is 2000 $MW_e$ at 40% efficiency and load factor of 0.8. $\nu = 3$ and $\eta = 2.45$ available for next fission reaction. Calculate the doubling times in years, if the breeding ratio varies from 1.1 to 1.5 in steps of 0.1.

| [BR | = | 1.1 | 1.2 | 1.3 | 1.4 | 1.5 |
|---|---|---|---|---|---|---|
| BG | = | 0.1 | 0.2 | 0.3 | 0.4 | 0.5 |
| $T_d$ | = | 16.8 | 8.4 | 5.6 | 4.2 | 3.36 yr] |

11. Using the equation $R = R_0\, A^{1/3}$ for the radius of a nucleus, calculate the radii of the following light elements taking $R_0$ = 1.25 fm.

   (a) $^1_1$H; (b) $D = {}^2_1$H; (c) $T = {}^3_1$H; (d) $^6_3$Li
   [1.25; 1.575; 1.803 ; 2.2714 fm].

*CHAPTER 3*

# Solid State Physics and Photo Voltaic Power Generation

## 3.1 Introduction

Conversion of limitless energy from the Sun to usable electrical energy depends on the use of solar cells. The process is called Photo Voltaic Energy Conversion. The field of solid-state physics gives the basis for understanding the mechanism of operation, design requirements of individual solar cells and systems consisting of concentrators, panels, modules and arrays. Although the control of generated power and interconnection to an existing power grid system through conversion of generated dc to ac or to feed individual loads utilize solid-state devices, the electronic circuitry will not form the contents of this chapter. The practical application of solar cell arrays and control of generated power will be described following the physics of the solid state.

The successful operation of solar cells depends upon the following factors:

(a) Generation of a voltage by the device, which depends on the energy or band gap between valence and conduction bands of the charge carriers, and the barrier potential developed by a P-N junction.

(b) Generation of electron-hole pairs in the device by the energy of the photons in sunlight, which are then forced to flow in the external load.

(c) Understanding loss mechanisms in the device and minimizing to yield high efficiency. The efficiency of a solar cell rarely exceeds 20%.

The device used for photo-voltaic generation of voltage and current consists of a solid-state device. This can be of three forms:

(1) *Crystals*: These are symmetrical arrays of atoms located at lattice points. The electrons in the atoms move in a wave-like manner in between the nucleus of positive ions located at the lattice points. The entire operation of the solar cell depends on the electron orbitals based on quantum-mechanical considerations.

(2) *Polycrystalline Materials:* These consist of many subdivisions, but each part has a perfect crystalline structure. There exist differences in the divisions in crystal orientation or lattice separations. In essence each part behaves as a crystal.

(3) *Amorphous Solids:* These are non-crystalline and the atoms are arranged at random. They are not amenable to theoretical analysis to the same extent as crystalline materials, so that design of and performance characteristics are more difficult than crystals. However, on account of their lower cost, they have received a lot of attention in the past two decades.

The subject matter of crystals, their structures, and crystallography forms one of the most important and major fields of physics and the literature is so enormous that no attempt is made here to describe or discuss their properties, except the electronic structure for use in solar cells. We will restrict attention to the following topics, each one of which has immense literature on it available:

(1) Free electron Fermi gas model and energy levels

(2) Fermi-Dirac Distribution Function and Density of Electron States

(3) Electrical and Thermal Conductivities: Ohm's Law and Wiedeman-Franz Law

(4) Bonding in crystals

(5) Energy bands

(6) Semiconductor crystals

(7) Intrinsic carrier concentration and mobilities

(8) Junctions

(9) Recombination and carrier lifetimes

(10) PN junctions, heterojunctions, Shottky barrier and MOS solar cells

(11) Amorphous materials and liquid crystals

(12) Hall effect in semiconductors.

### 3.2 Free Electron Fermi Gas Model and Energy Levels

Solid state materials of interest here can be divided into three categories:

(a) *Simple Metals:* These consist of alkali metals $^{3}$Li, $^{19}$K, $^{37}$Ce and $^{55}$Rb. In these elements there exists 1 electron in the unfilled shells or subshells, which is free to move in the crystal as a conduction electron.

Others which contain 2 conduction electrons are: $^{4}$Be, $^{12}$Mg, $^{20}$Ca, $^{38}$Sr, $^{56}$Ba, $^{13}$Al, $^{31}$Ga, $^{49}$In, $^{81}$Tl, $^{30}$Zn, $^{48}$Cd, $^{80}$Hg, and $^{82}$Pb.

The noble metals $^{29}$Cu, $^{47}$Ag, $^{79}$Au and some others are not called simple metals, even though these form the best electrical conductors with 1 free electron available for conduction. All these characteristics result from the crystal structure.

(b) *Semiconductors:* These have 4 electrons which can form a bond with other elements. They form by far the most interesting elements for solar-cell work. They belong to Group IV in the Periodic Table of Elements. At extremely low temperatures, theoretically at 0 K, they are perfect insulators. Some of these are given later.

(c) *Insulators* : These are materials in which no conduction electrons exist with all valence band orbitals fully occupied.

Important materials for solar cells are the following, along with their group numbers in the Periodic Table:

| Ge, | Si, | InP, | GaAS, | CdTe, | AlSb, | GaP, | AlP, |
|---|---|---|---|---|---|---|---|
| IV | IV | III-V | III-V | II-VI | III-V | III-V | III-V |

| CdSe-Ge, | ZnSe-Ge, | GaAs-Ge, | Ga(1-x) Al(x) As -GaAs |
|---|---|---|---|
| II-VI-IV | II,VI-IV | III,V-IV | III III V III-V |

These are further classified as follows:

(a) Intrinsic semiconductors

(b) PN junctions in which one and the same basic semiconductor material is doped with impurities of P-type and N-type, and a junction is formed of these

(c) Heterojunctions in which a junction is formed of two different varieties of semiconductor materials, as for example, GaAs and Ge. We shall discuss the properties of these in a subsequent section and their application as solar cells later.

In the free electron gas model, atoms become positive ions by experiencing a deficiency in electrons, because the electrons in the outermost or most loosely coupled orbits have acquired sufficient energy to move freely. These positive ions are immersed in a sea of electrons. The conduction or free electron is accompanied by its matter or de Broglie wave and propagates freely in a periodic structure of positive ions at the lattice points. They are also subject to Pauli's exclusion principle.

The free-electron Fermi gas consists of free and non-interacting electrons obeying Pauli's exclusion principle.

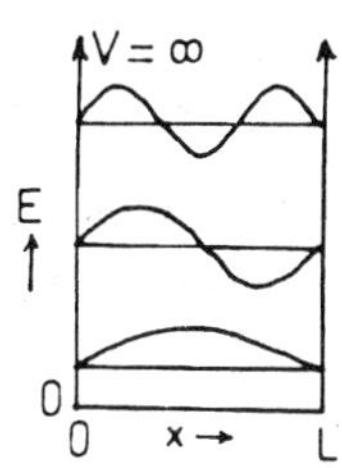

**Fig. 3.1** Electron wave function in infinite potential well

Figure 3.1 shows an electron with energy $E$ moving wave-like in between two infinitely high potential barriers by which the positive ions can be represented, separated by the lattice distance $L$ in one dimension. Since only discrete energy levels are allowed by quantum-mechanical rules, we obtain Schrodinger's equation for any orbit or energy level or wave-function as

$$-(\hbar^2/2m)\, d^2\Psi_n/dx^2 = E_n\Psi_n \tag{3.1}$$

The boundary conditions are $\Psi_n(0) = 0$ and $\Psi_n(L) = 0$. The solution or allowed value for $\Psi_n$ is

$$\Psi_n = A \sin \pi\, n\, x/L = A \sin 2\,\pi\, x/\lambda_n \tag{3.2}$$

Substituting Eq. (3.2) in Eq. (3.1), there results

$(\hbar^2/2m)\cdot(\pi\, n/L)^2 \cdot A \sin \pi\, n\, x/L = E_n A \sin \pi\, n\, x/L$, giving the energy as

$$E_n = (\pi^2 \hbar^2/2\, m\, L^2)\cdot n^2 \tag{3.3}$$

The wave length is $\lambda_n = 2L/n$, or, $\lambda_n/2 = L/n$ (3.4)

Therefore, within the periodic distance $L$, integral number of half wavelengths are supported. The value of $n$ can only be integers 1, 2, 3, ... By Pauli exclusion principle only 1 electron can occupy any given state. At each value of n or orbital number or quantum-mechanical state, there can exist 2 electrons, one with spin + ½ and another with – ½ times Planck's constant (up and down spins). These are denoted by quantum numbers $m_s = \pm$ ½ (see also chap. 1). Suppose there are 14 electrons. Then in the ground state of the system, the filled orbitals are described by $n = 7$ and $m_s = \pm$ ½, and they can be exhibited as follows:

| | | 1 | | 2 | | 3 | | 4 | | 5 | | 6 | | 7 | |
|---|---|---|---|---|---|---|---|---|---|---|---|---|---|---|---|
| | $n$ | 1 | | 2 | | 3 | | 4 | | 5 | | 6 | | 7 | |
| | $m_s$ | + ½ | – ½ | + ½ | – ½ | + ½ | – ½ | + ½ | – ½ | + ½ | – ½ | + ½ | – ½ | + ½ | – ½ |
| Electron occupied | | ↑ | ↓ | ↑ | ↓ | ↑ | ↓ | ↑ | ↓ | ↑ | ↓ | ↑ | ↓ | ↑ | ↓ |

For this case, $n = N/2 = 7$ is the top-most filled energy level. This is denoted as $n_F$. The energy corresponding to this topmost filled level is called the Fermi energy $E_F$ and forms the entire basis of electron conduction properties in a solid-state material.

Thus
$$E_F = \frac{1}{2\,m}(\pi\, n_F\, \hbar/L)^2 = \frac{1}{2\,m}(\pi\, N\, \hbar/2\, L)^2 \tag{3.5}$$

This applies in one dimension. In three dimensions, we are involved with a volume $V$ and the Fermi level is given by

$$E_F = \frac{1}{2\,m}\left(\frac{3\,\pi^2\,\hbar^3\,N}{V}\right)^{2/3} \tag{3.6}$$

Here $(N/V)$ = electron concentration per unit volume. Since no mention of temperature has been made, we assume this to be 0 degree absolute, or 0 $K$.

## 3.3 Fermi-Dirac Distribution Function and Density of States

When the temperature of the material increases, some energy levels that were occupied at 0 K become vacant and others which were vacant get occupied by an electron. The probability that an orbital of energy $E$ will be occupied in this ideal electron gas at thermal equilibrium is given by the Fermi-Dirac distribution function for spin-½ particle, the electron, as follows:

$$f_{FD}(E) = \left[ e^{(E-\mu)/kT} + 1 \right]^{-1} \tag{3.7}$$

where $E$ = energy of the orbital, Joule (or eV)

$\mu$ = chemical potential at which value of $E$, $f_{FD}$ = ½

$k$ = Boltzmann constant = $1.38066 \times 10^{-23}$ $J/K$ = $8.6174 \times 10^{-5}$ $eV/K$

and $T$ = temperature in $K$.

At $T = 0$, $\mu = E_F$, the Fermi energy level. Some examples of $f_{FD}$ are shown in Fig. 3.2.

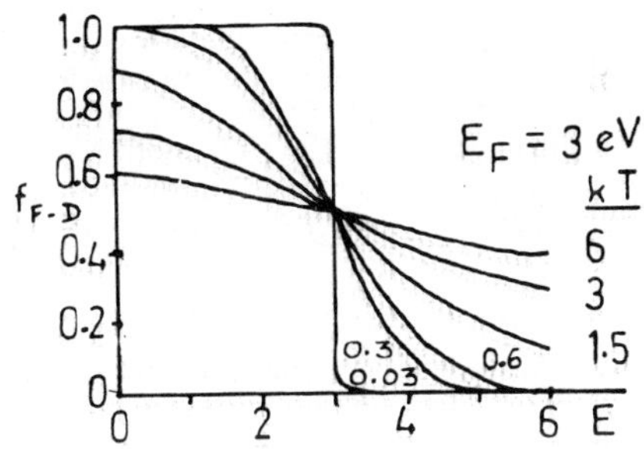


**Fig. 3.2** Fermi-Dirac distribution function

***Example 3.1***: The Fermi level in a crystal is 3eV. Calculate:

(a) the temperature $T_f$ corresponding to $E_F$, (b) plot the F-D distribution function for temperatures of 1%, 10%, 20%, 50%, 100% and 200% of $T_F$ as the energy $E$ is varied from 0 to $2E_F$.

***Solution***: (a) $E_F = k \cdot T_F$, or $T_F = E_F / k$

Therefore $T_F = 3 / 8.6174 \times 10^{-5} = 3481\ K$

$[\ ½\, m_e\, v_F^2 - 3\ eV - 3 \times 1.6022 \times 10^{19}$ J .

Therefore $v_F = 1.028 \times 10^6$ m / s = 0.3426 % c . ]

(b) The F-D distribution function is $f_{FD} = \left[ e^{(E-3)/kT} + 1 \right]^{-1}$

| $T/T_F$ = | 0.01 | 0.1 | 0.2 | 0.5 | 1 | 2 |
|---|---|---|---|---|---|---|
| $kT$ = | 0.03 | 0.3 | 0.6 | 1.5 | 3 | 6 eV |
| $E$ = 0 | ≈ 1 | 1 | 0.9933 | 0.8808 | 0.731 | 0.622 |
| 1.5 | ≈ 1 | 0.9933 | 0.924 | 0.731 | 0.622 | 0.562 |
| 3 | 0.5 | 0.5 | 0.5 | 0.5 | 0.5 | 0.5 |
| 4.5 | ≈ 0 | 0.0067 | 0.076 | 0.269 | 0.3775 | 0.438 |
| 6 | ≈ 0 | ≈ 0 | 0.0067 | 0.1192 | 0.269 | 0.3775 |

The plot of $f_{FD}$ against temperature and energy is shown in Fig. 3.2.

At $T = 0, f_{FD} = 0$ showing that there are no electrons in the conduction band and all orbits are filled in the valence band. For $(E - E_F) >> kT$, neglecting 1 in the denominator, $f_{FD} = e^{-(E - E_F)/kT}$.

At any value of energy, the number of orbitals per unit energy range is called the density of states, $D(E)$. The most interesting energy is the Fermi level, and at this energy $E_F$ we have

$$E_F = (\hbar^2 / 2\,m)\,[\,3\pi^2\,N / V\,]^{2/3} \tag{3.8}$$

This gives the number of states to be

$$N = (V / 3\,\pi^2) \cdot (2\,m\,E_F / \hbar^2)^{3/2} \tag{3.9}$$

or

$$\frac{3}{2}\frac{N}{E_F} = \frac{V}{2\,\pi^2}\left(\frac{2\,m}{\hbar^2}\right)^{3/2} E_F^{1/2} \tag{3.10}$$

Differentiating Eq. (3.9) with respect to $E_F$, there is

$$D\,(E_F) = d\,N / d\,E_F = (V / 2\,\pi^2) \cdot (2\,m / \hbar^2)^{3/2} \cdot E_F^{1/2} = 3\,N / 2\,E_F \tag{3.11}$$

Therefore the number of orbitals per unit energy at the Fermi energy = 1.5 × total number of conduction electrons/Fermi energy.

This expression is extremely useful in calculating the concentrations of electrons and holes in a semiconducting material as will be shown in Sec. 3.9. We also note that the density of states at Fermi energy level per unit volume is

$$D\,(E_F) / V = 3\,(N / V) / 2\,E_F \tag{3.12}$$

### 3.4 Electrical and Thermal Conductivities

The kinetic energy of a particle is $E = p^2/2m$, where $p$ = momentum. Recalling some ideas from Chap. 1, because of the wave-like nature of the electron in quantum mechanics, the momentum is

$$\boldsymbol{p} = \hbar\,\boldsymbol{k} = m\,\boldsymbol{v}$$

Therefore

$$E = \hbar^2\,k^2 / 2\,m = \hbar\,\omega \tag{3.13}$$

with $\omega = 2\,\pi\,\nu$ and $\nu$ = frequency of the wave. Also, the wave-function for a travelling or gliding wave obtained from the Schrodinger equation is

$$\Psi = A\,e^{i\,\boldsymbol{k}\cdot\boldsymbol{r}}\,e^{-i\,E\,t/\hbar} \tag{3.14}$$

We observe that the energy $E$ of any state is a function of $k$, the wave-vector or number. It is convenient to consider a k-space to describe energy states. The unit of $k$ is $m^{-1}$ since $(\boldsymbol{k} \cdot \boldsymbol{r})$ is dimensionless.

When an electric field is applied, the Newtonian force experienced by the electron of charge (–e) is

$$F = m\alpha = m\,dv/dt = \hbar \cdot dk/dt = -eE_a \quad (3.15)$$

upon using Eq. (3.11).

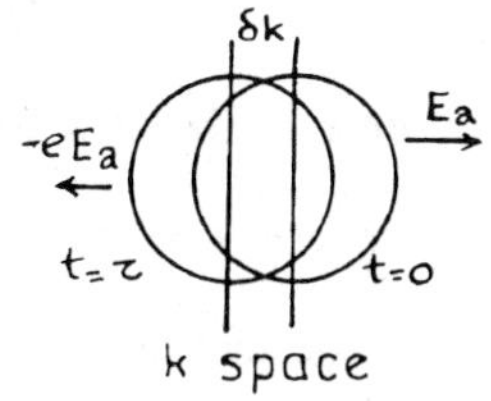

**Fig. 3.3** Motion of electron in $k$-space under applied electric field $E_a$

The term $(d\,k/d\,t)$ denotes the rate at which a sphere of radius $k$ is displaced. In this case, the displacement is against the direction of the applied electric field $E_a$, as shown in Fig. 3.3. If the electron experiences a collision after time $\tau$, the sphere stops at a value

$$\delta k = (dk/dt) \cdot \tau = -eE_a\tau/\hbar, \; m^{-1} \quad (3.16)$$

Also, the velocity acquired by the electron under the force $F$ is

$$dv = -eE_a\,dt/m = -eE_a\tau/m = \alpha\tau \quad (3.17)$$

This establishes a current because of the moving charge. Now, if $n$ = charge carriers per unit volume, the current density is

$$j = n \cdot e \cdot dv = ne^2 E_a \tau/m \quad (3.18)$$

Clearly, this is Ohm's law, from which the electrical conductivity is derived as

$$\sigma_e = j/E_a = ne^2\tau/m = (ne)\cdot(e/m)\tau \quad (3.19)$$

where $(ne)$ = charge density, $(e/m)$ = acceleration per unit applied field, and $\tau$ = collision time. The electrical resistivity is

$$\rho_e = 1/\sigma_e = m/(ne^2\tau) \quad (3.20)$$

The collision time $\tau$ indicates that at this time the electron velocity is zero. The mean free path between collisions is defined as

$$\left.\begin{aligned} l &= v \cdot \tau \\ \text{At the Fermi surface, } l_F &= v_F\tau \end{aligned}\right\} \quad (3.21)$$

The electrons involved are those near the Fermi surface since these are free to move. We note that both $\sigma$ and $\rho$ are independent of temperature $T$. The mean collision time is of the order of $\tau = 2 \times 10^{-9}$ sec.

*Thermal Conductivity*

Without going into the derivation, we quote the equation for thermal conductivity as a Fermi gas to be

$$\sigma_{th} = (\pi^2/3)\cdot(n/m)\cdot k^2 \cdot T \cdot \tau, \text{ Watt / K–m} \quad (3.22)$$

This depends on temperature and is called the Wiedeman-Franz Law. From Eqs. (3.18) and (3.22), there results

$$\sigma_{th} / \sigma_e = (\pi^2 / 3) \cdot (k / e)^2 \cdot T \tag{3.23}$$

With $k = 1.38066 \times 10^{-23}$ $J/K = 8.6174 \times 10^{-5}$ $eV/K$ and $e = 1.6022 \times 10^{-19}$ $c$,

there results $\sigma_{th}/\sigma_e = \pi^2 \times (8.6174 \times 10^{-5})^2$ $T/3 = 2.443 \times 10^{-8}$ $T$.

The constant factor $L = (\pi^2/3) \cdot (k/e)^2$ is called the Lorenz number. The ratio $\sigma_{th}/\sigma_e$ does not involve either the electronic concentration $n$ or the electron mass $m$. We will observe later that the mass of charge carriers moving in a crystal lattice is much less than the actual rest mass of the electron. This is known as the effective mass and is nearly 2% of the rest mass of the electron.

Although the Lorenz number is derived to be independent of temperature, measured values show some dependence on the temperature, increasing by 2% at 100°C of its value at 0°C in most metals. Some examples are given below:

| $L \times 10^8$ | Cu | Ag | Au | Sn | Zn | Pb |
|---|---|---|---|---|---|---|
| 0°C | 2.23 | 2.31 | 2.35 | 2.52 | 3.2 | 2.47 |
| 100°C | 2.33 | 2.37 | 2.40 | 2.49 | 2.33 | 2.56 |

In order to obtain an idea of the magnitude of quantities we are dealing with, the following example is provided.

***Example 3.2***: The following data refer to the metal $^{11}$Na:

Electron concentration, $n = 2.65 \times 10^{22}/\text{cm}^2 = 2.65 \times 10^{28}/\text{m}^3$.

Fermi energy, $E_F = 3.23$ eV; Fermi temperature, $T_F = 3.75 \times 10^4$ K;

Collision time, $\tau = 3.35 \times 10^{-14}$ sec. Calculate

(a) Average distance travelled by an electron at Fermi level between collisions; (b) The electrical conductivity in Siemens/m and resistivity in Ohm-m; (c) The thermal conductivity at 300 K; (d) The radius of the Fermi surface (The Fermi vector); (e) Displacement of Fermi surface, $\delta k$, under an applied field of 2 V/m and the drift velocity $v_d$.

***Solution***: $l_F = v_f \tau$ with $\frac{1}{2} m_e v_F^2 = E_F$.

(a) $v_F = (2 E_F / m_e)^{1/2} = [2 \times 3.23 \times 1.6022 \times 10^{-19} / 9.10956 \times 10^{-31}]^{1/2}$

$= 1.066 \times 10^6$ m/s

Therefore $l_F = v_F \tau = 1.066 \times 10^6 \times 3.35 \times 10^{-14} = 3.57 \times 10^{-8}$ m $= 357$ Å

(b) $\sigma_{el} = n e^2 \tau / m = \dfrac{2.65 \times 10^{28} \times 1.6022^2 \times 10^{-38} \times 3.35 \times 10^{-14}}{9.10956 \times 10^{-31}}$

(c) $\sigma_{th} =$ Lorenz number $\times\, \sigma_{el} \times$ temperature

$= 2.443 \times 10^{-8} \times 2.5 \times 10^7 \times 300 = 183.225 \text{W / K–m}$ .

(d) $k_F = m\, v_F / \hbar = 9.10956 \times 10^{-31} \times 1.066 \times 10^6 / 1.05459 \times 10^{-34}$

$= 9.2 \times 10^9\, m^{-1}$ . [Unit for $k_F$ = (kg–m / s) / J–s

= Newton / J = $m^{-1}$]

(e) $\delta k = -e E_a \tau / \hbar = -1.6022 \times 10^{-19} \times 2 \times 3.35 \times 10^{-14} / 1.0546 \times 10^{-34}$

$= -101.78\, m^{-1}$

$v_d = -e E_a \tau / m = 1.18 \times 10^{-2}$ m / s, opposite to direction of $E_a$.

Table 3.1 shows data for some well-known elements at room temperature.

**Table 3.1: Data for some common elements**

| Metal | Valency | $n$, $m^{-3}$ | $k_F$, $m^{-1}$ | $v_F$, m/s | $E_F$, eV |
|---|---|---|---|---|---|
| 1. Al | 3 | $18 \times 10^{28}$ | $1.75 \times 10^9$ | $2.0 \times 10^6$ | 11.63 |
| 2. Ag | 1 | $5.85 \times 10^{28}$ | $1.2 \times 10^9$ | $1.39 \times 10^6$ | 5.48 |
| 3. Au | 1 | $5.9 \times 10^{28}$ | $1.2 \times 10^9$ | $1.39 \times 10^6$ | 5.51 |
| 4. Ba | 2 | $3.2 \times 10^{28}$ | $0.98 \times 10^9$ | $1.13 \times 10^6$ | 3.65 |
| 5. Ca | 2 | $4.6 \times 10^{28}$ | $1.11 \times 10^9$ | $1.28 \times 10^6$ | 4.68 |
| 6. Cd | 2 | $9.28 \times 10^{28}$ | $1.4 \times 10^9$ | $1.62 \times 10^6$ | 7.46 |
| 7. Cu | 1 | $8.45 \times 10^{28}$ | $1.36 \times 10^9$ | $1.57 \times 10^6$ | 7.0 |
| 8. Ga | 3 | $15.3 \times 10^{28}$ | $1.65 \times 10^9$ | $1.9 \times 10^6$ | 10.35 |
| 9. In | 3 | $11.5 \times 10^{28}$ | $1.5 \times 10^9$ | $1.74 \times 10^6$ | 8.6 |
| 10. Na | 1 | $2.65 \times 10^{28}$ | $9.2 \times 10^9$ | $1.07 \times 10^6$ | 3.23 |
| 11. Zn | 2 | $13.1 \times 10^{28}$ | $1.57 \times 10^9$ | $1.82 \times 10^6$ | 9.39 |

## 3.5 Bonding in Crystals

A crystal is a stable structure with atoms located at lattice points and retained there by forces which act like bonds between neighbouring atoms. Because of forces of repulsion existing between positively-charged adjacent ions, as well as between negatively-charged electrons surrounding the nucleii, the atoms are held in their positions, and do not come any closer than determined by equilibrium conditions. These bonding forces depend on the number and arrangement of outermost orbiting electrons and we will discuss these in this section.

The more important types of bonding forces in crystals are the following: (a) Metallic bond; (b) Ionic bond; (c) Covalent bond; (d) Hydrogen bond; and (e) Van der Waals bond.

All of the above forces should be described by quantum-mechanical considerations, but we will omit these details and only describe the essential physical nature of the phenomena.

### *(a) Metallic Bond*

Metals are characterized by having one or more free electrons in the outermost orbital or unfilled shell or subshell which are free to move. See Table 3.1 for valency numbers. As has been described before, the atoms are immersed in a sea of electrons, and in this sense the free or conduction electron is shared by all the atoms. Since the electrons spend their time between positively-charged atoms (ions), they are attracted to them. This results in the atoms themselves being attracted to each other.

### *(b) Ionic Bond*

When a crystal is formed of two elements, in which one has an unfilled subshell lacking an electron and the other has an extra electron in its outermost shell or subshell, the extra electron can jump into the missing orbit in the first element thus forming stable shells or subshells. The loss of an electron makes the resulting atom a positive ion, while the absorption of an electron converts the second atom into a negative ion. The two ions now exhibit electrostatic attraction and a bonding force is created. These ions cannot come too close because of the force of repulsion between the electron clouds surrounding each nucleus.

Examples are $Na^+$ and $Cl^-$ in common salt. $^{11}$Na has 1 extra electron in the first subshell in the 3rd shell (2 + 8 + 1), while $^{17}$Cl has 1 electron lacking in the second subshell of the 3rd shell 2 + 8 + (2 + 5), which should have 6 electrons to form the closed subshell. Such bonding is prevalent in alkali-halides and other examples are as follows:

$^{3}$Li $^{9}$F, $^{3}$Li $^{17}$Cl, $^{11}$Na $^{9}$F, $^{11}$Na $^{17}$Cl, $^{19}$K F, K Cl, $^{55}$CsF,
(2+1), (10–1) (18–1) (10+1) (18+1) CsCl.

The 55 electrons in caesium are arranged as follows: 2, 8, 18, (2 + 6 + 10), (2 + 6 + 1).

### *(c) Covalent Bond*

This type of bond exists in semiconducting materials belonging to the IVth column of the Periodic Table of Elements. These have four electrons in the outer orbits, for example, $^{14}$Si (2 + 8 + 4), $^{32}$Ge (2 + 8 + 18 + 4), $^{6}$C (2 + 4). In order to have a stable closed shell or subshell, 8 electrons are necessary. This is made up by neighbouring atoms bonding together with their 4 outer electrons. Such bonds also exist when these materials are doped with impurities with 3 or 5 outer electrons, where 4 electrons form covalent bond with the (intrinsic) semiconducting material, leaving a hole (lack of electron) or an extra conduction electron, respectively. This is extremely important for solar-cell work, as will be seen in later sections.

Some elements belonging to the IIIrd column form covalent bonds with elements in the Vth column of the periodic table. Examples are Al, Ga, In with P, As, Sb. In such crystals, both ionic as well as covalent bonds exist. These are called III-V compounds.

*(d) Hydrogen Bond*

This is a variation of covalent bond and is particularly prominent in a compound such as water and ice. Because of quantum-mechanical considerations it transpires that the hydrogen atom is attracted towards one of the oxygen atoms in a molecule of water, and at other times by a second atom. Pictorially, we can view it as though a hydrogen atom describes a figure of 8 around two atoms of oxygen. This type of bonding is not very important for solar-cell work.

*(e) Van der Waals Bonding*

Because of existence of electric charge on electrons and the nucleus, they can induce charges on other particles, or in other words, can polarize them. The dipole moment caused by such polarization gives rise to an attractive force and contributes to inter-atomic bonding.

Some examples of energies involved per atom in different types of bonding are as follows:

Metallic : 1 - 5 eV (Tungsten is most tightly bound with 9 eV/atom)
Ionic : 5 eV
Covalent : 3 - 10 eV
Hydrogen : 0.3 - 1 eV .

## 3.6 Energy Bands

In a crystal the electrons move around their own atomic nucleii possessing energy levels generated and governed by the wave-function according to Schrodinger's equation subject to Pauli exclusion principle. Under externally applied forces such as temperature, electric fields, atomic vibrations, etc., these orbitals adjust themselves suitably. Due to collisions and atomic nucleii and the presence of other electrons, the wave-like behaviour of any electron is subject to Bragg reflection when it encounters other particles. This gives rise to the property that since the electron is constrained to move inside potential walls, it cannot have a continuous energy or frequency distribution, so that this results in gaps in energy. When the electron is constrained to move in an orbit around its own atomic nucleus, it stays (i.e. its orbital) in the valence band of energy. The electron farthest from the nucleus possesses the highest energy and occupies an orbit at the top of the valence band. In order to free this electron and make it take part in conduction, energy has to be supplied which increases the energy of the electron to make it occupy an energy level in the conduction band.

Furthermore, the electron wave is represented by the wave-function $\Psi = A\,e^{i \cdot k \cdot r} \cdot e^{-i \cdot \omega \cdot t}$ which represents a travelling or running or gliding wave. When this encounters the potential well represented by the positively-charged atomic nucleus, it is totally reflected if the potential barrier is considered infinitely high. The incident and reflected waves give rise to standing waves which possess a peak value and a minimum value of zero. Since the wave-function is the measure of probability of finding an electron in a given state, there are some positions at which the electron is not present and other positions where the probability of finding it in a given state (with given state variables or degrees of freedom) is maximum. Thus, some energy levels are not present while others are preferred.

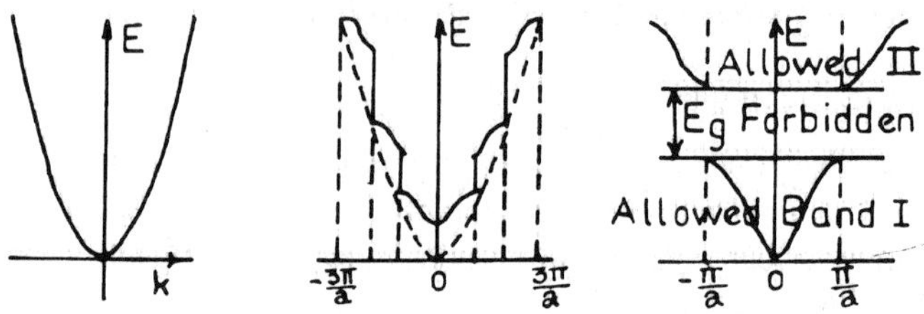


**Fig. 3.4** Energy gaps between valence and conduction bands in one dimension

Figure 3.4 shows the behaviour of energy levels as a function of *k* for a free electron*, and for an electron restricted to move between lattice atoms with separation distance *a*. It is a one-dimensional motion of the electron.

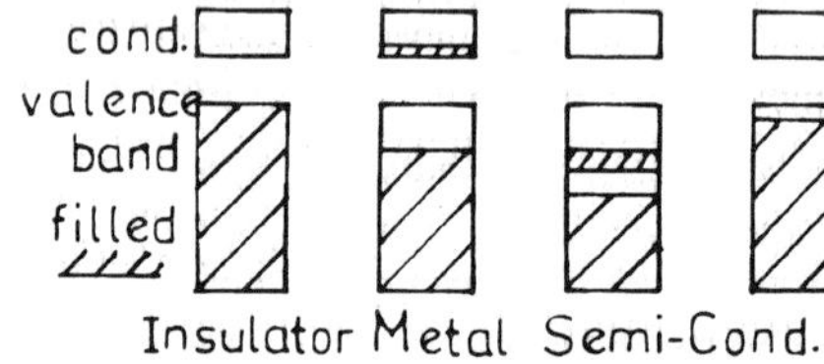


**Fig. 3.5** Energy bands in insulator, metal and semiconductors

If the valence electrons exactly fill one or more bands and others are empty, the crystal is a perfect insulator. No external electric field of reasonable value can cause them to move into the conduction band, and no electric current flows. In a metal, there are free electrons in the conduction band and the bands sometimes overlap. If there exists a definite

* The letter *k* has been used in standard literature in physics to denote Boltzmann's constant and wave number. This should cause no confusion from the context.

gap between valence and conduction bands, and furthermore some energy levels at the top of the valence band are empty and at the bottom of the conduction bands are filled, the crystal may belong to a semiconductor. A pictorial representation of energy bands of these three types of elements are qualitatively shown in Fig. 3.5.

For solar cells, semiconductors are the most useful of the three types and we now concentrate our attention on this material.

### 3.7 Semiconductor Crystals, Intrinsic Carriers

Figure 3.4 showed the energy gap between the valence and conduction bands in one-dimension. Since the electron moves in three dimensions, the allowed energies and orbitals look more like Fig. 3.6 in GaAs. The allowed energies experience still further differentiation, when we view the crystal along different lattice planes.

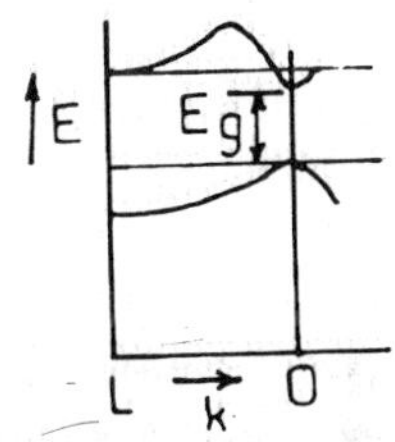


**Fig. 3.6** Permssible energy levels in three dimensions in GaAs

The band gap energy in semiconductors for solar cells ranges between 0.8 and 2.4 eV at 0 K. With increase in temperature, some valence-band electrons can acquire sufficient energy to move into the conduction band, leaving holes in the valence band. As we will observe later, adding impurities or doping these semiconductor materials can increase conduction properties by factors of $10^4$.

Table 3.2 gives values of energy gaps (band gaps) for several semiconductor materials used in solar cells, in eV.

**Table 3.2**

| | Ge | Si | InSb | GaAs | CdSe | CdTe | InP |
|---|---|---|---|---|---|---|---|
| 0 K | 0.74 | 1.17 | 0.23 | 1.52 | 1.84 | 1.61 | 1.29 |
| 300 K | 0.67 | 1.14 | 0.18 | 1.43 | 1.74 | 1.45 | 1.35 |

The density or concentration of electrons in the conduction band increases with increase in temperature. They vary from $10^{10}$ to $10^{14}$ conduction electrons/cm$^3$ as the temperature is increased from 200 to 300 K in Ge, and 280 to 450 K in Si, as shown in Fig. 3.7. In comparison, metals like Na, K and Cu have conduction electron concentrations of $10^{22}$ - $10^{23}$ per cc at room temperature as shown in Table 3.1. If the band gap is large, the concentration of intrinsic conduction charge carriers will be low. These are controlled to a large extent by $(E_g/kT)$.

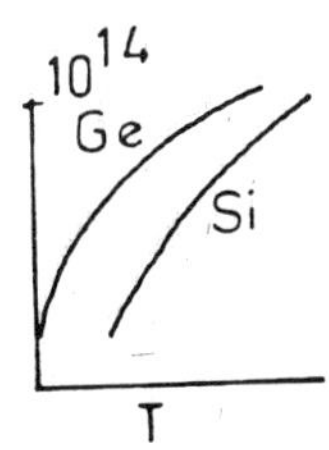


**Fig. 3.7** Density of electrons in conduction bands as a function of temperature

In semiconductors the chemical potential or Fermi level is midway between the top of the valence band and bottom of the conduction band. We usually measure energy from the top of valence band, see Fig. 3.8.

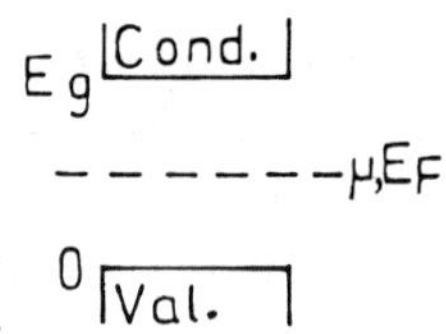


**Fig. 3.8** Fermi level in semiconductors

*Law of Mass Action and Generation of Electrons and Holes*

Equation (3.12) gave the density of states per unit volume and unit energy at the Fermi level. This is

$$D_e(E_F) = (1/2\pi^2)\cdot(2m_e/\hbar^2)^{3/2}\cdot E_F^{1/2} \tag{3.12}$$

At other energies; the number of orbitals with energy between $E$ and $(E + dE)$ is

$$D_e(E)\cdot dE = (1/2\pi^2)\cdot(2m_e/\hbar^2)^{3/2}\cdot(E-E_g)^{1/2}\cdot dE \tag{3.24}$$

The Fermi-Dirac distribution gives the probability of finding an electron at an energy level $E$, so that the concentration of electrons is

$$n_e = \int_{E_g}^{\infty} D(E)\cdot f_{FDe}(E)\cdot dE \tag{3.25}$$

Now, $$f_{FDe}(E) = [e^{(E-E_F)/kT} + 1]^{-1} \approx e^{-(E-E_F)/kT} \tag{3.26}$$

if $(E - E_F) >> kT$, in the conduction band. At room temperature $T = 300$ K, $kT = 8.6174\times10^{-5}\times300 = 2.585\times10^{-2}$ eV while $(E - E_F)\approx 1$ eV. Using Eq. (3.26) in Eq. (3.25), we obtain

$$n_e = \int_{E_g}^{\infty}(1/2\pi^2)\cdot(2m_e/\hbar^2)^{3/2}\cdot(E-E_g)^{1/2}\cdot e^{-(E-E_F)/kT}\cdot dE \tag{3.27}$$

Let $x = (E-E_g)/kT$, $dx = dE/kT$, so that

$$e^{-(E-E_F)/kT} = e^{(E_F-E_g)/kT}\cdot e^{-(E-E_g)/kT} = e^{(E_F-E_g)/kT}\cdot e^{-x}$$

Therefore

$$n_e = (1/2\pi^2)\cdot(2m_e/\hbar^2)^{3/2}\cdot e^{(E_F-E_g)/kT}\cdot(kT)^{3/2}\int_0^{\infty}x^{1/2}\cdot e^{-x}\cdot dx \tag{3.28}$$

The definite integral $\int_0^{\infty}x^{1/2}\cdot e^{-x}\cdot dx = \sqrt{\pi}/2$. Finally the concentration of conduction electrons or orbitals in the conduction band is

$$n_e = 2(m_e kT/2\pi\hbar^2)^{3/2}\cdot e^{(E_F-E_g)/kT} \tag{3.29}$$

We observe that above Eq. (3.29) involves a knowledge of the Fermi level. In order to circumvent this problem, we enquire what the hole concentration $n_h$ would be caused by vacant electron orbitals in the valence band. Having done this, we set

$$n_e = n_h = \sqrt{n_e\cdot n_h} \tag{3.30}$$

Now, since a hole means absence of an electron, the F-D distribution function for holes will become

$$f_{\text{FDh}} = 1 - f_{\text{FDe}} \approx e^{(E - E_F)/kT} \tag{3.31}$$

since,
$$1 - [e^{(E - E_F)/kT} + 1]^{-1} = e^{(E - E_F)/kT} \cdot [e^{(E - E_F)/kT} + 1]^{-1}$$

$$= [1 + e^{(E_F - E)/kT}]^{-1} \approx e^{(E - E_F)/kT}, \text{ for } (E_F - E) >> kT.$$

We note that energy levels for holes are negative. Then, the density of hole orbitals is

$$D_h(E) \cdot dE = (1/2\pi^2) \cdot 2\, m_h/\hbar^2)^{3/2} \cdot (-E)^{1/2} \cdot dE \tag{3.32}$$

where $(-E)$ is the energy from the top of the valence band.

Therefore $n_h = \int_{-\infty}^{0} D_h(E) \cdot f_{FDh} \cdot dE$

$$= (1/2\pi^2) \cdot (2\, m_h/\hbar^2)^{3/2} \int_{-\infty}^{0} e^{(E - E_F)/kT} \cdot (-E)^{1/2} \cdot dE \tag{3.33}$$

Following the steps as before, there results

$$n_h = 2\,(m_h\, kT/2\pi\hbar^2)^{3/2} \cdot e^{-E_F/kT} \tag{3.34}$$

Multiplying $n_e$ and $n_h$ from Eqs. (3.29) and (3.34), there results

$$n_e \cdot n_h = 4\,(kT/2\pi\hbar^2)^3 \cdot (m_e\, m_h)^{3/2} \cdot e^{-E_g/kT} \tag{3.35}$$

This depends only on the energy gap $E_g$ and does not involve the Fermi level $E_F$ in the semiconductor. Since the concentration of electrons in the conduction band must equal the concentration of holes in the valence band, we obtain

$$n_e = n_h = \sqrt{n_e \cdot n_h} = 2\,(kT/2\pi\hbar^2)^{3/2} \cdot (m_e \cdot m_h)^{3/4} \cdot e^{-E_g/2kT} \tag{3.36}$$

Furthermore, if $m_e = m_h$, the above expression is simplified further.

***Example 3.3***: Given that $E_g$ = 1 eV and $T$ = 300 K, calculate $n_e$ and $n_h$. Also compare with $E_g$ = 1.5 and 2 eV for the band gap.

$$[\,k = 1.38066 \times 10^{-23} \text{ J/K} = 8.6174 \times 10^{-5} \text{ eV/K}.$$

$$m_e = m_h = 9.1095 \times 10^{-31} \text{ kg},\ \hbar = 1.05459 \times 10^{-34} \text{ J–s}\,]$$

***Solution***:

$$\underline{E_g = 1}: n_e = n_h = 2\left(\frac{1.38066 \times 10^{-23} \times 300 \times 9.1095 \times 10^{-31}}{2\pi \times 1.05459^2 \times 10^{-68}}\right)^{3/2} \times$$

$$e^{-1/2 \times 8.6174 \times 10^{-5} \times 300}$$

$$= 2 \times 12.546445 \times 10^{24} \times e^{-19.340714}$$

$$= 25.093 \times 10^{24} / 2.5094 \times 10^{8} = 10^{17} / \text{m}^3$$

$$= 10^{11} \text{ charge carriers / cm}^3 .$$

$$\underline{E_g = 1.5} : n_e = n_h = 25.093 \times 10^{24} / (2.5094 \times 10^{8})^{1.5}$$

$$= 0.631245 \times 10^{12} / \text{m}^3 .$$

$$\underline{E_g = 2} : n_e = n_h = 25.093 \times 10^{24} / (2.5094 \times 10^{8})^{2}$$

$$= 3.985 \times 10^{8} / \text{m}^3 .$$

Note the reduction in concentration as $E_g$ increases, with temperature remaining constant.

*Fermi level in Semiconductor*

From Eqs. (3.29) and (3.34), taking $n_e = n_h$, there results

$$m_e^{3/2} \cdot e^{(E_F - E_g)/kT} = m_h^{3/2} \cdot e^{-E_F/kT}, \text{ giving}$$

$$e^{2E_F/kT} = (m_h / m_e)^{3/2} \cdot e^{E_g/kT} \tag{3.37}$$

or

$$2 E_F = E_g + (3\,kT/2) \cdot \ln (m_h / m_e) \tag{3.38}$$

If we take $m_h = m_e$, which is nearly valid, the Fermi level is $E_F = ½\, E_g$, i.e. it lies in the middle of the forbidden gap.

*Mobility*

Upto now we have taken the mass of an electron and of a hole equal to the rest mass of the electron. However, when an electric field is applied, due to the wave-like motion of the electron, the mass against which the force acts and does work results in a lowering of the actual mass of the charge carrier to an "effective mass". This is shown as follows:

The wave function is $\Psi = A\, e^{ikx} \cdot e^{-iEt/\hbar} = A\, e^{i(kx - \omega t)}$ (3.39)

The group velocity is defined by

$$v = d\omega / dk = d(E/\hbar)/dk = (1/\hbar) \cdot dE/dk \tag{3.40}$$

The phase velocity of the wave is $v_{ph} = dx/dt = \omega / k = \lambda\,\omega / 2\pi$, since $k = 2\pi/\lambda$, the wave vector number. It has unit of $m^{-1}$.

The acceleration caused by an external applied force is

$$\alpha = \frac{dv}{dk} \cdot \frac{dk}{dt} = dv/dt \tag{3.41}$$

Now, the energy $dE = F \cdot dx = F \cdot v \cdot dt$ (3.42)

Therefore $dE/dt = F \cdot v = F \cdot (1/\hbar) \cdot dE/dk$, or, $F = \hbar \cdot dk/dt$ (3.43)

Thus $$\alpha = dv/dt = (dv/dk) \cdot (F/\hbar) = \frac{1}{\hbar^2}\frac{d^2E}{dk^2} \cdot F \quad (3.44)$$

upon using Eq. (3.40). We observe that $\left(\frac{1}{\hbar^2}\frac{d^2E}{dk^2}\right)^{-1}$ is in the form of an effective mass, if we denote $\alpha = F/m_e^*$.

In so far as the solid is concerned, an electron in it can be assumed to have a mass equal to $m_e^*$. Similarly for holes.

The velocity acquired under the application of an electric field is

$$v_e = \mu_e E, \text{ and } v_h = \mu_h E \quad (3.45)$$

where $\mu_e$ and $\mu_h$ are mobilities of electron and hole, respectively. Since resistance is caused by collisions, the mean time for collision is given by taking force = mass × acceleration, or

$$eE = m_e^* v_e/\tau, \text{ or, } v_e = eE\tau/m_e^*, \text{ or, } \mu_e = e\tau/m_e^* \quad (3.46)$$

The electrical conductivity is caused by the motion of both electrons and holes, so that

$$\sigma = n_e e \cdot \mu_e + n_h e \cdot \mu_h = n_e e^2 \tau/m_e^* + n_h e^2 \tau/m_h^* \quad (3.47)$$

Table 3.3 gives examples of electron and hole mobilities in some semiconductors at room temperature.

**Table 3.3**

| | Si | Ge | InSb | InP | InAs | |
|---|---|---|---|---|---|---|
| $\mu_e$ | 1300 | 4500 | 77000 | 4600 | 33000 | cm/s per V/cm |
| $\mu_h$ | 500 | 3500 | 750 | 150 | 460 | = $cm^2$/V-s |

## 3.8 Junctions

The successful operation of a solar cell depends on electric fields created by the charge carriers and this requires that two or more materials be fused into junctions during the manufacturing process. Ge and Si belong to group IV of the periodic table, while group III elements are In, Ga, Al, and group V are As, P, Sb. We also have Cd, Zn in group II, and Te, Se in group VI. When semiconductors are formed by combining elements belonging to different groups, we obtain compounds such as IV-V, III-IV, III-V, II-VI, etc.

Group IV-V semiconductors are known as N-type, since group V element contributes 1 more free electron than the number of completed covalent bonds of 4.

Group III-IV materials are P-type, since group III element lacks 1 electron to form a completed covalent bond. The lack of an electron is obviously the presence of a hole. This can move under an applied electrical force and thus forms a current flow. Similarly, II-V compounds yield an extra electron and hole as demanded by a covalent bond of 4.

When a donor (of an electron), or group V material is combined with the intrinsic semiconductor and a free electron is present, it lowers the conduction band and the energy gap decreases. Similarly, the acceptor material (group II or III) yields holes which raises the valence band energy and also lowers the net energy gap. Figure 3.9 depicts pictorially what happens. ($E_C - E_D$) and ($E_A - E_V$) are of the order of kT, which at room temperature is 0.026 eV (= 8.6174 × $10^{-5}$ × 300). As donors are added to the intrinsic semiconductor material, the electron concentration is increased, while the hole concentration is decreased. Similarly, for a material doped with acceptor impurity, the hole concentration is increased. Normally, the ratio of charge carriers of donors and acceptors to intrinsic charge carriers is ($N_D$ or $N_A$)/$n_i$ ≈ $10^4$ to $10^5$.

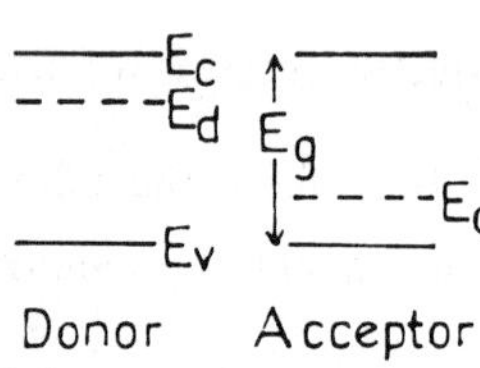


**Fig. 3.9** Energy bands with donor and acceptor impurities

Now, let us observe what happens when a P material has a junction with the N-material. At the junction, the Fermi levels are equalized. Figures 3.10 and 3.11 show the sequence of events. The Fermi level in the N-type is closer to the donor level, while in P-type it is closer to the acceptor level. When a junction is formed, equalization of the Fermi levels requires that in the P-type both the valence band energy $E_V$ and

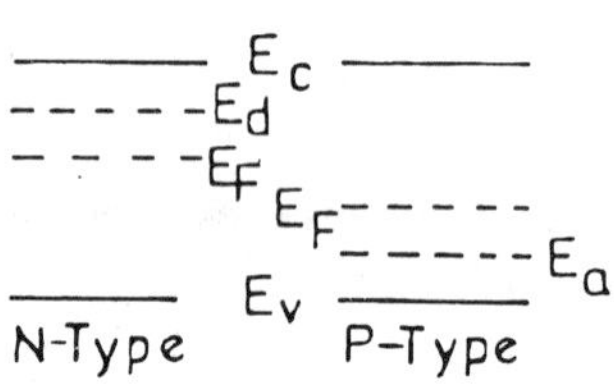


**Fig. 3.10** Fermi levels in N-type and P-type semiconductors

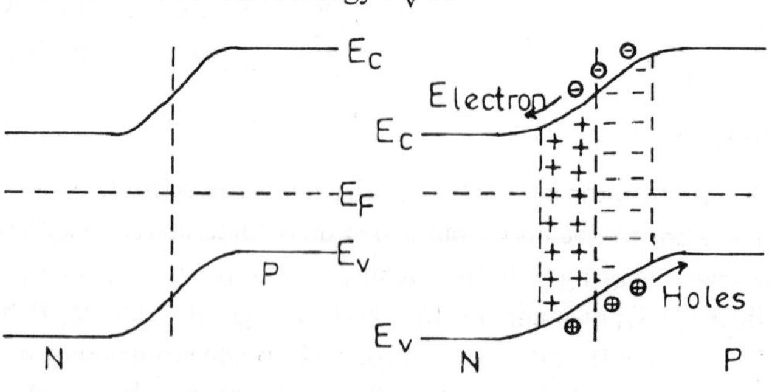


**Fig. 3.11** Barrier layer at P-N junction

conduction band energy $E_C$ be raised above those for the N-type. On account of this rise, any electron due to energy acquired at room temperature from the N-type will drift into the P-type across the junction to form a negative space charge. Similarly, some holes will drift from the P-type across the junction to form a positive space charge in the N-type material near the junction. This creates an electric field. Accumulation of space charge will prevent further drifts of charge carriers of the appropriate type. A junction or barrier potential or contact potential is generated, which is entirely responsible for the operation of a solar cell to generate a voltage across the externally-connected load. Because electrons on the P-side recombine with some holes, and holes on the N-side with electrons, there is a depletion layer across the junction. By shining light across the junction, sufficient energy is imparted for electrons to flow into the N-side and holes into the P-side of the solar-cell junction. We will discuss this mechanism in more detail later on.

### 3.9 Recombination and Carrier Lifetimes

When energy is imparted to the junction of the right type, say by shining light in a photo-voltaic cell, electron-hole pairs are created and these are separated to flow in an external load, electrons from the N-type material and holes from the P-type material. However, not all of the electrons and holes created in the bulk of the material of the solar cell can flow out to the load. Some percentage recombine in the material itself, given the time required, called the recombination time or carrier lifetime. The success of a solar cell to provide a load current depends on sweeping the electrons and holes into the load in a time less than the time of recombination. Recombination in the bulk material occurs in traps caused by defects. Note that recombination of electrons in N-type means that minority carrier holes are present to some extent in this material. Similarly, holes generated in P-type recombine with electrons, which are minority carriers in P-type material.

In addition to this type of recombination in the bulk of the semiconductor used in solar cells, there are other types of recombination which are briefly as follows:

(a) Recombination on the surface of the crystal on which radiation photons strike the cell. This surface region is 20 to 100 Å thick.

(b) Radiative recombination occurring when electrons cross the energy gap from conduction to valence band to fill a hole and releasing a photon.

(c) At higher energies, the carriers recombine in a process called Auger recombination.

Table 3.4 shows some minority carrier lifetimes (sec) for low levels of donor and acceptor impurity. ($N_D = N_A = 10^{14} - 10^{15}$ carriers/cm$^3$). The lifetimes of minority carrier electrons in P-type is generally equal to the lifetime of minority carrier holes in N-type. ($\tau_n = \tau_p$).

**Table 3.4: Minority Carrier Lifetimes (sec) in Solar Cell Semiconducting Materials**

| Si | Ge | InP | GaAs | GaP | CdTe | CdSe | AlSb |
|---|---|---|---|---|---|---|---|
| $0.8 \times 10^{-4}$ | $0.5 \times 10^{-4}$ | $4 \times 10^{-8}$ | $4 \times 10^{-8}$ | $4 \times 10^{-8}$ | $16 \times 10^{-8}$ | $16 \times 10^{-8}$ | $9 \times 10^{-8}$ |

The minority carrier lifetimes are given by the following equations based on Shottky-Read-Hall theory:

$$\tau_p = \tau_n = (\sigma\, v_{th}\, N_t)^{-1} \qquad (3.48)$$

where $\sigma$ = capture cross-section of electrons and holes in traps, i.e crystal defects

$v_{th}$ = average thermal velocity of carriers

$$= (3\,\mathrm{kT}/m^*)^{1/2} \approx 10^7\ \mathrm{cm/s}\ ;\ (m^*\, v_{th}^2 = 3\,\mathrm{kT}) \qquad (3.49)$$

and $N_t$ = density of traps.

## 3.10 PN Junction-, Hetero Junction-, Shottky Barrier-, and MOS Solar Cells

The principles of operation and electrical characteristics of solar cells will be very briefly discussed here. Practical uses will be discussed later in Sec. 3.18. In all of these, an electric field must be created by using the energy gap between valence and conduction bands, and the barrier potential at the junction.

(1) A *PN* junction is created by a P-material (III-IV) and an *N*-material (IV-V), where the intrinsic semiconductor is the same for both types (group IV). The energy levels are shown in Fig. 3.12.

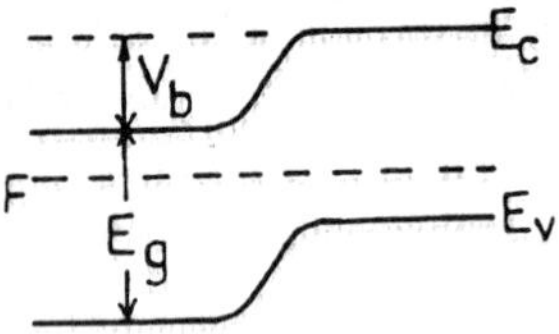


**Fig. 3.12** Energy levels in P-N junction

Intrinsic semiconductors are Si and Ge. Donor impurity atoms are P, As, Sb. Acceptor atoms are B, Al, In, Ga.

(2) A hetero-junction is made from two different types of semiconductors. Examples are:

| ZnSe - Ge, | GaAs - Ge | $Ga_{1-x}\ Al_x$ As - GaAs |
|---|---|---|
| (II,VI)-(IV) | (III,V)-(IV) | (III, III, V)-(III,V) |

The energy levels are shown in Fig. 3.13. Note that the energy gaps may be different on the two sides of the junction, but the Fermi levels are equal.

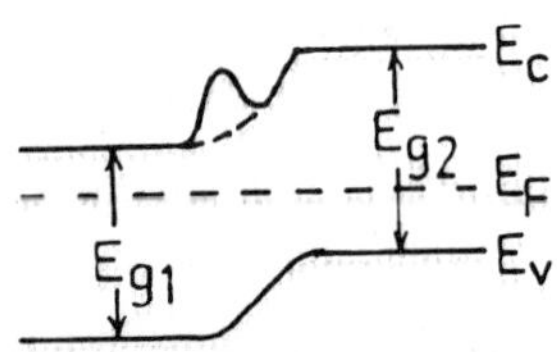


**Fig. 3.13** Energy levels in heterojunction materials

(3) The Shottky barrier material consists of a metal and an *N*-type semiconductor. Figure 3.14 shows a sketch of the energy levels.

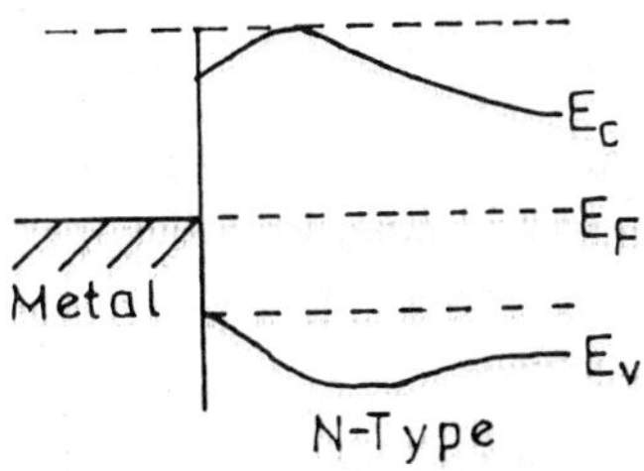


**Fig. 3.14** Energy levels in Shottky barrier material

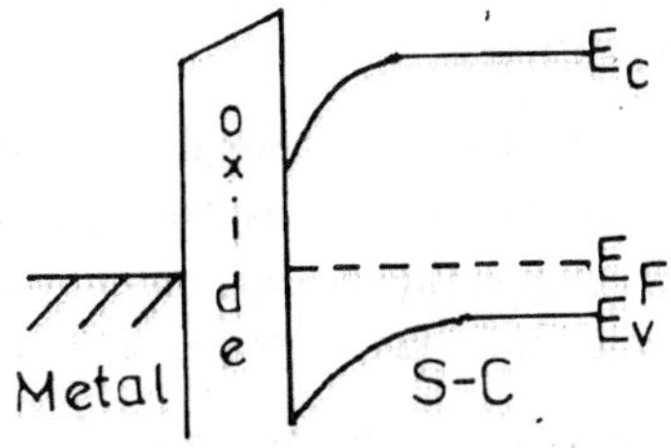


**Fig. 3.15** Energy levels in MOS material

(4) In a metal-oxide semiconductor, *MOS*, an oxide layer is interposed between the metal and semiconductor, one example being aluminium oxide and P-type silicon semiconductor. Normally, the barrier voltage is 0.4 V for Al on Si. But with the interposed oxide, this rises to 0.85 V. Figure 3.15 depicts the energy levels. Tunnelling is very much the mode of current flow through the interface.

### 3.11 Amorphous Materials and Liquid Crystals

Amorphous silicon has received a great deal of attention as material for solar cells. Depending on the manufacturing technique used, band gaps of about 1.5 eV are obtained, but on account of defects, recombination is high and efficiency lower than for crystalline-material photovoltaic cells. Fabrication costs, when large areas of solar arrays are required, are lower than for crystalline materials. These are known as (a- Si: H) films for amorphous silicon hydrogenated.

Discussion of physics of amorphous state is beyond the scope of the intended purpose of this book. Atomic positions in this material do not follow periodicity over a long range. But the average distribution of atoms from any chosen atom can be found using the very immense calculating abilities of large-memory digital computers. Once a pattern emerges (which is random) for the arrangement of atoms, other characteristics are predicted based on methods available for crystalline solids.

Solar cells fabricated from amorphous solids have the following forms:

(a) Shottky barrier cells have undoped a-Si:H deposited on molybdenum and a thin film of palladium on top of the silicon film.

(b) MIS cell has an insulating (I) layer of titanium oxide sandwiched between a metal, usually Pt, and the a-Si:H. Sunlight enters through the very thin film of metal and insulating layer and falls on the amorphous Si.

(c) PIN solar cells have a P-type material consisting of a-Si:H doped with boron, which is deposited on steel which is next to undoped a-Si:H layer and then an N-material which is usually a-Si:H doped with P (group V).

*Liquid Crystals*

A liquid crystal is a material that combines the properties of crystal-like behaviour or order, and amorphous disorder. These are organic molecules whose positions can be regular in one direction and disordered in another. There are two types of liquid crystals: (a) Lyotropic; and (b) Thermotropic.

Lyotropic liquid crystals are rod-like with lengths of about 300 Å and diameters of 20 Å. They are synthetic molecules. Soaps are one type of lyotropic liquid-crystals of alkaline molecules, which become positive ions in solution and then order themselves.

Thermotropic liquid crystals are known as nematic and three types of smectic (A, B, C). Nematic means thread-like and smectic stands for soap-like in Greek. Figure 3.16 shows molecules in a liquid crystal. The nematic type molecules do

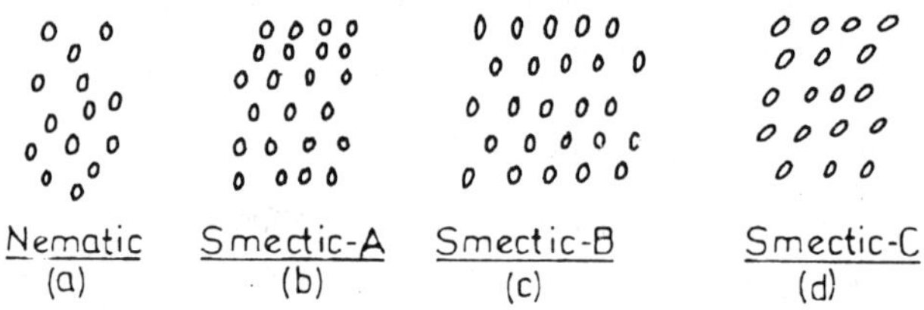


**Fig. 3.16** Arrangement of molecules in liquid crystals:
(a) Nematic: Molecules aligned. No long-range order in positions
(b) Smectic *A*: Molecules in layers and aligned perpendicular to layers
(c) Smectic *B*: Molecules form two-dimensional crystals. Positions on different layers not related.
(d) Smectic *C*: Molecules in layers, but long dimension not perpendicular to layers

not exhibit a long-range order in their positions, but nevertheless the molecules are aligned. In smectic type, they are concentrated in layers with three different configurations.

*Smectic A*: The molecules are aligned at right angles to layers.

*Smectic B*: Molecular positions on different layers are unrelated.

*Smectic C*: Molecules are disposed in layers and are aligned with their long dimension inclined to the layers and not perpendicular to them.

At high temperature, all four are nematic. At lower temperatures the molecules arrange themselves in layers, the molecules showing amorphous structure to begin with and become periodic as the temperature is lowered still further, and ends up as smectic B phase when it crystallizes completely. The reflectivity of these molecules depends on their orientation so that they are used in display devices. Applied electric fields, magnetic fields, temperature and pressure can

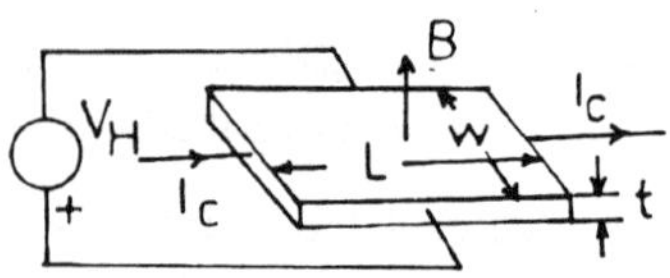


**Fig. 3.17** Hall effect in semiconductor

control these orientations and hence the colours. Furthermore, they can be used as pressure and temperature sensors.

### 3.12 Hall Effect and Hall-Effect Devices

In Fig. 3.17 is shown a semiconductor chip of dimensions ($w \times t \times L$). A magnetic field of strength $B$ Tesla is applied along $t$. A current $I_c$ is made to flow from an external source along $L$. If electrodes are connected across the remaining two perpendicular faces of area ($L \times t$), a voltage is generated across them. This is because a Lorenz force acts on the electrons both inside the semiconductor and the externally-pumped electrons.

If $u$ = velocity of electron, m/s, the Lorenz force is

$$F = e\,u\,B, \text{ Newton} \tag{3.50}$$

This force acts along the direction of $w$, and the electron now has a velocity in this direction. The voltage gradient due to this by Faraday's law will be

$$e_H = u \cdot B, \; V/m \tag{3.51}$$

The voltage measured will be

$$V_H = w \cdot e_H = w\,u\,B \tag{3.52}$$

The control current is $I_c = j\,w\,t$ (3.53)

where $j$ = current density in the material = $n\,e\,u$

and $n$ = electron or charge carrier concentration/m$^3$

Therefore $I_c = n\,e\,u\,w\,t$ (3.54)

Consequently $B = V_H / w\,u = V_H\,n\,e\,t / I_C = (1/R_H) \cdot (V_H/I_c) \cdot t$ (3.55)

where $R_H = 1/n\,e = 1/\text{charge density}$ (3.56)

This is known as the Hall coefficient which clearly depends on the doping level of the semiconductor.

A Hall-effect probe is eminently used for measuring the following:

(a) Flux density in a magnetic circuit when a control current is sent into the material and the Hall voltage is measured. The thickness of a typical chip is only 0.1 mm and the area is 1.5 × 3 mm. The probe is first calibrated in a known B-field to determine ($R_H/t$) for the particular chip used.

(b) The doping level ($n\,e$) in the material is measured if $B$, $V_H$ and $I_c$ are known.

The Hall-effect device has four terminals: two for connecting to a dc power supply to impress the control current $I_c$, and the remaining two for connecting a high-impedance voltmeter to measure the Hall voltage $V_H$. These devices can operate from –270 to +100°C, and measure fields up to several Teslas.

## OBJECTIVE TYPE QUESTIONS

1. Solar cells are made from materials which are: (a) crystalline; (b) polycrystalline; (c) amorphous; (d) all three.

2. Solid state materials are: (a) simple metals; (b) semiconductors; (c) insulators; (d) all three.

3. Simple metals are alkaline, like: (a) Li; (b) K; (c) Rb; (d) all three.

4. Noble metals include: (a) Cu; (b) Ag; (c) Au; (d) all three.

5. Bivalent simple metals include: (a) Mg; (b) In; (c) Ga; (d) Hg; (e) all four.

6. Important materials for solar cells can be: (a) Si; (b) Ga-As; (c) CdTe; (d) InP; (e) all four.

7. When an electron of energy $E$ is moving between two infinitely high potential barriers, the Schrödinger equation is:

   (a) $-(2\,m/\hbar^2)\cdot d^2\,\Psi_n/d\,x^2 = E_n\,\Psi_n$;
   (b) $d^2\,\Psi_n/d\,x^2 = -(2\,m/\hbar^2)\cdot E_n\cdot\Psi_n$;
   (c) $d^2\,\Psi_n/d\,x^2 = -(\hbar^2/2\,m)\cdot E_n\cdot\Psi_n$;
   (d) $d^2\,\Psi_n/d\,x^2 = (\hbar^2/2\,m)\cdot E_n\,\Psi_n$.

8. The Fermi-Dirac probability distribution function at any given electron energy and temperature is: (a) $1+e^{E/kt}$; (b) $1+e^{(E-\mu)/kT}$; (c) $e^{(E-\mu)/kT}$; (d) $[1+e^{-(\mu-E)/kT}]^{-1}$.

9. The energy μ in question 8 is the energy at which the probability of occupied states is: (a) $e^{-1}$; (b) 0.5; (c) 1/3; (d) 1/kT.

10. The electrical conductivity of a material is proportional to: (a) charge density (*ne*) of electrons; (b) the ratio (*e*/*m*) of the electron; (c) collision time τ of the electron; (d) all three.

11. The thermal conductivity is: (a) dependent on temperature; (b) independent of temperature; (c) follows Wiedeman-Franz law; (d) both (b) and (c) are true; (e) both (a) and (c) are true.

12. The ratio of $\sigma_{th}/\sigma_e$ depends upon: (a) Boltzmann's constant; (b) temperature; (c) Lorentz number; (d) all three.

13. The bond of atoms in crystal can be: (a) metallic; (b) ionic; (c) covalent; (d) hydrogen-like; (e) all four.

14. In order of increasing energy, bonding is generally arranged as follows: (a) Metallic; ionic, covalent, hydrogen; (b) Hydrogen, metallic, ionic, covalent; (c) Metallic, hydrogen, covalent, ionic; (d) Hydrogen, covalent, ionic, metallic.

15. Which of the bonds is used most in solar cell work? (a) metallic; (b) ionic; (c) covalent; (d) hydrogen-like; (e) Van der Waals.

16. Which type of material is most useful for solar cell work? (a) metals; (b) insulators; (c) semiconductors; (d) liquid crystals.

17. Solar cells can be: (a) PN junction type; (b) hetero-junction type; (c) Shottky barrier type; (d) MOS; (e) all four.

18. Energy gap usually denotes energy difference between: (a) conduction and valence band; (b) bottom of valence band and bottom of conduction band; (c) top of valence band and bottom of conduction band; (d) none of the three, since energy levels have to form a continuous band.

19. Examples of n-type semiconductors are: (a) Groups IV-V; (b) III-IV; (c) III-V; (d) Si-As; (e) both (a) and (d).

20. Examples of p-type semiconductors are: (a) Groups III-IV; (b) III-V; (c) Si-In; (d) Ga-As; (e) all four.

21. Which statements are valid? (a) Hall coefficient = reciprocal of charge density; (b) Hall gradient = velocity of charge × flux density; (c) Flux density = Hall voltage × material thickness/(Hall coefficient × control current); (d) all three are true.

22. A lyotropic liquid crystal (a) has rod-like organic molecules; (b) is designated as smectic; (c) has thread-like molecules; (d) none of the three.

23. Thermotropic liquid crystals (a) are soap-like; (b) are designated as smectic; (c) have thread-like organic molecules; (d) none of the three are true.

24. Solar cells are made of junctions of: (a) GaAs; (b) InP; (c) CdTe; (d) GaP; (e) all four.

25. Which quantities are most useful for solar cells? (a) High energy gap; (b) high temperature withstand; (c) low internal resistance; (d) all three are contributing and desirable factors.

[***Answers***: 1. (d); 2. (d); 3. (d); 4. (d); 5. (e); 6. (e); 7. (b); 8. (d); 9. (b); 10. (d); 11. (e); 12. (d); 13. (e); 14. (b); 15. (c); 16. (c); 17. (e); 18. (c); 19. (e); 20. (e); 21. (d): 22. (a); 23. (b); 24. (e); 25. (d).]

## REVIEW QUESTIONS AND PROBLEMS

1. What is common to the following sets of metals? (a) Li, Na, K, Ce, Rb, Cu, Ag, Au; (b) Be, Mg, Ca, Sr, Ba; (c) Al, Ga, In, Tl, Zn, Cd, Hg, Pb; (d) C, Si, Ge.
   Explain through shells, subshells, free electrons, etc.
   [(a) They all have 1 extra electron in the last subshell and shell. (b) These

have two free elctrons. (c) They have 2 conduction electrons. (d) These have 4 valence electrons.]

2. List 10 materials which have been considered as best for use as solar cells. Give their group numbers in the periodic table.
[Ge (IV), Si (IV), In-P (III-V), Ga-As (III-V), Cd-Te (II-VI), Al-Sb (III-V), Cd-Se (II-VI), Ga-P (III-V), Al-P (III-V), ZnSe-Ge (II,VI-IV), GaAs-Ge (III,V-IV).]

3. List three elements which form *n*-type semiconductor with Si, and three elements which give p-type material.
[n-type: P, As, Sb with Ge and Si; p-type; In, Ga, Al with Ge and Si.]

4. Derive Schrödinger's equation (3.1) for the wave-function of an electron moving in an infinite potential well. Then derive Eq. (3.3) for the permissible energy levels.

5. The Fermi level $E_F$ in a crystal is 2.5 eV. Calculate: (a) the temperature equivalent of $E_F$. (b) Write the Fermi-Dirac distribution function using this value of $E_F$. (c) Calculate the probabilities at (kT) = 0.2, 0.4, 0.8, 1.25 and 2.5 eV.

[(a) 2.5 eV = 29,000 K; (b) $f_{FD} = [1 + e^{(E-2.5)/8.6174 \times 10^{-5} T}]^{-1}$; (c) 0.076, 0.2227, 0.3486, 0.4013, 0.45.]

6. Explain the importance of Wiedeman-Franz law and the Lorenz number.

7. An X-ray used for determining crystal structure has a wavelength of $\lambda = 1.542$ Å. Find its energy in keV, degree K, Joule.
[$E = 14.384 \times 10^7$ K, 12.4 keV, $19.8786 \times 10^{-16}$ J]

8. A copper wire of 2.5 mm diameter carries a current of 12.5 A. (a) Calculate the drift velocity of electrons. (b) Find the average time $\tau$ between collisions. Assume concentration density of electrons = $8.5 \times 10^{28}/m^3$ at the temperature of the problem and electrical resistivity of copper as $\rho = 1.56$ μ-ohm-cm.
[(a) $v_d = 0.187 \times 10^{-3}$ m/s = 0.187 mm/s; (b) $2.676 \times 10^{-14}$ s]

9. (a) Explain clearly the Hall effect and show that the Hall voltage gradient is $\mathcal{E}_H = -\boldsymbol{v}_d \times \boldsymbol{B}$ for electrons. (b) Give the definition of Hall coefficient. (c) Calculate the Hall coefficients for Na, Al, and Cu, if the densities of electrons are ($2.52 \times 10^{28}$, $18.2 \times 10^{28}$ and $8.5 \times 10^{28}/m^3$) for the three materials, respectively. Give proper unit and sign.
[Na: $-248 \times 10^{-12}$; Al: $-34.3 \times 10^{-12}$; Cu: $-73.4 \times 10^{-12}$.
Unit: $R_H = (\text{coulomb/m}^3)^{-1} = \text{m}^3/\text{coul}$.]

10. In a piece of copper with $n = 8.45 \times 10^{28}$ charge carriers/m$^3$, the Fermi energy $E_F = 7$ eV. The collision time is $3 \times 10^{-14}$ s between encounters.

Calculate: (a) Fermi temperature $T_F$; (b) Average distance $l$ travelled by an electron at Fermi level between collisions; (c) The electrical and thermal conductivities at $T$ = 300 K. (d) Radius of Fermi surface (Fermi wave vector); (e) Displacement of Fermi surface $\delta k$ under an applied electric field of 3 V/m; and (e) the drift velocity $v_d$. (f) Compare some of these values with those given in Table 3.1.
[(a) $8.12 \times 10^4$ K; (b) $4.71 \times 10^{-8}$ m; (c) $\rho_e = 1.48 \times 10^{-8}$ ohm-m; $\sigma_{th}$ = 523.5 W/K-m = 5.235 W/K-cm; (d) $13.55 \times 10^9$ m$^{-1}$; (e) $-15.826 \times 10^{-3}$ m/s = $-1.5826$ cm/s]

11. Explain the differences between the five types of bonds existing in crystals: Metallic, ionic, covalent, hydrogen-like, Van der Waals.

12. Find the electron and hole concentrations in a semiconductor at two temperatures $T$ = 300 K and 400 K at energy gaps of $E_g$ = 1 and 2 eV. Discuss the effect of varying $T$ and $E_g$ on the concentration levels.

| [$E_g$ $T \rightarrow$ | 300 | 400 | |
|---|---|---|---|
| 1 eV | $10^{17}$ | $1.54 \times 10^{17}$ | /m$^3$ |
| 2 eV | $4 \times 10^8$ | $6.135 \times 10^8$ | /m$^3$] |

## II. PHOTO VOLTAIC POWER GENERATION

### 3.13 Introduction

Direct conversion of solar energy into electrical energy takes place through solar cells using semiconductor materials. We have discussed the physics aspects of these materials in the previous sections under Soild State Physics and now embark on the engineering aspects of photo voltaic power generation. The essential events in the direct energy conversion process are as follows: (a) If sunlight falling on the semiconductor has sufficient energy (short wavelength) to equal or exceed the band gap $E_g$ between valence and conduction bands, electrons will be stimulated to jump from valence band to conduction band creating electron-hole pairs. (b) The band gap gives the maximum voltage which can appear across external connected load. (c) The electrons and holes are separated to flow through the load as a current. This separation must occur in a time less than the recombination time (See Table 3.4). (d) Anti-reflection coating is applied on top of the bulk material of semiconductor, which improves performance.

Semiconductors used for solar cells have the following values shown in Table 3.5 of energy gap in eV, and maximum photo-current densities ($J_{ph}$) at sea level and above the atmospheric height. These are known as AM-1 and AM-0 conditions, where AM stands for Air Mass.

**Table 3.5**

| | Si | InP | GaAs | CdTe | CdSe | AlSb | |
|---|---|---|---|---|---|---|---|
| $E_g$, eV | 1.06 | 1.29 | 1.39 | 1.45 | 1.7 | 1.63 | (300 K) |
| $J_{ph}$, mA/cm$^2$ | 28 - 30 | 6 - 28 | 17 - 25 | 19 - 25 | 10 - 19 | 16 - 19 | (AM-1) |
| | 35 - 38 | 8 - 37 | 23 - 32 | 25 - 33 | 12 - 24 | 20 - 25 | (AM-0) |

The range is given for various types of solar-cell configurations which will be described later. There are other materials also which will be enumerated later.

Solar cells or photovoltaic cells, simply known as PV systems, are being developed and utilized on a large scale and the progress achieved in both materials and engineering applications is improving by leaps and bounds. Several countries have initiated PV roof-top programmes. Some examples are worth mentioning. (kWp = kilowatt peak).

(a) In Japan, upto the end of 1997, more than 10,000 small grid-connected systems with an average capacity of 3 kWp were installed.

(b) In Germany, plant installations completed in 1995 had over 2000 roofs equipped with PV systems of an average size of 2.6 kWp.

(c) In Austria, the Austrian Ministry of Research and Transport funded the development of a 2000 kWp PV roof-top programme, with a total of 100 PV systems with an average installed capacity of 2.28 kWp.

(d) In northern New York State in the U.S.A., on the Canadian border, (which is considered one of the coldest places in the U.S.A.) an innovative hybrid system is installed which includes (i) an 850 W PV array, (ii) 25 kWh of battery storage, and (iii) a 4 kW propane gas generator. The insolation level is on the average 20 $mW/cm^2$.

(e) In Australia, a hybrid system involving a PV array, battery and diesel-engine-driven DC or AC generator has been extensively studied, especially the computer-control of the entire system-operation for optimum performance. The battery takes care of the peak load demand while the diesel generator is adequate for meeting the peak load demand and charging the battery simultaneously.

(f) Countries such as Australia, Canada, China, Malaysia, Indonesia, Mexico, Russia and India have currently installed hybrid PV systems of one type or another.

## 3.14 Spectral Distribution of Energy in Solar Radiation

Table 3.6 shows the average wavelength, frequency and energy in sunlight which should provide an idea of its utility in semiconductor solar cells.

**Table 3.6 Energy Content of Solar Radiation, etc.**

| λ, μm | ν, GHz | *E*, eV | λ, μm | ν, GHz | *E*, eV |
|---|---|---|---|---|---|
| 1.0 | 0.3 | 1.24 | 0.5 | 0.6 | 2.5 |
| 0.9 | 0.333 | 1.38 | 0.4 | 0.75 | 3.1 |
| 0.8 | 0.375 | 1.55 | 0.3 | 1.0 | 4.14 |
| 0.7 | 0.43 | 1.78 | 0.2 | 1.5 | 6.22 |
| 0.6 | 0.5 | 2.07 | 0.2 - 0 | | 6.22 - ∞ |

$[\nu = c/\lambda, E = h\upsilon, c = 3 \times 10^8\ m/s, h = 6.62618 \times 10^{-34}\ J\text{–}s$

$= 4.1357 \times 10^{-15}\ eV\text{–}s]$

Due to absorption of energy in the atmosphere, the available power in $mW/cm^2$ at sea level is less than that above the atmosphere. The average measured powers per unit area, called the insolation level, are as follows:

$$\left.\begin{array}{ll} \text{AM–0: Above atmosphere} & : 135\ mW/cm^2 \\ \text{AM–1: At sea level} & : 107\ mW/cm^2 \end{array}\right\} \text{Total at all wavelengths}$$

Solar cells have a maximum efficiency of about 20%, so that the actual developed electrical power are 27 and 21.4 $mW/cm^2$. Thus, 1 $m^2$ of solar cell panel area can generate a maximum of 214 Watts at sea level. This energy will only be available during sunlight hours of the day at sea level, while it is available for 24 hours above the atmosphere.

With 200 W/m$^2$, the estimated areas for solar-cell arrays are as follows:

| | | |
|---|---|---|
| Residence: | 20 kW peak load | 100 m$^2$ area |
| Small Residential Development: | 2 MW = 2000 kW | $10^4$ m$^2$ area = 0.01 km$^2$ |
| Central Station: | 1000 MW | 5 km$^2$ area. |

There are interesting speculations about having a geocentric or stationary satellite or space station orbiting at 36,000 km from the earth, where the insolation level is nearly 10 times that on earth and 24 hours of the day (less an hour or so during some months). PV panels are proposed for developing 10,000 MW or more, converting the generated dc to microwave power and beaming this to earth.

***Example 3.4***: Taking a solar power content of 1 W/cm$^2$ at the space-station location, calculate the area of solar panels required at 20% efficiency of conversion for powers of 2000 MW, 5000 MW, 10000 MW and 15000 MW.

***Solution***: 1 km$^2$ of solar cell array will generate a power of
$0.2\ (\text{W/cm}^2) \times 10^{10}\ (\text{cm}^2) \times 10^{-6}\ (\text{MW/W}) = 2000$ MW.

Therefore areas required are = 1 km$^2$ for 2000 MW;
= 2.5 km$^2$ for 5,000 MW;
= 5 km$^2$ for 10,000 MW;
= 7.5 km$^2$ for 15,000 MW.

The design of such huge solar-powered energy converters, launching them into space, etc., can stagger any engineer's imagination, but not impossible for the human spirit and endeavour if such arrangements are absolutely necessary for the energy-hungry civilization and money is forthcoming.

### 3.15 Solar Cell Configurations

Figures 3.18 - 3.23 show usual configurations of solar cells fabricated up to now. Section 3.11 has described some aspects of PN junction, hetero junction, Shottky barrier, and MOS solar cells, while Sec. 3.12 has dealt with amorphous material, chiefly a-Si:H (hydrogenated amorphous silicon). Cells using non-silicon materials are also manufactured.

A P-N junction consists of a junction of a P-type semiconductor (Si or Ge doped with trivalent element B, Al, In), and an N-type semiconductor (Si or Ge doped with pentavalent element P, As, Sb). The intrinsic semiconductor is the same in both P and N type, which is either Si or Ge. Si is preferred because of its availability and high-temperature characteristics as well as larger band gap voltage than Ge. Therefore, we will not deal with Ge-based semiconductors. Other P-N junction solar cells are made of InP, GaAs, CdTe, CdSe and AlSb.

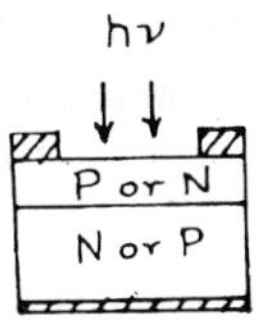


**Fig. 3.18** Vertical configuration of P and N materials in a solar cell

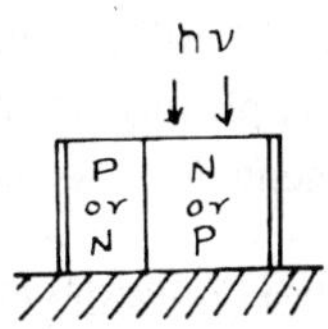


**Fig. 3.19** Horizontal configuration solar cell

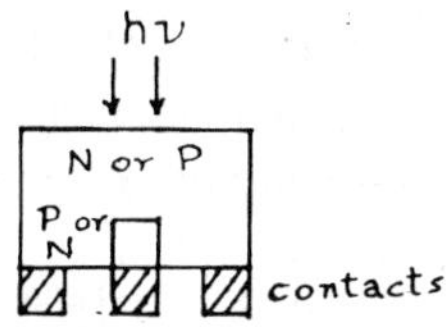


**Fig. 3.20** Island configuration of junction in solar cell

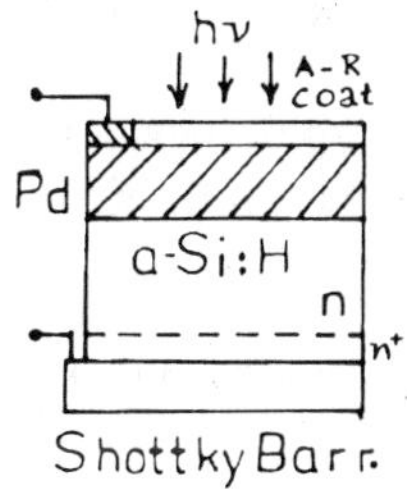


**Fig. 3.21** Shottky barrier solar cell

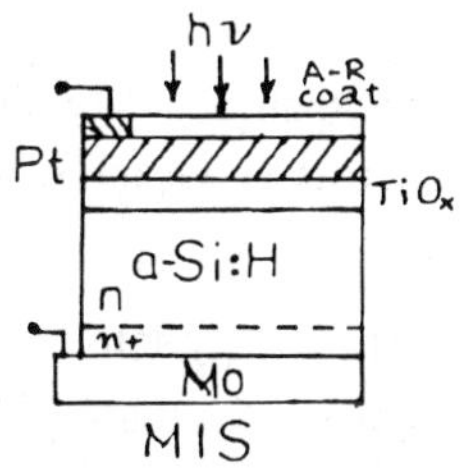


**Fig. 3.22** MIS solar cell

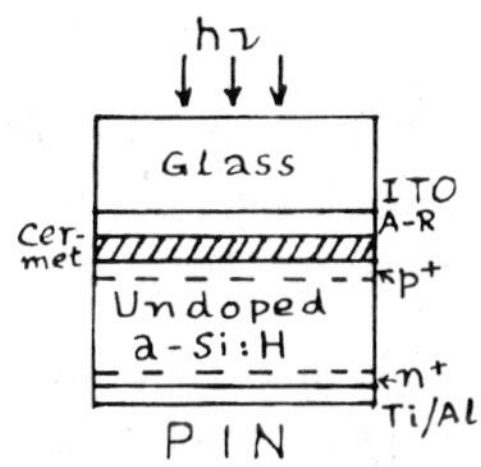


**Fig. 3.23** PIN solar cell

Hetero junctions use two types of s-c, such as GaAs - AlGaAs.

For solar-cell work, energy gaps greater than 1 eV are preferable.

*Reflection and Anti-Reflection Coating*

Sunlight travels in free space or air, while the solar cell is a solid material with a refractive index $n$ which is different from air. The reflection factor for air-solid interface is

$$r = (n-1)^2/(n+1)^2 \tag{3.57}$$

The refractive index is usually a complex number, so that the reflection factor has both a magnitude and a phase shift. But the bulk behaviour of the s-c does not depend on the phase but only on the magnitude.

The transmission factor is: $t = 1 - r = 2\,n/(n+1)^2$ (3.58)

***Example 3.5***: Reflection coefficients of some semiconductors are: Si = 0.3, CdTe = 0.21. Calculate the indices of refraction for them.

***Solution***: $r = (n-1)^2/(n+1)^2$, giving $r(n^2 + 2n + 1) = n^2 - 2n + 1$.

Therefore $n^2(1-r) - 2n(1+r) + (1-r) = 0$.

This gives $n = [(1+r) \pm \sqrt{2}\,r]/(1-r)$.

*For Si*, $r = 0.3$. Therefore $n_{Si} = (1.3 \pm \sqrt{0.6})/0.7 = 2.9637$ or $0.7506$.

For solids, $n > 1$. Therefore $n_{Si} = 2.9637$.

For CdTe, $r = 0.21$. Therefore $n_{CT} = (1.21 \pm \sqrt{0.42})/0.79 = 2.352$.

When an anti-reflection coating of $SiO_2$ is given to decrease the reflected energy of sunlight, there is a 50% improvement in most cases. Table 3.7 shows average values of reflection coefficients for uncoated and coated solar cells.

**Table 3.7: Reflection Coefficients for Solar Cells**

| | Si | InP | GaAs | CdTe | CdSe | GaP | AlSb |
|---|---|---|---|---|---|---|---|
| *Uncoated* | 0.3 | 0.26 | 0.29 | 0.21 | 0.18 | 0.29 | 0.27 |
| *$SiO_2$ Coated* | 0.15 | 0.12 | 0.14 | 0.08 | 0.065 | 0.15 | 0.13 |

Reflection losses as low as less than 10% are aimed in high-efficiency cells. These are made from materials such as $Ta_2O_5$ on Si, $TiO_2$ on MIS cells of Si, $TiO_2$ and $Si_3N_4$ on GaAs cells.

While increasing the transmitted energy into the cell, anti-reflection coatings also contribute some disadvantages, chief among which are:

(a) Chemical changes are induced by powerful sunlight, when concentrators are used, which can deteriorate the performance of solar cells over 3 or 4 years;

(b) Chemicals in the air also degrade the material;

(c) Any damage to the semiconductor due to deposition of anti-reflection coating acts as traps which increases surface recombination resulting in lowering of module efficiency;

(d) The anti-reflection coatings must exhibit same reflection coefficients at all wavelengths in the sunlight. However, they do not do so. Therefore, a single layer of coating is inadequate. Up to seven layers have been tried on practical solar cells to date. For solar-cell work the wavelengths used lie between 0.2 and 1.3 μm (2000 - 13,000 Å).

## 3.16 Voltage Developed by Solar Cell

There exist two types of voltages in the solar cell: (1) the energy band-gap between valence and conduction bands, which refers to the same semiconductor; and (2) the barrier voltage or junction voltage when a P-N junction is formed. The load is connected externally between P and N materials, positive at P and negative at N, through which electrons will flow out to the load.

It is clear that no charge carriers can flow inside the bulk material when a barrier voltage is established due to the accumulation of space charges at the junction of the P-N materials. This represents an open-circuit voltage of the system. Therefore, a mechanism must be built into the solar-cell semiconducting material for creating electric fields. These depend on doping levels.

From the requirement that the Fermi levels on the P and N sides must be equal, there results the barrier voltage

$$V_B = (kT/q)\ \ln\ (N_D N_A / n_i^2)$$

where $N_D$, $N_A$ = concentrations of donors and acceptors in the N-type and P-type materials forming the junction,

and $n_i$ = concentration of intrinsic charge carriers in the semiconductor at the given temperature.

Figures 3.9 through 3.15 should be referred for energy levels at the junction.

Another item of interest affecting the cell performance is the width of the barrier or depletion layer, which separates the hole-electron pairs at the junction. Because of the narrow μm-width of the layer or distance between space charges on either side of the barrier, the field intensity is extremely high. This can cause field breakdown of the bulk material and make the cell ineffective.

The depths of this barrier in the N- and P-type materials are given by the following relationship, which is given here without derivation:

$$x_n = \left( \frac{2\,\varepsilon_o\,\varepsilon_r\,V_B}{q\,N_D} \frac{1}{1 + N_D/N_A} \right)^{1/2} \tag{3.60}$$

$$x_p = x_n \cdot N_D / N_A \tag{3.61}$$

where $x_n$, $x_p$ = width of barrier inside the N-type and P-type from the junction layer, respectively,

$N_D$, $N_A$ = concentration of donor charge carriers in N material and acceptor charge carriers in the P material, respectively,

$\varepsilon_o$ = permittivity of free space = $8.842 \times 10^{-12}$ F/m,

$\varepsilon_r$ = relative permittivity of intrinsic semiconductor, (12 for Si),

$V_B$ = barrier potential in volts,

and $q$ = electronic charge = $1.6022 \times 10^{-19}$ coulomb.
(Note: In previous sections, the letter *e* was used for this).

Therefore barrier width is $x_b = x_n + x_p$ (3.62)

For the case when $N_D = N_A$, this becomes

$$x_b = 2\,x_n = [\,4\,\varepsilon_o\,\varepsilon_r\,V_B / q\,N_D\,]^{1/2} \tag{3.63}$$

Thus the average electrical stress in the layer is

$$\mathcal{E}_b = V_B / x_b = (q\,N_D\,V_B / 4\,\varepsilon_o\,\varepsilon_r)^{1/2} \tag{3.64}$$

Because of the distribution of charges, the maximum stress is usually double the average value, since it is zero at the depletion layer's edge and increases nearly linearly as we proceed inward towards the junction proper. Therefore,

$$\mathcal{E}_{max} = 2\,\mathcal{E}_{av} = 2\,\mathcal{E}_b = (q\,N_D\,V_B\,/\,\varepsilon_o\,\varepsilon_r)^{1/2} \qquad (3.65)$$

An example will show the magnitude of all these characteristics at the barrier.

***Example 3.6***: At 300 K in Silicon, the intrinsic carrier concentration is $n_i = 1.45 \times 10^{16}/\text{m}^3$. ($n_i^2 = 2.1 \times 10^{32}/\text{m}^6$). The impurity charge-carrier concentrations are $N_D = N_A = 10^5\ n_i$. Estimate (a) the barrier voltage, $V_B$; (b) the barrier width, $x_b$; and (c) the maximum electric field across the barrier.
[$k = 1.38066 \times 10^{-23}$ J/K $= 8.6174 \times 10^{-5}$ eV/K, $q = 1.6022 \times 10^{-19}$ coul, $\varepsilon_o = 8.842 \times 10^{-12}$ F/m, $\varepsilon_r = 12$ for Si]

***Solution***: $kT/q = 8.6174 \times 10^{-5} \times 300 = 2.58522 \times 10^{-2}$.

(a) $\ln (N_D\,N_A/n_i^2) = \ln 10^{10} = 23.026$.

Therefore from (3.59), the barrier voltage is $V_B = 2.58522 \times 0.23026 = 0.5953$V.

(b) $$x_b = \left[\frac{4 \times 8.842 \times 10^{-12} \times 12 \times 0.5953}{1.6022 \times 10^{-19} \times 1.45 \times 10^{21}}\right]^{1/2} = 1.04\ \mu\,m = 10{,}400\ \text{Å}$$

(c) $\mathcal{E}_{max} = 2\,V_B/x_b = 2 \times 0.5953/1.04 \times 10^{-6} = 1.1448 \times 10^6$ Volts/metre.

Note that if the energy gap for Si is 1.2 eV, the barrier voltage of 0.5953 amounts to nearly 50% of the band gap voltage of $E_g$.

### 3.17 The Photo Current and Load Current

We will now consider current flow across the junction which results from the solar radiation proper, which imparts sufficient energy for charge carriers to flow into the external load. First we consider the types of current which flow across the junction. These are:

(a) Recombination and generation currents due to electrons, and

(b) Same for holes.

Figures 3.24 (a - d) show the energy levels and flow of electrons and holes. Consider the flow of electrons first. Some electrons on the N-side present in the conduction band can get sufficient energy to climb the barrier potential $V_B$ and reach the conduction band on the P-side. Here, they recombine with the majority carrier holes present in the valence band. This is called recombination current, and

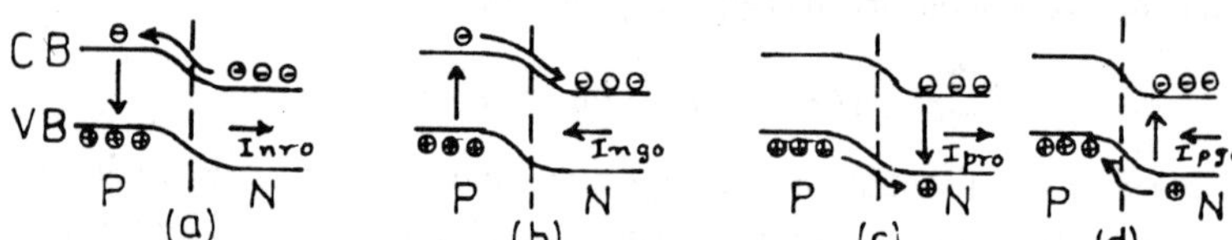


**Fig. 3.24** Recombination and generation currents for electrons and holes in PN junction

since this is due to negative charges, it is denoted as $I_{\text{nro}}$ flowing in a direction opposite to the direction of the charge carriers (conventional current flow).

Additionally, an electron present in the valence band on the P-side can obtain enough energy to surmount the energy gap $E_g$ and enter the conduction band on the P-side itself, leaving a hole behind. Due to the natural potential gradient, this electron is helped to reach the N-side. This increases the net electron concentration on the N-side and forms a generation current shown as $I_{\text{ngo}}$ in a direction opposite to the flow of electron.

Under equilibrium conditions the total current across the junction is zero. Therefore, $I_{\text{nro}} = I_{\text{ngo}}$.

In a similar manner, as shown in Figures 3.24 (c) and (d), holes in the valence band of *P*-side can slide into the valence band of *N*-type (minority carriers) where recombination will take place. This current is denoted as $I_{pro}$ and since it is due to the flow of positive charge carriers, is denoted in the same direction as the hole flow. The final current is $I_{pgo}$ which is due to an electron in the *N*-type acquiring enough energy to surmount the barrier voltage $V_B$ and enter the *P*-type material, increasing hole concentration thereby forming a generation current. Under equilibrium conditions, $I_{pro} = I_{pgo}$.

When an external voltage is applied so as to alter the barrier voltage, $(V_B + V_a)$ for negative bias and $(V_B - V_a)$ for positive bias, the charge carrier concentrations are altered. The currents now are:

$$\left.\begin{aligned} &\text{Recombination current for electron flow : } I_{nr} = I_{nro}\, e^{qV_a/kT} \\ &\text{Recombination current for hole flow : } I_{pr} = I_{pro}\, e^{qV_a/kT} \end{aligned}\right\} \tag{3.66}$$

On the other hand, the generation currents are unaffected since they are thermally generated and cross the junction no matter how large the barrier is, as they travel ''downhill''. Therefore,

$$I_{ng} = I_{ngo}, \text{ and } I_{pg} = I_{pgo}$$

The total current is now given by

$$\begin{aligned} I &= I_{pr} + I_{nr} - (I_{pg} + I_{ng}) = (I_{pro} + I_{nro}) \cdot (e^{qV_a/kT} - 1) \\ &= (I_{pgo} + I_{ngo}) \cdot (e^{qV_a/kT} - 1) \end{aligned} \tag{3.67}$$

We denote the generated current in the dark as $I_o$ which is also known as the ''saturation current''. Therefore, the current flowing across the junction for any applied voltage $V_a$ is

$$I = I_o\,(e^{qV_a/kT} - 1) \tag{3.68a}$$

If the polarity of $V_a$ is reversed, i.e. for reverse-biased condition,

$$I = I_o\,(e^{-qV_a/kT} - 1). \tag{3.68b}$$

***Example 3.7***: In a semiconductor, given that $I_o = 10\ \mu A$ at T = 300 K, calculate and plot the current when $V_a$ varies from –5 to +0.4 Volts.

***Solution***: $q/kT = 1.6022 \times 10^{-19}/1.38066 \times 10^{-23} \times 300 = 38.68$. The calculations of $I$ are shown in the following tabular form.

| $V_a$ | –5 | –4 | –3 | –2 | –1 | 0 | +0.1 | +0.2 | +0.3 | +0.4 |
|---|---|---|---|---|---|---|---|---|---|---|
| $e^{q V_a / kT}$ | ≈ 0 | ≈ 0 | ≈ 0 | ≈ 0 | ≈ 0 | 1 | 47.94 | 2298 | $0.11 \times 10^6$ | $5.283 \times 10^6$ |
| $e^{q V_a / kT} - 1$ | –1 | –1 | –1 | –1 | –1 | 0 | 46.94 | 2297 | $0.11 \times 10^6$ | $5.283 \times 10^6$ |
| $I$ | –10 μA | –10 μA | –10 μA | –10 μA | –10 μA | 0 | 470 μA | 23 mA | 1.1 A | 52.83 A |

Figure 3.25 shows the plot. Note the change in current scales. For reverse bias, the operation of the device is in the 4th quadrant, since both voltage and current are negative.

We observe that the current $I_{pgo}$ is due to flow of holes in $N$-type in the valence band of $P$-type semiconductor. So also, $I_{ngo}$ is due to flow of electrons from $P$-type to $N$-type semiconductor. They are minority carrier currents. The expressions for these are as follows, but expressed as current densities:

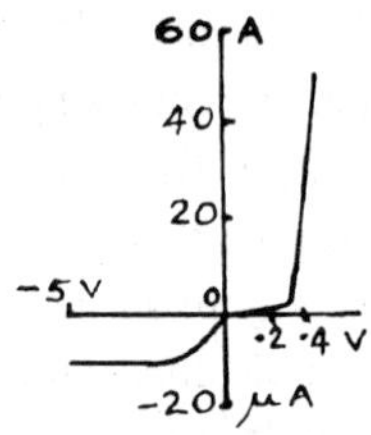


**Fig. 3.25** Current-voltage diagram in reverse and forward biased PN junction

$$J_o = q\,D_p\,p_{no} / l_p + q\,D_n\,n_{po} / l_n = J_{pgo} + J_{ngo} \tag{3.69}$$

where $J_o$ = dark current density across junction

$J_{pgo}, J_{ngo}$ = minority carrier current densities

$D_p, D_n$ = hole and electron diffusion constants

$p_{no}$ = density of holes on the $N$-side of junction at thermal equilibrium

$n_{po}$ = density of electrons on the $P$-side.

Also, we have $L_p, L_n$, hole diffusion length on $N$-side, and electron diffusion length on $P$-side, respectively.

The expressions for $p_{no}$, $n_{po}$, $L_p$, $L_n$, $D_p$ and $D_n$ are as follows:

$$p_{no} = n_i^2 / N_D, \text{ and } n_{po} = n_i^2 / N_A \tag{3.70}$$

The Einstein relations for diffusion constants are

$$D_p = kT\,\mu_p / q, \text{ and } D_n = k\,T\,\mu_n / q \tag{3.71}$$

where $\mu_p, \mu_n$ = hole and electron mobilities, respectively.

$$L_p = \sqrt{\tau_p D_p}\ ,\ L_n = \sqrt{\tau_n D_n} \tag{3.72}$$

where $\tau_p, \tau_n$ = hole and electron lifetimes as minority carries (Eq. (3.48)).

Now, consider what happens to the current across the junction when solar radiation is incident on the junction. Figure 3.26 shows the barrier voltages to be negotiated by the charge carriers. The photo voltage is $V_{ph}$ which lowers the barrier voltage to $(V_B - V_{ph})$. The Fermi levels are now separated by the photo voltage $V_{ph}$. For values of $V_{ph}$, see Table 3.6.

Prior to the junction being illuminated, the following conditions exist (Fig. 3.26):

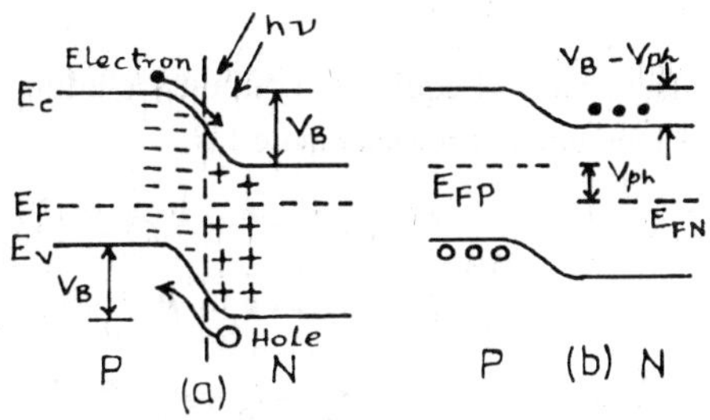


**Fig. 3.26** PN junction solar cell under illumination

(a) The conduction band energy level $E_c$ on the $P$-side is higher by the barrier voltage $V_B$ (in eV) than the conduction-band energy level on the $N$-side.

(b) Similarly for the valence-band energy levels.

(c) This is caused by Fermi levels in the two materials to be at the same height.

(d) Some minority carrier electrons from the $P$-type diffuse into the $N$-type, while some holes from the $N$-type diffuse into the $P$-type.

(e) On the $P$-side of the barrier, negative space charge exists, while on the $N$-side a positive space-charge region exists. Because of barrier voltage caused by these two space charges, the Fermi levels become equal.

(f) In the intrinsic semiconductor itself, the Fermi level is at the centre of the energy gap, but the moment a $P$-$N$ junction is formed, in the $N$-type the Fermi level moves closer to the conduction band because of donor atoms having contributed electrons and lowered the conduction band from that of the intrinsic semiconductor. Similarly, the Fermi level in the $P$-type moves closer to the valence band.

Now consider what happens when the junction is illuminated. The photo voltage contributes to a lessening of height of conduction-band levels in the $N$- and $P$-types by $V_{ph}$, so that the difference becomes $(V_B - V_{ph})$. The Fermi levels on the $N$-side and $P$-side experience a shift by $V_{ph}$. Holes can surmount the barrier easier and there is an increase in hole-electron pair generation. This is still a reverse-biased condition, but the reverse bias voltage now decreases from $V_B$ to $(V_B - V_{ph})$. The resulting photo current density becomes

$$J_{ph} = J_0\left[e^{-q(V_B - V_{ph})/kT} - 1\right] \tag{3.73}$$

This is clearly higher than $J_d = J_0\,(e^{-qV_B/kT} - 1)$ (3.74)

which is known as dark or diode current density.

The photo voltage is thus so biased that the diode current and load current equal the photo current in the device. Figure 3.27 shows the behaviour of dark and photo currents. In the 4th quadrant there is an increase in current. The equivalent circuit of the photo cell can thus be represented as in Fig. 3.28, where the load-current density is

$$J_L = J_0 \, e^{q V_{ph}/kT} \tag{3.75}$$

The practical equivalent circuit including all resistances is shown in Fig. 3.29. The load current for such a cell is

$$I_L = (1 + R_s / R_{sh})^{-1} \, [I_{ph} - I_d - V_L / R_{sh}] \tag{3.76}$$

$$[\, I_{ph} - I_d = I_L + (V_L + R_s I_L) / R_{sh} \text{, or , } I_L (1 + R_s / R_{sh})$$

$$= I_{ph} - I_d - V_L / R_{sh} \,].$$

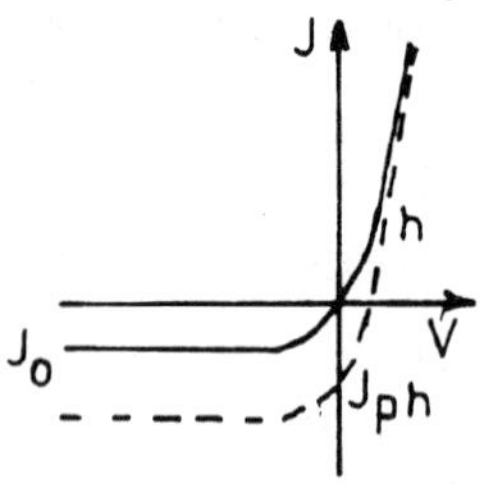


**Fig. 3.27** Dark and photo current densities under illumination

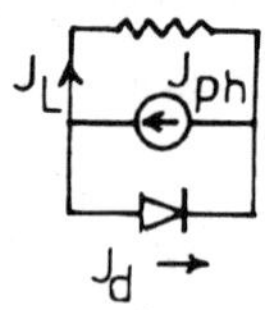


**Fig. 3.28** Equivalent circuit of photo cell

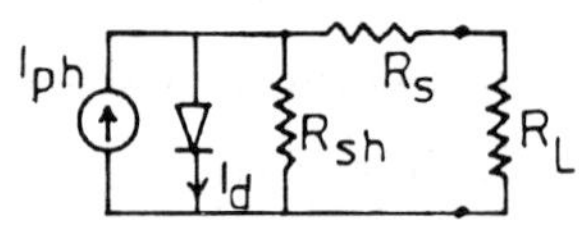


**Fig. 3.29** Equivalent circuit of photo cell (solar cell) with resistance load

### 3.18 Practical Solar Cell Performance

When a solar cell is illuminated, its ability to absorb the spectral components of energy in the sunlight is of paramount importance. Experiments have shown that only about 40% of the energy in the sunlight available at all wavelengths is absorbed by the material to produce electron-hole pairs. The rest serves to vibrate the atoms and is known as phonon energy.

Table 3.8 gives average values of usable absorption as solar-cell power output.

**Table 3.8: Solar Cell Usable Power**
(Incident power from Sun at sea level = 100 mW/cm$^2$)

| Si | InP | GaAs | CdTe | CdSe | AlSb | |
|---|---|---|---|---|---|---|
| 42 | 40.5 | 39 | 39 | 35 | 35 | mW/cm$^2$ |

Solar cells are usually manufactured in 150 μm thickness. The photo current density is $J_{ph} = q\,N_{ph}$ where $N_{ph}$ = photons reaching the bulk materials per cm$^2$ per second. This is based on the assumption that each photon is successful in generating one electron-hole pair. But this is never the case. Since each electron-hole pair has a maximum energy of $E_g$ eV, the maximum power density generated by the cell is

$$P_m = E_g J_{ph} \text{ with } E_g \text{ in Volts}$$
$$= N_{ph} E_g, \text{ with } E_g \text{ in eV} \quad (3.77)$$

Since the energy gap $E_g$ is fixed for any semiconductor material, the only way to increase the power density is to intensify the solar radiation falling on the cell by using concentrators. This unfortunately increases the temperature (phonon vibration) of the bulk material and increases losses. Therefore, there are optimum conditions to be satisfied in the design of a solar-cell array in practice.

The resistance of bulk material is given by

$$R_s = (l/A) \cdot (1/q\,\mu\,N_s), \text{ ohm} \quad (3.78)$$

where $l$ = length of substrate ($\approx$ 150 μm)

$A$ = area of the solar cell in $m^2$

$\mu$ = majority carrier mobility, $m^2$/V-s

and $N_s$ = hole or electron concentration ($10^{21}/m^2$ nearly).

Therefore $R_s A = l/q\,\mu\,N_s$ ohm–$m^2$ (3.79)

This is based on uniform impurity concentration in the substrate. There are schemes to grade the concentration exponentially, since the solar radiation penetration intensity varies with the depth. Values of mobility μ are given in Table 3.3. To observe the order of magnitude of series resistance, the following example is given.

***Example 3.8***: Given $l$ = 100 μm, $q$ = 1.6022 × $10^{-19}$ coul, mobility μ = 1000 $cm^2$/V-s, and charge carrier concentration $N_s = 10^{15}/cm^3$, calculate resistance-area, $R_s A$.

***Solution***: Converting all quantities to SI units,

$$R_s A = 100 \times 10^{-6} / 1.6022 \times 10^{-19} \times 0.1 \times 10^{21} = 6.242 \times 10^{-6} \text{ ohm–m}^2$$
$$= 0.06242 \text{ ohm–cm}^2.$$

Looking back at Eq. (3.76), we observe that when $R_{sh}$, $R_s$, $I_{ph}$, and $I_d$ are constant and independent of voltage $V_L$, the $I_L - V_L$ is a straight line with negative slope of $-(R_s + R_{sh})^{-1}$. However, the quantities $I_{ph}$ and $I_d$ are highly voltage-dependent as shown by Eqs. (3.73) and (3.74). In a practical solar cell, the $I - V$ characteristic is nearly as shown in Fig. 3.30. The maximum available power occurs at a current $I_m$

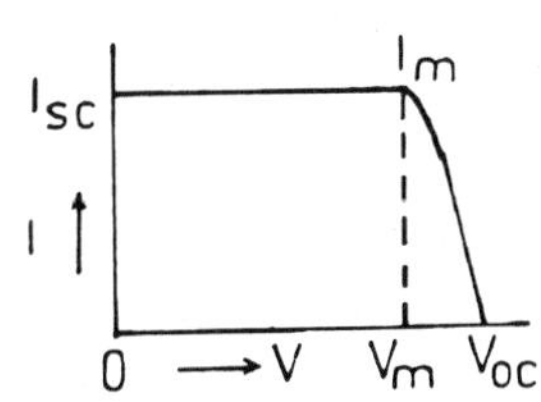

**Fig. 3.30** I - V characteristic of practical solar cell

at a voltage shown as $V_m$. The short-circuit current is $I_{sc}$ and the open-circuit voltage $V_{oc}$, as shown on the figure.

The input power in the solar radiation is $P_{in}$ which is the power density ($mW/cm^2$ or other unit) times the area $A_s$ of the cell on which the radiation falls.

The efficiency at maximum power availability is

$$\eta = I_m \cdot V_m / P_{in} \tag{3.80}$$

Now we define a term called Fill Factor by the relation

$$FF = (I_m V_m)/(I_{sc} V_{oc}) \tag{3.81}$$

Therefore

$$\eta = FF \cdot I_{sc} \cdot V_{oc} / P_{in} \tag{3.82}$$

Values of $J_{sc}$ range to a maximum of about 30 $mA/cm^2$ at sea level conditions for all types of solar cells made from *Si* substrate with $TiO_2$ anti-reflection coating. For other types of semiconductors, it is a little less, ranging from 20 to 25 $mA/cm^2$ for CdTe and InP cells. The open-circuit voltages range from 0.6 to 1 V for Silicon-silicon P-N junction cell and other cells such as $Ga_{1-x}$ $Al_x$ As - GaAs heterojunction cells. Fill factors are in the order of 0.8, but this depends upon the series resistance which controls $I_{sc}$.

Generally-observed efficiencies range from as low as 12.5% to 23% for Si cells to heterojunction cells.

Single-wafer solar cells are manufactured in 5 × 3.8 cm and 2 × 2 cm. Circular cells are made with diameters of 2.5, 5, 5.7 and 7.6 cm.

For a home with an available roof-top area of 100 $m^2$, at 200 $mW/m^2$ developed power, about 20 kW peak power can be developed if the array is arranged to track the Sun's position. For a fixed array, the power developed varies as cos $\phi$, so that the average output reduces to 0.637 (= $2/\pi$) times the maximum available, when the Sun is directly overhead or perpendicular to the array surface. Thus the average power reduces to about 12.5 kW. Even this is available only during sunlight hours and is used mainly for storing the energy in batteries for later use, or connecting it to the town power supply to feed energy into the utility, and buying power from the utility during dark hours. At nearly $100/$m^2$, the cost of the installation would run to $10,000 for the peak power of 12.5 kW. We will discuss more about the costs under commercialization of PV power next.

Concentrators in the form of parabolic mirrors, lenses of the conventional and Fresnel types increase the solar radiation on arrays from 10 to 100 Suns. Some concentrators have been tried to yield up to 2000 Suns, but these are for experimental purposes in order to investigate the high-temperature characteristics of the solar-cell material. Terrestrial-based solar cells operate at a maximum temperature of 100°C and require heat-sinking and cooling of the substrate.

***Example 3.9***: A domestic solar array of 100 $m^2$ area generates an average of 10 kW power during an average duration of 12 hr/day. The cost of the array is \$10,000. Calculate the unit cost of energy (¢/kWh) if the working life is 5 years.

***Solution***: Energy produced/year = $10 \times 12 \times 365 = 43{,}800$ kW-h.

Therefore energy produced in 5 years = 219,000 kW-h.

Thus, unit cost or cost per kW-h = \$10,000/219,000 = 4.566 ¢.

Note that this is based on the assumption that the sky is clear all through the year. If cloud cover amounts to say 30% of the time on an average, the unit cost would be 4.566/0.7 = 6.52 ¢.

Photovoltaic conversion of solar radiation directly into electrical energy offers a lot of benefits, especially in hot countries of Asia, Africa and many areas of the world, including Arctic and Antarctic, where sunlight is available practically without limit. Many national and international agencies are working on this problem. Unfortunately, in these very countries the menace of birds perching on such attractive installations on a long-term basis puts a severe restriction in cutting down the duration of sunlight falling on the array, since bird droppings are the biggest nuisance to the coating of the solar cell surface, which become opaque and make any such systems ineffective over time. This is also true in industrial environments and desert areas where wind-blown solid particles can be deposited on the array surface.

Countries where solar radiation is abundant have not yet manufactured solar cells in quantities commensurate with the possible extent of use. However, rapid progress in manufacture is taking place, as for example in India at the BHEL with technological help from Germany and other well-developed countries. Most of the recent studies in solar cell technology, as in every other energy game, is to increase efficiency, lower the cost, develop digital computer models for large array systems, computer control of installations for optimum performance, and develop materials or improve existing materials such as purity, etc.

As an example of an enterprising PV system in Ireland, a dairy with 250 heads of cattle consists of 50 kWp solar array, 600 A-h lead-acid battery, 30 kVA inverter for loads, 50 kVA inverter to deliver excess power to the utility grid. Micro-computers control all operations. The array works at 4% efficiency (= dc output of array/input radiation).

***Example 3.10***: A 2 cm × 2 cm × 0.05 mm solar cell has the following I - V characteristic with approximate $I_{sc} = 0.166$ A and $V_{oc} = 0.6$ V. The I - V characteristic is constant at 0.166 A up to 0.5 V, as shown in Fig. 3.31. Calculate the Fill Factor *FF* assuming $P_m$ to occur at the intersection of the two straight lines.

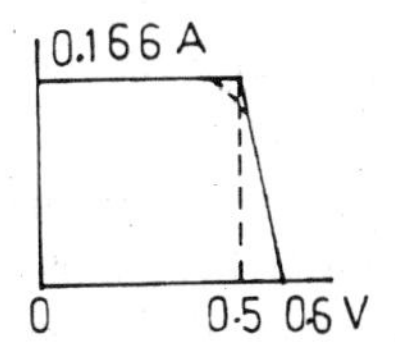


**Fig. 3.31** Example 3.10

***Solution***: $V_{oc} I_{sc} = 0.6 \times 0.166 = 0.0966$ W

$P_m = 0.5 \times 0.166 = 0.083$ W

Therefore $FF = 0.083 / 0.0966 = 5/6 = 0.833 = 83.3\,\%$.

This example shows the best possible output that can be attained at 135 mW/cm$^2$ solar radiation at AMO condition above the atmosphere.

Total incident power $P_i = 135 \times 10^{-3} \times 2 \times 2 = 0.54$ W.

Therefore cell efficiency $\eta_m = 0.083 / 0.54 = 0.1544 = 15.44\,\%$.

This PV system is obviously located inside an orbiting satellite.

## 3.19 Commercial Photo Voltaic Systems

Since the 1970s, PV systems have found increasing use for remote commercial applications such as microwave stations, signalling buoys, highway patrol communications, railroad-crossing signals, high voltage transmission-line communication using optical fibres using transmitters and receivers that require electrical power, refrigerating units in remote arctic environment to "freeze" the ground underneath pipe-line supports which otherwise would sink and damage the pipe during ground-thaw on warm days in summer, power supply to homes remote from existing power grids, and so on. The PV panels, of course, were developed in a very big way for space applications to power electrical systems aboard satellites, space stations, space telescopes, and so on.

A PV module consists of several crystalline cells or a single thin-film sheet, and are fabricated in various sizes and shapes to suit the application from small electronic watches and devices to generating electrical power in remote homes and agricultural or dairy operations. Typically a power module could be 4000 cm$^2$ in size, comprising 40 single-crystal silicon cells, and generating about 50 W at 17 V. Mirrors and lenses focus the sunlight in terrestrial applications thereby increasing efficiencies to nearly 15-20%.

Total sales of PV modules all over the world have been 80 MW and showing a trend of 12.5% increase every year. Costs range from US$ 7.00 per Watt for off-grid or remote applications. Crystalline cells make up nearly 50% of world markets, with polycrystalline Si cells 30% and amorphous Silicon 20%. A small percentage (less than 2%) are made up of advanced cells such as ribbon Si, silicon film and cadmium telluride, CdTe. If and when crystalline and polycrystalline module prices become as low as $ 2.50 per watt, new markets will open up for PV use and compete with grid-connected bulk power-supply from power companies.

Many world-wide financial organizations are helping underdeveloped countries to encourage the use of PV systems. Some important examples are as follows (Dracker and DeLanquil):

(a) The World Bank through Global Environmental Fund (GEF) has established a $ 50 million fund to commercialize PV, wind, and hydro technologies by aiding the IREDA, the Indian Renewable Energy Development Agency, with $ 5 million or 10% allocated to PV energy.

(b) The United Nations Conference on Environment and Development (UNCED) has helped

(i) Mexico for PV energy to be supplied to 60,000 villages;

(ii) Indonesia to bring electricity to 30,000 villages;

(iii) Sri Lanka for electrification of 20,000 villages; and

(iv) Brazil for rural electrification.

In India, the Ministry for Non-Conventional Energy Sources, along with the Government of Rajasthan, are planning the creation of Solar Energy Zone (SEZ) to offer solar power-plant developers with land at favorable lease prices, part of the installation cost and find guaranteed markets for use and sale of the PV electrical power.*

An estimate of the trend in decrease of cost of generating electricity through PV systems is as follows:

| 1976 | 1980 | 1985 | 1990 |
|---|---|---|---|
| US $ 3 per kW-h | US $ 0.75/kW-h | US $ 0.25/kW-h | US $ 0.20/kW-h = 20¢ |

Ever since the year 1990, the cost has almost levelled off.

As a matter of comparison with conventional power, in the province of British Columbia in Canada, unit price of electric power for domestic use now stands (year 2000) at Can 6¢ (US 4.5¢). The bulk of the power in this province is supplied by hydro-electric power stations by the BC HYDRO company. This shows that conventional electric power is nearly 20% of the cost of these alternative or renewable sources of electric power. This is the primary reason why PV and other sources of power have not shown the rapid rate of development and research that is aimed at. However, when fossil-fuels (but not hydro) are depleted, the world has

* One of the experiences this author had in India in dealing with energy planning was that foreign aid from world organizations as well as private companies was forthcoming in plenty. However, India being a very vast country and with so many state power boards as well as central government power authorities involved, local planning exists on a regional basis but nationwide planning requires a long time and good coordination.

to depend upon the perennial sources of power such as PV, wind, ocean and others, in spite of the higher costs, including nuclear power.

***Example 3.11***: In the Austrian roof-top PV development, the following costs per kWp are quoted, at 1990 prices including a 20% inflation rate. Calculate and compare the percentage decrease in cost of the three components mentioned here in the 6 years based on 1990 prices.

| Year | PV Modules | Inverter | Others | Total System |
|---|---|---|---|---|
| 1990 | 107,500 | 50,000 | 57,500 | 215,000 Schillings |
| 1996 | 67,500 | 12,500 | 25,000 | 105,000 Schillings |

**Note**: In order to get US $ prices, divide the above figures in Austrian currency by 12.

***Solution***:

| | PV Modules | Inverter | Others | Total Cost |
|---|---|---|---|---|
| Decrease in cost: | 40,000 | 37,500 | 32,500 | 110,000 |
| % Decrease in cost: | $\frac{40}{107.5} \times 100$ | $\frac{37.5}{50} \times 100$ | $\frac{32.5}{57.5} \times 100$ | $\frac{110}{215} \times 100$ |
| | = 37.2% | = 75% | = 56.5% | = 51% |

***Example 3.12***: In the above example, calculate the cost of various components as % of total cost of the system.

***Solution***:

| | 1990 | 1996 |
|---|---|---|
| (i) PV Modules | 107.5/215 = 0.5 = 50% | 67.5/105 = 0.643 = 64.3% |
| (ii) Inverter | 50/215 = 0.2326 = 23.26% | 12.5/105 = 0.119 = 11.9% |
| (iii) Others | 26.74% | 23.8% |

We observe that in this example, the largest share of improvement has been in the inverter cost which in 1996 is almost 50% of the cost in 1990. But the % cost of the PV Module has actually shown an increase percentagewise (64.3% against 50% of the total cost).

### Efficiency of Solar Cells

With constant improvements in technology taking place, it can be expected that efficiency of solar cells also show improvements. As a guide, Fig. 3.32 shows a projected trend in increase in efficiency of crystalline solar cells.

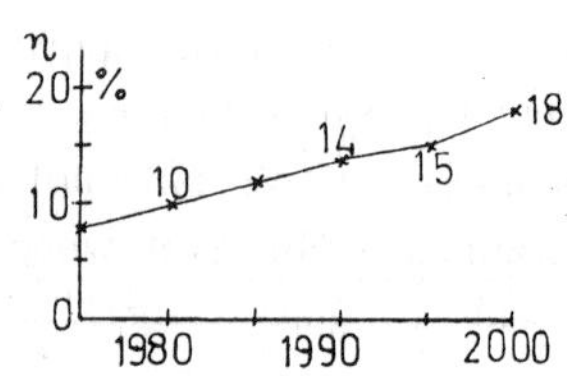


**Fig. 3.32** Efficiency of solar cells. 1975 to 2000.

Average 1990 efficiencies for different types of PV cells are:

(1) Crystalline Si Solar Cells: 14.5 - 23.5%

(2) Amorphous Si Cells, a-Si: H: 12%

(3) Multijunction a-Si: H cells: 10.5 - 17%

(4) Polycrystalline Thin-Film cells: 11 - 14%

(5) With concentrators: 100 Suns: 27% (experimental)

125 Suns: 25% (experimental)

20% (commercial)

160 Suns: 20% (commercial)

Some of the largest manufacturers of solar cells are the following with the list not complete:

*Japan* : Sanyo, Kanegufuchi, Kyocera, Taiyo Yuden

*U.S.A.* : ARCO Solar, Solarex (AMOCO), Chronar (French - US)

*India* : CEL, BHEL

*Germany* : AEG, SIEMENS

*England* : BP Solar

It is noteworthy that some of the largest manufacturers of solar cells are associated with petroleum companies. Of course it is needless to say that electrical machines manufacturers are also heavily involved in the PV industry.

### 3.20 Test Specifications for PV Systems

According to the European Communities Test Specifications for PV Modules, there are 20 control tests specified. The purpose of these tests is to provide data on the performance rating of PV modules and to identify (a) environmental factors, and (b) design features which could affect their durability.

1. The following 20 test specifications are given:

(1) Visual Inspection

(2) Dimensions and Weight

(3) Robustness of Terminations

(4) Mounting Twist Test

(5) Insulation Test

(6) Electrical Performance at Standard Test Condition

(7) Determination of Nominal Operating Cell Temperature (NOCT)

(8) Electrical Performance at NOCT

(9) Hot-Spot Heating Test

(10) Temperature Cycling Test

(11) Humidity-Freezing Test

(12) Hail Resistance Test

(13) Mechanical Loading Test

(14) Damp Heat Long Exposure Test

(15) High Temperature Long-Exposure Test

(16) UV Test

(17) $O_3$ Test

(18) $SO_2$ Test

(19) Salt Mist Test

(20) Ice Formation Test

A look at this list of tests will enable the readers to understand the need for these tests. In this chapter, only test #s (5), (6) and (8) will be described in detail.

**Insulation Test**

A voltage of 1000 Volts shall be applied between the shorted output terminals and the metal frame. The insulation resistance cannot be less than 100 MΩ after application of the test voltage for a duration of 1 minute. This test applies only to modules designed for systems operating at a voltage of 50 V and higher.

There should be no evidence of dielectric breakdown or surface tracking.

**Electrical Performance at Standard Test Condition (STC)**

These tests must be conducted at a temperature of 25°C and at illumination levels of E = 100 W/m$^2$ = 100 mW/cm$^2$, and E = 800 W/m$^2$ = 80 mW/cm$^2$.

The voltage-current characteristics of the module should be measured at these two values of illumination. The values of $I_{sc}$, $V_{oc}$ and $I_L$ should in no case be less than the relevant minimum values quoted by the manufacturer. $I_L$ = current at nominal operating voltage.

**Electrical Performance at NOCT**

This test is performed on the module at the nominal operating ceil temperature (NOCT) and at an irradiance level of 800 W/m$^2$ (80 mW/cm$^2$). The voltage-current characteristics of the cell must be measured.

Alternatively, the measurements carried out at 25°C and 800 W/m$^2$ can be transposed to NOCT using the following formulas:

$$I_2 = I_1 + \alpha (T_2 - T_1), \text{ and } V_2 = V_1 + \beta (T_2 - T_1);$$

where $I_1, V_1$ = measured values at $T_1 = 25°C$,

$I_2, V_2$ = transposed values at $T_2$ = NOCT,

and $\alpha, \beta$=current and voltage temperature coefficients of the module as quoted by the manufacturer.

**Determination of Internal Series Resistance $R_s$ of the Cell**

$R_s$ is determined very simply in simulated sunlight. The I-V characteristic at two different irradiation levels and at the same temperature in the range 23°C to 27°C are first traced.

A point on each characteristic is chosen, preferably near the "knee" of the curve, where the current is the same decrement ΔI below the short-circuit current $I_{sc}$. Then, measure the voltage displacement ΔV between these two points, as shown in Fig. 3.33.

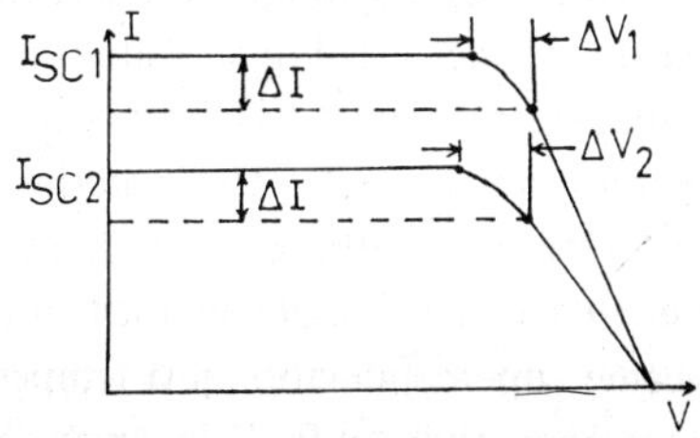


**Fig. 3.33** Calculation from measurements of I-V characteristics of series resistance $R_s$ of solar cells.

The value of $R_s$ is calculated from the expression: $R_s = \dfrac{\Delta V}{I_{sc1} - I_{sc2}}$

Then the same procedure is repeated using a third irradiance level at the same temperature. The three values of $R_s$ are thus calculated. The actual value of $R_s$ to be used is the mean of the three calculated values.

**Note**: The procedure for designing simulated sunlight is very involved, which uses Xenon lamps in indoor laboratory set-ups and will not be described here.

## III. APPLICATION OF SUPERCONDUCTING MATERIALS IN ELECTRICAL EQUIPMENT AND SYSTEMS

### 3.21 Introduction

In the year 1911, the Dutch Nobel-Prize winner Kammerling Onnes discovered the property of superconductivity in certain types of metals when cooled to extremely low temperatures, close to absolute zero or 0 K. His original work was carried out for discovering a method for liquifying Helium gas at 4.2 K (–269°C or –450°F). Immediately, he immersed metals in the liquid Helium to find that some materials showed the ability to conduct electric current with no resistance. This led to the concept of the possibility of transmitting electrical power without losses. Until 1986, research failed to discover metals which become superconductors at temperatures above 23 K. The materials used up to then were mercury (Hg), NbC, $Nb_3Sn$, $Nb_3Ge$, LaBaCu-O. Higher temperature superconductors were discovered after 1986 consisting of ceramic compounds, which are normally insulators. These became superconductors at a temperature of 30 K. However, the discovery of superconductivity at 94 K in a new ceramic called Yttrium Barium Copper Oxide resulted in the possibility of using liquid Nitrogen which can be liquified at 77 K. The further addition of Bismuth compounds and Thallium compounds raised the temperature to 125 K. Thus, cooling-system costs were brought down tremendously.

In addition to temperature, superconductivity applications in electrical apparatus was soon found to depend upon three physical properties of the materials which are interrelated:

(1) A Critical Temperature, $T_c$, which is the highest or maximum temperature at which the property of superconductivity can be maintained, and above which the property of superconductivity vanishes. The transition between these two stages is usually accompanied by a sudden explosion.

(2) A Critical Magnetic Field, $H_c$, which is the maximum value of magnetic field strength at which superconductivity can be maintained. Above this value, the material loses the property of superconductivity. A superconductor exhibits the property that at a lower critical value of H, usually called $H_{c2}$, the material rejects the penetration of the magnetic field while still remaining a superconductor.

(3) Critical Current Density, $J_c$ which is the maximum current density which a superconductor or the material in its superconducting state can conduct. Above this current density, the material loses its state of superconductivity. In other words, one cannot push a current density beyond this critical value.

These are the constraints under which superconducting materials have to be used in electrical machines and other applications. It is one of the strong points of superconducting materials that once a current is ''pumped'' into them, the current will keep circulating in them even when the voltage source is disconnected. However, certain conditions exist under which when the critical values are exceeded, the loss of superconducting property can take place with powerful explosions. This is especially important from the point of view of designing mechanical supporting structures.

## 3.22 Some Applications

It should be at once evident that the use of superconductors in motors, transformers and transportation will decrease losses and will save energy. It will also decrease oil consumption. Superconductors are applied for generating very high magnetic fields, in excess of 2 Teslas, while conventional copper or aluminium coils are limited to less than this on account of enormous power requirements. Higher the field strengths used, smaller and cheaper the equipment. Such high fields also eliminate the need for iron cores in generators, motors, transformers and other magnet-applications. We will observe later on that generation of power by MHD (Magneto Hydrodynamics, see Chapter IV) require very high magnetic fields. Also, energy storage systems use superconductors and are known as Superconducting Magnetic Energy Storage Systems (SMES). (See also Chapter 11: Wind Energy Conversion System, Sec. 11.3.4 for further description of SMES).

In medical applications such as MRI (Magnetic Resonance Imaging) for scanning the brain for tumours, field strengths as high as 7 T are used and they require superconducting magnets.

Low values of critical temperatures to achieve superconductivity require very large refrigeration systems whereas high $T_c$ reduces the power required in the cryogenic (liquid Helium) refrigeration systems. For example, operation at 80 K would require 100 times less energy than at 4 K.

### (1) Power System Application

Industrial research has come up with the applications of superconducting materials in transmission cables and energy storage systems. Liquid-cooled cables have been manufactured and put into practical use. The limitation is the refrigerating units for long lengths of cables which have to be located at the ends.

When using intermittent sources of energy, such as wind turbines, wave and tidal schemes, energy needs to be stored to match generation with the load requirements. Also, certain stability considerations of operating long transmission lines in parallel with each other require enormous energies to be stored and released instantaneously in order to prevent power swings. These require SMES for very large energy. These systems may be nearly 50 metres in diameter, buried underground and supported very rigidly even in earthquake-prone areas, carrying currents of the order of 50,000 Amps and store upto 100 Mega-watt-seconds

(MWs) of energy. Conventional copper windings are unthinkable for this application.

**(2) Generators and Motors**

Generators with liquid-cooled windings have been in existence for over 80 years, including liquid Nitrogen inside the stator bars. Therefore, superconducting materials are a natural extension of this concept, provided the materials can be properly shaped. Generators and motors are based upon the principle of two or more interacting magnetic fields, so that higher the field strength values used, smaller will be their size for generating or delivering the same power. Superconducting wires can generate higher field strengths than conventional copper conductors which will heat up due to the resistance loss, thus damaging the insulation. It is estimated that a generator or motor of the same output will cost 2 or 3 times lower when wound with superconducting coils than with copper coils. The material used in these machines is NbTi superconductors which can be shaped properly. Sizes for central station generators upto 300 MW can be achieved as is presently done with conventional copper windings.

High-temperature superconductors are proposed for use in ship propulsion systems by getting rid of propellers but by using electromagnetic thrusters. The principle involved is that the sea water is made conducting and passed through high magnetic field by channelling the water between the pole faces which, according to the usual motor-action principle according to Ampere and Fleming's rule, provide a thrust to the water. This principle can also be utilized for pumping water, thereby doing away with mechanical pumps. This is particularly useful for pumping liquid metals, corrosive and dangerous liquids such as radioactive liquids.

**(3) Magnetic Levitation**

Superconductors have found extensive application in transportation using very high land speeds, upto 500 or 600 km/hour. The most famous of these are the existing and projected "bullet" trains in Japan. The use of powerful magnets permits a vehicle to be lifted above the guide rails by gaps of 10-15 cm, thereby eliminating friction and increasing the speed without increasing the power in motors. Such fast or super fast trains can supplement short-distance aircraft between major cities, reducing or eliminating the need for airports near cities and also the time involved for travel between the city and the airport. The trains can also carry a high density of passenger traffic. Linear Induction Motors (LIM and LLM) also use high magnetic fields for propulsion and for magnetic levitation (MAGLEV).

This topic is in a very exciting stage of research and development, and will not be expanded any further here.

## OBJECTIVE TYPE QUESTIONS

1. Match the given symbols for solar cell materials with the group numbers from the Periodic Table.

| | | | | **Answers** | |
|---|---|---|---|---|---|
| (a) | Ge | (i) | III III V - III V | (a) | xi, xii |
| (b) | Si | (ii) | III V - IV | (b) | xi, xii |
| (c) | InP | (iii) | II VI - IV | (c) | iv, v, vii, ix, x |
| (d) | GaAs | (iv) | III V | (d) | iv, v, vii, ix, x |
| (e) | CdTe | (v) | III V | (e) | vi, viii |
| (f) | CdSe | (vi) | II VI | (f) | vi, viii |
| (g) | AlSb | (vii) | III V | (g) | iv, v, vii, ix, x |
| (h) | AlP | (viii) | II VI | (h) | iv, v, vii, ix, x |
| (i) | GaP | (ix) | III V | (i) | iv, v, vii, ix, x |
| (j) | GaAs - Ge | (x) | III V | (j) | ii |
| (k) | ZnSe - Ge | (xi) | IV | (k) | iii |
| (l) | GaAlAs - GaAs | (xii) | IV | (l) | i |

2. The Fermi-Dirac distribution function for spin-1/2 particles is:

   (a) $e^{-(E_F - E)/kT}$; (b) $e^{(E - E_F)/kT}$;

   (c) $1 + e^{(E - E_F)/kT}$; (d) $[1 + e^{(E - E_F)/kT}]^{-1}$;

3. The probability of finding the electron occupying energy level $E_F$ is: (a) $e^{-1}$; (b) 0.25; (c) 0.5; (d) 0.8.

4. The Fermi level in a crystal is 3.3 eV. The corresponding temperature is: (a) 23,200 K; (b) 38,280 K; (c) 11,600 K; (d) 50,000 K.

5. The electrical conductivity of a solar cell crystal depends upon: (a) charge density in material; (b) acceleration of electron per unit electric field applied; (c) mean collision time; (d) all three are true.

6. In sodium, with electron concentration $n_e = 2.5 \times 10^{28}/\text{m}^3$ with a charge density of $4 \times 10^9$ coul/m$^3$, and collision time $\tau = 3 \times 10^{-14}$ *s*, the electrical conductivity is with $(e/m) = 0.176 \times 10^{12}$ for electron: (a) $2.112 \times 10^7$ mho/m; (b) 2.112 mho/cm; (c) 2.112 mho/m; (d) 2.112 ohm-m.

7. The bond between atoms existing in a crystalline solar cell is mainly: (a) ionic; (b) hydrogen-like; (c) covalent; (d) metallic.

8. Solar cell materials have: (a) energy gap $\gg$ 5 eV; (b) no energy gap; (c) between 0.7 eV and 1.7 eV at room temperature; (d) valence and conduction bands overlap.

9. Solar cells are made from: (a) crystalline materials; (b) amorphous materials; (c) polycrystalline materials; (d) all three types of materials.

10. Structurally, solar cells can be: (a) PN junctions; (b) heterojunctions; (c) Shottky barrier; (d) metal oxide semiconductors; (e) all four.

11. Solar radiation of 1 μm wavelength corresponds to which set of frequency and energy? (a) 1 GHz, 1.24 eV; (b) 0.6 GHz, 3 eV; (c) 0.3 GHz, 1.24 eV; (d) none of the three.

12. At sea level, which amount of power in solar radiation is most reasonable? (a) 214 W/m$^2$; (b) 100 W/m$^2$; (c) 1.07 kW/m$^2$; (d) 1.35 kW/m$^2$.

13. At sea level, for a 20 kW peak load for a residence, approximately how much area of solar-cell panels is required? (a) $10^4$ m$^2$; (b) 10 m$^2$; (c) 100 m$^2$; (d) 1000 m$^2$.

14. In a space satellite, 1 m$^2$ of solar panel will generate approximately how much power? (a) 1 kW; (b) 2 kW; (c) 10 kW; (d) 1 MW.

15. Anti-reflection coatings given for solar cells are compounds like: (a) $SiO_2$; (b) $Ta_2O_5$; (c) $TiO_2$; (d) $Si_3N_4$; (e) all four and more.

16. Disadvantages of anti-reflection coatings are: (a) increase of traps and loss of efficiency; (b) dependence on wavelength of solar radiation; (c) degradation due to chemicals in the air; (d) all three.

17. The barrier voltage of a solar cell is given by: (a) $(q/\mathrm{kT}) \cdot \ln (n_i^2 / N_D N_A)$; (b) $V_B = (q/\mathrm{kT}) \cdot \ln ( N_D N_A / n_i^2 )$; (c) $V_B = ( N_D / N_A / n_i^2 ) \cdot e^{q/\mathrm{kT}}$; (d) none of the three.

18. The Fill factor of a solar cell is given by: (a) $V_m \cdot I_m / V_{oc} \cdot I_{sc}$; (b) $V_m / V_{oc}$; (c) $I_{sc} / I_m$; (d) $I_{sc} \cdot V_{oc} / I_m \cdot V_m$

19. The Fill factor is also known as: (a) reflection factor; (b) refractive index; (c) efficiency; (d) short-circuit factor.

20. In a heterojunction solar cell, the materials are: (a) *N* and *P* types on same substrate material; (b) *N* and *P* types with different substrate materials; (c) a metal and *P*-type material; (d) a metal and *N*-type material.

**Answers**: 2. (d); 3. (c); 4. (b); 5. (d); 6. (a); 7. (c); 8. (c); 9. (d); 10. (e); 11. (c); 12. (c); 13. (c); 14. (b); 15. (e); 16. (d); 17. (d); 18. (a); 19. (c); 20. (b).

## REVIEW QUESTIONS AND PROBLEMS

1. List 6 semiconductor junction solar cells giving the approximate energy gaps, current densities allowed at sea level and outside the atmosphere. Give their units.

2. (a) Show that a wavelength of $\lambda = 1$ μm solar radiation corresponds to an energy of 1.24 eV. Give all assumptions made.

(b) Explain the symbols AMO and AMI levels. Give the values of power densities available in solar radiation at these two levels.

(c) Explain the terms: 1-Sun; 10-Suns, and 100-Suns when referring to solar-cell work.

(d) Calculate the energy available across loads in a year at AM0 and AM1 levels. Make suitable assumptions. Use 5-cm diameter cell.

[**Answers**: *AMO*: 135 mW/cm$^2$, area = 20 cm$^2$, $\eta$ = 20%, all year, about 17 MJ;

*AMI*: 107 mW/cm$^2$ input, 20 cm$^2$ area, $\eta$ = 20%, 12 hr/day of sunshine, energy output about 6.75 MJ = 1.875 kWh.

3. The average measured total power density over the entire spectral content in solar radiation can be taken as 1070 W/m$^2$ at sea level and 1350 W/m$^2$ above the atmosphere. Taking an efficiency of cell as 18% for the cells, calculate the areas required for powers of (a) 20 kW; (b) 1 MW; (c) 1000 MW at sea level and above atmosphere. Is the last one practical?

   [**Answers**: (a) 103.3 m$^2$, 82.3 m$^2$; (b) 5165.3 m$^2$, 4115 m$^2$;
   (c) 5.1653 km$^2$, 4.115 km$^2$; (d) appears possible.]

4. A factory has solar panels over its roof and the factory peak load is expected to be 200 kW. Design a suitable solar-cell array using reasonable values.

   [**Answer**: Assume the roof is flat. Approximate area required from previous problem is 1030 m$^2$ made from 10 m wide × 100 m long panel or 10 panels each of 10 m by 10 m.
   If the roof is sloping, only half the panel is in sunlight, if the faces are oriented to face east and west. With roof sloping at 45°, the area required for each face = 1000 $\sqrt{2}$ m$^2$. Total solar-cell area required = 2800 m$^2$; etc.]

5. (a) Give the names of three elements which give rise to *P*-type semiconductor when doped in Si. Give three elements which yield *N*-type material with Si.

   (b) Give the names of five other PN-junction materials.

   (c) What are the materials in a heterojunction solar cell?

6. The reflection coefficients of several solar-cell materials are given in Table 3.7. Determine the refractive indices of any five of them for uncoated condition.

| [ | Si | InP | GaAs | CdTe | CdSe | GaP | AlSb |
|---|---|---|---|---|---|---|---|
| uncoated $r$: | 0.3 | 0.26 | 0.29 | 0.21 | 0.18 | 0.29 | 0.27 |
| ref.ind. $n$: | 2.964 | 2.68 | 2.9 | 2.35 | 2.17 | 2.9 | 2.75 |

Note that $n \approx 10.r$ for most materials.]

7. (a) Explain the difference between band gap and barrier voltage in a solar cell.

   (b) The intrinsic carrier concentration in a material is $n_i = 2 \times 10^{16}/\text{m}^3$ while the impurity concentrations are $N_D = N_A = 10^4$. $n_i$ on the $n$- and $p$-type semiconductors forming the junction. At 320 K, calculate: (i) the barrier width $x_b$ with $\varepsilon_r = 10$; (ii) the barrier voltage $V_B$; (iii) the maximum electric field strength across the barrier on open circuit.

   [$x_b = 2.368$ μm; $V_B = 0.508$ V; $\mathcal{E}_{\text{max}} = 4.29$ kV/cm = 429 kV/m]

8. (a) Explain the meaning of the terms: (i) Dark current; (ii) Photo current; (iii) Load current.

   (b) Derive Eq. (3.67) for total current when an external voltage $V_a$ is applied.

   (c) In a semiconductor the dark or saturation current is $I_o = 5$ μA at 350 K. Calculate the current at forward-bias voltages of 0.2 and 0.4 V.

   (3.786 mA, 2.8735 A)

   (d) Calculate the energy in solar radiation in order to yield a bias of 0.4 V. Express the energy in Joules, K, and eV.
   [eV = 0.4 = 4640 K = $0.6409 \times 10^{-19}$ J]

9. The values of hole and electron lifetimes as minority carriers ($\tau_p$, $\tau_n$) and mobilities of holes and electrons at room temperature of 300 K for some solar-cell materials are given. Calculate: (a) the diffusion constants for holes and electrons; (b) hole diffusion length on N-side and electron diffusion length on *P*-side of the junction. Give proper units.

| | Si | InP | GaAs | CdTe | |
|---|---|---|---|---|---|
| [$\tau_p = \tau_n$ | $10^{-7}$ | $10^{-10}$ | $10^{-10}$ | $10^{-9}$ | $s$ |
| $\mu_p$ | 66 | 600 | 3000 | 800 | cm$^2$/V-s |
| $\mu_n$ | 132 | 200 | 150 | 60 | cm$^2$/V-s |
| (a) $D_p$ | 1.706 | 15.51 | 77.56 | 20.68 | cm$^2$/s |
| $D_n$ | 3.412 | 5.17 | 3.878 | 1.55 | cm$^2$/s |
| (b) $L_p$ | $4.13 \times 10^{-4}$ | $3.95 \times 10^{-5}$ | $8.8 \times 10^{-5}$ | $1.438 \times 10^{-4}$ | cm |
| $L_n$ | $5.84 \times 10^{-4}$ | $2.274 \times 10^{-5}$ | $1.97 \times 10^{-5}$ | $0.394 \times 10^{-4}$ | cm |

10. In the previous problem, the density of minority carriers $p_{no}$ and $n_{po}$ are $10^{20}/\text{m}^3$. Calculate the dark current density across the junction for the four materials. ($J_0$: 0.16 100 176 29.3 mA/cm$^2$)

11. For a solar-cell array the bulk series resistance of the system is $R_s = 0.5$ ohm, and shunt resistance $R_{sh} = 500$ ohm. The photo current density is 20.5 mA/cm$^2$, while the cell area is 50 cm$^2$. The dark current density is

$0.5\ \mu A/cm^2$. For a load current of 1 A, calculate the load voltage and power density. Refer to Fig. 3.29. ($V_L = 12.5$ V, PD = 0.25 W/cm$^2$.)

12. (a) Explain the term fill factor and its importance as a performance parameter for a solar cell.

    (b) The short-circuit current density in a InP solar cell is 25 mA/cm$^2$, and the open-circuit voltage is 1 V. The fill factor is 0.8. Find the maximum power density of the cell. (20 mW/cm$^2$)

    (c) If the incident power density from solar radiation at sea level (AM1 condition) is 107 mW/cm$^2$ for production of photo current, calculate the efficiency in part (b). (18.7%)

*CHAPTER 4*

# Plasma Physics, Nuclear Fusion Power and Magnetohydrodynamics

## 4.1 Introduction

The study of plasma physics is essential for developing electrical energy through nuclear fusion and magneto-hydrodynamics. The former requires very advanced concepts of physics. Magneto hydro dynamics (MHD) on the other hand, is based on simpler concepts and we will restrict to this aspect of plasma physics. Nuclear fusion involves extremely high-temperature plasma (of the order of millions of degrees)* and uses such concepts as shock waves in plasmas, Landau damping, magnetic mirrors, containment of extremely high-temperature plasma, nonlinear effects, in addition to the concepts present in MHD. These latter are: (a) ionization; (b) conductivity; (c) Debye shielding; (d) trajectories of electrically charged particles in electric and magnetic fields; (e) Faraday and Hall effects and their engineering applications; (f) kinetic theory of gases; and (g) fluid mechanics. We will concentrate our discussion of plasma physics mainly on these items.

In an introductory way, a plasma is a gas containing neutral atoms, molecules, positively and negatively charged ions, and electrons. Their general behaviour under applied non-electromagnetic forces is collective, so as to present the properties of a neutral gas, but contain enough charged particles, so that under applied electromagnetic forces these charged particles behave independent of the neutral atoms and molecules, except through collisions. We will give a more scientific definition of a plasma in Sec. 4.3.

For a gas to become an electrical conductor, some of its atoms have to be ionized and the only way to do this is through thermal ionization. For useful MHD power generation, the temperature is in excess of 2500 $K$. Ionization of the main gas is aided by including a gas which has a low ionization potential (4 to 5.5 eV)

* We will not enter into the feasibility of developing nuclear fusion power at low temperatures, which has become a "hot" topic in recent years.

such as alkali gases (Na, K, Cs, Li). The main gas can consist of A, He, N or O, rocket exhaust, but in practical MHD systems which have to be cost-competitive and use easily available fuels, these gases can be and usually are (kerosene + oxygen), coal gas, flu gases, or liquid Na used in LMFBRs (liquid metal fast breeder nuclear fission reactors). Inclusion of a low-ionization-potential gas is called "seeding" the main gas.

Plasmas are not restricted to laboratory or industry. The entire universe consists of plasma in one form or another. Our Earth exhibits brilliant northern and southern lights at latitudes between roughly 50° to 80° (Aurora Borealis and Aurora Australis) caused by trapping of charged particles arriving from solar flares inside the earth's magnetic field. A little further out in space the Earth displays two radiation belts, called the inner and outer Van Allen belts, discovered as recently as 1958 at heights of a few thousand kilometres for the inner (> 1000 km) and between 20,000 to 30,000 km for the outer. In between the Auroras and the inner Van Allen belt is the Ionosphere discovered by Heaviside-Kennely and Appleton and others. The space in between the Earth and Sun consists of fast-moving electrically-charged particles thrown out by the Sun as flares, whose intensity is increased during sun-spot activity. The force required to eject such gigantic amounts of charged gas (some of them many times the size of the Earth) arises by MHD processes, in which the extremely powerful magnetic field generated by the high-velocity electrons inside the Sun interacts with the ionized gases He and H. The sunspots themselves are consequences of intense MHD effects, as theorized by Alfven in Sweden. Stellar interiors and interstellar hydrogen consist of plasmas. The plasma is therefore rightly named "the fourth state of matter" and is very abundant in nature. A study of the engineering aspects of MHD should certainly lead a young enquiring mind to understand the larger workings of the solar system, the stars and their formation, and indeed the vast and glorious subject of galaxy formation, and ultimately to the birth of our Universe with a study of gravitation and elementary particle physics.

Plasmas used in power generation by direct energy conversion contain particles which are non-relativistic. Also, their collective behaviour can be described by laws of classical mechanics and do not require use of quantum mechanics for the present.

## 4.2 Temperature and Ionization

In a gas the average kinetic energy of a particle, moving in one dimension or possessing one degree of freedom, is ½kT, Joule, where $k$ = Boltzmann constant $= 1.38066 \times 10^{-23}$ J / K, and $T$ = temperature in K. This is based on a Maxwellian distribution of particle velocities and is derived as follows:

The probability $p(u)$ of the number of particles in unit volume possessing velocity $u$ is given by Maxwell to be

$$p(u) = A\, e^{-mu^2/2kT} \tag{4.1}$$

where $\frac{1}{2} mu^2$ = kinetic energy of particle, and $A$ is to be determined as yet.

Therefore, in the velocity range $u$ and $(u + du)$, the number of particles per unit volume $(m^3)$ will be

$$p(u) \cdot du = A\, e^{-mu^2/2kT} \cdot du \tag{4.2}$$

The total number of particles in $1m^3$ will then be

$$n = \int_{-\infty}^{\infty} p(u) \cdot du = A \int_{-\infty}^{\infty} e^{-mu^2/2kT} \cdot du = 2A \int_0^{\infty} e^{-mu^2/2kT} \cdot du$$

$$= 2\, A \int_0^{\infty} e^{-a^2u^2} \cdot du \tag{4.3}$$

where $\qquad a^2 = m/2kT, \quad \text{or,} \quad 1/a = \sqrt{2kT/m} \qquad (4.4)$

But $\qquad \int_0^{\infty} e^{-a^2u^2} \cdot du = \sqrt{\pi}/2a = \frac{1}{2}\sqrt{2\pi kT/m} \qquad (4.5)$

Therefore $\qquad n = A\sqrt{2\pi kT/m}$, giving $A = n\sqrt{m/2\pi kT} \qquad (4.6)$

The average kinetic energy of the particles is

$$\varepsilon_{av} = \left[\int_{-\infty}^{\infty} \tfrac{1}{2} m\, u^2 \cdot p(u) \cdot du\right] \Big/ \left[\int_{-\infty}^{\infty} p(u) \cdot du\right]$$

$$= (m/2a^2)\left[\int_0^{\infty} a^2u^2 e^{-a^2u^2} \cdot du\right] \Big/ \left[\int_0^{\infty} e^{-a^2u^2} \cdot du\right]$$

Let $x = au$, giving $du = dx/a$.

Therefore $\varepsilon_{av} = (m/2\,a^3)\left[\int_0^{\infty} x^2 \cdot e^{-x^2} \cdot dx\right] \Big/ \left[\int_0^{\infty} e^{-x^2} \cdot dx\right]$

$$= m/4a^2 = m/(2m/kT) = \tfrac{1}{2} kT \tag{4.7}$$

The temperature of a particle is therefore defined in terms of the average kinetic energy it possesses. For one degree of freedom, $T = 2\varepsilon_{av}/k$. For three degrees of freedom, $\varepsilon_{av} = 3\,kT/2$, so that $T = 2\,\varepsilon_{av}/3k$.. For an energy of $1eV = 1.6022 \times 10^{-19}$ J, $T = 1.6022 \times 10^{-19}/\,1.38066 \times 10^{-23} = 1/8.6174 \times 10^{-5} = 11603.15\,K \approx 11600\,K$. For MHD work, $T$ is in the range 2000 – 3000 $K$ and $n \approx 10^{19}/\text{m}^3$. For nuclear fusion and other laboratory experiments, $T$ can reach $10^7\,K$ and $n = 10^{34}/\text{m}^3$.

### Thermal Ionization

Plasmas contain charged particles in addition to neutral atoms. Due to the high temperature, the electrons in the outermost orbits acquire enough energy to become free of the neutral atom, thereby converting the atom into a positive ion. We will restrict ourselves only to single ionization. To release a second electron from the atom (doubly-ionized) it is apparent that more energy has to be applied. Table 4.1 shows first ionization energy levels, $\varepsilon_i$, of typical gas atoms in eV and corresponding temperatures in degree K.

**Table 4.1: Ionization Potentials and Temperatures (1 eV = 11,600 K)**

| Element | Li | Na | K | Cs | He | Ne | A |
|---|---|---|---|---|---|---|---|
| $\varepsilon_i$, eV | 5.39 | 5.14 | 4.34 | 3.89 | 24.6 | 21.6 | 15.8 |
| $T \times 10^{-5}$, K | 0.6254 | 0.5964 | 0.5036 | 0.4535 | 2.854 | 2.506 | 1.833 |
| Gas | $H_2$ | $O_2$ | $N_2$ | NO | $CO_2$ | | |
| $\varepsilon_i$, eV | 15.6 | 12 | 15.6 | 9.26 | 14.4 | | |
| $T \times 10^{-5}$, K | 1.81 | 1.392 | 1.81 | 1.074 | 1.67 | | |

Note that cesium (Cs) has the lowest ionization potential of 3.89 eV and corresponding temperature of $4.5135 \times 10^4$ K = 45,135K. At this temperature all atoms are singly ionized. But in a hot gas seeded with Cs, a condition in which there are as many free electrons as there were neutral atoms is not essential. Even a fraction, say 0.1, is sufficient to increase the conductivity of the seeded gas to $10^4$ mho/m. This is nearly $10^{-4}$ times that of copper.

The degree of ionization of a gas, with $n_s$ neutral seed atoms, as a function of temperature is given by Saha's equation. This equation applies when all particles, (neutral atoms, positive ions and electrons) obey Maxwellian distribution. Saha's equation for thermal ionization is nearly

$$n_e \cdot n_i/n_s - [m_e kT/2\pi\hbar^2]^{3/2} \cdot e^{-e\varepsilon_i/kT} \qquad (4.8)^*$$

Here, $n_e = n_i =$ electron and ion concentration/m$^3$, $n_s$ = neutral atom concentration/m$^3$. The constant $(m_e k / 2\pi\hbar^2)^{3/2} = (1.8 \times 10^{14})^{3/2} = 2.414839 \times 10^{21}$. Therefore $n_e^2 / n_s = 2.41484 \times 10^{21} \cdot T^{3/2} \cdot e^{-11603\, \varepsilon_i / T}$ with $\varepsilon_i$ in volts. Also, $n_i = n_e$.

***Example 4.1:*** At 3000 *K* and ionization potential of 4 eV ($\varepsilon_i = 4V$), calculate $n_e$ or $n_i$ when $n_s = 10^{19}$ atom/m$^3$ in the neutral seed gas.

* The use of *e* for both base of Naperian logarithm and electronic charge has become unavoidable and should be clear from the context. The Naperian logarithm is being kept at Roman alphabet *e* in future also.

***Solution:*** $n_i^2 = 2.41484 \times 10^{21} \times 3000^{1.5} \cdot e^{-11603 \times 4/3000} \cdot 10^{19} = 7.492 \times 10^{38}$.

Therefore $n_e = n_i = 2.73715 \times 10^{19} / m^3$. The ratio $(n_e/n_s) = 2.73715$, showing that the number of neutral atoms remaining at this temperature is 1/2.73715 = 36.53% of seed atoms.

***Example 4.2:*** Repeat the previous example at $T = 2000$ K.

***Solution:*** $n_i^2 / n_s = 2.41484 \times 10^{21} \times 2000^{1.5} \cdot e^{-11603 \times 4/2000}$

$= 1.8035 \times 10^{16}$, giving $n_i = 4.24678 \times 10^{17} = 4.247\% \ n_s$.

Note the strong dependence of $n_i$ or $n_e$ on temperature $T$.

$\left[\text{At } T = 2500\ K,\ n_i^2 / n_s = 26.134 \times 10^{17}, \text{ giving } n_i = 5.112 \times 10^{18} / m^3\right]$.

### 4.3 Debye Length or Radius

When there is a concentration $n_e$ of electrons with a total charge density of $\rho = -(e\, n_e)$ coulomb / m$^3$, an electric field is set up which acts on the electrons. In addition to this, an electron at a temperature $T$ has an average kinetic energy of ½ $kT$ with one degree of freedom. The electric field is $E$ and given by solving Poisson's equation

$$\nabla^2 \phi = -dE/dx = -(-e\, n_e)/\varepsilon_o \text{ with } E = -\nabla \phi \tag{4.9}$$

where $\varepsilon_o$ = permittivity of free space = $8.842 \times 10^{-12}$ F / m

Therefore $$E = -e\, n_e\, x / \varepsilon_o \tag{4.10}$$

If the energy of an electron equals the mean kinetic energy due to thermal velocity, then the electrostatic field has no effect on the electron within a certain distance $\lambda_D$, called the Debye length. The kinetic energy shields the electron from experiencing the force due to the electric field. Its value is determined as follows:

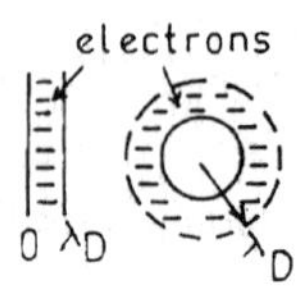


**Fig. 4.1** Debye length and radius

Work done in moving an electron over a distance $\lambda_D$ is (Fig. 4.1)

$$W = -\int_0^{\lambda_D} e\, E\, dx = e^2\, n_e\, \lambda_D^2 / 2\, \varepsilon_0 \tag{4.11}$$

Equating this to ½ kT, we obtain

$$\lambda_D^2 = \varepsilon_0\, k\, T / e^2\, n_e, \text{ or, } \lambda_D = \sqrt{\varepsilon_0\, k\, T / e^2 n_e} \tag{4.12}$$

As temperature increases, the shielding distance increases, since the thermal energy is high and the electrostatic field of the negative charges of $(e\, n_e)$ has less effect than at a lower temperature. Similarly, higher concentration $n_e$ lowers the

Debye shielding distance because of more intense electrostatic field which it sets up. The constant

$$(\varepsilon_0\, k\, /\, e^2)^{1/2} = (8.842 \times 1.38066 \times 10^{-35} / 1.6022^2 \times 10^{-38})^{1/2} = 68.97 \approx 69$$

Therefore $\lambda_D = 68.97\sqrt{T / n_e}$ (4.13)

Normally, $\lambda_D$ is a few micro-metres ($10^{-6}$m).

***Example 4.3:*** In Examples 4.1 and 4.2, $n_e$ was calculated to be $2.73715\times 10^{19}$ and $4.24678 \times 10^{17}$ per m$^3$ at 3000 *K* and 2000 *K*, respectively. Calculate (a) the Debye lengths for these two cases, and (b) the number of electrons $N_D$ in a sphere with radius $\lambda_D$.

***Solution:*** (a) (i) $n_e = 2.73715 \times 10^{19} \cdot T = 3000\ K$

$$\lambda_{D1} = 68.97\sqrt{3 \times 10^3\ / 2.73715 \times 10^{19}} = 72.2 \times 10^{-8}\ \text{m} = 0.722\ \mu\text{m}$$

(ii) $n_e = 4.24678 \times 10^{17}$, $T = 2000\ K$

$$\lambda_{D2} = 68.97\sqrt{2 / 4.24678} \times 10^{-7} = 4.73\ \mu\text{m}$$

[At $n_e = 5.112 \times 10^{18}$ and $T = 2500\ K$, $\lambda_{D3} = 1.526\ \mu$m]

(b) $N_{D1} = \dfrac{4}{3}\pi \times 0.722^3 \times 10^{-18} \times 2.73715 \times 10^{19} = 43$

Similarly, $N_{D2} = 188$, and $N_{D3} = 76$ in sphere of radius $\lambda_D$.

*Definition of Plasma*

The number of particles in a sphere of radius equal to the Debye radius is

$$N_D = 4\,\pi\,\lambda_D^3\, n\, /\, 3 = \frac{4}{3}\pi \times 68.97^3\, T^{3/2}\, n^{-1/2} = 1.37426 \times 10^6\, T^{3/2} n^{-1/2} \quad (4.14)$$

In the previous example we found values of 43, 76, 188 charged particles within spheres equal to Debye radii. These are much greater than 1, ($N_D >> 1$). If the dimension $L$ of the container of the gas is large, then $L >> \lambda_D$. When $N_D >> 1$, the particles exhibit collective behaviour and not individual behaviour. We now define a plasma as follows:

A plasma is an ionized gas in which $N_D >> 1$ and $\lambda_D << L$, and in which the ionized particles collide with neutral atoms sufficiently frequently that the motion can be described by hydrodynamic laws.

## 4.4 Cyclotron Frequency under Applied B - Field

When a charged particle with charge $q$ moves at a velocity **u** m / s in a magnetic field B Tesla, a Lorentz force acts on it equal to $\mathbf{F} = q\,\mathbf{u} \times \mathbf{B}$, where ($q$ **u**) is the current. Its equation of motion is consequently

$$m\,\alpha = m\,d\mathbf{u}/dt = q\,\mathbf{u}\times\mathbf{B} \qquad (4.15)$$

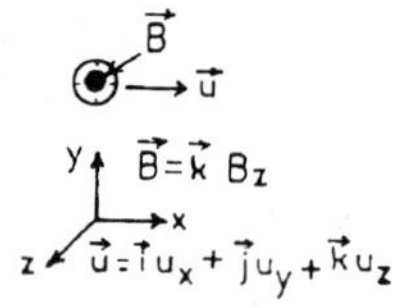


**Fig. 4.2** Magnetic field B and charge-carrier velocity *u*

In MHD, work, the direction of B-field is normal to the plane containing $\mathbf{u}$. (See Fig. 4.2).

Let $\mathbf{B} = B_z\,\mathbf{k}$ and $\mathbf{u} = \mathbf{i}u_x + \mathbf{j}\,u_y + \mathbf{k}\,0$.

Then

$$\mathbf{u}\times\mathbf{B} = \begin{vmatrix} i & j & k \\ u_x & u_y & 0 \\ 0 & 0 & B \end{vmatrix} = \mathbf{i}\,B\,u_y - \mathbf{j}\,B\,u_x + \mathbf{k}\,0 = [\,B\,u_y, -B\,u_x, 0] \qquad (4.16)$$

From Eq. (4.15), $du_x/dt = (q\,B/m)\,u_y$, and $du_y/dt = -(q\,B/m)\,u_x$ (4.17)

The resulting trajectory of particle in the x-y plane can be found if we determine $u_x$ and $u_y$. The quantity $(q\,B/m)$ is denoted by $\omega_c$ and is known as the cyclotron frequency in radian/sec.

[$qB/m$ = Coulomb × Tesla/kg = Coul × (Volt-sec/m$^2$) /kg

= (Joule/m) × sec/[kg-m/s$^2$] × sec$^2$ = Newton/(Newton-sec) = sec$^{-1}$]

Now, $$d^2 u_y/dt^2 = -\omega_c \cdot du_x/dt = -\omega_c^2\,u_y\,.$$

Therefore $$u_y = A\cos\omega_c t + B\sin\omega_c t = C\sin(\omega_c t + \varphi) \qquad (4.18)$$

where $A$, $B$, $C$ are constants, independent of $t$

$$C = (A^2 + B^2)^{1/2} \text{ and } \tan\varphi = A/B. \qquad (4.19)$$

Then, using eq. (4.17)

$$du_x/dt = \omega_c\,u_y = C\,\omega_c\,\sin(\omega_c t + \varphi - \pi/2) \qquad (4.20)$$

Therefore $$u_x = -C\cos(\omega_c t + \varphi) = C\sin(\omega_c t + \varphi - \pi/2) \qquad (4.21)$$

$$= A\sin\omega_c t + B\cos\omega_c t \qquad (4.22)$$

This yields for the velocity trajectory of the particle to be

$$u_x^2 + u_y^2 = (A^2 + B^2)(\sin^2\omega_c t + \cos^2\omega_c t) = C^2 \qquad (4.23)$$

Thus, $u_x$ and $u_y$ describe a circle in the *x-y* plane perpendicular to the direction of the *B*-field, with an amplitude *C*. We can take the phase $\varphi$ as zero, giving $u_x = C\sin(\omega_c t - \pi/2)$ and $u_y = C\sin\omega_c t$. Since $C$ denotes a velocity, we observe that $\omega_c$ can be written as $C = \omega_c \cdot r_L$, where the radius $r_L$ is called the Larmour radius.

In order to find the trajectory of the particle, we use

$$\left.\begin{aligned} u_x &= dx/dt = C\sin(\omega_c t - \pi/2) = -C\cos\omega_c t, \\ \text{and } u_y &= dy/dt = C\sin(\omega_c t) \end{aligned}\right\} \qquad (4.24)$$

$$\left.\begin{aligned} \text{Therefore } x - x_0 &= \int -C \cos \omega_c t \cdot dt = -(C/\omega_c) \sin \omega_c t = -r_L \sin \omega_c t \\ \text{and} \quad y - y_0 &= \int C \sin \omega_c t \cdot dt = -r_L \cos \omega_c t \end{aligned}\right\} \tag{4.25}$$

where $x_0$ and $y_0$ are the coordinates of a reference point for the particle. From Eq. (4.25) we observe that

$$(x - x_0)^2 + (y - y_0)^2 = r_L^2 \tag{4.26}$$

This shows that the charged particle is moving or rotating on a circle in the x-y plane perpendicular to $B$-field direction with radius equal to the Larmour radius, $r_L = C/\omega_c = C\,m/q\,B$. This radius is (a) directly proportional to the velocity $C$ of particle, (b) directly proportional to the mass m of the particle, but (c) inversely proportional to the charge $q$ of the particle, and the applied field $B$. Consequently, a heavier particle such as a proton or an ion has a larger radius of rotation than a lighter particle such as an electron. This is shown in Fig. 4.3.

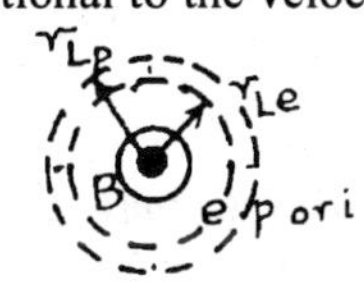

**Fig. 4.3** Larmour radius for positive and negative charge carriers in a magnetic field

In order to find the direction of rotation, we observe that the magnetic field produced by the rotating charged particle must oppose the externally applied $B$ field. These directions are shown in Fig. 4.4 for negative and positive charges. Since the main field is weakened, the moving charge produces a diamagnetic effect.

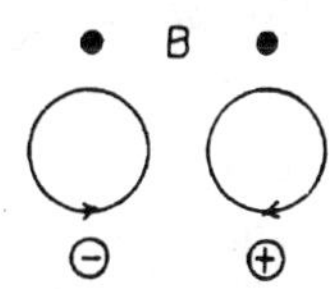


**Fig. 4.4** Directions of precession of positive and negative charge carriers in a magnetic field

## 4.5 Motion of Charged Particle in Combined E and B Fields

If in addition to the $B$-field, an electric field also acts on the charged particle, the velocity of the particle experiences a change in time, or in other words an acceleration is present due to the force exerted by the $E$-field on the charge. The particle now moves in the $B$-field in the $z$-direction and an electric field as shown in Fig. 4.5. The Lorentz force is

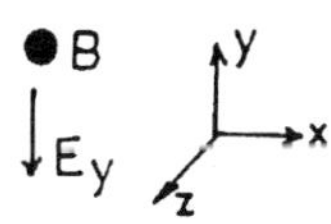


**Fig. 4.5** Particle motion in a magnetic field

$$m \cdot \mathbf{du}/dt = q\,(\mathbf{E} + \mathbf{u} \times \mathbf{B}) \tag{4.27}$$

This has two components:

$$m \cdot d\,\mathbf{u}_1 \;/\, dt = q \cdot \mathbf{E}, \text{ and } m \cdot d\mathbf{u}_2 \,/\, dt = q\,\mathbf{u} \times \mathbf{B}$$

We already know that the velocity $\mathbf{u}_2$ is in the $x$-$y$ plane if $\mathbf{B} = \mathbf{k}\,B_z$ and $\mathbf{u} = \mathbf{i}\,u_x + \mathbf{j}\,u_y + \mathbf{k}\,0$. The charged particle moves on a circle at centre $(x_0, y_0)$, its radius is the Larmour radius $r_L$, and velocity is $C = r_L/\omega_c$, where the cyclotron frequency is $\omega_c = qB/m$.

Let the electric field be in the (-$y$) direction, i.e. $\mathbf{E} = -\mathbf{j}\,E_{y.}$ Then the component of velocity $\mathbf{u}_1$ due to the electric field is, with $\mathbf{E}$ independent of time $t$

$$\mathbf{u}_1 = (q/m)\,\mathbf{E}\,t + \mathbf{u}_{10}\,,\ \text{or}\,,\ u_y = -(q/m)\,E_y\,t + u_{y0} \tag{4.28}$$

The guiding centre $(x_0\,, y_0)$ now moves in the direction of the E-field. This has occurred because the electric field **E** is perpendicular to the magnetic field **B**.

As a second case, let **E** have components only in the $x$- and $z$-directions with $E_y = 0$. Then

$$m \cdot d\,\mathbf{u}/dt = q\,(\mathbf{E} + \mathbf{u} \times \mathbf{B})\,,\ \text{giving}$$

$$du_{x1}/dt = (q/m)\ E_x\ \text{and}\ du_{z1}/dt = (q/m)\,E_z\,.$$

Therefore

$$du_x/dt = (q/m)\,E_x + \omega_c\,u_y\,,\ du_y/dt = -\,\omega_c\,u_x\,,\ du_z/dt = (q/m)\,E_z \tag{4.29}$$

These yield (a) $u_z = (q/m)\,E_z\,t + u_{z0}$, having an acceleration $(q\,e_z/m)$ in the direction of the $B$-field.

(b) $d^2u_x/dt^2 = \omega_c \cdot du_y/dt = -\,\omega_c^2 \cdot u_x$, giving as before

$$u_x = C\ \sin\ (\omega_c - \pi/2) \tag{4.30}$$

(c) $d^2u_y/dt^2 = -\,\omega_c \cdot du_x/dt = -\,(\omega_c\,q/m)\,E_x - \omega_c^2\,u_y$

$$= -\,\omega_c^2\,(u_y + E_x/B)\,,\ \omega_c = qB/m \tag{4.31}$$

Since $E_x$ is a constant, we can write

$$d^2u_y/dt^2 = d^2(u_y + E_x/B)/dt^2 \tag{4.32}$$

Therefore $u_y + E_x/B = C\sin\omega_c\,t$, or , $u_y = C\sin\omega_c\,t - E_x/B$ (4.33)

We observe that the particle velocity in the $y$-direction is changed while its velocity in the $x$-direction is unchanged from Sec. 4.4. It is obvious that the circle on which the particle is moving in the $x$-$y$ plane experiences two new velocites:

(1) In the direction of $B$-field it experiences an acceleration $(qE_z/m)$.

(2) In the $y$-direction, the circle moves down with velocity $(-E_x/B)$. These are shown in Fig. 4.6.

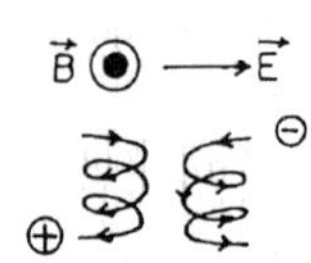


**Fig. 4.6** Helical motion of charged particles in combined B and E fields

From the above analysis it should be obvious that the trajectory of a particle to be analyzed follows a case-by-case structure. In the MHD case, if the gas velocity $u$ is in the $x$-direction and the $B$-field in the $z$-direction, because of the $(\mathbf{u} \times \mathbf{B})$ force, a voltage is induced in the $y$-direction and the charged particles experience a velocity in the $y$-direction. The $y$-component of velocity acting on the $B$-field induces a voltage in the $x$-direction as a consequence, i.e. in the direction of the original gas movement into the duct but opposing it or retarding the gas motion. This is known as the Hall voltage, whereas the induced voltage at right angles to both the velocity of gas and the $B$-field is known as the Faraday voltage. The Faraday voltage is what develops mainly in a conventional rotating generator using copper bars, since the Hall voltage is extremely low.

### 4.6 Conductivity in the Presence of B-Field

In Chap. 3, the conductivity of a solid was derived considering electric and hole mobilities. In plasma work, the conductivity is mainly due to electrons in the presence of applied electric and magnetic fields, which influence its velocity.

Under the influence of electric field only, an electron experiences an acceleration given by $\alpha_e = eE/m_e = 0.17585 \times 10^{12} E$. In the presence of random thermal motion, it collides with other particles in the gas such as molecules, neutral atoms, positive ions and electrons. The mean free time between collisions is

$$\tau = 1/n\sigma_c v_{th} \tag{4.34}$$

where $n$ = number density of atoms and molecules,
$\sigma_c$ = momentum-transfer cross-section of atom or molecule,
and $v_{th}$ = thermal velocity.

Now $$\tfrac{1}{2} m_e v_{th}^2 = kT \tag{4.35)*$$

[*Note*: *Some authors prefer Maxwellian velocity distribution and write $\tfrac{1}{2}m_e v_{th}^2 = 4kT/\pi$ while others use $\tfrac{1}{2}mv_{th}^2 = kT$. In Sec. 4.2, we observed that the average energy was $\tfrac{1}{2}kT$ and $\tfrac{3}{2}kT$ for 1- and 3-dimensional degrees of freedom.]

This gives $$v_{th} = (2kT/m_e)^{1/2} = 0.5503 \times 10^4 T^{1/2} \tag{4.36}$$

Table 4.2 shows average values of momentum-transfer cross-sections for some gases, which are in the wide range of $(0.35 \text{ to } 400) \times 10^{-16} \text{cm}^2$. For alkali metals it is extremely high.

**Table 4.2: Values of $\sigma_c$ for T = 2000 - 3000 K. (cm²)**

(Electron - Molecule Momentum-Transfer Cross-section)

| A | He | K | Cs | H | N | O | Air | Kerosene + O | |
|---|---|---|---|---|---|---|---|---|---|
| 0.35 | 5.4 | 400 | 300 | 13.8 | 6.5 | 3 | 8 | 40 | $\times 10^{-16}$ |

If at each collision the electron loses all its velocity, its average drift velocity is

$$u_d = \alpha_e \tau = eE/(m_e n \sigma_c v_{th}) \tag{4.37}$$

$$= \mu_e E \tag{4.38}$$

where $\mu_e$ = electron mobility $= e\tau/m_e = e/(m_e n \sigma_c v_{th})$ (4.39)

If the electron concentration is $n_e$ per $m^3$, which has been derived by Saha's equation (4.8), the current density is

$$j = e\, n_e\, u_d = n_e\, e^2\, \tau\, E / m_e \qquad (4.40)$$

Hence, the conductivity in the presence of only the $E$-field will be

$$\sigma_e = j / E = n_e e^2\, \tau / m_e = n_e\, e^2 / (m_e\, n\, \sigma_c v_{th}) = 0.0974\, n_e / (n\, \sigma_c\, T^{1/2}) \qquad (4.41)$$

where $e^2 / 2\ \text{k} m_e^{1/2} = 0.0974.$

Note that $n_e$ is proportional to $[T^{3/4} \cdot e^{-e\mathcal{E}_i / 2kT}]$ from Eq. [4.8], so that the electrical conductivity of a gas depends on temperature, unlike a solid.

In the presence of an applied magnetic field of strength $B$ Tesla, the electron has been shown to describe a circular orbit of radius $r_L$, the Larmour radius, and having a cyclotron frequency $\omega_c = eB / m_e$, rad/s.

Therefore $\quad \omega_c \tau = e\, B / (m_e\, n\, \sigma_c\, v_{th}) = 3.196 \times 10^7\, B / (n\sigma_c\, T^{1/2}) \qquad (4.42)$

The quantity is dimensionless and is known as the Hall parameter of the gas. The conductivity is, following Eq. (4.41)

$$\sigma_B = n_e\, e^2 / (m_e\, n\, \sigma_c\, v_{th}) = n_e\, e\, \omega_c \tau / B \qquad (4.43)$$

$$= \frac{\text{(charge density)} \times \text{(cyclotron frequency)} \times \text{(mean free time between collisions)}}{\text{magnetic field strength}}$$

$$(1)\, e / m_e v_{th} = (e / m_e) \cdot (m_e / 2kT)^{1/2} = (e / \sqrt{2k\, m_e}) \cdot T^{-1/2} = 3.196 \times 10^7 / T^{1/2} \qquad (4.44)$$

$$(2)\ n_e e / B = (\text{coul} / \text{m}^3) / \text{Tesla} = \text{coul} / [\text{m}^3 \times (\text{volt–sec} / \text{m}^2)]$$

$$= \text{Amp–sec} / \text{Volt–sec–m} = 1 / \text{ohm–m} = \text{Siemens} / \text{m} = \text{mho/ m}.$$

***Example 4.4:*** A gas has charged particles, moving with a velocity of 331.2 m/s (Mach 1) in a magnetic field of strength $B$= 2 T. Calculate : (a) the cyclotron frequency; and (b) Larmour radius for electrons and positive ions. Mass of atom of gas $= 10\, u$. $1\, u = 1.660566 \times 10^{-27}$ kg $= 931.502$ MeV. $m_e = 9.11 \times 10^{-31}$ kg $= 5.485803 \times 10^{-4}\, u$.

***Solution:*** $q_e$ = charge of electron $= 1.6022 \times 10^{-19}$coul.

Therefore $\omega_{ce} = 1.6022 \times 10^{-19} \times 2 / 9.11 \times 10^{-31} = 0.3517 \times 10^{12}$ rad / s

Frequency of gyration $f_{ce} = \omega_{ce} / 2\pi = 55.975 \times 10^9$ Hz

$$r_L = 331.2 / 0.3517 \times 10^{12} = 942.85 \times 10^{-12} \text{m}$$

*For positive ion :* $q_i = 1.6022 \times 10^{-19}$ coul , $m_i = 1.660566 \times 10^{-26}$ kg

Therefore $\omega_{ci} = 2 \times 1.6022 \times 10^{-19} / 1.660566 \times 10^{-26} = 1.9295 \times 10^7$ rad / s

$$f_{ci} = 3.071 \times 10^6 \text{ Hz}.$$

$$r_L = 331.2 / 1.9295 \times 10^7 = 171.86 \times 10^{-7} \text{ m}.$$

*Notes:*

(1) $m_i / m_e = 10 / 5.485803 \times 10^{-4} = 1.8229 \times 10^4$.

(2) $\omega_c$ is inversely proportional to $m$ for same $q$ and $B$.

(3) $r_L$ is proportional to $m$ for same $q$, $B$, and $u$.

(4) The velocity of a gas in medium of density $\rho$, pressure $p$, and ratio of specific heats $c_p / c_v = \gamma$, is $u = (\gamma p / \rho)^{1/2}$, m / s. For air, $\gamma = 1.4$, $p = 101{,}325$ *Pa*, $\rho = 1.293$ kg/m$^3$. This gives the velocity to be $u = 331.2$ m/s, which is the velocity of sound at standard atmospheric conditions.

***Example 4.5:*** A gas at 2500 *K* has a momentum-transfer cross-section $\sigma_c = 300 \times 10^{-16}$ cm$^2$. An electric field of 2 kV/m and a magnetic field of 1.5 T are applied. The number density of atoms involved in collision with electrons is $n = 10^{22} / \text{m}^3$, and the % ionization is 1%, ($n_e = 10^{20} / \text{m}^3$).

Calculate: (a) thermal velocity of electrons; (b) collision time, $\tau$; (c) acceleration of electrons in the electric field; (d) average drift velocity of electrons; (e) electron mobility; (f) electrical conductivity in the electric field only; (g) the Hall parameter; and (h) electrical conductivity in the magnetic field only.

***Solutions :***

(a) Thermal velocity: $v_{th} = (2\,kT / m_e)^{1/2} = 0.5503 \times 10^4 \times 50$

$$= 27.5 \times 10^4 \text{ m/s}$$

(b) Time between collisions:

$$\tau = 1 / (n\sigma_c\, v_{th}) = [\,10^{22} \times 300 \times 10^{-16} \times 10^{-4} \times 27.5 \times 10^{-4}\,]^{-1}$$

$$= 1.212 \times 10^{-10} \text{ s} = 0.1212 \; ns \;\; (n = \text{nano} = 10^{-9}).$$

(c) Acceleration : $\alpha_e = eE / m_e = 0.17585 \times 10^{12} \times 2 \times 10^3$

$$= 0.3517 \times 10^{15} \text{ m / s}^2$$

(d) Average drift velocity: $u_d = \alpha_e \tau = 0.3517 \times 1.212 \times 10^5$ m/s

$$= 4.2626 \times 10^4 \text{ m/s}$$

(e) Electron mobility: $\mu_e = e\tau / m_e = 0.17585 \times 10^{12} \times 1.212 \times 10^{-10}$

$$= 0.213 \times 10^2 \text{ m}^2 / \text{V–s} = 0.213 \times 10^6 \text{ cm}^2 / \text{V–s}$$

(f) Electrical conductivity: $\sigma_e = n_e e^2 \tau / m_e$

$$= 10^{20} \times 1.6022^2 \times 10^{-38} \times 1.212 \times 10^{-10} / 9.11 \times 10^{-31}$$
$$= 0.3414 \times 10^3 \text{ mho / m, or, Siemens / m.}$$

(g) Hall parameter $= \omega_c \tau$

$$\omega_c = eB / m_e = 0.17585 \times 10^{12} \times 1.5 = 0.263775 \times 10^{12} \text{ rad / s}$$

Therefore $\omega_c \tau = 0.3197 \times 10^2$.

(h) Electrical conductivity in magnetic field:

$$\sigma_B = n_e e \omega_c \tau / B = 10^{20} \times 1.6022 \times 10^{-19} \times 0.3197 \times 10^2 / 1.5$$
$$= 341.44 \text{ mho/m, or, Siemens/m.}$$

## OBJECTIVE TYPE QUESTIONS

1. Plasma physics is necessary as a background for understanding (a) Nuclear fusion; (b) MHD; (c) Cosmology; (d) Sun's energy output; (e) All four.
2. In a gas having particles with one degree of freedom, Maxwell's distribution function of velocities $p(u)$ is:

   (a) $Ae^{-3mu^2/kT}$; (b) $A\,e^{-3mu^2/2kT}$; (c) $A\,e^{-mu^2/kT}$; (d) $A\,e^{-mu^2/2kT}$
3. With one degree of freedom, the temperature of the particle is: (a) 11,600$K$; (b) 11,600 $E$, $K$ with $E$ in volts; (c) 11,600 $\mathcal{E}$, K with $\mathcal{E}$ in eV; (d) $2\,\mathcal{E} / k$, with $\mathcal{E}$ in Joule and $k$ = Boltzmann's constant; (e) Both (c) and (d) are true.
4. Which statements are true? (a) In nuclear fusion, $T \approx 10^6$ K and $n = 10^{28} / \text{cm}^3$; (b) In MHD work, $T \approx 2500$ K and $n = 10^{19} / \text{m}^3$; (c) Boltzmann's constant $k = 8.6174 \times 10^{-5}$ eV / K; (d) All three are true.
5. Ionization means: (a) transforming a neutral atom to one with electron deficiency; (b) transforming a neutral atom to one with electron excess; (c) transforming an unfilled subshell into a completely-filled one; (d) both (a) and (b) are true.
6. Which statement(s) is (are) true? (a) Electrical conductivity of $Cu \approx 0.6 \times 10^8$ / ohm–m; (b) Electrical conductivity of a hot gas is about $10^4$ / ohm–m; (c) Saha's equation for thermal ionization is $n_e^2 / n_s = 2.415 \times 10^{21}\, T^{3/2} . e^{-11603\mathcal{E}_i / T}$ with $\mathcal{E}_i$ in volts; (d) All are true.

7. The Debye shielding length (a) increases with temperature; (b) increases with electron concentration; (c) increases with electron energy; (d) both (a) and (c) are true.

8. A gas is considered a plasma if: (a) the Debye radius $\lambda_D > 1$ cm; (b) the number of charges in a sphere of radius $\lambda_D$ is much higher than 1; (c) $\lambda_D$ << size of container; (d) the behaviour of particles can be described by hydrodynamic laws; (e) all are true except (a).

9. When a charged particle of mass m and charge q moves in a magnetic field of strength B, the cyclotron frequency is: (a) $m/Bq$ ; (b) $B/mq$ ; (c) $qB/m$ ; (d) $1/mqB$.

10. The electrical conductivity $\sigma_e$ of a hot gas in plasma state is: (a) directly proportional to electron concentration/m$^3$; (b) directly proportional to electron mobility; (c) dependent on temperature; (d) all three are true.

11. The electrical conductivity $\sigma_B$ of a hot gas in plasma state when a *B*-field is applied is: (a) proportional to charge density/m$^3$/; (b) proportional to mean free time between collisions of charges; (c) proportional to cyclotron frequency $\omega_c$; (d) inversely proportional to *B*; (e) all the four are true.

12. The force $q\,\mathbf{v} \times \mathbf{B}$ on a charge q moving at a velocity **v** in a magnetic field **B** is called: (a) Maxwell's force: (b) Saha's force; (c) Einstein's force; (d) Lorentz force.

13. When a charged particle moves in a uniform magnetic field *B*: (a) its motion is along the *B*-field; (b) its motion is perpendicular to the direction of *B*-field; (c) it moves in a circle in a plane perpendicular to the direction of *B*-field; (d) follows the Larmour orbit; (e) all are true except (a).

14. If an *E*-field is applied in the same plane as *B*-field (*x*-*y* plane), an electron will move: (a) in a direction opposite to the *E*-field in the *x*-*y* plane; (b) in the *z*-direction perpendicular to both *E* and *B* field directions; (c) will have a gyrating motion about *z*-direction as axis; (d) will describe a helix; (e) both (c) and (d) are true.

15. A magnetic mirror is used in: (a) nuclear fusion experiments; (b) MHD work; (c) Lasers; (d) Ion engines.

16. The Auroras (Borealis and Australis) are caused by: (a) Cosmic rays; (b) ozone layer; (c) ionosphere; (d) charged particles in solar wind trapped by Earth's magnetic field; (e) Earth's rotation.

[***Answers***: 1.(e); 2.(d); 3.(e); 4.(d); 5.(d); 6.(d); 7.(d); 8.(e); 9.(c); 10.(d); 11.(e); 12.(d); 13.(e); 14.(e); 15.(a); 16.(d).]

## REVIEW QUESTIONS AND PROBLEMS

1. Give the definition of a plasma, explaining all quantities.
2. (a) Commencing from Eq. (4.1) show that for a particle with one degree of freedom, the average energy is $\mathcal{E}_{av} = \frac{1}{2} kT$, Eq. (4.7).

   (b) Then show that 1 eV = 11,600 *K*.
3. A gas has an ionization potential $\mathcal{E}_i = 5\ V$ and the seeding concentration is $n_s = 10^{20}$ atom / m$^3$. At a temperature of T = 4000 K, find the degree of thermal ionization by Saha's equation. $[n_e = 1.755 \times 10^{20} / \text{m}^3]$
4. In the previous problem, calculate: (a) the Debye radius $\lambda_D$ in *m*, *μm*, and Å; (b) the number of electrons in the Debye sphere of radius $\lambda_D$; (c) Does this satisfy the definition of a plasma?

   [(a) $\lambda_D = 3.2927 \times 10^{-7}$ m, 0.32927 μ m, 3293 Å; (b) $N_D = 26.243 >> 1$; (c) Yes $\lambda_D << L$, $N_D >> 1$]
5. (a) An electron is moving with velocity $\boldsymbol{u} = i\ u_x + \boldsymbol{j}\ u_y + \boldsymbol{k}\ u_z$ in a magnetic field $\boldsymbol{B} = \boldsymbol{k}\ B_z$. Find the three components of its acceleration.

   $[\alpha_x = -\omega_c u_y;\ \alpha_y = \omega_c u_x;\ \alpha_z = 0.]$

   (b) Explain why there is no acceleration or force in the *z*-direction, even though $u_z$ and $B_z$ are present. Describe the motion of the electron with suitable diagrams.

   (c) Taking $u_x$ = 300 m/s, $u_y$ = 100 m/s, $u_z$ = 50 m/s, and $B_z$ = 2.5*T*, calculate the accelerations and the cyclotron frequency $\omega_c$ in Hz.

   $[\alpha_x = -0.44 \times 10^{10}\ \text{m/s}^2;\ \alpha_y = +1.32 \times 10^{10}\ \text{m/s}^2;$
   $\omega_c = 0.44 \times 10^{12}\ \text{rad/s} = 0.07 \times 10^{12}\ \text{Hz}]$
6. The velocity of gas in a medium of density ρ, pressure *p*, and $\gamma = c_p / c_v$ is given by $u = (\gamma \cdot p / \rho)^{½}$ m / s. Calculate the velocity of gas under the following conditions, taking γ = 1.4 and $\rho = 3.4855\, p / T$, kg / m$^3$, with *p* in *kFa* and *T* in degree *K*.

   (a) Air at 1 atmosphere at 0 °C;

   (b) MHD gas at 20 atm and 2500 K. Assume gas to be air.

   (c) Air at 0.2 atm at –40 °C (which is true at about 9,000 m where a jet flies); (d) Give your comments and convert the velocities into Mach numbers. Mach 1 = 331.225 m/s.

   [(a) 331.225 m/s = Mach 1; (b) 1481.3 m/s = 4.472 Mach; (c) 305.9 m/s = 0.9235 Mach. Note that in an MHD duct, the velocity of gas is generally supersonic.]

7. The mean time between collisions of electrons randomly moving in a gas is $\tau = (n\,\sigma_c\,v_{th})^{-1}$, Eq. (4.34). Show that the electrical conductivity is $\sigma_e = 0.0974\, n_e / n\,\sigma_c\, T^{½}$, where $n_e$ = electron concentration and $n$ = concentration of atoms and molecules in gas.

8. A hot gas at $T = 3000$ K is seeded with caesium whose ionization potential is $\mathcal{E}_i = 3.89$ eV. Its momentum-transfer cross-section is $\sigma_c = 300 \times 10^{-16}$ cm$^2$. The degree of ionization by Saha's equation gives $n_e = 10^{19}$ electrons/m$^3$ in the gas with concentration of neutral atoms of $n = 10^{27}$atom/m$^3$. Calculate the electrical conductivity, mobility and velocity under an applied electrical field of 100 V/m. Give their units.

   [$\sigma_e = 5.9276 \times 10^6$ mho/m; $\mu_e = 1.945$ cm$^2$/V–s; $u_d = 1.945$ cm/s .]

9. In the previous problem, find the mean time between collisions of electrons with atoms. [$\tau = 1.106 \times 10^{-15}$ s]

10. A gas has charged particles moving with a velocity of Mach 4 = 1325 m/s, in which a magnetic field of 2.5 T is applied. Calculate: (a) the cyclotron frequency of the electron; (b) Larmour radius; (c) Hall parameter, if time between collisions is $\tau = 1.2 \times 10^{-10}$ s . Give units for all quantities.

    [$\omega_c = 0.44 \times 10^{12}$ rad / s; $r_L = 3 \times 10^{-9}$ m; H.P. = 52.8 rad]

11. (a) Prove that the Larmour radius and Hall parameter satisfy the relation $r_L \cdot H_p = u \times \tau$ = velocity × collision time.

    (b) Prove that the electrical conductivity $\sigma_B$ under an applied magnetic field $B$ is

    $\sigma_B$ = charge density × Hall parameter/magnetic field strength.

    (c) In Problem 10, calculate the electrical conductivity under the applied $B$-field if $n_e = 10^{19} / m^3$. [$\sigma_B = 33.84$ mho/ m].

## II. NUCLEAR FUSION

### 4.7 Basic Mechanism

When the nucleii of two light elements (up to $A \leq 56$) are fused together or collide, the resulting re-arrangement of nucleons releases energy. This may produce useful power for generation of electricity if harnessed suitably. As will be shown, the lightest elements—hydrogen, helium and lithium—and their isotopes are the preferred fuels. In principle, heavy hydrogen in the form of deuterium ($^2_1H$ or D) and tritium ($^3_1H$ or T) release an energy up to 17.6 MeV. The (D + T) reaction releases an $\alpha$-particle and a neutron. In order to provide enough initial energy for the fuel nucleii to collide, very high density laser beams are used. This is necessary in order to overcome the coulomb barrier or repulsion between protons in the two nucleii, which prevents the charged nucleii from colliding. In nuclear fission, on the other hand, the bullet particle was an uncharged neutron and does not experience an electrostatic force preventing the neutron from colliding with the target nucleus.

In a conceptual power generation station, the fuels are introduced into a container at which very high-powered laser beams are directed as shown in Fig. 4.7. The resulting high-energy neutrons are made to collide with $^6_3$Li-atoms which are heated. The liquid lithium raises steam in a heat exchanger using ordinary water and drives a conventional steam turbine and alternator unit. The most serious problem to be overcome is the containment of the hot fuel and products inside the container at temperatures in the range $10^{10}$ to $10^{11}$ K. If no suitable measures are taken to keep the fuel compressed, the resulting heat of reaction will melt the container. Two methods that have been tried are: (a) Magnetic-field containment; and (b) Mechanical or inertial containment by high pressure using high-power-density laser beams. We will discuss these two methods in Sec. 4.11.

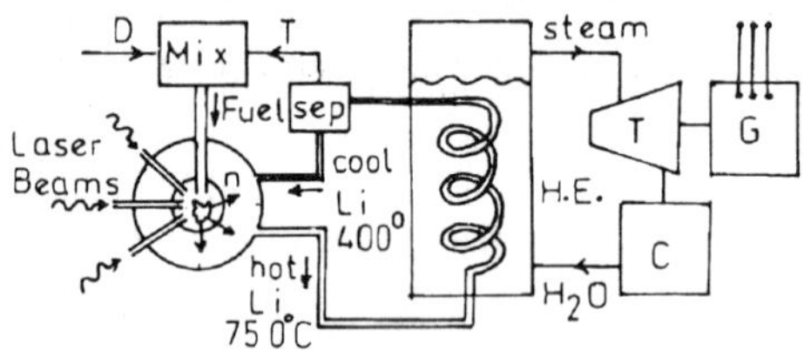


Fig. 4.7 Nuclear fusion reactor with steam station

### 4.8 Coulomb Barrier and Energy Reactions

The usual fuel elements and reaction products yielding an energy $Q$ are shown by the following equations:

$$D + D \longrightarrow {}^3_2He + n + Q \tag{4.45}$$

$$D + D \longrightarrow T + p + Q \tag{4.46}$$

$$\text{D} + \text{T} \longrightarrow {}_2^4\text{He} + n + \text{Q} \tag{4.47}$$

$${}_3^6\text{Li} + n \longrightarrow {}_2^4\text{He} + \text{T} + \text{Q} \tag{4.48}$$

$${}_3^6\text{Li} + \text{D} \longrightarrow 2 \times {}_2^4\text{He} + \text{Q} \tag{4.49}$$

The second of these reactions, Eq. (4.46) generates tritium (T , ${}_1^3$H) which can be used in reaction (4.47) as fuel. However, both reactions (4.45) and (4.46) are equally probable. We will calculate energy released $Q$ for all these reactions now. The atomic masses and other data are as follows:

$p = 1.0072765\ u$, $n = 1.008665\ u$, $D = {}_1^2\text{H} = 2.014102\,u$, $T = {}_1^3\text{H} = 3.016049\ u$, ${}_2^3\text{He} = 3.016029\ u$, ${}_2^4\text{He} = 4.002603\ u$, $k = 8.6174 \times 10^{-11}$ MeV / $K$, 1 $u = 931.502$ MeV, 1 MeV = $1.6022 \times 10^{-13}$J .

*Energy Release (Q value)*

(1) $m\,(\text{D} + \text{D}) = 4.028204$ u, $m\,({}^3\text{He} + n) = 4.024694$ u, $\Delta m = 0.00351$ u, Q = 3.27 MeV.

(2) $m\,(\text{T} + \text{p}) = 4.023305$ u, $\Delta m = 0.0049$ u, Q = 4.56435 MeV.

(3) $m\,(\text{D} + \text{T}) = 5.030131$ u, $m\,({}^4\text{He} + n) = 5.011268$ u, $\Delta m = 0.018863$ u, Q = 17.57 MeV.

(4) $m\,({}^6\text{Li} + n) = 7.023786$ u, $m\,({}^4\text{He} + \text{T}) = 7.018652$ u, $\Delta m = 0.005134$ u, Q = 4.78232 MeV.

(5) $m\,({}^6\text{Li} + \text{D}) = 8.029223$ u, $m\,(2 \times {}^4\text{He}) = 8.005206$ u, $\Delta m = 0.024017$ u, Q = 22.372 MeV.

*Note:* The reader should check all these values before proceeding further.

*Coulomb Barrier*

Consider two nucleii with atomic numbers $Z_1$ and $Z_2$ just touching. Their atomic mass numbers are $A_1$ and $A_2$, which determine the nuclear radii according to the equation

$$R = (1.2 \sim 1.4)\ A^{1/3}\ ,\ \text{fm}\ (10^{-15}\ \text{m}) \tag{4.50}$$

Using $A = 2$ for deuterium, $A = 3$ for tritium, and $A = 6$ for lithium, the following values for radii are obtained:

$$R_\text{D} = (1.2 \sim 1.4) \times 1.26 = 1.512 \sim 1.764\ \text{fm}$$

$$R_\text{T} = (1.2 \sim 1.4) \times 1.442 = 1.7307 \sim 2.019\ \text{fm}$$

and

$$R_\text{L} = (1.2 \sim 1.4) \times 1.817 = 2.18 \sim 2.544\ \text{fm}$$

When two nucleii with charges $(+Z_1e)$ and $(+Z_2e)$ are just touching and are separated by the distance $(R_1 + R_2)$, the electrostatic force of repulsion is

$$F = Z_1Z_2e^2/4\pi\varepsilon_0 (R_1+R_2)^2 \text{ Newton} \tag{4.51}$$

The corresponding electrostatic potential is

$$B_c = Z_1 Z_2 e^2 / 4\pi\varepsilon_0 (R_1+R_2), \text{ Joule} \tag{4.52}$$

This is the minimum amount of energy that has to be provided by an external source before the nucleii can collide. Due to quantum-mechanical effects, somewhat less energy is sufficient for the nucleons to penetrate the barrier. Using minimum values for the nuclear radii, the coulomb barriers for the D-D, D-T, and Li-D reactions have the following values:

(1) *D - D Reaction :* $R_1 = R_2 = 1.512 \times 10^{-15}$ m. $Z_1 = Z_2 = 1$,
$4\pi\varepsilon_o = 10^{-9}/9$, $e = 1.6022 \times 10^{-19}$ c, 1 MeV $= 1.6022 \times 10^{-13}$ J,
1 eV = 11,600 K

$$B_c = 1.6022^2 \times 10^{-38} \times 9/10^{-9} \times 10^{-15} \times 3.024 = 7.64 \times 10^{-14} \text{ J}$$
$$= 0.4768 \text{ MeV} = 477 \text{ keV} = 5.53 \times 10^9 \text{ K}.$$

(2) *D - T Reaction :* $R_1 = 1.521 \times 10^{-15}$, $R_2 = 1.7307 \times 10^{-15}$ m

$$B_c = 23.10336 \times 10^{-14}/3.2427 = 7.125 \times 10^{-14} \text{ J}$$
$$= 0.4447 \text{ MeV} = 444.7 \text{ keV} = 5.1585 \times 10^9 \text{ K}$$

(3) *Li - D Reaction :* $R_1 = 1.512 \times 10^{-15}$ m, $R_2 = 2.18 \times 10^{-15}$ m

$$B_c = 23.10336 \times 10^{-14} \times 3/3.692 = 18.77 \times 10^{-14} \text{ J}$$
$$= 1.172 \text{ MeV} = 1172 \text{ keV} = 13.6 \times 10^9 \text{ K}$$

Even though the coulomb barrier is nearly 0.5 - 1 MeV and corresponding temperatures are between $10^9$ and $10^{10}$ K, because of wave-mechanical effects and random velocity distribution, usually 10 - 100 keV energies and $10^8$ - $10^9$ K temperatures create conditions favourable for thermonuclear fusion process to take place and the resulting energy release is sufficient to continue the process. For the D-D collisions of Eqs. (4.45) and (4.46), we observe that for an input energy of about 0.5 MeV in each atom or a total of 1 MeV at temperature of 5.5 X $10^9$ K, the energy released is 3.27 MeV or a ratio of 3.3/1.

## 4.9 Kinetic Energy of Products

When an energy of $Q$ MeV is released in a thermonuclear reaction, it is shared by the product nucleii which are eventually utilized in a heat exchanger to raise steam. The energy carried away by each species of daughter nucleus can be calculated, for which we assume the momenta of the product nucleii are equal and oppositely directed, and the total kinetic energy is equal to the $Q$ value. If $a$ and $b$ refer to the two nucleii, then we have the following relations:

$$m_a v_a = m_b v_b, \text{ and } \tfrac{1}{2} m_a v_a^2 + \tfrac{1}{2} m_b v_b^2 = Q \qquad (4.53)$$

Therefore

$$Q_a = \tfrac{1}{2} m_a v_a^2 = Q / (1 + m_a / m_b), \text{ and } Q_b = Q - Q_a = Q/(1 + m_b / m_a) \quad (4.54)$$

$$\left.\begin{aligned} &\text{Also } v_a / v_b = m_b / m_a, v_a = \sqrt{2 Q_a / m_a}, v_b = \sqrt{2 Q_b / m_b} \\ &Q_a + Q_b = \tfrac{1}{2} m_a v_a^2 (1 + m_a / m_b) = \tfrac{1}{2} m_b v_b^2 (1 + m_b / m_a) = Q \\ \text{and } &Q_a / Q_b = \tfrac{1}{2} m_a v_a^2 / \tfrac{1}{2} m_b v_b^2 = m_b / m_a \end{aligned}\right\} \qquad (4.55)$$

Let us now compute these for the five reactions (4.45) through (4.49).

(1) $D + D \longrightarrow {}^3\text{He} + 3.27$ MeV

$m_a = m({}^3\text{He}) = 3.016029\ u$, $m_b = m(n) = 1.008665\ u$,

$1\ u = 1.660566 \times 10^{-27}$ kg $m_a / m_b = 2.99$, and $m_b / m_a = 0.3344$.

Therefore $\quad Q_{\text{He}} = Q / 3.99 = 0.81955 \text{ MeV} \approx 25\%\ Q$;

$\quad Q_n = Q / 1.3344 = 2.4505 \text{ MeV} \approx 75\%\ Q$.

The lighter nucleus carries higher kinetic energy in the inverse ratio of the masses of the two daughter or product nucleii.

*Velocities* :

$$v_{\text{He}} = [2 \times 0.81955 \times 1.6022 \times 10^{-13} / 3.01609 \times 1.660566 \times 10^{-27}]^{1/2}$$
$$= 0.724 \times 10^7 \text{ m/s} = 2.41\% \text{ of light velocity.}$$

*Neutron* : $v_n = v_{\text{He}} (m_{\text{He}} / m_n) = 2.1652 \times 10^7$ m/s $= 7.217\%$c.

The resulting temperatures of the products are:

*He* : $Q_{\text{He}} = 0.81955 \times 10^6 \times 11600 = 9.5 \times 10^9$ K;

$n : Q_n = 28.5 \times 10^9$ K.

(2) $D + D \longrightarrow T + p + 4.56435$ MeV

$m_T = 3.016049\ u$, $m_p = 1.0072765\ u$. $m_T / m_p = 2.99424$, and $m_p / m_T = 0.334$.

Therefore

$$Q_T = 4.56435 / 3.99424 = 1.14273 \text{ MeV, and } Q_p = 3.42162 \text{ MeV.}$$

*Velocities* : $v_T = 1.38914 \times 10^7 \sqrt{1.14273 / 3.016049} = 0.855 \times 10^7$ m/s.

and $\quad v_p = 2.56 \times 10^7$ m/s $= 8.534\%$ light velocity.

*Temperatures* : $Q_T = 1.14273 \text{ MeV} = 13.256 \times 10^9 \text{ K};$

$$Q_p = 3.42162 \times 10^6 \times 11600 = 36.69 \times 10^9 \text{ K}$$

(3) $D + T \longrightarrow {}^4\text{He} + n + 17.57 \text{ MeV}$

$$m_{\text{He}} / m_{\text{n}} = 4.002603 / 1.008665 = 3.9682$$

$$Q_{\text{He}} = 17.57 / 4.9682 = 3.5365 \text{ MeV} = 41 \times 10^9 \text{ K}.$$

$$Q_{\text{n}} = 14.0335 \text{ MeV} = 162.8 \times 10^9 \text{ K}$$

(4) ${}^6\text{Li} + D \longrightarrow 2 \times {}^4\text{He} + 22.372 \text{ MeV}$

Energy of each helium nucleus $= 11.186 \text{ MeV} = 129.76 \times 10^9 \text{ K}.$

***Example 4.6*** : Consider the possible reactions with deuterium yielding a total of $(3.27 + 4.56 + 17.57 + 22.37) = 47.77 \text{ MeV} \approx 48 \text{ MeV}$ utilizing 6 nucleii of $D$. Calculate the energy released from 1 gram of $D = {}^2_1\text{H}$. Give the answer in MeV, Joules, kW-h, MW-h, and MW-d.

***Solutions*** : $m(D) = 2.0135532\, u = 1875.628 \text{ MeV}$, since $1\, u = 931.5 \text{ MeV}$. $1\, u = 1.660566 \times 10^{-27}$ kg, 1 MeV $= 1.6022 \times 10^{-13}$ J, 1 kW–h $= 3.6$ MJ.

The number of nucleii contained in 1 g of $D$ is

$$10^{-3} / (2.0135532 \times 1.660566 \times 10^{-27}) = 0.3 \times 10^{24}.$$

Therefore energy released $= 48 \times 0.3 \times 10^{24} / 6 = 2.4 \times 10^{24}$ MeV

$$= 3.84528 \times 10^{11} \text{ J} = 1.068 \times 10^5 \text{ kW–h}$$

$$= 106.8 \text{ MW–h} = 4.45 \text{ MW–d}$$

[*Note*: 1 g of ${}^{235}$U generates about 1 MW-d in fission.]

In a conceptual nuclear fusion power-generation system, all the four possible reactions with deuterium take place.

### 4.10 Plasma Condition and Radiation Loss

In a fusion reactor, the thermo-nuclear fuel is provided with enough energy from an external source to heat the fuel pellet to temperatures of the order of $10^8$ K, or since 1 eV = 11,600 K, an energy of 10/1.16 = 8.62 keV, or about 10 keV. This is carried out through bombardment with high-energy laser beams, and is maintained for a sufficiently long time for fusion reaction to occur, which can be about 1 milli second or less. Since only 13.645 eV are necessary to ionize a hydrogen atom completely, an energy of 10 keV strips all atoms of electrons and sets them free. The resulting fuel or product is a mixture of positive ions and negative electrons inside the fusion container.

In such a plasma, the Debye length is, according to Eq. (4.12)

$$\lambda_d = (\varepsilon_0\, k\, T / e^2\, n)^{½} \tag{4.12}$$

Consider values of $n = 10^{22} / m^3$ and $kT = 10^4$ eV $= 1.6 \times 10^{-15}$ J

Then, $\lambda_D = (8.842 \times 10^{-12} \times 1.6 \times 10^{-15} / 1.6022^2 \times 10^{-38} \times 10^{22})^{½}$

$= 0.7434 \times 10^{-5}$ m $= 7.434$ μm

The number of charge carriers in a sphere with radius equal to $\lambda_D$ will be

$$N_D = (4\,\pi / 3) \times 0.7434^3 \times 10^{-15} \times 10^{22} = 1.72 \times 10^7 .$$

Thus, $\lambda_D <<$ container dimension $L_c$, and $N_D >> 1$. According to Sec. 4.3, these criteria satisfy the conditions for considering the resulting charge carriers as a plasma and apply all equations of performance governing plasma behaviour.

Because the electrons flow freely and are subjected to attractive forces by the positive ions, they experience bremsstrahlung or braking radiation. This is a source of loss, and the energy released in the fusion reaction must exceed this loss as well as provide energy for overcoming the coulomb barrier. Without resorting to detailed derivation, the energy loss of electron by bremsstrahlung is

$$BR_{\text{loss}} = \frac{4\pi n_i\, n_e\, Z^2\, e^6\, v_e}{3\,(4\pi\,\varepsilon_0)^3\, m_e\, \hbar\, c^3}\ \text{W / m}^3 \tag{4.56}$$

where $n_i, n_e$ = number density of positive ions and electrons per $m^3$, respectively,

and $v_e$ = average electron velocity given by $½\, m_e\, v_e^{\,2} = 3\,\text{kT} / 2$

With $e = 1.6022 \times 10^{-19}$ coulomb, $4\,\pi\,\varepsilon_0 = 10^{-9} / 9$, $\hbar = 1.054589 \times 10^{-34}$J-s, $c = 2.9979246 \times 10^8$ m / s, $m_e = 9.109538 \times 10^{-31}$ kg, $k = 1.38066 \times 10^{-23}$ J / K,

and $v_e = \sqrt{3\, kT / m_e} = 6.743 \times 10^3 \sqrt{T}$, there results

$$BR_{\text{loss}} = 1.34564 \times 10^{-40} \times n_i\, n_e\, Z^2 \sqrt{T}, \text{W / m}^3 \tag{4.57}$$

For example, if $n_i = n_e = 10^{22}$, $Z = 1$, $T = 10^8$ K, the bremsstrahlung loss will be $BR_{\text{loss}} = 1.34564 \times 10^8$ W / m$^3$ = 135 MW / m$^3$ nearly.

If (kT) is in keV, since 1 keV $= 1.6022\ 10^{-16}$ J

$v_e = \sqrt{3 \times 1.6022 \times 10^{-16} / m_e}\ (\text{kT})^{½}$, with kT in keV,

$= 2.297 \times 10^7\ (\text{kT})^{½}$

Therefore $BR_{\text{loss}} = 1.34564 \times 10^{-40} \times (2.297 \times 10^7 / 6.743 \times 10^3)\, n_i\, n_e\, Z^2 \sqrt{kT}$

$$= 0.4584 \times 10^{-36}\, n_i\, n_e\, Z^2\, (\text{kT})^{½}_{\text{keV}} \tag{4.58}$$

For example, as before, for

$$T = 10^8 \text{ K}, \ (\text{kT})_{\text{keV}} = 10^8 / 11.6 \times 10^6 = 8.62 \text{ keV}.$$

Therefore $BR_{\text{loss}} = 0.4584 \times 10^{-36} \times 10^{44} \times \sqrt{8.62} = 1.346 \times 10^8 \text{ W / m}^3$

Furthermore, if (kT) is in Joules, then

$$BR_{\text{loss}} = 0.362 \times 10^{-28} \, n_i \, n_e \, Z^2 \, (\text{kT})_{\text{J}}^{1/2} \tag{4.59}$$

This is left as an exercise for the reader.

For $T = 10^8$ K, kT $= 1.38066 \times 10^{-23} \times 10^8 = 1.38066 \times 10^{-15}$ J and $(\text{kT})^{1/2} = 3.7157 \times 10^{-8}$. Thus, $BR_{\text{loss}} = 0.362 \times 3.7157 \times 10^8 = 1.345 \times 10^8$.

The input energy supplied for sustaining the nuclear fusion reaction must exceed the bremsstrahlung and other losses. These include, among others, the cyclotron and synchrotron radiation when a magnetic field is applied for containment of the plasma.

Example 4.7 : Laser beams of $10^{-6}$ m diameter are used for heating a pellet of D-T mixture inside a nuclear fusion container. If 10 beams are used and the power is to be a minimum of 135 MW/m$^2$, and the efficiency of each laser unit is 1%, find the power in each laser.

Solution: Input power = $135 \times 10^6 / 0.01 = 135 \times 10^8$ MW / m$^2$. Let $P_L$ = power of each laser unit or beam. Then the power density is

$$P_{\text{L}} / [10 \times (\pi \times 10^{-12} / 4)] = 1.2734 \times 10^{11} \, P_{\text{L}}, \text{MW / m}^2$$

Therefore $\quad P_{\text{L}} = 135 \times 10^8 / 1.2734 \times 10^{11} = 0.106 \text{ MW}.$

## 4.11 Confinement of Plasma

In order to confine the extremely hot plasma inside the container, two methods are being adopted for the present:

(a) Magnetic-field confinement; and (b) Inertial confinement by mechanical pressure. This is carried out by high-powered lasers which also provide the energy required in the fuel for overcoming the coulomb barrier, $\text{BR}_{\text{loss}}$ and other losses. Magnetic-field confinement provides instabilities or breaking up the plasma by oscillations, but can be overcome by proper design of the field distribution and strength. All methods involve non-linear effects and shock waves.

### *4.11.1 Magnetic Confinement*

We observed earlier that a charged particle exhibits a cyclotron frequency and Larmour radius when a magnetic field is applied, the orbit being in a plane at right angles to the direction of the B-field direction. The cyclotron frequency is

$\omega_c = qB/m$, and the Larmour radius $r_L = v/\omega_c$ where $v$ is the amplitude of velocity perpendicular to B (see Eq. (4.17) and Fig. 4.4). The charged particles of both kinds give rise to intense electric fields, so that they have a spiral loci under the influence of both B- and E-fields as shown in Fig. 4.6. If the negatively-charged particles were to flow all in one bunch, then they would represent a current of one type which would attract each other electromagnetically and repel each other electrostatically. If the electromagnetic attraction exceeds the repulsion, then the filaments tend to come close to each other and there will be some type of self-confinement of the particles. This is known as the "pinch effect". The same holds for positively-charged ions. However, in the plasma, both types of charged particles are in a mixture and the pinch effect is not the primary force to contain the plasma and prevent it from spreading and coming into contact with the cool walls of the container or burning it due to the extremely high temperature.

In order to contain the particles in their orbits, a doughnut-shaped container is used which is called a toroid. Two types of field are applied with two coils whose axes are at right angles. One is along the circumference of the toroid called the "toroidal field", and the other round the smaller dimension of the doughnut which is called the "poloidal field", as shown in Fig. 4.8.

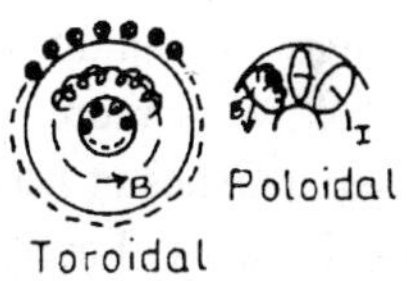


**Fig. 4.8** Toroidal and poloidal magnetic fields for containment of hot plasma

In a linear arrangement of the container, magnetic, mirrors are employed. These have a lower field strength at the middle and high *B*-field at the ends, Fig. 4.9. The spirals on which the charged particles move are squeezed closer since $r_L = v\,m/qB$, so that a high $B$ value gives a smaller Larmour radius $r_L$. This makes the particles reflect back into the low-B region and the arrangement acts like a mirror and a bottle where the particles are trapped. However, some particles leak through the strong-B region at the ends, which cannot be avoided in such an arrangement.

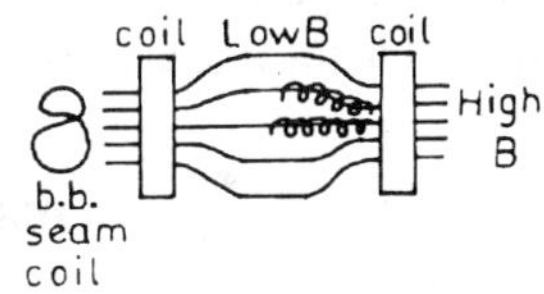


**Fig. 4.9** Magnetic mirror confinement of plasma

To minimize this loss and improve performance, a series of mirrors or coils are utilized called a "Tandem Mirror" and at the ends a base-ball seam-like coil or figure of 8 is provided which reflects any particles that leak at the ends, as shown in Fig. 4.10.

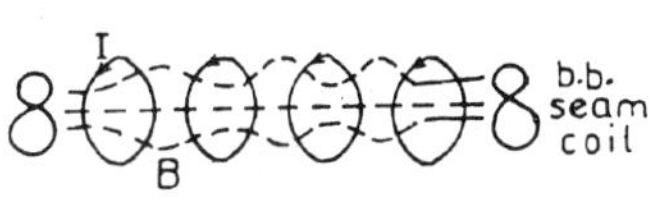


**Fig. 4.10** Tandem mirror arrangement in nuclear fusion experiments

All magnets are made from superconducting material and the field strength used is a minimum of 2 Tesla.

Another arrangement is known as "Field-Reversing System". In one form the principle is to utilize the diamagnetic property of a stream of charged particles in a B-field sufficiently strong to reverse the applied field inside the ring. The current flowing along the circumferential direction induces a poloidal field which confines the hot plasma.

### *4.11.2 Inertial Confinement*

As shown in Fig. 4.7, pellets of fuel with *D* and *T* are introduced at a rate between 10 and 100 per second having sizes from 0.1 to 1 mm diameter. In the combustion chamber, high-powered laser pulses are directed at the pellets, which heat them to high temperature as required by the fusion reaction and at the same time compress them, not allowing them to blow apart within the time required for the reaction. This time is as low as $10^{-9}$ s and could extend to 1 ms. An energy of 10 keV corresponds to $1.6 \times 10^{-15}$ J, so that the power required can be as high as $1.6 \times 10^{-6}$ W for each reaction. In a reactor, the total energy involved may be as high as $10^5$ J in the totality of reactions, so that the power required in pulsed form is $10^{14}$ W or more. With lasers having efficiencies of 1 - 10% the power in the lasers reaches at least $10^{15}$ W. Such high power in pulsed form provide intense shock waves. Lasers for this high powers are not available yet.

Another scheme is to obtain very high energy charged particles, namely protons and electrons, in accelerator-type machines and inject them on the pellets. This is now under investigation. This scheme may require a particle accelerator to go alongside the nuclear fusion generating scheme.

## OBJECTIVE TYPE QUESTIONS

1. The temperature required to overcome coulomb barrier in fusion power generation is in the range of:
   (a) $10^6$ - $10^7$ K; (b) $10^9$ - $10^{10}$ K; (c) $10^{11}$ - $10^{12}$ K; (d) none of the three.
2. The plasma in a nuclear fusion generator can be contained by: (a) Magnetic field; (b) high-powered lasers; (c) toroidal field; (d) poloidal field; (e) all four.
3. In a conceptual nuclear fusion reactor, the reactions taking place are:
   (a) $\mathrm{D + D \longrightarrow {}^3_2He} + n + 3.27\ \mathrm{MeV}$;
   (b) $\mathrm{D + D \longrightarrow T} + p + 4.56\ \mathrm{MeV}$;
   (c) $\mathrm{D + T \longrightarrow {}^4_2He} + n + 17.6\ \mathrm{MeV}$;
   (d) $\mathrm{{}^6_3Li + D \longrightarrow 2 \times {}^4_2He + 22.4\ MeV}$;
   (e) All four.

***Answers:*** 1.(b); 2.(e); 3.(e).

## REVIEW QUESTIONS AND PROBLEMS

1. Calculate the coulomb barriers in Joules, MeV and degree K for the following two reactions: (a) D - T reaction; (b) Li - D reaction.

   [(a) $6.843 \times 10^{-14}$ J = 0.4271 MeV = $4.954 \times 10^{9}$ K;
   (b) $17.01 \times 10^{-14}$ J = 1.0617 MeV = $12.316 \times 10^{9}$ K].

2. Explain the significance of the coulomb barrier in nuclear-fusion generation of power.

## III. MAGNETOHYDRODYNAMICS — MHD

### 4.12 Principles of MHD Power Generation

In a rotating dynamo discovered by Faraday a conductor moves at right angles to the direction of an applied magnetic field of strength $B$ at a velocity $v$. A voltage is thereby induced in the third perpendicular direction having the magnitude

$$e = B\,v\,,\ V/m \tag{4.60}$$

where $B$ is in Tesla and $v$ in m/s. If the velocity of conductor is not at right angles to $B$, only that component of velocity at right angles to $B$ will be used in Eq. (4.60). The polarity of voltage, i.e., the direction in which a current will flow out to a

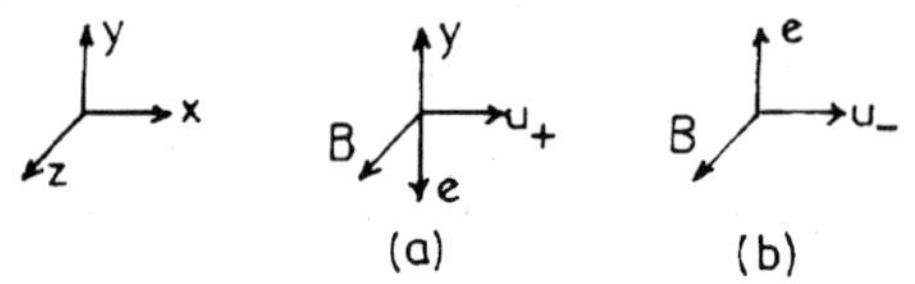


**Fig. 4.11** Illustrating Fleming's rule for positive and negative charge carriers in a B-field

connected load is given by Fleming's right-hand rule, Fig. 4.11(a), with (a) the fore finger pointing along the direction of $B$, or, the flux density vector, (b) the middle finger pointing in the direction of current flow I, and (c) the thumb pointing in the direction of torque or turning of the conductor. The conventional flow of current is taken to be of positive charges, i.e., against the direction of electron flow. The general vector expression is

$$\mathbf{e} = \mathbf{v} \times \mathbf{B} \tag{4.61}$$

However, if the solid conductor normally used in a conventional Faraday, dynamo is replaced by a conducting gas with free electrons, the left-hand rule of Fleming would be used as shown in Fig. 4.11(b) and the direction of induced voltage will be opposite as compared to the solid-conductor case. In an MHD generator, shown schematically in Fig. 4.12, a magnetic field $B$ is applied in a direction at right angles to the flow of gas containing electrons (negatively-charged particles in general), with the result that an emf $V_F$ is induced, whose polarity is such that it drives conventional current in the third perpendicular direction as shown. This is called the Faraday Configuration of the MHD generator.

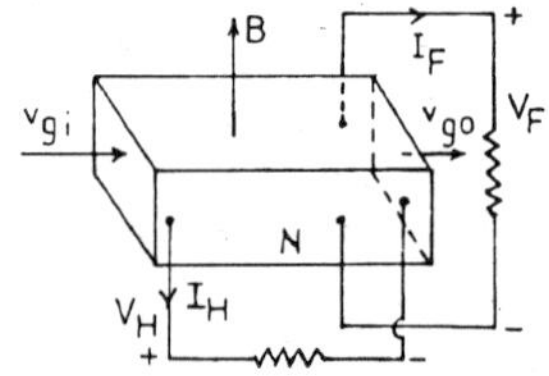


**Fig. 4.12** MHD duct with Faraday and Hall voltages and loads

As discussed earlier an electron (or charged particle) moving in a magnetic field is deflected. This results in a velocity component at right angles to the gas-flow direction. The electrons experience a Lorentz force which tries to concentrate them on the down-stream side of face N. This part acquires a negative potential with respect to the upstream side as in Fig. 4.12, so that a voltage develops along the direction of gas flow. This is known as the Hall voltage.

The main parts of an MHD generator are consequently as follows:

(i) A duct through which high-temperature ionized gas flows at a very high velocity;

(ii) A magnetic field in a direction at right angles to the gas flow, produced by suitable coils; and

(iii) Electrodes located suitably to carry the current to external loads in the Faraday and/or Hall configurations.

The generator is capable of producing extremely high specific power outputs (power/$m^3$ volume of duct) of 100 $MW/m^3$ or of that order. But the high temperature, the high magnetic field and the electrode material present problems that are very severe and much more difficult to handle than in conventional electromagnetic generators with copper conductor, copper magnetic field coils and copper commutator and brushes for current collection. Material problems have restricted the use of this extremely attractive power-generation method. Faraday himself in the 1830's was searching for a suitable gas with good conductivity to generate a voltage and having a low internal voltage drop; but it was over a century later that an acceptable MHD mode of power generation became feasible and acceptable for industrial use by Kantrowitz and his co-workers at Cornell University and later at AVCO. MHD power generation or the research and development of it has now become world-wide. (In India, the Bharat Heavy Electricals have an MHD plant at their high-temperature equipment works at Tiruchirapalli).

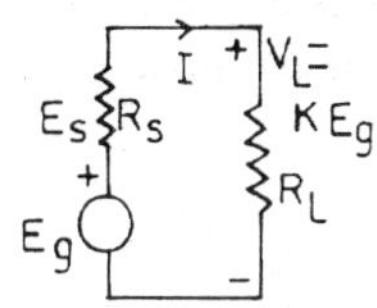

**Fig. 4.13** Thevenin equivalent of MHD generator on load

By applying power from an external source, it is evident that a gas can be propelled to very high velocities (high Mach numbers) giving motor effect in the MHD duct. This has been used mainly for research purposes. The development got a boost when the possibility of using rocket exhaust as the high-temperature gas was investigated successfully.

## 4.13 Ideal MHD - Generator Performance

First consider Fig. 4.12 in which is shown a source of emf $E_g$, having an internal resistance $R_s$, connected to a load $R_L$. We are assuming the voltage developed to be dc. The load voltage is $V_L$ and the current in the circuit is $I$. Let $K = V_L / E_g$, so that the internal voltage drop in the emf source is $E_s = I \cdot R_s = (E_g - V_L) = (1 - K)\, E_g$. Then

$$R_s = (1 - K)\ E_g / I \tag{4.62}$$

If $a$ = area in the source that is conducting current,
$l$ = length of current path in source,
and $\sigma$ = conductivity of material inside the source,
then $R_s = l/\sigma a = (1-K)\,E_g/I$, ohm (4.63)

This expression yields the current density inside the source to be

$$j = I/a = \sigma\,E_g\,(1-K)/l = \sigma\,E_i\,(1-K)\,,A/m^2 \tag{4.64}$$

where $E_i = E_g/l$ = electric field intensity inside the source, V/m.

$E_i = u\,B$, with $u$ = velocity of conductor which for now is taken to be perpendicular to the direction of applied magnetic field $B$ (Fig. 4.14). This applies when $u$ represents velocity of positively-charged particles.

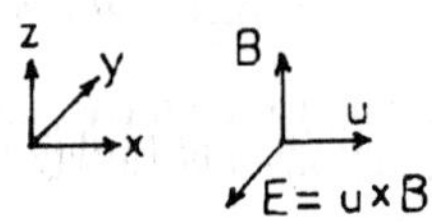

Fig. 4.14 Faraday voltage in MHD duct

The quantity $E = V_L/l = K\,E_i = K\,u\,B$ is the electric field intensity set up by the load voltage, as it were, inside the generator. Therefore

$$j = \sigma\,(u\,B - E) \tag{4.65}$$

We can now transfer these ideas to the MHD duct, with the difference that the velocity of the conducting ionized gas represents the velocity of electrons in it. The voltage gradient generated is

$$|\mathbf{E_i}| = |\mathbf{u}\times\mathbf{B}| = u\,B\,,\mathrm{V/m} \tag{4.66}$$

Taking $u = u_x$ and $B = B_z$, the generated voltage is in the $y$-direction with magnitude $(u_x\,B_z)$, since from Fig. 4.15 we have

$$\mathbf{u}\times\mathbf{B} = \begin{vmatrix} i & j & k \\ u_x & 0 & 0 \\ 0 & 0 & B_z \end{vmatrix} = [0, -u_x\,B_z\,,\,0]$$

Let $\quad E = V_L/l\,,\mathrm{V/m}$ and $E/uB = K$ (4.68)

K is known as the Performance Coefficient. Then the current density is

$$j = \sigma\,(E_i - E) = \sigma\,u\,B\,(1-K)\,,\mathrm{A/m^2} \tag{4.69}$$

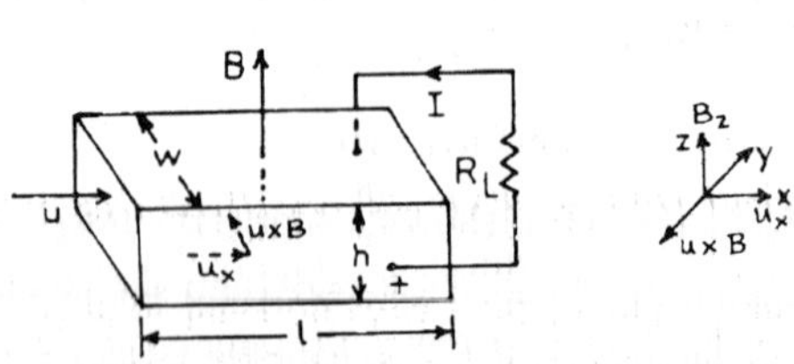

Fig. 4.15 MHD duct in Faraday configuration

The power density delivered to load, or the specific output, is

$$P_0 = j\,E = \sigma\,u\,B\,(1-K)\cdot K\,u\,B = \sigma\,u^2\,B^2\,K(1-K)\,,\mathrm{W/m^3} \tag{4.70}$$

For the same current flowing through load and source, the efficiency is

$$\eta = \text{load voltage / source voltage} = K \quad (4.71)$$

Therefore power density generated in duct is

$$P_g = P_0 / \eta = \sigma u^2 B^2 (1 - K) \quad (4.72)$$

The electrical power is generated at the expense of pressure difference in the gas at inlet and outlet. Thus we obtain the force due to pressure difference in the duct to be

$$f = P_g / u = \Delta p = \sigma u B^2 (1 - K), \text{ Newton/m} \quad (4.73)$$

The force on gas is opposed by power developed. Therefore $\mathbf{f} = \mathbf{j} \times \mathbf{B} = \sigma u B^2 (1 - K)$, and the work done is $(f u) = \sigma u^2 B^2 (1 - K)$. The open-circuit voltage gradient is $E_{ioc} = u B$, and the corresponding voltage across load is

$$V_{oc} = u B w \quad (4.74)$$

where $w$ = width of duct at right angles to $u$ and $B$ in the direction of $E_i$, Fig. 4.15.

The short-circuit current density is $j_{sc} = \sigma u B$, with $K = 0$, and the corresponding current will be

$$I_{sc} = \sigma u B w h \quad (4.75)$$

Therefore $\quad E_i j_{sc} = \sigma u^2 B^2 \quad (4.76)$

Maximum power delivered to load can now be obtained from Eq. (4.70):

$$dP_o / dK = \sigma u^2 B^2 [(1 - K) - K] = \sigma u^2 B^2 (1 - 2K) \quad (4.77)$$

This is zero when $K = 0.5$. Consequently, the maximum power density delivered to load is

$$P_{max} = 0.25 \sigma u^2 B^2 = 0.25 E_{ioc} j_{sc}, W/m^3 \quad (4.78)$$

Efficiency at maximum power delivered to load is $K = 0.5$. But this does not mean that the efficiency of the system cannot be higher than 50%, but the power delivered will be lower than maximum possible. Fig. 4.16 shows the relationship between $K$ and $(P_0 / \sigma u^2 B^2) = K(1 - K)$. The latter is symmetrical about $K = 0.5$.

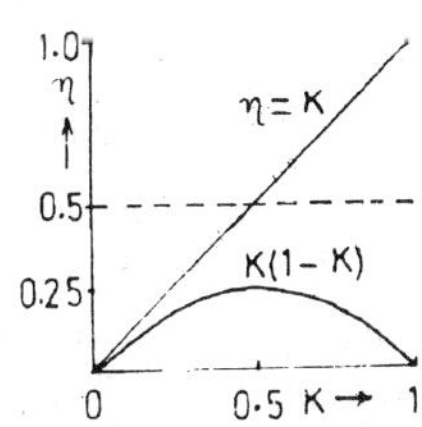


**Fig. 4.16** Power output variation with coefficient of performance K

We can also write the power density developed inside the duct or generator from Eqs. (4.72) and (4.76), as follows:

$$P_g = \sigma u^2 B^2 (1 - K) = (1 - K) E_{ioc} j_{sc} \quad (4.79)$$

Referring to Fig. 4.16:

(a) The total power developed is

$$W_g = P_g \times \text{duct volume} = \sigma u^2 B^2 (1 - K)\cdot(w\,h\,l),\ W \qquad (4.80)$$

(b) Current flowing in duct in the y-direction is

$$I = j\,(l\,h) = \sigma\,u\,B\,(1-K)\cdot(l\,h),\ A \qquad (4.81)$$

(c) The generated voltage is

$$E_g = l\,E_i = u\,B\,w \qquad (4.82)$$

(d) The resistance of the duct will be

$$R_d = (1/\sigma)\cdot w/(l\,h), \text{ and conductance } G_d = \sigma\,l\,h/w \qquad (4.83)$$

All the equations (4.65) through (4.83) are based on the assumption that the charged particles in the gas have a velocity only along the direction of gas flow, which has been taken to be along the $x$-direction, at right angles to the direction of the applied magnetic field $B$. This is known as the Faraday configuration.

The current from the generator duct to the load will be collected across the faces perpendicular to the $y$-direction of area $(l\,h)$ in the $x$-$z$ plane.

The maximum power developed per $m^3$ of duct at $\sigma = 10$ mho/m, $B = 1$ T, $u = 100$ m/s at $K = 0.5$ works out as

$$P_{gu} = 10 \times 10^4 \times 1 \times (1 - 0.5) = 0.05 \text{ MW} = 50 \text{ kW}.$$

For $\sigma = 10$, $B = 5$ T, $u = 500$ m/s and $K = 0.5$, it is $P_{gu} = 6.25$ MW/m$^3$.

In order to appreciate the extremely large power densities obtainable, the following examples are provided. Conductivities of gases used for MHD work at temperatures between 2000 and 3000 K range from 10 to 50 mho/m. Flux densities using superconducting magnets range from 2 to 8 Tesla, while gas velocity can range from 200 to 800 m/s. [Note: Velocity of sound in air at 0°C and 1 atm pressure is 331.6 m/s at sea level. The main gas velocities in the MHD duct come close to Mach 1 in the gas to prevent shock waves.]

***Example 4.8***: An MHD duct has the dimensions $w = 0.6\ m$, $h = 0.35\ m$ and $l = 1.7\ m$. (Volume = 0.357 m$^3$). The magnetic field strength is $B = 4.2\ T$ along $h$, and the gas velocity is $u = 600$ m/s along $l$. At a performance coefficient of K = 0.65, calculate:

(a) Generated voltage and its gradient $E_i$ inside the duct;

(b) Indicate the direction of flow of conventional current in the load and the polarities of the electrodes of the generator (duct);

(c) Load voltage and the gradient $E$ caused by it inside the duct.

Solution : Assume $u = u_x$ and $B = B_z$.

(a) Generated voltage gradient: $E_i = u\,B = 600 \times 4.2 = 2520$ V / m. Generated voltage, $V_g = u\,B\,w = 1512\ V$. This is also the open-circuit voltage.

(b) Positive electrode is at the far end and negative electrode is at the near end in Fig. 4.15

(c) Load voltage, $V_L = K\,u\,B\,w = 0.65 \times 1512 = 983$ V.

Gradient, $E = K\,u\,B = 0.65 \times 2520 = 1638$ V/m. Also, $V_L / w = 1638$.

Example 4.9 : The ionized gas in the previous example has a conductivity of $\sigma = 60$ mho / m. Calculate:

(a) Current density and current in the system;

(b) Short-circuit current density and current generated;

(c) Power density and current generated in the duct;

(d) Total power generated; (e) Power delivered to load;

(f) Joule heating loss in duct; (g) Efficiency at this load;

(h) Maximum possible power delivered to load.

Solution

(a) $j = \sigma\,u\,B\,(1 - K) = 60 \times 2520 \times 0.35 = 52{,}920\ \text{A / m}^2 = 5.292\ \text{A / cm}^2$

$I = j\,h\,l = 52{,}920 \times 0.35 \times 1.7 = 31{,}487.4\ \text{A} = 31.4874\ \text{kA}$

(b) S-C current density, $j_{Sc} = 60 \times 2520 = 151.2\ \text{kA / m}^2 = 15.12\ \text{A / cm}^2$

$I_{sc} = j_{sc}\ h\,l = 90$ kA

(c) $P_g = \sigma\,u^2\,B^2\,(1 - K) = 52{,}920 \times 2520\ \text{W / m}^3 = 133.36\ \text{MW / m}^3$.

(d) Total power generated $= P_g \times$ volume of duct

$$W_g = \sigma\,u^2\,B^2\,(1 - K) \cdot (w\,h\,l) = 133.36 \times 0.357 = 47.61\ \text{MW}$$

(e) Power delivered to load, $W_0 = K\,W_g = 30.95$ MW at $K = 0.65$.

(f) Joule heating loss in duct

$$W_h = W_g - W_o = 16.66\ \text{MW} = 0.35\ W_g \cdot\ (1 - K) = 0.35.$$

Also, $$w_h = j^2 / \sigma = 52.92^2 / 60 = 46.68\ \text{MW / m}^3.$$

Therefore $W_h = w_h \times$ volume of duct $= 46.68 \times 0.357 = 16.66$ MW

(g) Efficiency $\eta = K = 65\%$.

(h) Maximum power density delivered to load

$$P_{max} = 0.25\,\sigma\,u^2\,B^2 = 0.25\,E_{ioc}\,j_{sc} = 0.25 \times 60 \times 2520^2 \times 10^{-6}$$

$$= 95.256\ \text{MW / m}^3$$

$$W_{max} = \sigma u^2 B^2 (1-K) \cdot (w\,h\,l) = E_{ioc} j_{sc}\ (w\,h\,l)$$

$$= 60 \times 2520^2 \times (1 - 0.5) \times 0.357 = 68 \text{ MW}$$

Therefore efficiency at maximum power $= 34 / 68 = 0.5 = 50\%$.

Example 4.10 : For delivering a power of 2000 MWe at $K = 0.5$, for $\sigma = 10, B = 5\ T$, and $u = 300$ m / s, calculate:

(a) the volume of duct; (b) the diameter and length of cylindrical duct with $l / d$ ratio of 5.

Solution : $P_g = \sigma u^2 B^2 (1 - K) = 10 \times 9 \times 10^4 \times 25 \times 0.5 = 11.25 \text{ MW / m}^3$

Therefore volume of duct required $= 2000 / 11.25 = 177.8 \text{ m}^3$

or $\pi d^2 l / 4 = 1.25 \pi d^3 = 177.8$, giving $d = 3.564$ m.

The corresponding length of duct is $l = 5\,d = 17.82$ m (= 58.45 feet).

Note the very large dimensions over which a uniform magnetic field is to be impressed in a non-magnetic medium. Even with superconducting coils used, magnets weigh about 2000 Tonnes. Attendant refrigerating equipment, etc., weigh an equal amount.

## 4.14 Practical MHD Generator: Faraday and Hall Configurations

In the previous section, the velocity of electrons was equal to the gas velocity and was assumed to be along the gas flow. This was considered to be in the $x$-direction, while the applied magnetic field is in the $z$-direction at right angles to the direction of gas flow. A Lorentz force acts on the electrons which is

$$\mathbf{F} = -q\,\mathbf{u} \times \mathbf{B} \tag{4.84}$$

This force is such as to deflect the electrons in the $+y$ direction (Fig. 4.11) by using Fleming's right-hand rule for the electron (–ve charge). The electron velocity is now given by

$$\mathbf{u} = \mathbf{i}\,u_x + \mathbf{j}\,u_y + \mathbf{k}\,0 \tag{4.85}$$

Consequently, the voltage gradient induced inside the duct is

$$\mathbf{e} = -\mathbf{u} \times \mathbf{B} = [-u_y B_z, u_x B_z, 0] \tag{4.86}$$

We now observe that in addition to the Faraday voltage gradient ($u_x B_z$) in the $y$-direction at right angles to both gas velocity $u$ and magnetic field $B_z$, there is a voltage gradient in the (- $x$) direction, i.e., opposing the gas flow. Its value is ($u_y B_z$) and is called the Hall voltage gradient.

If the electrodes which collect current in the Faraday configuration of dimensions ($l\,h$) are solid, they will act as short circuit for the Hall voltage. A very heavy current flows in the electrodes as a consequence. Therefore, to drive loads due to Hall voltage, the electrodes are made discontinuous or segmented. This is shown in Fig. 4.17.

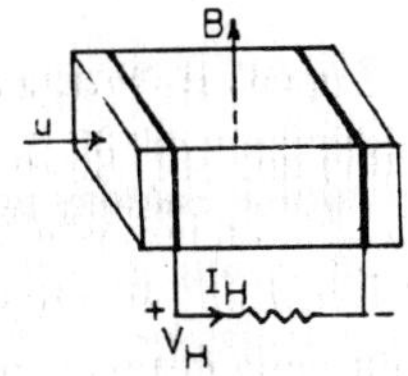


Fig. 4.17 MHD duct in Hall configuration

We now observe that there are several voltage gradients induced inside the duct. Let $\mathcal{E}_e = i\,\mathcal{E}_x + j\,\mathcal{E}_y + k\,\mathcal{E}_z$ and the voltage induced due to velocity u and magnetic field $B$ be equal to $\mathcal{E}_u = -\mathbf{u} \times \mathbf{B}$, caused by electrons. We observed earlier in this chapter, Eq. (4.44), that electronic motion in a magnetic field gave rise to a conductivity

$$\sigma_B = n_e\, e\, \omega_c \tau / B \text{ , mho / m} \tag{4.87}$$

where $n_e\, e$ = total charge of electrons, $\omega_c = e\,B / m_e$ ,and $\omega_c \tau$ = Hall parameter. The current density is therefore

$$j = \sigma_e \mathcal{E} - \sigma_B\, \mathbf{u} \times \mathbf{B} \tag{4.88}$$

But $\quad \sigma_B\, \mathbf{u} = n_e\, e\, \mathbf{u} \cdot \omega_c \tau / B = \omega_c \tau j/B \qquad (4.89)$

This gives an equation for the current density:

$$\mathbf{j} = \sigma_e \mathcal{E} - (\omega_c \tau / B) \cdot \mathbf{j} \times \mathbf{B} \tag{4.90}$$

Now, with $\quad B = B_z,\ \mathbf{j} \times \mathbf{B} = [j_y B, -j_x B, 0] \qquad (4.91)$

Therefore, we obtain the three components of curent density to be, from Eq. (4.90) by using Eq. (4.62) as follows:

$$\left.\begin{aligned} j_x &= \sigma\, \mathcal{E}_x - \omega_c \tau j_y \\ j_y &= \sigma\, \mathcal{E}_y + \omega_c \tau j_x \\ \text{and} \qquad j_z &= \sigma\, \mathcal{E}_z \end{aligned}\right\} \tag{4.92}$$

Upon solving for $j_x$ and $j_y$ explicitly, there results

$$\left.\begin{aligned} j_x &= (\mathcal{E}_x - \omega_c \tau\, \mathcal{E}_y) \cdot \sigma / (1 + \omega_c^2 \tau^2) \\ \text{and} \qquad j_y &= (\mathcal{E}_y + \omega_c \tau\, \mathcal{E}_x) \cdot \sigma / (1 + \omega_c^2 \tau^2) \end{aligned}\right\} \tag{4.93}$$

Thus we observe that $\mathcal{E}_x$ = Hall voltage gradient, and $\mathcal{E}_y = u\,B$.

Therefore $\quad j_x = (\mathcal{E}_x - \omega_c \tau\, u\, B) \cdot \sigma / (1 + \omega_c^2 \tau^2) \qquad (4.94)$

Thus, the open-circuit voltage gradient in Hall configuration is

$$\mathcal{E}_{x0} = \omega_c \tau\, u\, B, \text{ with } j_x = 0 \tag{4.95}$$

The effective velocity is increased by the Hall parameter $(\omega_c \tau)$. The short-circuit current density is

$$j_{xs} = \sigma\, \omega_c \tau\, u\, B / (1 + \omega_c^2 \tau^2),\ \mathcal{E}_x = 0 \tag{4.96}$$

For $\omega_c \tau >> 1, j_{xs} = \sigma u B/(\omega_c \tau)$

For the Faraday generator we obtained

$$\mathcal{E}_{y0} = u B, \text{ and } j_{ys} = \sigma u B \tag{4.97}$$

Therefore, Hall open-circuit voltage gradient $= \omega_c \tau \times$ Faraday gradient. Hall s-c current density = Faraday s-c current density $\times \omega_c \tau/(1 + \omega_c^2 \tau^2)$.

Let the Hall generator performance-coefficient be defined as

$$K_h = \mathcal{E}_x / \omega_c \tau u B = \text{load voltage/o–c voltage} \tag{4.98}$$

Then, the specific power output is

$$P_{oh} = -j_x E_x = \frac{\sigma \omega_c^2 \tau^2}{1 + \omega_c^2 \tau^2} u^2 B^2 K_h (1 - K_h), \text{ W/m}^3 \tag{4.99}$$

We note that if $\omega_c \tau >> 1$, $P_{oh} = \sigma u^2 B^2 K_h (1 - K_h)$. This has the same expression as for the Faraday generator, Eq. (4.70).

Example 4.11 : An MHD duct consists of gas (with electrons) of velocity $\mathbf{u} = 600\,\mathbf{i} + 100\,\mathbf{j} + 0\,\mathbf{k}$. A magnetic field $B = 3.2\ T$ is applied in the $\mathbf{k}$-direction. The gas conductivity is $\sigma = 60$ mho / m. The mean collision time of the electrons with neutral atoms in gas is $\tau = 10^{-10}$ s. The coefficient of performance in Hall configuration is $K_h = 0.65$. Calculate: (a) The cyclotron frequency; (b) Hall parameter; (c) Hall current density $j_x$; (d) Power density delivered to load at $K_h = 0.65$; (e) Short-circuit current density; and (f) Open-circuit voltage gradient. (g) Compare with Faraday configuration.

Solutions :

(a) $\omega_c = e B / m_e = 1.6022 \times 10^{-19} \times 3.2 / 9.11 \times 10^{-31}$

$= 0.56272 \times 10^{12}$ rad/s

(b) Hall parameter: $\omega_c \tau = 56.272$ (dimensionless)

(c) $$-u \times B = -\begin{vmatrix} i & j & k \\ u_x & u_y & u_z \\ 0 & 0 & B \end{vmatrix} = [-u_y B,\ u_x B,\ 0]$$

Hall current density $j_x = \sigma(\mathcal{E}_x - \omega_c \tau\ u_x B)/(1 + \omega_c^2 \tau^2)$

$$|j_x| = 60\,|\,(100 \times 3.2 - 56.272 \times 600 \times 3.2)\,|\,/(1 + 56.272^2)$$

$$\approx \sigma u_x B / (\omega_c \tau) = 60 \times 600 \times 3.2 / 56.272 = 2047.2 \text{ A/m}^2.$$

(d) $P_{oh} = \sigma \omega_c^2 \tau^2 u^2 B^2 K_h (1 - K_h) / (1 + \omega_c^2 \tau^2)$

For $\omega_c \tau >> 1$, $P_{oh} = \sigma u^2 B^2 K_h (1 - K_h) = 60 \times 1920^2 \times 0.65 \times 0.35$

$$= 50.32 \times 10^6 \text{ W / m}^3 = 50.32 \text{ MW / m}^3$$

(e) S-C current density

$$j_{xs} = \sigma \omega_c \tau u_x B / (1 + \omega_c^2 \tau^2) \approx \sigma u_x B / \omega_c \tau$$

$$= 2047.2 \text{ A / m}^2 \approx 2.05 \text{ kA / m}^2$$

(f) Open-circuit voltage gradient

$$E_{xo} = \omega_c \tau u B = 56.272 \times 600 \times 3.2 = 108 \text{ kV / m}$$

(g) For Faraday generator

$$E_{yo} = u B = 1920 \text{ V / m} = 1.92 \text{ kV / m}$$

$$j_{ys} = \sigma u B = 115.2 \text{ kA / m}^2$$

For the Faraday generator $E_{yo} j_{ys} = 221.2 \text{ MW / m}^3$

For the Hall generator $E_{xo} j_{xs} = 108 \times 2.05 = 221.4 \text{ MW / m}^3$.

From the above example, we observe the following salient properties:

(a) In the Faraday configuration, voltage gradient is low but current density is very high.

(b) In the Hall configuration, voltage gradient is very high but current density is low.

(c) The power densities are nearly equal.

(d) An MHD duct with given dimensions can develop the same power density (MW/m$^3$) in either configuration.

(e) The Faraday configuration is useful for lower voltage, higher current than in Hall configuration, which is used for high voltage — low current application.

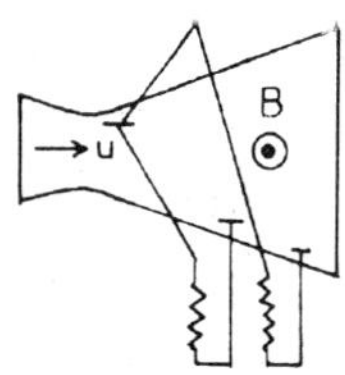

**Fig. 4.18** Diagonal electrode arrangement in MHD duct

In order to take advantage of both the voltages induced in the direction of gas flow and at right angles to it in a plane perpendicular to the applied B-field, electrodes are fixed in a diagonal direction as shown in Fig. 4.18. Voltages are of the order of 10, 20, 40 kV, which are tapped and fed to their own individual loads, which could be connected through inverters and transformers which step up the voltages to 132 kV, 230 kV, or even 500 kV. This is the preferred configuration for generators designed for a predicted power in the range 1000 to 2000 MW, electrical. Overall efficiencies of such conceptual devices are of the order of 45%, so that the thermal power is a little over twice the electrical power output. The angle of inclination of the electrode configuration to the gas flow direction is 45° or more.

In the next section we will describe some of the MHD technology envisaged in future, and which has been achieved until now, based on the theoretical discussion presented earlier.

### 4.15 MHD Technology

From what can be imagined, MHD generating stations of large capacity are very expensive and technologically use very difficult concepts, while material problems at high temperature themselves involve very stringent properties. These are all easier said than done in practice. However, with progress of time it is envisaged that MHD power plants equalling the output of conventional thermal or nuclear plants can be made available at costs approaching 1 billion ($10^9$) dollars.

Faraday's discovery of electromagnetic induction took place in 1831 and 30 years later Edison had designed, built and operated central stations using dc supply. With the discovery of the three-phase ac system by Tesla soon after and its adoption by Westinghouse, power station sizes increased by leaps and bounds. Unfortunately, the same type of progress has not been achieved with MHD in spite of huge amounts of money spent on research and development. What Faraday, Edison, Tesla and even Bell achieved by working in isolation with their own financial resources and some backing by others in their "wax, twine, tin-can" laboratories, modern high-pressure research and development has lacked the same progress from conception to realization. The fields of MHD and Nuclear Fusion depend on harnessing high temperatures and man has not yet shown progress in these fields as has been the case with low temperatures. This is a great stumbling block. MHD has seen the most development in the USA, Russia, and to some extent in Japan. But European countries have shied away from this power source for reasons of lack of financial resources for R and D that it entails. So we can imagine what success or achievement less fortunate countries can achieve in the MHD field, even with best of intentions and ingenuity.

Historically, the feasibility of obtaining enormous specific power outputs by MHD was conceived after the Second World war in the 1950's. The main agencies which could encourage this concept and fund the research and development were Defence, Space, and Science Departments at Government levels, and not at individual or even corporate levels, although giant manufacturing firms in the electrical industry did help initially. Since these agencies are very volatile, the moment funds were withdrawn all development came to a halt. During the course of 40 years, MHD generators built and tried achieved the following purposes, listed chronologically:

(a) Demonstrate the feasibility of MHD power generation. (These units operated for 10 s).

(b) Obtain fluid-mechanical data of high-pressure and high-temperature plasmas.

(c) Test materials for use in MHD ducts and electrodes.

(d) Exhibit rapid-starting capability of an MHD system to take up peak loads in an interconnected system.

(e) Develop MHD units capable of developing ac power directly from the duct.

All these systems were used in an unsystematic manner, subject to vagaries in research funding. But with cooperation between major countries becoming a reality, a systematic development was undertaken and the required ideas as well as equipment which were guarded secrets, were exchanged. We can say that we are in a position to describe MHD systems directed towards large-scale electrical power generation in combination with steam generating stations called the "bottoming cycle". With the advent of LMFBR's, the MHD generator can in turn become the bottoming cycle in a nuclear power station in the future. These are very advanced concepts and open up vast possibilities for utilizing MHD systems.

We realize the tremendous attraction of MHD of compactness, simplicity and high power density. Furthermore, theoretical Carnot efficiencies are as follows:

Inlet temperature = 3000 K, Outlet temperature = 300 K. Carnot efficiency $\eta_c$ = (3000 – 300) / 3000 = 0.9 = 90%.

Such a high efficiency is an ideal to be aimed at, but MHD systems even at the development stages have overall efficiency of less than 50%, which is still higher than thermal stations at the highest steam pressures and temperatures used (2500 psi and 1000°F). The highest temperature used in the MHD duct is about 2850 $K \approx 2600°C$= 4700 F.

Some of the salient points of design, plant description are given below:

(a) *Fuel used* : Modern MHD systems use dried and pulverized coal, with less than 20% ash content, which is injected at the input end through coal-injection equipment. This is mixed with pre-heated air at about 1400°C in nearly equal ratio giving a combustion gas. In the combustor seed material in $K_2CO_3$ powder form is combined. This gives a potassium content of about 1% by weight in the combustion gas. $K_2CO_3$ is desirable as it combines with sulphur in coal and precipitates it at the outlet. Some portion of the heat in combustion gas is also used for drying coal to remove moisture. Air is compressed and heated before being fed to the combustor utilizing heat in the exhaust gases of the MHD generator.

Those countries who possess vast natural-gas deposits used this gas directly in the initial stages of development, but are gradually converting to coal. Several countries have tried kerosene, indigenous vegetable oils, etc., but coal is still the preferred fuel. In research MHD systems, argon and helium gases were used but for large-scale power production these are impractical.

(b) *MHD Generator:* An average value of magnetic field strength is 5 Tesla. The inlet pressure of gas in duct is nearly 10 atm and outlet pressure 1 atm (1 atm $\approx 10^5$ N / m$^2$). The gas velocity is in excess of 500 m/s (1.5 Mach).

For a 2000 MW.e plant size planned, the MHD duct has inlet diameter of 6.5 m with an active length of 25 m. The magnet must be of this size, made in two halves, as shown in Fig. 4.19. It has an ampere-turns of about $50 \times 10^6$ with an average current density in its super-cooled winding of 20 A / mm$^2$. The *B*-field is suitably graded with approximately 2 to 3 *T* at inlet and exit ends, reaching 5 to 7 *T* maximum inside the duct. A superconducting magnet uses niobium-zirconium winding. The power consumption is about 5 W/tonne weight.

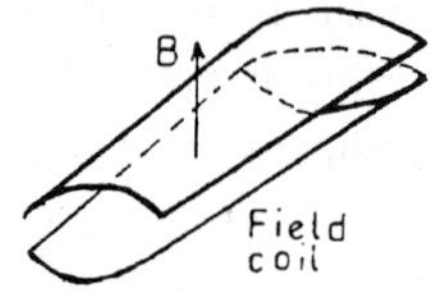


**Fig. 4.19** Field-coil shape for MHD generator

***Example 4.12*** : An MHD duct has an inlet pressure of 10 atm and discharges into the atmosphere.

(a) Find its volume for a length of 20 *m* and inlet diameter of 2 *m*, if the duct is of circular cross-section throughout, as well as the outlet diameter.

(b) Repeat for a square cross-section, if the inlet dimension is 1.5 *m* and duct length of 25 *m*.

***Solution :*** For both cases, outlet area = 10 × inlet area.

(a) Outlet dia $= \sqrt{10} \times$ inlet dia $= 2\sqrt{10} = 6.325$ m

Volume $= \pi\,(2 + 6.325)^2 \times 20 / 16 = 272.2\ m^3$

Inlet area $= \pi\, 2^2 / 4 = 3.1416\ m^2$

(b) Outlet dimension $= 1.5\sqrt{10} = 4.4743\ m$

Outlet area $=$ 10 × inlet area $= 10 \times 1.5^2 = 22.5\ m^2$

Volume of duct $= [(1.5 + 4.743) / 2]^2 \times 25 = 243.6\ m^3$

(c) *Duct and Electrode Materials*

These are strictly protected by patents. Broadly speaking, with temperatures reaching 3000 *K*, the walls of the duct have to be lined with high-temperature refractory material. Reinforced fibreglass composites have also been tried. The highest temperature bricks are made from zirconium oxide, the same as are used in the fuel rods of nuclear-reactor cores.

On account of high temperature and high gas velocity, electrodes inserted into the channel melt and vaporize, are eroded mechanically. A suitable material and a scheme for preserving the electrodes in position has consumed a major portion of research and development-time and effort. Many conflicting requirements have to be met. Copper is still the best material for the electrodes but melts in the heat. The resulting melted copper can short-circuit many pieces of equipment, especially those used for protection. Other materials tried are $Al_2O_3$-oxide coating on copper, $Zr_2O_3$ refractory coating and zirconium boride ($ZrB_2$). Because of erosion of the surface, an arrangement for continuously feeding the electrode rods must be used.

## OBJECTIVE TYPE QUESTIONS

1. When a conducting medium moves with a velocity **v** in a magnetic field **B** the induced voltage per metre length is: (a) **v.B**; (*b*) **B** ×**v** ; (*c*) **v** ×**B** ; (d) none of the three.

2. The voltage induced in a direction along the direction of one of the velocity components is known as: (a) Faraday voltage; (b) Hall voltage; (c) Lorentz voltage; (d) none of the three.

3. A hot gas has a velocity $u_x$ in a magnetic field $B_z$ , where the subscripts *x*- and *z* denote directions in a Cartesian coordinate system. The resulting generated voltage (a) is in the *y*-direction; (b) deflects electrons in the *y*-direction; (c) the deflected electrons give rise to a voltage in the opposite direction to the gas velocity; (d) all the three are true.

4. In Question 3, (a) the voltage induced in the y-direction is called the Faraday voltage; (b) the voltage induced in the direction opposite to the gas flow (- *x* direction) is called the Hall voltage; (c) the voltage induced in the *z*-direction is called Lorentz voltage; (d) both (a) and (b) are true.

5. The force on electron $\mathbf{F} = -q\,\mathbf{v}_e \times \mathbf{B}$ is known as: (a) Faraday force; (b) Hall force; (c) Lorentz force; (d) Maxwell force.

6. A conducting gas with conductivity $\sigma = 100$ mho/m moves at $u = 333.3$ m/s in a magnetic field $B = 3\ T$ and at right angles to it. The short-circuit current density in the duct is: (a) 1000 A/m$^2$ ; (b) 100 kA/m$^2$; (c) 33.33 kA/m$^2$ (d) none of the three.

7. In Question 6, the voltage gradient generated is: (a) 1 kV/m; (b) 3 kV/m; (c) 333.3 V/m; (d) none of the three.

8. In Questions 6 and 7, if a performance coefficient $K = 0.5$ is used, the voltage across load is: (a) 1.5 kV/m; (b) 50 V/m; (c) 500 V/m; (d) none of thc three.

9. The maximum power delivered in W/m$^3$ of duct is: (a) $0.5\ \sigma\ u\ B$; (b) $0.25\ u^2\ B^2$; (c) $0.25\ \sigma\ u^2\ B^2$; (d) $0.25\ E_{oc}\,j_{sc}$; (e) both (c) and (d) are true.

10. The resistance of an MHD duct with width $w$, length $l$ along which the gas flows and height $h$ along which the $B$-field is applied, is given by:

    (a) $R_d = \sigma \cdot w \cdot l \cdot h$; (b) $R_d = (1/\sigma) \cdot w \cdot l \cdot h$; (c) $R_d = w / \sigma l \cdot h$; (d)$R_d = l / \sigma w \cdot h$.

11. An MHD generator delivers a power of 2000 MWe at $K = 0.6$ with $\sigma = 20$ mho / m $= 2.5\ T$, and gas velocity $u = 200$ m/s. The volume of the duct is nearly: (a) 10 $m^3$; (b) 2600 $m^3$; (c) 200 $m^3$; (d) 1000 $m^3$.

12. Modern commercial generating MHD systems are fuelled with: (a) kerosene, (b) high pressure air seeded with caesium gas; (c) low ash content dried pulverized coal mixed with hot air and seeded with $K_2CO_3$ powder; (d) hot liquid sodium from LMFBRs; (e) all four are used to some extent.

    Answers: 1. (c); 2. (b); 3. (d); 4. (d); 5. (c); 6. (d); 7. (a); 8. (d); 9. (e); 10. (c); 11. (b); 12. (e).

## REVIEW QUESTIONS AND PROBLEMS

1. (a) A conducting gas is blown into an MHD duct at velocity $u_x$ m/s across a magnetic field of $B_z$ Tesla. Prove that the electrons in the gas are deflected in the $+y$ direction.

   (b) With electron velocity given by $\mathbf{u} = \mathbf{i}\ u_x + \mathbf{j}\ u_y + \mathbf{k}\ 0$, show that: (i) the Faraday voltage gradient is $u_x\ B_z$ V/m; (ii) the Hall voltage gradient is $-\ u_y\ B_z$ V/m.

   (c) Show by diagrams how the Faraday voltage and Hall voltage can be connected to loads.

2. What is meant by the term "Segmented Electrodes"? Give reasons why such an electrode arrangement is necessary in an MHD generator. Are segmented electrodes necessary for the Faraday configuration or Hall configuration, or both in a combined Faraday-Hall generator?

3. (a) The internal resistance of an MHD duct is $R_d = 2.5$ m-ohm. At a performance factor of $K = 0.5$, what is the value of load resistance?

   (b) If the generated voltage is 1500 $V$, what are the current and load power delivered?

   (c) Calculate the efficiency of the generator.

   [(a) 2.5 m–ohm; (b) $I = 600$ kA, $P = 450$ MW; (c) $\eta = 0.5$.]

4. Derive Eq. 4.70 for the power density delivered to the load in terms of $\sigma$ and $u$ of the gas, $B$-field, and performance coefficient $K$. Give all units properly. Then show that maximum power density delivered to load occurs when $K = 0.5$.

5. An MHD duct has the idealized dimensions of width = 0.5 *m*, height = 0.5 *m* , $l$ = 2*m*. The magnetic field $B = 3$ *T* along *h*, while gas velocity is $u$ = 400 *m/s* along $l$ . Take $K = 0.55$. Calculate: (a) Generated voltage along *w*; and (b) load voltage. [(*a*) 600 *V*; (*b*) 330 *V*.]

6. In Prob. 5, the ionized gas has a conductivity of $\sigma$ = 50 mho / m. Calculate:

   (a) Current density and current flowing in the duct

   (b) S-C current density and s-c current in the duct

   (c) Joule heating loss in the duct under load.

   [(a) 27 kA / m$^2$ , 27 kA (b) $j_{sc}$ = 60kA / m$^2$ ,$I_{sc}$ = 60kA
   (c) $R_d$ = 0.01 ohm, loss = 7.29 MW ]

7. In the previous problems, calculate:

   (a) Power density generated in the duct (32.4 MW/m$^3$)

   (b) Total power generated (16.2 MW)

   (c) Power delivered to load (8.91 MW)

   (d) Efficiency (55%)

   (e) Maximum power delivered to load. (18 MW)

8. The velocity of gas with electrons in an MHD duct is $\mathbf{u} = 300\,\mathbf{i} + 50\,\mathbf{j} + 0\,\mathbf{k}$, while the applied magnetic field is $B = 3$ *T* along the **k**-direction. The coefficient of performance in Hall configuration is K = 0.6. The gas conductivity is $\sigma$ = 40 mho / m, while the mean collision time of electrons with the gas atoms is $\tau = 10^{-9}$ s. Calculate: (a) The cyclotron frequency of electrons about the *B*-field; (b) The Hall parameter, (c) Hall current density $j_x$;

   [(a) $8.3973 \times 10^{10}$ Hz; (b) 527.62 rad; (c) 68.23 A / m$^2$]

9. In prob. 8, calculate:

   (a) Power density delivered to load; (b) Short-circuit current density; and (c) Open-circuit Hall voltage gradient

   [ (a) 8.1 MW / m$^3$ ; (b) $j_{xs}$ = 68.23 A / m$^2$; (c) 474.86 kV / m]

10. In Prob. 8, for Faraday configuration, calculate; (a) Open-circuit voltage gradient; (b) Short-circuit current density; (c) Power density in duct at short circuit. Compare all the values with Hall generator.

    [(a) 900 V / m; (b) $j_{ys}$ = 36 kA / m$^2$;
    (c) $E_{yo} j_{ys}$ = 32.4 MW / m$^3$; $E_{xo} j_{xs}$ = 32.4 MW / m$^3$.]

## CHAPTER 5

# Wind Energy Conversion

### 5.1 Power From Wind

Power from wind is converted to electrical form through a wind turbine coupled to an electrical generator. This can be (1) a dc generator connected through a solid-state inverter to the local ac load or an existing electrical system, or, (2) a synchronous alternator with or without frequency conversion, or, (3) an asynchronous induction generator connected to an electrical distribution system from which it derives its excitation, or, (4) very special generators designed specially for wind-electric generation of ac power, converting variable-frequency to fixed-frequency voltage. Such generators have names like "field-modulated generator" and Roesel generator, etc.

Detailed properties of air and wind are of importance in wind-power application and will be described in the next section.

The wind turbine consists of blades mounted either on a horizontal axis (wind axis) or on a vertical axis (cross-wind axis). The basic quantitative theory of power extracted from the wind by a turbine was first developed by J. Rankine, W. and R.E. Froude, and C. Betz. However, with rapid advances made in propeller and airfoil theory, and aerodynamics, wind-turbine designs have become very advanced and the interested reader should refer to exhaustive literature on such topics.

Based on Rankine-Froude-Betz theories, the following salient properties can be summarized. These are derived later on in this section. Figure 5.1 shows three circular planes at inlet, turbine and the exit where the wind velocities are $v_i$, $v_t$, and $v_e$, respectively. At the Betz condition when maximum power is being extracted from the wind, the following relations hold:

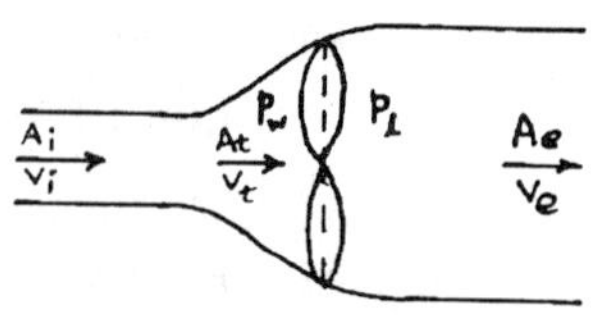

**Fig. 5.1** Theory of wind-energy conversion (ideal case)

(1) Area over which wind flows over turbine is

$$A_t = 3A_i/2\text{, or, } A_i = 2A_t/3 \qquad (5.1)$$

(2) Area over which wind exits from the system is

$$A_e = 3\,A_i = 2\,A_t \tag{5.2}$$

(3) From the relations $A_i\,v_i = A_t\,v_t = A_e\,v_e$, the velocities are

$$v_t = 2\,v_i/3\,,\ \text{and}\ v_e = v_i/3 \tag{5.3}$$

(4) Therefore $v_t = ½\,(v_i + v_e)$ (5.4)

Wind velocity at turbine = average of inlet and exit velocities. These velocity changes occur because the turbine rotor is partly obstructing the free flow of wind.

(5) Kinetic energy in input wind, $e_i = ½\ \rho\,A_i\,v_i^2$ (5.5)

where ρ = density of air = 1.293 kg/m$^3$ at 760 mm Hg and 0°C.

Total power available in input wind: $P_{it} = ½\,\rho\,A_i\,v_i^3\,,\ W$ (5.6)

Power available in input wind at turbine-blade location

$$P_i = ½\ \rho\,A_t\,v_i^3 \tag{5.7}$$

(6) Power of turbine $P_t = ½\,\rho\,A_t\,v_t\,(v_i^2 - v_e^2)$ (5.8)

(7) Power in wind still present at outlet of system

$$P_e = ½\,\rho\,A_t\,v_t\,v_e^2 = ½\,\rho\,A_e\,v_e^3 \tag{5.9}$$

(8) Coefficient of performance $C_p = P_t/P_i = 4\,a^2\,(1 - a)$ (5.10)

where $a = v_t/v_i$.

(9) Maximum possible power extracted by ideal turbine from wind (5.11)

$$C_{\text{pmax}} = 16/27 = 0.593 \text{ when } a = 2/3$$

This is called the Betz coefficient. It is at this condition that

$A_t = 1.5\,A_i\,,\ A_e = 3\,A_i\,,\ v_t = 2\,v_i/3\,,\ v_e = v_i/3\,,$ and $v_t = ½\,(v_i + v_e)$.

Therefore, an ideal turbine cannot extract more than about 60% of the energy in the free wind present at the turbine-rotor location.

(10) Efficiencies or coefficients of performance usually do not exceed 50% due to various losses such as vortex creation, turbulence, blockage of wind, non-optimum designs because of mechanical constraints etc.

(11) At maximum $C_p$, pressure difference across turbine is

$$\Delta p = \rho\,v_t\,(v_i - v_e) = 4\,\rho\,v_i^2/9 \tag{5.12}$$

The distribution of pressure is shown in Fig. 5.2.

These relations are now derived for an ideal turbine. It is assumed that only the wind blowing in the area $A_i$ is blown over the turbine and it is streamlined. There are ways of augmenting this area such as mounting the wind turbine on a ridge, whose angle with the horizontal is about 30°, which will help blow most of the wind under the turbine onto the blades, as shown in Fig. 5.3 (a). Also, Fig. 5.3(b) shows augmenters which are used for increasing the pressure difference between the inlet and outlet sides of turbine rotor. Such augmenters are usually thermal, where air on the downstream side is heated by burning waste. One such arrangement is called a Tornado.

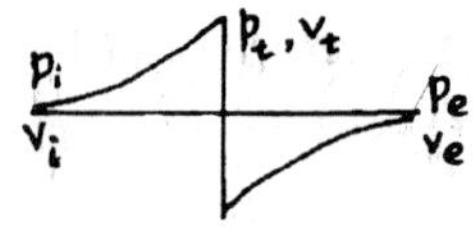


**Fig. 5.2** Pressure distribution across wind turbine

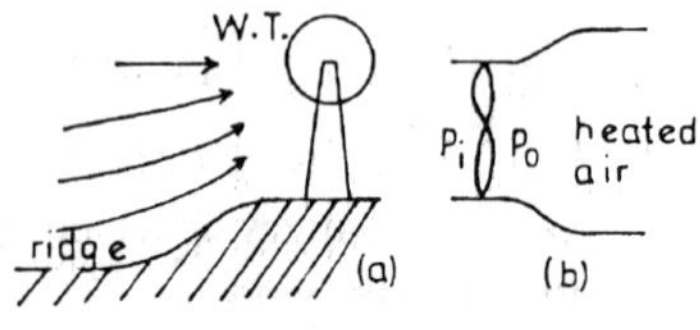


**Fig. 5.3** Augmenters for increasing power extraction from conventional wind turbines

Referring to Fig. 5.1, the following properties hold:

(1) Mass of air flowing past an area $A_i$ per second = density × volume involved per second,

or, $$m_i = \rho\, A_i\, v_i = \rho\, A_t\, v_t, \text{ kg} \tag{5.13}$$

(2) Therefore, the kinetic energy per second = power available in wind

$$P_i = ½\, m_i\, v_i^2 = ½\, \rho\, A_i\, v_i^3, \; W \tag{5.14}$$

(3) Power still present in the wind at exit is

$$P_e = ½\, \rho\, A_e\, v_e^3 = ½\, \rho\, A_t\, v_t\, v_e^2 \tag{5.15}$$

(4) The power developed by an ideal turbine is therefore

$$P_t = P_i - P_e = ½\, \rho\, A_t\, v_t\, (v_i^2 - v_e^2) \tag{5-16}$$

(5) We can eliminate $v_e$ by making the following assumptions:

Let $$a = v_t / v_i \tag{5.17}$$

and $$v_t = ½\, (v_i + v_e) \text{ giving } v_e = 2\, v_t - v_i \tag{5.18}$$

Also $$v_i^2 - v_e^2 = (v_i + v_e) \cdot (v_i - v_e) = 2\, v_t \cdot 2\, (v_i - v_t)$$

$$= 4\, a\, (1 - a)\, v_i^2 \tag{5.19}$$

(6) Therefore $$P_t = ½\, \rho\, A_t\, v_i^3 \cdot 4\, a^2\, (1 - a) \tag{5.20}$$

At the velocity $v_i$ and area $A_t$, the power available in wind is

$$P_i = ½\, \rho\, A_t\, v_i^3 \tag{5.21}$$

(7) Therefore the coefficient of performance is defined as

$C_p$ = power developed by turbine/power available in wind at turbine

or, $$C_p = P_t / P_i = 4\, a^2\, (1 - a) \tag{5.22}$$

(8) As the ratio $a = v_t/v_i$ = wind velocity at turbine/wind velocity at inlet varies, the coefficient of performance also varies. To find the value of $a$ at maximum $C_p$, there is

$$dC_p / da = 0 = 4[2a(1-a) - a^2] = 4a(2-3a) \quad (5.23)$$

This gives $a = 0$, for minimum $C_p$, or $a = 2/3$ for maximum $C_p$ (5.24)

(9) Substituting this value in Eq. (5.22), we obtain the Betz criterion

$$C_{pmax} = 4 \times (4/9) \times (1/3) = 16/27 = 0.593 \quad (5.25)$$

(10) At this maximum performance condition

$$v_t = a\, v_i = 2\, v_i/3\,,\ v_e = v_i/3\,, A_i = 2\, A_t/3\,, A_e = 2\, A_t \quad (5.26)$$

(11) Maximum mechanical power extracted from wind

$$P_{max} = P_i - P_e = ½\, \rho\, (A_i\, v_i^3 - A_e\, v_e^3) = ½\, \rho\, A_i\, v_i^3\, (1 - 3/3^3)$$
$$= ½\, \rho\, A_i\, v_i^3 \times (8/9) \quad (5.27)$$

(12) In terms of undisturbed wind speed $v_i$ and turbine area $A_t$,

$$P_{max} = ½\, \rho\, (2\, A_t/3) \cdot v_i^3 \times 8/9 = ½\, \rho\, A_t\, v_i^3 \cdot 16/27\,,\ W \quad (5.28)$$

(13) This shows that an ideal turbine in practice cannot extract more than 59.3% of the power in an undisturbed wind of area $A_t$ = turbine-blade swept-area and inlet velocity $v_i$, which is normally measured at any location through suitable instruments.

(14) Now, the power $P_t = ½\, \rho\, A_t\, v_t\, (v_i^2 - v_e^2)$ = force × distance moved by wind per second.

Therefore the force $F = ½\, \rho\, A_t\, (v_i^2 - v_e^2)$, Newton

This is called the Thrust. This force is caused by the difference in pressure on the two sides of the rotor.

Therefore $F = A_t\,(p^+ - p^-) = A_t \cdot \Delta p$

Thus $$\Delta p = ½\, \rho\, (v_i^2 - v_e^2) = \rho\, v_t\, (v_i - v_e) \quad (5.29)$$

At maximum value of $C_p$, $v_t = 2\, v_i/3\,,\ v_e = v_i/3$

Therefore $$\Delta p_{max} = \rho \frac{2}{3} \times \frac{2}{3} v_i^2 = \frac{4}{9} \rho\, v_i^2\,, \text{ Pascals (Newton/m}^2) \quad (5.30)$$

[$(\text{kg/m}^3) \times (\text{m}^2/\text{s}^2) = \text{kg/m-s}^2 = (\text{kgm/s}^2)/\text{m}^2 = \text{Newton/m}^2$ = Pascal.]

(15) If the rotor speed is $\omega_m$ rad/s, the torque acting on the rotor is

$$T_{av} = P_t / \omega_m = ½\, \rho\, A_t\, v_i^3 \cdot C_p / \omega_m \quad (5.31)$$

since $$P_t = ½\, \rho\, A_t\, v_i^3 \cdot C_p$$

(16) Consider Fig. 5.4 showing a blade of radius $R$. If the blade or propeller cross-section is the same from hub to tip, then at a given wind speed every unit length of the blade develops the same force, $f$. Then the average torque is

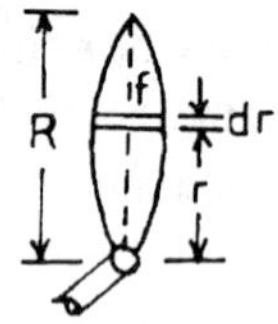


**Fig. 5.4** Force and torque generation by a turbine blade

$$T_{av} = \int_0^R f \cdot r \cdot dr = \tfrac{1}{2} f R^2 \qquad (5.32)$$

Therefore $f = 2\, T_{av} / R^2 = (2\, C_p / \omega_m) \cdot \tfrac{1}{2} \rho\, (\pi R^2 / R^2) \cdot v_i^3$ (5.33)

where $\pi R^2 = A_t$ = swept-area of turbine blade. Thus, the coefficient of performance $C_p$ can be written as

$$C_p = f \omega_m / \pi \rho v_i^3 \qquad (5.34)$$

From aerodynamic principles, the force $f$ developed per metre of blade can be calculated, so that $C_p$ can be obtained for a given rotor angular velocity $\omega_m$ and wind speed $v_i$. The most important property is that the coefficient of performance $C_p$ depends on wind speed $v_i$, since the rotor speed $\omega_m$ is kept constant at all wind speeds by control of pitch angle of blade from the plane of rotation. The force developed by the propeller depends upon wind speed in a complicated manner, so that we cannot write $C_p \propto 1 / v_i^3$.

Equation (5.33) holds even when the bottom of the propeller blade is at a distance $R_o$ from the hub or axis of rotation, since

$$T_{av} = \int_{R_o}^{R} f \cdot r \cdot dr = \tfrac{1}{2} f (R^2 - R_o^2) = f \cdot A_t / 2\pi$$

where $A_t$ = swept area of turbine rotor

For a 2-blade turbine, $T_{av} = f \cdot A_t / \pi$, where now

$A_t$ = swept area of each blade = $\pi\, (R^2 - R_o^2)$.

Therefore $\quad C_p = 2 f \omega_m / \pi \rho v_i^3$ (5.35)

In general, for $n$ blades, $C_p = n f \omega_m / \pi \rho v_i^3$ (5.36)

This clearly indicates that as the number of blades on the rotor is increased, the coefficient of performance and hence the power developed also increases in proportion to the number of blades. But because turbulence increases, the power is seldom if ever proportional to the number of blades.

(17) From the equation for the power developed, $P_t = \tfrac{1}{2} \rho A_t \cdot v_t \cdot v_i^2 \cdot C_p$, at maximum $C_p$, $v_t = 2\, v_i / 3$ and $C_{pmax} = 0.593$. Therefore

$$P_{tmax} = \tfrac{1}{2} \times 1.293 \times \frac{2}{3} v_i^3 \times \frac{16}{27} \times \frac{\pi}{4} D^2 = 0.2\, D^2 v_i^3 \qquad (5.37)$$

where $D$ = diameter of rotor. This is given as

$$D = \sqrt{P_{\text{tmax}}/0.2\, v_i^3} \tag{5.38}$$

Several typical examples will serve to illustrate the power developed by a wind turbine and its properties.

***Example 5.1***: Construct a table showing the rotor diameters required for developing maximum powers of 10, 15, 50, 100, 200 kW at undisturbed wind speeds of 5, 10, 15, 20 m/s. Take $C_p$ = 0.593, the Betz value.

***Solution***: From Eq. (5.38), for a wind speed of 10 m/s and power of 10 kW, the required rotor diameter turns out to be

$$D = \sqrt{10{,}000/0.2 \times 10^3} = \sqrt{50} = 7.07 \text{ m} \quad (23.2 \text{ ft.})$$

Other diameters are proportional to $\sqrt{P_t/v_i^3}$

The table of rotor diameters is then constructed as shown below:

**Rotor Diameters at Values of $P_t$ (kW), in Metre**

| $v_i$ \ $P_t$, kW | 10 | 15 | 50 | 100 | 200 |
|---|---|---|---|---|---|
| 5 m/s | 20 | 24.5 | 44.7 | 63.25 | 89.4 |
| 10 | 7.07 | 8.66 | 15.81 | 22.35 | 31.6 |
| 15 | 3.85 | 4.72 | 8.61 | 12.2 | 17.2 |
| 20 | 2.5 | 3.06 | 5.6 | 7.9 | 11.2 |

As an example of a practical wind turbine manufactured with 2 blades, the following details are given:

Horizontal axis; Rated power 100 kW; Rated speed 40 rev/min; Blade diameter 38.1 m (125 feet); Rated wind speed 10 m/s (21.7 mph). Comparing with the table given above, we observe that the $C_p$ value for the designed turbine is lower than the maximum value of 0.593 for the ideal turbine.

***Example 5.2***: At sea level and 0°C, calculate the power available in undisturbed wind with speed $v_i$ = 10 m/s and turbine rotor swept area of 100 m$^2$ (D = 11.28 m = 37 ft.)

***Solution***: $P_i = \frac{1}{2}\rho A v_i^3 = \frac{1}{2} \times 1.293\, A v_i^3 = 0.6465 \times 100 \times 10^3$

$= 64.65$ kW

***Example 5.3***: Calculate the drop of pressure across a wind turbine rotor operating at the Betz value for $C_p$ = 0.593, when the undisturbed wind speed is $v_i$ = 5, 10, 15, 20 m/s. Take $\rho$ = 1.293 kg/m$^3$. Express the answer in Pascals, mm-Hg, and atm.

***Solution***: From eq. (5.30), we obtain

$$\Delta p_{\max} = \frac{4}{9}\rho v_i^2 = 0.5747\, v_i^2, \text{ Pascal}$$

For $v_i$ = 10 m/s, $\Delta p$ = 57.47 Pascal. [760 mm-Hg = 101.3 k-Pascal = 1 atm which we will derive in the next section. 760/101.3 = 7.5]

The following table gives all values:

| $v_i$, m/s | 5 | 10 | 15 | 20 | |
|---|---|---|---|---|---|
| $\Delta p_{max}$ | 14.37 | 57.47 | 129.3 | 230 | Pascal |
| | 0.108 | 0.431 | 0.97 | 1.725 | mm-Hg |
| | 0.014% | 0.057% | 0.128% | 0.227% | atm |

We note that the pressure drop across the turbine rotor is a very small percentage of atmospheric pressure. For other wind speeds,

$$\Delta p = \rho v_t (v_i - v_e) .$$

***Example 5.4***: The undisturbed wind speed at a location is $v_i$ = 30 mile/hr ,the speed at turbine rotor is 60% of this value, and the speed at exit is 30% of $v_i$. The rotor diameter is 9 m (30 feet). $\rho$ = 1.293 kg/m$^3$. Calculate: (a) $v_i$ in m/s; (b) Power available in undisturbed wind at the turbine rotor; (c) Power in the wind at outlet; (d) Power developed by turbine; and (e) the value of $C_p$.

***Solution***: (a) 1 m/s = 3.28 ft/s = 3.28 × 3600 ft/hr = 3.28 × 3600 / 5280 mile/hr = 2.23636 mph

Therefore 30 mph = 13.415 m/s [10 m/s = 22.36 mph, 10 mph = 4.472 m/s]

(b) Power available in wind at turbine-rotor inlet is

$$P_i = \tfrac{1}{2} \rho A_t v_t v_i^2 , \text{ W} = 0.50776 D^2 v_t v_i^2$$
$$= 0.50776 \times 9^2 \times 0.6 \times 13.415^3 W = 59.6 \text{ kW} .$$

(c) Power in the wind at outlet = $\tfrac{1}{2} \rho A_t v_t v_e^2$

$P_e = 0.50776 \times 9^2 \times (0.6 \times 13.415) \times (0.3 \times 13.415)^2 = 27$ kW

(d) Power available at rotor, $P_i - P_e$ = 32.6 kW

(e) $C_p$ = 32.6/59.6 = 0.547

## 5.2 Properties of Air and Wind

In order to locate a wind turbine at some elevation above ground terrain, the properties of wind at the turbine location must be known in order to evaluate the power that can be developed, as well as mechanical forces, to which the entire installation is subjected. In the previous section, the density of air was taken to be $\rho$ = 1.293 kg/m$^3$, which applies only to dry air at standard atmospheric conditions of 0°C, 760 mm-Hg (273.15 K, 101.33 kPa). When these are varied, we must have the basic equations for variation of wind speed with elevation, and air density at given temperature and atmospheric pressure. These are now discussed.

The laws that pertain to pressure, volume and temperature of ideal gases are:

(1) Boyle's Law: $p\ V$ = constant. Therefore $p_1\ V_1 = p_2\ v_2$ (5.39)

(2) Charles's Law : $V/T$ = constant. Therefore $V_1/T_1 = V_2/T_2$ (5.40)
The volume occupied by a gas becomes zero at $T = 0\ K = -273.15°C$.

(3) Combining Boyle's law and Charles's law, there results

$$p\,V = n\,R\,T \tag{5.41}$$

where $p$ = pressure in Pascal or Newton/m$^2$

$V$ = volume in m$^3$

$T$ = temperature in K

$R$ = universal gas constant = 8314.5 J/kmole - K

and $n$ = 22.414 m$^3$/kmole at 0°C and 1 atm.

Condition (3) is known as Gay-Lussac law and the value of $n$ is the same for all ideal gases. This corresponds to Avagadro's number for atoms which we encountered for solids. When $n$ = 22.414 m$^3$/kmole - K, this also means $n$ = 22.414 litres/g-mole - K, which value was postulated by Gay-Lussac originally.

***Example 5.5***: Calculate the density of air at the following temperatures given in degrees centigrade:

$t$ = –30, –20, –10, 0, 10, 20, 30°C. Take pressure = 1 atm.

***Solution***: At 0°C and 1 atm, atmospheric pressure is with $R$ = 8314.5, $n$ = 22.414, $T$ = 273.15,

$$P_{atm} = 8314.5 \times 273.15 / 22.414 = 101{,}325 \text{ Pascal}$$

$$= 101.325 \text{ kPa} = 0.101325 \text{ MPa}. \ [1 \text{ MPa} = 10 \text{ atm, roughly}]$$

Mass of 22.414 m$^3$ of air = 22.414 × 1.293 = 29 kg

From Boyle's law, $p\,V = p \cdot m/\rho = n\,R\,T$.

Therefore at the same pressure and mass $\rho \propto 1/T$.

Thus, $\rho = 1.293 \times 273.15/T - 353.183/T$, or, $\rho T$ = constant – 353.183.

The following table gives all values:

| $t$, °C | –30 | –20 | –10 | 0 | 10 | 20 | 30 |
|---|---|---|---|---|---|---|---|
| $T$, K | 243.15 | 253.15 | 263.15 | 273.15 | 283.15 | 293.15 | 303.15 |
| $\rho = 353.183/T$ | 1.4525 | 1.395 | 1.342 | 1.293 | 1.247 | 1.205 | 1.165 |
| % atm pressure | 112 | 108 | 104 | 100 | 96.5 | 93.2 | 90 |

Since the power developed by a wind turbine depends on air density, at any given location when the temperature varies from –30 to +30°C, the power output can vary by as much as 20% for the same wind velocity.

Air density can also be expressed as

$$\rho = m/V = m\,p/n\,R\,T \tag{5.42}$$

At $p = 101.33$ kPa = 760 mm-Hg and $T = 273.15$ K, $\rho = 1.293$ kg/m$^3$

This gives the value of $(m/n\,R)$ to be

$$m/n\,R = \rho\,T/p = 1.293 \times 273.15/101.33 = 3.4855, \text{ with } p \text{ in kPa.}$$

When $p$ is in mm-Hg, $(m/n\,R) = 353.183/760 = 0.4647$.

Therefore, the air density at any given pressure and temperature will be

$$\left.\begin{aligned}\rho &= 3.4855\,p/T, \text{ with } p \text{ in } kPa \\ &= 0.4647\,p/T, \text{ with } p \text{ in mm–Hg}\end{aligned}\right\} \quad (5.43)$$

[As a check, 3.4855 × 101.33/273.15 = 1.293; 0.4647 × 760/273.15 = 1.293. Also, 3.4855/0.4647 = 7.5 = 760/101.33]

### 5.2.1 Variation of Atmospheric Pressure with Altitude

The drop of atmospheric pressure with increase in altitude is almost linear. At about 16,000 feet ≈ 5,000 m height above sea level, flyers have experienced an atmospheric pressure of 50% of sea-level value. Thus, it is 380 mm-Hg or about 50 kPa at 5,000 m elevation. Other observational data yield the following values of pressure:

| $H =$ | 0 | 1000 | 2000 | 3000 | 5500 | m above sea level |
|---|---|---|---|---|---|---|
| $p =$ | 101.33 | 92 | 80 | 70 | 50 | kPascal |

Assuming a relation $p = a + b\,H$, and using values at $H = 0$ and 5500 m, there result $a = 101.33$, and $b = (50 - 101.33)/5500 = -9.33 \times 10^{-3}$. Thus, an equation for the pressure variation with elevation above sea level is, with $H$ in metres,

$$p = 101.33 - 9.33 \times 10^{-3}\,H, \text{ kPa} \quad (5.44)$$

[If $p$ is in mm-Hg, since 1 kPa = 7.5 mm-Hg, $p_{mm} = 760 - 70 \times 10^{-3}\,H$, mm-Hg, with $H$ in metres.]

From Eq. (5.43), since air density is directly proportional to $p$ at the same temperature, the density change with elevation can be obtained. But as the temperature also changes with altitude, we will consider both effects a little later.

### 5.2.2 Variation of Temperature with Altitude

For an adiabatic process, the variation of temperature with pressure follows the relation

$$T/T_0 = (p/p_0)^{0.286} \quad (5.45)$$

where the factor 0.286 = (1.4 – 1)/1.4, the well-known constant.

Therefore, upon using Eq. (5.44) for pressure variation with height, we obtain the relationship for temperature variation with height.

$$T = [(101.33 - 9.33 \times 10^{-3}\, H) / 101.33]^{0.286}\; T_0$$
$$= (1 - 92.1 \times 10^{-6}\, H)^{0.286}\; T_0 \tag{5.46}$$

Here, $T_0$ = temperature at $H = 0$ or at sea level, and $H$ is in metres above sea level.

From practical observations, the temperature is known to fall 10°C for every 1000 m increase in elevation. The approximate formula based on this rule becomes

$$t = t_{gr} - 0.01\, H, \text{°C} \tag{5.47}$$

This applies for low altitudes (< 1000 m).

***Example 5.6***: Using Eqs. (5.46) and (5.47), compute and compare the temperature of air at $H$ = 100 m, 200 m, 500 m, 1000 m, and 2000 m, if the sea-level temperature is 20°C = 293 K.

***Solution***

| $H$ = | 100 | 200 | 500 | 1000 | 2000 m |
|---|---|---|---|---|---|
| $T/293$ = | $(1 - 0.0092)^{0.286}$ | $0.9816^{0.286}$ | $0.954^{0.286}$ | $0.908^{0.286}$ | $0.816^{0.286}$ |
| | = 0.9973 | 0.9947 | 0.9866 | 0.9728 | 0.9435 |
| $T$, K | 292.2 | 291.4 | 289.4 | 285 | 276.4 |
| $t$, °C | 19.2 | 18.4 | 16.4 | 12 | 3.4 |

According to Eq. (5.47), $t = 20 - 0.01\, H$, °C.

| $H$ = | 100 | 200 | 500 | 1000 | 2000 | m |
|---|---|---|---|---|---|---|
| $t = 20 - 0.01\, H$ | 19 | 18 | 15 | 10 | 0 | °C |
| $T$ | 292 | 291 | 288 | 283 | 273 | K |

In practice, the fall in temperature is nearly

$$T = T_{gr} - K'\, H \tag{5.48}$$

where the constant $K' \approx$ 8 to 10 degree K/1000 m change in elevation.

### *5.2.3 Variation of Air Density with Altitude*

Equation (5.43) gave the variation of density with pressure and temperature, both of which vary with height $H$ above sea level. Equation (5.44) can be written as

$$p = (1 - 92.1 \times 10^{-6}\, H)\; 101.33\;, \text{kPa}$$

while $$T = (1 - 92.1 \times 10^{-6}\, H)^{0.286}\; T_0, \text{K}$$

Therefore $$\rho = 3.4855\, p / T = 3.4855\, (1 - 92.1 \times 10^{-6}\, H)^{0.714} \times 101.33 / T_0 \tag{5.49}$$

At $H = 0$ and $T_0 = 273.15$, $\rho = 3.4855 \times 101.33/273.15 = 1.293$

At $H = 0$ and $T_0 = 293.15$, $\rho = 3.4855 \times 101.33/293.15 = 1.205$ kg/m$^3$

***Example 5.7***: Calculate the air density at $H = 0$, 100, 200, 500, 1000 and 2000 m above sea level if the sea-level temperature is $T_0 = 293.15$ K.

***Solution***:

| $H =$ | 0 | 100 | 200 | 500 | 1000 | 2000 |
|---|---|---|---|---|---|---|
| $1 - 92.1 \times 10^{-6} H$ | 1 | 0.9908 | 0.9816 | 0.954 | 0.908 | 0.816 |
| $(1 - 92.1 \times 10^{-6} H)^{0.714}$ | 1 | 0.9934 | 0.9868 | 0.967 | 0.9334 | 0.865 |
| $\rho = 1.205 \times (1 - 92.1 \times 10^{-6} H)^{0.714}$ | 1.205 | 1.197 | 1.189 | 1.165 | 1.125 | 1.042 |

The power developed by a wind turbine is proportional to ρ.

### *5.2.4 Variation of Wind Speed with Height*

For low changes in height up to 120 m, wind loadings on buildings have been measured very carefully. An empirical formula for wind-velocity ratio at two different heights is

$$v_2 / v_1 = (H_2 / H_1)^{1/7} \tag{5.50}$$

This is known as the 1/7th power law.

***Example 5.8***: Calculate the wind velocities at heights of 20, 40, 60, 80, and 120 m above ground if the velocity at $H_1 = 10$ m is $v_1 = 10$ m/s.

***Solution***:

| $H =$ | 20 | 40 | 60 | 80 | 120 | m |
|---|---|---|---|---|---|---|
| $H_2/H_1 =$ | 2 | 4 | 6 | 8 | 12 | |
| $v_2 = 10(H_2/H_1)^{1/7}$ | 11 | 12.2 | 12.92 | 13.5 | 14.27 | m/s |
| Powers: $P_H/P_{10} = (v_2/v_1)^3$ | 1.33 | 1.825 | 2.16 | 2.46 | 2.9 | |

The power developed varies as cube of wind speed. We notice that at 120 m height, the increase in wind velocity from 10 m gives nearly 3 times the developed power by the turbine, which is 300% at 10 m height. The advantage of locating a wind generation system at high elevation is now obvious.

## 5.3 Types of Wind Turbines

Wind turbines can operate with their axes directed along the wind or at right angles to it, although in both cases the blade profile is parallel to the wind direction. With turbines having their axes inclined to the wind direction of other than 0° or 90° are rare, although such have been designed and operated. Horizontal axis turbines can have one, two or more blades or propellers, but to minimize stresses impressed on supporting structures, it is usual to mount a minimum of two blades on the rotor. Vertical axis turbines have been designed with two or more blades.

Most modern blades or propellers have a twist given to them which varies from hub to tip. The majority of turbines for power production operate at a constant angular velocity $\omega_m$ rad/s, or constant speed of $n$ rev/min ($\omega_m = 2\pi\, n/60$). This is achieved by twisting the entire blade by a control mechanism actuated by the wind speed. Therefore, the linear velocity of the blade varies from hub to tip by the relation $v = r\,\omega_m$. When this velocity is combined vectorially with the wind speed across the blade, the relative velocity changes with radius $r$, so that the forces trying to rotate the propeller, called the Lift Force of an airfoil or wind-turbine rotor,changes from hub to tip. This changes the Angle of Attack of the wind on the blade section resulting in lowering of the efficiency of the turbine. The best operating condition is to have the angle of attack constant from hub to tip, and not allow it to vary with the radius $r$. Thus a twist is given to the propeller. This is more expensive to fabricate than untwisted blades, so that not all installations might use blades with a twist. We consider the lift force later on.

Wind turbines are also classified according to the original inventor's name, although modern developments have advanced the original designer's ideas, as is the case with all engineering developments. Some important and typical ones are shown in Fig. 5.5. These are: (a) Savonius rotor; (b) Darrieus rotor; (c) Savonius-Darrieus rotor; (d) Smith-Putnam rotor with two, three and six blades; (e) Gedser 3-blade rotor with connecting spars; (f) Hutters wind turbine with alternator and control gear at ground level driven by a long shaft. There are over a hundred designs patented by inventors, so that the reader can also attempt one.

V. Daniel Hunt, Director of the Energy Institute, has classified wind turbines according to their function and given descriptions of Wind Energy Conversion Systems (WECS) under the following categories:

(1) *Water-Pumping Windmills:* Some details are as follows:

Rotor blade dias : 4.2 - 16 feet (1.28 - 4.88 m)

Number of blades : 2 - 18 (multi-blades). Horizontal axis.

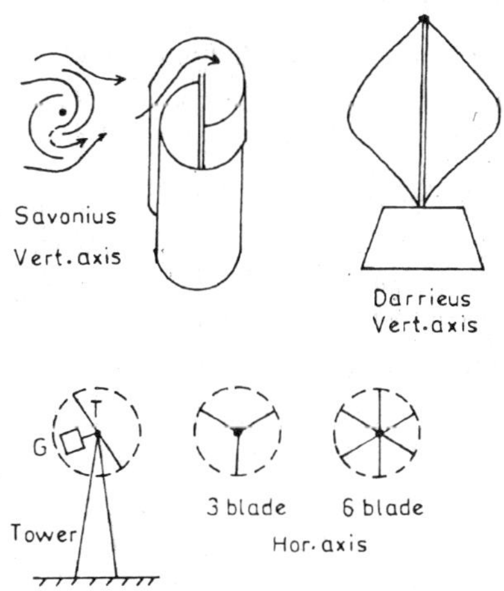


**Fig. 5.5** Types of wind turbines: Vertical and horizontal axis machines

Water pumping rate : Up to 3300 US gal/hour.

$$[1 \text{ US gal} = \frac{5}{6} \text{ Imp. gal} = 3.8 \text{ litres}]$$

No standard design parameters are available. Some manufacturers keep speed constant at 150 rev/min with blade diameters ranging from 6 to 12 feet with standard diameters of 6, 8, 10 and 12 feet. Some other windmills have the product of speed at rated output × blade diameter at 750 - 900.

Blade material : Galvanized steel, cast aluminium.
Wind speed : Rated 15 - 20 mph; Cut-in 5 - 9; Cut-out 25 - 50 mph.
Overspeed control : Blade feathering, brake, rotor turns sideways into wind.
Type : Upwind

(2) *Electricity producing WECS*

These are manufactured in sizes from a few Watts to 2.5 MW (2500 kW). Wind speeds at rated power range from 15 to 35 mph (6.7 to 15 m/s). The number of blades go from 2 to 6 (2, 3, 4, 6). Speeds of rotor at rated output range from 17.5 rpm for the 2.5 MW unit, 35 rpm for 2 MW machine, 40 to 60 rpm for sizes in the range 40 to 200 kW, and higher for lower outputs. (The power is given as electrical output at the generator terminals.)

Blade diameters: 12 ft for 1.5 kW; 16 to 38 ft for 6 to 40 kW; 160 to 200 ft for 200 kW machine; and 300 ft for 2500 kW 2-blade unit.

Material for rotor blades: Wood up to 10 kW; aluminium and its alloys for sizes up to 2000 kW and steel for the largest sizes are required. With the constant developments in aircraft and spaceships, propeller designs and materials do not pose a problem in wind turbines.

## 5.4 Operating Characteristics

A wind turbine requires a certain minimum wind velocity called "cut-in" wind speed to commence rotation against the inertia and static friction in the rotating parts. Beyond this, the power generated varies as the $v^3$-law. The rated power output is reached at the designed wind velocity and thereafter by proper control of pitch angle of the blade, the rated output power is maintained constant up to a wind speed called the "cut-out" speed. Beyond this speed, the mechanical forces on the turbine exceed safe values, so that the turbine is either stalled by brakes or feathered by turning the blades in such a way that no power is generated, as shown in Fig. 5.6.

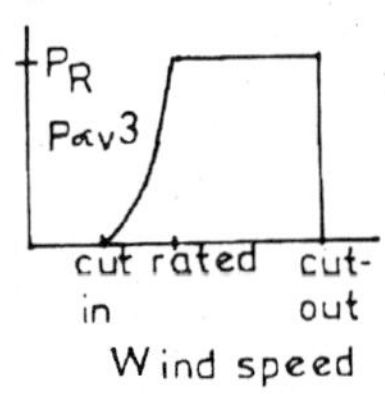


**Fig. 5.6** Power output variation with wind speed, illustrating cut-in speed, rated speed, and cut-out speed

Representative values for Rated/Cut-in/Cut-out wind speeds are as follows:

*Horizontal axis*: 6 kW - 30/7/50 mph; 100 to 200 kW - 21.7/13/40 mph; 2000 kW - 35/5/40 mph; 2500 kW - 18/15.7/42.5 mph

*Vertical axis Darrieus*: 25/10/80 mph

The Darrieus type has its vertical axis supported from a heavy structure near ground (usually 3 m above ground level to clear obstacles and operating personnel), so that an electric motor is used for starting the turbine. In horizontal-axis machines, this is not possible as the turbine is located on tall towers.

A quantity that is of importance is the tip-speed ratio. This is defined as

$$\text{Tip-speed ratio,} = \frac{\text{speed at tip of rotor}}{\text{wind speed}} = \frac{R\,\omega_m}{v_i} \tag{5.51}$$

The coefficient of performance $C_p$ depends on this ratio. If the turbine rotor rotates slowly, it is evident that it will interfere with wind and produce less than maximum possible power. The linear speed of rotor tip is kept higher than wind speed by factors ranging from 4 to 10. A typical performance curve is shown in Fig. 5.7. Since $R$ and $\omega_m$ are constant for a given turbine, the $C_p$ versus $v_i$ variation can also be plotted, as shown in Fig. 5.8. Representative curves for several types of turbine are shown in Fig. 5.9 for horizontal-axis, Darrieus and Savonius rotors.

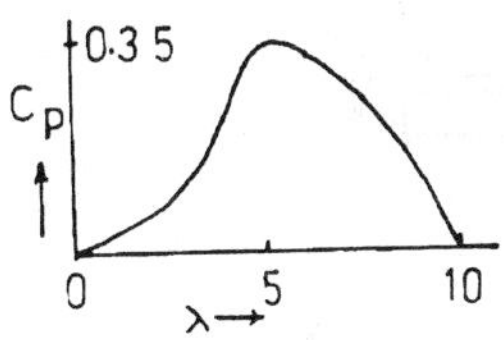


**Fig. 5.7** Coefficient of performance as a function of tip-speed ratio for average wind turbine

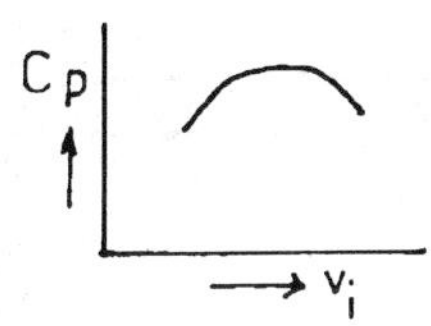


**Fig. 5.8** Coefficient of performance as a function of input wind velocity

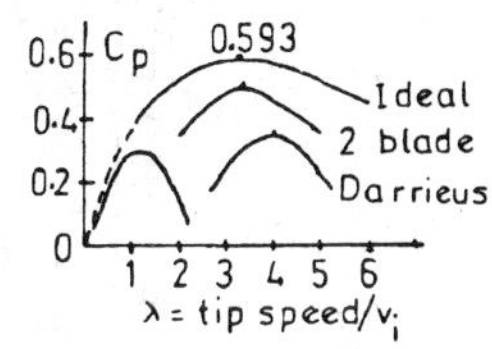


**Fig. 5.9** Comparison of coefficient of performance $C_p$ as a function of tip-speed ratio, λ, for several types of wind turbines

## 5.5 Basics of Airfoil Theory and Lift Force

The design and operation of a propeller having a cross-section of an airfoil, similar to the one on aircraft, is quite complicated and considered beyond the scope of a book such as this on energy conversion problems. But it is believed that some basic ideas will help the reader to appreciate the problem and this discussion is only an introduction to airfoil theory producing a lift and a drag force. The lift gives the forc to the blade to rotate it in a plane essentially at right angles to the wind, while the drag is a force essentially along the wind direction and affects the design of the supporting structure. In this discussion, only lift is considered.

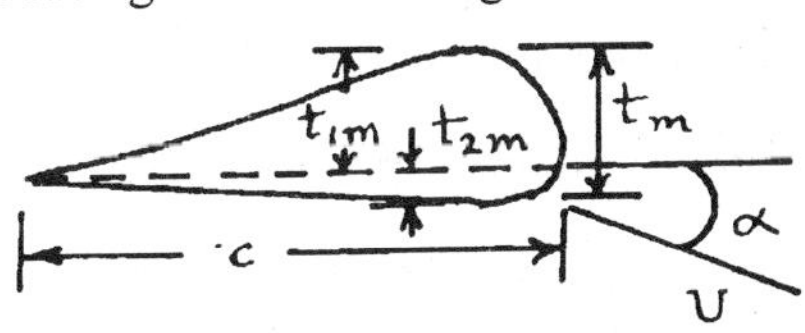


**Fig. 5.10** Airfoil profile and wind direction with chord

Figure 5.10 shows the basic form of an airfoil called the Zhukovsky profile, which was the forerunner of the modern propeller. We will restrict discussion to this profile. The main properties of this airfoil shape or profile are as follows:

$c$ = chord, $t_m$ = maximum thickness,
$t_{1m}$ = point at maximum thickness above chord line,
$t_{2m}$ = point at maximum thickness below chord line,
$t_m = t_{1m} + t_{2m}$
$\alpha$ = angle between chord and wind direction, $U$ = wind velocity.

Other parameters not shown are:

$K$ = strength of a circulation or vortex field which contributes to the lift. This has a minimum value of $K = 4\,\pi\,a\,U \sin(\alpha + \beta)$ (5.52)

where $a = 0.25\,c\,(1 + 0.77\,t_m/c) = 0.25\,c + 0.1925\,t_m$ (5 53)
$\beta$ = a parameter (angle) described in detail in Appendix. (See Fig. 5.11)

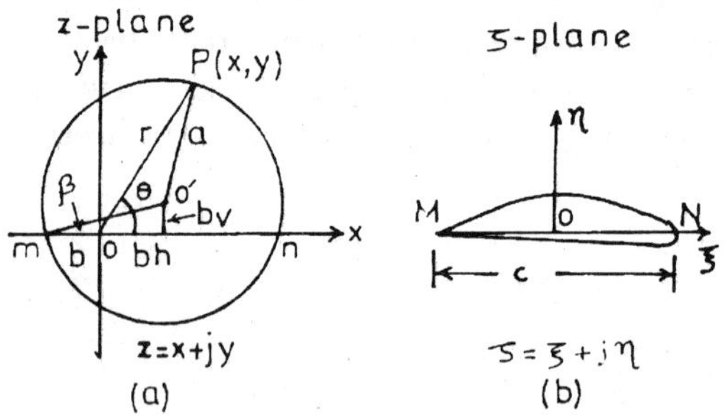


**Fig. 5.11** Katta-Zhukovsky transformation of a circle into airfoil profile

The lift force for unit span (1 metre length of propeller) is

$$L = \rho\,U\,K = 4\,\pi\,\rho\,U^2\,a \sin(\alpha + \beta)\,, \text{ Newton/m} \qquad (5.54)$$

Then, the total lift is $L_T = L\,R$, Newton (5.55)

Average torque for each blade will be $T_{av} = ½\,L\,R^2$ (5.56)

If $n_r$ = rotor speed in rev/min, the angular velocity is $\omega_m = 2\,\pi\,n_r/60$.

Therefore, the power is $P = N\,T_{av}\,\omega_m$, $W$ (5.57)

where $N$ = number of blades on rotor.

In the Appendix are derived these expressions in as simple a way as possible for the famous Katta-Zhukovsky transformation of a circle into the airfoil profile. Several numerical examples are also provided there to relate the pov er developed to all the quantities affecting the wind turbine.

## APPENDIX:
## PROPERTIES OF THE KATTA-ZHUKOVSKY PROFILE

The derivation of the properties of the airfoil profile based on the Katta-Zhukovsky theory is based on the method of Conformal transformation in the complex variable planes. We take two planes called the $z$-plane and the $\zeta$-plane, designated as planes 1 and 2, respectively, or the original and the transformed plane, as shown in Fig. 5.11. From chosen origin of coordinate axes, we write $z = x + jy = r e^{j\theta}$ in the original plane ($j = \sqrt{-1} = e^{j\pi/2}$) and $\zeta = \xi + j\eta$ in the transformed plane.

*Step 1*: Consider a circle of radius $a$ in the $z$-plane whose centre $O$ is displaced by the distance $(bh)$ and $(bv)$ in the $x$- and $y$-directions. The quantities $h$ and $v$ are known as the eccentricity parameters and $b$ is called the transformation parameter, which is the distance $\overline{mo}$ as shown.

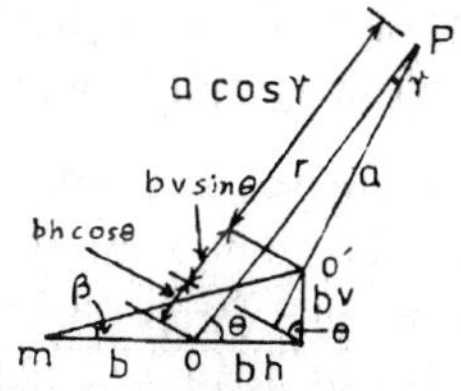


**Fig. 5.12** Details of dimensions for Fig. 5.11

*Step 2*: The radius vector $r$ from the origin $O$ to a point $P(x, y)$ is first expressed in terms of the quantities $b$, $h$, $\beta$ and the angle $\theta$ as follows, by referring to Fig. 5.12, and taking $h << 1$ and $v << 1$:

$OP = a \cos\gamma + b\, v \sin\theta + b\, h \cos\theta$. Confining to small values of eccentricity, there are:

$$\left.\begin{aligned} b\,v &= (b + b\,h)\tan\beta \approx b\,\beta \\ a &\approx (b + b\,h)\sec\beta \approx b\,(1 + h) \end{aligned}\right\} \tag{5.58}$$

$$\cos\beta \approx 1\,,\quad \cos\gamma \approx 1$$

Now,
$$\begin{aligned} r &= a\cos\gamma + b\,v\sin\theta + b\,h\cos\theta \\ &= b\,(1+h) + b\,v\sin\theta + b\,h\cos\theta \end{aligned} \tag{5.59}$$

Therefore
$$r/b = 1 + h + h\cos\theta + v\sin\theta \tag{5.60}$$

We also form the quantity

$$b/r = [\,1 + h\,(1+\cos\theta) + v\sin\theta\,]^{-1} \approx 1 - h\,(1+\cos\theta) - v\sin\theta \tag{5.61}$$

where we use the property that $(1+\varepsilon)^{-1} \approx 1 - \varepsilon$ when $\varepsilon << 1$, and $\varepsilon = h\,(1+\cos\theta) + v\sin\theta$.

*Step 3*: We now take the important function called the Katta-Zhukovsky transformation

$$\zeta = z + b^2/z \tag{5.62}$$

Letting $z = r e^{j\theta}$, we obtain

$$\zeta = \xi + j\eta = r e^{j\theta} + b^2/r e^{j\theta} = r(\cos\theta + j\sin\theta) + \frac{b^2}{r}(\cos\theta - j\sin\theta)$$

$$= b\,(r/b + b/r)\cos\theta + j\,b\,(r/b - b/r)\sin\theta \tag{5.63}$$

Therefore $\xi = b\,(r/b + b/r)\cos\theta$, and $\eta = b\,(r/b - b/r)\sin\theta$ (5.64)

where we have separately equated the real and imaginary parts to $\xi$ and $\eta$, respectively.

*Step 4*: Now, $(r/b + b/r) = 2$,

and $$(r/b - b/r) = 2\,h\,(1 + \cos\theta) + 2\,v\sin\theta \quad (5.65)$$

Therefore, $\xi = 2\,b\cos\theta$, $\eta = 2\,b\,[\,h(1 + \cos\theta) + v\sin\theta\,]\sin\theta$ (5.66)

*Step 5*: With $b$, $h$, and $v$ or $\beta$ constant, by varying $\theta$ we can find $\xi$ and $\eta$, and trace the profile in the transformed $\zeta$-plane into which the circle in the $z$-plane is "transformed" under the Katta-Zhukovsky transformation function of Eq. (5.62). The resulting profile or airfoil is shown in Fig. 5.11(b).

*Step 6*: When $\theta$ is varied from 0 to $\pi$, i.e. from $n$ to $m$ on the top portion of the circle, the point $P$ moves from $\xi = +2b$ to $\xi = -2b$ on the horizontal. Similarly, when $\theta$ varies from $\pi$ to $2\pi$, on the bottom portion of the circle (or from 0 to $-\pi$) the locus of $P$ is the curve connecting $\xi = -2b$ to $\xi = +2b$. The extreme points are shown as $M$ and $N$ in the $\zeta$-plane corresponding to the points $m$ and $n$ in the z-plane. The length $MN$ is called the chord of the airfoil, $c$. Thus

$$c = 4\,b = 4\,a/(1 + h) \quad (5.67)$$

Similarly, as $\theta$ varies, so also $\eta$. At $\theta = 0$ and $\pi$, $\eta = 0$ so that the points $M$ and $N$ fall on the horizontal or $\xi$-axis. Also, the quantity $(2\,b\,v\sin\theta)$ is positive from $0 < \theta < \pi$, while it is negative for $\pi < \theta < 2\pi$. Therefore, the top portion of the circle is transformed into the top half of the airfoil, since $2\,b\,h\,(1 + \cos\theta)$ is positive for $0 < \theta < \pi$. The sign of $\eta = 2b\,[\,h\,(1 + \cos\theta) + v\sin\theta\,] \times \sin\theta$ for the region $\pi < \theta < 2\pi$ depends upon the ratio $(h/v)$. For example, at $\theta = 3\pi/2$, $\cos\theta = 0$ and $\sin\theta = -1$. This gives $\eta = 2b\,(v - h)$ which can be positive, negative or zero. $\eta = 0$ when $\theta = \pi$ and $2\pi$, or when $\theta = \cot^{-1}[(h^2 - v^2)/2\,h\,v]$, since $h\,(1 + \cos\theta) + v\sin\theta = 0$ when $(1 + \cos\theta)/\sin\theta = -v/h$, giving $\operatorname{cosec}\theta + \cot\theta = -v/h$. Using the relation $\operatorname{cosec}^2\theta = 1 + \cot^2\theta$, and solving for $\cot\theta$, we obtain $\cot\theta = (h^2 - v^2)/2\,h\,v$. Therefore, by controlling the ratio $(h/v)$ of the eccentricity parameters, we can alter the shape of the top and bottom portions of the airfoil from $M$ to $N$.

*Step 6*: The thickness of the airfoil is the difference between $\eta$-values at $\theta$ and $-\theta$, since the value of $\xi = 2\,b\cos\theta$ is the same at these two angles. Denoting by $\eta_t$ and $\eta_b$ the two values, the thickness of the airfoil is $t = \eta_t - \eta_b$.

Now $$\eta_t = 2\,b\,[\,h\,(1 + \cos\theta) + v\sin\theta\,]\sin\theta \quad (5.68)$$

and $$\eta_b = -2\,b\,[\,h\,(1 + \cos\theta) - v\sin\theta\,]\sin\theta \quad (5.69)$$

Therefore $$t = 4\,b\,h\,(1 + \cos\theta)\sin\theta = c\,h\,(1 + \cos\theta)\sin\theta \quad (5.70)$$

This gives the thickness-to-chord ratio to be

$$t/c = h(1+\cos\theta)\sin\theta \tag{5.71}$$

This ratio is maximum when

$$\frac{d}{d\theta}[(1+\cos\theta)\sin\theta] = 2\cos^2\theta + \cos\theta - 1 = 0 \tag{5.72}$$

Therefore $\cos\theta = 0.5$ or $-1$. At $\cos\theta = -1$, $\theta = \pi$, so that $t = 0$, i.e. minimum value. The maximum $(t/c)$ value occurs at $\theta = 60°$, and has the value $(t_m/c) = h(1+0.5)\sqrt{3}/2 = 3\sqrt{3}\,h/4 = 1.3\,h$. From Eq. (5.67), $c = 4\,b\,h$, so that

$$t_m = 4 \times 1.3\,b\,h = 5.2\,b\,h \tag{5.73}$$

Note (a) that when $h = 0$, namely when the centre of the circle in the $z$-plane has no horizontal eccentricity and therefore lies on the vertical or $y$-axis, the thickness of the airfoil is zero, so that the top and bottom curves merge, and (b) when $v = 0$, i.e. the centre of circle lies on the $x$-axis both $\eta_t$ and $\eta_b$ are symmetrical about the horizontal axis in the $\zeta$-plane. A symmetrical profile results. When (c) both $h$ and $v$ are zero, so that the centre of the circle is not moved from the origin, $\eta = 0$ and the circle transforms into a flat plate of width $4b$. These three cases are shown in Fig. 5.13.

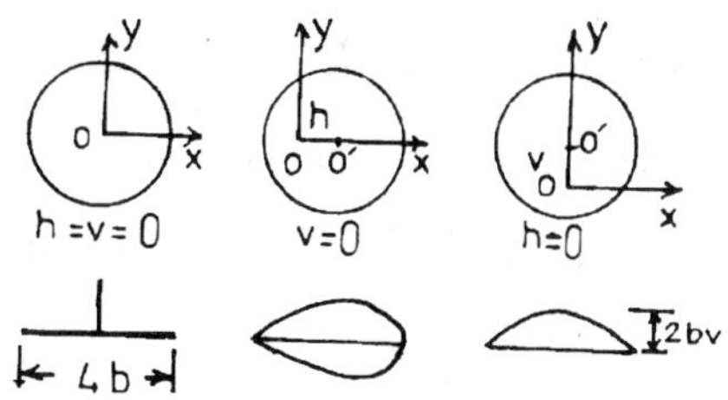


**Fig. 5.13** Transformation of circle into various types of profiles under Katta-Zhukovsky trnsformation of circle: Flat plate, Symmetrical profile, and Segment

*Step 7*: The mean camber line of the airfoil is the locus of points $\frac{1}{2}(\eta_t + \eta_b) = 2\,b\,v\sin^2\theta$, which is obtained trom Eq. (5.69). The percentage camber is defined as

$$\%\gamma = [\tfrac{1}{2}(\eta_t + \eta_b)_{max}/\text{chord}] \times 100\,\% = \tfrac{1}{2}v(\sin^2\theta)_{max} \times 100\,\%$$
$$= \tfrac{1}{2}v \times 100\,\%, \text{ since } (\sin^2\theta)_{max} = 1 \text{ at } \theta = \pi/2 \tag{5.74}$$

*Step 8*: We can also determine the horizontal and vertical eccentricity parameters $h$ and $v$ in terms of the (thickness/chord) ratio and $(t_{1t}/t_{1b})$–ratio at maximum thickness. From Eq. (5.73),

$$t_m/c = 3\sqrt{3}\,h/4 = 1.3\,h, \text{ or}, h = 0.77\,t_m/c \tag{5.75}$$

From eq. (5.69), at $\theta = \pi/3 = 60°$,

$$t_{1t} = \eta_{1t} = 2\,b\,(1.5\,h + \sqrt{3}\,v/2)\sqrt{3}/2 = 1.5\,b\,(\sqrt{3}\,h + v) \tag{5.76}$$

and $\quad t_{1b} = \eta_{1b} = -2\,b\,(\,1.5\,h - \sqrt{3}\,v/2\,)\,\sqrt{3}\,/2 = 1.5\,b\,(\,v - \sqrt{3}\,h\,)$ (5.77)

Also $\quad t_{1t}/t_m = 1.5\,b\,(\,\sqrt{3}\,h + v\,)/(\,3\,\sqrt{3}\,hc/4\,)$

$$= 1.5\,b\,(\,\sqrt{3}\,h + v\,)/(\,3\,\sqrt{3}\,h\,b\,) = (\,\sqrt{3}\,h + v\,)/(2\,\sqrt{3}\,h\,)$$

$$= 0.5 + 0.289\,v/h \tag{5.78}$$

Since $\quad t_{1t} < t_m$, $0.289\,v/h < 0.5$, or, $v/h < \sqrt{3}$ (5.79)

This gives an important design limit for the ratio of the two eccentricity parameters.

*Step* 9: Going back to Eq. (5.54), the lift force on the airfoil can be calculated as follows:

$$L = 4\,\pi\,\rho\,U^2\,a\sin(\,\alpha + \beta\,),\ \text{Newton / m}$$

Here, $\rho$ = air density, kg/m$^3$

$U$ = wind velocity, m/s

$a$ = radius of circle in the $z$-plane, m

$\alpha$ = direction of wind from the chord line $MN$

$\beta \approx v$, the vertical eccentricity of centre of circle for small $v$

Now $\quad a = b\,(\,1 + h\,) = 0.25\,c\,(\,1 + 0.77\,t_m/c\,) = 0.25\,c + 0.1925\,t_m$ (5.80)

Also $\quad ½\,\rho\,U^2$ = kinetic energy of wind per $m^3$.

The lift $L$ is written in terms of the chord length $c$ using a lift coefficient $C_L$, as follows:

$$L = ½\,\rho\,U^2 \cdot c \cdot C_L \tag{5.81}$$

giving $$C_L = \frac{4\,\pi\,\rho\,U^2\,b\,(\,1 + h\,)\sin(\,\alpha + \beta\,)}{½\,\rho\,U^2 \cdot 4\,b} = 2\,\pi\,(\,1 + h\,)\sin(\,\alpha + \beta\,) \tag{5.82}$$

It depends only on $h$, $\beta$ (= $v$), and $\alpha$. The factor $\sin(\alpha + \beta)$ is a measure of the wind-velocity component at right angles to the chord direction, as shown in Figs. 5.10 and 5.11.

***Example 5.9***: In the $z$-plane a circle of radius $a = 27.5$ cm has its centre displaced, such that $h = v = 0.1\,b$. Plot the airfoil section resulting from the transformation $\zeta = z + b^2/z$.

***Solution***: $a = b(1 + h)$. Therefore $b = 27.5/1.1 = 25$ cm $= 0.25$ m. From Eq.(5.66), $\xi = 2\,b\cos\theta = 0.5\cos\theta$, and

$$\eta = 2\,b\,[\,h\,(\,1 + \cos\theta\,) + v\sin\theta\,]\sin\theta = 0.05\,(\,1 + \cos\theta + \sin\theta\,)\sin\theta\,.$$

We calculate $\xi$ and $\eta$ values at every $0.1\,\pi = 18°$.

| θ, rad | 0 | 0.1 π | 0.2 π | 0.3 π | 0.4 π | 0.5 π | 0.6 π | 0.7 π |
|---|---|---|---|---|---|---|---|---|
| θ, deg | 0 | 18 | 36 | 54 | 72 | 90 | 108 | 126 |
| ξ | 0.5 | 0.475 | 0.405 | 0.294 | 0.1545 | 0 | –0.1545 | –0.294 |
| $\eta_t$ | 0 | 0.0348 | 0.0704 | 0.0968 | 0.108 | 0.1 | 0.078 | 0.0494 |

| θ, rad | 0.8 π | 0.9 π | π | 1.1 π | 1.2 π | 1.3 π | 1.4 π | 1.5 π |
|---|---|---|---|---|---|---|---|---|
| θ, deg | 144 | 162 | 180 | 198 | 216 | 234 | 252 | 270 |
| ξ | –0.405 | –0.475 | –0.5 | –0.475 | –0.405 | –0.294 | –0.1545 | 0 |
| $\eta_b$ | 0.023 | 0.0055 | 0 | 0.004 | 0.0116 | 0.016 | 0.012 | 0 |

| θ, rad | 1.6 π | 1.7 π | 1.8 π | 1.9 π |
|---|---|---|---|---|
| θ, deg | 288 | 306 | 324 | 342 |
| ξ | 0.1545 | 0.294 | 0.405 | 0.475 |
| $\eta_b$ | –0.017 | –0.032 | –0.036 | –0.0252 |

$$t = \eta_t - \eta_b = \eta_t(\theta) - \eta_b(2\pi - \theta)$$

| θ, deg | 0 | 18 | 36 | 54 | 72 | 90 | 108 | 126 | 144 | 162 | 180 |
|---|---|---|---|---|---|---|---|---|---|---|---|
| $t$ | 0 | 0.06 | 0.1064 | 0.128 | 0.124 | 0.1 | 0.066 | 0.0332 | 0.0112 | 0.0015 | 0 |

Maximum thickness occurs at $\theta = \pi/3 = 60°$, where $b = 0.25$ m.

Therefore $\eta_t = 0.05\,(1 + 0.5 + 0.866) \times 0.866 = 0.1024\ m$ ; $(\sqrt{3}/2 = 0.866)$

and $\eta_b = -\,0.05\,(1 + 0.5 - 0.886) \times 0.866 = -\,0.0276\ m$

Therefore the maximum thickness is $t_m = 0.13$ m. Also, $t_m/c = 1.3\ h = 0.13$.

At maximum thickness, i.e. at $\theta = \pi/3 = 60°$, the ratio $t_1/t_m = 0.1024/0.13 = 0.7875$. Equation (5.78) gives $t_1/t_m = 0.5 + 0.289\ v/h = 0.789$, since $v/h = 1$.

Figure 5.14 shows the resulting profile.

***Example 5.10***: A wind turbine has 2 blades with rotor diameter 10m, chord $c = 0.5$m, and rotor speed at rated power of 100 rev/min. Other details are $(t_m/c) = 0.3$, and $v = h$. The wind speed is 10 m/s. Calculate the power generated when the directlon of wind with the chord makes angles of 10°, 20°, and 30°.

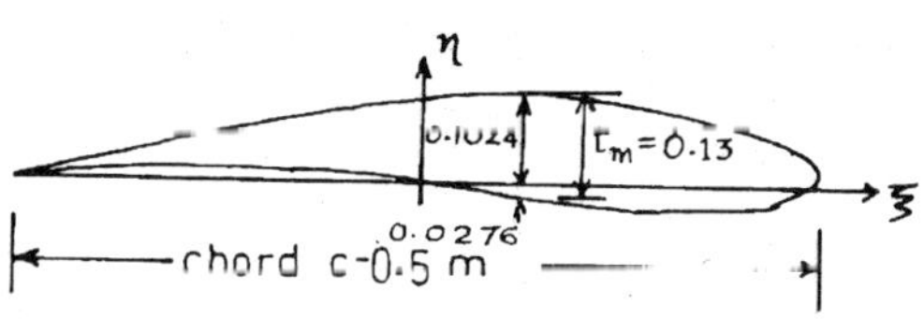


**Fig. 5.14** Airfoil profile for Example 5.9

***Solution***: $c = 0.5$ m, $t_m/c = 0.3$. Therefore $t_m = 0.15$ m

Now from Eq. (5.80), $a = 0.25\ c + 0.1925\ t_m = 0.1539$ m. Also, $\beta = v$, from Step 9. Since $t_m/c = 1.3$ h from Eq. (5.75), and $h = v$ in this problem,

$$\beta = v = h = 0.77\ t_m/c = 0.77 \times 0.3 = 0.231 \text{ rad} = 13.235°.$$

Therefore from Eq. (5.54), the lift per metre of blade length is

$$L = \tfrac{1}{2}\rho U^2 a \sin(\alpha + \beta) = \tfrac{1}{2} \times 1.293 \times 10^2 \times 0.1539 \sin(\alpha + 13.23°)$$
$$= 9.95 \sin(\alpha + 13.23°),\ \text{Newton / m}$$

Rotor radius $R = 5$ m. Number of blades $N = 2$.

Average torque $T_{av} = ½\, N\, L\, R^2 = ½ \times 2 \times 9.95 \times 25 \sin(\alpha + 13.23°)$

$= 248.75 \sin(\alpha + 13.23°)$, Newton–metre .

Rotor speed = 100 rev/min. Therefore $\omega_m = 2\pi n_r / 60 = 10.47$ rad/sec. Therefore the developed power is

$$P = T_{av}\,\omega_m = 248.75 \times 10.47 \sin(\alpha + 13.23°)$$

$$= 2604.4 \sin(\alpha + 13.23°),\ \text{W}$$

*For* $\alpha = 10°$ : $P_{10} = 1027$ W

*For* $\alpha = 20°$ : $P_{20} = 1427$ W

*For* $\alpha = 30°$ : $P_{30} = 1784$ W

The angle $\alpha$ can be arranged to have any desired value by giving the blade a twist.

The tip-speed ratio is $\lambda = R\,\omega_m/U = 5 \times 10.47/10 = 5.235$.

***Example 5.11***: A wind turbine with 3 blades has a rated power of 1500 W at 22 mph (10 m/s) wind speed. The rotor diameter is 13.2 ft (4 m) and its speed at rated power is 170 rev/min. The chord of the blade airfoil profile is $c = 1.2$ m and the ratio of eccentricity parameters is $(h/v) = 1$. Take $\rho = 1.22$ kg/m$^3$. Calculate the required blade thickness at maximum-thickness point using the Katta-Zhukovsky model, and $\alpha = 15°$.

***Solution***: From Eqs. (5.56) and (5.57), $P = ½\, N\, L\, R^2\, \omega_m$

$$\omega_m = 2\pi \times 170/60 = 17.6 \text{ rad/s} .\ R = 2\,m,\ N = 3,\ P = 1500 \text{ W} .$$

Therefore $L = 1500 \times 2 / (3 \times 2^2 \times 17.8) = 14.04$ N / m

$$a = c\,(0.25 + 0.1925\, t_m / c) = 1.2\,(0.25 + 0.1925\,\gamma),\ (\gamma = t_m / c)$$

$$= 0.3 + 0.231\,\gamma$$

$$h = 0.77\, t_m / c = 0.77\,\gamma .$$

$$L = ½\,\rho\, U^2\, a \sin(\alpha + \beta)$$

$$= ½\ 1.22 \times 10^2 \times (0.3 + 0.231\,\gamma) \times \sin(15 + 44.1\,\gamma)°$$

Therefore $14.04 = 61\,(0.3 + 0.231\,\gamma) \sin(15 + 44.1\,\gamma)°$

giving $(0.3 + 0.231\,\gamma) \sin(15 + 44.1\,\gamma)° = 0.23$ .

This is solved by trial and error for $\gamma = t_m/c$.

| $\gamma =$ | 0.1 | 0.2 | 0.3 | 0.4 | 0.45 | 0.5 |
|---|---|---|---|---|---|---|
| *LHS* | 0.107 | 0.14 | 0.175 | 0.2116 | 0.231 | 0.25 |

Therefore $t_m / c = 0.45$, and $t_m = 0.45 \times 1.2 = 0.54\ m$

$$h = 0.77\ t_m / c = 0.3465 = v, \text{ the eccentricity parameters}$$

Practical airfoil designs are more complicated than the simple shape resulting from the Katta-Zhukovsky transformation.

## OBJECTIVE TYPE QUESTIONS

1. A wind is blowing at a velocity $v$ through an area at right angles to it. The density of wind is $\rho$. The kinetic energy of the wind is:
   (a) $\rho A v^3$; (b) $\rho A v^2$; (c) $½ \rho v^3 / A$; (d) $½ \rho A v^2$.
2. The coefficient of performance of a wind turbine is defined as: (a) Power available in input wind at turbine/Total power available in wind; (b) $C_p = 1 - v_e^2 / v_i^2$, with $v_e$ = velocity at exit and $v_i$ = velocity at inlet; (c) $C_p = 4 a^2 ( 1 - a)$, with $a = v_t/v_i$; (d) all three are true.
3. The value of $a = (v_t/v_i)$ at maximum $C_p$ is: (a) 0.35; (b) 16/27; (c) 2/3; (d) 0.5.
4. The Betz crlterion of maximum or optimum performance has the value of $C_p$ equal to: (a) 0.35; (b) 16/27; (c) 2/3; (d) 0.5.
5. At maximum value of $C_p$: (a) $v_t = 2 v_i / 3$; (b) $v_e = v_i / 3$; (c) $v_t = ½ ( v_i + v_e )$; (d) all three are true.
6. In terms of maximum $c_p$, the rotor diameter is:
   (a) $D = \sqrt{P_{\text{tmax}} / v_i^3}$; (b) $D = \sqrt{5\ P_{\text{tmax}} / v_i^3}$; (c) $D = \sqrt{P_{\text{tmax}} / 5\ v_i^3}$;
   (d) none of the three are true.
7. At a wind speed of 10 m/s and 100-*kW* turbine output, the rotor diameter is nearly: (a) 63 m; (b) 11.2 m; (c) 22.35 m; (d) 90 m.
8. A pressure of 1 atm at 0°C is equal to: (a) 0.101325 MPa; (b) 101.325 kPa; (c) 14.7 lbs/in$^2$; (d) 760 mm-Hg; (e) all are true.
9. A pressure of 1 bar = $10^6$ dyne/cm$^2$ and 1 MPa = $10^6$ N/m$^2$. What is the atmospheric pressure in bars? (a) 1 bar; (b) 0.101325 bar; (c) 1.01325 bar; (d) 1000 bar; (e) none of the four.
10. The air density in kg/m$^3$ at pressure $p$ and temperature $T$°$K$ is given by: (a) 3.4855 $p/T$, with $p$ in kPa; (b) 0.4647 $p/T$ with p in mm-Hg; (c) 1.293 at 0°C and 1 atm; (d) all are true.
11. The atmospheric pressure at altitude $H$ metre above sea level is nearly: (a) $p = 101.3 - 9.33 \times 10^{-3}$ H, kPa; (b) $p = 760 - 0.07\ H$, mm-Hg;

(c) Roughly decreases by 10 kPa for each 1000 m increase in altitude; (d) all three are true.

12. The temperature of air decreases with altitude roughly as: (a) 8 to 10°C/1000 m; (b) 8 to 10 K/1000 m; (c) 281 to 283 K/1000 m ; (d) 14.4 to 18°F/1000 m; (e) all are true except (c).

13. The wind velocity with altitude: (a) increases; (b) decreases; (c) stays same; (d) follows one-seventh power law; (e) both (a) and (d) are true.

14. Vertical axis wind turbines are known by name(s) such as: (a) Smith-Putnam; (b) Savonius; (c) Darrieus; (d) Both (b) and (c).

15. The tip speed ratio refers to (a) ratio of wind speed at turbine and undisturbed wind speed; (b) speed at middle of rotor/wind speed; (c) speed at tip of rotor/wind speed; (d) none of the three.

16. A turbine speed is given as 15/5/25 mph. They represent which sequence? (a) Rated/cut-in/cut-out speeds; (b) Normal/minimum/maximum speeds; (c) wind speeds at turbine, exit, and input; (d) both (a) and (b) are true.

17. When the speed exceeds cut-out speed, the turbine is protected from damage by: (a) Using brakes; (b) Rotor is made to turn sideways into wind; (c) Blades are feathered; (d) any or all three are used.

18. Generators used in wind turbine power systems are: (a) DC synchronous generators; (b) DC induction generators; (c) AC commutator generators; (d) none of the three.

19. A wind turbine connected to a synchronous AC generator must have: (a) Constant speed; (b) Constant power output; (c) Constant frequency; (d) Governor control; (e) All four.

20. For a system with variable speed of turbine, the generator used can be (a) AC induction type; (b) Field-modulated type; (c) Roesel type; (d) Any of the three.

21. The Katta-Zhukovsky transformation function : (a) transforms a flat plate into an airfoil type; (b) transforms a circle into a flat plate; (c) transforms an airfoil into a flat plate; (d) transforms a circle into an airfoil shape.

22. In order for an airfoil to have a lift force, the fluid must have turbulence: (a) true; (b) false.

23. Lift force is generated by: (a) stream line flow; (b) vortex flow; (c) combination of stream line and vortex flows; (d) wind must blow at rignt angles to chord of airfoil.

[**Answers**: 1. (d); 2. (d); 3. (c); 4. (b); 5. (d); 6. (b); 7. (c); 8. (e); 9. (c); 10. (d); 11. (d); 12. (e); 13. (e); 14. (d); 15. (c); 16. (d); 17. (d); 18. (d); 19. (e); 20. (d); 21. (d); 22. (b); 23. (c)]

## REVIEW QUESTIONS AND PROBLEMS

1. Based on Rankine-Froudes-Betz theory for an idealized wind turbine, show that the following relations are valid:

   (a) Power developed by ideal turbine is $P_t = ½ \rho A_t v_t (v_i^2 - v_e^2)$ where subscripts *i*, *t*, *e* refer to inlet, turbine and exit

   (b) $P_t = ½ \rho A_t v_i^3 \cdot 4 a^2 (1 - a)$, where $a = v_t/v_i$

   (c) At maximum $C_p = P_t/P_i$, the Betz coefficient is $C_p = 16/27$ at $a = 2/3$. Give all assumptions on which the theory is based.

2. The inlet and exit velocities for a wind turbine system are 24 m/s and 8 m/s, respectively. At sea level and 0°C, calculate the pressure difference across the turbine. Give the values in $N/m^2$, *Pa*, atm, mbar, and mm-Hg. [331 $N/m^2$, 331 *Pa*, 0.00327 *atm*, 3.31 *mbar*, 2.483 *mm-Hg*]

3. At the Betz value for $C_p$, $\rho = 1.293$ kg/m$^3$ at 0°C and 1 atm, inlet velocity $v_i = 24$ m/s and rotor angular velocity of 83 rpm, calculate:

   (a) the force developed by blade per metre;

   (b) the rotor blade radius if the tip speed ratio is 6;

   (c) the average torque developed by 2 blades; and

   (d) the power develped. Give all units.

   [(a) 3831 N/m; (b) 16.57 m; (c) $1.052 \times 10^6$ N-m; (d) 2.91 MW]

4. Calculate the rotor diameters required for 50, 100, and 200 kW at undisturbed wind speeds of 10 and 20 m/s at 0°C and sea level using $C_p = 0.4$. Take $v_t = 0.6\, v_i$.

| [$v_i$ $P_t$ | $50 \times 10^3$ | $100 \times 10^3$ | $200 \times 10^3$ | W |
|---|---|---|---|---|
| 10 m/s | D = 12.81 | 18.1 | 25.62 | m |
| 20 m/s | D = 4.528 | 6.4 | 9.055 | m] |

5. With these rotor diameters and wind speeds in Prob. 4, find the powers developed at a height of 1000 m and 0°C. Repeat for $H = 2000$ m and $t = -10$°C. $\rho = 0.4647\ /p/T$ with *p* in mm-Hg and 3.4855 $p/T$, with *p* in kPa.

   [(a) H = 1000 m, p = 92 kPa, ρ = 1.1746 = 90.8% of 1.293.
   Therefore powers will be reduced to 90.8% of previous values.

   *10 m/s*: D = 12.81 m, $P_t$ = 45.4 kW; 18.1 m/90.8 kW; 25.62 m/181.6 kW.
   *20 m/s*: 4.528 m/45.4 kW; 6.4 m/90.8 kW; 9.055 m/181.6 kW.

   (b) $H = 2000$ m, $p = 80$ kPa: $\rho = 3.4855 \times 80/263 = 1.06$ kg/m$^3$
   = 82% of 1.293.

   *10 m/s*: 12.81 m/41 kW; 18.1 m/82 kW; 25.62 m/164 kW
   *20 m/s*: 4.528 m/41 kW; 6.4 m/82 kW; 9.055 m/164 kW]

6. (a) Plot tne variation of atmospheric pressure with height $H$ above sea level, for $0 < H < 5000$ m.

   (b) Plot the variation of atmospheric temperature with height $H$ above sea level, if the temperature at sea level is 20°C. On the same graph, plot the relation $t = t_{gr} - 0.01\ H$, °C for comparison.

   (c) Assuming $T = T_{gr} - K.H$, find the average value of K in °C/1000 m from $H = 1000$ to 5000 m.

   (d) Using these two variations of $p$ and $T$ with altitude, plot the variation of air density wlth altitude.

| [$H =$ | 0 | 1000 | 2000 | 3000 | 4000 | 5000 | m |
|---|---|---|---|---|---|---|---|
| $p =$ | 101.33 | 92 | 82.67 | 73.34 | 64.01 | 54.68 | kPa |
| $T_o =$ | 293 | 285 | 276.4 | 267.1 | 257 | 245.9 | K |
| $t =$ | 20 | 12 | 3.4 | –5.9 | –16 | –27 | °C |
| $t_{gr} - 0.01\ H$ | 20 | 10 | 0 | –10 | –20 | –30 | °C |
| $K =$ | | 8 | 8.3 | 8.667 | 9 | 9.4 | |

$K_{av}$ = 8.68 between $H = 1000$ m and 5000 m.]

7. (a) Plot the variation of wind velocity ratio $(v_2/v_1)$ as a function of height taking $H_1 = 20$ m and varying $H_2$ from 10 m to 100 m.

   (b) On the same graph plot the ratio of powers $(P_2/P_1)$.

   (c) If a wind turbine develops rated power of 10 kW at $H = 10$ m, how much power can it develop at $H = 30$ m?

8. Draw the figures of: (a) Horizontal axis downwind 4-blade wind turbine. (b) Darrieus turbine with 2 blades; (c) Savonius turbine with 2 hemi-cylinders.

9. A wind turbine rated for 100 kW has the specification 21.7/13/40 mph. Explain what these figures mean. Convert these mph values into m/s. How much power does the turbine develop between 21.7 and 40 mph? Assuming a cubic relation, how much power does it develop at 17 mph? (100 kW, ≈ 50 kW)

10. Explain how the energy produced by a wind turbine can be stored for re-use. What are the arrangements used for starting a Darrieus wind turbine?

11. A wind turbine has 3 blades with rotor diameter of 20 m, chord $c = 0.75$ m, and rated speed of 60 rpm for rated power. $t_m/c = 0.25$ for the airfoil profile and equal eccentricity parameters $v = h$ for the centre of the circle in the z-plane. At a wind speed of 15 m/s and $\rho = 1.2$ kg/m$^3$, calculate the power generated by turbine when the wind blows on the chord at an angle of $\alpha = 30°$. [Total lift = 594 N; $T_{av} = 2970$ N-m; $p = 18.66$ kW]

*CHAPTER 6*

# Ocean Energy Conversion

Oceans of the world have practically unlimited energy and if harnessed suitably can supply all of mankind's energy needs. Three such potential energy sources until now are:

(1) Tidal energy; (2) Wave energy; and (3) Ocean thermal energy.

Tides occur up to heights of 12 m in latitudes between 40 and 50 deg. on the earth and lesser heights elsewhere. These are caused by the gravitational effects of the Sun and moon and the centrifugal forces of the earth's rotation on its axis. The scheme involves storing sea water when the tide is rising behind a barrage in a reservoir extending up to 30 km behind the embankment which may be up to 10 km in length. This can be augmented by pumping from seaward side into the reservoir. During low-tide periods this stored water is led through turbines and drive electric generators. Power potential up to 20,000 MW exist at any one location, but the largest tidal plant operating to date is at the La Rance in northern France for 240 MW.

Waves caused by winds in the open sea and off-shore provide potential sources of power. A wave has both a vertical movement and a horizontal motion of water particles. Both these can be utilized for conversion to translatory motion of pistons in cylinders to pump pressure oil, which can in turn be used for running turbines. In other devices, air is compressed and rarified which can drive air turbines. Wave energy is still in experimental stages and no power production for commercial use is available.

The ocean thermal energy conversion (OTEC) utilizes the natural thermal gradient between 25 - 30°C at the surface and 4 - 5°C at the ocean depth. A heat exchanger converts freon or $NH_3$ into gas, which drives a turbine and the cool water is used in a condenser as in a conventional thermal unit. This is also in experimental stages.

# I. TIDAL POWER DEVELOPMENT

## 6.1 Tides and Tidal Power Stations

Gravitational and rotational forces exerted on the sea water give rise to tides with varying heights during a day which have exercised considerable influence on the lives of people living on sea coasts. In roughly 25 hours there are two high tides and two low tides. Tidal power development uses periods of high tide to fill a reservoir behind an embankment or barrage, and during low-tide periods this stored water is made to flow through turbines coupled to electric generators. The heads can go up to 15 m, but useful heads must have a minimum of about 5 m. Data about several possible developments and those that have already been built are given in Sec. 6.3 in Table 6.1.

Tides at any particular location are caused by the gravitational pull exerted by the Sun and the moon. The moon rotates around the earth's equitorial plane, as shown in Fig. 6.1. At the time of high tide, the sea rises due to this pull as well as the gravitational effect of the Sun, and water flows from the poles towards the equator. At the same time, there is a corresponding high tide on the opposite side of the earth. Although the moon's pull is on one side, due to the centrifugal forces exerted by the rotation of the earth, a corresponding balancing force is exerted on the diametrically opposite side of the equator. Therefore, there are two high tides during the period of rotation of the moon around the earth, which is 24 hours 50 minutes.

**Fig. 6.1** Generation of tides on earth due to gravitational effect of moon

The highest amplitude for the high tide occurs during full moon and new moon days; these are known as "spring tides". The height decreases as days progress towards the quarters and are lowest on the days of first and third quarters, when the Sun is on the opposite side to the earth from the moon. The Sun's effect on tides is about 50% of the moon's effect. These low amplitudes for the high tides are known as "neap tides". Fig. 6.2 shows typical variation of amplitude in the tide from spring tide to neap tide and back over a 15-day period (bi-weekly). Due to narrowness of bays and river mouths called estuaries, very high amplitudes for tides can be achieved in practice. This phenomenon is known as "resonance".

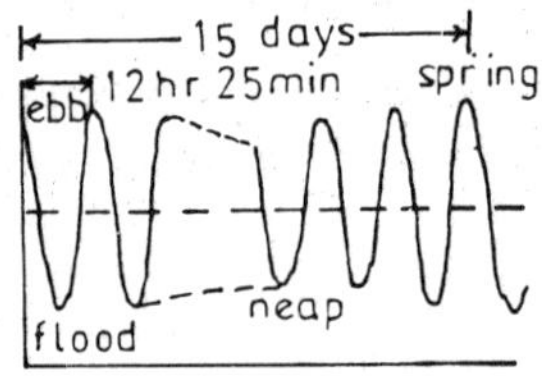

**Fig. 6.2** Spring- and neap-tide cycles, and ebb- and flow-tides

The period of earth's rotation on its axis is about 23 hours 56 minutes while the moon's period of rotation round the earth is 24 hours 50 minutes. Consequently, the high tides do not occur at the same time by the clock on all days, but are delayed by 54 minutes each day. There is a change in phase between generation of power at a tidal power station on account of this, which follows tidal timings, and the load cycle during the day on the electrical system to which the station is connected, which depends on the solar day.

Due to the intermittent nature of power generation from a tidal scheme, there must exist a way of storing the power and use it when necessary. One such storage scheme is as follows:

If several hydro-electric power stations exist on the system along rivers nearby, the power generated by a tidal power station can be used to run pumps to store more water in the reservoir and use this extra water through the turbines at the dams, in addition to the water stored naturally in the river. Thus, the stations work as pumped-storage plants. Several other possibilities exist for utilizing the power generated by a tidal power development, the simplest and most direct of which consisting in synchronizing it with an existing power system when its generators are developing power (in the tidal station). All such schemes require starting, synchronizing and shutting down twice a day. With the use of main computers in the overall control scheme at the control room and mini-computers at the power station, these operations can be programmed and the desired operational procedures can be automated in the schedule.

### 6.2 Modes of Operation of Tidal Project

During one tidal cycle of about 12 hours 25 minutes, commencing with a high tide when the tidal level is maximum, the level goes through a decrease in height called the ebb tide reaching its minimum height after about 6 hours 12.5 minutes, and then the tide rises once again to reach maximum height after about 6 hours 12.5 minutes. Using this behaviour of tides, several possibilities suggest themselves for using them for power generation. These are known as ''generating modes''.

(a) *Ebb Generation*: When the tide is falling on the seaward side of the embankments, stored water in the basin is allowed to flow through the turbine, after closing the sluices through which the basin was filled during the rising portion of tidal activity.

(b) *Flood Generation*: When the tide is rising, water can be sent through the turbine chute. This is opposite to ebb generation.

(c) *Two-way Generation*: Here, the generation can be both during flood and ebb tides. This is not very different from flood generation.

(d) *Pumping and Turbining*: Water can be pumped in addition to natural rise of tide from seaward to basin, to obtain an increase in head. Then during ebb tide, the turbine functions as the prime mover to the generator, which acted as a motor during the pumping operation earlier.

Of these, only the first and last are used. At the La Rance project in France, the latter is utilized to build up more head (13.5 m) than available naturally, which is 8.4 m. Pumping usually commences after the basin level has reached tidal maximum.

For ebb generation, a barrage or embankment built across the bay or estuary is equipped with sluice gates to permit water to fill the basin and one-way turbine-generators which operate when the tide decreases, and until the operating head becomes too low in the basin. This occurs sometime later than low water.

For two-way or double-effect generation, both ebb and flood tides are utilized. This has the advantage that power can be produced over a longer period than only ebb generation. This will more nearly match the load requirement connected on the system. The main disadvantage is that, the turbine must be designed for two-way flow, which usually reduces the turbine efficiency, as well as the fact that the operational head is much lower than in ebb generation. It is estimated that the energy output is less than for one-way ebb generation by 10-15%.

On the other hand, pump-turbine operation can increase energy production over both types of generation given before, namely, ebb generation only and two-way generation.

An example of single-effect and double-effect generation is given below for proposed tidal power scheme at the Severn Barrage in England, which will have 140 turbine-generators of 60 MW each.

| Tidal Range, m | No. of Hours of Power Generation | | Average Turbine head, m | | Maximum Power Output, MW | |
|---|---|---|---|---|---|---|
| | S.E. | D.E. | S.E. | D.E. | S.E. | D.E. |
| 6.5 | 3.5 | 10.3 | 4.5 | 2.7 | 4500 | 2100 |
| 8.5 | 4.7 | 10.8 | 5.4 | 3.4 | 6100 | 3500 |
| 11.5 | 5.7 | 11.5 | 6.8 | 4.4 | 8400 | 3750 |

Note that the maximum power generated during single-effect operation and ebb generation is nearly double that for double-effect operation and both ebb-flow generation. The number of hours of operation for double-effect is nearly twice that for single-effect operation, so that energy produced is nearly the same for both types. But on account of lower head for double-effect generation and two-way operation of the turbine, design of turbines poses more problems and higher expense than for single-effect ebb generation.

Figure 6.3 shows pictorially the energy output during one tide of about 6 hours when ebb-generation, or flood-generation, or two-way generation is used. They are also shown for spring and neap tides.

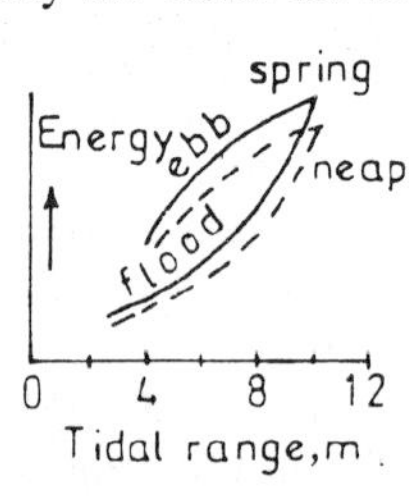


**Fig. 6.3** Energy output in one tidal cycle of about 6 hr

The same effect as two-way generation can also be achieved with two-basin schemes. Here, some of the machines operate as pump-motors to fill a second basin by using part of the power developed during ebb generation of the main turbine-generators from the first basin instead of allowing the water to go to waste in the sea. The stored water in the second basin is then used for power generation during the period in which the main power station is idle. This scheme prolongs the duration of power supply to the connected power system and follows the load requirement based on solar-day cycle. But most tidal development schemes prefer the single ebb-generation schemes, with or without additional pumping.

Operation of all such schemes is pictorially represented in Fig. 6.4. In the simple and straightforward single-effect ebb generation, the basin water level is built up. There is a period of wait until the natural tide on the seaward side falls to nearly its minimum level before generation commences. It stops when the basin level is allowed to fall to the minimum value. This minimum is made necessary by the operation of the turbine, which requires a certain minimum head at its outlet or draft tube to prevent 'negative pressure' and cavity formation that damages the turbine metal.

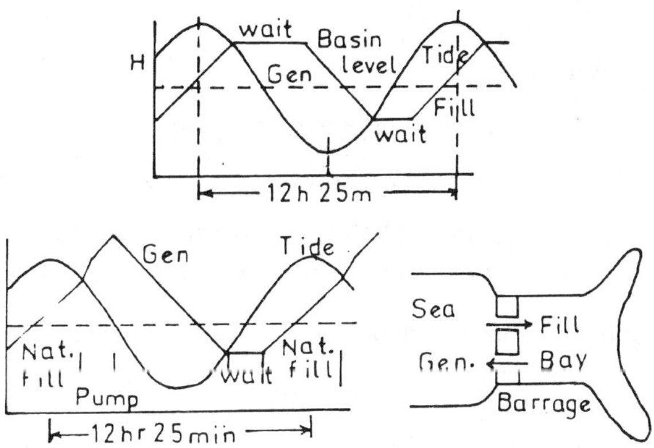


**Fig. 6.4** Operational sequence of a tidal power generation scheme

When pumping is resorted to, as is done in the french La Rance estuary development, there is a wait period while the basin level is rising to its maximum. The generator-turbine unit is now working in the motor-pump mode. After the maximum designated level is built up, the machines are reversed for normal generator-turbine mode of working.

## 6.3 Examples of Tidal Power Systems

In this section we will describe some examples of tidal power development schemes, in order to give an idea of the magnitude of different parameters and quantities involved in such schemes. Since we are dealing with as vast a natural phenomenon as the sea and trying to harness a part of its enormous power, it can be expected that the civil works, mechanical equipment needed to control the forces of nature, and the electrical power equipment will be of gigantic proportions and sometimes unique to the situation. However, the technology of harnessing power is available already from other branches of engineering development such as building dams, laying caisson foundations under water, design of water turbines and generators, etc.

The quantities to be described are: (a) Reservoir volume; (b) Reservoir surface area; (c) Head of sea water; (d) Quantity of water flow through turbine; (e) Generator rating and number. This discussion is based on simple assumptions which should be basic to all tidal development, the details varying from scheme to scheme. The density of sea water is taken to be 1025 kg/m$^3$, compared to 1000 kg/m$^3$ for fresh water.

The power input in watts at the turbine inlet in the water is

$$P = \text{generator output/turbine-generator efficiency} \quad (6.1)$$

In terms of density of sea water, head, quantity of flow per second, and acceleration due to gravity, the turbine power is

$$P = \rho q g h, W \quad (6.2)$$

where $\rho$ = density, kg/m$^3$

$q$ = quantity of flow, m$^3$/s, ($\rho q$ = kg/s)

$g$ = acceleration due to gravity = 9.81 m/s$^2$,

and $h$ = head in metres, usually from water surface behind the turbine to the center of the turbine runner.

(Note that $\rho q g h$ = total potential energy in water at height $h$).

Therefore, $P = \rho q g h$ = generator output/efficiency (6.3)

If there are $N$ identical units in the power station, then the total quantity of flow per second is

$$Q = NP/\rho g h \quad (6.4)$$

Several considerations are very special to tidal power. They are:

(a) The head $h$ is variable from the maximum at the commencement of generation to nearly zero at the end of generation. We assume this to decrease linearly.

(b) The power generated also decreases linearly from a maximum to zero. The maximum is taken equal to the rated output of the generator.

(c) The reservoir bottom is considered flat and to rise steeply at the banks. The slope of the bank does not alter the volume of water from the assumption of vertical banks, as is definitely the case with a reservoir created by a dam across a river. The cross-section of reservoir in a tidal project is therefore rectangular and not trapezoidal.

(d) No pumping is assumed. However, alterations caused by the turbine operating as a pump will be indicated in the discussion.

***Example 6.1***: A tidal power scheme has 140 generators rated 60 MW output each, and the turbine operates at a maximum designed head of 10 m. The minimum head at the end of generation is 2 m. The number of hours of generation is on the average 6 at every tidal cycle, (12 hours a day). Assume power to decrease linearly and the reservoir to have a rectangular cross-sectional area. The length of embankment is 16 km. The efficiencies of turbine and generator are 93% each. Calculate:

(a) The quantity of water flowing through each turbine at maximum output in $m^3/s$ (cumsecs).

(b) The surface area of reservoir in $km^2$.

(c) The wash behind the embankment at full reservoir capacity.

(d) Energy produced in TW-h per year. ($1 \text{ TW-h} = 10^3 \text{ GW-h} = 10^6 \text{ MW-h} = 10^9 \text{ kW-h} = 10^{12} \text{ W-h} = 3.6 \times 10^{15} \text{ J}$)

***Solution***: $\rho = 1025 \text{ kg/m}^3 = 1.025 \text{ tonne/m}^3$

$$P = 60 \times 10^6/(0.93 \times 0.93) = 9.81 \times 1.025 \times 10^3 \times 10 \times q.$$

(a) Therefore $q = 690 \text{ m}^3/\text{s} = 707 \text{ tonne/s}$
Through 140 turbines, the flow is $Q = 10^5 \text{ m}^3/\text{s}$, nearly.

(b) Since the flow is constant for 6 hours (as the turbine opening is constant even though the head is changing), the total reservoir capacity above the minimum head of 2 metres will be

$$10^5 \text{ (m}^3\text{/s)} \times (6 \times 3600) \text{ (s)} = 2.16 \times 10^9 \text{ m}^3 = 2.16 \text{ km}^3.$$

Height of reservoir = 10 m. Therefore the surface area is $0.216 \times 10^9 \text{ m}^2 = 216 \text{ km}^2$.

(c) Assuming the reservoir to have equal width throughout its height, the wash behind the embankment of 16 km will be 216/16 = 13.5 km.

(d) Energy produced at 12 hours of operation per day is:
Output at 10 m head = 60 MW, maximum.
Output at end of 6 hours = 0.
Therefore average output during a cycle = 30 MW.
Energy output per day = 30 MW × 12 hr = 360 MW-h
Energy output per year = 360 × 365 MW-h/generator.
For 140 generator units, total energy output per year
$= 360 \times 365 \times 140 \times 10^{-6} = 18.4$ TW-h

(At an average of 1 ¢ per kW-h, the total revenue for the power company will be $184 million annually).

This example corresponds closely to the proposed Severn Barrage Tidal development in the United Kingdom near Bristol.

***Example 6.2***: A tidal project has installed capacity of 2176 MW in 64 units each of 34 MW rated output. The head at rated output is 5.52 m. The embankment is 4 miles long = 6.4 km. Again assume 93% efficiency for both turbine and generator. The generation is 5 hours twice a day. Calculate

(a) The quantity of water flowing through each turbine and the total flow out of the tidal basin.

(b) The surface area of reservoir behind the embankment, and the wash.

(c) Energy produced in TW-h per year.

***Solution***:

(a) $P = 2176 \times 10^6/0.93 \times 0.93 = 9.81 \times 1025 \times 5.52 \times Q$

Therefore $Q = 45.33 \times 10^3$ m³/sec in 64 units

and $q = 708$ m³/s through each turbine

(b) Surface area of reservoir $= 45.33 \times 10^3 \times 5 \times 3600/5.52$

$$= 14.78 \times 10^7 \text{ m}^2 = 147.8 \text{ km}^2.$$

Therefore wash behind the embankment = 147.8/6.4 = 23.1 km

(c) Energy produced per day $= 0.5 \times 2176 \times 10 = 10{,}880$ MW-h

Therefore energy generated per year $= 10{,}880 \times 365$ MW-h

$$= 10.88 \times 0.365 \text{ TW-h} = 3.97 \text{ TW-h}.$$

This example corresponds to one of the possible power development sites studied for Bay of Fundy in Canada.

***Example 6.3***: A tidal power station has 24 generators each of 10 MW operating at a maximum head of 13.5 m. It generates for two 6-hour periods per day. Calculate the basin capacity in $m^3$, and annual energy production. Again assume 93% efficiencies.

***Solution***:

$$Q = 240 \times 10^6/(9.81 \times 13.5 \times 1025 \times 0.93 \times 0.93) = 2044 \text{ m}^3/\text{s}.$$

For 6 hours, total quantity involved is

$$2044 \times 6 \times 3600 = 44.15 \times 10^6 \text{ m}^3$$

Annual energy production $= 0.5 \times 240 \times 12 \times 365 \times 10^{-6}$ TW-h/yr

$$= 0.5256 \text{ TW-h} = 525.6 \text{ GW-h}$$

This example corresponds to the La Rance development in northern France. The basin capacity is quoted by them as $184 \times 10^6$ m$^3$ and annual energy generation is 540 GW-h.

Table 6.1 shows overall details of proposed tidal power schemes from all over the world. Only those schemes capable of providing over 200 MW are included.

**Table 6.1: Details of Tidal Power Projects of the World (Partial)**

| | Average Head, m | Average Potential Power, MW | Annual Energy Potential, TW-h* |
|---|---|---|---|
| *North America* | | | |
| *Bay of Fundy, Canada* | *Total* | 29,000 | 255 |
| Annherst | 10.7 | 250 | 2.25 |
| Annapolis | 6.4 | 760 | 6.7 |
| Cobscook | 5.5 | 720 | 6.3 |
| Cumberland | 10.0 | 1,700 | 15 |
| Memtaincook | 10.7 | 590 | 5.2 |
| Menas-Cobequid | 10.7 | 20,000 | 175 |
| Passamaquoddy | 5.5 | 1,800 | 16 |
| Pentcodiac | 10.7 | 800 | 7 |
| Shepody | 9.8 | 2,500 | 22 |
| *Europe* | | | |
| *England*:: Severn | 9.8 | 1,700 | 15 |
| *France* Total | | 11,300 | 98 |
| Aurguenon | 8.4 | 450 | 3.9 |
| La Rance | 8.4 | 350 | 3 |
| Mont St.Michel | 8.4 | 10,000 | 85 |
| Somme | 6.5 | 470 | 4.1 |
| *USSR* (former) Total | | 16,000 | 140 |
| Lumbovskii Bay | 4.2 | 280 | 2.43 |
| Mezen Estuary | 6.6 | 1,400 | 12 |
| White Sea | 5.6 | 14,400 | 126 |
| *South America* | | | |
| *Argentina*: San Jose' | 6 | 5,900 | 51.5 |

* Annual energy potential, TW-h = Average potential power MW × 8760 h × $10^{-6}$

## 6.4 Turbines for Tidal Power Generation

Turbines for tidal power stations have to operate under special circumstances and possess the following characteristics:

(a) For single-effect ebb-generation schemes, they are usually the conventional Kaplan type. (See Chapter 8).

(b) For double-effect ebb- and flood-generation, the turbines must generate power when water flows in both directions.

(c) For pump-turbine operation, the same runner must be capable of functioning as both a turbine and a pump as well.

(d) The same holds for double-basin schemes.

(e) They must operate at low heads, below 10 m, and in many cases not above 15 m.

(f) They handle vast amount of sea-water. Some examples have already been given in the previous section.

(g) The head of water is variable from a maximum at high-water level in the basin to practically zero at the end of generation.

(h) The turbine runner must always be submerged in water and must discharge into a cushioning tank called the tail-race tank or draft tube. If at any time, especially during low tide on the seaward side, the runner has a chance of being exposed, cavitation sets in and blade erosion takes place.

(i) Since the runner operates in saline water, corrosion is a severe problem. This is prevented by "cathodic protection". This involves immersing zinc rods in the turbine casing and connecting them to a negative potential with respect to the turbine steel proper. Corrosion is thereby limited to zinc rods, which have to be replaced at regular intervals after inspection.

Other characteristics of the entire turbine unit consist mainly of the following:

(a) Because of the enormous flow, the turbine diameter is also considerable of the order of 7.5 to 9 m.

(b) In most cases, turbines have fixed speeds. Some examples are: 253 rev/min at La Rance, 56 rev/min at Severn barrage, 50 to 60 rev/min at proposed Bay of Fundy schemes.

(c) When variable speed is used, the generated ac is rectified to dc and re-converted to 50 or 60 Hz to suit the electrical system to which the station is tied.

(d) A turbine consists of vanes fixed to a distributor connected through heavy rods to the governor servomotor. The opening between vanes controls the amount of water let into the turbine casing and the runner.

(e) The blade on the runner is normally either fixed or its pitch can be varied in order to keep the speed constant at all heads.

(f) A combination of variation of distributor vane angle and runner blade angle can provide a large range of speed and power output at variable heads. The best combination must be selected for each tidal development scheme, always keeping costs in mind.

(g) The number of turbines in these schemes is very large, unlike normal hydro-electric power stations built across rivers.

(h) The turbines are also relatively of low output for the large quantity of water flowing in them. For hydro stations, 200 MW is usual for single units, whereas for tidal stations the power is normally between 10 MW and 60 MW, electrical, for each machine.

(i) Turbines are classified according to distributor, blade and speed as follows: FD-FB-FS; FD-FB-VS; VD-FB-VS; FD-VB-FS; VD-FB-FS; FD-VB-VS; VD-VB-FS; VD-VB-VS; and so on, where the letters are $F$ = fixed, $V$ = variable, $D$ = distributor, $B$ = blade, $S$ = speed.

(j) From studies made of turbines for low variable-head operation, FD-FB-VS and VD-FB-FS are the best suited for providing energy at lowest cost. For maximum power, it is desirable to vary any two of the variables.

(k) Pump-turbines require special attention.

Turbines used for tidal power generation are further classified into four types, depending upon their location and connection to the generator through the drive shaft. The design of generator is governed by the type of turbine to which it is coupled. These are:

(1) Vertical axis Kaplan turbine

(2) Bulb turbine with horizontal shaft

(3) Tubular turbine with either horizontal or inclined shaft

(4) Straight flow (STRAFLOW) turbine with a rim generator.

These four types are shown in Fig. 6.5 (a) to (e). A brief description of each type is provided below. Because the head is low, the machinery should provide least obstruction to water flow in order to minimize flow losses.

(1) *Vertical-Axis Kaplan Turbine*

The use of this type of turbine requires that water should come into the casing from a horizontal direction, undergo a right angle bend in the turbine proper and discharge again in a horizontal direction. Because these provide obstructions to normal flow of water, such turbines are never used, even though arranging the generator above the turbine out of the water is a great advantage.

(2) *Bulb Turbine*

The generator is on the upstream side of the turbine runner and is directly coupled or driven through a gear to increase the speed of generator. The generator is housed in a steel casing which makes the entire unit take on the appearance of a bulb. The bulb is normally 15-20% larger in diameter than the turbine runner and its length is about $2D$, with $D$ = turbine-runner diameter. Installing such horizontal units requires less excavation than vertical-axis turbines.

(3) *Tubular Turbines*

The generator is located outside the water passage, so that the shaft is very long. This causes serious vibration problems, especially as all low-head turbines have a

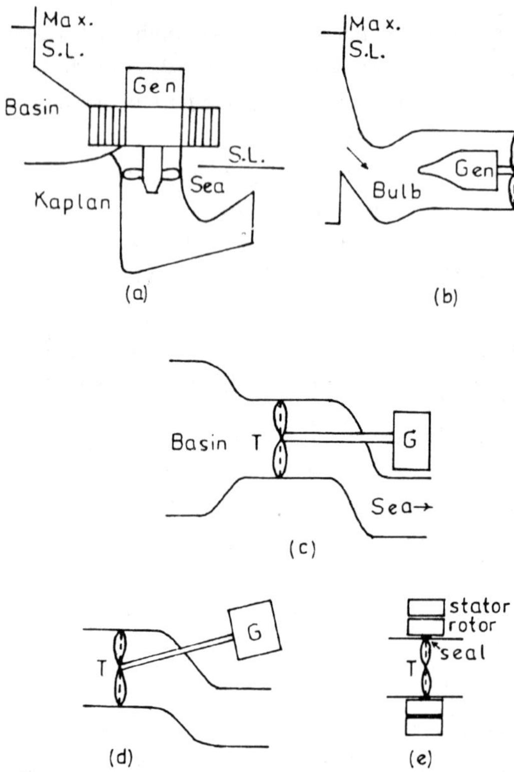


**Fig. 6.5** Types of turbines and generators for tidal power schemes:
(a) Vertical axis Kaplan type (not used much); (b) Bulb turbine (c) Tubular turbine with horizontal shaft; (d) Tubular turbine with inclined shaft; (e) Straflow turbine with rim generator.

high runaway speed in the event of malfunction of the governor, which may fail to close the distribution vanes at no load. A long shaft has low critical speed if sufficient stiffness is not built into it. If this speed falls below runaway speed, the shaft experiences severe stresses by bending into a sinusoidal shape between the bearings. Both the horizontal shaft and inclined shaft tubular turbines suffer from this problem.

(4) *Straflow Turbines*

As shown in Fig. 6.5(e), there are no bends in the straight flow or STRAFLOW turbine and water flows horizontally with least obstruction. The generator rotor is fixed to the turbine runner and is located outside the water passage. It is called a "rim generator". Because of this, the turbine runner has fixed blades. While offering lot of advantages, the main limitation is the very large-diameter seal required, in order that water may not leak into the generator. Such a turbine-generator unit is being tried on an experimental basis at the Bay of Fundy tidal development in Canada for 20 MW, where the turbine runner is 7.6 m in diameter.

The preferred choice for most tidal development projects is the Bulb Turbine, since these have been built by many manufacturers in the world since a long time, and the vast number of turbines required in short time does not permit new designs to be tried *in situ*.

## 6.5 Generators for Tidal Power Generation

Figure 6.5 shows the different possible locations of generators coupled to bulb turbines, tubular turbines and straflow turbines. These are the main types preferred for tidal stations. The generators used are polyphase synchronous type, which are most suitable for such high outputs. The details of design are governed by turbine types. The generator is normally directly coupled to the turbine, or in cases of powers of 20 MW or less they can be geared to run at a speed higher than turbine speed.

### *6.5.1 Bulb Type Direct-Driven Generator*

Here, the generator is enclosed by a water-tight steel bulb upstream from the turbine. Both turbine and generator are placed in the centre of the stream, as shown in Fig. 6.5(b). As mentioned earlier, if $D$ = diameter of turbine runner, because of severe space restriction, the generator is about (1.1-1.2)$D$, while the length of the bulb is about 2$D$.

The runner diameter can reach a maximum of 9 m and the rotational speed is in the range 50-60 rev/min. The number of poles will be very high, in the range 120-100 for 50 Hz and 144-120 for 60 Hz. For efficient cooling, the conductors can either be gas cooled or air cooled or even water cooled. Inner cooling of conductor is found necessary, because the heat generated is much more than conventional generators. If water cooling is used, it is clear that the temperature of the winding must be kept below 100°C. Air cooling at a pressure of 2-3 atmosphere is usually recommended, with the hot air cooled by liquid in a heat exchanger. Dry air is preferred, because the entire generator operates constantly in a wet atmosphere.

One major problem associated with all generating systems, which is complicated further by having an extremely large number of generators operating in parallel which have to be synchronized to the electrical system, is the problem of stability. This can be steady-state, transient- and dynamic stability, when slow load changes, and fast load changes occur. To improve dynamic stability, both the turbine governor and the electrical voltage regulator operate simultaneously, the turbine governor also being of the electronic type.

Stability is governed both by the mechanical moment of inertia of the rotating parts and the transient reactance included in the generator electrical design. To design a generator in a restricted space to obtain a high output, the flux density and current density must be higher than when such a restriction is not present. These are reflected in what are known as ''magnetic loading'' which is equal to the flux acting on the armature periphery (= $P\,\phi_p$), and the ''electric loading'' equal to the total current flowing in the machine (= number of conductors × current in each conductor). With a small diameter, the specific magnetic and electric loadings per unit area or unit length along the periphery is high, giving rise to excessive heat in the machine.

Another factor is that, to achieve high output in a restricted space, leakage fluxes must be minimized. However, the transient reactance to some extent depends on the leakage flux, so that reducing one decreases the other. Lowering the transient reactance increases short-circuit current on the machine winding giving rise to excessive mechanical forces and contributes to lower margins of stability.

On the mechanical side, if moment of inertia per unit MVA is reduced, the machine hunts under load changes and this is detrimental to stability of an alternator when it has to operate in parallel with other alternators. Design details indicate that only 20% of inertia constant can be incorporated in bulb generator units as compared to conventional salient-pole generators used for hydro-electric stations which do not pose space-restriction problems other than the normal requirement to keep the size down as far as possible. Details of generator design are beyond the scope of this book.*

### *6.5.2 Gear-Driven Bulb Generators*

By using epicyclic gears, generator speed can be raised so that 8-10 poles may be sufficient (600-750 rpm for 50 Hz, and 720-900 rpm for 60 Hz).

The high speed effectively reduces the diameter of the generator and the design can be more conventional as well as improving conditions of water flow to the turbine runner. The gear box is also enclosed in the bulb. Power transmission up to 50-60 MW through a gear is still to be achieved but not impossible.

### *6.5.3 Tubular-Type Turbine-Generators*

As shown in Figs. 6.5(c) and (d), the generator is outside the water channel and design poses very few problems which are common to all generators of the conventional type.

### *6.5.4 Rim-Type Generator*

The rim-type generator has the poles rotating with the turbine runner, and the generator rotor is placed outside the water passage, as shown in Fig. 6.5(e). This

* Some aspects of synchronous-machine operation, dynamics and design are given in the author's book, *Electromechanical Energy Conversion with Dynamics of Machines*, New Age Publishers International (P) Ltd., New Delhi, 1997.

type of generator was invented by Harza in the US in the 1920's to go with low-speed large-diameter Kaplan turbines. This scheme permits larger moment of inertia to be incorporated in the rotor than for bulb-type generators. Since the stator is outside the water passage, design of generator is more conventional. A large machine of 7.6 m diameter is being tried out at the Bay of Fundy tidal development in Canada.

As pointed out earlier, the large diameter seal to prevent water from reaching the generator rotor is all-important. Some of these rotors for machines can weigh as much as 800 tonne. These have to be very frequently brought to rest, then started, speeded up, and synchronized to the electrical system, which pose more severe problems than a machine running continuously for a year or more at constant speed.

# II. WAVE ENERGY CONVERSION

## 6.6 Introduction

Waves in the sea possess practically unlimited energy and if properly harnessed can supply an equivalent of a country's entire power requirement, in the same way as solar or wind energy conversion processes. But the engineering complexity and effort involved taxes the ingenuity of man to the farthest extreme, since we are dealing with raw nature at its worst. However, with extremely large structures already erected in roughest of seas for oil exploration and drilling platforms, the problem of using similar structures has opened up the possibility of the energy in the waves to be harnessed for production of power for running industrial wheels on shore, or for erecting small-scale factories out on the sea itself. We will describe in a later section 6.8 the details of wave-energy harnessing schemes, and some uses for the power at the site itself, other than transmission of the generated power to the shore either in the form of pumped pressurized fluid (oil) or as electricity through cables.

Broadly speaking, the potential power existing in 1 m length of a wave is expressed by the relations

$$P = (1/64\,\pi)\cdot \rho\, g^2 \cdot H_w^2 \cdot T_w\,,\ W/m \tag{6.5}$$

where $\rho$ = density of sea water = 1025 kg/m$^3$

$g$ = acceleration due to gravity = 9.81 m/s$^2$

$H_w$ = height of wave in metres

and $T_w$ = period of wave in seconds

The factor ($\rho\, g^2/64\,\pi$) = 490.6 kg/m-s$^4$. We will give definitions of wave height and period in more detail later on in Sec. 6.7.

As an example, with $H_w$ = 7 m, $T_w$ = 10 s, the potential power per metre length of wave will be given by

$$P = 1025 \times 9.81^2 \times H_w^2 \times T_w / 64\pi = 490.6 H_w^2\, T_w = 0.4906 H_w^2\, T_w\,, \text{kW/m}$$

$$= 0.4906 \times 7^2 \times 10 = 225.7\,\text{kW/m} \tag{6.6}$$

For inshore schemes, the power varies from a low of 10 kW/m to 100 kW/m, since wave characteristics depend very much on wind speeds, storms, etc. Wave properties, as can be imagined, are extremely random, so that they have to be described through spectral power density S(f), m$^2$/Hz. We will consider this problem later. Because of the randomness in property of every factor entering into assessing the potential power in the wave, which are naturally based on experimental results, no two investigators agree on the exact variations in these properties. They depend on observations carried on with instruments placed inside wave-rider buoys or in weather ships, combined with wind-speed records from local meteorological offices. Thus, no general rules can be given and long-term observations must be carried out at the probable site where wave-energy conversion station will be ultimately located. Data extending over a short-term and borrowing from published literature will not help design a satisfactory power plant. This is particularly important in those countries where wave-energy development is being planned, and for obvious reasons, quick results are aimed at.

Waves are broadly classified as "wind" and "swell". The latter is due to winds and storms very far from the wave location, while wind-sea is caused by local winds.

Before discussing wave properties relevant to energy harnessing, a brief summary of principles of possible devices will be described, which have been developed during the past 25 years. We will restrict to seven of them. The actual engineering details will be reserved for Sec. 6.8. These are broadly classified as (a) Terminators; (b) Attenuators; and (c) Point Absorbers (see Fig. 6.6).

*Terminators*

Such devices use waves incident on them, or experience the pressure indirectly, to convert wave motion into reciprocating motion. This drives pistons to fill pressurized oil from the pump into a container, or create differential air pressure to drive air turbines and electric generators coupled to them. In every case there must be a stationary part, relative to which the movable part has a translatory motion. Four major devices of this type are as follows:

(1) *The Bristol Cylinder*

This is a cylinder submerged fully below the still water level of the sea and moored to the sea bed. The cylinder is rotated by the wave. Power is extracted through hydraulic pumps connected between the moving cylinder and the stationary mooring structure. Since the cylinder is fully submerged, it is free of destructive effect from storms.

(2) *The Salter Duck*

This device has a cam-shaped assymmetric cylinder which is hinged to a heavy immovable 'spine' or rod moored to the sea bed. A wave's up-and-down motion is translated into a rotary motion over an arc which once again actuates hydraulic pumps.

(3) *The Cockerell Raft*

This has two large hinged flaps or surfaces connected to an immovable raft moored to the sea bed. The wave motion in the vertical direction is converted to reciprocating motion, which has the same effect as the spine and duck.

(4) *The Oscillating Water Column*

Air is trapped between two columns of water in an inverted U-tube of large dimensions, which moves due to the pressure difference created by the rising and falling wave external to the tube or tank. An air turbine is placed in the air passage which drives an electric generator.

*Attenuators*

These devices are aligned parallel to the incident wave instead of at right angles to it as is the case with Terminators.

(5) *The Flexible Bag*

There are many bags containing air which are squeezed by the wave as it travels past. This air-circulation in properly-designed passages drives air turbines and electric generators.

(6) *Masuda Device*

This has the form of a ship open at the bottom and closed at the top, with many compartments underneath open to the sea. The rise and fall of water compresses or rarifies trapped air and this helps to drive air turbines and electric generators.

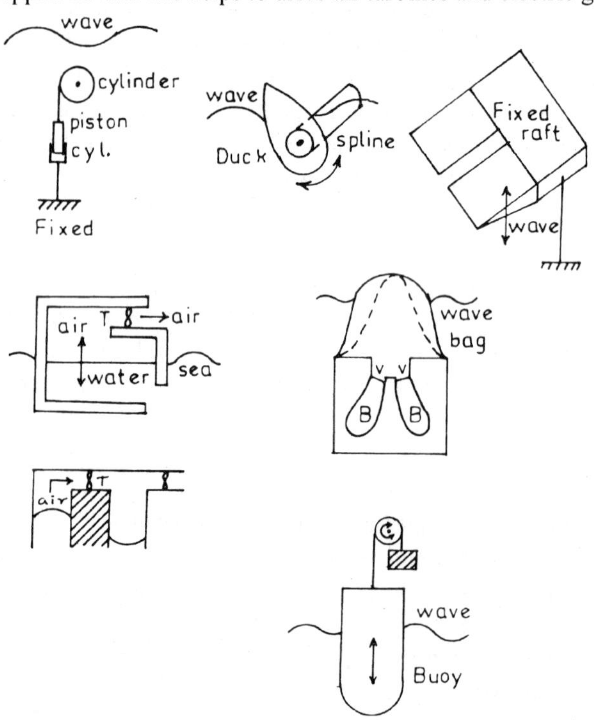


**Fig. 6.6** Seven types of wave-energy conversion schemes:
(a) Bristol cylinder; (b) Salter's ducks; (c) Cockerell's three-raft scheme;
(d) Oscillating water column; (e) Flexible bag; (f) Masuda device; (g) Buoy

*Point Absorbers*

(7) These consist of many small components with no connection between them. They move up and down vertically. This can take the shape of resonant air duct and absorbs the wave energy.

Figure 6.6 shows schematic diagrams of all the seven devices.

## 6.7 Properties of Waves and Power Content

As an introduction, a formula was given in the previous section, Eq. (6.5), from which the power in a wave-energy conversion device can be estimated. We will enlarge on this topic as well as dwell on significant properties of waves.

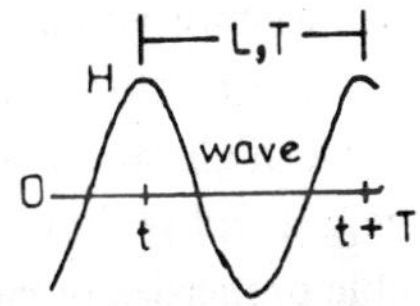


**Fig. 6.7** Wave motion

Waves are created in the open sea or near the shore line by the power in the wind. The kinetic energy is imparted to particles of water on the surface and results in change in potential energy which causes the particles of water to move up and down. When at maximum height above still water, the potential energy is maximum with value ($\rho\, g\, H_w$) per $m^3$. Due to gravity, the wave height decreases to still-water level, but because of inertia the water level decreases still further. When this happens, the potential energy is transferred to neighbouring particles, so that the water level increases and the wave crest moves to a new location. In open water, there exists no damping force, so that the wave travels or propagates as shown in Fig. 6.7. The wave length is $L = c\,T$, where $c$ = phase velocity and $T$ = periodic time. Note that by the time the particle of water at any location moves from crest through still-water level to trough, the second wave-crest has formed.

From the theory of potential flow pertaining to incompressible homogeneous fluids like sea water, the following properties are obtained (see Refs. 15 and 16 in Bibliography) with $d$ = depth of sea bed below still-water surface in metres.

$$\text{Phase velocity, } c = [(g\,L/2\,\pi)\cdot \tanh(2\,\pi\, d/L)]^{1/2}\text{, m/s} \tag{6.7}$$

where $L$ = wave length.

For infinite depth, $d \to \infty$, $\tanh(2\,\pi\, d/L) \to 1$, and the phase velocity becomes

$$c_\infty = (g\,L/2\,\pi)^{1/2} = 1.25\sqrt{L}\text{, m/s} \tag{6.8}$$

However, sea waves do not occur in singles because the wave generated at any one location consists of summation of an infinite number of small waves caused by a continuous flow of wind and so continuous transfer of potential energy to the water. The frequency of these multitude of waves is not constant, but they have their own amplitude-frequency spectrum. We therefore have to resort to the use of random variables and a group velocity.

Experimental results have indicated that the group velocity is

$$c_g = ½\, c\,[1 + (4\,\pi\, d/L)/\sin h\,(4\,\pi\, d/L)] \tag{6.9}$$

where $c$ = phase velocity given by Eq. (6.7).

In deep water, as $d \to \infty$, $x/\sinh x \to 0$ with $x = 4\,\pi\, d/L$.

Therefore
$$c_g = ½\, c_\infty \tag{6.10}$$

A typical record of wave height and time at an experimental station may look like Fig. 6.8. Such records are taken over a number of years continuously at 3-hour intervals typically, so that seasonal or monthly variations are determined. It is clear that during stormy months, waves can be expected to be highest. With such a random variation of height and period between crests, certain manageable properties or parameters must be defined. These are

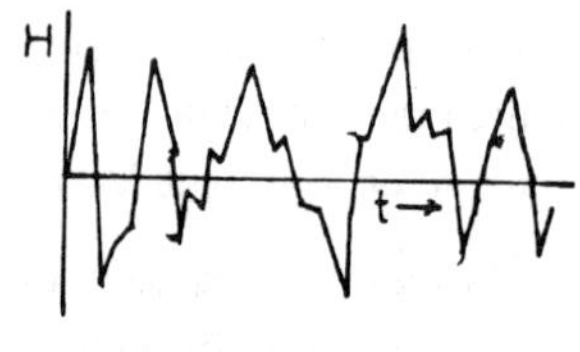


**Fig. 6.8** Wave height variation with time over a long period

(1) $$T_{zc} = \frac{\text{duration of long–time records in seconds}}{\text{number of times water level is at peak value}} \tag{6.11}$$

This is the average period of the wave or zero crossing time.

(2) Spectral density of energy, $S(f)$, denoting the energy within a unit bandwidth. Its unit is $m^2/Hz$. A typical spectral density plot is shown in Fig. 6.9.

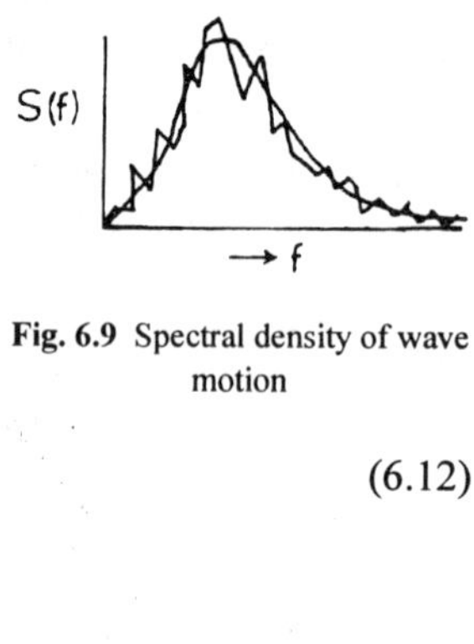


**Fig. 6.9** Spectral density of wave motion

(3) We denote by $S$ the height caused by summing the energy of all frequency components in the wave caused by the wind. This is in actuality the mean square height, thus

$$S^2 = \int_0^\infty S(f) \cdot df \tag{6.12}$$

(4) This is also called the 0-th moment

$$M_o = S^2 = \int_0^\infty S(f) \cdot df \tag{6.13}$$

where we define the nth moment as

$$M_n = \int_0^\infty f^n \cdot S(f) \cdot df \tag{6.14}$$

(5) The 'significant wave height' for evaluating the energy is defined as $H_w = 4\,S$, so that

$$H_w^2 = 16\,S^2 = 16\,M_o = 16\int_0^\infty S(f) \cdot df \tag{6.15}$$

(6) We also note that if $h_i$ is the measured wave height on instruments located in a buoy or other wave-rider platform, and $n$ such readings are taken in a time interval $\tau$, say one or two or more years at 3-hour intervals then the mean-square value is

$$S^2 = \frac{1}{n} \sum_{i=1}^{n} h_i^2 \tag{6.16}$$

(7) Since the sensitivity of instruments determine the accuracy of recorded observations, it is quite often the practice to select only those wave heights that fall between the maximum and two-thirds the maximum, i.e. only 33.3% of the highest recorded wave heights are chosen. This defines the significant height at one-third height as

$H_{1/3}$ = average height of the highest one-third of the waves

and $T_{1/3}$ = average period of these waves

(8) The zero-crossing time is then given from a large number of observations to be

$$T_{zc} = 1.12\, T_{1/3} \tag{6.17}$$

(9) In terms of $H_{1/3}$ and $T_{1/3}$, the equation for power potential in the wave per metre length is

$$P = (1.12/64\,\pi) \cdot \rho\, g^2\, H_{1/3}^2 \cdot T_{1/3}$$

$$= 550\, H_{1/3}^2 \cdot T_{1/3}\,, \text{ W/m} \tag{6.18}$$

In eq. (6.5), $T_w = T_{zc}$, so that in terms of the zero-crossing period, the power is, with $H_w = H_{1/3}$,

$$P = (1/64\,\pi) \cdot \rho\, g^2\, H_w^2\, T_w = 490.6\, H_w^2\, T_w\,, \text{ W/m} \tag{6.19}$$

(10) The group velocity is

$$c_g = g\, T_e/2\,\pi\,, \text{ m/s} \tag{6.20}$$

where $T_e = T_{1/3}$ and is called the energy period.

(11) In terms of the wind velocity, based on the theory of hydrodynamic potential theory of incompressible homogeneous fluids, it has been established that for infinite depth of sea

$$H_w^2 = 4.545 \times 10^{-4}\, V_w^4\,, \text{ m}^2 \tag{6.21}$$

and

$$T_w = 0.51862\, V_w\,, s \tag{6.22}$$

For example, if $H_w = 10$ m, $V_w = 21.66$ m/s ($\approx$ 50 mph) and $T_w = 11.23$ s. Here, $V_w$ = wind speed causing the wave in m/s. The decrease in wave height is accompanied by higher frequency.

(12) Therefore, in terms of wind speed $V_w$, the power is

$$P = 490.6 \times 4.545 \times 10^{-4} \times 0.51862\, V_w^5 = 0.11565\, V_w^5\,,\ \text{W/m} \quad (6.23)$$

Also $$H_w^2\, T_w = 4.545 \times 10^{-4} \times 0.51862\, V_w^5 = 2.357 \times 10^{-4}\, V_w^5\,,\ \text{m}^2\text{–s} \quad (6.24)$$

The potential power per metre varies as the 5th power of wind speed causing the wave.

(13) The spectral power density is given among other formulas by Pierson and Moskowitz as

$$S(f) = 5 \times 10^{-4} f^{-5}\, e^{-4.4/(f V_w)^4}\,,\ m^2/\text{Hz} \quad (6.25)$$

(14) Another formula by Gledenning is

$$S(f) = A f^{-5}\, e^{-B/f^4} \quad (6.26)$$

where $$A = H_w^2 / 4\pi T_w^2 \text{ and } B = 1/\pi T_w^4 \quad (6.27)$$

Comparing with Eq. (6.25), there results

$$T_w^4 = V_w^4 / 4.4\pi \text{ giving } T_w = 0.51862\, V_w \quad (6.28)$$

and $$H_w^2 = 5 \times 10^{-4} \times 4\pi T_w^4 = 4.545 \times 10^{-4}\, V_w^4 \quad (6.29)$$

***Example 6.4***: Referring to Fig. 6.9, the spectral density for square of wave height is given approximately by a triangle with maximum amplitude of 7.4 m$^2$/Hz within the frequency range 0.05 to 0.2 Hz. It is zero elsewhere. Calculate the significant wave height.

***Solution***: $S^2 = \int_0^\infty S(f) \cdot df = ½ \times 7.4 \times 0.15 = 0.555$

Therefore $S = 0.745$, and $H_w = 4S = 2.98$ m

***Example 6.5***: For the above example, the energy period is 10.75 s. Calculate the power potential per metre length of the wave.

***Solution***: $P = 490.6\, H_w^2\, T_e = 490.6 \times 2.98^2 \times 10.75$, W / m

$= 46.835$ kW / m

We observe that the peak of the spectral energy density is between 0.05 and 0.2 Hz, which corresponds to 5 to 20 s. The spectral density graph gives nearly all the information required to estimate the power content in the wave.

## 6.8 Vortex Motion of Waves

In addition to the vertical motion of the water particles, they are also subjected to rotatory motion causing a vortex. Once again, from hydrodynamic theory of incompressible homogeneous fluids, the particle motion in the ($x$-$y$) plane or horizontal plane is an ellipse, the dimensions (major and minor axes) decrease exponentially with depth from the free surface. If the water is infinitely deep, the motion becomes circular, as shown in Fig. 6.10.

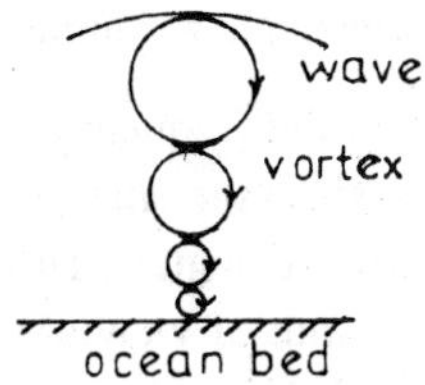

**Fig. 6.10** Vortex motion of water particle in wave motion from surface to sea bed

This type of motion results because of the boundary conditions, namely, that on the sea bed the particle velocity has to be zero while it follows the wind speed at the surface. With increasing depths, the hydrostatic pressure increases and Bernoulli's equation combined with potential-flow theory yields vortex motions with decreasing amplitudes. This can also be seen in everyday life, when in a bucketfull of water the surface experiences a force. This force is transmitted to the entire volume of water resulting in a swirling motion.

## 6.9 Device Descriptions and Applications

Schematic sketches of wave-energy conversion devices have been given in Fig. 6.6. The block diagram for conversion of wave energy into electrical energy eventually, and supplying customers is shown in Fig. 6.11. A typical frequency

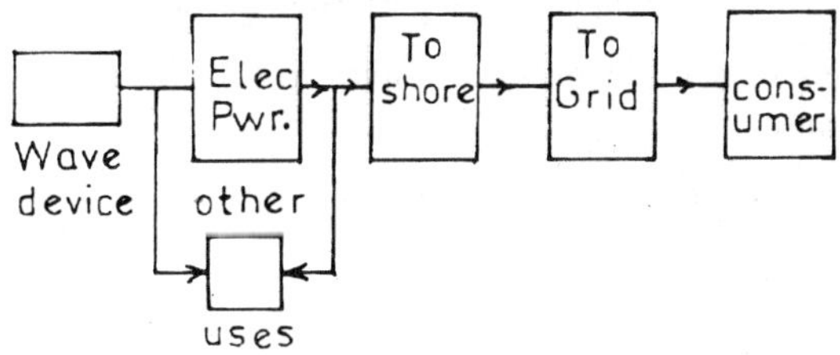

**Fig. 6.11** Block diagram of wave-energy conversion system

spectrum of spectral density for sea waves (wind sea) and swell waves are shown in Fig. 6.12. Waves at the device location arrive from distant sources. The lower frequency waves with their longer periods arrive before those of higher frequency, since the velocity is higher as given by Eqs. (6.7) and (6.9), where the wavelength $L$ is larger for lower frequency. The group velocity is given in general by

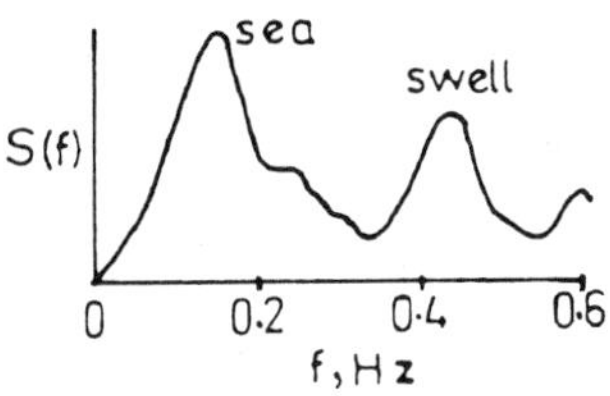

**Fig. 6.12** Frequency spectra of sea and swell waves

$$c_g = \tfrac{1}{2}\, c = g / 4\pi f \qquad (6.30)$$

where the phase velocity is $c = g/2\,\pi\,f$ (6.31)

(Note that $c.f$ is in m/s$^2$).

From the frequency spectrum, it is easy to distinguish between swell and sea waves, since the latter occur with high amplitude and low frequency. This is important from the design point of view of suitable devices, to convert the fluid-mechanical power in waves to other forms. This is done by properly assessing the "wave climate", which denotes the average kW/m available in each month. A typical "wave climate" plot looks like Fig. 6.13.

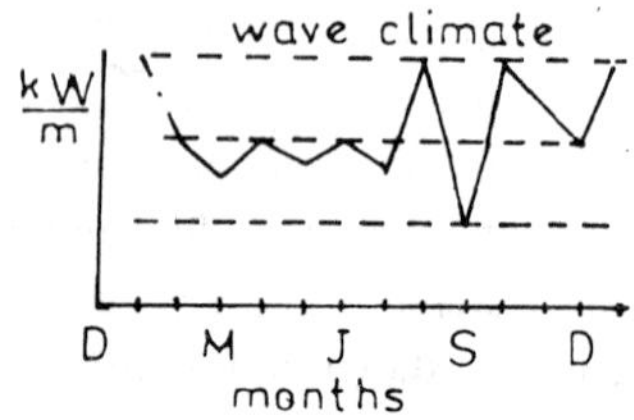


**Fig. 6.13** Wave climate over one year

Reference 2 has given a very extensive and clear description of many types of devices of five "generations", commencing with the historical wave-energy devices to the modern times. Some of these are listed here:

1. Three-raft system of Cockerell
2. Buoys with diaphgrams or air turbines
3. Masuda's ship with open bottom and closed top
4. Salter's nodding duck using gyroscope. (The gyroscope keeps the floating system stationary and does not require a fixed spine)
5. Oscillating water column (following Masuda's ship)
6. The rectifier which uses one-way valves to fill reservoir and use this in water turbines
7. Lancaster flexible bag
8. Bristol cylinder
9. Submerged resonant duct
10. Lanchester clam energy converter
11. Point absorbers of Norwegian origin

There are many more devices which have been patented. (Nearly 500 to date).

In order to utilize the energy in the wave for use at consumer location, electrical power can be generated at site and transmitted through cable to shore, preferably by dc, since ac cables for long lengths can cause reactive-power problems. The generated electricity at site can also be used for electrolysis of water, desalination, or manufacturing synthetic fuels. One of the most energy intensive products is extraction of uranium fuel from sea water. This is also one of the applications of Ocean Thermal Energy conversion Schemes described next.

## III. OCEAN THERMAL ENERGY CONVERSION SCHEMES

### 6.10 Introduction

In the tropical regions of the oceans the surface water is heated by the sun to not less than 20°C, while the ocean depths are nearly at 4°C. This temperature difference can be utilized for extracting energy. For practical purposes it is estimated that a temperature difference $\Delta T$ of at least 19°C is necessary from the economic and technological points of view. This is available near the equatorial regions. The total area of the oceans having this $\Delta T$ is estimated at $50 \times 10^6$ km$^2$, and the total available power per km$^2$ is estimated at 800 kW, and per m$^2$ it is 0.8 W or nearly 1 W. This represents an enormous amount of power equal to $40 \times 10^6$ MW = 40 TW. As mentioned earlier, the average measured power from the Sun available for photo-voltaic power generation at sea level is 107 mW/cm$^2$ $\approx$ 1 kW/m$^2$. However, power from the ocean is available continuously and utilizes known technology, unlike solar radiation as sunlight is intermittent.

In principle, a working fluid such as freon or ammonia is pumped at very high pressure of more than 10 atm into a heat-exchanger evaporator, where the warm surface water converts it to gaseous form. This is used for driving a turbine which exhausts into a condenser where the working medium is cooled by the ocean-depth cool water. The liquid is pumped back to the evaporator, thus forming a closed Rankine cycle. Other schemes utilize an open cycle, in which the working fluid is the sea water itself. We will discuss the details later on. Thus in theory, it is practicable to extract the energy inherent in the temperature difference between the warm surface water heated by the Sun and the cold ocean-depth water.

### 6.11 Types of OTEC Systems

There are basically two important types of Ocean Thermal Energy Conversion (OTEC) systems that have been studied. Prototype experimental models for only the closed cycle have been built and operated to date.

Figures 6.14 and 6.15 show block diagrams for the closed-cycle and open-cycle systems.

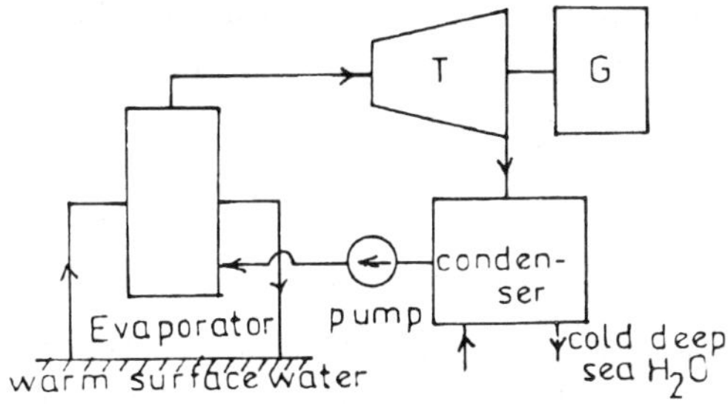


**Fig. 6.14** Block diagram of closed-cycle OTEC power generation scheme

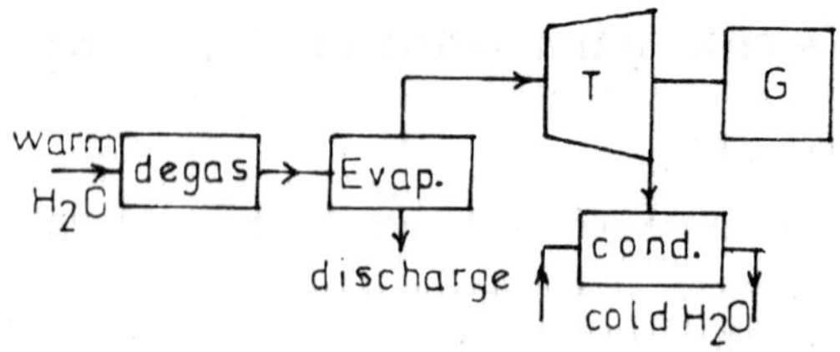


**Fig. 6.15** Block diagram of open-cycle OTEC scheme

*Closed-Cycle System*

The warm water at the surface between 22°C and 30°C is pumped into a heat exchanger, where the working fluid can be either freon or $NH_3$. Other working fluids considered are $SO_2$, propane, isobutane and methyl alcohol. At the exhaust of the turbine, cold sea water from depths of 1 km is pumped into a condenser at temperature between 8 and 4°C. This gives a theoretical Carnot efficiency between 70 and 80%. However, the efficiency of such OTEC projects rarely exceeds 15% in practice, since most of the generated power is used in driving house-service pumps.

*Open Cycle System*

Sea water itself is used as the working fluid which is first de-gassed and then flash evaporated in vacuum, so that the turbine uses de-salinated steam at low pressure. A turbine for generating 100 MW (which is a usual output in a land power station) is estimated to have a diameter of 60 m.

OTEC plants may be shore based or tower-mounted in the open sea or floating offshore. A fourth type is called 'grazing', which moves freely in the open ocean to obtain maximum possible $\Delta T$. These can operate hundreds or thousands of kilometres from shore and be on a constant move if necessary.

## 6.12 Application of OTEC Systems

Primarily, an OTEC system is used for generating electric power. For economically viable systems, the power range is estimated to be between 200 MW and 400 MW. This power can be used for various applications. These are as follows:

(a) By desalination of sea water it is estimated that 3 million litres of fresh water can be won per MW of input electric power. One scheme uses salt water sprayed on heated pans.

(b) The desalinated water can be electrolyzed to obtain $H_2$ and $O_2$ which can be further utilized for many processes. One use is production of $NH_3$ itself for the working fluid from a portion of the power, like a breeder process.

(c) $CO_2$ from sea water can be converted to methanol fuel. Other types of synthetic fuels can also be made on site, but this requires shipping carbon-containing compounds (coal or limestone) to the OTEC platform.

(d) The cold deep-sea water used for cooling is rich in nitrogen and phosphorous. This water can be used for breeding oysters, clams and other shell fish varieties. These can also convert organic material into proteins.

(e) The electric power can be used, as in wave-energy schemes, to win uranium from the sea water.

## 6.13 Examples of OTEC Systems Studied to the Present

We will describe some quantitative studies carried out to date and computer projections of possible future OTEC schemes based on results and theoretical predictions of existing projects.

A team of scientists from Japan established a 100 kW unit on the equator in the Pacific using freon at 10.6 atm (abs). Some relevant details are as follows:

*Working Medium*: Freon-22 at 25°C, 74 ton/hr, 1 $m^3$/min

*Warm Surface Water*: Inlet temperature 29.8°C into the evaporator 1450 ton/hr; Pump uses 28 kW.

*Cold Ocean-Depth Water*: Inlet temperature to condenser = 8.1°C, 1410 ton/hr, Pump uses 43 kW. Height of pumping = 700 m. Intake pipe: Polyethylene 700 mm diameter, Thickness of wall: 30-35 mm.

*Output power*: 100 kW

*Total Inhouse Power* consumed for services: 85 kW

*Efficiency*: 15%

Based on their studies they have proposed a 2500 kW commercial plant with the following details:

*Working Medium*: Freon-22 at 25°C, 1350 ton/hr, 18 $m^3$/min

*Warm Surface Water*: 29.8°C, 27,000 ton/hr, 440 $m^3$/min

*Cold water*: 6.3°C, 26,000 ton/hr, height 700 m, Polyethylene intake pipe 2.1 m diameter. Two in number.

*Output Power*: 2,500 kW

*Inhouse Power*: 50% of output power

As another example of a very large scheme studied in the USA, the following details are given:

*Output Power*: 15 MW gross, 10.5 MW net

*Sea Water Temperatures*: Warm: 26.7°C; Cold: 4.4°C.

*Water Flow Rates*: Evaporator: 34 ton/s;
Condenser: 31.5 ton/s (1 ton = 2240 lb)

*Working Fluid*: Ammonia; Evaporator: 21°C; Condenser: 10°C
Flow rate: 800 lb/s (363 kg/s)

*Evaporator*: Titanium; 24,167 sq.m

*Condenser*: Titanium; 27,420 sq.m

Materials considered for heat exchangers are titanium, stainless steel, copper-nickel alloys and aluminium alloys. Cold water pipe is the most critical of all components. It may be as enormous as 20-30 m in diameter. Pipe materials considered are steel, polyethylene, and fibre-reinforced plastic. Concrete has not been found suitable.

OTEC plants are environmentally very clean with no waste products, and do not cause pollution.

## OBJECTIVE TYPE QUESTIONS

1. Tides are caused by: (a) gravitational effects of sun and moon; (b) centrifugal forces due to earth's rotation; (c) flow of water from polar to equatorial regions; (d) all three are true.
2. Tidal cycles at any location have a periodic time of: (a) 24 hr; (b) 24 hr 50 min; (c) 6 hr 12.5 min; (d) 12 hr 25 min.
3. Spring tides occur at: (a) full-moon days; (b) new-moon days; (c) first quarter; (d) last quarter; (e) both (a) and (b) are true.
4. Neap tides occur at: (a) full-moon days; (b) new-moon days; (c) first quarter; (d) last quarter; (e) both (c) and (d) are true.
5. Spring tides are higher than neap tides. (a) true, or (b) false.
6. Ebb tides and low tides have a time interval between them of: (a) 24 hr; (b) 24 hr 50 min; (c) 6 hr 12.5 min; (d) 12 hr 25 min.
7. Water from tides is stored during the time of: (a) spring tide; (b) neap tide; (c) ebb tide; (d) all are true.
8. Ebb generation means generating electric power when: (a) Tide is rising and filling the reservoir; (b) Tide is falling and reservoir water is flowing to the bay; (c) Both when tide is rising and falling; (d) none of the three.
9. Flood generation means generating power when: (a) Tide is rising; (b) Tide is falling; (c) Both when tide is rising or falling; (d) none of the three.
10. A turbine-generator unit can be operated as: (a) turbine-motor unit; (b) pump-motor unit; (c) pump-generator unit; (d) none of the three, since a turbine must always operate as turbine and generator as generator.

11. The disadvantage of two-way generation is: (a) turbine must handle water both ways in opposite directions; (b) efficiency is lower than one-way generation; (c) energy output is 10-15% less than for one-way ebb generation; (d) all are true.

12. Two-basin systems: (a) use pump-motors for filling one basin while power is developed at the other; (b) require more water-storage area than single-basin schemes; (c) follow generation schedules more closely with load requirements; (d) all are true.

13. The power output of a hydraulic generation scheme is: (a) $P_0 = \rho\ q/gh$; (b) $P_0 = \eta\rho\ q/gh$; (c) $P_0 = \eta\rho\ q\ g\ h$; (d) none of the three.
[$\eta$ = efficiency of turbine-generator unit, $\rho$= density of water, $g$ = acceleration due to gravity, $h$ = hydraulic head, $q$ = quantity of water flow].

14. The maximum head in a scheme is 12 m and minimum 3 m, falling linearly. The quantity of flow is constant at 300 $m^3/s$. How much energy is developed by the turbine in one tidal cycle of operation of 6.25 hr? Assume turbine efficiency $\eta$ = 95%. (a) 300 kW-h; (b) 981 kW-h; (c) 134 kW-h; (d) 1 MW-h.

15. Turbines used or planned for tidal power stations can be: (a) Vertical axis Kaplan turbine; (b) Straflow with conventional ac generator; (c) Bulb turbine with vertical shaft; (d) none of the three.

16. Wave generating schemes are classified as: (a) Point absorbers; (b) Terminators; (c) Attenuators; (d) all three.

17. Taking $H_{1/3}$ as average height of highest 33.3% of waves, and $t_{1/3}$ as average period of these waves, the power potential in watts for unit length (metre) is: (a) $P = 550\ H\ t$; (b) $490.6\ H^2\ t$; (c) $550\ H^2\ t$; (d) none of the three.

18. For an infinite length of sea, which statement is most nearly correct? (a) Height of wave = $2.132 \times 10^{-2}\ V_w^2$; ($V_w$ = wind velocity in m/s); (b) Period of wave = $0.51862\ V_w$; (c) Power potential per metre length of wave = $0.11565\ V_w^5$, $W$; (d) all three are true.

19. Sea waves (a) occur with high amplitudes; (b) have low frequency, (c) originate in the open sea, (d) all three are true.

20. Wave energy can be used for: (a) Electric power generation; (b) desalination; (c) production of synthetic fuels from raw materials; (d) extraction of uranium; (e) all of these and many more.

21. An OTEC system uses: (a) evaporator; (b) turbine; (c) generator; (d) condenser; (e) all the four.

22. The working fluid in an OTEC system can be: (a) steam; (b) ammonia; (c) refrigeration fluid; (d) liquid sodium; (e) all except (d).

23. The Salter Duck system has: (a) a flat platform to which are hinged two smaller flaps to nod like ducks; (b) a buoy which bobs up and down like a duck; (c) air bags which get compressed and expanded; (d) none of the three.

24. The efficiency of an OTEC system is nearly: (a) 50%; (b) 15%; (c) 5%; (d) 30%.

25. Cold deep-sea water can be used for: (a) breeding shell fish; (b) convert organic materials into proteins; (c) cooling water in condenser; (d) all the three purposes.

[*Answers*: 1. (d); 2. (d); 3. (e); 4. (e); 5. (a); 6. (c); 7. (d); 8. (b); 9. (a); 10. (b); 11. (d); 12. (d); 13. (c); 14. (c); 15. (d); 16. (d); 17. (c); 18. (d); 19. (d); 20. (e); 21. (e); 22. (e); 23. (d); 24. (b); 25. (d)]

## REVIEW QUESTIONS AND PROBLEMS

1. The average radius of the earth is 6400 km. Calculate: (a) its volume; (b) surface area; (c) Taking 71% of the surface as oceans, find the surface area of the oceans and land. (d) Water on the earth's surface is divided as follows by volume in $10^6$ km$^3$: Oceans - 1370, Ice caps and glaciers - 29, Ground water - 9.5; Lakes - 0.125, Soil moisture - 0.065, Atmosphere - 0.013, Rivers - 0.0017, Biosphere - 0.0006. Calculate them as percentages of total volume of water on earth. (e) Calculate the centrifugal force on 1 m$^3$ of water at the equator. Density of sea water = 1025 kg/m$^3$.

[*Answers*: (a) $1.1 \times 10^{12}$ km$^3$; (b) $510 \times 10^6$ km$^2$; (c) $362 \times 10^6$, $148 \times 10^6$; (d) 97.25, 2.05, 0.68, $10^{-2}$, $5 \times 10^{-3}$, $1 \times 10^{-3}$, $1 \times 10^{-4}$, $0.4 \times 10^{-4}$; (e) $m\,\omega^2\,r = 34.692$ Newton]

2. Describe the following schemes for tidal generation, with suitable figures: (a) Ebb generation; (b) Flood generation; (c) Two-way generation; (d) Single-basin scheme; (e) Two-basin scheme.

3. (a) Describe the difference between spring tides, neap tides, high tide, and low tide.

   (b) Discuss the possible reasons why energy output in double-effect generation is usually lower than for single-effect generation.

4. (a) Derive Eq. (6.2) for generator output in a hydraulic generation scheme.

   (b) A tidal power development has total installed generation of 7500 MW operating at a maximum head of 8 m. The minimum head at the end of cycle of generation is 2.5 m after 5 hours. Assume two cycles of generation in 24 hr. The generated power decreases linearly from 7500 MW to zero. The turbine and generator have efficiencies of 93% and 97%, respectively. The length of embankment is 20 km. Calculate:

(a) Quantity of water flowing through the turbines at maximum output in $m^3/s$. $(0.10443 \times 10^6\ m^3/s)$

(b) Surface area of reservoir in $km^2$. $(306\ km^2)$

(c) Wash behind the embankment at maximum reservoir capacity. (15.3 km)

(d) Energy delivered per year at a load factor of 0.8. (21.9 TW-h)

5. (a) Describe some schemes used for storing electrical power generated by tidal power stations for re-use later.

   (b) In spite of the attractiveness of tidal power generation, discuss why tidal schemes are not being developed in the world as fast as one would like to talk about them. Compare nuclear power, as an example.

6. Draw figures showing layout of tidal schemes with: (a) Vertical axis Kaplan turbine; (b) Bulb turbine with horizontal shaft; (c) Straflow turbine with rim generator.

7. (a) Describe the difference, if any, between the one-third height $H_{1/3}$ and wave height $H_w$, used for estimating power potential in a wave.

   (b) Using Eqs. (6.17) through (6.19), derive a relation between $H_{1/3}$ and $H_w$.

   (c) Discuss why $H_{1/3}$ is important for estimating the potential power per metre of wave and not all the measured wave heights.

8. The wind speed at a location is $V_w = 20$ m/s. Calculate: (a) the wave height $H_w$; (b) the wave period $T_w$; (c) power in W/m in the wave. (d) Using eqs. (6.21) and (6.22), find the relation between $T_w$ and $H_w$.
[(a) $H_w = 8.5276$ m; (b) $T_w = 10.372$ s;
(c) $P = 370$ kW/m; (d) $T_w = 3.552\sqrt{H_w}$]

9. Describe the principle of operation of the following wave-energy conversion systems and devices: (a) Salter's nodding duck; (b) Cockerell's three-raft system; (c) Oscillating water column.

10. The temperature difference between ocean surface water and deep-sea water is 20°C at a location. Estimate the thermal energy available in the water per $m^3$ in calories, Joules, and kW-h. Assume a linear temperature gradient. (Av. temp. = 10°C. Energy = $10.25 \times 10^6$ cal = $42.9 \times 10^6$ J $\approx 12$ kW-h).

11. Describe the working of a closed cycle OTEC system using $NH_3$ as the working fluid.
12. Describe *four* applications for which OTEC systems can be utilized. Why are OTEC systems not yet in operation in the world's oceans for commercial power generation?

CHAPTER 7

# Fossil Fuel Power Generation

## 7.1 Introduction

Fossil fuels used for generation of electric power include (a) coal; (b) oil; (c) natural gas; and (d) synthetic derivatives. The machinery used are steam turbines, gas turbines and reciprocating engines. In steam stations, which belong to the largest capacities in existence, a high-pressure boiler forms the heart of the operation. An idea of the capabilities of the largest design for a single unit is given below:

*Boiler-Turbine-Generator*

*Generator*: 960 MVA, 0.9 p.f. (lag), 3-phase, 60 Hz, 3600 rev/min, 26 kV, conductor cooled, 0.5 short-circuit radio, maximum hydrogen pressure 75 psig.

*Exciter*: 2910 kW, 510 V, soild-state control.

*Turbine*: 2400 psig, 1000° F, 3600 rev/min, tandem-compound, reheat to 1000°F, last stage buckets 0.851 m (33.5") height. Condenser 38.1 mm-Hg absolute exhaust pressure. Feedwater heated 7 times.

*Steam Generator*: Single reheat of steam. At the superheater, outlet steam has 2640 psig and 1007°F. Normal feedwater temperature 496°F. Flow rate at continuous load $6.15 \times 10^6$ lb/hr.

*Fuel*: Sub-bituminous coal. Heating value 10,000 Btu/lb.

*Cooling Water*: $334 \times 10^3$ gallon/min.

An example of a large modern gas turbine is given below.

*Generator output*: 100 MW; *Turbine-generator efficiency*: 33%

*Turbine heat rate*: 10,880 kJ/kW-h (1 kW-h = 3600 kJ)

*Inlet and Exhaust Temperatures*: 1040°C and 540°C

*Pressure Compression ratio*: 10.6

*Fuel Flow*: $5 \times 10^4$ lb/hr (6.24 kg/s)

*Exhaust Flow*: 355 kg/s (Air/Fuel ratio = 56/1)

From a look at the specifications of the boiler-turbine-generator unit, we can formulate the sequence of operations from the cold water stage to the turbine exhaust stage. This is called the ''power extraction process''.

(a) Clean feedwater from a source (river or lake) in addition to the condensed steam in the condenser is pumped into the boiler or steam generator. During the passage, the water is warmed in heat exchangers which use hot steam tapped from intermediate turbine stages between the high-pressure (H.P. or h.p.) first stage and the low-pressure (L.P. or l.p.) last stage. There could be as many as seven such heat exchangers in a very large unit such as a 800 MW turbine.

(b) The heated water is converted to steam in the boiler which can be fired by coal, oil, or natural gas, or synthetic fuels. The steam leaving the boiler is free from water vapour, which is obtained by a steam separator in addition to heating the dry saturated steam to high temperatures, say, 1000°F (538°C).

(c) The dry steam runs the H.P. turbine stage. In large units, the steam is brought back to the boiler for reheating to the original temperature of say 1000°F using the heat of the gases at the boiler exhaust or radiated heat from the flame underneath the water.

(d) The reheated steam is taken back to the next stage, which is usually the intermediate stage (I.P. or i.p.). No further reheating is normally carried out, but there may be exceptions.

(e) The turbine usually has an impulse stage at the front and reaction stages at the back. The impulse stage is necessary to reduce the steam pressure, as we will observe later on. Most of the energy from steam to mechanical motion is converted in the reaction stages. These two are known as ''velocity-compounding'' and ''reaction compounding''. The turbine is then known as tandem compounded.

(f) At the exhaust from the last stage the steam with 10-12% water vapour flows or is sucked into a condenser which operates at vacuum pressures (less than atmospheric) of 25 to 75 mm-Hg. Here, cooling water heat-exchanger condenses the steam into water at 10 to 40°C depending on the vacuum. The heat in the exhaust steam which condenses could amount to 40% of the total heat in steam at the entrance to the H.P. stage, which cannot be recovered and is thus lost.

(g) The feedwater from the condenser is then pumped back to the boiler as in Step (a). The cycle is now complete.

Figures 7.1 (a) to (c) show typical cycles of operation for feedwater heating and steam heating. It is clear that in addition to availability of fuel, enormous amount of fresh water is necessary as well as land for the operation of a fossil-fueled generating station.

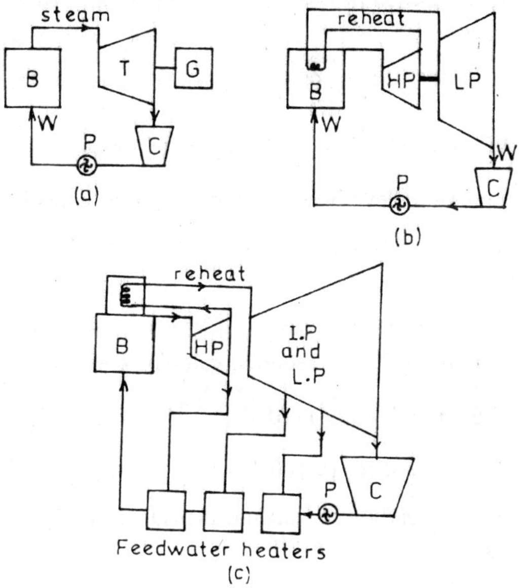


**Fig. 7.1** Steam plant block diagrams: (a) Without reheat of steam; (b) With one reheat cycle; (c) Multiple reheat cycle

Table 7.1 gives the variation of boiling temperature of water with pressure, and Table 7.2 the temperature of steam corresponding to vacuum pressures in the condenser. The following units are used while dealing with steam: 1 atm absolute (ata) = 1 kg/cm$^2$ = 736 mm-Hg = 14.226 psia. 760 mm-Hg = 1.03 ata. 1 kg/cm$^2$ = $10^4$ kg/m$^2$ = $9.81 \times 10^4$ N/m$^2$ or Pa = 0.981 bar. 1 bar = 0.1013 MPa.

**Table 7.1 Boiling Temperature of Water with Pressure**

| *ata* | 1.03 | 5 | 10 | 20 | 40 | 60 | 80 | 100 | 150 | 200 |
|---|---|---|---|---|---|---|---|---|---|---|
| *psia* | 14.65 | 71.1 | 142.26 | 284.5 | 569 | 853.6 | 1138 | 1422.6 | 2134 | 2845.2 |
| $T_b$, °C | 100 | 151 | 179 | 211 | 249 | 274 | 293 | 309 | 341 | 364 |
| $T_b$, °F | 212 | 304 | 354.2 | 412 | 480 | 525.2 | 559.4 | 588.2 | 646 | 687.2 |

**Table 7.2 Temperature of Condensed Steam in Condenser at Vacuum**

| $P_c$, *ata* | 0.01 | 0.02 | 0.03 | 0.05 | 0.1 | 0.15 | 0.25 | 0.5 |
|---|---|---|---|---|---|---|---|---|
| $P_c$, *mm-Hg* | 7.4 | 14.7 | 22.1 | 36.8 | 73.6 | 110.3 | 184 | 368 |
| $T_s$, °C | 6.7 | 17.2 | 23.8 | 32.6 | 45.4 | 53.6 | 64.6 | 80.9 |

***Example 7.1***: Feedwater enters a boiler at 500°F (260°C). If the water is not to boil in the feedwater line, calculate the minimum pressure of the pump which operates between condenser and boiler.

***Solution***: At 40 ata, $T_b$ = 249°C, and at 60 ata $T_b$ = 274°C. Therefore the minimum pressure required lies between 40 and 60 ata. By linear interpolation, required pressure is

$$P_{fw} = 40 + (60 - 40) \cdot (260 - 249) / (274 - 249) = 48.8 \text{ ata}$$

$$= 48.8 \text{ kg/cm}^2 = 4.7873 \text{ MPa} = 694 \text{ psia}$$

Note that the pressure developed by pump has to be considerable.

***Example 7.2***: The vacuum in a condenser is 0.07 ata. Calculate the temperature of the condensed steam.

***Solution***: At a pressure of 0.05 ata, $T_s$ = 32.6°C, and at 0.1 ata, $T_s$ = 45.4°C. Therefore by linear interpolation, required value of $T_s$ is

$$= 32.6 + (45.4 - 32.6) \cdot (0.07 - 0.05) / (0.1 - 0.05) = 32.6 + 5.12$$

$$= 37.72°\text{C} \approx 38°C \ (\approx 100°\text{F})$$

***Example 7.3***: Corresponding to vacuum pressures of 25, 50, and 75 mm-Hg, calculate ata, psia.

| ***Solution***: | | | | | |
|---|---|---|---|---|---|
| | *Pc* | = | *25 mm-Hg* | *50 mm-Hg* | *75 mm-Hg* |
| | *ata* | = | 25/736 = 0.034 | 0.068 | 0.102 |
| | *psia* | = | 0.034 × 14.226 = 0.4837 | 0.9674 | 1.451 |

Since the entire operation of the system depends upon properties of steam, we will take up a discussion of these separately later on.

Most, if not all, large steam turbines are of the reaction type. Details of working of a turbine are dealt with in the next section. The cycle of operation from condenser-boiler-turbine-condenser involves heat additions and losses. The ideal cycle in such heat machinery is called the Carnot cycle. However, because of change of state or phase of the working medium, the actual cycle is known as the Rankine cycle. We will deal with these in Sec. 7.3. In a gas turbine, the gas does not change its character from inlet to exhaust and the cycle is known as the Brayton cycle.

## 7.2 Principles of Impulse and Reaction Steam Turbines

The quantities involved in extracting power from high-pressure steam are mainly the following:

(a) Total heat or enthalpy, also called internal heat, *i*;

(b) Temperature $T$, entropy $S$, pressure of steam $P$, and volume $V$;
$i = T \times S + P \times V$

(c) Velocity of steam entering and exiting the turbine blades, both stationary and moving.

(d) Rotor speed or velocity of runner blade.

The energy extracted from steam with given entrance conditions and exit conditions can be utilized to yield maximum efficiency under the severe thermal and mechanical constraints by arranging the turbine internal structure suitably. The extraction of energy and converting to useful rotary form can take place in two most important ways, and the turbines or turbine stages are known as (a) Impulse Turbine, and (b) Reaction Turbine.

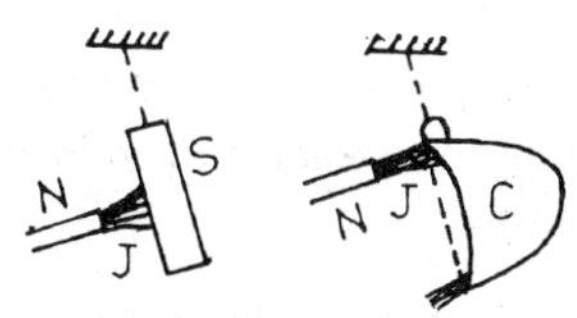

**Fig. 7.2** Principles of impulse and reaction turbines. Saucer and cup model

The difference in concepts can be very simply explained by the well-known cup-and-saucer experiment. Figure 7.2 shows these two. If a jet of fluid from a nozzle is directed to the centre of a suspended flat saucer, it will deflect by absorbing the full force in the jet. The energy of water issuing from the nozzle at velocity $v\ (= \frac{1}{2} m\, v^2)$ is arrested instantaneously, which is imparted to the flat saucer to move it. The velocity of fluid distributed or scattered after impact is zero. Both the pressure and velocity change, and this gives an impulse to the flat saucer.

On the other hand, as in Fig. 7.2(b), if the jet is directed towards one side of the curved cup, there is a continuous loss of pressure and velocity as the fluid flows along the curvature of the cup. Due to the reaction of fluid on the cup, the cup will experience a deflection, or in other words there is a gradual but continuous exchange of energy from the jet to the cup. The velocity of fluid at exit will be low and even zero. It is clear that whether the energy exchange is in impulse form or a continuous reaction depends upon the shape of the object on which the jet is impinging. In steam turbines, the following essential mechanisms occur between the steam, its passage and the blade profiles.

*Impulse Turbine*

Figure 7.3 shows the shape and arrangement of fixed and movable blades, called the nozzle and runner. There are two stages: (a) Velocity stage or compounding; and (b) Pressure stage or compounding. Steam at high pressure is expanded to final low pressure in the nozzle of the stationary part. Due to this pressure drop, the potential energy is converted to kinetic energy, since there is no motion or losses. This increases the steam velocity. In the rotor blade the pressure is constant, but due to the conversion of energy into the motion of the rotor, the energy and hence the steam velocity decreases. The difference between initial and final kinetic energies comes out as mechanical motion of rotor and hence useful work for power generation.

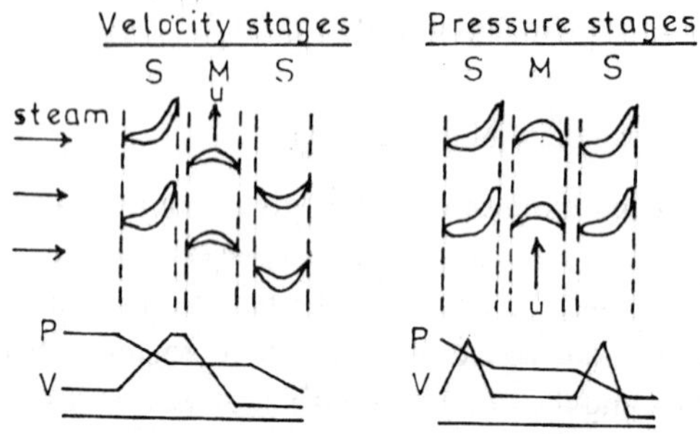


**Fig. 7.3** Impulse turbine blading: Velocity and pressure stages

In the pressure stage, the blades are so shaped that while there exists a pressure drop as the steam moves in the nozzles, its velocity first increases and then decreases.

Such compounding is found necessary in order to make the turbine operate at maximum or optimum efficiency, as also to keep the speed in manageable limits. If the velocity stage is not provided, the runner might have to run at 10,000 rev/min if not restrained within limits. Note that the pressure conversion occurs only in the fixed blades.

*Reaction Turbine*

Figure 7.4 shows the general blade profiles for the stationary and moving parts. In front of the reaction stages there is a velocity stage. In this stage pressure drop is continuous as the steam flows on the movable blade, but stays constant along the stationary nozzle blades. On the other hand, the velocity increases as the pressure drops and on account of mechanical energy generated the exit velocity is lower than maximum.

The shape of blades in the reaction part is different, so as to yield a velocity drop in the movable blades, thereby transforming the kinetic energy of steam to

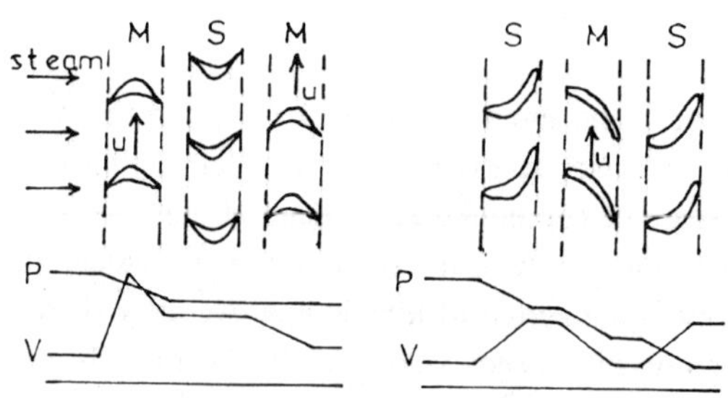


**Fig. 7.4** Reaction turbine blading: Velocity and reaction stages

mechanical motion of rotor. The pressure drop occurs both in the fixed and movable blades as shown in the reaction turbine.

*Energy Transfer*

Figure 7.5 shows a turbine blade moving at velocity **u** in the tangential direction. The inlet and exit velocities of the steam following the contour of the blade tips are $\mathbf{W}_i$ and $\mathbf{W}_e$, respectively. The actual steam velocities at the two ends will be, as in Fig. 7.5, given by

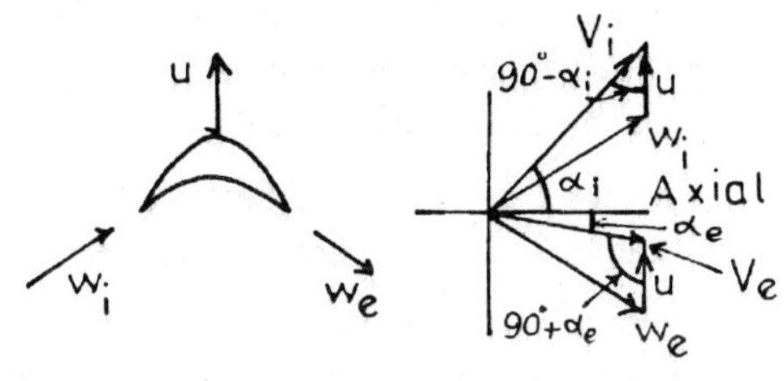


**Fig. 7.5** Velocity details of input steam, blade velocity and exit steam

$$\mathbf{V}_i = \mathbf{W}_i + \mathbf{u}, \text{ and } \mathbf{V}_e = \mathbf{W}_e + \mathbf{u} \tag{7.1}$$

We denote by $\alpha_i$ and $\alpha_e$ the angles of steam at the inlet and exit from the axial direction of the turbine. Then the mechanical energy involved per unit weight of steam will be

$$E_m = u \cdot V_i \cdot \sin \alpha_i + u \cdot V_e \cdot \sin \alpha_e \tag{7.2}$$

where we take $\alpha_e$ to be negative and $\alpha_i$ to be positive, according to usual convention for angles. From the triangles, there result

$$W_i^2 = V_i^2 + u^2 - 2\,u \cdot V_i \cdot \sin \alpha_i, \text{ and } W_e^2 = V_e^2 + u^2 + 2\,u \cdot V_e \cdot \sin \alpha_e \tag{7.3}$$

Therefore $\quad E_m = \frac{1}{2}\,[\,(V_i^2 + u^2 - W_i^2) + (W_e^2 - V_e^2 - u^2)\,]$

$$= \tfrac{1}{2}\,[\,(V_i^2 - V_e^2) - (W_i^2 - W_e^2)\,] \tag{7.4}$$

In the turbine it is so arranged that the velocities $W_i$ and $W_e$ have equal magnitudes, and $V_e$ is minimum ($\alpha_e = 0$), so that it is all in the axial direction for maximum energy transfer. Under these conditions, the energy transferred is

$$E_m = \tfrac{1}{2}\,(V_i^2 - V_e^2) \tag{7.5}$$

This shows that the energy transferred as mechanical motion is equal to the difference in kinetic energies in steam at the inlet and outlet per unit weight.

## 7.3 Carnot and Rankine Cycles

Most turbo machines operate in the Rankine cycle or Brayton cycle. The former applies to steam-turbine operation, while the Brayton cycle applies to gas turbines. The major difference between the two lies in the property that in the Rankine cycle the phase of the working medium changes from the inlet to the outlet, being dry steam at the boiler exit to wet water at the condenser. On the other hand, in a gas turbine the working medium is gas at both the inlet and outlet ends of the turbine.

Considering an ideal turbo machine we observe four stages as shown in Fig. 7.6 on a temperature-entropy ($T-S$) diagram. The operation is as follows:

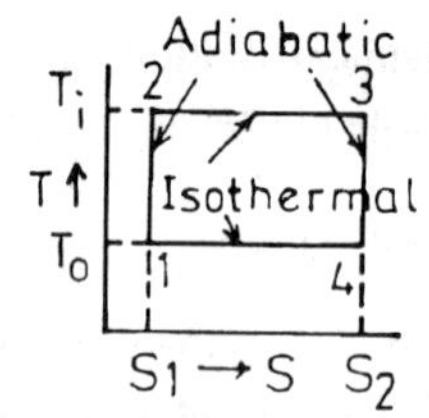


**Fig. 7.6** Carnot cycle

*Process 1-2*: The working medium is compressed to raise its temperature from $T_o$ to $T_i$ at constant entropy and is adiabatic.

*Process 2-3*: Additional heat is given at temperature $T_i$ and is an isothermal process. Total heat is $i_3$.

*Process 3-4*: The working medium expands and its heat as well as temperature decrease at constant entropy. Heat still retained is $i_4$.

*Process 4-1*: The working medium condenses at constant temperature and loses heat as an isothermal process. For steam this is the latent heat in it.

The mechanical work converted by the ideal turbine is $(i_3 - i_4)$, while the heat added is $(i_3 - i_1)$. The Carnot thermal efficiency is

$$\eta_{ic} = (i_3 - i_4)/(i_3 - i_1) = (T_i S_2 - T_o S_2)/(T_i S_2 - T_o S_1) \qquad (7.6)$$

If the ideal machine has $S_1 = 0$, then the ideal Carnot efficiency becomes

$$\eta_{ic} = (T_i - T_o)/T_i \qquad (7.7)$$

The Rankine cycle applies to a steam turbine for which the $T-S$ diagram belongs to steam and water. (See Fig. 7.14 in Appendix to this chapter). This is shown in Fig. 7.7, when the steam is not reheated, i.e. there is no bleeding after the first H.P. stage. Heat is added to water with initial heat $i_w$ until it is converted to saturated steam at temperature $T_i$ which is mostly the latent heat of evaporation at the constant temperature $T_i$ and the heat required to raise temperature of water from $T_o$ to $T_i$. The total heat in steam is $i_1$, which may also consist of any heat added to superheat the steam. It then expands in the turbine until its heat falls to $i_2$, where it is still in vapour form. Then it loses further heat in the condenser to become water at the same temperature $T_o$. The latent heat lost is $(i_2 - i_w)$ in the condenser, which cannot be recovered. Superheating of steam is necessary in order to avoid excessive wetness in steam in the last L.P. stages. This also increases the efficiency as will be observed later on. Unlike in Carnot cycle, the increase of pressure and temperature from $T_o$ to $T_i$ is not adiabatic but takes place with increase in entropy.

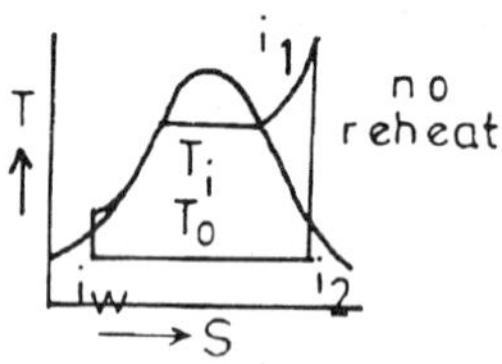


**Fig. 7.7** Rankine cycle with no reheat

The theoretical Rankine thermal efficiency is

$$\eta_R = \text{energy output/energy input} = (i_1 - i_2)/(i_1 - i_w) \qquad (7.8)$$

Figure 7.8 shows the *T-S* diagram of the complete Rankine cycle with one reheat.

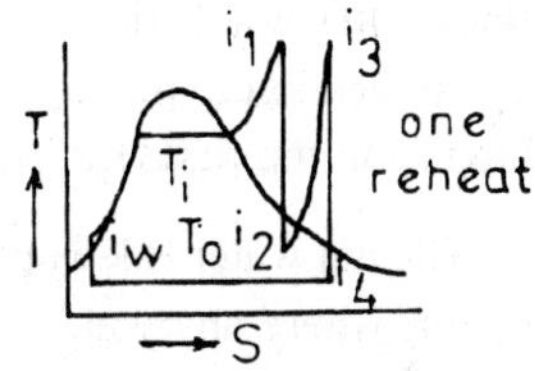


**Fig. 7.8** Rankine cycle with one reheat

***Example 7.4***: High pressure dry saturated steam issues from a boiler at 700°F (371°C) at 500 psia (35.147 ata). Find the degree of superheating of the dry steam using Table 7.1.

***Solution***: Using linear interpolation we obtain, since temperature of dry steam at 20 ata = 211°C and at 40 ata = 249°C, temperature at 35.147 ata is

$$211 + (249 - 211) \cdot (35.147 - 20)/(40 - 20) = 239.8°C \approx 240°C = 464°F$$

Therefore degree of superheat = 371 – 240 = 131°C (700 – 464 = 236°F).

Steam tables given in appendix give the temperature of dry saturated steam at 500 psia as 467°F.

***Example 7.5***: The above steam condenses at a vacuum of 1 psia. The total heat in superheated dry steam at 500 psia and 700°F is 1357 Btu/lb. At 50 mm-Hg (≈ 1 psia) temperature of water is 38°C = 100.4°F. Calculate the ideal Rankine efficiency of the system. The heat in steam at 1 psia = 1106 Btu/lb.

***Solution***: $i_1 = 1357$, $i_2 = 1106$, $i_w = 100.4$ Btu/lb

Therefore $\eta_{iR} = (1357 - 1106)/(1357 - 100.4) = 0.2 = 20\%$.

### 7.4 Overall Operation of Boiler

A boiler consists of very complicated maze of tubes carrying clean water and steam at very high pressures. A water-tube boiler could be as tall as a 10-storey building. But the overall operation, omitting mechanical and structural details, can be explained with reference to Fig. 7.9. Feedwater is pumped into the lower cylindrical vessel called the "evaporator" underneath which the flame from combustion of fuel is applied. The fuel could be coal, pulverized coal, oil or gas. Depending upon the type of fuel, the burners differ. A fan blows the air necessary for combustion after being heated. The fuel and air then ignite and cause the hot

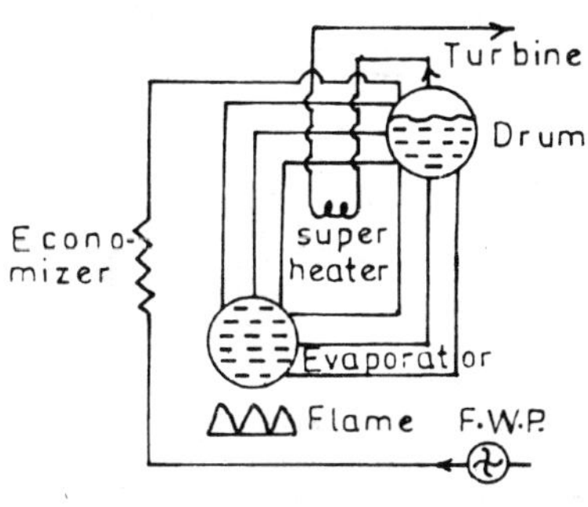


**Fig. 7.9** Schematic diagram of a boiler or steam generator

flame. In some boilers called "mixed flow", some of the heat from the flame rises by convection to the top to aid in superheating and then reheating steam drawn or bled from the first H.P. stage.

The hot water is led up to the steam separator or drum, perched on the top of the boiler, where any water condenses and is led back down to the evaporator. The steam issuing from the drum is thus in dry saturated condition and is superheated as it flows out, in a separate cylindrical vessel.

The most annoying problem in very huge boilers is the control of dangerous effluents, if not their complete removal. The flue gas contains very toxic components such as sulphur oxides, nitrous oxides and others. Nearly all improvements in modern days are concentrated on removal of these acidic oxides. We will consider this problem in Chapter 12 under "Environment Effects". The flue gases also contain carbon particles. These are collected by electrostatic (e.s.) precipitators before the gases are permitted to enter the tall chimney and escape into the atmosphere. Any malfunction of the e.s. precipitators is not only detrimental to the environment but the coal and other conducting solid particles in the effluents will choke the free passage. This reduces the capability of the steam generator.

## 7.5 Gas Cycle and Gas Turbine

In a gas engine or turbine the working medium is compressed air into which fuel is burnt or ignited to deliver its heat. A complete cycle of operations usually consists of four processes: (1) Suction of charge; (2) Compression; (3) Ignition of compressed gas; and (4) Exhaust.

These four can occur under different conditions and are classified by the name of its inventor. These are mainly:

(a) Otto Cycle; (b) Diesel Cycle; (c) Brayton or Joule Cycle; (d) Sterling and Ericsson Regenerative Cycles. The Brayton cycle, shown in Fig. 7.10, has the four processes occurring under the following conditions:

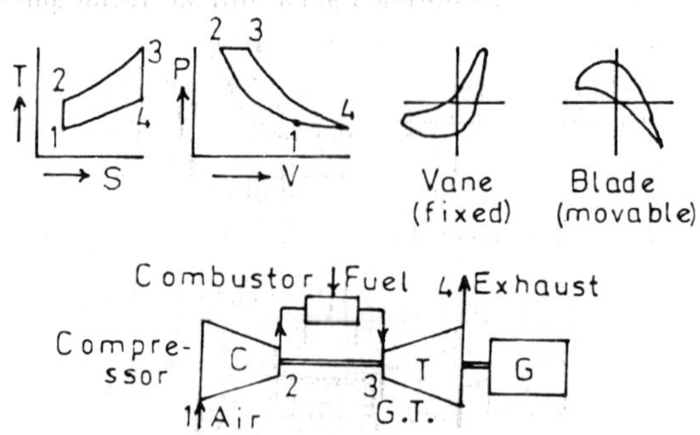


Fig. 7.10 Temperature-Entropy and Pressure-Volume diagrams with blade profiles of a Brayton cycle gas turbine.
C: Compressor, T: Turbine, G: Electric generator

*Process 1-2*: Air is compressed in an adiabatic or isentropic manner without addition of heat. However, a part of the turbine output (15 to 20%) is used to drive the air compressor.

*Process 2-3*: Heat from the fuel is given through combustion with the compressed air. This occurs at constant high pressures of 6 to 10 atm.

*Process 3-4*: The gas expands adiabatically at constant entropy. The pressure drops to its initial value at compressor input.

*Process 4-1*: Heat is removed at constant pressure and the gas reaches its initial state. The exhaust gas still contains quite a bit of heat and in the open cycle, is not recovered. However, in recent times this heat is taken to a heat exchanger to raise steam and run a steam turbine plant as a bottoming plant. This could give up to 20% of the gas-turbine output. This is called co-generation or combined cycle.

For an ideal gas, the specific heat at constant pressure is $c_p$ = 1.004 kcal/kg-°C (or K). Also the ratio of specific heats is $c_p/c_v$ = 1.4. However, for the working medium in actual use in a gas turbine, $\gamma = c_p/c_v$ has a lower value of about 1.2.

During the expansion process from 3 to 4, the temperatures and pressures have the relation

$$T_3 / T_4 = (P_3 / P_4)^{(\gamma - 1)/\gamma} \tag{7.9}$$

This is derived as follows: Now for any gas

$$P_3 V_3 = R T_3, \text{ and } P_4 V_4 = R T_4 \tag{7.10}$$

where $R$ = universal gas constant.

Also $$P_3 V_3^\gamma = P_4 V_4^\gamma \text{ (for adiabatic change)} \tag{7.11}$$

Therefore $$P_3 / P_4 = (V_4 / V_3)^\gamma \tag{7.12}$$

Consequently $$T_3 / T_4 = (P_3 / P_4) \cdot (V_3 / V_4) = (P_3 / P_4) \cdot (P_4 / P_3)^{1/\gamma}$$

$$= (P_3 / P_4)^{1 - 1/\gamma} = (P_3 / P_4)^{(\gamma - 1)/\gamma}$$

We define the compression ratio as $r = V_1/V_2$ (7.13)

Now $$P_1 V_1^\gamma = P_2 V_2^\gamma, \text{ giving } (P_2 / P_1) = (V_1 / V_2)^\gamma = r^\gamma \tag{7.14}$$

Since $P_3 = P_2$ and $P_4 = P_1$, we also have

$$P_3 / P_4 = P_2 / P_1 = r^\gamma \tag{7.15}$$

Consequently, from Eq. (7.9), the temperature ratios are

$$T_2 / T_1 = T_3 / T_4 = r^{\gamma - 1} \tag{7.16}$$

This results from the relation

$$P_1 V_1 = R T_1 \text{ and } P_2 V_2 = R T_2 \text{ as well as } P_1 V_1^{\gamma} = P_2 V_2^{\gamma}$$

giving $T_2 / T_1 = (P_2 / P_1) \cdot (V_2 / V_1) = (P_2 / P_1) \cdot (P_1 / P_2)^{1/\gamma} = r^{\gamma - 1}$ (7.17)

- The heat added per kg of air is

$$i_3 - i_2 = c_p (T_3 - T_2) \tag{7.18}$$

while the heat rejected is

$$i_4 - i_1 = c_p (T_4 - T_1) \tag{7.19}$$

Therefore the work done $= c_p [ (T_3 - T_2) - (T_4 - T_1) ]$ (7.20)

The efficiency of the Brayton cycle is

$$\eta_b = [ (T_3 - T_2) - (T_4 - T_1) ] / (T_3 - T_2) = 1 - (T_4 - T_1) / (T_3 - T_2) \tag{7.21}$$

Now $T_4 / T_3 = T_1 / T_2 = (T_4 - T_1) / (T_3 - T_2) = 1 / r^{\gamma - 1}$ (7.22)

Therefore $\eta_b = 1 - 1 / r^{\gamma - 1} = 1 - 1 / (P_2 / P_1)^{(\gamma - 1)/\gamma}$ (7.23)

The actual efficiency $\eta_a$ is less than the theoretical $\eta_b$ by the amount of power from the turbine used for running the compressor in relation to the input power. The following example will give the magnitude of quantities involved.

***Example 7.6***: A gas turbine has an output of 100 MW electrical with an actual efficiency of 33%. Temperatures at inlet and exhaust are 1040 and 538°C, respectively. The compression ratio is $r = 10.6$. Exhaust pressure $P_1 = 1$ atm. The fuel rate is 6.23 kg/s. Calculate: (a) the value of $\gamma$; (b) other losses; (c) pressure at inlet to turbine; and (d) calorific or heating value of fuel at $\eta = 33\%$.

***Solution***: $T_2/T_1 = (1040 + 273)/(538 + 273) = 1.62$.

(a) If $r = 10.6$ and $T_2/T_1 = 1.62$, then

$10.6^{\gamma - 1} = 1.62$, or, $(\gamma - 1) \log 10.6 = \log 1.62$

giving $\gamma = 1 + \log 1.62/\log 10.6 = 1.204$.

(b) $\eta_b = 1 - 1 / 10.6^{0.204} = 0.3822$.

Input $= 100/0.3822 = 261.6$ MW.

But $\eta_a = 0.33$. Therefore input $= 100/0.33 = 303$ MW.

Consequently, other losses $= 303 - 261.6 = 41.4$ MW.

(c) $P_2/P_1 = r^{\gamma}$ with $P_1 = 1$ atm.

Therefore the inlet pressure $P_2 = 10.6^{1.204} = 17.158$ atm $= 1.7386$ MPa

$= 252$ psia. (1 atm $= 0.10133$ MPa $= 14.7$ psi).

(d) Fuel flow = 6.23 kg/s.

Heat flow = 303 MW = 303 × $10^6$ J/s = 303 × $10^6$/4.186 × $10^3$ kcal/s.

Therefore the calorific value of compressed air and fuel is

$$= 303 \times 10^6 / (4.186 \times 10^3 \times 6.23) \text{ kcal / kg} = 11{,}620 \text{ kcal/kg}$$

$$= 20{,}910 \text{ Btu / lb.} \ (1 \text{ cal} = 4.186 \text{ J}; 1000 \text{ kcal / kg} = 1800 \text{ Btu / lb}).$$

## 7.6 Combined Cycle or Co-generation

Figure 7.11 shows a gas-turbine topping plant whose exhaust gases contain sufficient heat to raise steam in a regenerative heat boiler. This can run a steam-turbine plant called the bottoming cycle. A typical rating of the combined-cycle plant, with some more addition of steam from a second boiler, is as follows:

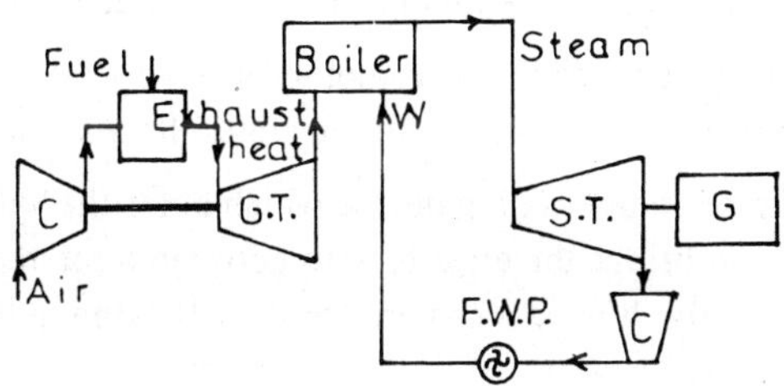


**Fig. 7.11** Combined-cycle gas-steam electrical generating system

*Gas Turbine* : 25 MW, 490°C (915°F). 16-stage compressor with compression ratio 6.5.

*Steam Plant* : 2200 psi (150 atm = 15.15 MPa), 1000°F (538°C). 200 MW steam turbine. H.P. stage 1800 psi, 1000°F.

***Example 7.7***: A gas turbine with a compression ratio of 6/1 has maximum cycle temperature $T_3$ = 600°C. Air enters the compressor at 15°C at the rate of 15 kg/s. Take $c_p$ = 1.005 kJ/kg-K, and $\gamma$ = 1.4 for both compression and expansion. Calculate the heat rejected in the exhaust.

***Solution***: The temperatures are first calculated.

$$T_1 = 15°\text{C} = 288 \text{ K}, \ T_3 = 600°\text{C} = 873 \text{ K}. \ P_2/P_1 = 6^{1.4} = 12.3.$$

$$T_2/T_1 = 6^{(1.4-1)/1.4} = 1.67. \text{ Therefore } T_2 = 481 \text{ K} = 208°\text{C}.$$

$$\text{Heat input } i_3 - i_2 = m\, c_p (T_3 - T_2) = 15 \times 1.005 \times (873 - 481)$$

$$= 5849 \text{ kg / s}$$

$$\text{Brayton efficiency of turbine} = 1 - 1/r^{\gamma-1} = 1 - 1/6^{0.4} = 0.51164.$$

$$\text{Therefore, heat rejected} = 5849\,(1 - 0.51164) = 2856 \text{ kJ/s} = 682.4 \text{ kcal/s}.$$

This represents a power of 2.856 × $10^6$ $W$ = 2.856 MW.

## 7.7 Governing of Steam Turbines

A steam or gas turbine driving an alternator must run at its rated speed irrespective of the magnitude of load from zero to full value. If load increases the speed of the unit drops, which should result in admission of more steam or gas by opening the throttle or inlet valve a little wider. When the input adjusts itself equal to the output, the speed should increase and reach the normal rated value. But because of inertia of rotating parts, the speed increases slightly above the rated value which will act on the governing mechanism. After a few oscillations the speed settles down to the rated value. This hunting is minimized in modern units suitably. All this is automatically accomplished by some type of governor. Its parts are as follows:

(a) Speed-responsive device, either mechanical or electrical

(b) A power element called the servomotor, which operates in response to the speed-responsive device and in turn operates the main steam valve

(c) A follow-up or compensating device which holds the valve opening at the new value and brings the error to zero between a reference value and the speed of the unit. It must also perform its duty without hunting.

*Speed-Responsive Device*

This takes several forms:

(i) Pair of spring-loaded flyballs which are driven from the turbine shaft either directly or by gear

(ii) The flyballs (or weights) are driven by a separate electric motor whose speed is proportional to the turbine speed. This can be accomplished if the motor is fed with a voltage by the alternator whose frequency responds to speed changes

(iii) A permanent-magnet generator or an equivalent which measures turbine speed. This is known as a tachometer generator. The signals from this generator are transmitted to the electrical portion of the governor-actuating mechanism.

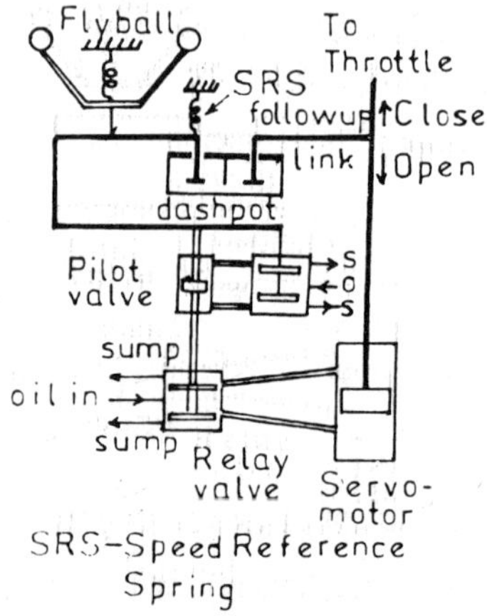


Fig. 7.12 Details of a speed-governing mechanism for turbines

*Power Element or Servomotor*

This is a pressure-oil operated cylinder-piston arrangement which operates the turbine inlet valve. Figure 7.12 shows the servomotor with two input ports, in between which a heavy piston is located. Admission of pressure oil to the top pushes the servomotor piston downward, which will open the throttle and increase steam flow to the turbine. The oil-admission is carried out by a valve which is actuated by the speed-responsive device, either directly (very rarely) or as is usual through a relay valve controlled by a pilot valve, thereby using more power to move the heavy mechanical parts of the governor itself.

*Compensating Device*

Once the steam-valve actuating rod connected to the servomotor piston has reached a position which corresponds to rated speed at the new load, further movement of relay valve must stop and all mechanisms except the servomotor piston must return back to their initial positions to respond to further load and speed change. This is carried out by a dashpot. For example, if the link from the servomotor to butterfly valve has moved down to open the throttle, a cross piece called "follow up" also moves down, which will change the pressure of oil in the dashpot. As soon as a pressure difference develops, the piston in the dashpot moves and returns to its stable initial position. The viscosity of oil in dashpot is used for preventing hunting. One of the chief causes of hunting of a turbine is due to air bubbles trapped in the dashpot. This must be prevented and the dashpot must operate smoothly. The manufacturer usually provides all maintenance procedures. The governor is a very sensitive and sophisticated mechanism which controls all operations.

In a completely electric governor, the parts may consist of the following:

(i) A tachometer generator responsive to turbine speed and developing electrical voltage signals which are proportional to the speed in magnitude and frequency

(ii) A transmitting medium of the above information to the electrical part of the governor

(iii) A comparator actuated by a reference signal and the tachometer signal; an error signal is developed

(iv) The error signal operates an electrical motor which helps pump pressure oil to the suitable compartment of the servomotor

(v) The servomotor finally operates the inlet fuel valve and the speed of the turbine adjusts to rated value at the new load. The error signal is then zero and the servomotor stops in its new stable position.

Electrical governors with their electronic control circuitry can operate with a delay of only milliseconds and the "dynamic stability" of the alternator is improved considerably. This means that the system can adjust to new load conditions, even with wide changes in magnitude, quicker and without hunting. The same governing principles are applied to gas turbines and hydraulic turbines which we will consider in Chap. 8.

### 7.8 Miscellaneous Worked Examples

[1 ata = 1 kg/cm$^2$ = 736 mm-Hg = 14.226 psia = 0.981 bar = 0.0981 MPa.
1000 Btu/lb = 555.5 kcal/kg = 2325.3 kJ/kg. 1 kcal = 4.186 kJ]

***Example 7.8***: Steam enters the H.P. stage from a boiler at 50 bar (51 ata = 725 psia), and exhausts into a condenser at 0.04 bar (30 mm-Hg). Calculate: (a) Carnot efficiency using wet steam; (b) Rankine efficiency with dry saturated steam at the boiler exit. (Refer also to steam tables given in appendix).

***Solution***:

(a) From Table 7.1, at 40 ata, $T_b = 249°C$ and at 60 ata, $T_b = 274°C$.

Therefore at 51 ata, $T_b = 249 + (274 - 249) \cdot (51 - 40) / (60 - 40)$

$= 262.75°C = 536\ K$.

Saturation temperature at 0.04 bar (30 mm-Hg):

From Table 7.2, $t_s$ at 0.03 ata is 32.6°C and at 0.05 ata, $t_s = 23.8°C$.

Therefore at 0.04 ata, $t_s = 23.8 + (32.6 - 23.8) \cdot (0.04 - 0.03) / (0.05 - 0.03)$

$= 28.2°C = 301.35$ K.

Therefore, Carnot efficiency $\eta_c = (536 - 301.35) / 536 = 0.438 = 43.8\ \%$

(b) Rankine efficiency $\eta_R = (i_1 - i_2) / (i_1 - i_w)$

Heat $i_1$ in dry steam at 725 psia = 1200 Btu/lb = 667 kcal/kg = 2791 kJ/kg.

Wet steam at 0.04 bar (0.58 psi) has

$i_2$ = 1099.3 Btu/lb = 610.72 kcal/kg = 2656.5 kJ/kg

(This value is calculated from Table 7.4 in appendix as

$$1096.6 + (1101 - 1096.6) \cdot (0.6982 - 0.580)/(0.698 - 0.507)$$
$$= 1096.6 + 2.7 = 1099.3 \text{ Btu/lb})$$

Condenser water at 28.2°C has heat of 28.2 kcal/kg = 50.76 Btu/lb = 118 kJ/kg

Therefore, $\eta_R = (667 - 610.72)/(667 - 28.2) = 0.088 = 8.8\%$

***Example 7.9***: Steam at 2400 psia has a temperature of 1000°F (538°C) when it enters the H.P. stage from the boiler. From Table 7.1, determine if the steam is superheated and if so the degree of superheating.

***Solution***: 2400 psia = 168.7 ata. At 150 ata, $T_b$ = 341°C, and at 200 ata, $T_b$ = 364°C. Therefore $T_b$ at 168.7 ata will be

$T_b = 341 + (364 - 341) \cdot (168.7 - 150)/(200 - 150) = 349.6°C = 661.3°F.$

Therefore the steam is superheated.

Degree of superheat = 538 – 349.6 = 188.4°C = 339°F, (1000 – 661).

Table 7.3 in Appendix gives $T_b$ to be

$$635.8 + (668.13 - 635.82) \cdot (2400 - 2000)/(2500 - 2000) = 661.6°F$$

***Example 7.10***: In the previous example, the plant efficiency is 33% with an output of 500 MW at the generator terminals. The steam exhausts into a condenser at 50 mm-Hg. Calculate the rate of flow of steam from the boiler.

***Solution***: From worked example 7.3 in Sec. 7.1, the vacuum corresponding to 50 mm-Hg is 0.9674 psia ≈ 1 psia. (Heat in vapour is 1106 Btu/lb = 614.4 kcal/kg = 2572 kJ/kg).

Heat in dry superheated steam at 1000°F at 2400 psia will be:

At 2000 psia, $i$ = 1474.5 Btu/lb, and at 2500 psia, $i$ = 1458.4 Btu/lb.

$$\begin{aligned}\text{Therefore at 2400 psia, } i &= 1474.5 - (1474.5 - 1458.4) \cdot (2400 - 2000)/500 \\ &= 1474.5 - 12.9 = 1461.6 \text{ Btu/lb} = 812 \text{ kcal/kg}\end{aligned}$$

Therefore, heat converted in turbine = 812 – 614.4 = 197.6 kcal/kg
= 827.1 kJ/kg

This represents 500/0.33 = 1500 MW = $1.5 \times 10^9$ J/s = $1.5 \times 10^6$ kJ/s.

So, rate of steam flow = $1.5 \times 10^6/827.1$ = 1813 kg/s.

[1 kg/s = $2.205 \times 3.6 \times 10^3$ lb/hr = $7.938 \times 10^3$ lb/hr. Therefore, $1.8136 \times 10^3$ kg/s = $14.4 \times 10^6$ lb/hr.]

***Example 7.11***: If the condenser vacuum is 25 mm-Hg in the previous example instead of 50 mm-Hg, calculate the new flow rate.

***Solution***: Latent heat of steam at 25 mm-Hg = 1050 Btu/lb = 2441.8 kJ/kg = 583.3 kcal/kg (1 kcal = 4.186 kJ).

Heat converted in turbine = 812 – 583.3 = 228.7 kcal/kg = $12.44 \times 10^6$ lb/hr = 1567 kg/s. This is 86.4% of the flow at 50 mm-Hg vacuum in the previous case.

***Example 7.12***: In the previous example, sub-bituminous coal with a heating value of 10,000 Btu/lb is used to fire the boiler. Calculate the quantity of coal consumed per year in tons (1 ton = 2240 lb) if the annual load factor is 0.7.

***Solution***: The average efficacy of power generation = load factor × installed capacity. Therefore, average power delivered = 350 MW. Consequently,

energy input = (350/0.33) × 8760 = $9.2 \times 10^6$ MW-h.

1 MW-h = $10^6 \times 3.6 \times 10^3$ J = $3.6 \times 10^6$ kJ = $0.86 \times 10^6$ kcal.

10,000 Btu/lb = 5,555 kcal/kg = $5.555 \times 10^6$ kcal/tonne.

Therefore, amount of coal consumed annually

$$= 9.2 \times 10^6 \times 0.86 \times 10^6 / 5.555 \times 10^6 \; = \; 1.424 \times 10^6 \text{ tonne.}$$

But 1 tonne = 1000 kg = 2205 lb = 0.9844 ton.

Therefore coal consumed = $1.40175 \times 10^6$ tons annually.

***Example 7.13***: Steam enters the H.P. stage from the boiler in superheated condition at 1000 psi and 800°F. Its saturation temperature is 544.6°F as given in steam table in the appendix, Table 7.3. It expands in the H.P. stage and is just saturated when it enters the first reheater, where its temperature is again raised to 800°F. It then exhausts into the condenser with a vacuum of 50 mm-Hg. Calculate the cycle efficiency with and without the reheat. (See Fig. 7.13).

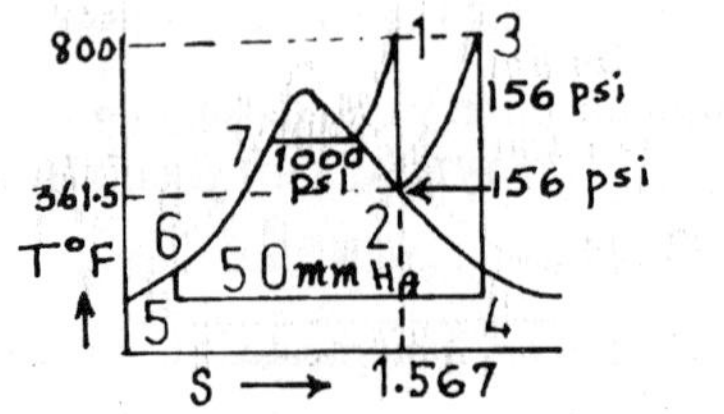


**Fig. 7.13** Temperature-entropy (T – S) diagram for Example 7.14 with one reheat

***Solution***:

(a) *With reheat*: At 1000 psi and 800°F, Table 7.3 in appendix gives $i_1$ = 1389.2 Btu/lb. In Fig. 7.13, at point 1 the steam has an entropy of 1.567. From point 1 to 2, the expansion takes place isentropically. The temperature and pressure drop but the entropy stays constant. From steam tables, the entropy of 1.567 for just dry saturated steam is obtained for 156 psia and 361.5°F. The heat is $i_2$ = 1195.1 Btu/lb.

The heat at Point 3 is at 156 psia and 800°F. This is $i_3$ = 1426.6 Btu/lb. At Point 4, the steam is wet at 50 mm-Hg ≈ 1 psia, and the heat content is $i_4$ = 1106 Btu/lb at a temperature of 101.74°F. Therefore, $i_5 = i_w$ = 101.74. The work done in turbine = $(i_1 - i_2) + (i_3 - i_4)$

$$= 1389.2 - 1195.1 + 1426.6 - 1106 = 194.1 + 320.6 = 514.7 \text{ Btu/lb}$$

$$\text{Heat supplied} = \; (i_1 - i_5) + (i_3 - i_2) \; = \; 1389.2 - 101.7 + 1426.6 - 1195.1$$

$$= \; 1519 \text{ Btu/lb}$$

Therefore, cycle efficiency with one reheat = 514.7/1519 = 0.339 = 33.9%.

Note the large output obtained by the reheat.

(b) *Without Reheat*

$$\text{Heat supplied} = \; i_1 - i_5 \; = \; 1389.2 - 101.7 \; = \; 1287.5 \text{ Btu / lb}$$

Work done $= i_1 - i_4 = 1389.2 - 1106 = 283.2$ Btu / lb

Therefore, efficiency = 283.2/1287.5 = 0.22 = 22%.

***Example 7.14***: A gas turbine receives air at atmospheric pressure and 25°C. The maximum allowable gas temperature is 1000°C. The compression ratio is r = 5. Per kg of air, calculate: (a) turbine work; (b) compressor work; (c) nett work; and (d) efficiency. $\gamma = 1.4$ and $c_p = 1.004$ kJ/kg-K.

***Solution***: Temperature at exit of compressor

$$T_2 = T_1 \cdot (P_2 / P_1)^{(\gamma - 1)/\gamma} = 5^{0.4/1.4} \cdot (25 + 273) = 5^{0.286} \cdot 298$$

$$= 472 \text{ K} \qquad (5^{0.286} = 1.58455).$$

Temperature at turbine exit

$$T_4 = T_3 \cdot (P_3 / P_4)^{-0.286} = (1000 + 273) / 1.58455 = 803.6 \text{ K}$$

(a) Turbine work: $i_3 - i_4 = 1.004\ (1273 - 803.6) = 471.3$ kJ/kg

(b) Compressor work: $i_2 - i_1 = 1.004\ (472 - 298) = 175$ kJ/kg.

(c) Nett work available for power generation = 471.3 – 175 = 296.3 kJ/kg

(d) Heat supplied = $c_p\ (T_3 - T_2) = i_3 - i_2$

$$= 1.004\ (1273 - 472) = 804 \text{ kJ / kg}$$

Therefore, efficiency = 296.3/804 = 0.3684 = 36.84%

Also, $\eta = 1 - 1/r^{(\gamma - 1)/\gamma} = 1 - 1/1.58455 = 0.3689$.

Full details of electric generators used with steam turbines known as Turbo-alternators or smooth air-gap machines or non-salient-pole machines or cylindrical-rotor machines are described in Chap. 9.

# APPENDIX

## Partial Steam Tables (for Problem-Solving only)

Table 7.1 contains boiling temperature of water with pressure, and Table 7.2 contains temperature of condensed water in condenser vacuum. Some more relevant data are given below.

**Table 7.3: Properties of Superheated Steam: Enthalpy and Entropy**

| Pressure (psia) | | Temperature of Dry Steam (Sat. Temp.)°F | | | | |
|---|---|---|---|---|---|---|
| | | 400 | 600 | 800 | 1000 | Sat. Temp. |
| 100 | Enthalpy, Btu/lb | 1227.6 | 1329 | 1429 | 1530.8 | 327.81 |
| | Entropy | 1.652 | 1.758 | 1.844 | 1.9193 | 1.6026 |
| 200 | | 1210.3 | 1322 | 1425 | 1528 | 381.8 |
| | | 1.5594 | 1.677 | 1.7655 | 1.8415 | 1.5453 |
| 300 | | — | 1368.3 | 1472.8 | 1578 | 417.3 |
| | | | 1.6268 | 1.7184 | 1.7954 | 1.5104 |
| 400 | | | 1307 | 1416.4 | 1522.4 | 444.6 |
| | | | 1.5894 | 1.6842 | 1.7623 | 1.4844 |
| 500 | | | 1298.6 | 1412 | 1519.6 | 467 |
| | | | 1.559 | 1.657 | 1.7363 | 1.4634 |
| 800 | | | 1270.7 | 1398.6 | 1511 | 518.23 |
| | | | 1.4863 | 1.5972 | 1.68 | 1.4153 |
| 1000 | | | 1249 | 1389.2 | 1505 | 544.6 |
| | | | 1.445 | 1.567 | 1.6525 | 1.39897 |
| 1200 | | | 1223.5 | 1379.3 | 1499.2 | 567.2 |
| | | | 1.405 | 1.541 | 1.6293 | 1.3667 |
| 1400 | | | 1193 | 1369.1 | 1493.2 | 587.1 |
| | | | 1.364 | 1.518 | 1.6093 | 1.3454 |
| 1600 | | | — | 1358.4 | 1487 | 604.9 |
| | | | | 1.4964 | 1.5914 | 1.325 |
| 1800 | | | | 1347.2 | 1480.8 | 621 |
| | | | | 1.4765 | 1.5752 | 1.305 |
| 2000 | | | | 1335.5 | 1474.5 | 635.8 |
| | | | | 1.4576 | 1.56 | 1.285 |

**Table 7.4: Properties of Water and Steam (Partial Table)**
**Temperature °F, Pressure psia**
**Enthalpy Btu/lb, Entropy Btu/lb – °F**

| Temp. | Press. | Enthalpy | | Entropy | |
|---|---|---|---|---|---|
| | | Sat. Liquid | Sat. Vapour | Sat. Liquid | Sat. Vapour |
| 32 | 0.0885 | 0.00 | 1075.8 | 0.00 | 2.188 |
| 40 | 0.1217 | 8.05 | 1079.3 | 0.0162 | 2.16 |
| 50 | 0.1781 | 18.07 | 1083.7 | 0.0361 | 2.1264 |
| 60 | 0.2563 | 28.06 | 1088 | 0.0555 | 2.0948 |
| 70 | 0.3631 | 38.04 | 1092.3 | 0.0745 | 2.0647 |
| 80 | 0.507 | 48 | 1096.6 | 0.0932 | 2.036 |
| 90 | 0.6982 | 58 | 1101 | 0.1115 | 2.009 |
| 100 | 0.9492 | 68 | 1105.2 | 0.1295 | 1.9826 |
| 120 | 1.6924 | 88 | 1113.7 | 0.1645 | 1.934 |
| 140 | 2.889 | 107.9 | 1122 | 0.1984 | 1.889 |
| 160 | 4.741 | 127.9 | 1130.2 | 0.2311 | 1.8585 |
| 180 | 7.51 | 147.9 | 1138 | 0.263 | 1.811 |
| 200 | 11.53 | 168 | 1146 | 0.294 | 1.776 |
| 212 | 14.7 | 180 | 1150.4 | 0.312 | 1.7566 |
| 250 | 29.825 | 216.5 | 1164 | 0.3675 | 1.7 |
| 300 | 67 | 269.6 | 1180 | 0.437 | 1.635 |
| 350 | 134.6 | 321.6 | 1192.3 | 0.503 | 1.5783 |
| 400 | 247.3 | 375 | 1201 | 0.5664 | 1.5272 |
| 450 | 422.6 | 430 | 1204.6 | 0.628 | 1.4793 |
| 500 | 680.8 | 488 | 1201.7 | 0.689 | 1.4325 |
| 600 | 1543 | 617 | 1165.5 | 0.8131 | 1.331 |
| 700 | 3093.7 | 823.3 | 995.4 | 0.9905 | 1.139 |
| 705.4 | 3206.2 | 902.7 | 902.7 | 1.058 | 1.058 |

Figure 7.14 shows a plot of these values.

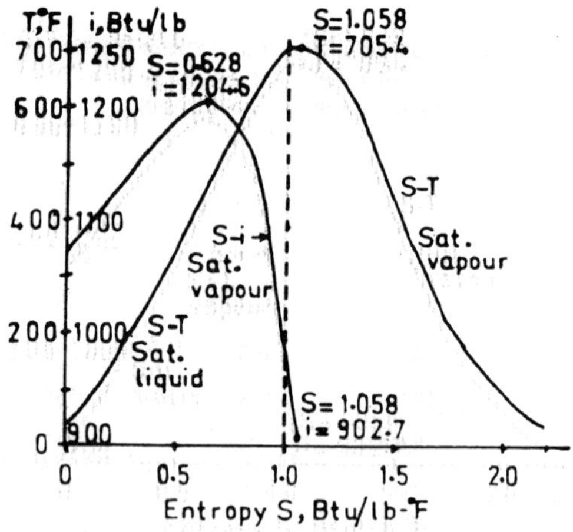


Fig. 7.14 Steam charts or diagrams for saturated vapour: temperature-entropy and enthalpy-entropy diagrams

## OBJECTIVE TYPE QUESTIONS

1. The inlet temperature of steam to the H.P. stage of a turbine is 550°C and the exhaust is at 50°C. The Carnot efficiency is: (a) 50%; (b) 91%; (c) 80%; (d) none of the three.

2. The total heat of dry superheated steam into a turbine is 1400 Btu/lb and exhausts into a condenser with total heat in steam of 1000 Btu/lb. In the condenser at 25 mm-Hg vacuum, the condensed water is at a temperature of 27°C. The Rankine efficiency of the cycle is: (a) 25%; (b) 27%; (c) 30.3%; (d) none of the three.

3. High pressure steam at exit of boiler is at 1000°F at 1000 psia. The saturation temperature at this pressure is 545°F. The degree of superheating is: (a) 252.8°C; (b) 455°F; (c) 252.8 K; (d) all three are true.

4. The effluents from coal-fired boilers without control are: (a) $SO_2$; (b) $N_2O$; (c) NO; (d) all three and many more.

5. Acid rain near fossil-fuel power plants contains: (a) $H_2SO_4$; (b) $NHO_3$; (c) $H_2CO_3$; (d) all three and some more.

6. For a combustion gas turbine, the inlet and outlet gas temperatures are 1000 and 400°C, respectively, at a compression ratio of 10. The Carnot efficiency is: (a) 60%, (b) 40%; (c) 50%; (d) none of the three.

7. A pressure of 1 ata corresponds to: (a) 1 kg/cm$^2$; (b) 736 mm-Hg; (c) 14.226 psia; (d) 10 tonne/m$^2$; (e) 98.1 kPa; (f) 0.981 bar; (g) all six are true.

8. A pressure of 1 atm at sea level and 0°C corresponds to: (a) 1.03 ata; (b) 1.0104 bar; (c) 760 mm-Hg; (d) 0.101 MPa; (e) all four are true.

9. A condenser operates at 50 mm-Hg vacuum. Which statement is correct? (a) The pressure is 0.068 kg/cm$^2$; (b) 0.9674 psia; (c) 6.671 kPa; (d) all three are true.

10. Steam turbines operate on: (a) Carnot cycle; (b) Rankine cycle; (c) Brayton cycle; (d) Joule cycle; (e) both (c) and (d) are true.

11. Gas turbines operate on: (a) Carnot cycle; (b) Rankine cycle; (c) Brayton cycle; (d) Joule cycle; (e) both (c) and (d) are true.

12. The heating value of fuel for a gas turbine is 20,000 Btu/lb. Which statement is most valid? The heating value is: (a) 10,000 kcal/kg; (b) 36,000 kcal/kg; (c) 11,111 kcal/kg; (d) none of the three is true.

13. Combined cycle means having: (a) steam turbine as topping plant and gas turbine as bottoming plant; (b) nuclear station as topping plant and MHD as bottoming plant; (c) steam turbine as bottoming plant and gas turbine as topping plant; (d) all three are true.

14. Which statement is most valid? (a) Compression ratio in a gas turbine is about 10/1; (b) Inlet pressure in an air compressor for a gas turbine is about 1 atm; (c) Exhaust temperature from a gas turbine is about 500°C; (d) all three are true.

15. A governing mechanism for a turbine consists of: (a) Speed responsive and sensing device; (b) Power element or servomotor; (c) Compensating device; (d) All three.

16. 1 tonne of coal with calorific value of 10,000 Btu/lb burnt with an efficiency of 50% has an output of about: (a) $11 \times 10^6$ Btu; (b) $2.774 \times 10^6$ kcal; (c) 3.225 MW-h; (d) all three are true.

17. A steam station has an output of 2100 MWe. Its efficiency is 35%. Coal used has a heating value of 5,000 kcal/kg. The amount of coal used per year at a load factor of 0.75 will be nearly: (a) 6.78 million tonne; (b) $9.04 \times 10^6$ tonne; (c) $2.373 \times 10^6$ tonne; (d) none of the three.

[***Answers***: 1. (b); 2. (c); 3. (d); 4. (d); 5. (d); 6. (a); 7. (g); 8. (e); 9. (d); 10. (b); 11. (e); 12. (c); 13. (d); 14. (d); 15. (d); 16. (d); 17. (a).]

## REVIEW QUESTIONS AND PROBLEMS

1. Draw the block diagram of a steam-turbine plant with one reheat cycle of steam. Show all parts from boiler feed water input to exhaust from condenser.

2. Draw the block diagram of a combined cycle plant with gas turbine topping cycle and steam plant bottoming cycle.

3. The input steam to a turbine is 2000 psig, 1000°F. The condenser vacuum is 25 mm-Hg. Convert these quantities to ata, and °C. (141.62 ata; 538°C; 0.034 ata).

4. On a temperature-entropy diagram, draw approximately the following cycles: (a) Carnot; (b) Rankine cycle without superheat; (c) Rankine cycle with one superheat; (d) Brayton cycle.

5. A steam plant has a boiler pressure of 50 atmospheres absolute and a condenser pressure of 25 mm-Hg. The input heat in the steam is 800 kcal/kg while the temperature of steam in condenser vacuum is 24°C. At the entrance to condenser, the steam still has a heat of 500 kcal/kg. Calculate the Rankine efficiency. (38.66%)

6. Feedwater enters a boiler at 200°C. If the water is not to boil in the feed line, estimate the minimum pressure required in the feed-water pump in psig and ata. (220.9 psig, 16.56 ata).

7. (a) Describe the difference in action between an impulse turbine and a reaction turbine.

   (b) What are pressure compounding and velocity compounding stages?

8. The temperature and pressure of dry steam issuing from a boiler are 900°F and 1000 psia. Calculate the degree of superheating in the steam in °F and °C. (355°F, 197.2°C).

9. Steam at 1500 psia has a temperature of 900°F (482.2°C) when it enters the H.P. stage of turbine. The steam exhausts into a condenser at 25 mm-Hg. The output at generator is 200 MW at an efficiency of plant operation of 30%. Calculate rate of steam flow from the boiler in kg/s and lb/hr. Use steam tables given. (861 kg/s = $6.835 \times 10^6$ lb/hr).

10. A steam turbine plant has a rating of 2100 MWe at an efficiency of 35%. Coal with calorific value of 5000 kcal/kg is used. The annual plant load factor is 0.75. Calculate the tonnes of coal consumed per year by this plant. (This is representative of the largest single steam plant at Singrauli in India in the Dhanbad coal belt). ($6.78 \times 10^6$ *t*).

11. Superheated steam at 1500 psia and 900°F enters the H.P. stage of a turbine, where it expands until it is just dry. It is then bled and reheated to the original temperature of 900°F. It then expands in the L.P. stage and exhausts into a condenser at a vacuum of 25 mm-Hg. Calculate the cycle efficiency with and without reheat. Draw the temperature-entropy diagram.

[*With reheat*: Entropy at 900°F = 1.5563. This is found at 180.8 psia and 371.4°F. Heat after first expansion = 1196 Btu/lb. Total heat at 1500 psia and 900°F is 1427.5 Btu/lb. Therefore, heat at 180.8 psia and 900°F is 1477.2 Btu/lb. Heat in steam at condenser inlet = 1096 Btu/lb. Temperature of water at 25 mm-Hg = 77°F. Therefore, $\eta$ = 612.7 × 100/1631.7 = 37.5%.

*Without reheat*: $\eta$ = 331.5 × 100/1350.5 = 24.55%].

12. Derive all equations from (7.9) through (7.23).

13. A gas turbine operates between 30°C and 970°C. The ratio of specific heats is $\gamma$ = 1.25 and $c_p$ = 1 kJ/kg at constant pressure. The compression ratio is $r$ = 7. Calculate:

    (a) Temperature at exit of compressor; (b) Temperature at exit of turbine; (c) Turbine work; (d) Compressor work; (e) Power generated; (f) Heat supplied; (g) Efficiency; Take weight of gas = 1 tonne.
    [(a) 447.16 K; (b) 842.3 K; (c) 95.72 × $10^3$ kcal/tonne; (d) 34.44 × $10^3$ kcal/tonne; (e) 61.28 × $10^3$ kcal/tonne; (f) 190.16 × $10^3$ kcal/tonne; (g) $\eta$ = 32.22%. ($1 - 7^{-0.2} = 0.3224$).]

14. Describe with neat sketches the operation of a govenor for a steam turbine unit. Show the pilot valve, relay valve, servomotor, dashpot and follow-up, and describe their functions.

CHAPTER 8

# Hydro-Electric Power Generation

## 8.1 General Introduction

Rivers flow from their sources, usually mountainous regions, through hilly valleys and finally discharge their waters into the sea or a lake in plains. They carry enormous amount of power, which has been properly harnessed since the seventies of the nineteenth century for generation of electric power in a big way for the benefit of mankind, ever since Tesla discovered the 3-phase system. The power is usually transmitted at very high voltages (220 kV to 1200 kV ac and dc) over long distances, since giant power stations are located in mountainous regions far away from load centres.

The flow of water in a river varies from season to season, so that a large dam has to be built to store the total flow over a year in an extensive reservoir, allowing for flood discharge. This immerses a lot of forest and agricultural land, and changes animal life patterns and the ecology of the area. Environmental groups are very conscious of this situation and a dam with a reservoir is built only after extensive hearings from all concerned groups, including international meetings. However, industrial economy is ultimately benefited by the electric power and other facilities that go with the construction of the scheme. In addition, floods are controlled, by and large, ground-water levels are lifted in the reservoir neighbourhood by rise in water table, and recreational facilities are created. In very large dams, however, when the reservoir spreads over porous rocks, the resulting pressure of water lets it seep through these rocks to reach the hot underground magma generating steam, whose pressure causes fissures increasing the seepage. With time, this causes earthquakes where there were none prior to building the dam and reservoir. Another stumbling block in some rivers is the enormous amount of silt carried by the swift-flowing water, especially in mountainous areas. This will settle in the reservoir and reduce the quantity of stored water, making the entire water-power development ineffective with passage of time, which may be as short as half a century or as long as one century. These and many other limitations have to be recognized before a hydro-electric power project is undertaken for execution.

The fact that water power is perennial and not exhaustible like fossil fuel is very attractive and speaks well for it, since it is also pollution-free. Extensive and accurate land surveys (usually from the air) are required for estimating reservoir capacity and hence the potential annual power available. This also involves keeping good records of daily runoff quantities of water in the river or rivers draining into the proposed reservoir. Records for over 25 years prior to building the dam are necessary, since weather, climate and flow properties exhibit their own cyclic behaviour over long periods of time.

Hydropower developments are classified into three broad categories:

(a) Storage reservoir with one-way flow from reservoir to power house located at a lower level.

(b) Pumped-storage plants in which certain parts of the 24-hour day (usually at nights when system load is low) power generated by other stations in an interconnected system or grid is utilized to pump water from the down-stream side of the dam or power station back to the reservoir to raise its storage capacity. In this case, the generator usually works as a motor and the hydraulic turbine in the pump mode. There are, however, cases where a separate pump is used or even a separate pumping station.

(c) Run-of-the-river plants in which the water in the river can be diverted by a retaining wall to flow through the turbine utilizing low head but large quantity of water. In some countries such a power potential can amount to 25% of the total power consumption while 50% can be developed by building high dams.

In recent times the development of micro-hydel plants is becoming popular for local electric supply. There are many mountain streams whose potential goes unused in areas remote from the main power scheme of the province. For such areas, even as little as 50 kW can bring a lot of benefits to a community.

The size of single turbine-generator unit has gone to 500 MW or more, with runner diameters of 9 m. Since the cost of a hydro-electric development is high and civil works have to be built in one step in most cases, power station sizes are on the increase. Some examples of giant schemes are:

| | |
|---|---|
| *Russia*: | 6000 MW (12 × 500) built in 1967 at Krasnoyarsk |
| | 6400 MW at Sayano-Shusensk in 1980 |
| | 4500 MW and 4300 MW on the Angara River |
| | 7500 MW to be built on River Yenisey |
| *Canada*: | 11340 MW on La Grande River in James Bay area. |

With the increasing development of nuclear power plants, hydro-electric power plants are generally on the decline since they have to be located far from civilization and furthermore they have to be constructed underground in very cold areas, thereby increasing the cost still further.

Hydro-electric plants are classified according to their purpose. Broadly speaking, these are:

(a) Base-load stations.

(b) Peak-load stations in a system where steam stations carry the base load, since it is more expensive to have these as spinning reserve to supply peak loads only during the day.

(c) Combined-load where some units in a hydro-power station are kept as spinning reserve on purpose.

(d) Isolated power station with no interconnection. Such stations have low capacity. Micro-hydel stations are examples.

Power development is also categorized according to head of water available at a site. These are:

(a) High head, generally in excess of 500 m

(b) Medium head of 40 to 500 m, and

(c) Low head, less than 40 m.

There are no clear-cut distinctions between these values of head and there is always some overlapping. High heads usually go with low water quantity, while low-head developments carry maximum quantity of water, since they most closely resemble run-of-the-river concept.

Hydraulic turbines for these three ranges of head are classified as follows, with some overlapping, dictated by circumstances peculiar to the project:

(a) Pelton Wheel or Impulse Turbine for high heads

(b) Francis Turbine or Reaction Turbine for medium heads

(c) Kaplan Turbine or Variable-Pitch Propeller Turbine for low heads

(d) Pump Turbine or Reversible Turbine, and

(e) Bulb Turbine.

Details of principles of construction and operation of all these turbine types are discussed later.

## 8.2 Power-Plant Development Types

Figure 8.1 shows three types of hydro-electric development schemes used in practice. In Fig. 8.1(a) is shown a dam across a river to impound the flow of water throughout the year. At the dam, the expected amount of water for the generating pattern or load cycle is diverted in a channel usually a tunnel, or pipe made of

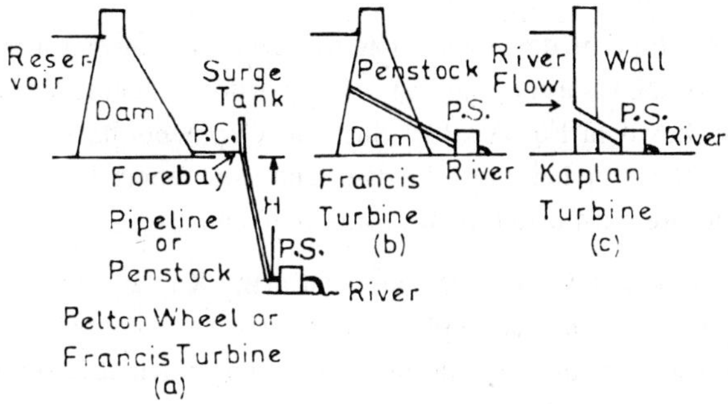


**Fig. 8.1** Schematic diagram of hydro-electric developments:
(a) High-head Pelton wheel; (b) Medium-head Francis turbine at dam site;
(c) Low-head Kaplan turbine. (There is usually some overlapping).

concrete or steel, or any open water channel (canal). If the tunnel or pipe runs full, there is no loss of head from the dam to the power station. These water passages follow the hill sides and their slope is very gentle. The water then discharges into a lake called the Forebay, in case no pressure channel is used. From the forebay the actual pipeline or penstock laid along the hill slope to the turbine at the bottom of the hill carries the water on to the rotor of the machine proper. After being used by the turbine, the water usually discharges into the river at the lower level. The power station site is generally selected to be on the river, so that the tail race or draft tube discharges into the natural channel of the river and flows further downstream. The height of water involved in power generation is the difference in the water level from the forebay to the centre of the turbine runner. At the top of the hill and entry into the penstock, a surge tank is provided. This is necessary to serve as an outlet to the water backing up, when the load on the turbine-generator decreases suddenly and the water passages in the turbine are suddenly blocked (fully or partially by the action of a governor), thus creating a surge of water. This is known as Water Hammer.

The turbines used in such developments are either Pelton Wheels or Francis Turbines, since the head is usually high to medium. Because the head H is quite considerable, early power developments took place near water falls, with the power channel and penstock bypassing the sudden decrease in height of the topography. (In fact there was a misconception in early days that the turbine wheel was located right under the falls to be rotated by the falling water!). However, a sudden vertical fall of the river is not quite necessary, but only a difference in level of water between the dam and the power house located a few kilometres away. The natural gradient can be utilized equally profitably in the same way as a water fall with sudden vertical fall of water, although the development is less scenic and requires a very long water channel, either closed or open as the situation requires. There are also schemes where the water of one river is taken to a forebay a few kilometres away and the water from the power station is discharged into another river after flowing through the turbines.

The second type of development is to locate the power station immediately downstream of the reservoir and dam. The penstock is embedded inside the dam structure as shown in Fig. 8.1(b). Such developments have heads of between 100 m and 250 m (the height of the dam) and use Francis Turbines. By far such developments are most usual in the world in all countries.

The third type is low-head development using Kaplan Turbines, as shown in Fig. 8.1(c). There is some attempt to store the river's water behind a low dam and lead the large quantity of water through the turbine. Such developments use heads of less than 40 m. For very low heads, Bulb Turbines with horizontal shaft are used, similar to tidal power stations described in Chap. 6. It is not repeated here.

Whatever be the type of development, environmental effects must be investigated with great care.

The amount of power potential at a site is calculated as follows from the rate of flow $Q$ and head $H$:

The density of water is $\rho = 1$ g/cm$^3 = 10^3$ kg/m$^3$ = 1 tonne/m$^3$. Thus, the rate of flow of water is $M = 10^3\,Q$, kg/s. When this weight of water is at a height $H$ metres above the turbine runner, its potential energy is

$$P = MgH = 10^3\,g\,Q\,H, \text{ Joule/s or Watt,} \tag{8.1}$$

where $g$ = acceleration due to gravity = 9.81 m/s$^2$.

The output obtained from the turbine from this quantity of flow and head is

$$P_0 = 10^3\,g\,Q\,H\,\eta, \text{ Watt} = 9.81\,Q\,H\,\eta, \text{ kW} \tag{8.2}$$

where $\eta$ = efficiency of the turbine. This is usually 90 to 95% for turbines of good design.

***Example 8.1***: A hydro power plant with 1050 MW output has an efficiency of 93%. The plant load factor is 65%. It operates at a constant head of 60 m. Calculate:

(a) The maximum flow rate required, and (b) the quantity of water to be stored behind a dam to cater for a year's load requirement.

***Solution***: (a) Maximum output = 1050 MW and input = 1050/0.93 = 1129 MW

Therefore $9.81 \times 60 \times Q \times 10^{-3} = 1129$

giving $Q = 1.92 \times 10^3 = 1920$ m$^3$/s = 1920 tonne/s.

(b) Average power output during the year = 1050 × 0.65 = 682.5 MW.

Therefore $Q = 0.65 \times 1920 = 1248$ m$^3$/s. Consequently, total quantity of water to be stored for a year's load requirement is

$$1248 \times 3600 \times 24 \times 365 = 39.357 \times 10^9 \text{ m}^3 = 39.357 \text{ km}^3.$$

There are several ways in which this amount of water may be stored or the total quantity realized:

(1) The amount of water stored will depend upon the outflow to the power house and inflow in the natural stream of the river. During flood times, the flow in the river is usually much more than the outflow to the power house. Therefore, the capacity of the actual reservoir is not as large as the previous example indicates.

(2) If the site is suitable for pumped-storage development, water from the downstream side of the power house can be pumped during light-load hours of the night to replenish the reservoir capacity. However, the power for pumping must be available from another source, usually the connected grid system. For example, if the pumping takes place for 8 hr at full capacity, only two-thirds the required quantity need be stored in the reservoir.

The above example applies nearly to a development such as Niagara Falls on the Canadian side of the river. It is a pumped-storage plant with part of the water from the head of the famous 50 m falls diverted through a pressure tunnel situated underground right below the township of Niagara Falls Ontario. A separate pumping station with its own large reservoir is located at a higher level than the forebay, from where the power station is fed during normal operation. Thus, even with a gigantic amount of water flowing in the river, a pumped-storage plant is utilized and found necessary.

***Example 8.2***: In the previous example, assume the reservoir capacity to be 39.357 $km^3$. Take the length of dam as 2 km. The height of dam is 100 m and the maximum and minimum levels of the reservoir are 80 and 20 m from the river bed. If the banks of the lake thus formed are vertical, and the reservoir fans out from 2 km to 8 km at the outermost stretch on a straight line, calculate the wash behind the dam. Neglect gradient of river bed.

***Solution***: Height of water = 80 – 20 m = 0.06 km.

Average cross section = 0.06 (2 + 8)/2 = 0.3 $km^2$.

Then, $0.3 \times L = 39.357$, giving the length of wash = 131.2 km.

In normal reservoirs, the shoreline is not straight but widens out from the dam, so that the wash is not as long as has been calculated. Also, a more accurate calculation should take into account the gradient of the river bed. These details are beyond the scope of the book, but the reader can realize that the amount of land submerged in the water is quite important.

## 8.3 Hydraulic Turbines

Turbines adopted for harnessing the energy in the incoming water and converting to mechanical rotary motion are classified according to the following types:

(1) High head, low quantity, impulse type known as the Pelton Wheel after its inventor. The runner has a fixed shape.

(2) Medium head, larger quantity of water generally (than Pelton), reaction type known as Francis Turbine after its inventor. Runner is fixed in shape in this also.

(3) Low head, enormous water quantity, propeller type known as Kaplan Turbine after its inventor. The pitch of the propeller blades is varied to suit load and to run at constant speed.

(4) Very low head, enormous water quantity, run-of-the-river turbine known as Bulb Turbine.

(5) Less familiar turbines are Tubular Type and Rim Type. These will not be discussed here. Please refer to Tidal Power in Chap. 6.

### *8.3.1 The Pelton Wheel*

The casing in which the runner is located in the Pelton Wheel is at atmospheric pressure. Therefore, the total potential energy of water is converted to velocity head in the turbine. The water issues in one or more jets to hit the runner periphery on which are mounted several pairs of "buckets" or bowl-like rotor vanes. The quantity of water striking the buckets is varied by controlling the opening between a needle valve and the water pipe, thereby varying the size of the jet, as shown in Fig. 8.2.

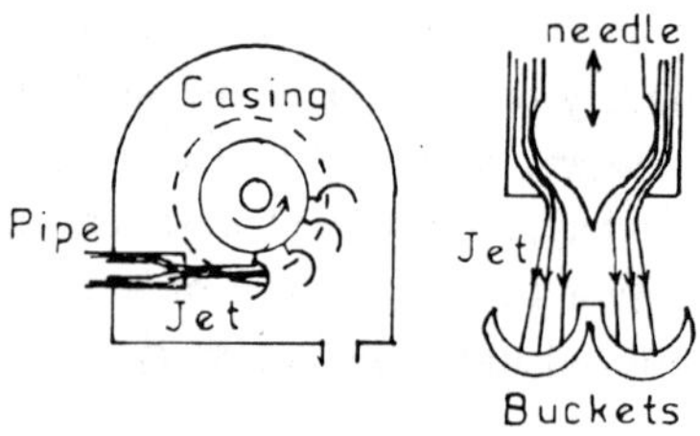

Fig. 8.2 Pelton wheel showing buckets, jet, and needle valve

When load changes occur, especially during lowering of output, it is not possible to reduce the water quantity by the needle valve acting alone, since the pressure of water is considerable because of the high head behind the turbine, and because the inertia of water is much higher than that of a working medium such as steam. The mechanism to reduce water quantity falling on the bucket consists of a baffle or thick steel plate, which the governor servomotor inserts in front of the buckets thereby deflecting the water from the jet away from the buckets. In a short time the needle-valve opening adjusts itself to the new load condition and the baffle is moved away. During load increases, the deflector or baffle is not normally required to stop the water.

ince the water surface at the intake to the penstock is exposed to atmospheric pressure at the forebay and the turbine casing is also at the same pressure, the entire potential energy of the water at height $H$ between intake level and turbine runner is converted to kinetic energy on the buckets.

Therefore, $\frac{1}{2} M v^2 = M g H$, giving $v = \sqrt{2 g H}$, m/s (8.3)

***Example 8.3***: The effective head of water in a Pelton-Wheel development is 500 m from the forebay to the turbine runner. Calculate the velocity of water in the jet in m/s and km/hr.

***Solution***: P.E. of water per kg = $g H = 9.81 \times 500$. K.E. = $\frac{1}{2} v^2$.

Therefore, $v = \sqrt{(2 g H)} = 9810^{1/2} = 99$ m/s $\approx 360$ km/hr.

It is not possible to operate a Pelton Wheel as a pump, so that if a pumped-storage plant with high head is used, a separate pump impeller has to be coupled to the electrical machine which will operate as a synchronous motor, receiving power from the rest of the electrical system. One such typical scheme is the Super Bissorte power development in France. Its specifications are as follows:

| | | |
|---|---|---|
| Total installed capacity | : | 750 MW (4 × 187.5 MW), |
| Maximum pumping head | : | 1217 m (1120 to 1217 m), |
| Pumps | : | 4 × 187.5 MW, 5 stages, 600 rev/min. |
| Turbine net head | : | 1072 to 1194 m, |
| Turbine output | : | 130 to 156 MW, |
| Pump power consumption | : | 148 to 158 MW, |
| Pelton Wheel | : | 150 MW, 500 rev/min. |

***Example 8.4***: In Example 8.3, the Pelton Wheel consists of 2 jets each of 15 cm diameter. Estimate the power developed, taking the velocity to be 100 m/s (see Fig. 8.3).

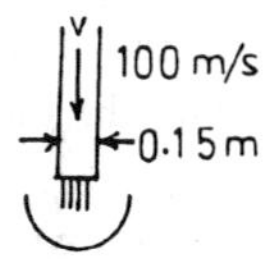


**Fig. 8.3** Details for Example 8.4

***Solution***: Voume of water issuing from each jet per second

$= \pi \times 0.15^2 \times 100/4$ m$^3$/s = 1.767 m$^3$/s. Weight of water – 1767 kg/s.

Energy/sec = $\frac{1}{2} \times 1767 \times 100^2 = \frac{1}{2} \times 17.67 \times 10^6$ W .

Therefore, in two jets, power = 17.67 MW.

A Pelton Wheel is mostly designed with a horizontal shaft, with the wheel rotating in a vertical plane. There are exceptions, however, and installations with vertical axis are also used but are less common than horizontal-axis machines.

### *8.3.2 The Francis Turbine*

In the Pelton Wheel or Impulse Turbine, the entire pressure head $H$ in the water is converted to velocity head $v = \sqrt{2 g H}$. In the case of the Francis or Reaction

Turbine, as in the case of the steam turbine, there is a pressure head still remaining in the water just before it enters the turbine casing, which is fully submerged in the water and supports a ''draft head'' of a few metres before the water surface is exposed to atmospheric pressure. In the vanes of the rotor, both decrease in pressure and increase in velocity take place. The pressure head ''pushes'' or causes an acceleration to the water and the curved buckets change the direction of flow of water through it, creating a reaction. The schematic of a Francis-Turbine runner is shown in Fig. 8.4.

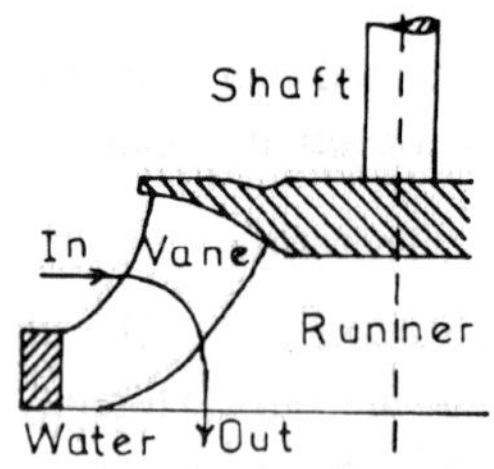


**ig. 8.4** Francis turbine runner with vanes and water flow

The water enters at right angles to the shaft and leaves in the axial direction, giving a thrust to the curved blades cast integrally to the runner structure. Unlike in the impulse turbine, the water passage is completely filled with water until the exit called the draft tube. Movable wicket gates mounted on the scroll or stationary part are controlled from the governor servomotor to regulate the gate opening and control the amount of water to suit the load on the turbine. The runner is inside a volute scroll, which has a large diameter at the penstock entry end and gradually decreases since the quantity of water is less as it flows round on the runner. This is shown in Fig. 8.5.

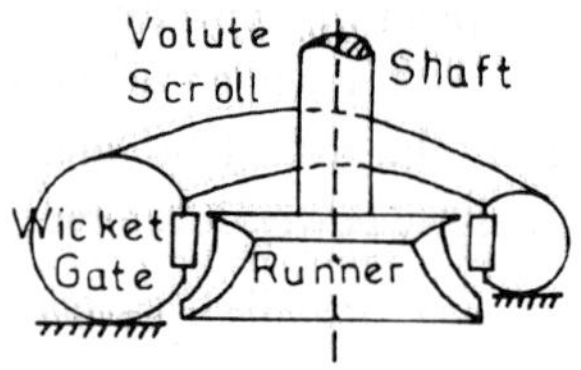


**Fig. 8.5** Volute scroll casing, wicket gates, and runner for Francis reaction turbine

Francis Turbines can have their shaft either horizontal or vertical, the latter being the most common for larger units. Unit sizes have reached 500 MW and larger, requiring very highly specialized design in thrust bearings which have to carry the weight of rotors of turbine, generator and exciter. These weigh hundreds of tonnes.

### *8.3.3 The Kaplan Turbine*

This is used for low-head (< 40 m), large-quantity developments. The runner consists of huge blades which are hydraulically movable by governor control to maintain constant speed under load variations. The wicket gates or guide vanes control the amount of water flow to suit the load, being actuated by the servomotor of the speed-governing mechanism. Figure 8.6 shows a Kaplan-Turbine schematic.

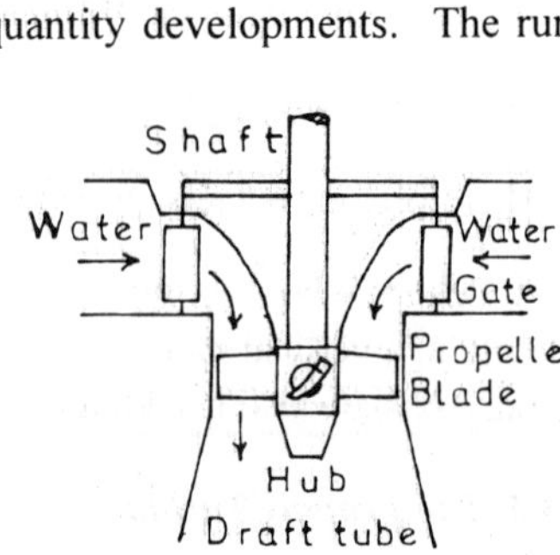


**Fig. 8.6** Water flow, wicket gates, runner, and draft tube for Kaplan turbine installation

Water enters radially, takes a vertical turn and discharges axially, the flow being inward. The angle of the propellers to the direction of flow of water generates thrust and torque. Once again, the entire water passage is filled with water. A few metres of head are lost (about 3 m), because of the draft tube. Any exposure of the blades creates negative pressures and causes cavitation, which loosens the metal of the propeller blades and pits them badly. This not only reduces the strength of the metal but with progress of time the blades cause turbulence and reduce the effectiveness of the runner. Cavitation is a problem even in Francis Turbines.

## 8.4 Turbine Parameters and Models

### *8.4.1 Turbine Parameters*

We have already seen in Eq. (8.2) that the output of a turbine is

$$P_0 = 9.81\, Q\, H\, \eta\,, \text{kW}$$

where $9.81$ = acceleration due to gravity, $\text{m/s}^2$

$Q$ = rate of water flow, $\text{m}^3/\text{s}$

$H$ = head above the turbine, m

and $\eta$ = efficiency.

A designer uses several quantities which have been known to stay within certain limits based on wide practice and experience.

*Throat Diameter and Velocity*

If the diameter at runner entrance is *d*, and water velocity is *v*, then the quantity of water flowing per second is $Q = \pi d^2 v/4$.

Then $$P_0 = 9.81 \times 0.7854\, d^2\, v\, H\, \eta \tag{8.4}$$

Taking $\eta = 0.93$, this becomes

$$P_0 = 7.165\, d^2\, v\, H, \text{ kW} \tag{8.5}$$

Therefore $$\text{kW}/d^2 = P_0/d^2 = 7.165\, v\, H \tag{8.6}$$

From a large number of reaction turbines built, the ratio ($\text{kW}/d^2$) is fairly well given in terms of head as

$$P_0/d^2 = 50\, H^{1.17} \tag{8.7}$$

This yields $$v = 50\, H^{1.17}/7.165\, H = 6.98\, H^{0.17} \tag{8.8}$$

In a Pelton Wheel, however, $v \approx \sqrt{2\,g\,H} = 4.43\, H^{0.5}$ (8.9)

The runner receives its impulse from jets, so that there is no relation between runner diameter and velocity of water.

*Turbine Variables and Models*

Turbine designers use three important "variables" which are defined as follows:

(1) *Flow Coefficient*: $\phi = Q / n\, d^3$ (8.10)

where $n$ = speed of rotor in rev/s. This could also be converted to $\omega = 2\,\pi\, n$, rad/s. When $Q$ is in $m^3/s$, $d$ is in $m$, and $n$ in $s^{-1}$, the flow coefficient $\phi$ is dimensionless.

(2) *Head Coefficient*: $\Psi = g\, H / n^2\, d^2$ (8.11)

With $g$ in $m/s^2$, $H$ in m, $n$ in $s^{-1}$, and $d$ in $m$, the quantity $\Psi$ is dimensionless since $g\, H/n^2\, d^2 = (m/s^2) \times m/s^{-2} \times m^2$.

(3) *The Specific Speed*

$$n_s = \phi^{0.5} \times \Psi^{-0.75} = n\, Q^{0.5}\, (g\, H)^{-0.75} \tag{8.12}$$

This is also dimensionless. $(m^{1.5}\, s^{1.5}/m^{1.5}\, s^{1.5})$.

Although dimensionless, turbine engineers use another expression for specific speed. This is

$$n_q = n\, Q^{0.5}\, H^{-0.75} \tag{8.13}$$

in which $n$ is in rev/min, $Q$ in $m^3/s$, and $H$ in $m$.

Experience has shown that the specific speed given by Eq. (8.12) has the following properties:

(a) For a head $H = 1\ m$ and $Q = 1\ m^3/s$, the specific speed $n_q = n$, the speed of turbine in rev/min.

(b) Turbine specific speeds have the following range of values:

| | | |
|---|---|---|
| *Pelton Turbines* | : | Up to 13 (for heads from 250 to 2000 m) |
| *Francis Turbines* | : | $n_q$ = 20 to 140 (30 to 600 m heads). |
| *Pump Turbines* | : | $n_q$ = 25 to 120 (30 to 600 m heads). |
| *Kaplan Turbines* | : | $n_q$ = 100 to 300 (8 to 60 m heads). |
| *Bulb Turbines* | : | $n_q$ = 140 to 400 (4 to 25 m heads). |

In the Pelton Turbine, $Q$ is low and $H$ is high, so that $n_q$ is low. In the Kaplan Turbine, $Q$ is very high and $H$ is low giving a large value for $n_q$. The specific speed is also an indication of the runaway speed (in relation to normal speed) when the governor fails to operate to close the wicket gates. The Kaplan Turbine and Bulb Turbine have very high runaway speeds. In practice this can be 250 to 300% of normal speed.

A relation between head and specific speed for turbines built and in operation is as follows:

*Pelton Turbine* : $H = 38{,}500\ n_q^{-2}$

*Francis Turbine* : $H = 58{,}370\ n_q^{-1.53}$

*Pump Turbine* : $H = 377{,}120\ n_q^{-2.02}$

*Kaplan Turbine* : $H = 920{,}630\ n_q^{-2.06}$

*Bulb Turbine* : $H = 69{,}180\ n_q^{-1.6}$

[See F. Schweiger and J. Gregori: Water Power and Dam Construction, May 1989]

***Example 8.5***: A Pelton Wheel operates at a head of 800 m. Estimate its specific speed $n_q$. Give its units.

***Solution***: $n_q^2 = 38500/H = 38500/800 = 48.125$. Therefore, $n_q = 6.94$.

$$\text{Units: } n_q = n\,Q^{0.5}\,H^{-0.75} = (\text{rev/min}) \times (m^3/s)^{1/2} \times m^{-0.75}$$

$$= (\text{rev/min}) \times m^{0.75} \times s^{-0.5} = 60 \times (\text{rev/s}) \times m^{0.75} \times s^{-0.5}$$

$$= 60 \times (m/s^2)^{0.75}$$

However, $n_s$ as defined in Eq. 8.11 has no dimensions.

### *8.4.2 Turbine Models*

Model testing of hydraulic turbines is accepted as preliminary to designing the extremely large machines used in practice. Thus, scaling laws are used based on valid engineering assumptions. For hydraulic turbines, the most important coefficients are:

(a) *Power Coefficient*: $C_p = P_0 / \rho\ \omega^3\, d^5$ (8.14)

This is held constant between model and actual turbine.

(b) *Flow Coefficient*: $\phi = Q / \omega\, d^3$ (8.15)

or, $\phi = Q / n\, d^3$ (8.16)

This is constant between model and actual turbine.

(c) *Head Coefficient*: $\Psi = g\,H / \omega^2\, d^2$ (8.17)

This is also held constant between model and actual turbine.

These three coefficients give all information necessary for dimensioning model turbines.

***Example 8.6***: A turbine for 100 MW operating at a head of 100 *m* and running at 120 rev/min at an efficiency of 93% is to be scaled down 40/1 for model testing. (Scale factor = diameter of actual turbine/diameter of model). The head available at the model-testing laboratory is 25 *m*. Estimate:

(a) the probable speed of model; (b) flow rate in model; and
(c) power produced by model.

*Solution*: The flow rate $Q$ in the actual turbine is first calculated.

Now, $100 \times 10^6 / 0.93 = 9.81 \times 10^3 \times 100 \times Q$

giving $Q = 10^3 / 0.93 \times 9.81 = 109.61 \text{ m}^3/s$ .

Now, between the actual and model turbine, the following relations hold:

$$Q_a / n_a d_a^3 = Q_m / n_m d_m^3 \text{, and } g H_a / n_a^2 d_a^2 = g H_m / n_m^2 d_m^2$$

Therefore,

$$109.61 / (120 \times d_a^3) = Q_m / (n_m d_m^3) \text{, or , } (Q_m / n_m) = 109.61 / (120 \times 40^3)$$

and $$100/(120^2 d_a^2) = 25/(n_m^2 d_m^2)\text{, or, } n_m^2 = 25 \times 120^2 (d_a/d_m)^2/100$$

$$= 25 \times 120^2 \times 16 = 2400^2$$

Therefore, speed of model, $n_m = 2400$ rev/min.

Then $Q_m = 109.61 \times 2400 / (120 \times 40^3) = 34.25 \times 10^{-3} \text{ m}^3/\text{s}$ .

$$[Q_a / Q_m = 109.61 / 34.25 \times 10^{-3} = 3200 \text{, } n_a / n_m = 120 / 2400 = 0.05]$$

(c) Power generated by model: $P_m = 9.81 \times 10^3 \times 34.25 \times 10^{-3} \times 25 \text{ W}$

$$= 8.4 \text{ kW} .$$

***Example 8.7***: Repeat the above example for a scaling-down ratio of 20/1.

***Solution***: $n_m^2 = 25 \times 120^2 \times (d_a / d_m)^2 / 100 = 3600 \times 20^2$ .

Therefore, $n_m = 1200$ rev/min .

$$Q_m = 109.61 \times 1200/ (120 \times 20^3) = 34.25 \times 10^{-3} \times 16 = 0.548 \text{ m}^3/\text{s}.$$

$$P_m = 9.81 \times 10^3 \times 0.548 \times 25 \; W = 134.4 \text{ kW}$$

### 8.5 Micro-Hydel Developments

Very small hydro-electric power stations from as low as 10 kW to about 1000 kW are now being developed for supplying power to villages and small townships in hilly areas, which cannot be fed from a large electric-supply grid. Places like coffee and tea plantations had their own water-power stations using the natural run-off in mountain streams for a century now for the plantation operations and electrifying bungalows of the owners and staff quarters. However, in modern days because of talk of economy (above all else) and competitive costs of energy supply between micro-hydel stations and a very large regional interconnected network, the basic idea of giving benefits of electricity to remote areas is forgotten. Even railroads have suffered from this philosophy in some parts of the world. However, in spite of the cost of energy, micro-hydel developments are on the increase due to various reasons.

A small hydro-station requires a fairly steady flow of water in the stream, which does not necessitate a large storage reservoir. Such streams usually carry melted snow and do not dry up. A low diversion wall is all that is necessary as well as a good fall in the topography.

***Example 8.9***: A micro-hydel power station for 50 kW has a head of 60 *m*. At an efficiency of 85% for the unit (turbine 93% and generator 91%), calculate the quantity of water required, assuming a load factor of 100%.

***Solution***: The load is continuous at 50 kW. Turbine input = 50 kW/0.85 = 58.8 kW. Therefore, from Eq. (8.2).

$$58.8 = g H Q = 9.81 \times 60 \times Q, \text{ giving } Q = 0.1 \text{ m}^3/\text{s} = 10^5 \text{ cm}^3/\text{s} .$$

Referring to Fig. 8.7(a), if $H_m$ is the head in metres, the pressure on the pipe at turbine level is, since 1 $m^3$ of water weighs 1000 kg = 1 tonne,

$$P = 1000 H_m, \text{ kg/m}^2 = H_m, \text{ tonne/m}^2 \qquad (8.18)$$

On the other hand, if the head is $H'$ feet, the pressure in $lb/in^2$ will be (since 1 cu. ft. of water weighs 62.42 lb, and 1 sq. ft. = 144 sq. in.) given by

$$P = (62.42/144) H' = 0.43347 H', \text{ lb/in}^2 \qquad (8.19)$$

Steel pipes usually support 200 lb/in$^2$ pressure for 1 inch (2.54 cm) thickness with ample margin of safety. This is nearly 14 kg/cm$^2$ for 2.54 cm thickness. For a head of 200 feet (60 *m*), the pressure is 86.7 lb/in$^2$ (6.07 kg/cm$^2$) requiring a thickness in pipe of nearly 0.435 inch = 1.1 cm. Also, 6.07 × 2.54/14 = 1.1.

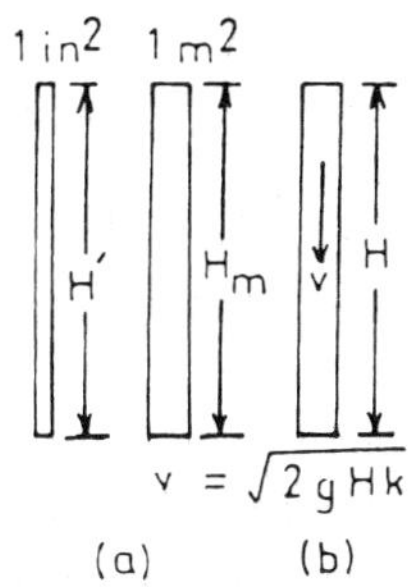

**Fig. 8.7** Pressure head and velocity head details referring to a micro-hydel development project

Furthermore, when the total pressure head is converted to velocity head at the turbine, $v = (2\,g\,H)^{1/2}$, m/s. Therefore, if the pipe area is $A\ m^2$, the quantity of water flowing per second is

$$Q = A v = A (2\,g\,H)^{1/2}, \text{ m}^3/\text{s} \qquad (8.20)$$

Therefore, required area of pipe is $A = Q/(2\,g\,H)^{1/2}$, m$^2$ (8.21)

In Example 8.9, for the 50 kW, 60 m development, the pipe area will be a minimum of

$$A = 0.1/(2 \times 9.81 \times 60)^{1/2} = 29 \times 10^{-4}\ \text{m}^2 = 29\ \text{cm}^2$$

This yields a pipe diameter $d = (4\,A/\pi)^{1/2} = 6.1$ cm $= 2.4$ in

Now, $P_0 = g\,Q\,H\,\eta = g\,H\,A\,(2\,g\,H)^{1/2}\,\eta$

giving $A = P_0/\eta\,\sqrt{2\,g^3\,H^3} = 0.023\,P_0/\eta\,H^{1.5}$ (8.22)

and corresponding diameter $d = (4\,A/\pi)^{1/2}$ (8.23)

If only a partial pressure head is converted to velocity at the turbine, a larger pipe area has to be provided. Let

$k$ = fraction of pressure head converted to velocity head ($k \leq 1$).

Then $v = (2\,g\,H\,k)^{1/2}$. Therefore, $A = Q/v = Q/(2\,g\,h\,k)^{1/2}$.

Thus $P_0 = g\,H\,Q\,\eta = g\,H\,A\,\eta\,\sqrt{2\,g\,H} \cdot \sqrt{k}$ (8.24)

This gives $A = 0.023\,P_0/\eta\,H^{1.5}\,k^{0.5}$ (8.25)

For example, if $k = 0.5$, then $0.5^{-0.5} = \sqrt{2} = 1.414$. The pipe area is increased by 41.4% over the value required for $k = 1$. The diameter will be about 20% larger than that calculated by Eq. (8.23).

***Example 8.10***: A mini-hydel plant for developing 500 kW to supply a small town operates under a head of 80 *m* (about 250 feet). The efficiency is $\eta = 90\%$. Assume $k = 0.5$. Calculate the diameter and thickness of pipe required, and the quantity of water flow per second at full load.

***Solution***: $Q = P_0/\eta\,g\,H = 500/0.9 \times 9.81 \times 80 = 0.708\ \text{m}^3/\text{s}$.

$$A = Q/\sqrt{2\,g\,H\,k} = 0.708/\sqrt{2 \times 9.81 \times 80 \times 0.5} = 0.0253\ \text{m}^2.$$

$$d = \sqrt{4\,A/\pi} = 0.18\ \text{m} = 18\ \text{cm}.$$

Pressure $p = 0.43347 \times 80 \times 3.28 = 113.74\ \text{lb/in}^2 = 7.97\ \text{kg/cm}^2$.

Required thickness of pipe $t = 113.74/200 = 0.569$ inch $= 1.445$ cm.

## 8.6 Miscellaneous Worked Examples

***Example 8.11***: A Francis Turbine for $H = 63$ *m* has a power output of 15 MW at the generator terminals. The turbine efficiency is 92% and generator efficiency 93%. Calculate the following:

(a) Quantity of water flowing per second

(b) Assuming 50% of pressure head to be converted to velocity head at the runner entrance, determine the diameter of pipe required

(c) Estimate the thickness of pipe required, if the safe stress is 14 kg/cm$^2$.

***Solution***: $P_0 = 9.81\, Q\, H\, \eta$ , kW

(a) Therefore $Q = 15 \times 10^3 / 9.81 \times 0.93 \times 0.92 \times 63 = 28.37$ m$^3$/s

(b) From Eq. (8.25).

$$A = Q / \sqrt{2\, g\, H\, k} = 0.023\, P_0 / \eta\, H^{1.5}\, k^{0.5} = 0.023 \times 15 \times 10^3 / 302.526$$

$$= 1.14 \text{ m}^2 \text{, giving } d = \sqrt{4\, A / \pi} = 1.2 \text{ m for the diameter .}$$

(c) $p = 0.43347 \times (63 \times 3.28) = 89.565$ lb/in$^2$ $= 6.27$ kg/cm$^2$

Using 200 lb/in$^2$ or 14 kg/cm$^2$ stress, required $t = 0.448$ in $= 1.375$ cm.

***Example 8.12***: A high-head Francis turbine develops 50 MW at a head of $H = 450$ m at efficiency of turbine-generator unit of 90%. The entrance diameter of pipeline is 1.2 m. Calculate: (a) the quantity of water flowing per second; (b) value of k; and (c) thickness of pipe at the turbine.

***Solution:***

(a) $Q = P_0 / 9.81\, \eta\, H = 50 \times 10^3 / 9.81 \times 0.9 \times 450 = 12.6$ m$^3$/s .

(b) $A = Q / \sqrt{2\, g\, H\, k}$ , or , $k = (Q / A)^2 / 2\, g\, H$ .

Therefore $k = [12.6 / (\pi \times 1.2^2 / 4)]^2 / 2 \times 9.81 \times 450 = 0.014$

Note that only a very small part of pressure head is converted to velocity head.

(c) $p = 0.43347 \times (3.28\, H_m)$ , lb/in$^2$ $= 639.8$ lb/in$^2$

$$= 0.43347 \times (3.28 \times H_m) \times 0.07 \text{ , kg/cm}^2 = 0.0995\, H_m \text{ , kg/cm}^2$$

$$\approx 0.1\, H_m \text{ , kg/cm}^2 = 45 \text{ kg/cm}^2 .$$

Therefore $t = (45/14) \times 2.54 = 8.164$ cm. Also, $639.8/200 = 3.2$ in $= 8.164$ cm.

***Example 8.13***: Using Eq. (8.18), construct a table showing thickness of pipe required for heads ranging from 100 m to 1000 m in steps of 100 m.

***Solution***:

| $H_m =$ | 100 | 200 | 300 | 400 | 500 | 600 | 700 | 800 | 900 | 1000 |
|---|---|---|---|---|---|---|---|---|---|---|
| $p \approx 0.1\, H_m$ | 10 | 20 | 30 | 40 | 50 | 60 | 70 | 80 | 90 | 100 |
| $\frac{t}{\text{cm}} = \frac{2.54\, p}{14}$ | 1.81 | 3.63 | 5.44 | 7.26 | 9.07 | 10.9 | 12.7 | 14.5 | 16.3 | 18.1 |

***Example 8.14***: A Francis Turbine unit for an output of 250 MW at the generator terminals at an efficiency of 90% operates at a head of 100 m and runs at 125 rev/min. It is to be scaled down 30/1 for model tests. Calculate: (a) Quantity of water, (b) speed, and (c) output of model turbine if the laboratory head is 25 m. The water for the test flows down from an overhead tank.

***Solution***: For the actual turbine, the flow rate is

$$Q_a = 250 \times 10^6 / 0.9 \times 9.81 \times 10^3 \times 100 = 283.16 \text{ m}^3/\text{s}.$$

The flow coefficient is $\phi = Q / n\, d^3 = \text{constant}$.

The head coefficient is $\Psi = H / n^2 d^2 = \text{constant}$.

Therefore,

$$283.16 / (125 \times d_a^3) = Q_m / (n_m \times d_m^3), \text{ and } 100 / (125^2 \times d_a^2) = 25 / (n_m^2 \times d_m^2)$$

or, $$n_m^2 = (H_m / H_a) \cdot (d_a / d_m)^2 \cdot n_a^2 = (25 / 100) \times 30^2 \times 125^2$$

or, $$n_m = 0.5 \times 30 \times 125 = 1875 \text{ rev/min}$$

$$Q_m = (n_m / n_a) \times (d_m / d_a)^3 \times Q_a = (1875 / 125) \times (1 / 30)^3 \times 283.16$$

$$= 0.1573 \text{ m}^3/\text{s}.$$

$$P_m = 9.81 \times 0.1573 \times 25 \text{ kW} = 38.6 \text{ kW} = 51.7 \text{ HP}.$$

***Example 8.15***: A Kaplan Turbine operates at rated head of 20 *m* and has an output of 108 MW at the generator at a speed of 72 rev/min. Calculate:

(a) Specific speeds $n_s$ and $n_q$ according to Eqs. (8.12) and (8.13).

(b) Check with the expression $H = 920{,}630\, n_q^{-2.06}$

***Solution***: $$P_0 = 9.81 \times Q \times H \times \eta \text{, kW} = 108 \text{ MW} = 108 \times 10^3 \text{ kW}$$

Therefore, $$Q = 108 \times 10^3 / 9.81 \times 20 = 550 \text{ m}^3/\text{s}.$$

(a) $$n_s = n\, Q^{0.5} (g\, H)^{-0.75} = (72 / 60) \times 550^{0.5} \times (9.81 \times 20)^{-0.75}$$

$$= 1.2 \times 23.452 / 52.423 = 0.537.$$

$$n_q = 72 \times 550^{0.5} \times 20^{-0.75} = 178.54.$$

(b) $$n_q^{2.06} = 920{,}630 / H = 920{,}630/20 = 46{,}031.5.$$

Therefore $2.06 \log n_q = \log 46{,}031.5$ giving $\log n_q = 2.26362$.

or $$n_q = 183.5 \text{ as against } 178.54 \text{ of part (a)}.$$

Full details of electric generators used with hydraulic turbines, known as salient-pole machines or alternators, are described in Chap. 9, next.

## OBJECTIVE TYPE QUESTIONS

1. The major components of a hydro-electric scheme are:
(a) A dam; (b) Pipeline; (c) Turbine-generator station; (d) Tail race; (e) All four.

2. Hydraulic turbines are classified into: (a) Pelton Wheel; (b) Francis Turbine; (c) Kaplan Turbine; (d) Bulb Turbine; (e) All four.

3. High-head developments usually use: (a) Pelton Wheel; (b) Francis turbine; (c) Kaplan turbine; (d) Bulb turbine; (e) All four.

4. Kaplan turbines are classified as: (a) Impulse turbines; (b) Reaction turbines; (c) Propeller turbines; (d) None of the three.

5. Francis turbines are ciassified as: (a) Impulse turbines; (b) Reaction turbines; (c) Propeller turbines; (d) None of the three.

6. Generators used for hydro-electric power stations are: (a) AC induction type; (b) AC synchronous type; (c) DC commutator type; (d) Rim type; (e) None of the four.

7. A hydro-electric scheme operates at a head of 100 m and the water flow is 2000 $m^3/s$. The power potential is: (a) 1962 kW; (b) 2000 MW; (c) 1200 MW; (d) 1962 MW.

8. In the previous problem, the plant efficiency is 90% and annual load factor is 0.68. The average output over a year is: (a) 1962 kW; (b) 2000 MW; (c) 1200 MW; (d) 1962 MW.

9. The effective head of water in a Pelton-wheel development is 800 m. If all the potential energy is converted to kinetic energy in the turbine, the velocity of water is: (a) 40 m/s; (b) 125.3 m/s; (c) 88.6 m/s; (d) none of the three.

10. A micro-hydel plant for 500 kW has a head of 50 *m*. At an efficiency of 80% and load factor of 0.8, the average quantity required is: (a) 1.02 $m^3/s$; (b) 3670 tonne/hr; (c) 2160 $ft^3/min$; (d) all three are true.

11. Based on maximum power, the diameter of pipe required in Question 10 is nearly: (a) 0.228 *m*; (b) 9 *in*; (c) 0.747 *ft*; (d) all three.

12. A surge tank is used for relieving: (a) Surge of electric power when large loads are switched on; (b) Surge of water when large loads are switched on; (c) Surge of water in pipe line when large loads are thrown off; (d) To protect damage during floods.

[**Answers**: 1. (e); 2. (e); 3. (a); 4. (c); 5. (b); 6. (b); 7. (d); 8. (c); 9. (b); 10. (d); 11. (d); 12. (c).]

## REVIEW QUESTIONS AND PROBLEMS

1. Draw the schematic diagrams of the following types of hydraulic power generation schemes: (a) high-head Pelton wheel and generation unit with storage reservoir located 40 km from the power station; (b) medium head Francis turbine development with power station located at the dam; (c) low-head Kaplan turbine development; (d) tidal power development using bulb turbine unit.

2. (a) Discuss why surge tanks are necessary for short- to medium-length pipe lines in a hydro-electric development.
(b) What is the function of a forebay?
(c) What is a tail race? Why is a draft head necessary at the turbine runner above the tail race, except for Pelton wheels?

3. A medium-size hydro-electric plant for 600 MWe output has 8 identical units at an efficiency of 95% and an annual plant load factor of 0.8. The head is constant at 90 *m*. Calculate: (a) The maximum flow required; (b) The diameter of pipe; (c) The amount of water to be stored behind a dam in a reservoir to cater for 300 days of power generation.
[$Q_m$ = 715.35 $m^3/s$; $d$ = 1.646 m; 14.83 $km^3$]

4. Draw the cross-sectional views of: (a) A Pelton wheel showing buckets and two jets; (b) A Francis turbine showing scroll casing, wicket gates and runner; (c) A Kaplan turbine.

5. What is a guide bearing for large turbine-generator unit? What is the function of a thrust bearing?

6. Describe environmental effects, both beneficial and detrimental, of a hydro-electric development.

7. Derive Eq. (8.2) for output power of a hydro-electric development.

8. The effective head of water behind a turbine is 200 *m*. Find the velocity of water at the turbine rotor if the percentage of static head converted to velocity head is: (a) 100%; (b) 50%; (c) 10%. (62.64, 44.3, 19.8 m/s).

9. The effective head of a high-head single-jet Pelton wheel hydro-station is 700 m. The velocity head at the turbine is 100% of static head. The jet diameter is 0.25 m. Calculate the power potential in water at the turbine runner. (39.5 MW ≈ 40 MW)

10. Define the terms: (a) Flow coefficient; (b) Head coefficient; (c) Specific speed. Give their units.

11. (a) A Pelton wheel operates at a head of 1000 *m*. Estimate its specific speed. (b) If the speed of the runner is 600 rev/min, estimate the quantity of water flowing. (c) Estimate the power potential at this specific speed.
(6.205; 3.382 $m^3/s$; 33.2 MW).

12. In a Francis turbine developing 75 MW at the generator output at a head of 300 m, the efficiency is 0.9375. The velocity head developed at the inlet to the runner is 50% of the static head ($k = 0.5$ in Eqs. (8.24) and (8.25)). Calculate the following:

    (a) Entrance diameter of pipe into the turbine (≈ 0.8 m)

    (b) The quantity of water flowing per second (27.183 $m^3/s$)

    (c) Thickness of pipe required (5.44 cm)

    (d) The specific speed, $n_q$, if the actual speed is 500 rev/min (38.6)

    (e) Check with the relation: $H = 58{,}370.\ n_q^{-1.53}$ (31.34)

13. A turbine for 300 MW has to operate under a head of 250 *m* and run at 200 rev/min at an efficiency of 0.9375. It is to be scaled down to 50/1 for model testing. The head available at the model-testing lab is 30 *m*. Estimate: (a) The probable speed of model. (b) Flow rate in model.
($n_m$ = 3464 rev/min. (Closest for 50 Hz operation is 3000 rev/min and for 60-Hz operation, 3600 rev/min). $Q_m = 0.013\ m^3/s$; $P_m = 3.826$ kW).

14. A Kaplan turbine has an output of 70 MW at the generator terminals with an efficiency of 0.933 at a head of 15 m, and runs at 60 rev/min. Calculate the following: (a) its specific speed $n_q$; (b) the quantity of water flow; and (c) check $n_q$ with the formula $n_q = (920{,}630/H)^{1/2.06}$.
($n_q = 177.7$; $Q = 509.7\ m^3/s$; $n_q = 211$).

CHAPTER 9

# Electrical Equipment for Energy Conversion

## 9.1 AC-DC Conversion and DC-AC Inversion

### *9.1.1 Phase-Controlled Converter Circuits*

When power in alternating form is to be converted to direct form, rectifiers or converters are utilized. The heart of the controller is a controlled thyristor (also known as silicon controlled rectifier, SCR) consisting of a cathode and an anode to conduct the main current in one direction only, and a gate which turns the device on when it receives a pulse, but not turn it off with a pulse fed to the gate. The remaining part of the circuit turns the thyristor off. Figure 9.1 shows a load $L$

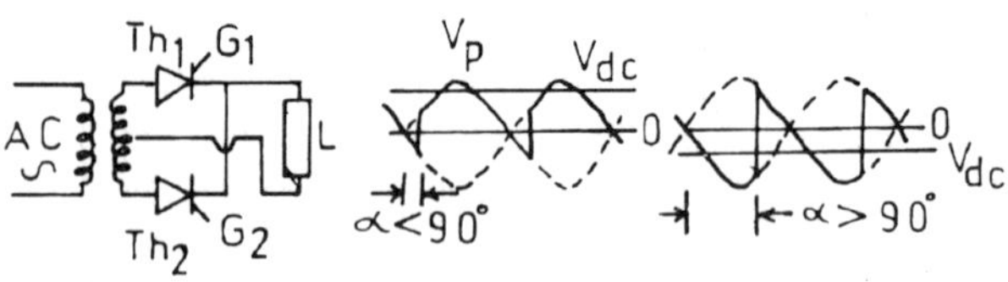


**Fig. 9.1** Single-phase thyristor bridge for converter and inverter, showing output waveforms

which receives unidirectional (dc) voltage and conducts a current $I_{dc}$ from an ac source. The gate-firing pulse can be given at any point on the ac voltage wave to vary both the magnitude and polarity of the dc voltage in relation to the current. This arrangement is known as a phase-controlled mid-point two-pulse converter operating from a single-phase ac source. The figure also shows resulting load-voltage waveforms (as well as current for a purely resistive load). At full conduction, the firing angle $\alpha$ is zero. When $\alpha = 90°$, the load voltage is zero, while for $\alpha > 90°$, the device acts as an inverter. Such converters are used in battery-chargers, electrolysis of water, etc.

Let the rms value of ac-side voltage be V and peak value $V_p = \sqrt{2}$ V, frequency $f$, and firing from $\alpha$ to $(\alpha + 90°)$. Then the dc-side voltage is the average over one-half cycle and given by

$$V_{dc} = \frac{1}{\pi} \int_{\alpha}^{\pi + \alpha} \sqrt{2}\, V \sin 2\pi f t = (2\sqrt{2}/\pi)\, V \cos \alpha$$

$$= 0.9\, V \cos \alpha = 0.637\, V_p \cos \alpha \qquad (9.1)$$

Table 9.1 gives the ratio ($V_{dc}/V$) and ($V_{dc}/V_p$) as a function of the gate-firing angle $\alpha$.

**Table 9.1: DC Voltage as a Function of Firing Angle $\alpha$ (degrees)**

| $\alpha =$ | 0 | 15 | 30 | 45 | 60 | 75 | 90 |
|---|---|---|---|---|---|---|---|
| $\cos\alpha$ | 1 | 0.966 | 0.866 | 0.707 | 0.5 | 0.259 | 0 |
| $V_{dc}/V$ | 0.9 | 0.87 | 0.78 | 0.636 | 0.45 | 0.233 | 0 |
| $V_{dc}/V_p$ | 0.637 | 0.615 | 0.55 | 0.45 | 0.3185 | 0.165 | 0 |
| | ← Rectification → | | | | | | |
| $\alpha =$ | 105 | 120 | 135 | 150 | 165 | 180 | |
| $\cos\alpha$ | –0.259 | –0.5 | –0.707 | –0.866 | –0.966 | –1 | |
| $V_{dc}/V$ | –0.233 | –0.45 | –0.636 | –0.78 | –0.87 | –0.9 | |
| $V_{dc}/V_p$ | –0.165 | –0.3185 | –0.45 | –0.55 | –0.615 | –0.637 | |
| | ← Inversion → | | | | | | |

When 3-phase ac has to be converted to unidirectional dc, more thyristors are required and the secondaries of transformers must match the number of thyristors used. These are known as 3-pulse, 6-pulse, and 12-pulse convertors and shown in Fig. 9.2 (a)-(c). The 3-pulse converter requires a transformer with six secondary windings arranged in a zig-zag connection. Such connection eliminates circulation of dc in the transformer magnetic circuit. The 6-pulse converter also requires six secondaries and a heavy inductor (reactor) known as the inter-phase reactor to prevent circulating current between the two sets of 3-phase converters and the troublesome harmonics in the undulating current. In the 12-pulse converter, the two secondaries are connected in Wye and Delta to obtain phase difference of 30° between voltages. As many as 12 thyristors are required and gate pulses are given 30° apart. The large number of phases or pulses helps to keep the ripple down in the dc-side voltage, the lowest harmonic frequency being (12 × power frequency). This requires smaller smoothing reactors to filter the dc-side voltage. Later on we will observe how high-voltage dc transmission uses these ac-dc converters and dc-ac inverters.

## 9.2 Phase-Controlled Inverter Circuits

In many situations such as Wind Energy Conversion, the generated dc has to be converted to ac in order that the generator may be connected to an existing 3-phase power-frequency ac system. Inverters are also used in electric cars, propulsion systems such as trains, and for electric-motor controls. Figure 9.3 shows a bridge type 3-phase inverter and the points on the dc voltage where gate-firing pulses should be given. The pulses are displaced by 180° for the thyristors belonging to

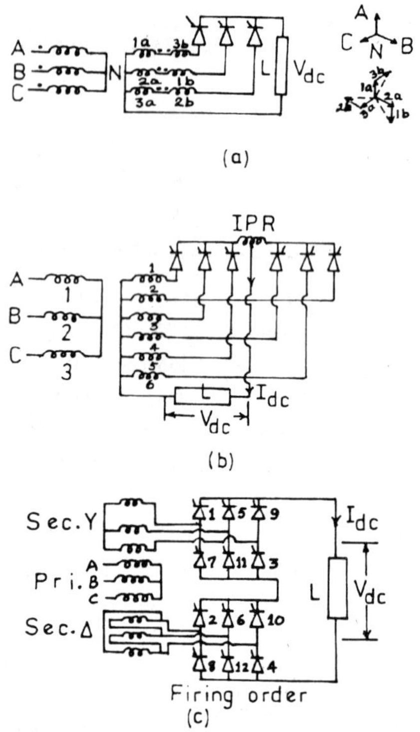


**Fig. 9.2** Converters for ac-dc conversion: (a) 3-pulse; (b) 6-pulse; (c) 12-pulse

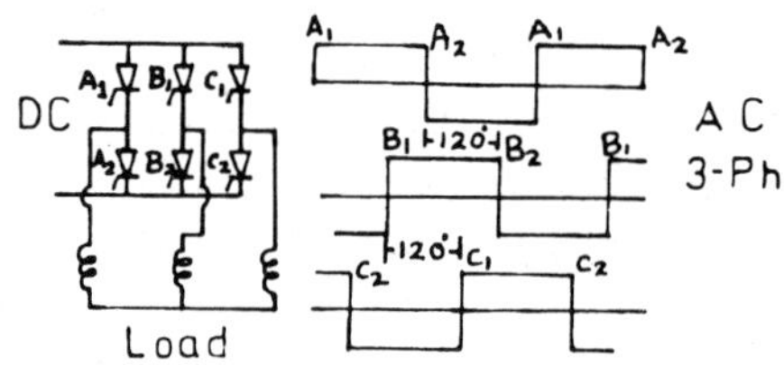


**Fig. 9.3** Inverter schematic

one phase, but displaced 120° between phases. The arrangement delivers "blocks" of unidirectional voltage displaced 120° from each other, to the loads connected to the ac side. The gate-circuit firing comes from ring-counters or switching transistors controlled by suitable clocks. These non-sinusoidal rectangular but periodic voltages can be expressed as a composite wave (Fourier series), with $V_{dc}$ = dc-side voltage,

$$e(t) = (4\,V_{dc}/\pi)\cdot\left[\sin 2\pi f t + \frac{1}{3}\sin 3\times 2\pi f t + \frac{1}{5}\sin 5\times 2\pi f t + \ldots\right] \quad (9.2)$$

which contains the fundamental component $(4V_{dc}/\pi)\sin 2\pi\,\text{ft} = 1.274\,V_{dc}\sin 2\pi\,\text{ft}$, and all its odd-multiple harmonics, whose amplitudes decrease in proportion to the order of harmonic. Thus, the amplitude of the 5th harmonic is 20% of the fundamental. By filtering these harmonics, a pure sine wave at the desired fundamental frequency can be obtained. Inversion is also necessary in high-voltage dc transmission involving enormous amounts of power. They are used for evacuating power from large thermal- and hydro-power stations over very long distances, such as 400 to 1000 km with powers up to 10,000 MW. We discuss dc transmission later.

## 9.3 Transformers

Central steam-station and hydro-electric generators or alternators generate 13.2 to 15 kV (or a little higher) in their windings. These voltages cannot be utilized directly; they have to be either stepped up or stepped down. There are also many interconnections in a large electric power system using many voltage levels. Power utilization at loads requires transformation of voltages from one level to another of a different voltage. All these require transformers for the multifarious duties imposed upon them. They use coils wound on the same magnetic circuit (air or steel) linking nearly the same flux, with the voltage induced in a coil being proportional to the number of turns in the coil.

The most usual number of coils or windings is either two or three. There exist single-winding transformers also called auto-transformers from very small dimmers of a few watts to the largest sizes used in power transmission (≈ 1000 MVA). The auto-transformer has a conducting path from the high- to the low-voltage circuits, while the two- and three-winding transformers isolate the two sides electrically, as shown in Fig. 9.4. Auto-transformers are used where the voltage levels on the two sides have a ratio less than 3. Multi-winding (2,3) transformers have no such restriction on the voltage levels of the two sides, such as the auto-transformer has.

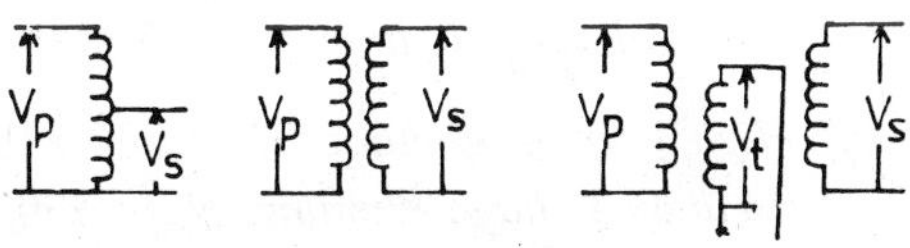

**Fig. 9.4** Transformer windings: Single-winding (auto-) transformer; Two-winding transformer; Three-winding transformer

### *9.3.1 Two-Winding Transformer*

Figure 9.5 shows the equivalent electrical circuit of a two winding transformer with a voltage $V_p$ applied to one side called the Primary, and a load $L$ connected to the second winding called the Secondary. The two windings have a turns ratio $a/1$. Usually the number of turns in each winding is determined by the oil-soaked paper insulation or compound-soaked cambric insulation, which can support no more than 10 V between turns. All voltages unless specifically mentioned are effective or rms values.

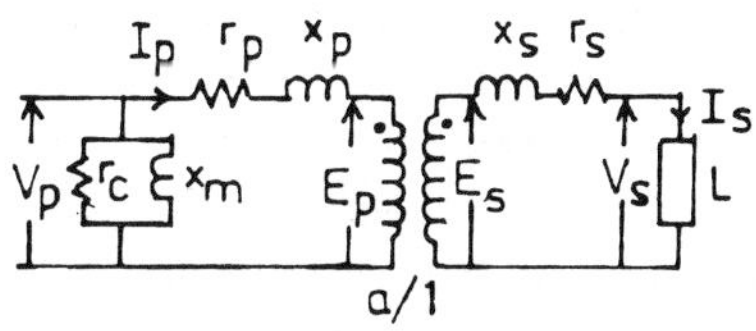

**Fig. 9.5** Equivalent electrical circuit of two-winding transformer

***Example 9.1***: Transformer windings are used for the following voltage levels and connection given below. Using 6 V per turn, calculate the number of turns required in each winding (see Fig. 9.6).

(a) Single-phase: 133 kV/7.62 kV; (b) Three-phase: 345 kV Wye/33 kV Delta; (c) Three-phase: 500 kV Wye/230 kV Wye/13.8 kV Delta.

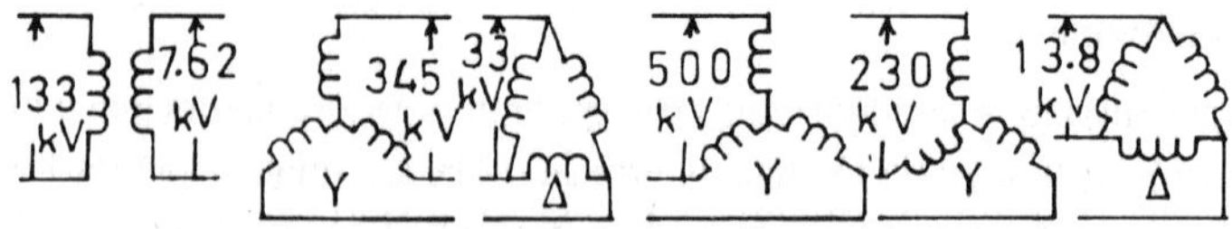


**Fig. 9.6** Transformer winding details of Example 9.1

***Solution***:

(a) *High Voltage Winding*: $N_h = 133 \times 10^3/6 = 22{,}167$ turns
*Low Voltage Winding*: $N_l = 7620/6 = 1270$ turns

(b) *High Voltage Winding*: $N_h = 345 \times 10^3/6\sqrt{3} = 33{,}200$ turns
*Low Voltage Winding*: $N_l = 33 \times 10^3/6 = 5{,}500$ turns

(c) *High Voltage Winding*: $N_h = 500 \times 10^3/6\sqrt{3} = 48{,}112$ turns
*Medium Voltage Winding*: $N_m = 230 \times 10^3/6\sqrt{3} = 22{,}132$ turns
*Low Voltage Winding*: $N_l = 13.8 \times 10^3/6 = 2{,}300$ turns

Note in all cases that the ratio of number of turns in any two windings of the same transformer is proportional to their voltages.

Referring back to Fig 9.5, the impedance components are described now. At the entrance to the primary is placed a resistance $r_c$ which draws a current in phase with $V_p$ denoting the power loss (heating) in the magnetic iron of the transformer. These losses are caused by ''hysteresis'' and ''eddy currents'' in the magnetic circuit. The reactance $x_m$ draws a pure inductive current which is necessary to magnetize the core, lagging behind $V_p$ by 90°.

The resistances $r_p$ and $r_s$ are the copper-winding resistances at power frequency (about 140% of their dc resistance values). The two reactances, $x_p$ and $x_s$, are called ''leakage reactances''. In an non-ideal practical transformer, not all the flux set up by the primary-winding current $I_p$ links the secondary winding. The flux that does not link the secondary but flows in other paths is a leakage as far as the winding is concerned. The reactance due to this is shown as $x_p$, which develops a voltage drop $I_p x_p$. Similarly, $(I_s x_s)$ represents a voltage drop in the secondary due to secondary-winding current and leakage flux. The voltage appearing across the load is then found as follows, denoting phasors by bold-face letters:

$$\mathbf{E}_p = \mathbf{V}_p - \mathbf{I}_p(r_p + j\,x_p)\,;\ \mathbf{E}_s = \mathbf{E}_p / a\,;$$

$$\mathbf{V}_L = \mathbf{E}_s - \mathbf{I}_s(r_s + j\,x_s) = \frac{1}{a}[\mathbf{V}_p - \mathbf{I}_p(r_p + j\,x_p)] - \mathbf{I}_s(r_s + j\,x_s) \quad (9.3)$$

Therefore, $a\,\mathbf{V}_L = \mathbf{V}_p - \mathbf{I}_p(r_p + j\,x_p) - a\,\mathbf{I}_s(r_s + j\,x_s)$ (9.4)

The portion ($E_p/E_s$) is called an ideal transformer with no voltage drops or losses. Also, $E_p = a \cdot E_s$. Thus, any voltage on the secondary side when multiplied by the turns ratio denotes an equivalent voltage on the primary side. Also, for an ideal transformer, volt-amperes input to one winding must equal the volt-ampere output at the other winding.

Therefore $\quad E_p I_p = E_s I_s \qquad (9.5)$

giving $\quad I_p / I_s = E_s / E_p = 1/a$, or, $I_p = I_s / a$ and $I_s = a\, I_p \qquad (9.6)$

The currents therefore transform inversely as the turns ratio. Using this in Eq. (9.4), there results

$$a\,\mathbf{V}_L = \mathbf{V}_p - \mathbf{I}_p (r_p + j\,x_p) - \mathbf{I}_p\, a^2 (r_s + j\,x_s)$$

or

$$\mathbf{V}_{Lp} = \mathbf{V}_p - [\,(r_p + a^2 r_s) + j\,(x_p + a^2 x_s)\,]\,\mathbf{I}_p$$

$$= \mathbf{V}_p - (R_p + j\,X_p)\,\mathbf{I}_p \qquad (9.7)$$

where now all quantities are referred or ''transformed'' to the primary side. The new quantities now are the following:

$\mathbf{V}_{Lp}$ = load voltage referred to the primary winding = $a\,\mathbf{V}_L$

$R_p$ = $r_p + a^2 r_s$ = resistance of primary + (turns ratio)$^2$ × sec. res.
= series resistance of transformer referred to primary

$X_p$ = $x_p + a^2 x_s$ = series leakage reactance of tranformer referred to the primary winding

A similar transformation can be made referring all quantities to the secondary winding, as follows:

$$\mathbf{V}_L = \mathbf{V}_p / a - (1/a)\,\mathbf{I}_p (r_p + j\,x_p) - \mathbf{I}_s (r_s + j\,x_s)$$

$$= \mathbf{V}_{ps} - [\,(r_p / a^2 + r_s) + j\,(x_p / a^2 + x_s)\,]\,\mathbf{I}_s = \mathbf{V}_{ps} - (R_s + j\,X_s)\,\mathbf{I}_s \qquad (9.8)$$

where $\mathbf{V}_{ps}$ = applied voltage to the primary referred to the secondary

$= \mathbf{V}_p / a$

and $R_s$, $X_s$ = equivalent series resistance and leakage reactance of transformer referred to the secondary winding

***Example 9.2***: A medium-sized 100 kVA, (33/√3) kV/440 V transformer with turns ratio $a = 43.3$ (33000/440√3) has the following details:

Load voltage $V_L$ = 440 V

Power supplied to motor and lighting load: 100 kVA at 0.9 p.f. lagging

Resistances: Core loss, $r_c$ = 181.5 kohm on h.v. side
Primary winding, $r_p$ = 36.3 ohm
Secondary winding, $r_s$ = 19.36 mohm = 0.01936 ohm

Reactances: Magnetizing, $x_m$ = 72.6 kohm on h.v. side
Primary leakage reactance, $x_p$ = 72.6 ohm
Secondary leakage reactance, $x_s$ = 39 mohm = 0.039 ohm

Calculate the following:

(a) The full rated currents on the two sides based on 100 kVA, 440 V, $a = 43.3$

(b) Load current drawn at 100 kVA, 440 V and 0.9 p.f. lag on l.v. or secondary side, and the corresponding current on the primary h.v. side.

(c) The voltage $V_p$ to be applied on the primary or h.v. side for this load

(d) The referred values of series resistances and leakage reactances to the two windings

(e) The voltage drops in these series elements of impedances

(f) Power loss in the winding resistance elements and in the core

(g) Input power to the primary h.v. side and efficiency based on watts

(h) If the load is reduced to zero (load terminals open) holding the primary applied voltage constant at $V_p$ as in part (c), calculate the voltage across the load terminals on the secondary l.v. side.

***Solution***:

(a) $I_s$ = 100 kVA/0.440 kV = 227.3 A. $I_p$ = 227.3/43.3 = 5.25 A

(b) We take $V_L$ = 440 V as reference. Thus, $\mathbf{V}_L = 440\underline{/0^\circ}$
$\mathbf{I}_s = 227.3\,(0.9 - j\,0.436) = 204.6 - j\,99 = 227.3\underline{/-25.84^\circ}$
$\mathbf{I}_p = 5.25\underline{/-25.84^\circ} = 4.725 - j\,2.29$

(c) By Eq. (9.7)

$$\mathbf{V}_p = [440 + (204.6 - j\,99)\cdot(0.01936 + j\,0.039)]\cdot 43.3 + (4.725 - j\,2.29)\cdot(36.3 + j\,72.6) = 19{,}728.36 + j\,265.93$$

$$= 19{,}730\underline{/0.772^\circ}\ V$$

(d) $R_p = r_p + a^2 r_s = 36.3 + 43.3^2 \times 19.36 \times 10^{-3} = 36.3 + 36.3 = 72.6$ ohm

$X_p = x_p + a^2 x_s = 72.6 + 43.3^2 \times 39 \times 10^{-3} = 72.6 + 73.12 = 145.72$ ohm

$Z_p = R_p + j\,X_p = 72.6 + j\,145.72 = 162.8\underline{/63.5^\circ}$

$R_s = r_p/a^2 + r_s = 38.72 \times 10^{-3}$ ohm , $X_s = x_p/a^2 + x_s = 77.22 \times 10^{-3}$ ohm

$Z_s = R_s + j\,X_s = (38.72 + j\,77.72)\,10^{-3} = 86.83 \times 10^{-3}\underline{/63.5^\circ}$

*Check*: $Z_s\,a^2 = 86.83 \times 10^{-3} \times 43.3^2 = 162.8 = Z_p$

(e) *Voltage drops*:

Referred to l.v. secondary: $227.3\angle{-25.84°} \times 86.83 \times 10^{-3} \angle{63.5°}$
$= 19.736 \angle{37.7°}\ V.$

Referred to h.v. primary: $5.25 \angle{-25.84°} \times 162.8 \angle{63.5°} = 854.7 \angle{37.7°}\ V.$

*Check*: 854.7/43.3 = 19.74

(f) Power loss in primary-winding resistance = $5.25^2 \times 36.3 = 1000$ W
Power loss in secondary-winding resistance = $227.3^2 \times 0.01936 = 1000$ W
Core loss: $V_p^2 / r_c = 19730^2/181.5 \times 10^3 = 2145$ W (see part (c) for $V_p$)

(g) Input power = 100,000 × 0.9 + 1000 + 1000 + 2145 = 94,145
$W$ = 94.145 kW
Output power = 90,000 W = 90 kW

Therefore, efficiency = 90/94.145 = 0.956 = 95.6%

(h) When load is thrown off and primary voltage is held at 19,730 V, since no load-current flows, series voltage drops are zero. Therefore, load voltage = 19,730/43.3 = 455.66 $V$
Voltage rise = 455.66 – 440 = 15.66 V
As a percentage of full-load voltage, this represents a rise of 15.66 × 100/440 = +3.56%. This is called ''regulation'' and is positive for an inductive or lagging power-factor load.

*Percentage Voltage Drops*

It is convenient always to carry out performance calculations of a transformer by referring all quantities to any one of the windings. In doing so, the following properties can be kept in mind:

(a) The voltages transform as the turns ratio of the windings;

(b) The currents transform inversely as the turns ratio;

(c) Impedances transform as the square of the turns ratio. Values are higher when referred to the high-voltage winding by $a^2$, ($a > 1$).

(d) Powers remain the same on both sides of a two-winding transformer. Instead of working with actual values of the voltage and current and the impedances which vary widely in transformers used in practic from as low as 1 kVA to as immense as 1,000,000 kVA = 1,000 MVA, it is convenient to use percentage values, especially for impedance drops. Later on we will extend this idea by utilizing per unit values for all quantities, namely, voltage, current, impedance and power.

Let $I$ = current flowing when referred to any of the windings, and $Z$ the series impedance referred to the same winding. If $I_f$ = full rated current of the transformer, $\%I = (I/I_f)100$ or, fractional current $I = I/I_f$. The voltage drop is $V_{ser} = I.Z$.

At full rated current it is $I_f Z$. If $V_r$ = rated voltage, then $I.Z/V_r$ = fractional series voltage drop with the rated voltage as reference. This value of the fractional voltage drop stays fairly within narrow ranges for all transformers used in practice from the smallest to the largest.

***Example 9.3***: In the previous example, calculate:

(a) The fractional and percentage voltage drops in series impedance when referred to the primary and to the secondary. Show that they are equal.

(b) The percentage voltage drops in individual windings.

(c) The primary voltage applied to the h.v. winding by using fractional values.

***Solution***: $\mathbf{I}_s = 227.3\underline{/-25.84°}\,A$, $\mathbf{V}_{\text{rated}} = 440\underline{/0°}\,V$

(a) $Z_s = 86.33 \times 10^{-3}\underline{/63.5°}$ ohm

$I_s \cdot Z_s / V_{\text{rated}} = 0.04486\underline{/37.66°} = 4.486\underline{/37.66°}\,\%$

$\mathbf{I}_p = 5.25\underline{/-25.84°}\,A$, $Z_p = 162.8\underline{/63.5°}$ ohm, $V_{\text{prated}} = 33/\sqrt{3}$ kV

Therefore,

$$I_p \cdot Z_p / V_{\text{prated}} = (5.25 \times 162.8 / 19{,}053)\underline{/37.66°} = 0.04486\underline{/37.66°}$$

$$= 4.486\underline{/37.66°}\,\%$$

(b) $I_p r_p / V_{\text{prated}} = (5.25 \times 36.3 / 19{,}053)\,100 = 1\%$

$I_p x_p / V_{\text{prated}} = (5.25 \times 72.6 / 19{,}053)\,100 = 2\%$

$z_p = 0.01 + j\,0.02$ at full rated current

$I_s r_s / V_{\text{srated}} = 227.3 \times 19.36 \times 10^{-3} / 440 = 0.01 = 1\%$

$I_s x_s / V_{\text{srated}} = 227.3 \times 39 \times 10^{-3} / 440 = 0.02 = 2\%$

$z_s = 0.01 + j\,0.02$

Total impedance drop $Z_{\text{series}} = z_p + z_s = 0.02 + j\,0.04 = 0.04472\underline{/63.5°}$

(c) $\mathbf{V}_L = 1\underline{/0°}$, $\mathbf{I}_s = 1\underline{/-25.84°}$, $z_s = 0.01 + j\,0.02$

$\mathbf{I}_p = 1\underline{/-25.84°}$, $z_p = 0.01 + j\,0.02$

Therefore, $\mathbf{V}_p = 1 + j\,0 + (0.9 - j\,0.436) \cdot (0.01 + j\,0.02) + (0.9 - j\,0.436) \cdot (0.01 + j\,0.02)$

$$= 1 + j\,0 + (0.9 - j\,0.436) \cdot (0.02 + j\,0.04) = 1.0358\underline{/1.5°}$$

Rated primary voltage $V_{pr} = 33{,}000/\sqrt{3} = 19{,}053\,V$

Therefore, primary voltage required for the load condition is

$V_p = 1.0358 \times 19{,}053 = 19{,}735\,V$, which is the same as was obtained in Example 9.2 earlier in part (c). But note that we have been able to convert all q antities into small values between 0 and 1, which are easier to handle.

*Per Unit Values*

Per unit values denote fractional values of power, voltage, current and impedances referred to "base quantities" at the many different voltage levels involved in a system. Because of the need to preserve the turns ratio, the base quantities at two voltage levels are related to each other and not independent of each other. However, at the same voltage level, two of the above four quantities can be chosen independently, since there are inter-relationships between the four.

Refer to Fig. 9.7, in which all impedance elements are shown in their places. We select two quantities, say the voltage and current on one of the voltage levels (the low-voltage side in this case) indicated as $V_B$ and $I_B$. These form the base or reference quantities to which all other quantities in the system are referred. The base impedance is then given by

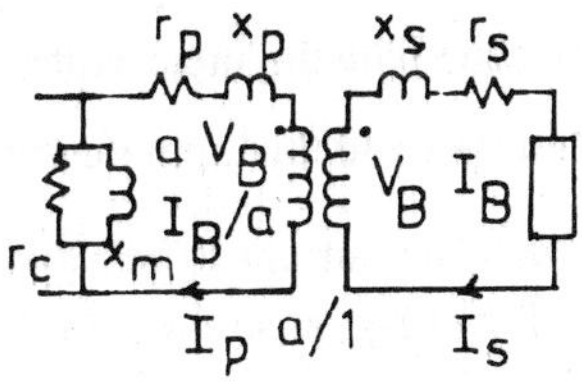


**Fig. 9.7** Two-winding transformer equivalent circuit showing impedances, voltages, and currents in their respective places

$$Z_{B1} = V_{B1} / I_{B1} \tag{9.9}$$

The base power becomes $W_{B1} = V_{B1} \cdot I_{B1}$ (9.10)

These refer to winding 1, which is taken to be the secondary side.

Having selected $V_{B1}$ and $I_{B1}$ at one voltage level as the bases, the base quantities at other level or levels will be automatically determined or fixed by the turns ratio of the transformer. Thus, at the high-voltage level, (taken as winding 2), we have:

$$\left.\begin{array}{ll}
\text{Base voltage} & V_{B2} = a \cdot V_{B1} \\
\text{Base current} & I_{B2} = (1 / a) \cdot I_{B1} \\
\text{Base impedance} & Z_{B2} = V_{B2} / I_{B2} = a^2 (V_{B1} / I_{B1}) = a^2 \cdot Z_{B1} \\
\text{Base power} & W_{B2} = V_{B2} \cdot I_{B2} = a\, V_{B1} \cdot (1 / a)\, I_{B1} = V_{B1} \cdot I_{B1} = W_{B1}
\end{array}\right\} \tag{9.11}$$

Note that the base volt-amperes is constant throughout the system.

All impedance are converted to per unit values by dividing by the base impedance at that voltage level. Similarly, all voltages and currents are suitably converted to per unit values. Such a representation gives all quantities near unity or decimals, which is easier to handle and more importantly to visualize their order of magnitudes. It is easier to talk about 1% or 0.01 per unit value of series resistance drop or 5% or 0.05 per unit than actual voltage drop in volts. The following procedure for solving Examples 9.2 and 9.3 will serve to illustrate the convenience of using per unit (or, p.u.) values.

***Example 9.4***: In the previous examples, take $V_{B1} = 440\ V = 1$ p.u., and $I_{B1} = 227.3\ A = 1$ p.u. on the low-voltage or load side. Turns ratio $a = 43.3$.

(a) Calculate base voltage, current, impedance and power on both sides.

(b) Convert the given impedance elements, $r_s$, $r_p$, $x_s$, $x_p$, $x_m$ and $r_c$ to per unit values on the chosen bases.

(c) Re-draw the circuit at the two voltage levels on a single voltage level using the per-unit values.

(d) Calculate the input voltage at the h.v. side in p.u. and actual kV.

(e) Calculate the input power in p.u. and volt-amperes.

(*Note*: The current to be used for the calculation is $1\underline{/-25.84°} = 1$ p.u. at 0.9 power factor lag, as in the previous examples).

***Solution***:

(a) *L.V. Side*: $V_{B1} = 440\ V = 1$ p.u. $I_{B1} = 227.3\ A = 1$ p.u. These two quantities have been arbitrarily selected and may correspond to rated values, but this is not essential for applying the per-unit value method.
$Z_{B1} = 440/227.3 = 1.9358$ ohm $= 1$ p.u.
$W_{B1} = 440 \times 227.3 = 100{,}000$ V-A $= 100$ kVA $= 1$ p.u.

We note that $Z_{B1}$ and $W_{B1}$ cannot be arbitrarily selected. They depend on the other two quantities selected as bases, in this case, $V_{B1}$ and $I_{B1}$.

*H.V. Side*: Since the turns ratio is $a = 33{,}000/440\sqrt{3} = 43.3$, we obtain:

$$V_{B2} = a \cdot V_{B1} = 43.3 \times 440 = 19{,}052\ V = 19.052\ kV = 1 \text{ p.u.}$$
$$I_{B2} = I_{B1}/a = 227.3/43.3 = 5.2494\ A = 1 \text{ p.u.}$$
$$Z_{B2} = a^2 \cdot Z_{B1} = 3629.4 \text{ ohm} = 1 \text{ p.u.}$$
$$W_{B2} = W_{B1} = 100 \text{ kVA} = 1 \text{ p.u.}$$

(b) $r_s = 0.01936$ ohm $= 0.01936/1.9358 = 0.01$ p.u., since $Z_{B1} = 1.9358$ ohm.
$r_p = 36.3$ ohm $= 36.3/3629.4 = 0.01$ p.u., since $Z_{B2} = 3629.4$ ohm.
$x_s = 0.039$ ohm $= 0.039/1.9358$ p.u. $= 0.02015$ p.u. $\approx 0.02$ p.u.
$x_p = 72.6$ ohm $= 72.6/3629.4$ p.u. $= 0.02$ p.u.
$r_c = 181.5 \times 10^3$ ohm $= 181.5 \times 10^3/3.6294 \times 10^3 = 50$ p.u.
$x_m = 72.6 \times 10^3$ ohm $= 72.6/3.6294 = 20$ p.u.
$r_s + r_p + j(x_s + x_p) = 0.02 + j\,0.04 = 0.044856\underline{/63.52°}$ p.u.

(c) Figure 9.8 shows the re-drawn equivalent circuit in p.u. representation. Note that the turns ratio has disappeared.

(d) When load voltage $\mathbf{V}_L = 1\underline{/0°}$ p.u. and $\mathbf{I}_L = 1\underline{/-25.84°}$, input voltage to h.v. side is $\mathbf{V}_h = 1 + j\,0 + 1\underline{/-25.84°} \times 0.044856\underline{/63.52°} = 1 + 0.044856\underline{/37.68°}$

$$= 1.0355 + j\,0.02742 = 1.035863\underline{/1.516°}$$

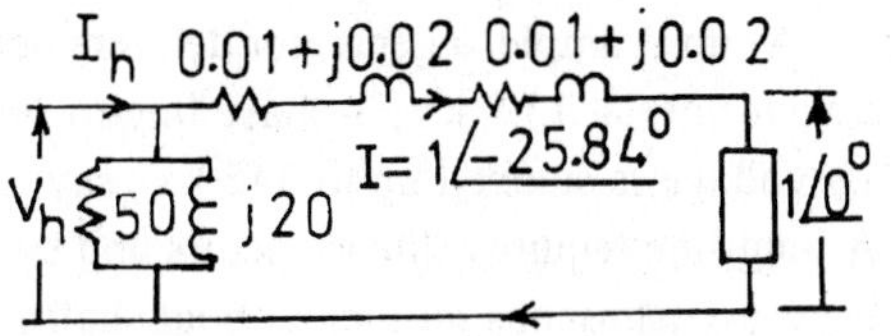


**Fig. 9.8** Equivalent circuit of transformer for Example 9.4 showing all quantities referred to one of the windings in per-unit values

Since base voltage is $V_{B2}$ = 19.052 kV, actual applied voltage is $V_h$ = 1.035863 × 19.052 = 19.7353 kV.

(e) Current in $r_c$ = 1.035863/1.516° / 50 = 0.0207/1.516° p.u.
Current in $x_m$ = 1.035863/1.516° / $j$ 20 = 0.0518/–88.484°, ($j$ 20 = 20/90°)
Therefore, input current = 1/–25.84° + 0.0207/1.516° + 0.0518/–88.484°

= 0.92214 – $j$ 0.048713 p.u. = 1.043/–27.84°

Base current $I_{B2}$ = 5.2494 $A$ on h.v. side.

Therefore, input current $I_h$ = 5.2494 × 1.043/–27.84° = 5.475/–27.84°
= 4.8407 – $j$ 2.557 $A$

Input power

$$W_h = V_h \cdot I_h^* = 1.035863\underline{/1.516°} \times 1.043\underline{/+27.84°} = 1.0804\underline{/29.356°}$$

$$= 0.94167 + j\,0.52965 \text{p.u.}$$

(*Note*: $I_h^*$ = complex conjugate of $I_h$). The difference in phase between voltage and current is $\phi_2$ = 1.516 + 27.84 = 29.356°.

Base power $W_{B2} = W_{B1}$ = 100 kVA in both windings.

Therefore, input power = 94.167 + $j$ 52.965 kVA = 108.04 kVA at a power factor of $\cos^{-1}$ (0.94167/1.0804) = 0.8716 lag = cos 29.356°.

The input reactive power is inductive as shown by the fact that the current $I_h$ is lagging behind the voltage $V_h$. Also, the sign of reactive power is positive in $W_h$. This is by convention. However, there are other conventions, chiefly in electronic circuits, where the reactive power with positive sign should be taken to mean capacitive. But for this book, the convention followed is that inductive reactive power is taken as positive, as followed by power system requirements.

Efficiency = 90 kW/94.167 kW = 0.956 = 95.6%

Total losses = 4.167 kW, with 1000 W = 1 kW in copper-loss in each winding and 2.167 kW in the core.

### *9.3.2 Three-Winding Transformers*

A large power system consists of either fossil-fuel or nuclear or hydro-electric generating stations which feed into high voltage (up to and including 230 kV) or extra high voltage (up to and including 750 kV) or ultra high voltage (> 750 kV) transmission systems. As an example, a generator delivers power to the low-voltage winding of its transformer at 13.8 kV, 3-phase line-to-line ($13.8/\sqrt{3} = 8$ kV, line-to-neutral). This voltage is stepped up to 345 kV, say, and fed to the e.h.v. transmission line. A long line requires shunt reactors and switched capacitors or synchronous condensers (synchronous motors without shaft load but used only to supply Vars of both types at zero power factor lagging or leading) for voltage control of the long line. This "line compensating" equipment usually works at 33 kV, especially the capacitors and synchronous condensers. They can be connected to a third winding on the same core, where the 13.8 kV and 345 kV windings are wound. In such a case, the three-winding transformer has 13.8 kV low-voltage/345 kV high-voltage/33 kV medium-voltage windings called the Primary, Secondary, and Tertiary windings, respectively.

If any one of the three windings is used as a reference and base quantities are selected on it, this choice determines the base quantities at all voltage levels in the entire system. A large system may consist of 20 e.h.v. stations along with a lower-voltage system consisting of over a hundred or even a thousand transformer locations with feeders supplying loads. Modern digital computers can perform all system calculations in a single step. Power system analysis is a highly specialized field and no discussion of this topic is presented in this book. Only the method of dealing with a single three winding transformer is discussed.

In the case of the two-winding transformer, the equivalent circuit shown in Fig. 9.8 can be re-drawn with only one series impedance $Z_s = R_s + j X_s$ between the input and the load. In a 3-winding transformer, three impedance elements are connected in a Y as shown in Fig. 9.9 with the subscripts *p*, *s*, *t* denoting primary, secondary and tertiary, respectively. Loads are shown connected to the secondary and tertiary windings. The primary is fed from a source of power to which it is connected.

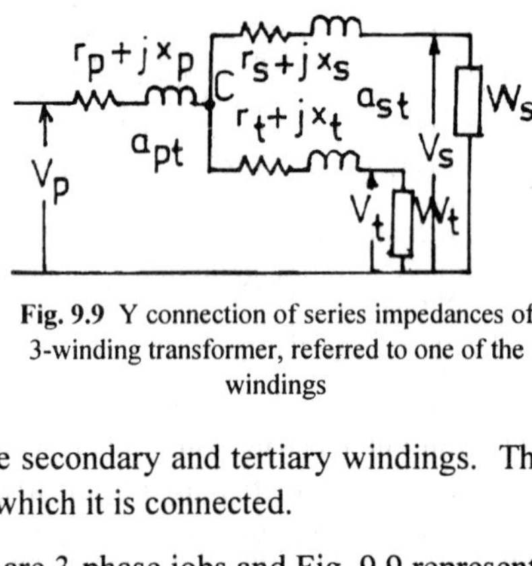

**Fig. 9.9** Y connection of series impedances of 3-winding transformer, referred to one of the windings

Normally, three-winding transformers are 3-phase jobs and Fig. 9.9 represents only one phase of the 3-phase transformer. When the load volt-amperes with power factor is given in the secondary and tertiary, and the voltage across only one of them is also specified, then the voltages, currents and powers can be calculated as shown by the following example, in which all quantities are given in per-unit values referred to one of the three windings.

***Example 9.5***: A 3-winding transformer is rated 500 kV wye/230 kV wye/33 kV delta, and is used at a receiving station to tie a 500-kV transmission network with a 230-kV network. The low-voltage winding feeds line-compensating equipment at the station. Series impedances are given as per-unit values on the 500-kV side base values, Fig. 9.10.

The secondary 230-kV side is feeding a load of 1 p.u. at 0.9 power factor lag at 1 p.u. voltage, and $V_s = 1\underline{/0°}$ the reference voltage. The tertiary is loaded to 1 p.u. load at 0.9 p.f. lead.

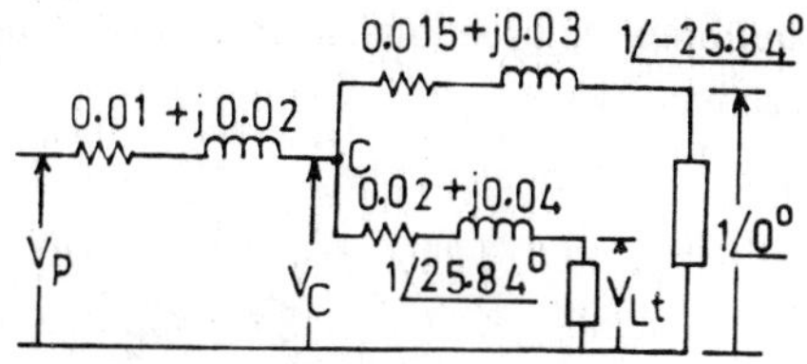

**Fig. 9.10** Details of 3-winding transformer for Example 9.5

Calculate the voltages to ground at the common point $C$, the tertiary load $V_{Lt}$, and the primary $V_p$ (see Fig. 9.10).

***Solution*:**

Voltage $V_C$ of the common or star point $C$:

$$V_C = 1\underline{/0°} + 1\underline{/-25.84°} \times (0.015 + j\,0.03) = 1 + j\,0 + 0.03354\underline{/37.6°}$$

$$= 1.02657 + j\,0.02046 = 1.0268\underline{/1.142°} \text{ p.u.}$$

Therefore, voltage across load connected to the tertiary is lower and is

$$V_{Lt} = V_C - 1\underline{/25.84°} \times (0.02 + j\,0.04) = 1.0268\underline{/1.142°} - 0.04472\underline{/89.28°}$$

$$= 1.026 - j\,0.02426 = 1.0263\underline{/-1.3545°} \text{ p.u.}$$

Voltage across primary terminal and ground:

$$V_p = 1.0268\underline{/1.142°} + (0.01 + j\,0.02) \cdot (1\underline{/-25.84°} + 1\underline{/25.84°})$$

$$= 1.0268\underline{/1.142°} + 0.02236\underline{/63.44°} \times 1.8\underline{/0°} = 1.04457 + j\,0.0567$$

$$= 1.046\underline{/3.1°} \text{ p.u.}$$

## 9.4 Synchronous Generators and Motors

### *9.4.1 High Speed Turbo Alternators*

An alternating-current generator, or alternator as it is known, generates a pure sine wave of output voltage at power frequency $f$ = 50 or 60 Hz. When a conductor moves past two poles on the alternator, a north and a south pole, the voltage goes through one cycle. Therefore for generating 50 or 60 Hz, the conductor should have gone through 100 or 120 pole pitches. If there are $P$ poles on the machine, the number of revolutions per second is $100/P$ or $120/P$, or in general $2f/P$. In one minute this corresponds to

$$n_s = 120\,f/P, \text{ rev/min} \tag{9.12}$$

This speed is known as the synchronous speed for the given number of poles and frequency of the generated voltage. It does not matter if the poles rotate and conductors are stationary, or the conductors rotate and the poles are stationary.

The former is used in all alternators except for laboratory demonstration-type, for less than 5 kVA.

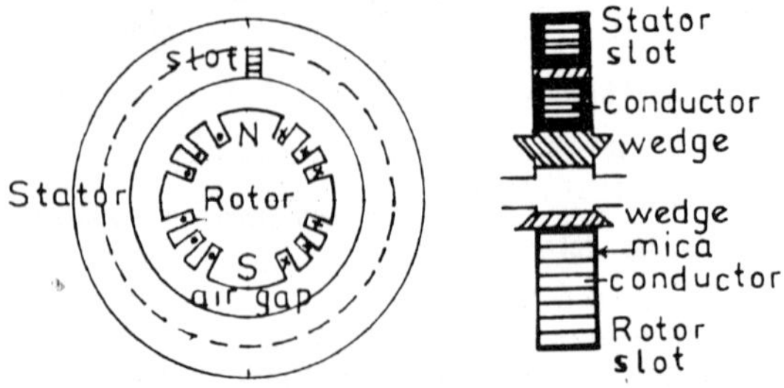


**Fig. 9.11** Turbo-alternator rotor and stator details

In turbo alternators driven by steam turbines, the speed of the 2-pole rotor is 3000 or 3600 rpm for 50 or 60 Hz systems, and 1500/1800 rpm for 4 poles. Figure 9.11 shows a cross-sectional drawing of a smooth-rotor or uniform airgap turbo-alternator with two poles. Four-pole turbo alternators are not as widely used as 2-pole machines, because steam-turbine speeds cannot be reduced and the cost of the machine is higher for the lower speeds. The rotor carries a dc field winding embedded in deep slots, whose openings are covered by a wedge after assembling the mica-insulated copper-bar conductors. The field coils are supplied with current from an exciter, which now-a-days is another alternator whose output is rectified and smoothed. The voltage generated by the exciter is altered by changing its field current (see Fig. 9.16). In order to maintain the voltage output of the main alternator constant at all loads, the generated voltage is suitably changed by varying the flux through the field current supplied by the main exciter, whose voltage in turn is controlled by the automatic voltage regulator. Figure 9.12 shows a block diagram of an alternator and its excitation system.

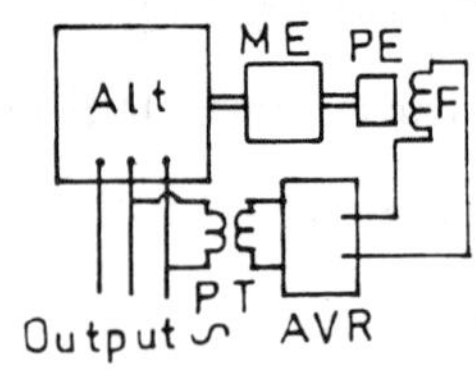


**Fig. 9.12** Block diagram of excitation system for a large alternator showing the alternator, main exciter, pilot exciter, automatic voltage regulator (AVR)

The alternator is a voltage source with winding resistance $r$, and because of the flux generated by the load current $I$ the winding has a reactance $x_s$. Therefore, its Thevenin equivalent circuit consists of an ideal variable source $E$ feeding a load at a fixed terminal voltage $V\angle 0^\circ$ and current $I\angle\phi$ through a series impedance $Z_s = r + j\,x_s$. The reactance

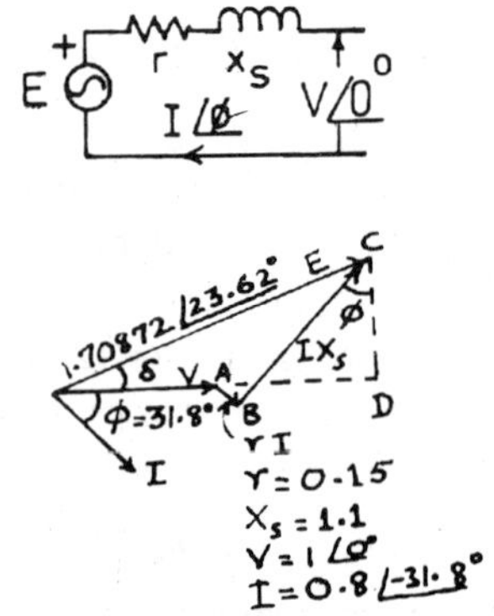


**Fig. 9.13** Phasor diagram of round-rotor alternator on load

$x_s$ is called the Synchronous Reactance and is at power frequency. Figure 9.13 is the equivalent circuit and phasor diagram, from which all performance characteristics are obtained easily, the main aim is to determine the field current necessary for a given load condition. Again, it is most convenient to work with per-unit values.

***Example 9.6***: A 2-pole 3-phase Y-connected turbo alternator has the following details:

3-phase kVA: 100,000, rated kV = 13.8 kV line-to-line, rms;

$r = 0.015$ p.u. on machine rating, $x_s = 1.1$ p.u. on machine rating.

Load: 0.8 full load at 0.85 p.f. lag ($\cos^{-1} 0.85 = 31.8°$)

Field current required generates 60,000 ampere-turns for 20 kV at line terminals on open circuit. Assume magnetic circuit to be linear.

Calculate:

(a) Base impedance on machine rating of 100 MVA and 13.8 kV

(b) Ohmic values of the armature resistance and synchronous reactance

(c) Generated voltage and field ampere-turns for the given load condition

(d) Draw the phasor diagram for one phase.

***Solution***:

(a) Rated phase current $I_r = 100{,}000 / \sqrt{3} \times 13.8 = 4{,}184\, A$

Rated phase voltage $V_{ph} = 13{,}800 / \sqrt{3} = 7{,}967\ V$

Therefore, base impedance on machine rating $Z_B = V_{ph}/I_r = 7{,}967/4{,}184$
$= 1.904$ ohm

We also note that

$$V_{ph} / I_r - (V_{L-L} / \sqrt{3}) / (W_{3-\phi} / \sqrt{3}\ V_{L-L}) - V_{L-L}^2 / W_{3\phi}$$

$$= 13{,}800^2 / 100{,}000{,}000 = 13.8^2 / 100 = 1.904 \text{ ohm}$$

Therefore, $Z_B = (kV)_{L-L}^2/3\text{-phase MVA}$, which is a very convenient formula.

(b) Ohmic values: $r = 0.15 \times 1.904 = 0.2856$ ohm

$x_s = 1.1 \times 1.904 = 2.0946$ ohm

Consequently, $Z_s = (0.15^2 + 1.1^2)^{1/2} / \underline{\tan^{-1} 1.1 / 0.15} = 1.11 \underline{/ 82.235°}$ p.u.

$- 2.113 \underline{/ 82.235°}$ ohm

(c) Generated voltage

$E = V_L + Z_s \cdot I_L = 1 \underline{/ 0°} + 1.11 \underline{/ 82.235°} \times 0.8 \underline{/ -31.8°}$

$= 1.5656 + j\,0.6846 = 1.70872 \underline{/ 23.62°}$ p.u. $= 23.58$ kV, line–to–line

This requires $23.58 \times 60{,}000/20 = 70{,}741$ field ampere-turns.

(d) To draw the phasor diagram, take $V = 1$ p.u. along a reference direction. Place load current $I_L = 0.8\underline{/-31.8^\circ}$ to a suitable scale. The resistance voltage drop is $r \cdot I_L = 0.15 \times 0.8 = 0.12$ on the voltage scale in line or in phase with $I_L$. The voltage drop in $x_s$ leads the current by 90° and has the value $x_s \cdot I_L = 1.1 \times 0.8 = 0.88$ p.u.

The excitation voltage $E$, which is the voltage developed by the machine winding behind the series impedance, is the phasor sum of $V_L$, $rI_L$ and $x_sI_L$. From the phasor diagram, this has a magnitude of 1.70872 and leads the terminal voltage $V_L$ by the angle 23.62°. This angle is known as the "power angle" for that load condition and denoted by δ.

We observe that the resistance voltage drop $rI_L$ is very small compared to the synchronous-reactance drop $x_sI_L$ and is at right angles to it. Thus, in all calculations, the resistance drop is neglected.

Then, $$E\underline{/\delta} - V\underline{/0^\circ} = I\underline{/-\phi} \times x_s\underline{/90^\circ} = I \cdot x_s\underline{/90^\circ - \phi} \tag{9.13}$$

or, $$E \cos \delta - V = x_s\, I \cdot \sin \phi, \text{ and } E \sin \delta = x_s\, I \cdot \cos \phi \tag{9.14}$$

We can solve for $E$ and δ in terms of output quantities $V$, $I$, ϕ and machine reactance $x_s$, thus (see Fig. 9.13):

and $$\left.\begin{aligned} \tan \delta &= I \cdot x_s \cdot \cos \phi / (V + I \cdot x_s \cdot \sin \phi) \\ E &= I \cdot x_s \cdot \cos \phi / \sin \delta = (V + I \cdot x_s \cdot \sin \phi) / \cos \delta \end{aligned}\right\} \tag{9.15}$$

In the previous example, $I = 0.8$, $\phi = 31.8^\circ$, $x_s = 1.1$, and $V = 1.0$.

Therefore, $\tan \delta = 0.8 \times 1.1 \times 0.85/(1 + 0.88 \times 0.527) = 0.4981$

giving $\delta = 26.48^\circ$, $\sin \delta = 0.4459$ and $\cos \delta = 0.895$

or, $E = 0.8 \times 1.1 \times 0.85/0.4459 = 1.6775$ p.u. Thus, in phasor form, $\mathbf{E} = 1.6775\underline{/26.48^\circ}$.

With the inclusion of the resistance drop, $\mathbf{E} = 1.7087\underline{/23.62^\circ}$.

In all calculations pertaining to excitation-current required, saturation in the magnetic circuit must be taken into account. But this is not considered in this book. See Ref. (1) at the end of the chapter.

### *9.4.2 Water-Wheel Driven Alternator — Salient-Pole Alternator*

Water-turbine-driven alternators have 4 or more poles, which are always even numbers. The number of poles will be $P = 120 \times 50/n$ for 50 Hz and $120 \times 60/n = 7200/n$ for 60 Hz machines. Thus, for a Kaplan turbine running at speeds as low as 40 rpm, $P = 150$ for 50 Hz and 180 for 60 Hz. These poles are fixed to the rotor by strong wedge-type keepers to resist the very heavy centrifugal forces. The air gap in such machines is non-uniform hence the name "salient-pole" machines or non-uniform air gap machines. Figure 9.14 shows a cross-sectional view of a salient-pole alternator. A special winding consisting of bars called the amortisseur or damper or pole-face winding is characteristic of these machines. The main field winding is wound on the pole structure and is fed by a source of dc by an exciter. The pole-face windings (usually in the form of bars embedded in slots) develop a motor torque whenever the rotor speed differs from synchronous speed because of currents induced in them by the magnetic field of the stator winding. This additional torque helps to reduce oscillations of the rotor when load changes take place. We will observe later on that a synchronous motor requires this winding to make it self-starting.

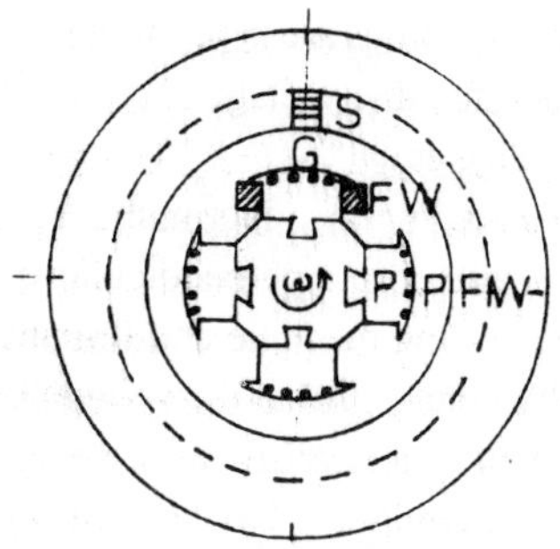


**Fig. 9.14** Cross-section of salient-pole alternator

As the rotor rotates with its salient poles, the effective length of airgap between stator winding and field-excitation coils varies from a minimum to a maximum, so that the flux or flux density also change with the position of the rotor. If the flux-density variation were a pure sinusoid, then the voltage generated by a coil on the stator which this flux links will also be sinusoidal at the fundamental frequency $f = n.P/120$. Otherwise, the voltage contains odd-multiple harmonics present in the flux density. These higher harmonics are undesirable, as they interfere with telephone and other signalling communications, and when motor loads are fed by these higher harmonics, the motor rating is reduced due to torques generated in a direction opposite to that generated by the fundamental-frequency component of voltage.

This difference in flux conditions as the rotor rotates was first analyzed by Blondel in France who considered or resolved the salient-pole machine into two independent machines called the "direct-axis" and "quadrature-axis" machine. The armature reactance has a maximum $X_d$ when the centre of the pole with minimum airgap length is aligned with the centre of the stator-phase winding of any phase. It is called the direct-axis or polar-axis synchronous reactance. Similarly, a quarter cycle later, when the airgap length is maximum, the reactance (due to the decrease in flux linkage) is at its minimum. This is called the quadrature-axis or inter-polar axis synchronous reactance, $X_q$. The resulting phasor diagram is shown in Fig. 9.15, omitting the small resistance drop in the armature or stator winding in large machines. The phasor diagram is described briefly here.

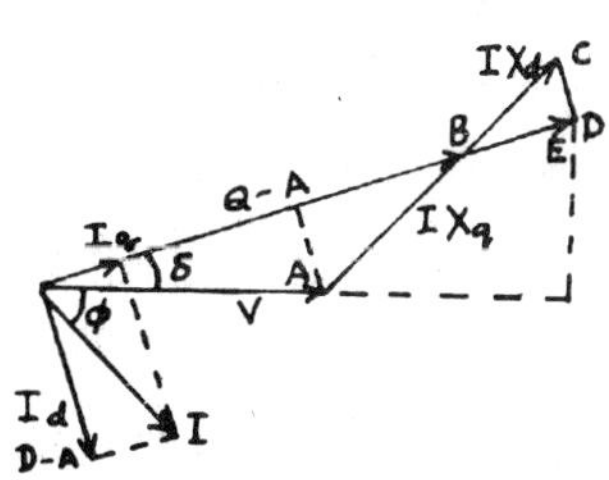


**Fig. 9.15** Phasor diagram of salient-pole alternator on load, showing direct- and quadrature-axis quantities

The terminal conditions are denoted by $V$, $I$, and $\cos\phi$. A lagging power factor (inductive) load is shown on Fig. 9.15.

All quantities are in per-unit values on selected base quantities, which are normally the rated line voltage and rated MVA of the large alternator. From the tip of $V$, a voltage equal to $(I \cdot X_q)$ is drawn leading $I$ by 90°. Join AB and extend it to C, such that AC $= I \cdot X_d$. Normally, $X_d \approx 1$ p.u. and $X_q \approx 0.7$ p.u. on machine ratings. Join OB and drop a perpendicular from C on to this line. OB is called the quadrature axis of the machine and it makes the power angle $\delta$ with the terminal voltage $V$. The voltage OD is the voltage to be induced in the stator phase. From a magnetization characteristic of the magnetic circuit, the field current or ampere-turns can be determined. The load current $I$ is resolved into the direct-axis component $I_d$, which lags 90° behind E, and the quadrature-axis component of current $I_q$ in line with $E$. In order to determine the excitation voltage $E$ for a given load condition $V$, $I$, cos $\phi$, and the machine reactances $X_d$ and $X_q$, we proceed as follows:

(a) $\tan \delta = I \cdot X_q \cdot \cos \phi / (V + I \cdot X_q \cdot \sin \phi)$ (9.16)

(b) Knowing $\delta$, we use the relations

$$I_d = I \cdot \sin (\phi + \delta), \text{ and } I_q = I \cdot \cos (\phi + \delta) \quad (9.17)$$

(c) Then, $E = V \cdot \cos \delta + I \cdot X_d \cdot \sin (\phi + \delta) = V \cdot \cos \delta + I_d \cdot X_d$ (9.18)

This is called the excitation voltage.

An example will illustrate the manner in which $E$ is found.

***Example 9.7***: A 3-phase 30,000 kVA = 30 MVA alternator of the salient-pole type runs at 300 rpm for 50 Hz. Its rated voltage is 15 kV, line-to-line, rms value. The terminal load on the machine is 30 MVA (1 p.u.) on machine rating at 1 p.u. voltage of 15 kV. The reactances are $X_d = 1.1$ p.u. and $X_q = 0.7$ p.u. on machine rating. Calculate:

(a) Full rated current, $I$

(b) Ohmic values of $X_d$ and $X_q$

(c) Number of poles on machine

(d) Power angle $\delta$, and excitation voltage $E$ as well as $I_d$ and $I_q$

Work part (d) for power factors of 0.8 lag and 0.8 lead. Compare the working conditions of the alternator at the two power factors.

***Solution***: The load voltage is taken as reference: V = $1\angle 0°$ p.u. = $15\angle 0°$ kV.

(a) $I = 30{,}000/15\sqrt{3} = 1154.7$ A = 1 p.u. on machine quantities

(b) $Z_B = kV^2/MVA = 15^2/30 = 7.5$ ohm. Therefore,

$X_d = 1.1 \times 7.5 = 8.25$ ohm, $X_q = 0.7 \times 7.5 = 5.25$ ohm

(c) $P = 120 f/n$ giving $P = 6000/300 = 20$ poles

There are 10 north poles and 10 south poles arranged alternately on rotor.

(d) (i) *0.8 lag p.f.* $\phi = 36.87°$

$$\tan\delta = I \cdot X_q \cdot \cos\phi / (V + I \cdot X_q \cdot \sin\phi) = 0.7 \times 0.8 / (1 + 0.7 \times 0.6)$$

$$= 0.39437 \,.\; \delta = 21.52°$$

$$I_d = 1.0 \sin(21.52° + 36.87°) = 0.85166 \text{ p.u.}$$

$$I_q = 1.0 \cos 58.39° = 0.5241 \text{ p.u.}$$

$$E = V \cdot \cos\delta + I_d \cdot X_d = 1.0 \cos 21.52° + 0.85166 \times 1.1$$

$$= 1.8672 \text{ p.u.} = 28 \text{ kV, line-to-line.}$$

This is the excitation voltage required.

(ii) *0.8 lead p.f.* $\phi = -36.87°$

$$\tan\delta = 0.7 \times 0.8 / (1 - 0.7 \times 0.6) = 0.9655 \,.\; \delta = 44°$$

$$I_d = 1.0 \sin(44° - 36.87°) = 0.124 \text{ p.u. (still positive)}$$

$$I_q = 1.0 \cos 7.13° = 0.9923 \text{ p.u.}$$

$$E = 1.0 \cos 44° + 0.124 \times 1.1 = 0.8557 \text{ p.u.}$$

$$= 12.84 \text{ kV, line–to–line}$$

(e) *Comments*: From the above calculations, we can observe that when the alternator is supplying an inductive load at lagging power factor, the excitation voltage required is higher than when the machine is working at leading power factor, and therefore requires higher field current.

### 9.4.3 Excitation Control and Voltage Regulation

Synchronous generators are subject to changes in terminal operating conditions due to various reasons, and they have to adjust from one operating state to the next without losing synchronism. Some of the changes are the following, requiring excitation control which acts on the magnetic field of the alternator, and governor control which acts on the input/output of the prime mover:

(a) Gradual load changes in the course of normal operation. The stability of the synchronous machine is then called 'steady-state stability'.

(b) Sudden and violent change in terminal condition such as a short-circuit. These last for a few cycles only, but are violent enough to trip the machine and disconnect it from the lines when stability is lost or the short-circuit persists beyond about 20 cycles. This condition is known as 'transient stability'.

(c) Dynamic stability condition in which very large load changes occur and the operation of the machine is in the transient state. In order to restore the machine to the new load state and run at synchronous speed both the quick-acting voltage regulator and the governor function simultaneously, creating a dynamic condition.

Governors have been described in Chap. 7. The excitation system of a large alternator is shown in Fig. 9.16. The main generator field winding is fed by an

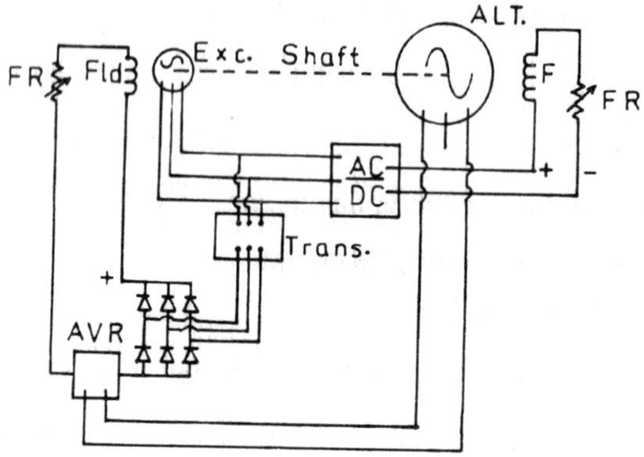


**Fig. 9.16** Details of excitation control of large alternator

AC/DC rectifier which receives its input from the exciter alternator, either mounted on the same shaft as the alternator or run by an induction motor at any desired speed. The exciter also feeds its own field winding through another rectifier circuit shown as exciter-field suppply, or by a small dc generator called a 'pilot exciter'. The alternator voltage is fed to an automatic voltage regulator AVR, in which a comparison is made with a reference voltage. The error voltage acts on a small motor which varies the exciter-field rheostat and thereby change the field current. This in turn will change the exciter voltage output, and control the current flowing in the main-alternator field winding. Solid-state exciters have very quick response time, typically a few milli-seconds as compared to rotating dc generators which take a few seconds to respond to changes.

### *9.4.4 Synchronous Motors*

Synchronous motors are constant-speed motors which run at their synchronous speed at all loads as given by $n_s = 120 f/P$, rev/min. Neglecting the resistance voltage drop in the armature windings and using cylindrical rotor theory discussed in Sec. 9.4.1, we observe from Fig. 9.13

$$I \cdot X_s \cdot \cos\phi = E \cdot \sin\delta\,, \text{ or },\ I \cdot \cos\phi = (E/X_s) \cdot \sin\delta \tag{9.19}$$

Therefore $P = V \cdot I \cdot \cos\phi = (V \cdot E/X_s) \sin\delta$ (9.20)

This shows that if two voltages $V$ and $E$ are connected through a reactance $X_s$ and the phase difference between $V$ and $E$ is $\delta$, the power flowing from $E$ to $V$ is given by the product of the two voltage magnitudes divided by the series reactance, and multiplied by the sine of the power angle. When the load applied to the shaft is given and $V$ and $X_s$ are known, the power angle $\delta$ and the power-factor angle vary when the excitation voltage $E$ in the machine developed by the field current varies. The synchronous motor utilizes this property, in that at a fixed shaft load $P$ ($W$ or $kW$ or $HP$) by varying the dc field excitation current, the current drawn from the ac mains can not only be varied in magnitude, but the power factor also changed during the operation of the motor. When a system consists of several loads, some of the motor loads drawing heavy lagging currents such as induction motors, a synchronous motor connected to the mains and operating at a leading power factor can improve the power factor of the overall system. The motor is said to work in over-excited condition, with normal excitation corresponding to unity power-factor condition of the motor. If the synchronous motor is under-excited, it will draw ac current from the mains at lagging power factor.

***Example 9.8***: The load on a $Y$-connected 3-phase 11 kV (line-to-line) system consists of the following loads connected in parallel:

(1) Lighting load of 1000 kW at 1.0 power factor

(2) Induction motor load of 2000 kW at 0.8 power factor lag

(3) Synchronous motor of 1000 kW

Calculate the leading power factor at which the synchronous motor must operate, so that the overall power factor is unity, as shown in Fig. 9.17. Calculate the total current drawn from the mains to supply the three loads.

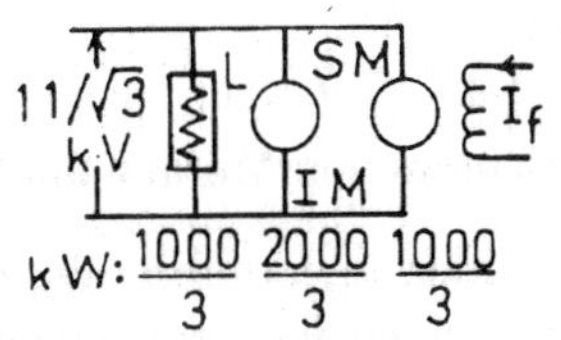


**Fig. 9.17** Load connection for Example 9.8

***Solution***:

Reactive power drawn by the induction motor = 2000 × 0.6/0.8 = 1500 kVAR lagging. To obtain unity power factor, the synchronous motor must draw 1500 kVAR leading. Therefore, its power is

$$W_{sm} = 1000 - j\,1500 = 1802.8\underline{/-56.31^\circ}\text{, kVA.}$$

This gives $\cos\phi_{sm} = \cos 56.31^\circ = 0.5547$ leading.

The total kW load at unity power factor is then = 1000 + 2000 + 1000 = 4000 kW. Therefore, current drawn from mains = $4000/11\sqrt{3}$ = 210 A, in phase with the voltage. This is the minimum current necessary to supply the loads.

Because of ease of control of VARS, unloaded synchronous motors are utilized in voltage control of the ends of a long transmission line in ac and dc transmission systems.

Synchronous motors do not have self-starting capability if both the ac supply to the armature and dc supply to the rotor field are switched on. The rotor must first be brought to very near synchronous speed before the dc voltage to the field is switched on. The interaction between the two fields will pull the rotor to synchronous speed and lock itself to the stator rotating field, which is rotating at synchronous speed with respect to the stationary armature conductors. Bringing the rotor to near full speed is carried out by any one of the methods as follows:

(a) Heavy pole-face windings are given on the rotor pole surfaces next to the air gap. When the rotor is at standstill, and 3-phase ac voltage is switched on to the stator winding, the force due to currents induced in these pole-face windings is sufficient to start the rotor and bring it to very near synchronous speed, as will be explained next under induction motors. The dc field is now switched on and the rotor pulls into "step".

(b) A small ac induction motor is mounted on the shaft of the very large synchronous motor, with the small motor helping to bring the large rotor of the synchronous motor close to synchronous speed. Then both the ac supply to the stator and dc supply to the rotor are switched on.

Synchronous motors are manufactured up to the largest sizes of 100,000 *HP* to drive giant pumps for pumped-storage plants, irrigation purposes, steel rolling mills, etc.

## 9.5 Induction Motors and Generators

Induction motors form the workhorses of industry, ranging in size from a few watts, fractional horse-powers, and as large as the largest built, of the order of 100,000 *HP*. There are many types of induction motors for single-phase use and two important types of the 3-phase variety. Single phase motors are classified as follows:

(1) Capacitor motor; (2) Split-phase motor; (3) Repulsion motor; (4) Shaded pole motor; (5) Series motor also called the universal or ac/dc motor; (6) Stepper motors and others for very small powers such as ac tachometers and drag-cup motors for control purposes, computer printers, etc.

*9.5.1* The single-phase winding generates only an oscillatory magnetic field and the inertia of the rotor prevents it from rotating from its position of rest. The motor has no self-starting capability. In order to make it self-starting, a second winding called the starting winding is provided, whose magnetization axis is at right angles to that of the main or running winding. To improve starting conditions, a capacitor is connected across the starting winding to make its current lead the running-winding current by 90° or nearly so in time. When the speed of rotor reaches about 80-90% of normal speed, a centrifugal cut-out operates to open the starting-winding circuit. In the split-phase motor, two windings with different magnetic axes and currents with different phases (both lagging behind the applied voltage) are placed on the stator giving a starting torque.

In the series motor or universal motor, a commutator is used which conducts current through brushes to the winding on the rotor. In most motors, the rotor carries a short-circuited set of bars called a squirrel cage winding. In the commutator motor, the winding on stator and rotor are connected electrically in series. Such motors run at speeds of the order of 10,000 rev/min and are used in vacuum cleaners, portable drills and other high-speed applications at home and office at low powers. The shaded-pole motor has two salient poles in which thick copper bars are embedded in slots, short-circuited upon themselves. The main single-phase ac winding induces voltage in the copper ring and its current generates a small magnetic field with its axis displaced from the main magnetic field. A low torque is thereby generated to make the motor self-starting and then keep it running. The shaded-pole motor is used for table fans, small blowers, etc., not exceeding 100 W.

We will now discuss 3-phase induction motor and generator in detail.

### *9.5.2 The 3-Phase Induction Motor*

On the stator of a 3-phase motor, there exists a winding divided under two adjacent poles into three distinct parts, each part consisting of two halves displaced by one pole pitch. The three phases are mechanically displaced by 120° or one-third pole pitch, thus generating magnetic fields whose axes are displaced 120° around the periphery, as shown in Fig. 9.18. They carry currents which are displaced 120° in time from one another as is usual in a 3-phase balanced system. The result is that even though the stator phase-windings are stationary and their currents are alternating in time, a continuously rotating magnetic field of constant magnitude is generated. Mathematically, we have the MMF of the windings equal to $F \cos \theta$, $F \cos (\theta - 120°)$, $F \cos (\theta + 120°)$, where $F$ – peak value of oscillating MMF and $\theta$ = angle on the stator periphery from a reference direction. The currents in the three windings giving rise to the MMF's are at frequency $f = \omega/2\pi$, and are $I_a = I \cos \omega t$, $I_b = I \cos (\omega t - 120°)$ and $I_c = I \cos (\omega t + 120°)$. The resulting total MMF at any point on the stator periphery will be, with $N$ = number of turns in the phase and $K$ = a constant for the winding:

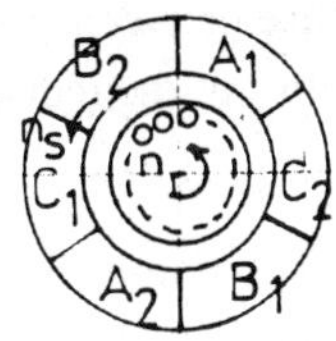


**Fig. 9.18** Distribution of stator phase windings and rotor conductors in 3-phase induction motor

$$F = K N I [\cos \theta \cdot \cos \omega t + \cos (\theta - 120°) \cdot \cos (\omega t - 120°) + \cos (\theta + 120°) \cdot \cos (\omega t + 120°)]$$

$$= K N \frac{I}{2} [\cos (\theta - \omega t) + \cos (\theta - \omega t) + \cos (\theta - \omega t) + \cos (\theta + \omega t) + \cos (\theta + \omega t - 240°) + \cos (\theta + \omega t + 240°)]$$

$$= \frac{3}{2} K N I \cos (\theta - \omega t) \tag{9.21}$$

since the sum of three equal phasors displaced 120° from each other is zero. This remarkable result shows that the total MMF and therefore the flux generated by the stationary 3-phase winding has a peak value of 1.5 times the peak value of MMF of each phase. Also, and most importantly, the field is rotating on the stator with respect to the conductors producing it, at the speed

$$d\theta/dt = \omega \text{ rad/sec} = 2\pi f \tag{9.22}$$

The mechanical speed for $P$ poles is

$$n_s = 120 \, . f/P, \text{ rev/min} \tag{9.23}$$

This is its synchronous speed.

When a closed winding is given on the rotor, the rotating field of the stator cuts past the rotor conductors and induces a voltage. The entire operation of the motor depends on this. The rotor can generate a voltage due to induction from the stator only if there is relative motion between the two. As such the rotor of an induction motor can never reach synchronous speed $n_s$, but a speed $n_r$ less than $n_s$. The difference between the stator field speed ($n_s$) and the rotor speed ($n_r$) is known as the "slip" of the induction motor, and is defined as follows:

(a) Slip, $s = n_s - n_r$

(b) Fractional slip, $s = (n_s - n_r)/n_s$

(c) Percentage slip, $\% s = 100\,(n_s - n_r)/n_s$

The magnitude $E_r$ and frequency $f_r$ of the induced voltage in the rotor are proportional to the slip $s$, since both are proportional to the relative speed or the speed difference $(n_s - n_r)$. Thus

$$E_r = s \cdot E_0, \text{ and } f_r = s \cdot f \tag{9.24}$$

where $E_0$ = voltage induced in rotor at standstill, and $f$ = frequency of voltage and current in rotor at standstill which is of course the frequency of applied voltage to the stator.

When load increases on the shaft of the motor, more current must flow in the rotor so that a higher voltage $E_r$ is necessary. This makes the rotor slow down or the slip increases as well as the frequency $f_r$. A motor usually has a full-load slip between 2.5% and 5%, so that the speed falls by these amounts from synchronous speed. Consequently an induction motor has a fairly constant speed from no-load to full-load but never equal to the synchronous speed as is the case with the synchronous motor which has a dc field on the rotor. Thus, an induction motor is called an asynchronous motor.

Figure 9.19 shows the equivalent circuit for one phase of a 3-phase induction motor, which is very nearly the same as Fig. 9.5 for a transformer, except that the reactance of the rotor varies as slip $s$, since the frequency changes. The rotor has

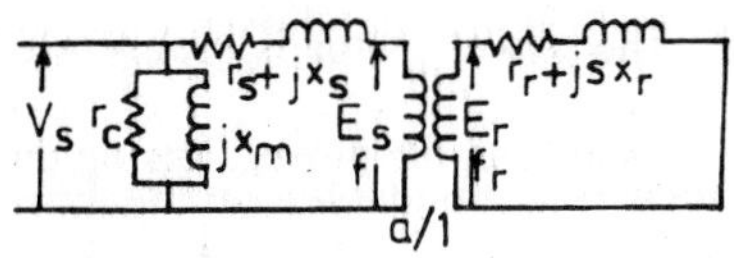


**Fig. 9.19** Equivalent circuit of one phase of an induction motor at slip *s*

a resistance $r_r$ and a leakage reactance $x_r$ at standstill ($s = 1$), when the frequency of rotor current is equal to the applied stator frequency $f$. Its value reduces to $f_r \cdot x_r/f = s \cdot x_r$ at other speeds. The current flowing in rotor winding at any slip is

$$\mathbf{I}_r = \mathbf{E}_r / \mathbf{Z}_r = s \cdot \mathbf{E}_0 / (r_r + j\, s \cdot x_r) \tag{9.25}$$

at the power factor given by $\cos \phi_r = \cos [\tan^{-1} (s \cdot x_r / r_r)]$ (9.26)

We can change things a bit and write Eq. (9.25) as follows:

$$\mathbf{I}_r = \mathbf{E}_0 / (r_r / s + j\, x_r) \tag{9.27}$$

This shows that $E_0$ and $x_r$ are at power frequency $f$ and only the resistance contains the slip term. It represents the $I^2 r_r$ heating plus a mechanical power developed due to the torque. Note that

$$r_r / s = r_r + r_r \cdot (1 - s) / s \tag{9.28}$$

Since $E_0$ is a voltage in the rotor at standstill frequency $f$ of the stator, it can be transformed by the turns ratio $a$ in the usual manner as was done for the transformer. Thus

$$\mathbf{E}_s = a \cdot \mathbf{E}_0 \,, \quad \text{and} \quad \mathbf{I}_s = \mathbf{I}_r / a \tag{9.29}$$

On the stator side, the applied voltage becomes

$$\begin{aligned} \mathbf{V}_s &= \mathbf{E}_s + \mathbf{I}_s (r_s + j\, x_s) = a \cdot \mathbf{E}_0 + (r_s + j\, x_s) \cdot \mathbf{I}_r / a \\ &= a \cdot (r_r / s + j\, x_r) \cdot \mathbf{I}_r + (r_s + j\, x_s) \cdot \mathbf{I}_r / a \\ &= [\,(r_s + a^2 \cdot r_r / s) + j\, (x_s + a^2 \cdot x_r)\,] \cdot \mathbf{I}_r / a \\ &= (R_s + j\, X_s) \cdot \mathbf{I}_r / a + \frac{1 - s}{s}\, a^2 \cdot r_r \cdot \mathbf{I}_s \\ &= (R_s + j\, X_s) \cdot \mathbf{I}_s + [\,(1 - s) / s\,] \cdot a^2 \cdot r_r \cdot \mathbf{I}_s \end{aligned} \tag{9.30}$$

where $\quad R_s + j\, X_s = (r_s + a^2 \cdot r_r) + j\, (x_s + a^2 \cdot x_r)$ (9.31)

This is the total resistance and leakage reactance of the motor referred to the stator and at power frequency. We can also denote $R_r = a^2 \cdot r_r$, the referred value of rotor resistance to the stator side, and $X_r = a^2 \cdot x_r$. Now

$$\mathbf{I}_s = \mathbf{V}_s / \mathbf{Z}_s = \mathbf{V}_s / [\,(r_s + R_r / s) + j\, (x_s + X_r)\,] \tag{9.32}$$

with magnitude $|\,\mathbf{I}_s\,| = V_s / [\,(r_s + R_r / s)^2 + (x_s + X_r)^2\,]^{1/2}$ (9.33)

The power factor is $\cos\phi = (r_s + R_r/s)/|\mathbf{Z}_s|$ (9.34)

Therefore, the power flowing through the airgap to the rotor will be

$$P_g = |\mathbf{I}_s|^2 \cdot R_r/s = V_s^2 \cdot R_r/s \cdot |\mathbf{Z}_s|^2$$

$$= V_s^2 \cdot R_r/s \cdot [\,(r_s + R_r/s)^2 + (x_s + X_r)^2\,] \tag{9.35}$$

The copper-loss in rotor is $P_c = I_s^2 \cdot R_r = s \cdot P_g =$ slip × airgap power (9.36)

The developed mechanical power is then

$$P_m = P_g - P_c = (1-s) \cdot P_g \tag{9.37}$$

Now, the synchronous speed is $\omega_s = 2\pi n_s/60$, and mechanical speed of rotor is $\omega_r = (1-s)\,\omega_s$ with $n_r = (1-s) \cdot n_s$. Consequently, the developed electromagnetic torque is *N-m* is

$$T_d = P_m/\omega_r = P_g/\omega_s = \frac{V_s^2}{\omega_s} \cdot \frac{R_r/s}{(r_s + R_r/s)^2 + (x_s + X_r)^2} \tag{9.38}$$

At starting, $s = 1$. The starting torque is then

$$T_{st} = (V_s^2 \cdot R_r/\omega_s) \cdot [(r_s + R_r)^2 + (x_s + X_r)^2]^{-1} \tag{9.39}$$

Note that a heavier starting torque can be obtained by having a high resistance $R_r$. But this will affect the running torque, since $R_r/s$ occurs in the denominator of Eq. (9.38) (see Example 9.9).

In the squirrel-cage motor, the bars are placed inside the rotor slots and connected permanently to end rings forming a cage-like structure, whose resistance cannot be varied. However, if the rotor also carries a 3-phase winding and the terminals are made available, an external resistance can be inserted at starting through slip rings to yield a high starting torque. This starting resistance can be cut out to yield a low-resistance rotor during running. Such motors are known as ''Wound Rotor Induction Motors'' or ''Slip Ring Motors''. These motors are used for cranes, locomotives and other situations where a high starting torque is necessary. Squirrel-cage motors find application where general loads such as fans, blowers, pumps, lathes, etc. are to be run.

### *9.5.3 Induction Generators*

An induction motor can be made to generate 3-phase power, if its rotor is driven by a prime mover at a speed in excess of the synchronous speed. In this case the slip is negative. In order to supply a magnetic field, the stator must be connected to an ac source which in early days was the electrical system. An induction generator therefore was unable to operate in isolation like a synchronous generator could, which of course requires a source of dc to supply its field current. The induction machine has several reactances which are inductive because of leakage fluxes and the main flux. If these lagging reactive powers can be compensated and exceeded by capacitive reactive powers, then the generator can be self-excited. This is easily carried out nowadays with capacitors controlled by high-power switching devices, such as thyristors. The most popular use of the induction generator is in wind energy conversion systems.

Figure 9.20 shows a connection diagram of self-excitation capacitors and a resistive load on an induction generator, whose rotor is driven by a prime mover. The equivalent circuit is shown at the side, in which the slip is a negative fraction.

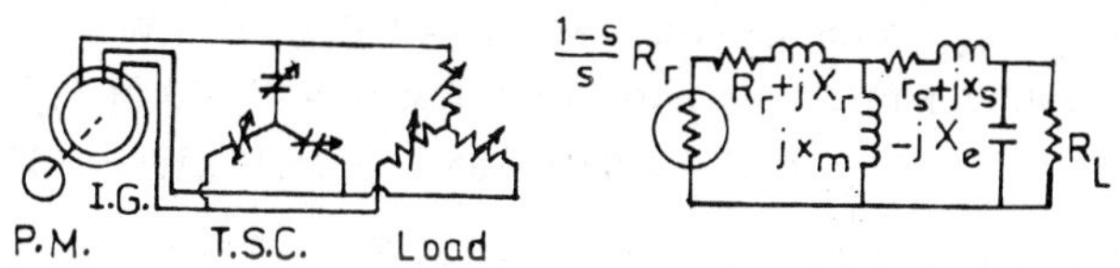


**Fig. 9.20** Connection diagram and equivalent circuit of induction generator showing rotor driven by prime mover, self-excitation capacitors (thyristor controlled) and resistive load

In order to observe the performance of an induction motor as a generator, consider the following examples.

***Example 9.9***: A 3-phase Y-connected 8-pole 50-Hz induction machine has the following details:

Stator applied voltage = 440 V (line-to-line) = 254 V, phase

$r_s = 0.1$, $x_s = 0.3$, $R_r = 0.1$, and $X_r = 0.3$ ohm, with all quantities referred to the stator side.

Using Fig. 9.19 for its equivalent circuit as a motor, calculate the following at full-load slip of 5%:

(a) Stator current, $I_s$

(b) Stator copper-loss and rotor copper-loss

(c) Input power and power factor

(d) Airgap power $P_g$, developed power $P_d$, and shaft output power, assuming rotational losses = 1% of input power to the motor

(e) Developed torque at full load

(f) Starting torque

(g) Efficiency, assuming core losses to amount to 400 *W*, 3-phase

(h) Magnetizing reactive power input assuming $x_m = 40$ ohm

***Solution***: Phase voltage = $254\angle 0°$ *V*, $R_r/s = 0.1/0.05 = 2$ ohm

(a) Impedance $Z_s = (r_s + R_r/s) + j(x_s + X_r) = 2.1 + j0.6 = 2.184\angle 15.95°$

Stator current $I_s = (254/2.184)\angle -15.95° = 116.3\angle -15.95°$

(b) Stator copper-loss = $3 \times 0.1 \times 116.3^2 = 4057.8$ W = rotor copper-loss.

(c) Input power $P_{in} = 3 \times 254 \times 116.3 \cos 15.95° = 85.2$ kW.
Power factor = cos 15.95° = 0.9615 lag.
The above figures have not taken core-loss and magnetizing power into account.

(d) Airgap power $P_g$ = Input – stator Cu-loss = 85.2 – 4.058 = 81.15 kW.
Also, $P_g = 3 \times I^2 \cdot R_r/s = 3 \times 116.3^2 \times 2$ W = 81.15 kW
Developed power $P_d = P_g -$ rotor Cu–loss $= (1 - s)\, P_g$
$= 0.95 \times 81.15 = 77.1$ kW
Also, $P_d = P_g -$ rotor Cu-loss = 81.15 – 4.058 = 77.1 kW
Shaft output power = $P_d -$ rotational losses $= P_d - 0.01\, P_{in}$
$= 77.1 - 0.01 \times 85.2 = 76.15$ kW = 102 HP

(e) Developed torque $T_d = P_d/(1 - s)\,\omega_s = P_g/\omega_s$
$\omega_s = 2\,\pi \times 750/60 = 78.5$ rad / sec, since synchronous speed for 50-Hz and 8 poles in $n_s = 120 \cdot f/p = 6000/8 = 750$ rev/min.
Therefore, $T_d$ = 81,150/78.5 = 1033.8 N-m.

(f) Starting torque, Eq. (9.39):

$$T_{st} = \frac{440^2}{78.5}\,\frac{0.1}{0.2^2 + 0.6^2} = 616.56 \text{ N–m} = 59.64\%\ T_d \text{ at full load.}$$

(g) Efficiency: Total input including core-loss = 85.2 + 0.4 = 85.6 kW.
Output = 76.15 kW. Therefore, efficiency = 76.15/85.6 = 0.89 = 89%.

(h) Magnetizing current = 254/40 = 6.35 *A*. Therefore,
reactive power in $x_m = 3 \times 254 \times 6.35 = 4{,}839$ VARS, lagging.
Total reactive power input to motor,
$Q_m = 4839 + 3 \times 254 \times 116.3 \times \sin 15.95°$
$= 29.19$ kVAR

***Example 9.10***: The rotor of the induction machine in the previous example is driven externally by a wind turbine. At a speed 5% in excess of the synchronous speed with slip = –5%, calculate the output of the generator. Neglect the core-loss and magnetizing branches $r_c$ and $x_m$. The terminal voltage is $V_s = 254$ *V*/phase = 440 *V*, line-to-line.

***Solution***: At slip = –5%, rotor speed = 787.5 rpm.

Apparent rotor resistance = $R_r/s = -0.1/0.05 = -2$ ohm.

Therefore, stator input current

$$\mathbf{I}_p = 254/(0.1 - 2 + j\,0.6) = -121 - j\,38.39\,A = 126.94\,\underline{/180° + 17.6°}$$

$$= 126.94\,\underline{/197.6°}$$

Power factor $\cos \phi = -121/126.94 = -0.9532$ (leading).

Output $P_0 = 3 \times 254 \times 121\ W = 92.2\ kW$

Reactive power = $3 \times 254 \times 38.39\ VAR = 29.25\ kVAR$. This is drawn from the ac system, to which the generator is connected. Or else, a 3-phase capacitor bank must be connected across the generator to supply the leading VARS necessary for self-excitation. As the speed changes these *VARS* also have to change and therefore thyristor-switched capacitors are necessary.

### *9.5.4 Starting of Induction Motors, and Starters*

If a 3-phase induction motor is switched on to the full supply voltage, it draws a very heavy current. In Example 9.9, the impedance at $s = 1$ i.e. at standstill, is $(0.2 + j\,0.6)$ ohm and the starting current will be $254/\sqrt{0.4} = 401.6\ A$ when the full-load current is $116.3\ A$. While starting the motor it is clear that a reduced voltage must be applied to the stator, or in the case of a wound-rotor motor a high resistance can be inserted in the rotor circuit, which also helps to deliver high starting torque at starting.

There are two types of starters adopted in practice for applying a reduced voltage: (a) Star-Delta starter; (b) Auto-transformer starter. Figure 9.21 (a) and (b) respectively show these two types. The former is used for motors up to 100 *HP* and the auto-transformer for large motors where the cost of the motor justifies the additional cost of the latter. Referring to Fig. 9.21(a), the starter handle is moved to *START* position, which connects the three phases of the motor stator winding in *Y*. A voltage equal to $1/\sqrt{3} = 0.577$ times the line voltage is applied. As the motor speeds up and reaches nearly synchronous speed ($s \approx 0$), the handle is moved to RUN position when the three phases are connected in delta. This applies full line voltage to the motor phase-windings.

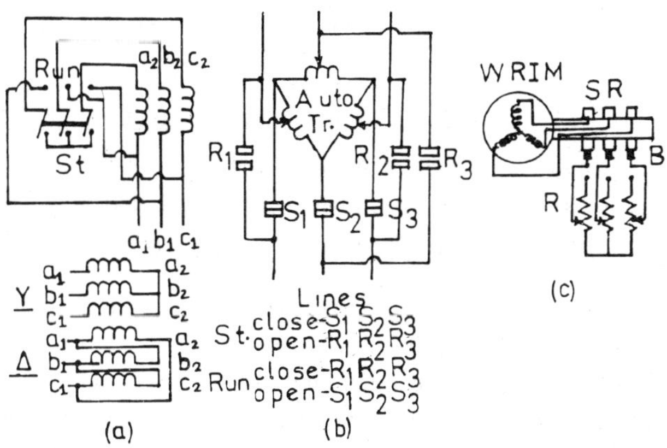


**Fig. 9.21** Starting methods for 3-phase induction motors: (a) Star-Delta starter; (b) Autotransformer starter; (c) Wound-rotor motor starter with rotor-resistance control

In the auto-transformer starter, the motor windings form the load on the secondary or low-voltage side of the transformer. Its turns ratio is adjusted to apply 60-65% of line voltage. Starting is carried out at this low voltage and when the motor speeds up, the lines are connected directly to the motor, bypassing the auto-transformer.

Figure 9.21(c) shows a schematic of starting condition of a *WRIM*. The rotor-resistance legs are fed through slip rings from the wound rotor winding and are inserted fully during starting, prior to connecting the full supply voltage to the stator. The rotor resistance is gradually decreased until it becomes zero. The WRIM can also work with shaft load connected, such as cranes, rolling stock, etc. It develops high pulling torque at standstill.

## 9.6 High Voltage Power Transmission — AC and DC

### *9.6.1 AC Transmission*

The highest voltage used for evacuating huge amounts of power from giant stations has now reached 1200 *kV* 3-phase ac and soon 1500 *kV* will be used. Once engineers confidently control the surges released under switching conditions, which art has reached near perfection, still higher voltages can be used, although certain insulating characteristics of very long airgaps such as used on towers indicate that ac transmission voltage has a ceiling value of about 1900 *kV*. Representative values of power that can be carried by a single 3-phase circuit are as follows, without using capacitors in series.

These values are based on the equation

$$P = V_s \cdot V_r \cdot \sin\delta / X_s \tag{9.40}$$

which is similar to Eq. (9.20). Normally, $\delta = 30°$ so that $P = V_s \cdot V_r/2 \cdot X_s$, *MW* when $V_s$ and $V_r$ are in *kV*, line-to-line, and $X_s$ is in ohms. In principle

| *System kV* | 230 | 400 | 525 | 750 | 1000 | 1200 | |
|---|---|---|---|---|---|---|---|
| 200 km | 325 | 1340 | 2420 | 5700 | 12,000 | 17,250 | *MW* |
| 400 | 162 | 670 | 1210 | 2860 | 6,000 | 8,625 | |
| 600 | 108 | 450 | 806 | 1900 | 4,000 | 5,750 | |
| 800 | 81 | 335 | 605 | 1430 | 3,000 | 4,310 | |
| 1000 | 65 | 270 | 484 | 1140 | 2,400 | 3,450 | |

by decreasing the series reactance $X_s$ between the sending- and receiving-end voltages, the power-handling capacity can be increased. For example, by using series capacitors with a reactance amounting to 50% $X_s$, the total series reactance is halved, and double the power of an uncompensated line can be pushed through. Because the shunt line capacitance draws a heavy charging current, the power station bus voltage on the high-voltage side of the transformer or the voltage at the entrance to the line, is lower than the voltage across the load if the load is low and inductive or for any amount of capacitive load. This rise in voltage is known as Ferranti Effect, first discovered in underground cables by that eminent engineer in England. Since then, voltage is controlled by using shunt reactors, which are now switchable by thyristors. When the system is loaded to draw high inductive reactive power, shunt capacitors are required at the load end usually connected to the tertiary winding of a three-winding transformer. An unloaded synchronous motor can provide both types of *VARS* by control of its excitation current to the dc field winding.

*AC* transmission lines used in the world are either (a) single-circuit, or, (b) double-circuit. There are one or two lines in Europe which have more than two circuits on the same tower, as shown in Fig. 9.22. For voltages up to 230 kV, wood-pole lines may be used in addition to steel towers, which are invariably used for 345 kV and above. Ground wires on top of the phase conductors are utilized to arrest lightning strokes to the line. Their locations on the tower top are governed by the need to have the angle between the ground wire and phase-conductor at its maximum swing limited to about 30°. This is called the 'shielding angle'. The overhead ground wires are connected to earth at the tower base at every tower in order to have a low resistance.

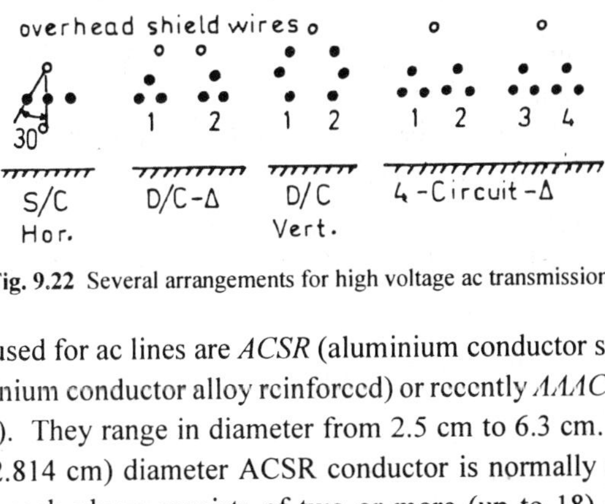


**Fig. 9.22** Several arrangements for high voltage ac transmission

Conductors used for ac lines are *ACSR* (aluminium conductor steel reinforced) or *ACAR* (aluminium conductor alloy reinforced) or recently *AAAC* (all aluminium alloy conductor). They range in diameter from 2.5 cm to 6.3 cm. For 230 kV, a single 1.108" (2.814 cm) diameter ACSR conductor is normally used, while for higher voltages each phase consists of two or more (up to 18) sub-conductors arranged in a circle and connected electrically by spacers. These are called bundled conductors and they give a lower series inductance $X_s$ in Eq. (9.40), as well as lower electric field gradient around the conductor. This is important from the point of view of lowering power loss due to corona discharges, audible noise emanating from the line during humid and rainy conditions, lowering interference to radio and television reception as well as not disturbing sleep during nights of residents living close to the line. Bundling also lowers the conductor resistance and keeps $I^2R$ heating loss down. Another important environmental aspect is the high electrostatic field in the line vicinity. This has to be kept within specified limit by providing adequate minimum height from ground to the lowest conductor at midspan between towers, taking into account the height of vehicles parked underneath the line. The rule recommended by the National Electrical Safety Code must be a minimum of 17 feet for 33 kV and then 1 foot for every 33 kV or part thereof, (5.183 m + 0.305 m for every 33 kV). According to this rule, the following minimum heights have to be maintained:

| *System kV* | 230 | 400 | 525 | 750 | 1000 | 1200 |
|---|---|---|---|---|---|---|
| *Height* | $17+\frac{197}{33}$ | $17+\frac{367}{33}$ | $17+\frac{492}{33}$ | $17+\frac{717}{33}$ | $17 + 29.3$ | $17 + 35.36$ |
| | = 23′ | = 29′ | = 32′ | = 38.73′ | = 46.3′ | = 52.36′ |
| | = 7.01 m | = 8.84 m | = 9.76 m | = 11.8 m | = 14.12 m | = 15.96 m |

There are other considerations involved based on switching surges. Average heights found in practice are: 230 kV – 10 m; 400 kV – 15 m; 750 kV – 18 m; 1000 kV – 21 m; 1200 kV – 21 m. This takes care of the height of a trailer-truck parked underneath the line. The limiting safe value of electrostatic field for a human being is 15 kV/m, rms, beyond which shock is experienced when the body discharges to a grounded object, such as a driver touching the chasis of his truck while standing on ground.

*Power Frequency Voltage Control*

Figure 9.23(a) shows an unloaded line, where $X_s$ is a lumped inductive reactance equalling the distributed inductive reactance of the line. The line also has distributed capacitance all along its length, but has been represented as two equal parts placed at the two ends. They have a reactance $X_{sh} = -j/\omega C_{sh}$. During normal operation if the load voltage is to be kept constant at the rated value of 1 p.u. or at any specified value $V_r\underline{/0°}$, the required voltage at the power station called the sending end will be as follows:

$$V_s\underline{/\delta} = V_r\underline{/0°} + (j\cdot\omega\cdot C_{sh}\cdot V_r)\cdot jX_s = V_r(1 - X_s/X_{sh}) \qquad (9.41)$$

The magnitude of $V_s$ is less than $V_r$ and in phase with it when resistance is neglected. This is Ferranti Effect. For example, a 400-kV line has 10 nF/km capacitance and 1 mH/km inductance. If the load-voltage is held at 400 kV,

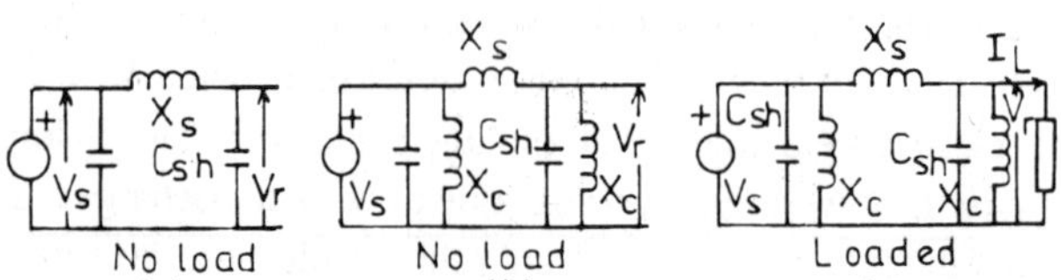


**Fig. 9.23** Equivalent circuits of unloaded and loaded ac transmission lines illustrating voltage control: (a) No load, no shunt-reactor compensation; (b) No load, with shunt-reactor compensation; (c) On load, with both shunt-reactor compensation for no-load and capacitor-compensation on load

line-to-line, $2 \cdot C_{sh} = 4000$ nF for a line of length of 400 km giving $X_{sh} = 1591.55$ ohm for half-length of line, and $X_s = 125.66$ ohm. Therefore, the sending-end voltage has to be kept at $V_s = 400\ (1 - 125.66/1591.55) = 0.921\ V_r = 368.4$ kV, line-to-line.

However, it is not usual to lower the power-station voltage by this much. The scheme adopted is to have both ends operate at nearly rated values of 400 *kV* in this case, by providing a compensating shunt reactance of value $X_c$, as shown in Fig. 9.23(b). If its value is equal to $X_{sh}$ of the line capacitive shunt reactance, placed at the load or receiving end, then it is clear that the current drawn by the receiving end is zero, and there will consequently be no voltage drop in the line reactance $X_s$. Thus, $X_c = 1591.55$ ohm giving an inductance at 50 Hz of 5.066 Henry. The reactive power drawn is $Q_c = 400^2/1591.55$ MVAR = 100 MVAR, 3-phase, drawing a current of 145 *A*. It is usual in practice to connect an equal amount of reactor for line compensation at both ends to take care of the distributed nature of line capacitance.

Consider what happens now at the other limit of full load, as shown in Fig. 9.23(c). From the power-handling capacity table for a 400-kV 400-km line, we observe that the full load is 600 MW. Let 600 MW at 0.9 p.f. lag be connected to the receiving end at $1\underline{/0°}$ voltage. Without the compensating reactors connected, the current flowing in the line is

$$[(600 / 0.9) \times 10^3 / 400\ \sqrt{3}]\ \underline{/-25.84°} + (400 \times 10^3 / 1591\ \sqrt{3})\ \underline{/90°}$$

$$= 908.5\ \underline{/-17.6°}\ A\ .$$

The resulting sending-end voltage will be $\mathbf{V}_s = 400 / \sqrt{3} + 908.5\ \underline{/-17.6°} \times 125.66\ \underline{/90°}\ V/\text{phase} = 286.9\underline{/22.3°}$ kV, phase, = 497 kV, line-to-line. But the voltage usually allowed by standard regulations can only be 5% higher than normal, or 420 kV in a 400-kV system. Thus we need additional reactive compensation equipment to bring the voltage from 497 kV down to 420 kV.

We have already seen that at no-load, in order to maintain the voltages at both ends at 400 kV, a shunt compensating reactor of 100 *MVAR* inductive was necessary. It is a normal practice not to change these voltages with load variation. This can be realized by sufficient and proper type of compensation to counteract the reactive power drawn by the load, which is usually inductive. Therefore, capacitive compensation is necessary, which takes the form of switched capacitor banks. Let $X_{CL}$ be the reactance of the shunt capacitors at load end. Then the total line current is

$$\mathbf{I}_L = 908.5\ \underline{/-17.6°} + (400 / \sqrt{3})\ 10^3 / 1591.55\ \underline{/90°} + j X_{CL}^{-1}\ (400 / \sqrt{3})\ 10^3$$

$$= 866 - j\,419.7 + j\,230.94 \times 10^3 / X_{CL}$$

Then

$$\mathbf{V}_s = 230.94\underline{/0^\circ} + j\,125.66\,\mathbf{I}_L = 230.94 + 52.74 - 29020/X_{CL} + j\,108.82$$

However, since $|V_s| = 400/\sqrt{3} = 230.94$, there results

$230.94^2 = (283.68 - 29020/X_{CL})^2 + 108.82^2$. Solving for $X_{CL}$, we have $X_{CL} = 29020/80 = 362.75$ ohm. This is capacitive and draws a current of $I_{CL} = 230.94/362.75 = 0.63664\ kA = 636.64\ A$. The 3-phase MVAR of the switched capacitor required is $400^2/362.75 = 441$ MVAR, 3-phase. These will be switched by thyristors whose gate-firing pulses are impressed through an automatic voltage regulator provided across the load to hold the voltage at the pre-determined value. Figure 9.24 shows the overall scheme. The above problem can be worked most conveniently by using per-unit values. This is left as an exercise for the reader at the end of the chapter.

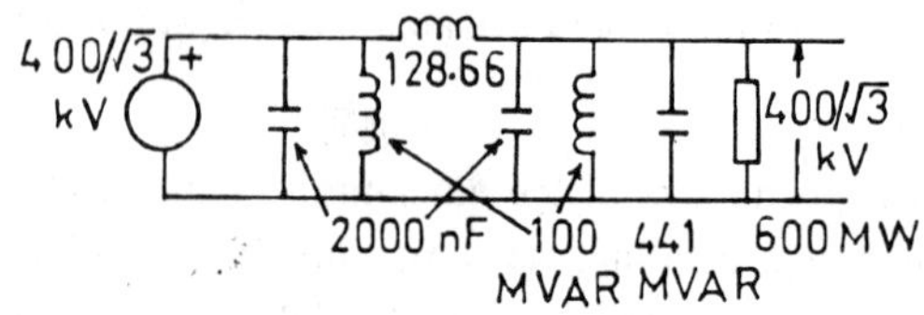


**Fig. 9.24** Equivalent circuit for voltage control of 400-kV line with shunt reactors for no-load voltage control and switched capacitors for voltage control on load

### *9.6.2 High Voltage DC Transmission*

Power is generated as ac and is utilized as ac. But in between, instead of transmitting the bulk power over long distances by ac, it can be done by high-voltage dc. The development of suitable rectifying and inverting high-voltage, high-current thyristors since 1950 and its predecessor the mercury-arc valve has made it possible to handle ± 600 kV to ground (1200 kV between lines or poles) and currents of the order of 2000 *A* and more. Thus, the dc transmission line is known as a "DC Link" between two ac systems, namely the generation and utilization systems. One advantage is the use of ground as possible return, including sea water in under-sea cable transmission, if proper precautions are taken at the electrode through which the large current enters the ground or sea water. Some deleterious effects are however the stunning of fish, deflection of navigating compasses on ships and boats, etc.

Conceptually, dc transmission can be carried out in three different ways called: (a) Monopolar, (b) Homopolar, and (c) Bipolar modes. They are shown in Fig. 9.25. In the bipolar mode, if the two poles are carrying equal currents, no current flows in the ground. But if one pole develops a fault, 50% of the rated power can still be fed from the healthy pole using ground return. In the monopolar and homopolar modes, the two poles are at high voltage and ground has to be used for the return current. In the homopolar mode, the two conductors are at the same

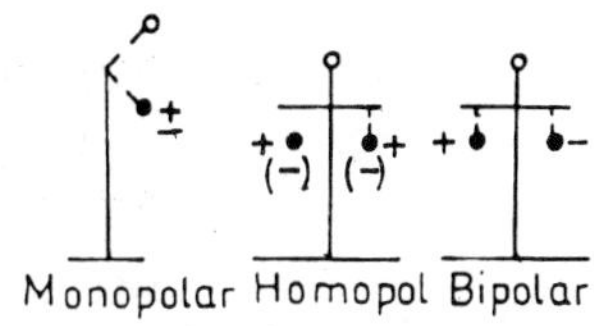


**Fig. 9.25** Three arrangements for high voltage dc transmission

potential and insulation clearances are lower than in the bipolar mode, thereby reducing the size of towers. Each pole in these three types of transmission may have a single conductor or a bundle as in ac transmission, determined by the current-carrying capacity and electric field gradient around the conductor. In general, interference fields at audible frequency, radio frequency and TV frequency are much less from dc lines, while the electrostatic field is more intense due to travel of ions of one polarity continuously from overhead conductor to ground, with increase of charge developed on the human body under the line and other objects.

In principle, all conversion and inversion circuits described in Sec. 9.1 can be used for dc transmission links. The most usual is the 12-pulse converter also known as the double 6-pulse bridge, or two phase-shifted (30°) bridges in parallel, as shown in Fig. 9.26. Series connection is also used for high voltages. The lowest harmonic developed is (12 × power frequency). These require heavy smoothing interphase reactors in order to deliver a smooth direct voltage to the line. At the load end, the thyristors work in the inverter mode and deliver ac to the load. The firing angles of the gates of thyristors determine the dc voltage which adjusts to load current. Figure 9.27 shows a schematic of a dc link including the two ac areas, bipolar transmission line, grounding, smoothing reactors and thyristor bridges.

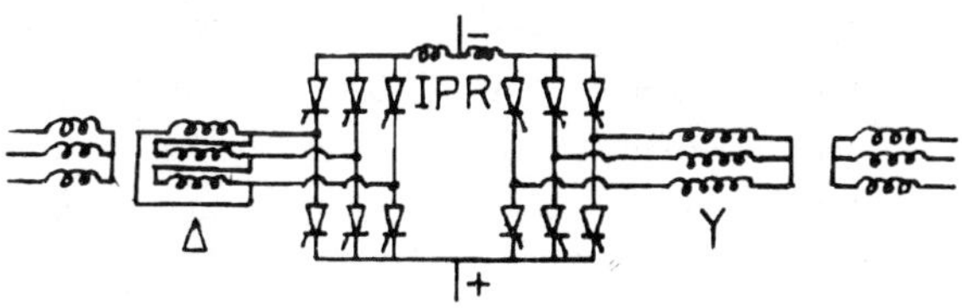


**Fig. 9.26** DC link using 12-pulse arrangement

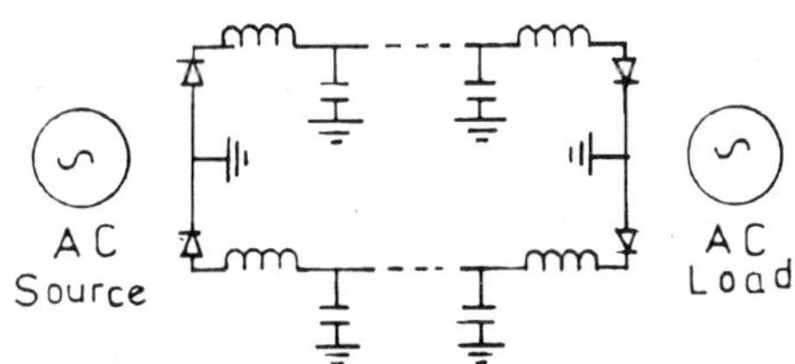


**Fig. 9.27** Details of dc transmission link between two ac areas

*Control of Voltage*

Figure 9.28 shows sine waves for a 6-phase system or 6-pulse converter. It is clear that each phase conducts for $2\pi/6 = 60°$. If the firing angle is $\alpha = 0$, then this corresponds to natural commutation and the average dc voltage is, with $V$ = rms value of ac input wave

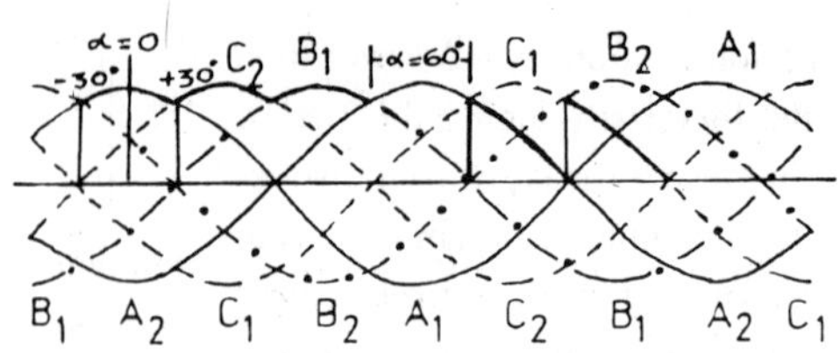


**Fig. 9.28** Output voltage waveform in 6-pulse converter for firing angle α = 0° and 60° (natural and forced commutation)

$$V_{dc} = \frac{\sqrt{2}\ V}{(\pi/3)} \int_{-30°}^{30°} \cos\theta \cdot d\theta = 3\sqrt{2}\ V/\pi = 1.35\ V$$

$$= 0.955\ V_p \tag{9.42}$$

where $V_p$ = peak value of ac voltage = $V\sqrt{2}$.

If the firing angle is delayed by α, this thyristor will continue to conduct for an angle of 60°, i.e. until (α + 60°), when the gate pulse to the next thyristor in the sequence is applied. The dc voltage is then

$$V_{dc} = \frac{\sqrt{2}\ V}{(\pi/3)} \int_{\alpha-30°}^{\alpha+30°} \cos\theta \cdot d\theta = 1.35\ V\cos\alpha$$

$$= 0.955\ V_p \cos\alpha \tag{9.43}$$

The following table shows ($V_{dc}/V$) and $V_{dc}/V_p$ for $0 \le \alpha \le \pi$:

| α = | 0° | 15° | 30° | 45° | 60° | 75° | 90° | |
|---|---|---|---|---|---|---|---|---|
| cos α | 1.0 | 0.966 | 0.866 | 0.7071 | 0.5 | 0.2588 | 0 | Convert |
| $V_{dc}/V$ | 1.35 | 1.304 | 1.169 | 0.955 | 0.675 | 0.349 | 0 | or |
| $V_{dc}/V_p$ | 0.955 | 0.922 | 0.827 | 0.675 | 0.458 | 0.247 | 0 | Rectify |
| α = | 105° | 120° | 135° | 150° | 165° | 180° | | |
| cos α | −0.2588 | −0.5 | −0.7071 | −0.866 | −0.966 | −1 | | |
| $V_{dc}/V$ | −0.349 | −0.675 | −0.955 | −1.169 | −1.304 | −1.35 | Inverting | |
| $V_{dc}/V_p$ | −0.247 | −0.458 | −0.675 | −0.827 | −0.922 | −0.955 | | |

If α > 90°, the polarity of dc voltage changes while the direction of current flow is unaltered, i.e. the system is inverting.

If there are *n* phases, then each phase conducts for (2π/*n*) radians. If the firing angle is delayed by α from the position of natural commutation or transfer of current to the most positive voltage without control of firing angle, the dc voltage becomes:

$$V_{dc} = \frac{\sqrt{2}\ V}{(2\pi/n)} \int_{\alpha-\pi/n}^{\alpha+\pi/n} \cos\theta \cdot d\theta = \sqrt{2}\ V \cdot \cos\alpha \cdot \frac{\sin(\pi/n)}{(\pi/n)}$$

$$= V_p \cos\alpha \cdot \frac{\sin(\pi/n)}{(\pi/n)} \tag{9.44}$$

For different number of phases, $n = 3, 6, 12, 24$, the following dc voltages are obtained from Eq. 9.44:

| $n =$ | 3 | 6 | 12 | 24 |
|---|---|---|---|---|
| $V_{dc}/V$ | $1.17 \cos \alpha$ | $1.35 \cos \alpha$ | $1.398 \cos \alpha$ | $1.41 \cos \alpha$ |
| $V_{dc}/V_p$ | $0.827 \cos \alpha$ | $0.955 \cos \alpha$ | $0.9885 \cos \alpha$ | $0.997 \cos \alpha$ |

As $n$ increases, $V_{dc}$ approaches the peak value of ac voltage $V_p$ for $\alpha = 0$. Also, the ripple content becomes low and smoothing is easier. However, at other firing angles the ripple is still high. When the firing angle increases to decrease $V_{dc}$ with a given number of pulses or phases $n$, the reactive power increases since the power factor $\cos \alpha$ decreases. Thus, the system must provide variable VARS. The filters used for smoothing the output voltage provide some part of this reactive power, but the thyristor controlled variable reactors must be used.

As an example, the ± 270 kV cross-channel link between England and France has a rated power of 2000 MW with 4 × 500 MW bipolar undersea cables (a total of eight cables) fed by 8 × 306 MVA 400 kV/118 kV transformers. There are 8 × 130 MVAR filters on the 400-kV bus and 200 MVAR controlled shunt reactors. In addition, 2 × 150 MVAR variable static compensators are provided.

Now, the current flowing in the line is

$$I_L = (V_s - V_r)/R \tag{9.45}$$

where $R$ = line resistance for dc. When load changes, the converter and inverter firing angles are controlled to have a suitable voltage drop $(V_s - V_r) = I_L \cdot R$.

## OBJECTIVE TYPE QUESTIONS

1. A single-phase transformer has a current ratio 100 A/5 A. The turns ratio is: (a) 4/1; (b) 1/20; (c) 20/1; (d) $1/\sqrt{20}$
2. The secondary voltage of the transformer above is 1000 V. The primary voltage is: (a) 20 kV; (b) 250 V; (c) 50 V; (d) 223.6 V
3. The kVA rating of the transformer above is (a) 2; (b) 5; (c) 2.236; (d) none of the three
4. A 230-kV Y-connected 3-phase transformer has a line-to-neutral voltage of: (a) 230 kV; (b) 400 kV; (c) 133 kV; (d) 76.7 kV
5. The 3-phase rating of the transformer in Q. 4 is 10,000 kVA. The line current is: (a) 25.1 A; (b) 43.48 A: (c) 100 A; (d) 230 A
6. The base impedance on 10 MVA 3-phase 230 kV (line-to-line) is: (a) 5290 ohm; (b) 230 ohm; (c) 23 ohm; (d) 10 ohm

7. A transformer has turns ratio of 20/1 and the resistance of the l.v. winding is 0.01 ohm. The resistance of the high-voltage winding is nearly: (a) 0.01 ohm; (b) 0.2 ohm; (c) 4 ohm; (d) 8 ohm

8. The total resistance of the above transformer referred to the low-voltage winding is: (a) 0.01 ohm; (b) 0.02 ohm; (c) 8 ohm; (d) 2 ohm

9. The % resistance drop referred to the low-voltage winding is 1% at full rated current for the previous transformer. The % resistance drop referred to the h.v. winding is: (a) 20%; (b) 1%; (c) 2%; (d) 4%

10. The rated voltage of the h.v. winding is 100 kV. The rated h.v. current for the previous transformer is: (a) 125 A; (b) 6.25 A; (c) 20 A; (d) 100 A

11. A high-speed 60-Hz turbo-alternator has 2 poles. The synchronous speed in rev/min is: (a) 3000; (b) 1500; (c) 3600; (d) 1800

12. The rating of a turbo-alternator is 240 MW 3-phase, and the line-to-line voltage is 13.86 kV, rms. The rated current is: (a) 17.32 kA; (b) 10 kA; (c) 30 kA; (d) None of the three

13. The base impedance of the above alternator on its rating is: (a) 192 ohm; (b) 80 ohm; (c) 0.8 ohm; (d) 20 ohm

14. The synchronous reactance drop at full rated current in the above alternator is 8 kV. The per-unit value of $X_s$ on machine rating is: (a) 1.1; (b) 1.0; (c) 2.0; (d) 0.5

15. The above alternator is loaded to rated load at 1 power factor at a terminal voltage of 1 p.u. The excitation voltage in p.u. is: (a) 2 p.u.; (b) 1.5 p.u.; (c) $\sqrt{2}$ p.u.; (d) 1.75 p.u.

16. The power angle $\alpha$ in Q. 15 is: (a) 45°; (b) 30°; (c) 25.8°; (d) 36.8°

17. Synchronous motors find application in: (a) Constant-speed work; (b) Provide power-factor correction possibilities; (c) Supply reactive VARS of both types; (d) All three purposes

18. An induction motor runs at 1710 rev/min from 60-Hz feeders. Its % slip is nearly: (a) 195%; (b) 5%; (c) 10%; (d) 15%

19. The airgap power fed to the rotor of an induction motor is 1000 kW at a slip of 7.5%. The rotor copper-loss is: (a) 50 kW; (b) 75 kW; (c) 7.5 kW; (d) 10 kW

20. The developed mechanical power above will be: (a) 925 kW; (b) 990 kW; (c) 950 kW; (d) 1000 kW

21. The motor runs at 570 rev/min at a slip of 5%. The developed torque is: (a) $50{,}000/\pi$ *N-m*; (b) $20{,}000/\pi$ *N-m*; (c) $10^5/\pi$ *N-m*; (d) None of the three

22. The line-to-line voltages at the two ends of an ac transmission line are $V_s = 230$ kV and $V_r = 240$ kV with a phase difference of 30°. The series reactance is 0.8 ohm/km and line length is 200 km. The power flow is nearly: (a) 300 MW; (b) 172.5 MW; (c) 230 MW; (d) 240 MW.

23. A high-voltage dc transmission line is called a dc link because: (a) It connects two ac systems (the source and the load); (b) It looks like a chain hung from towers; (c) Both are true; (d) Both are untrue

24. Ground can form the return path in which type(s) of dc transmission? (a) Monopolar; (b) Homopolar; (c) Bipolar; (d) All three

25. In bipolar transmission the two conductors or poles have same polarity of voltage with respect to ground. (a) True; (b) False.

[**Answers:**1. (b); 2. (c); 3. (b); 4. (c); 5. (a); 6. (a); 7. (c); 8. (b); 9. (b); 10. (a); 11. (c); 12. (b); 13. (c); 14. (b); 15. (c); 16. (a); 17. (d); 18. (b); 19. (b); 20. (a); 21. (a); 22. (b); 23. (a); 24. (d); 25. (b).]

## REVIEW QUESTIONS AND PROBLEMS

1. A single-phase controlled converter operates from 550 $V$, rms. Draw the circuit diagram of a bridge rectifier using thyristors with phase control. Sketch the output waveforms of load voltage for firing angles of $\alpha = 0°$, 30°, 60°, and 90°. Show the ac voltage across load and average dc output. Draw them to scale and indicate the dc voltage values properly.
   What is the voltage appearing across the thyristors in (a) conducting state, and (b) cut-off state?

2. Explain the principles of action of an inverter circuit using a bridge.

3. Draw the electrical equivalent circuit of: (a) an auto-transformer, (b) a two-winding transformer referred to one of the windings, and (c) a 3-winding transformer referred to one of the windings. Show all series resistances and leakage reactances, as well as the shunt branches.

4. The turn-to-turn insulation of transformers using oil-soaked Kraft paper can withstand 8 V. Calculate the number of turns in the windings of the following transformers:
   (a) Single-phase: 4.6 kV/240 V
   (b) Three-phase: 230 kV wye/13.8 kV delta
   (c) Three-winding 3-phase: 400 kV wye/132 kV wye/33 kV delta
   [(a) 575/30; (b) 16600/1725; (c) 28,868/9,526/4,125]

5. Derive Eq. (9.7).

6. A power transformer at a generating station has the rating 3-phase, 50,000 kVA, 13.8 kV delta/230 kV wye. Its constants for each phase (13.8 kV/230/$\sqrt{3}$ kV) are as follows: Series $r = 0.01$ p.u., leakage $x_s = 0.05$ p.u.,

core-loss resistance $r_c$ = 100 p.u., magnetizing reactance $x_m$ = 20 p.u. Calculate the following:
(a) Line currents on the two sides; (b) Winding currents on the two sides; (c) Turns ratio of the windings; (d) Ohmic values of all resistances and reactances. Base quantities are 13.8 kV, 50 MVA on l.v. side; (e) Draw the equivalent circuit for one phase indicating all values; (f) If the terminal load is 40 MW at 0.85 power factor lead at rated voltage, calculate the p.u. value of current as a phasor at rated voltage; (g) Calculate the load voltage phasor if the input voltage is $1\angle 0°$; (h) Find the core-loss and copper-loss at this load in kW; (i) Calculate the efficiency.

[(a) 2091.85 *A*, 125.51 *A*; (b) 1207.73 *A*, 125.51 *A*; (c) 93.3; (d) $Z_B$ = 38.09 ohm, $r_s$ = 0.381 Ω, $x_s$ = 1.904 Ω, $r_c$ = 3809 Ω, $x_m$ = 762 Ω; (f) **I** = 0.941 (0.85 + *j* 0.527) = $0.941\angle 31.8°$; (g) $\mathbf{V}_L$ = 1.0168 – *j* 0.045 = $1.0178\angle -2.53°$; (h) 0.5 MW, 2.214 MW; (i) input = 42.714 MW, efficiency = 93.65%].

7. Discuss why 3-winding transformers are necessary in a transmission system.

8. The Y-connected series branches of a 3-winding transformer have the following per-unit values: $Z_p$ = 0.01 + *j* 0.04, $Z_s$ = 0.015 + *j* 0.05, $Z_t$ = 0.01 + *j* 0.03. The tertiary is loaded to $1\angle 0°$ p.u. voltage at 0.8 p.u. current at 0.8 power factor lagging. Calculate:
   (a) The voltage of the common or star point *C*;
   (b) If the secondary is loaded to 1 p.u. current at 0.9 p.f. leading, find the secondary load voltage and the primary input voltage;
   (c) Calculate the efficiency of the transformer. Neglect no-load losses in the core. [(a) $V_C$ = $1.0209\angle 0.808°$; (b) $V_s$ = $1.0297\angle 2.065°$, $V_p$ = $1.04\angle 4.162°$; (c) Efficiency = 95.5%].

9. Draw the cross-sectional view of a 4-pole turbo-alternator showing slots on rotor carrying dc windings in six slots per pole. Show the directions of current to generate alternate North and South poles.

10. A large 2-pole 50-Hz 3-phase Y-connected turbo-alternator is rated 480 MVA, 13.8564 kV ( 8 kV line-to-neutral). The number of coils per phase is 3, connected in series. They are embedded in three stator slots under a pole with phase difference of 20° for adjacent slots. Calculate the voltage induced in each coil. (Add three equal phasors at 20° phase difference, to get a resultant whose value is the phase voltage of 8 kV).

    [$E_{ph}$ = 8 *kV* = $E_c$ [(1 + cos 20° + cos 40°)$^2$ + (sin 20° + sin 40°)$^2$]$^{1/2}$ giving $E_c$ = 2.78 kV].

11. In the previous question, calculate the rated winding current in kA and the base impedance on machine rating. (20 kA, 0.4 Ω).

12. (a) Explain the meaning of the term "Synchronous Reactance" of a uniform-airgap turbo-alternator.

    (b) The per-unit value of synchronous reactance of the alternator in Q 10 is 1.2 p.u. on machine rating. The alternator is loaded to 1 p.u. voltage and 0.75 p.u. load (MVA value) at 0.8 p.f. leading. Calculate the excitation voltage in stator per phase and the power angle δ. Draw a phasor diagram.

    ($I = 0.75\ (0.8 + j\ 0.6)$ $E = 0.8544\underline{/57.426°} = 6.8352$ kV phase, $\delta = 57.426°$)

13. In the above problem, check the power delivered with the equation $P = E \cdot V \cdot \sin \delta / X_s$. (0.6 p.u.)

14. Describe the difference in construction between a turbo-alternator and a water-wheel driven alternator in terms of speed, number of poles, pole construction, airgap distribution, diameter and length of rotor.

15. Describe the meanings of the terms "direct axis" and "quadrature axis". How are their armature-reaction characteristics different?

16. A 3-phase, 50-Hz salient-pole alternator has a full rating of 200 MVA and 18 kV, line-to-line. It has 100 poles. The synchronous reactances are $X_d = 1.2$ p.u. and $X_q = 0.75$ p.u. on machine ratings. Calculate:
    (a) Its synchronous speed in rev/min; (b) The full-load current;
    (c) Base impedance on machine rating; (d) Ohmic values of $X_d$ and $X_q$.

    [(a) 60; (b) 6.415 kA; (c) 1.62 Ω; (d) 1.944 Ω, 1.215 Ω]

17. The alternator in the previous question carries the following load: 200 MVA at 18 kV and 0.9 p.f. lag. Calculate:

    (a) The current supplied as phasor in Amps and p.u. value on machine ratings;

    (b) The same on bases of 250 MVA and 25 kV.

    (c) Draw the phasor diagram for this load condition. Use p.u. values on machine ratings.

    (d) Calculate the direct- and quadratur-axis currents $I_d$ and $I_q$.

    (e) Find the excitation voltage $E$.

    [(a) $0.9 - j\ 0.4359$ p.u. $= 5.7735 - j\ 2.7962$ kA; (b) Load = 0.8 p.u., voltage = 0.72 p.u., $I = 1 - j\ 0.483$ p.u. (d) $\tan \delta = 0.5087$, $\delta = 26.96°$, $I_d = 0.7967$, $I_q = 0.6045$ p.u. (e) $E = 1.8472$ p.u. = 33.25 kV, line-to-line]

18. Draw a schematic diagram of a governor for a hydraulic turbine and how the speed is made constant following a change in load.

19. Draw a schematic diagram of excitation control of a very large alternator showing alternator-exciter, voltage regulator and control of exciter output.

20. The load on a 3-phase 4.6 kV (line-to-line) system consists of the following components:

    (a) Lighting load of 500 kW at unity power factor;

    (b) Induction motor load of 1000 HP output working at 90% efficiency and 0.85 p.f. lagging;

    (c) Synchronous motor of 500 HP output working at 92% efficiency and 0.85 p.f. lead. Calculate:

    (i) The load on the system in kW, kVAR, and kVA for each load;

    (ii) The power input from the mains in kW and kVAR;

    (iii) The power factor of the overall system;

    (iv) If the overall power factor is to be improved to unity, calculate the new power factor of the synchronous motor whose dc excitation can be controlled. The other two loads remain same as before.

    (v) At this improved condition, calculate the line current.

[(i) Lighting: 500 kW, 0 kVAR; Ind. Mot.: 829 kW, 513.5 kVAR inductive; Syn. Mot.: 405.4 kW, 251.32 kVAR capacitive. (ii) Total: 1734 kW, 262.18 kVAR inductive, 1754.1 kVA; (iii) 0.989 lagging; (iv) Syn. Mot. kW = 405.4, kVAR = 513.5; kVA = 654.24, p.f. = 0.785 lead; (v) Total kW = 1734.4, kVAR = 0, $I = 217.7\ A$]

21. Describe the principle of action of an induction motor, clearly explaining how the stator and rotor rotating fields have the same speed in spite of the mechanical speed of the rotor not equalling the speed of the stator rotating field.

22. The slip of an induction motor is 7.5%. It has 8 poles and works from 60-Hz mains. Calculate:

    (a) Synchronous speed of the stator field; (b) Rotor mechanical speed; (c) Speed of rotor field with respect to rotor conductors; (d) Speed of rotor field with respect to stator conductors; (e) Speed of rotor field with respect to the stator rotating field. [900, 832.5, 67.5, 900, 0 rev/min]

23. A 3-phase Y-connected 50-Hz 10-pole induction motor has the following details:

    Phase voltage = 2656 $V$ (4.6 kV, line-to-line);

    Motor constants per phase:

    Resistances $r_s + R_r = 0.2$ ohm ($r_s = R_r = 0.1$ ohm);

    Leakage reactances $x_s + X_r = 1$ ohm;

    Core-loss resistance $r_c = 1500$ ohm;

    Magnetizing reactance $x_m = 375$ ohm

    Friction and windage loss: 120 kW total

At a slip of 3%, calculate the following performance characteristics: (a) Current drawn from the mains; (b) Input power in kW; (c) Airgap power $P_g$; (d) Rotor copper-loss; (e) Developed power and torque; (f) Shaft output power in HP; (g) Efficiency of operation; (h) Reactive power and kVA drawn from the mains, and the power factor.

[(a) $Z = 3.433 + j\,1 = 3.576\underline{/16.24°}$, $I' = 742.73\underline{/-16.24°}$, $I_c = 8.85$ $A$, $I_m = j\,35.4\ A$, $I = 722 - j\,243 = 761.8\underline{/-18.6°}\ A$; (b) $P_{in} = 5753$ kW; (c) $P_{\text{core}} = 70.517$ kW, stator Cu-loss = 165.5 kW; (d) $P_r = 165.5$. Also, 3% $P_g = 165.5$ kW; (e) $P_d = 5351.5$ kW, $\omega_s = 20\,\pi$, $T_d = 87{,}800$ N-m; (f) $P_{\text{out}} = 5231.5$ kW = 7010 HP; (g) $\eta = 90.935\%$; (h) 1936 kVAR, 6070 kVA, cos $\phi = 0.948$ lagging.]

24. In the previous question, the rotor is driven by a prime mover at 3% above synchronous speed. Calculate:
    (a) Output of the machine as an induction generator;
    (b) The reactive power and the kVA of capacitor bank to provide self-excitation.

    The stator is connected to an electrical supply system with line voltage of 4.6 kV (phase voltage = 2656 V).

    [(a) Stator input current $I_p = 1046.38\underline{/203.2°}$, Output = 7663.2 kW. (b) Reactive power = 3284.7 kVAR, Magnetizing kVAR = 282.2; Total = 3567 kVAR. Capacitor bank must supply this much.]
25. In the table of power capabilities of ac lines from 230 kV to 1200 kV given in Sec. 9.5.1, the lines are compensated for 50% of their series inductive reactance by providing series capacitor. Calculate the new power capabilities. (× 2)
26. Verify the minimum clearance at midspan given in the text for 400 kV, 525 kV and 750 kV lines.
27. Discuss why in an uncompensated ac line, the generating-station voltage is usually lower than the voltage at the load end unlike in dc transmission.
28. Describe how the voltage of a dc transmission line is controlled. Give an idea of how this is achieved by varying the firing angle $\alpha$ at the load or inverter end.

# CHAPTER 10

# Miscellaneous Energy Conversion Systems

In this chapter we will describe six important types of energy conversion systems which have considerable influence on the energy scenario of the future. They are:

(1) Coal Gasification and Liquefaction

(2) Biomass Energy Conversion

(3) Geothermal Energy

(4) Hydrogen Energy System

(5) Thermo Electric Energy Conversion and

(6) Fuel Cells and Batteries

## 10.1 Coal Gasification and Liquefaction

### *10.1.1 General*

Capacities of fossil-fueled power stations and amount of vehicular traffic on roads have increased enormously in recent years, which have contributed and will continue to contribute to

(a) fast depletion of fossil-fuel resources of the world, and

(b) increasing environmental (atmospheric and water) pollution.

A thermal power plant of 2000 MW releases about 80,000 tonne of sulphur oxide annually, which may amount to 70% of the toxic effluent due to all causes in the vicinity. Also, 24,000 tonne of nitrogen oxides are released annually. These form the bulk of acid gases in the atmosphere. Other sources are steel plants, nickel smelters, chemical industries, etc. Replacing coal by natural gas and nuclear power plants reduces $SO_x$ emission by one half. If coal is gasified or liquefied, nearly all potential pollutant material can be removed with cleaner exhausts. Furthermore, economic sanctions and oil embargos are increasingly becoming common in the world today, so that countries of necessity have to become self-reliant for their fuel requirements. Germany during the 1939-45 war and South Africa during recent decades are prime examples. Coal liquefaction and gasification yield clean fuels as substitutes for natural gas and fuel oils of various types (gasoline, diesel oil, etc.), and moreover existing coal- and oil-fired power generation equipment can use these with very little or no modifications.

Broadly speaking, a conventional coal-fired steam power station of 2000 MW output requires 6 M tonne of coal annually, which yields 1 M tonne of ash. In order to clean or desulphurize the flue gases, 0.3 M tonne of limestone and 25,000 tonne of $H_2SO_4$ are needed after combustion of coal in the boiler. This generates 50,000 tonne of $CaCl_3$ and gypsum each. However, if the coal is gasified by using 6 M tonne of coal with 0.6 M tonne of limestone, the ash content is the same, while in gas-purification process nearly 70,000 tonne of sulphur are recovered as a saleable product. The gas runs a gas turbine as a topping plant and a steam-turbine as a bottoming plant, using the heat in the exhaust gas. The flue gases are purer than in a conventional plant. Burning of limestone with coal in a fluidized bed (with char) absorbs about 90% of $SO_x$, converting it to $H_2S$, and the formation of $NO_x$ is also low.

Table 10.1 gives an idea of the average calorific values of coal and oil, and coal-derived substitute gases and liquids.

**Table 10.1: Heating Values of Hydrocarbon Fuels, kcal/kg**

| Gaseous | | Liquids | | Solids | |
|---|---|---|---|---|---|
| Natural gas | 12,000 | Methanol, $CH_3OH$ | 5,300 | Lignite | 4,000-5,000 |
| Methane, $CH_4$ | 13,000 | Gasoline | 11,000 | Coke | 8,000 |
| Producer gas | 1,200 | Diesel | 10,000 | Anthracite | 9,000 |
| Water gas | 4,300 | Crude shale oil | 10,500 | Bituminous coal | 6,500-9,000 |
| Coke-oven gas | 9,600 | | | Sub-bituminous coal | 5,500 |
| Hydrogen | 34,000 | | | | |

We observe that methane obtained from coal gasification has nearly the same or better calorific value than natural gas, and moreover has no pollutant. However, methanol obtained by liquifying coal-derived gas has only 50% of the calorific or heating value of gasoline. The cost of producing liquid fuels from coal is nearly double that for producing gasoline from crude oil. Natural gas contains 75 to 99% $CH_4$, methane. Other components are $H_2$, CO, $CO_2$. Also, $CH_4$ is a combination of CO and $H_2$. Coal gas contains $H_2$, CO, $CO_2$, $H_2S$, $N_2$, $NH_3$ and $CH_4$. Thus a cleaning process is necessary.

Methanol is derived from $CH_4 + H_2O \rightarrow CO + H_2$, $CO + 2\,H_2 \rightarrow CH_3OH$ by a catalytic process. Methanol can in turn be methanated by $CH_3 + H_2 \rightarrow CH_4 + H_2O$. $H_2O$ is in the form of steam. Depending on the process used, up to 25% of power generated in a station may be used for generating hydrogen required for coal gasification process.

We will now describe some processes used for coal gasification and liquifaction, which can then be pumped in pipelines or stored in barrels (for liquid only).

### *10.1.2 Coal Gasification Process*

[1000 Btu/ft$^3$ = 2670 kcal/m$^3$; 1000 Btu = 252 kcal;
1 kW-h = $3.6 \times 10^6$ J = 861.2 kcal = $3.42 \times 10^3$ Btu;
1000 Btu/lb = 555.5 kcal/kg = $2.322 \times 10^6$ J/kg;
1 atm = 14.7 lb/in$^2$ = 101.3 kPa $\approx$ 0.1 MPa;
100 psi $\approx$ 7 atm $\approx$ 0.7 MPa, 1 MPa = 9.8717 atm = 145 psi]

As can be imagined in a technology such as coal gasification and liquefaction, there are literally a hundred patented processes, some commercially viable, others in laboratory and pilot-plant stages, and many more in idea stages. The most widely used commercial process for coal gasification is the LURGI process and its improvements such as Koppers-Totzec, Wellman-Galusha, etc. Gasification is also necessary for further liquifaction which will be described in the next section.

*Lurgi Process and Others*

A typical Lurgi process generates substitute natural gas (SNG) with an efficiency of 55-60% based on heating value. As an example, for an input of $20.5 \times 10^9$ Btu/hr in coal (6000 kW) the resulting SNG has a heating value of $11.8 \times 10^9$ Btu/hr (3450 kW). Other products are tar, tar oils, phenols, naphtha, $NH_3$ and sulphur. High-temperature ash can amount to 25% weight of coal input.

The overall block diagram of the process is illustrated in Fig. 10.1 and the products in Fig. 10.2.

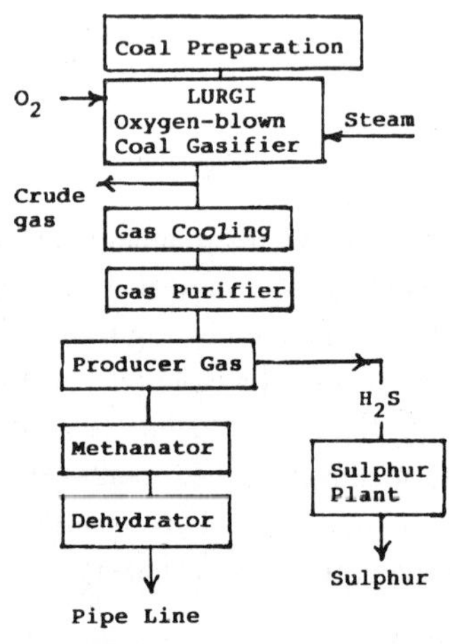


**Fig. 10.1** Block diagram of Lurgi-gasification process

Lignite or sub-bituminous coal in particle sizes of > 0.5 cm is fed through a hopper into a fixed-bed gasifier up to 3 MPa (420 psi) pressure. Steam and air or oxygen are also fed. The rate of production of gas is low. New and advanced fluidized-bed systems using a bed of char can produce eight times or more gas in the same duration.

The HYGAS process combines coal with $H_2$ to form $CH_4$ (methane) using lignite or sub-bituminous coal, which is heated at atmospheric pressure at about 400°C in a fluidized-bed reactor. This involves coal slurry with light oil and then pumped at

7-10 MPa. After gasification, the remaining oil is recovered and used over again. Production rate of gas is very fast.

There are many other gasification processes for special cases. These include the GEGAS process developed by General Electric Co., for power generation only.

### *10.1.3 Coal Liquefaction*

A block schematic of liquefaction process is shown in Fig. 10.3 Some typical processes are described below:

*Fischer-Tropsch Process*

This uses Lurgi gasifiers to obtain coal gas and a modification of the Bergius liquefaction process which was developed in Germany during World War II. This latter process uses hydrogenation and a catalytic-hydro-refining process carried out between 350 and 500°C and high pressures of 200-

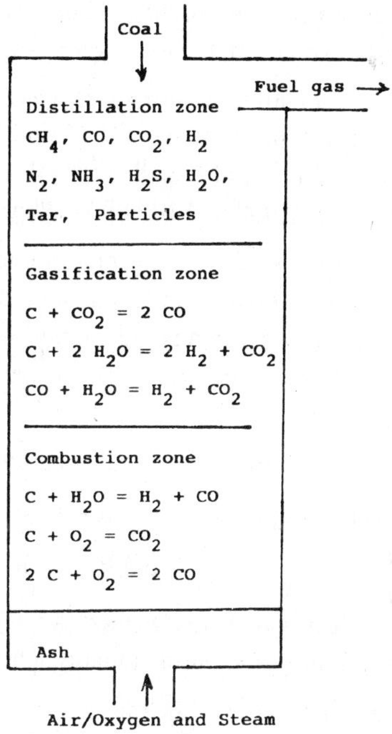


**Fig. 10.2** Details of chemical reactions in Lurgi process

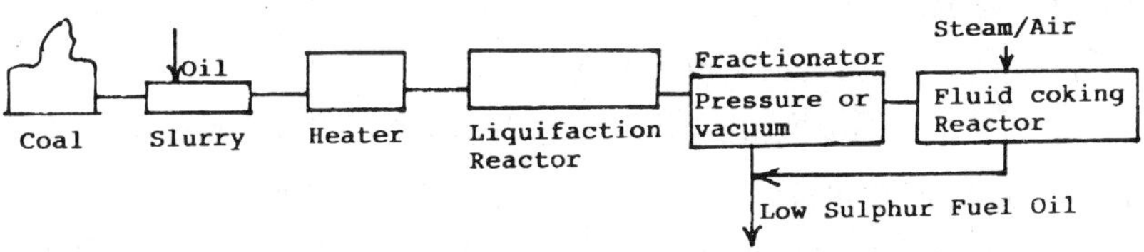


**Fig. 10.3** Coal liquefaction process

700 atm (21-70 MPa, 3000-10,000 psi). The process essentially breaks down the gas into carbon and recombines with $CH_4$ under temperature and pressure:

$$CO + 2\,H_2 \rightarrow CH_3OH, \text{ by catalytic process.}$$

In recent years, the SASOL process in South Africa has depended upon this process to obtain its fuel oil requirements.

In another process, developed by Char Oil Energy Co., small size (3 mm) coal is heated at slightly above atmospheric pressure (0.2 MPa) in steps from 300°C to 850°C by using combustion of char in oxygen. Oils are evolved and separated from the gases. The methanol is produced along with methane gas. This filtered crude synthetic oil (Syncrude) is combined with high temperature (400°C) high pressure (100 to 200 atm) hydrogen to remove sulphur, nitrogen and oxygen. Each ton of coal can produce about 1 barrel (42 gallon) of Syncrude and half a ton of char, which can be used over again.

There are other processes using pulverized coal slurried with oil. In all cases, hydrogen has to remove S, N, and O. Centrifuging removes solids. Yield can be up to 3 barrels (126 gallon) of oil per ton of coal used. The oil has a calorific value between 9,000 and 10,000 kcal/kg, comparable to gasoline and diesel.

***Example 10.1***: An average home consumes 1000 units (kW-h) of energy per month. If coal of 5500 kcal/kg (sub-bituminous coal with 10,000 Btu/lb heating value) is fired in a power station with an efficiency of 30%, estimate the amount of coal in tonnes (1000 kg) burnt in this station annually to supply this home (1 cal = 4.18 J).

***Solution***: 1000 kg of coal generate energy equal to

$$1000 \times 5500 \text{ kcal} = 5.5 \times 10^9 \text{ cal} = 23.0 \times 10^9 \text{ J} = 23 \times 10^9 / 3.6 \times 10^6 \text{ kW–h}$$
$$= 6{,}386 \text{ kW–h}$$

Electrical energy generated = 6386 × 0.3 = 1916 kW-h at the generator output. Therefore, coal burnt annually = 1000 × 12/1916 = 6.2636 tonne.

***Example 10.2***: If the power station is oil-fired with a heating value of 10,000 kcal/kg at the same efficiency, calculate the number of barrels of oil consumed annually to supply the average home. [1 US gallon weighs 3.5 kg, 1 barrel = 42 gal].

***Solution***: Energy consumed annually by the home

$$= 1000 \times 12 \text{ kW-h} = 4.32 \times 10^6 \text{ J} = 10.335 \times 10^6 \text{ kcal.}$$

Fuel required $= 10.335 \times 10^6/0.3 \times 10^4$ kg $= 3.445$ tonne

Therefore, gallons consumed annually = 3445/3.5 = 984 gal = 23.3 barrel.

## 10.2 Biomass Conversion

### *10.2.1 General*

Biomass is the name given to describe wood, bark, crops, food-processing wastes, municipal wastes and animal refuse. These can be used directly as fuels, or they can be converted to derived fuels such as methane gas, methanol and ethanol liquids. Biomass has specific gravities of 0.2 to 0.3 for crop waste to 0.35 to 0.65 for wood. Moisture content can be as high as 50% in wood and animal refuse, and 30% in municipal solid wastes (MSW). In addition, sewage from municipalities can be made to yield $CH_4$ (methane) gas by anaerobic (out of contact with air) digestion.

Analysis of some biomass fuels reveals the following constituents on the average, as shown in Table 10.2, and compared to bituminous coal. Moisture and metals in MSW are excluded.

**Table 10.2: Some Properties of Biomass Fuels**

| | Wood | Bark | Rice Hull | MSW | Coal |
|---|---|---|---|---|---|
| Carbon | 52 | 53 | 38.3 | 52 | 75.5 |
| Hydrogen | 6.5 | 5.8 | 4.4 | 5.6 | 5 |
| Oxygen | 40.6 | 38 | 34 | 42 | 5 |
| Nitrogen | 0.1 | 0.1 | 0.8 | 0.2 | 1.2 |
| Sulphur | | 0.1 | | 0.2 | 3.3 |
| Ash | 0.8 | 3 | 22.5 | | 10 |
| High Heating Value (HHV) | | | | | |
| Btu/lb | 9,000 | 9,000 | 6,000 | 8,000 | 13,800 |

(Note: 1000 Btu/lb = 555.5 kcal/kg = 2.33 MJ/kg.)

In addition, MSW may contain up to 20% metals on its weight.

From the table it can be observed that biomass fuels contain little or no sulphur, nitrogen, and ash. Whatever ash there is, is caused by dirt.

Municipal sewage, grass and water hyacinth have high ash content in addition to phosphorous. Their average compositions are shown in Table 10.3.

**Table 10.3: Properties of Biomass Wastes (excluding wood)**

| | Sewage | Grass | Water hyacinth |
|---|---|---|---|
| Carbon | 44 | 47 | 41 |
| Nitrogen | 4 | 2 | 2 |
| Phosphorous | 1 | 0.2 | 0.5 |
| Ash | 26 | 5 | 23 |
| Moisture | 25 | 45.8 | 33.5 |
| HHV: Btu/lb | 8,000 | 8,000 | 7,000 |
| kcal/kg | 4,444 | 4,444 | 3,890 |

It is estimated that in countries like India, China and African nations where people and cattle are plentiful and electricity or gas supply has not reached sufficiently plentifully to the villages where the bulk of the population lives, animal refuse can provide all the gas necessary for everyday domestic consumption for cooking and lighting. Five heads of cattle and crop refuse from 5 acres can provide enough fertilizers, while producing energy for a family of 5 to 6 members.

### *10.2.2 Conversion Process and Products*

The volatile products in biomass include $CO_2$, CO, $H_2$, $CH_4$, ethane, acetylene, methanol, phenol, in addition to other miscellaneous combustibles. In general, these volatiles are higher than that present in coal. Char is pure carbon. Biomass has 30 to 50% oxygen content as compared to less than 10% for coals. This, combined with low ash content, makes gasification easier, but the high moisture content dilutes the effluent gas. It acts as a heat absorber and retards chemical reactions.

Broadly speaking, conversion of biomass into useable fuels can be divided as follows which we will discuss later:

(1) *Biochemical Conversion*
  - (a) Anaerobic digestion, which is carried-out out of contact with air
  - (b) Aerobic digestion in the presence of air, also called composting
  - (c) Enzymatic fermentation by converting to glucose and fermenting

(2) *Thermal Conversion or Pyrolysis*

(3) *Thermo-Chemical Gasification*

*1 (a) Anaerobic Digestion*

The process converts basically cellulose material into $CH_4$ (methane) and $CO_2$:

$$C_6H_{10}O_5 + H_2O \rightarrow 3\ CH_4 + 3\ CO_2$$

In small digestors of earlier designs in industry and prevalent in villages, digestion is carried out at 35°C in the natural environment. This is known as Mesophilic Digestion. The retention time can be 15-30 days before re-fuelling with animal waste. However, in new designs, if the process is carried out at 55-60°C, called the Thermophilic Process, the retention time is reduced to less than 10 days. A balance between rate of input waste and rate of output gas must be struck in any given situation. Figure 10.4 shows typical digestors. For single-family use, the cost of the digestor can be very high, thereby preventing the valuable source of gas from reaching the family.

Municipal sewage is also converted to methane gas by anaerobic digestion in large underground reservoirs. The resulting gas is used for municipal waste-water treatment plants for the energy requirement. Some electricity is also produced in towns and cities.

In these processes, enzymes and acid-producing bacteria dissolve the carbohydrates to a soluble form and result in sugars, fatty acids and amino-acids. These are further digested to undergo metabolic changes to generate $CH_4$ and $CO_2$.

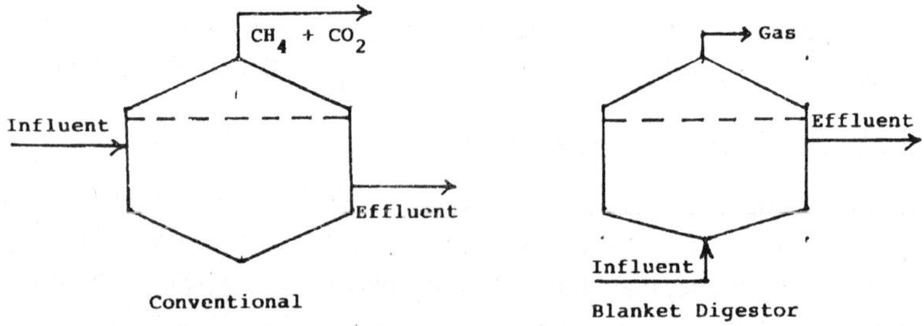


**Fig. 10.4** Anaerobic digestors for biomass energy converters

*1. (b) Aerobic Fermentation — Composting*

This is carried out with water when it is called wet composting, or, with heat called thermophilic fermentation. A sludge is formed with enough water and taken to a reactor. The microbial activity produces enough heat for the fermentation. The final product is mainly fertilizer, which can then be converted to gas in a proper digestor.

Landfills in backyards of homes in villages can produce gas by aerobic fermentation, but there is a risk of the gas spreading if not contained properly and cause fire hazards and accidents.

*(2) Thermal Conversion*

Municipal solid waste (MSW) can be pyrolized, which is a process of destructive distillation in the absence of air. Thereby, gas, fluid and solid fuels (mainly char) can be recovered. Wood can also be used and converted to wood oil. 1 ton of wood yields about 2.5 barrels (105 gallon) of oil.

The use of wood for domestic use needs no explanation, as this is the only fuel available for 80% of the world's population. Civilization and commercial supply of electricity and gas has not yet reached those unfortunate people. However, some attempts have been made to improve wood-burning stoves in rural areas. This is mostly the result of creating enough turbulence by the evolved gas to burn CO that would have otherwise escaped unburnt, as well as using high-temperature walls. Several examples are shown in Fig. 10.5.

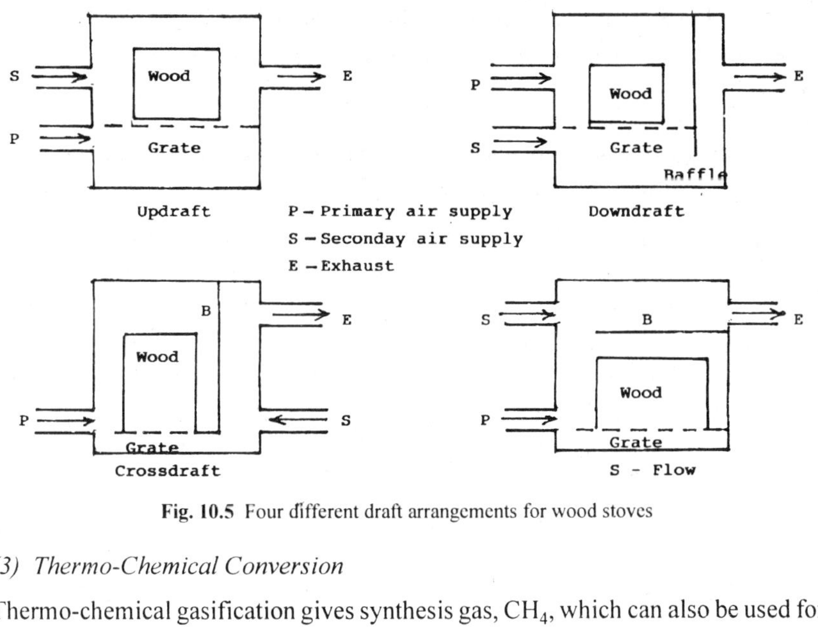


**Fig. 10.5** Four different draft arrangements for wood stoves

*(3) Thermo-Chemical Conversion*

Thermo-chemical gasification gives synthesis gas, $CH_4$, which can also be used for production of liquid fuels like methanol. The gas can be used for operating gas turbines and in boilers, while liquid fuels are used in internal combustion engines as well as boilers, which are originally designed for natural gas and petroleum.

Thermo-chemical gasification yields the following gases: CO, $CO_2$, $H_2$, $H_2O$ and $CH_4$, and their mixtures. Biomass containing quantities of components (like lignin and ash) cannot be used for anaerobic digestion, so that these as well as every other biomass can be made to yield gas by thermo-chemical process.

The gasifiction involves the following steps:

(a) Pyrolysis at high temperature leads to separation of energy-rich gases, water in the form of steam, and gives char.

(b) Hydrogenation, involving introducing $H_2$, results in formation of hydrocarbons.

(c) Oxygen gasification, whereby introduction of air or pure oxygen gives the high temperature required for the gasification process.

Thus, sources of hydrogen, steam and oxygen or air are necessary for the process.

Liquid fuels produced from biomass are generally methanol and ethyl alcohol (ethanol). The steps for the production of methanol are as follows:

(a) *Synthesis Gas Generation*: Biomass is converted to CO, $H_2$, $CO_2$, $H_2O$, C and other hydrocarbons. Biomass + $O_2$ = CO + $H_2$ + $CO_2$ + $H_2O$.

(b) The CO and $H_2$ react further in what is known as a "shift reaction" to produce $H_2$ and $CO_2$.

(c) Hydrogen is also generated from the reaction $CH_4 + 2H_2O = 4\ H_2 + CO_2$.

(d) Finally, the hydrogenation reaction gives methanol, $CH_3OH$:

$$CO + 2\ H_2 = CH_3OH;\ CO_2 + 3\ H_2 = CH_3OH + H_2O$$

The steps for production of ethanol involve fermentation, the key reaction being $C_6H_{12}O_6$ (hexose) $\rightarrow$ 2 $C_2H_5OH$ (ethanol) + 2 $CO_2$.

Any sugar-containing biomass can be fermented to yield $C_2H_5OH$ (ethanol). The schematic of the process is shown in Fig. 10.6. Thus corn, sugarcane, etc. can be used as raw inputs. As an example, the sugarcane juice after first crystallization is drawn off along with molasses to be converted to ethanol. The dry sugarcane bagasse is used to fuel the reactor (still), without using any other source for heat.

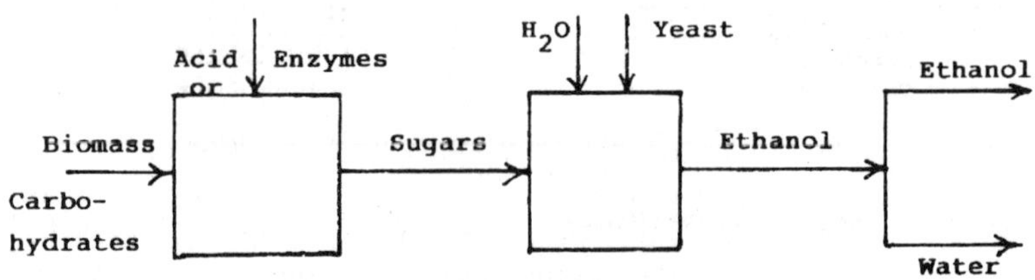


**Fig. 10.6** Ethanol production from biomass

## 10.3 Geothermal Energy

Mineral water from hot springs have been used since antiquity for baths and therapeutic purposes. Recent years are showing increased use of geothermal steam and water resources for power generation, residential and industrial heating, aquaculture, greenhouses, wood and paper industries, mining, production of salt and many local uses. Italy, New Zealand and USA have steam power plants of over 500 MW each. At the Geysers in California, Nevada and other hot-spots, power stations of 100 MWe are in operation.

The earth's inner core, consisting of Fe and Ni, is at a temperature of about 4500°C. The earth's crust, to a depth of nearly 50 km, consists of Si-Fe-Mg magma, whose temperature is about 1400°C. For this temperature to be useful, we look for hot dry rock nearer the surface which is accessible to drilling, extending between 2 to 6 km. Once shafts are sunk, water has to be injected artificially to bring the heat to the surface. Recently, nuclear explosives have been used for opening up vast natural-gas reservoirs and the same is used for tapping geothermal sources also.

At depths accessible to drilling (up to 10 km), geothermal gradient is between 10-50°C/km. But to be economically viable, the gradient should be high, in the region of 40°C/km. Porous rocks near volcanically active regions have temperature between 70 and 340°C. For power generation, temperature must be in excess of 150°C and nearer 200°C.

Pressure of steam issuing from water pumped to these dry hot rocks exceeds 1 MPa (10 atm). Young volcanic centres are the best sources.

The major geothermal resources in the world exist at the following locations:

*Asia*:

Tibet, Southern Siberian Mountains, Tashkent, Asia Minor, Japan, Kamachatka Peninsula, Indonesia, Phillippines and Taiwan

*Europe*:

Iceland, Italy, Southern Russia and Georgia

*Africa*:

Ethiopia and Somaliland

*N. America*:

Yellowstone and California

*C. and S. America*:

West Indies and Chile

*New Zealand*

There are everywhere pockets of hot springs which are used as sanatoriums and health resorts, but they have not been listed above.

Figure 10.7 shows a schematic of a geyser. Where it shows "rain", artificial pumping of water can be carried out in the fissures or shafts driven to bring out steam and hot water.

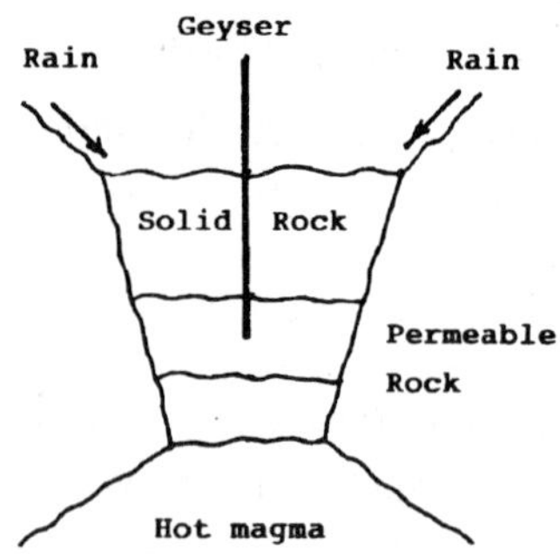


**Fig. 10.7** Principle of geothermal heat generation and extraction through a geyser

*Power Generation*

In 1981, the total power generation from geothermal sources was 2500 MW, but it has shown enormous growth at 15% annually. This means that in 1991 the installed capacity was 10,000 MW, and in 1996 it was 17,500 MW. Cost estimates show that the minimum capacity should be 7.5 MW at any one location, but nearer to 25-50 MW if transmission is necessary. Comparative costs for power plant are:

Geothermal - 100; Oil-fired - 125; Coal-fired - 200; Nuclear - 250.
Drilling of geothermal wells cost 2-4 times as much as oil and gas wells, since hot solid rock is encountered.

In practice, the issuing steam and water are separated, yielding low-pressure saturated steam and very hot water. Consequently, nearly 2.5 times the weight of steam is necessary as compared to high-pressure steam generated in coal or oil-fired boilers. Fossil-fuel plants operate up to 555°C and 250 atm (25 MPa) and heat necessary is 2100 kcal/kW-h. As compaıed to this, geothermal plants yield steam at 180°C, 1 MPa and require 5500 kcal/kW-h. Volume of steam is 50 times greater and weight of steam is 2.5 per kW-h generated, as compared to fossil-fueled power stations (1 kW-h = 861.2 kcal).

There are essentially four types of geothermal systems in commercial use in the world:

(a) Dry-steam plants which are similar to conventional steam plants.

(b) Single-flash plants: Here, the hot water after separation from the steam is evaporated by using part of the power and fed back to the steam plant.

(c) Double-flash plant: The hot water is evaporated to steam a second time, just as in the case of single-flash plants.

(d) Multiple-flash plants: The same is repeated several times until all hot water is used economically.

Other power generation schemes used are as follows:

(a) Binary Plants: Here, the hot water is utilized in heat exchangers to evaporate $NH_3$ or freon in a closed Rankine cycle, as has been discussed under OTEC is Chap. 6.

(b) Liquid turbines called Rotary Separator Turbines (RST) are developed, in which the mixture of water and steam is separated centrifugally. In such a process, the separated steam generates 5 times as much power as the water when used in proper turbines.

*Pollutants*

Because of the presence of water used in bringing the heat upwards and the sulphur content of volcanic activities, $H_2S$ is profusely generated. This gas paralyzes olefactory nerves. Waste heat is quite considerable and the atmosphere near geothermal plants is considerably hotter than otherwise.

Poisons in the underground rocks pollute the steam and water. Because of salinity, corrosion of equipment is very much the problem. Therefore, geothermal plants present dangers from water pollution, heat pollution, and corrosion in addition to air pollution.

However, when suitable precautions are taken, they provide inexpensive heat for many applications. Some of the more dramatic are: In Iceland, 80% of residents of the capital city of Reykjavik receive heat for space heating of homes. This is the most usual application in all countries other than power generation. In the far north in Russia, a complete weather station is operated by geothermal energy source.

## 10.4 Hydrogen Fuel

### *10.4.1 Introduction*

It has been foretold that ''the future fuel of the world will be liquified hydrogen obtained by electrolysis of water, with the energy source being the wind'' (J.B.S. Haldane, 1923). From predictions of world fuel resources, natural gas and petroleum have a short life of another 30 years (more in some countries) while coal will last for 200 years. Thereafter nuclear fusion and breeder fission reactors will serve part of the energy needs of the world. But hydrogen will last forever. Its use has already been demonstrated in many areas such as gas turbines, aircraft, rockets, and internal combustion engines, fuel cells, and industrial conversion of coal to methane or methanol.

The advantages of $H_2$ as a fuel are the following:

(1) It has an energy/gram ratio which is highest among all fuels, exceeding twice that of gasoline, being about 29,000 cal/g.

(2) Its combustion with oxygen results only in water as by-product. Pollutants are negligible.

(3) It can be burnt directly with $O_2$ in turbines.

(4) It can be oxidized with $O_2$ in fuel cells.

(5) It can desulphurize coal and petroleum to provide clean power.

(6) It can be pumped in pipelines, stored as gas, liquid or in solid hydrides. Hydrogen can also be transported in rail cars using double-walled Dewar tanks. Thus it is claimed that hydrogen is an energy carrier.

(7) Off-load-time power in conventional electrical power stations can be used for generating hydrogen, which can be stored properly for future use.

### *10.4.2 Production*

Five main categories for production of hydrogen, depending on the quantity required, are as follows:

(1) Chemical methods; (2) Electro-chemical methods; (3) Thermo-chemical methods; (4) Photo-chemical methods; (5) Biochemical methods.

(1) *Chemical Methods*:

The most widely used are:

(a) Steam-reforming of hydrocarbons

(b) Partial oxidation of hydrocarbons

(c) Coal gasification

In steam reforming, the reaction is $CH_4 + 2\ H_2O + \text{heat} \rightarrow CO_2 + 4\ H_2$. The process is carried out at 650-700°C, 7-48 atm using Ni catalyst, which is poisoned by any sulphur present in the hydrocarbon.

In partial oxidation of hydrocarbons, refinery residual oil is used. The process occurs at 1300-1400°C. A block diagram of the process is shown in Fig. 10.8.

The coal gasification process, Fig. 10.9, uses pulverized coal suspended in steam and $O_2$ in low-pressure Koppers-Totzek or the high pressure Shell-Koppers process, among others. The reaction is

$$3\ FeO + H_2O \rightarrow Fe_3O_4 + H_2$$

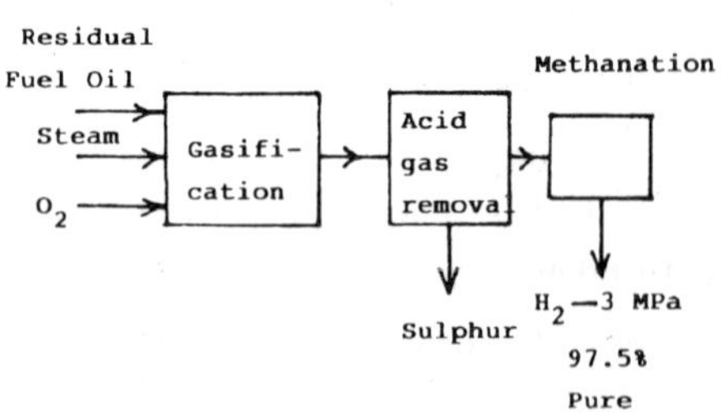


Fig. 10.8 Production of hydrogen by chemical methods from fuel oil

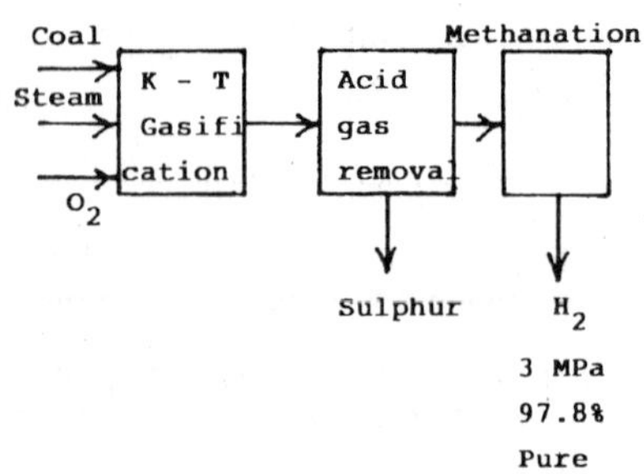


Fig. 10.9 Production of hydrogen from pulverized coal

*(2) Electro-Chemical Methods*

This is electrolysis of water, where $O_2$ and $H_2$ are separated at the electrodes ($O_2$ at anode and $H_2$ at cathode). The electrolyte is 25-30% acqueous KOH or NaOH. Typical voltage required is 1.47 V, although Gibbs free energy (see Sec. 10.6) at 25°C and 1 atm is $\Delta G$ = 56.69 kcal/gram-mole corresponding to E = 1.23 V as discussed under fuel cells and batteries.

Electrodes are Ni, NiO + Li, and NiCo for anode. The cathode is nickel steel. The process can take place in containers with suitable separators for the two gases, or in a filter-press type, where a series of thin cells are arranged side by side to collect the gases. The power consumption is between 4-5 kW-h/$m^3$ of $H_2$.

The other three processes (Thermo-, Photo-, and Biochemical) are still in experimental stages and produce only lab quantities of $H_2$, and will not be described here.

### *10.4.3 Applications*

Up until now the primary application as well as need for development of hydrogen has been in transportation. Starting with the zeppelins in the early part of this century (with disastrous results) to the rockets of the latter half, hydrogen has served as the primary fuel. Liquid $H_2$ is used in space programmes, even with some tragic loss of lives. Hydrogen as fuel in tanks of automobiles have been developed. Aircraft have used this lightest of fuels, since it weighs only 10% of hydrocarbon fuel and produces twice the power for equal weight. An aircraft therefore uses only 5% of weight in fuel and so has a range far in excess of hydrocarbon-fuelled aircraft. The first aircraft to be tested was in Russia in 1988. It is estimated that the range is 200% that of a conventional plane, showing that even though fuel weight is low, the rest of the structural parts are still comparable to existing aircraft.

As described later, hydrogen is used as a fuel with oxygen in a fuel cell for direct generation of electricity.

## 10.5 Thermo-Electric Energy Conversion

### *10.5.1 Seeback, Peltier, and Thomson Effects*

Thermo-electric energy conversion is a means of converting heat directly into electrical energy. Some familiar devices which have been most common are thermionic conduction in electronic devices, where a heated cathode at high temperature releases electrons from its surface, if the heat energy imparted is greater than the work-function of the material of the cathode. The thermionic "valve" can be called a "generator". However, the power has been very low, and moreover, the heated cathode requires electrical input from other sources. Recently, the advent of small nuclear reactors has provided industry and scientific community with compact and intense heat sources, which have changed the concept of thermo-electric generators and refrigerators, coupled with the development of high-temperature semiconductor materials of the *n*- and *p*-types.

Thermo-electric generation of power is usually considered as having been discovered in the early 1820's, when Thomas J. Seebeck applied heat to the junction of two dissimilar metals and found a potential difference between the cold ends of the metals. This is known as the Seebeck Effect. This was followed in the 1830's by the discovery of "heat pumping" by Jean Peltier, in which when an electric current is passed in a circuit containing two dissimilar metals, heat is evolved at one junction and absorbed at the other. This is also used as a thermo-electric cooler or refrigerator. The next and final discovery was by William Thomson (Lord Kelvin), who found that heat is absorbed or evolved in homogeneous conductor carrying an electric current in the presence of a temperature gradient.

Depending upon the capacity of the heat source, thermo-electric generators with powers of 50 kW have been built. The impetus was provided by space applications, one of the most dramatic being the deployment of a radio isotope generator of only 15 cm diameter and 15 cm height, using the α-decay of Polonium-210 on the lunar surface by astronauts, to power scientific equipment.

### *10.5.2 Seebeck Effect and Coefficient*

Figure 10.10 shows two dissimilar materials, whose junction receives heat at the rate of $Q$ at the higher temperature $T_h$. The others are at the lower temperature $T_c$ and remove heat at the rate $Q_c$. During this process, an emf appears across the two cold ends. Each material generates an emf $\Delta E$, which is given by the Seebeck relation

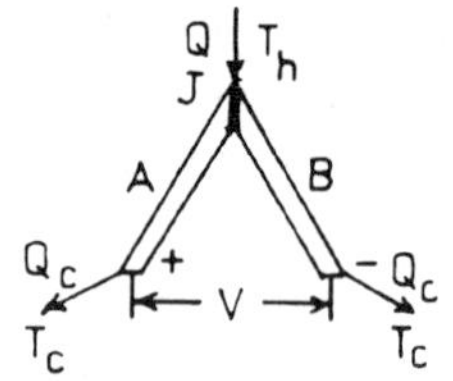


**Fig. 10.10** Seebeck effect and generation of emf between hot and cold junctions of dissimilar materials

$$\Delta E = S \cdot \Delta T \tag{10.1}$$

where $\Delta T = T_h - T_c$

and $S$ = Seebeck coefficient, $V/°C$ or $\mu V/K$, etc.

Some publications use the symbol α, since $S$ denotes entropy.

When the circuit is closed, a current will circulate and in Fig. 10.10 this is shown as left-to-right in an external load circuit and counter clockwise in the materials. For the two dissimilar materials

$$E_{AB} = (S_A + S_B) \cdot (T_h - T_c) \tag{10.2}$$

Normal values of Seebeck coefficients are as follows:

*Metals*:

80 $\mu V/K$;

*Semiconductors*:

50 - 1000 $\mu V/K$, + for *p*-type and – for *n*-type;

*Special metals*:

100 - 400 $\mu V/K$ (developed for thermo-electric application)

Equation (10.1) gives $S = dE/dT$ (10.3)

The simple device serves as a thermocouple for measuring the temperature of the junction.

### *10.5.3 Peltier Effect and Coefficient*

Figure 10.11 shows the junction of two dissimilar materials, usually *n*- and *p*-type semiconductors in recent years, across which an electric current I is passed from an external electrical source. The materials are carrying heats $Q_A$ and $Q_B$ per second, while heat $Q_r$ is removed from the junction to maintain the junction temperature at a constant value. The difference between heat removed and the $I^2R$ heating at the junction is known as the Peltier Effect.

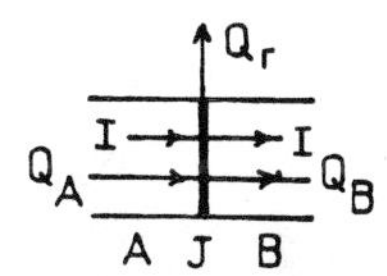


**Fig. 10.11** Peltier effect at junction of dissimilar materials

Depending upon the types of materials and direction of current flow, we can determine whether the Peltier heat must be added to the junction or removed from it. The latter will function as a cooler or refrigerator. In 1838, Lenz observed experimentally for the first time that water could be frozen into ice. Now, the rate of heat removed is

$$Q_r = Q_A + Q_B + I^2R_j \tag{10.4}$$

The heat generated in the materials due to current flow is

$I \cdot \Delta V_A = I\,T\,S_A$, and $I \cdot \Delta V_B = I\,T\,S_B$. Therefore

$$Q_r = I\,T\,(S_A - S_B) + I^2R_j \tag{10.5}$$

The term $[I\,T\,(S_A - S_B)]$ is called Peltier heating and denoted by $Q_p$.

This is written as

$$Q_p = I\,T\,(S_A - S_B) = \pi_{AB}\,I \tag{10.6}$$

where $\pi_{AB}$ is called the Peltier coefficient, $\mu V$ or V, etc.

If one material is *p*-type and the other is *n*-type

$$\pi_{AB} = \pi_p - \pi_n \tag{10.7}$$

### *10.5.4 The Thomson Effect and Coefficient*

In Fig. 10.12 is shown a junction, across which a potential difference $\Delta E$ exists due to Seebeck effect and a temperature difference $\Delta T$, so that a temperature gradient exists. An electric current is passed which will generate heat. If sufficient heat $Q_r$ is removed to maintain all temperatures constant at the value before passing the current, it is known as Thomson Effect. This effect is due to passage of electric current in the presence of a temperature gradient in the material.

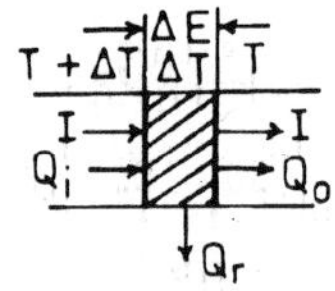


**Fig. 10.12** Thomson effect at junction with current flow and temperature gradiant

The magnitude and sign of Thomson effect are controlled by the materials, current $I$ and its direction in relation to the temperature gradient, and the temperature gradient. This is seen as follows:

The rate of heat removed is

$$Q_r = I \cdot \Delta E + I(T + \Delta T)\, S_A - I\, T\, S_B \tag{10.8}$$

But

$$S_A = S_B + (dS/dT)\, \Delta T \tag{10.9}$$

Therefore

$$Q_r = I \cdot \Delta E + I\left[\, (T + \Delta T)\, (S_B + \frac{dS}{dT} \Delta T) - T\, S_B\right]$$

$$= I \cdot \Delta E + I\, [S_B \cdot \Delta T + (dS/dT) \cdot T \cdot \Delta T + (\Delta T)^2 \cdot dS/dT] \tag{10.10}$$

If $\Delta T$ is small, and the last term is neglected, and $(S_B \cdot \Delta T)$ = voltage across the junction due to Seebeck Effect, the term $I \cdot (\Delta E + S_B \cdot \Delta T)$ represents the heat produced by the electrical resistance $R_e$. Therefore, heat to be removed becomes

$$Q_r = I^2 R_e + I \cdot T \cdot \Delta T \cdot (dS/dT) \tag{10.11}$$

The Thomson heating is consequently

$$Q_{Th} = I \cdot T \cdot (dS/dT) \cdot \Delta T \tag{10.12}$$

Since heat is removed from the system, we write this as

$$Q_{Th} = -I \cdot \tau \cdot \Delta T \tag{10.13}$$

where $\tau$ = the Thomson coefficient $= -T \cdot dS/dT = -Q_{Th}/I \cdot \Delta T$ (10.14)

Lord Kelvin also found the interrelationships between the three coefficients, which are as follows:

$$\left.\begin{aligned} S_A - S_B &= d\,E_{AB}/dT \\ \pi_{AB} &= T\,(S_A - S_B) \\ \text{and} \quad \tau_A - \tau_B &= -T\,(dS_A/dT - dS_B/dT) = -T\,dS_{AB}/dT \end{aligned}\right\} \tag{10.15}$$

When the Seebeck Coefficient $S = dE/dT$ is found, the Peltier Coefficient $\pi$ can be obtained as well as the Thomson Coefficient.

In conclusion, we observe the following:

(a) When the junction of two dissimilar materials is heated, a voltage is generated which can deliver energy to an external load. If no load is connected, the device acts as a thermocouple to measure the junction temperature in terms of a voltage.

(b) When a voltage much higher than Seebeck voltage is applied to a thermo-electric device, heat can be pumped from the cold junction to the hot junction. This is refrigeration or thermo-electric cooling. We consider these separately in detail now.

### *10.5.5 Thermo-Electric Generator*

*(1) Power Output*

The open-circuit voltage in Fig. 10.13 is

$$E_{oc} = S\,(T_h - T_c) \tag{10.16}$$

and the heating loss in the materials $= I^2 \cdot r_t$ (10.17)

where $r_t$ = total resistance of the two materials in series.

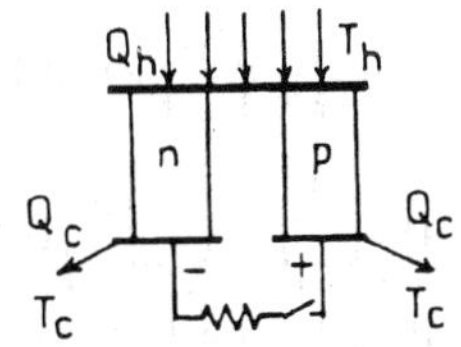

**Fig. 10.13** Schematic of a thermo-electric generator using *n*- and *p*-type semiconductors

Therefore, the power output is

$$P = I \cdot S\,(T_h - T_c) - I^2\, r_t \tag{10.18}$$

This varies with the current. At maximum power output

$$dP/dI = S\,(T_h - T_c) - 2\,I\,r_t = 0$$

which gives

$$I_{pm} = 0.5\,(S/r_t)\cdot(T_h - T_c) \tag{10.19}$$

Using this in Eq. (10.18), the maximum power output becomes

$$P_m = 0.25\,(T_h - T_c)\,S^2/r_t \tag{10.20}$$

***Example 10.3***: Consider the following data for a thermo-electric generator (Fig. 10.13):

| | |
|---|---|
| Lengths of materials | $L_n = L_p = 5$ cm |
| Areas of materials | $A_n = 1.5\ \text{cm}^2,\ A_p = 1\ \text{cm}^2$ |
| Hot and cold temperatures | $T_h = 500°\text{C},\ T_c = 30°\text{C}$ |
| Seebeck coefficients | $S_n = -300\ \mu V/°\text{C},\ S_p = 200\ \mu V/°\text{C}$ |
| Specific resistances | $\rho_n = 10^{-3}$ ohm–cm, $\rho_p = 8 \times 10^{-4}$ ohm–cm |

Calculate the following:

(a) The Seebeck open-circuit voltage of generator

(b) Resistance of the two materials

(c) Maximum power output and

(d) Current at maximum power output

***Solution***: $S = S_p - S_n = 500\ \mu V/^\circ C$ (or , K)

(a) O.C. voltage $= 500 \times 10^{-6} \times (500 - 30) = 0.235\ V$

In degrees Kelvin, 500°C = 773 K, and 30°C = 303 K. The difference between hot and cold ends is 773 – 303 = 470 K = 470°C

(b) $r_n = 10^{-3} \times 5 / 1.5 = 3.33 \times 10^{-3}$ ohm

$r_p = 8 \times 10^{-4} \times 5 / 1 = 4 \times 10^{-3}$ ohm

Therefore, $r_t = 7.33 \times 10^{-3}$ ohm for the two in series.

(c) $P_m = 0.25 \times (500 \times 10^{-6})^2 \times 470^2 / 7.33 \times 10^{-3} = 1.88\ W$

(d) $I_{pm} = 0.5 \times 500 \times 10^{-6} \times 470 / 7.33 \times 10^{-3} = 16.03\ A$

*(2) Thermal Efficiency*

The power output of the generator is given by Eq. (10.18). Now consider the rate of heat flow from the hot junction to the cold end along one of the arms. The heat input is $Q_h$ + heat in thermal conduction $- \frac{1}{2} I^2 r_t$ loss in one leg, i.e.

$$P_{in} = I S T_h + K (T_h - T_c) - 0.5 I^2 r_t \tag{10.21}$$

where $K$ = total thermal conductivity of the two legs in parallel.

Therefore, the thermal efficiency is

$$\eta_{th} = \frac{I S (T_h - T_c) - I^2 r_t}{I S T_h + K (T_h - T_c) - 0.5 I^2 r_t}$$

$$= \frac{T_h - T_c}{T_h} \quad \frac{I - (r_t / S) I^2 / (T_h - T_c)}{I - 0.5 (r_t / S) \cdot I^2 / T_h + (K / S) \cdot (T_h - T_c) / T_h} \tag{10.22}$$

We note that the term $(T_h - T_c) / T_h$ is the Carnot efficiency.

The total thermal conductivity is

$$K = k_n \cdot A_n / L_n + k_p \cdot A_p / L_p,\ W / K \tag{10.23}$$

and the total resistance is

$$r_t = L_n / A_n \sigma_n + L_p / A_p \sigma_p \tag{10.24}$$

where $k_n$, $k_p$ = thermal conductivities of *n*- and *p*-type materials in W/cm-K, or, W/m-K, etc.

$\sigma_n$, $\sigma_p$ = conductivities of the two materials, 1/ohm-cm or Siemens/cm

and $L_n$, $L_p$ = lengths of the two legs, cm.

As the current varies, i.e. the electrical heat input changes the thermal efficiency changes. As its maximum value, the current is given by $d\eta_{th}/dI = 0$. We also define a figure of merit as

$$Z = S^2 / K r_t \tag{10.25}$$

Carrying out the differentiation and equating to zero, we obtain

$$I_{\max} = (S/r_t) \cdot (T_h - T_c) [\sqrt{1 + Z(T_h - T_c)/2} - 1] / Z \cdot (T_h + T_c)/2$$

$$= (T_h - T_c) M \tag{10.26}$$

where $M$ is called the Coefficient of Merit.

The maximum thermal efficiency will then the

$$\eta_{thm} = \frac{T_h - T_c}{T_h} \cdot \frac{M - M^2 \cdot r_t / S}{M - M^2 \cdot r_t / 2 \cdot S \cdot T_h + K / S\, T_h} \tag{10.27}$$

The coefficient of merit $M$ depends on the factor $[Z \cdot (T_h + T_c)/2]$ = (Figure of merit) × (Average temperature between the hot and cold junctions).

***Example 10.4***: In the previous example, take the thermal conductivities as $k_n = k_p = 25$ mW / cm-°C. Calculate the following.

(a) Total thermal conductivity of the two materials in parallel, $K$

(b) The figure of merit, $Z$. Give its unit.

(c) The coefficient of merit at maximum thermal efficiency, $M$

(d) The current at maximum thermal efficiency, $I_{max}$. Compare with current at maximum power, $I_{pm}$

(e) Power output at maximum efficiency. Compare with maximum power output.

(f) The maximum thermal efficiency. Compare with Carnot efficiency of the system, and the efficiency at maximum power output.

***Solution***:

(a) $K = 25 \times 10^{-3} (1.5 + 1)/5 = 12.5 \times 10^{-3}$ W/°C (or, K)

(b) $Z = S^2 / K r_i = (0.5 \times 10^{-3})^2 / (12.5 \times 10^{-3} \times 7.33 \times 10^{-3}) = 2.73 \times 10^{-3}$

*Units*: $(\text{Volt/deg})^2/(\text{Watt} \times \text{ohm/deg}) = \text{Volt}^2 \times \text{deg}/(\text{Watt} \times \text{ohm} \times \text{deg}^2)$

$= 1 / \text{deg} = \text{deg}^{-1}$, since $\text{Watt} = \text{Volt}^2 / \text{ohm}$

(c) $M = (S/r_i) \cdot [\sqrt{1 + Z(T_h + T_c)/2} - 1] / Z \cdot (T_h + T_c)/2$

Now, $Z \cdot (T_h + T_c)/2 = 2.73 \times 10^{-3} \cdot (773 + 303)/2 = 1.46874$

Therefore,

$$M = (0.5 \times 10^{-3} / 7.33 \times 10^{-3}) \cdot (\sqrt{1.46874 + 1} - 1) / 1.46874$$

$$= 0.02653 \text{ , A / K}$$

(d) $I_{max} = M \cdot (T_h - T_c) = 0.02653 \times 470 = 12.47\ A$.

Current at maximum output is by Eq. (10.19) and Example 10.3, $I_{pm} = 16.03\ A$.

(e) Power output at maximum efficiency

$$P_{\eta m} = I S (T_h - T_c) - I^2 r_i$$

$$= 12.47 \times 0.5 \times 10^{-3} \times 470 - 12.47^2 \times 7.33 \times 10^{-3}$$

$$= 2.93045 - 1.13982 = 1.79063\ W$$

Maximum power output = 1.88 $W$.

(f) Maximum thermal efficiency, Eq. (10.27):

$(T_h - T_c) / T_h = 470 / 773 = 0.608$

$M^2 r_i / S = 0.02653^2 \times 7.33 \times 10^{-3} / 0.5 \times 10^{-3} = 0.01032$

$(M^2 r_i / S) \cdot (T_h - T_c)/2 \cdot T_h = 0.003135$

$K / S \cdot T_h = 12.5 \times 10^{-3} / (0.5 \times 10^{-3} \times 773) = 0.03234$

Therefore,

$$\eta_{tm} = 0.608 \times \frac{0.02653 - 0.01032}{0.02653 - 0.003135 + 0.03234} = 0.1768 = 17.68\%$$

Carnot efficiency $= 470/773 = 0.608 = 60.8\%$

At maximum power output, current $I_{pm} = 16.03\ A$. From Eq. (10.22)

$$\eta_{Pm} = 0.608 \times \frac{16.03 - (7.33 \times 10^{-3} \times 16.03^2)/(0.5 \times 10^{-3} \times 470)}{16.03 - \dfrac{7.33 \times 10^{-3} \times 16.03^2}{2 \times 0.5 \times 10^{-3} \times 773} + \dfrac{12.5 \times 10^{-3}}{0.5 \times 10^{-3}} \dfrac{470}{773}}$$

$$= 0.608 \times \frac{16.03 - 8.015}{16.03 - 2.43664 + 15.2} = 0.16924 = 16.924\%$$

Efficiencies obtained in practice do not exceed 8% because of

(a) heavy radiation losses, which have been neglected in the example,

(b) change in electrical and thermal conductivities with temperature, which range from 773 to 303 K (room temperature nearly) in this example.

Some typical thermo-electric units used or planned are given later.

### *10.5.6 Peltier Cooling*

The Peltier cooling, also called heat pumping, is very attractive because there are no moving parts, the operation is silent, size is small, weight is less, and there is a high degree of reliability of solid-state devices.

Figure 10.14 shows a schematic in which a cold junction of *n*- and *p*-type materials is maintained at the low temperature $T_c$ and rejected at the high temperature $T_h$ by providing electrical power input at voltage $V$ and current $I$. The quantities that control the operation of the heat pump are: (a) the heat-pumping capacity $Q$; (b) the pumping current $I$ to be supplied; (c) the temperature difference $\Delta T = T_h - T_c$ to be maintained; and (d) the efficiency, which is usually known as the coefficient of performance of the system.

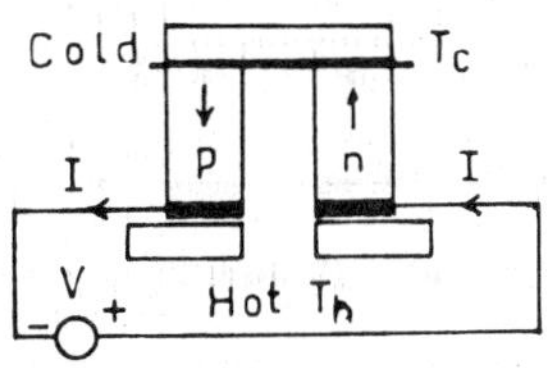


**Fig. 10.14** Peltier cooling (refrigeration) using *n*- and *p*-type semiconductor materials

Now, the rate of heat transfer from cold to hot junction by the Peltier effect, i.e., the Peltier heat, is

$$Q = \pi I = S \cdot T_c \cdot I \tag{10.28}$$

where $S$ = total Seebeck coefficient = $|S_n| + |S_p|$

Also, if electrical resistance $r_t$ of the two arms in series, and the thermal conductivity of the two arms in parallel, are constant, the $I^2R$ heat appearing at each of the hot junctions is $0.5\ I^2\ r_t$. [We omit the thermodynamic analysis to justify this]. The heat flowing from hot to cold junction is $K \cdot (T_h - T_c) = K \cdot \Delta T$ Therefore, rate of heat removal is

$$Q = S \cdot T_c \cdot I - 0.5\, I^2 r_t - K \cdot \Delta T \tag{10.29}$$

where $S \cdot T_c \cdot I$ = Seebeck potential at $T_c$ × current.

The current for maximum cooling is obtained from

$$dQ/dI = 0 = S \cdot T_c - I \cdot r_t,\ \text{giving},\ I_m = S \cdot T_c / r_t \tag{10.30}$$

Under this condition, the maximum cooling rate becomes

$$Q_m = S \cdot T_c \cdot I_m - 0.5\, I_m^2\, r_t - K \cdot \Delta T \tag{10.31}$$

The electrical power required to pump heat from $T_c$ to $T_h$ is

$$P = I \cdot S \cdot (T_h - T_c) + I^2 r_t \tag{10.32}$$

The coefficient of performance is denoted by

$$\phi = Q/P = \left[ \frac{I \cdot S \cdot (T_h - T_c) + I^2 r_t}{S \cdot T_c \cdot I - 0.5\, I^2 r_t - K \cdot \Delta T} \right]^{-1} \tag{10.33}$$

***Example 10.5***: The following data apply for a Peltier cooling system:

Seebeck coefficients : $|S_n| = |S_p| = 250\ \mu V/°C$

Electrical resistivities : $\rho_n = \rho_p = 1.5 \times 10^{-3}$ ohm-cm

Thermal conductivities : $k_n = k_p = 20 \times 10^{-3}$ W/cm-deg

Temperatures : $T_h = 27°C = 300$ K; $T_c = -10°C = 263$ K

Dimensions of couple : $A_n = A_p = 1.5\ cm^2$; $L_n = L_p = 1.2$ cm

At maximum cooling condition, calculate:

(a) Current required; (b) Electrical power input required; (c) Amount of heat at maximum cooling condition; and (d) The coefficient of performance.

***Solution:*** $S = 500 \times 10^{-6}\ V/°C = 0.5 \times 10^{-3}\ V/°C$ (or, K)

$$r_t = \rho_n L_n / A_n + \rho_p L_p / A_p = 2 \times 1.5 \times 10^{-3} \times 1.2 / 1.5$$

$$= 2.4 \times 10^{-3}\ \text{ohm}$$

$$K = k_n A_n / L_n + k_p A_p / L_p = 2 \times 20 \times 10^{-3} \times 1.5 / 1.2$$

$$= 50 \times 10^{-3}\ W/°C$$

(a) $I_m = S \cdot T_c / r_t = 0.5 \times 10^{-3} \times 263 / 2.4 \times 10^{-3} = 54.79$ A

(b) $P_m = I \cdot S \cdot (T_h - T_c) + I^2 r_t$

$$= 54.79 \times 0.5 \times 10^{-3} \times 37 + 54.79^2 \times 2.4 \times 10^{-3}$$

$$= 1.0136 + 7.205 = 8.2186\ W$$

(c) $Q_m = S \cdot T_c \cdot I_m - 0.5\, I_m^2\, r_t - K \cdot \Delta T$

$$= 0.5 \times 10^{-3} \times 263 \times 54.79 - 0.5 \times 54.79^2 \times 2.4 \times 10^{-3} - 50 \times 10^{-3} \times 37$$

$$= 7.205 - 3.6025 - 1.85 = 1.7525 \text{ W}$$

(d) Coefficient of performance = Heat removed/Electrical input

$$\phi = 1.7525 / 8.2186 = 0.213 = 21.3\%, \text{ ideally}.$$

### *10.5.7 Thermo-Electric Devices Using Nuclear Heat*

Practical thermo-electric devices use lead telluride as intrinsic semiconductor material doped with bismuth for *n*-type and sodium for *p*-type materials. These can operate at junction temperatures close to 700°C (≈1000 K or 1300°F). The heat source uses polonium - 210 isotope whose half-life is 138 days. In an α-particle radioactive decay, each reaction generates 5.3 MeV energy. Thus, when power is required for a short span of about 6 months, this source of heat is quite suitable, since after a period of time the polonium source becomes weak due to its disintegration and limited half-life period of days. An example of such a nuclear isotope power source has 27 p-n couples arranged radially from a small central container of Po-210, measuring only 5 cm diameter and 2.5 cm height. It gives 50 W with $T_h$ = 480°C and $T_c$ = 38°C. Electrical output is 3.4 W at an efficiency of 6.8%. This was used for space applications.

Other larger units for 5 kW output use $T_h$ = 700°C and $T_c$ = 500°C, with an efficiency of only 2%. The *n*- and *p*-type materials have sizes of 0.7 cm diameter and 0.6 cm length. There are 45 couples in the thermo electric generator. The reactor uses enriched uranium carbide fuel and works with fast neutrons.

## 10.6 Fuel Cells and Batteries

Fuel cells and batteries convert chemical energy directly to electrical energy and represent devices which do this at the highest possible efficiency of all energy-conversion devices, direct or indirect. There is no explicit need to describe the usefulness of storage batteries for energy storage coupled with other types of energy-conversion devices, such as wind and solar cells. We now discuss fuel cells and then storage batteries later on.

As the name implies, fuel cells use hydrogen as fuel and oxygen as oxidant. The two gases are pumped into a cell containing an anode, a cathode and an electrolyte as shown in Fig. 10.15. An electrical load is connected externally, through which electrons that are separated from the hydrogen nucleus at the anode flow, which constitutes the electric current. These electrons return to

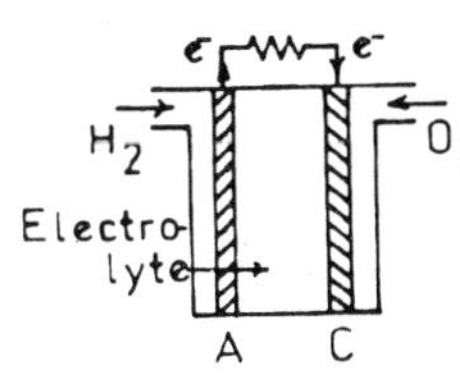

Fig. 10.15 H - O fuel cell

the cell at the cathode where they are absorbed by the hydrogen and oxygen ions to form $H_2O$. The electrolyte is necessary to conduct the positively-charged hydrogen ions from the anode electrode to the cathode electrode to complete the circuit.

Originally, as the fuel cell was manufactured for manned space missions (Gemini and Apollo of the USA) a few years after the end of the Second World War (1945), the hydrogen fuel and the oxygen were stored in their pure form as liquids, and the resulting combustion product, namely water, was then used for drinking by the astronauts. However, for terrestrial uses, in addition to utilizing the fuel and oxidant in liquified form, cheaper methods are also utilized. These involve using hydrogen-containing gases or liquids for the fuel at the anode, and of course air, containing oxygen at the cathode. Such cells are not as efficient as using $H_2$ and $O_2$ in pure form, but are a logical development.

Examples of hydrogen-containing gases and liquids which have been used, and can be possibly used, are given below. These are hydrocarbons and nitrogenous mixtures.

*Hydrocarbons*

| | | | | | |
|---|---|---|---|---|---|
| Methane | $CH_4$ | Butene | $C_4H_8$ | Hexane | $C_6H_{14}$ |
| Acetylene | $C_2H_2$ | Butane | $C_4H_{10}$ | Toluene | $C_7H_8$ |
| Ethylene | $C_2H_4$ | Pentane | $C_5H_{12}$ | Heptane | $C_7H_{16}$ |
| Ethane | $C_2H_6$ | Benzene | $C_6H_6$ | Octane | $C_8H_{18}$ |
| Propylene | $C_3H_6$ | Cyclohexane | $C_6H_{12}$ | Nonane | $C_9H_{20}$ |
| Propane | $C_3H_8$ | Kerosene | | Decane | $C_{10}H_{22}$ |
| Methanol | $CH_3OH$ | | | | |

*Nitrogenous*: Ammonia $NH_3$, Hydrazine $N_2H_4$.

The hydrocarbons are "cracked" with steam giving rise to CO, $CO_2$, and $H_2$. This is usually carried out outside the cell, but sometimes can be done inside also. However, the main product to serve as fuel is $H_2$.

When $H_2$ is blown through a porous metallic electrode consisting of catalysts such as platinum and noble metals, the hydrogen molecule containing two atoms in bondage through its electrons loses this bond and releases the two electrons ($2e^-$) becoming a doubly-charged molecule, $2H^+$. This is an oxidation process and does not involve internal energy, called Gibbs energy.

Because of electrons accumulating on the surface of the metallic anode and the electrolyte acquiring positively-charged ions adjacent to the electrode, a charge separation occurs resulting in a potential difference, positive on the electrolyte side and negative on the anode side, much like the plates of a capacitor. The $H^+$ ions pass through the electrolyte such as KOH, in which the bond is ionic with $K^+$ and $OH^-$ ions being present.

At the cathode, electrons returning back to the cell from the external circuit combine with oxygen and react with water in the KOH solution of the electrolyte to form hydroxyl ions: $O_2 + 4\,e^- + 2\,H_2O \rightarrow 4\,OH^-$

The oxygen suffers a reduction process through combining with the electrons. These enter the electrolyte and maintain the strength of the KOH, thereby forming a vehicle for transporting the electrons from the cathode to the anode. The $H^+$ and $OH^-$ ions combine to form $H_2O$ and go into solution.

The electrodes must be good electrical conductors and highly resistant to corrosive environment. They must also be catalytic to perform charge separation, but not take part in any chemical reaction themselves. Because fuel cells work best with platinum and other precious metals, nearly 25% of the cost of the cell is in these electrodes. The electrolyte is a carrier of charges and can be either acidic or alkaline, and be in liquid or solid state. Details of some fuel cells that have been developed and are in developmental stages are given in Sec. 10.8 later on. The basic necessities for bringing sizes and costs down are that the reactants must have a very high degree of reactivity. This may sometimes require fuel and oxidant in very pure forms, if they can be obtained at reasonable cost, or that the temperature and pressure must be raised. Regeneration in which the product materials can be re-converted to fuel and oxidant reduces costs, especially as the size for terrestrial and industrial applications is not a primary governing factor, as is the case for use in space applications.

## 10.7 Principles of EMF Generation

As mentioned earlier, the fuel cell generates an emf across the anode and cathode by chemical reaction, as against electromagnetic or thermal energy-conversion devices. No heat is added from an external source or a mechanical input given as in MHD or steam-turbine-driven alternators. We now discuss the generation of the emf by chemical means. Current flow due to the generated emf is caused by the electrons which have been detached from the hydrogen molecule at the anode.

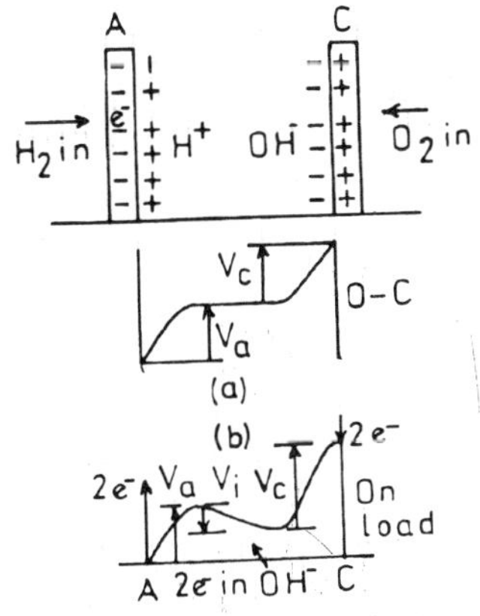


**Fig. 10.16** Electrode reactions in H-O fuel cell, and emf's on no-load and on load

The electric charge distributions near the anode and cathode are as shown in Fig. 10.16(a) when the cell is open-circuited and operating without load. At the anode which is the most negative terminal, electrons are accumulated; while adjacent to it inside the electrolyte, positive charges exist. This gives a potential difference $V_a$. The electrolyte being a conductor is at this potential. At the cathode, because of presence of $OH^-$ ions, the electrolyte is negative with respect to the cathode by the potential $V_c$. Therefore, the open-circuit voltage of the cell is $V_{oc} = V_a + V_c$..

When the cell carries a current, the voltage drop across the cell makes the cathode side of the electrolyte lower its voltage with respect to the anode, as shown in Fig. 10.16(b), creating an uphill gradient for the negative charges to flow, in a manner similar to solid-state devices as discussed in Chap. 3. Consequently, the voltage appearing across load drops from the open-circuit voltage. It is evident that one of the main contributions to this voltage drop comes from the internal resistance of the electrolyte. There are other causes for this voltage drop, which we will discuss later on since evolving of gases inside the cell will lower the rate of reaction at the electrodes. These are polarization effects present in all cells using chemical reactions.

We will now give quantitative values for these potentials which are generated from chemical reactions occurring at the anode due to the hydrogen fuel, and at the cathode due to the oxygen in a H-O fuel cell. Similar reactions occur in a storage battery or other types of electrode materials and electrolytes.

It will be appreciated that every chemical reaction involves energy which is in Joules or calories (1 cal = 4.186 J). In chemical reactions the unit of mass is the gram-mole or kg-mole, and the unit of energy is the calorie or kilocalorie. Thus, the SI unit is kcal/kg-mole. When charge separation occurs due to the energy, the result is a potential in volts, since $J = C \times V$.

The amount of charge is expressed in Faraday, where 1 Farady is the total charge of electrons equal to Avagadro's number. Thus

$$1\ \mathfrak{F} = 6.022045 \times 10^{23} \times 1.602189 \times 10^{-19} = 96{,}485\,\mathrm{C} \approx 96{,}500\ \mathrm{C}\,.$$

Also, 1 kcal = 4,186 J. Therefore, 1 kcal/1 Faraday = 4186/96500 J/C = 1/23.06 V. Every reaction involves its own characteristic internal energy. Table 10.1 gives values of Gibb's internal energy ΔG for some reactions which are important for fuel cells and batteries.

Some examples will show the voltages or emf's generated when energy is released in the chemical reaction. The basic equation is:

$$|\Delta G| = |n\,\mathfrak{F}V| \tag{10.34}$$

$$V = |\Delta G / n\,\mathfrak{F}| \tag{10.35}$$

For ΔG = 10 kcal/mole and $n = 1$, the emf generated is $V = 10/23.06 = 0.43365$ V, and for ΔG = 10 and $n = 2$, $V = 0.21682$ V.

**Table 10.1: Internal Energies ΔG for Chemical Reactions**

[+ energy denotes energy input to bring about the chemical reaction and the cell operates in the charging mode.
– energy denotes energy released and the cell is discharging].

| | Reaction | Internal Energy, kcal/mole |
|---|---|---|
| (1) | $Zn + Cu^{++} \rightarrow Cu + Zn^{++}$ | For $Zn^{++}$, $\Delta G = -35.18$<br>Cu, $\Delta G = +15.53$ |
| (2) | $Zn \rightarrow Zn^{++} + 2e^-$<br>$Zn^{++} + 2e^- \rightarrow Zn$ | $\Delta G = +35.18$ (Electrolyte is positive<br>$\Delta G = -35.18$ with respect to anode) |
| (3) | $Cu \rightarrow Cu^{++} + 2e^-$<br>$Cu^{++} + 2e^- \rightarrow Cu$ | $\Delta G = +15.53$<br>$\Delta G = -15.53$ |
| (4) | $O_2 + 2H^{++} + 4e^- \rightarrow 2H_2O$<br>$\frac{1}{2}O_2 + H^{++} + 2e^- \rightarrow H_2O$ | $\Delta G = -113.4$<br>$\Delta G = -56.7$ |
| (5) | $Li \rightarrow Li^+ + e^-$<br>$Li^+ + e^- \rightarrow Li$ | $\Delta G = -70.22$<br>$\Delta G = +70.22$ |
| (6) | Lead-acid Battery | |

Total reaction: $Pb + PbO_2 + 2H^+ + 2H_2SO_4^- \underset{\longleftarrow ch}{\overset{dis \longrightarrow}{\rightleftharpoons}} 2PbSO_4 + 2H_2O$

Anodic reaction: $Pb + HSO_4^- \underset{\longleftarrow ch}{\overset{dis \longrightarrow}{\rightleftharpoons}} PbSO_4 + H^+ + 2e^-$

Cathodic reaction: $PbO_2 + 3H^+ + HSO_4^- + 2e^- \underset{\longleftarrow ch}{\overset{dis \longrightarrow}{\rightleftharpoons}} PbSO_4 + 2H_2O$

Free energy changes are:
Anodic reaction: $\Delta G = +14$ kcal/mole
Cathodic reaction: $\Delta G = -75$ kcal/mole
Overall reaction: $\Delta G = -89$ kcal/mole

(1) *In a Daniell Cell*:

(a) For the reaction $Zn \rightarrow Zn^{++} + 2e^-$, with $\Delta G = 35.2$ and $n = 2$,
$V_a = 3.52 \times 0.21682 = 0.7632$ V.

(b) For the reaction $Cu^{++} + 2e^- \rightarrow Cu$, $\Delta G = -15.53$, and $n = 2$.
Therefore, $V_c = -1.553 \times 0.21682 = -0.33672$.

(c) This gives a total emf of $V_0 = 0.7632 + 0.3367 = 1.11$ V.

The value +0.763 indicates that the electrolyte is positive with respect to the anode, while –0.337 V indicates that the electrolyte is negative with respect to the cathode, as shown in Fig. 10.16.

(2) *In a lead-acid battery*:

(a) At the anode: $Pb + HSO_4 \rightarrow PbSO_4 + H^+ + 2e^-$
For $\Delta G = 14$ kcal/mole, $V_a = 1.4 \times 0.21682 = 0.30355$ V

(b) At the cathode: $\Delta G = -75$ and $n = 2$
Therefore, $V_c = -7.5 \times 0.21682 = -1.626$ V

(c) Total cell voltage $V_0 = 1.93$ V

(3) *For a Hydrogen-Oxygen fuel cell*:

(a) At the anode: $H_2 \rightarrow 2\,H^+ + 2\,e^-$. $\Delta G = 0$.

(b) At the cathode: $\frac{1}{2}\,O_2 + 2\,H^+ + 2\,e^- \rightarrow H_2O$. $\Delta G = -56.7$ kcal/mole and $n = 2$. Therefore, $V_c = -5.67 \times 0.21682 = -1.22937 = 1.23$ V

(c) Total cell voltage $V_0 = 1.23$ V

(4) *For a Lithium reaction*: $Li \rightarrow Li^+ + e^-$, $\Delta G = +70.22$ and $n = 1$.

Therefore, $V = 7.022 \times 0.43365 = +3.05$ V

For $Li^+ + e^- \rightarrow Li$, $V = -3.05$ V

All voltages are open-circuit voltages. On load, the anode-cathode voltages will be lower. As a last example in hydrazine and ammonia reactions, there are:

(5) $N_2H_4 + 4\,OH^- \rightarrow N_2 + 4\,H_2O + 4\,e^-$, $\Delta G = -107$ kcal/mole

Therefore, $V = -107/(4 \times 23.06) = -1.158$ V

(6) $4\,NH_3 + 3\,O_2 \rightarrow 2\,N_2 + 6\,H_2O + 12\,e^-$. $\Delta G = -305.2$ kcal/mole

Therefore, $V = -305.2/(12 \times 23.06) = -1.127$ V

This value is comparable to 1.23 V for a hydrogen-oxygen fuel cell, case (3).

## 10.8 Description of Fuel Cells

The status of development of fuel cells and research needs are described in detail in Ref. (44). The five types of cells developed to date are as follows:

(a) Phosphoric Acid Fuel Cell — PAFC

(b) Alkaline Fuel Cell — AFC

(c) Solid Polymer Electrolyte Fuel Cell — SPEFC

(d) Molten Carbonate Fuel Cell — MCFC and

(e) High Temperature Solid Oxide Fuel Cell — HTSOFC

Fuel cells possess the following desirable qualities over other types of energy conversion systems.

(a) Higher conversion efficiency of fuel into electricity. Figure 10.17 compares several systems.

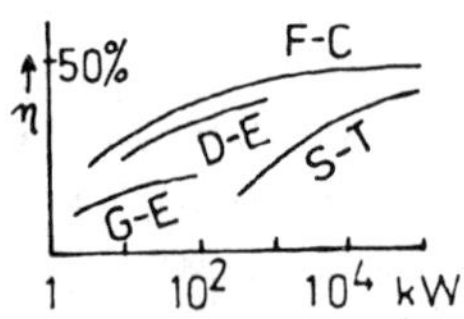


**Fig. 10.17** Efficiency-Load curves for different types of energy converters

(b) Modular construction where power is necessary, eliminating transmission lines.

(c) Pollutants, both thermal and chemical, are minimum.

(d) They can be combined with other systems and offer the possibility of co-generation which is more desirable than operating as a single system.

(e) Possibility of regeneration of fuel from products.

(f) Using well-known ''scrubber'' technology from the chemical industry to generate hydrogen fuel from hydrocarbons.

(g) Continuous power as long as fuel is fed.

The main disadvantage is still the high cost involved in having to use platinum and precious metals for electrode-catalysts (electrocatalysts). It is in the region of \$3000/kW. (About Rs. 1,20,000/kW).

### *10.8.1 PAFCs*

These are the most highly developed and are seeing the light of day in industrial power plants. They have been built in sizes of 1 MW at 13.8 kV, even though single cells generate about 0.8 V. The cell possesses good stability over a long period of operation. The cell operates at about 200°C and by using high pressure, efficiency is improved. Platinum is still the electro-catalyst. This is a $H_2$ - $O_2$ cell.

### *10.8.2 AFCs*

These were developed for space applications and require $H_2$ and $O_2$ in pure form. For terrestrial applications, the cost of $CO_2$ removal from hydrocarbons must be added. The electrolyte is KOH. The electrodes are made of porous Ni substrate, on which a mixture of Pt and PTFE are supported. [PTFE: Poly Tetra Fluoro Ethylene. It is for water-proofing purposes].

### *10.8.3 SPEFCs*

These operate at a low temperature of less than 100°C and use a high polymer electrolyte and Pt electro-catalyst. These were at first developed for space missions for supply of power to all systems other than propulsion. But for terrestrial use, the cost is much higher than PAFC.

### *10.8.4 MCFCs*

As mentioned before, high temperature and pressure increase the power density. But liquids boil off at temperatures higher than 500°C. The electrolyte therefore consists of molten carbonate of sodium or potassium ($NaCO_3$ or $KCO_3$). Electrodes are made of Ni for the anode and Ag for the cathode.

### *10.8.5 HTSOFCs*

For still higher temperatures of about 1000°C, a solid electrolyte is necessary. This is usually zirconia ($ZrO_2$).

### *10.8.6 Applications of Fuel Cells*

While originally fuel cells were developed for space missions, they are now used for terrestrial applications of the following types:

(a) Electric power generation; (b) Electric transportation; (c) Peaking power plants, with steam stations supporting base load at high efficiency.

As shown in Fig. 10.17, fuel cells maintain high efficiency at part loads, while the efficiency of a steam station falls off as load is decreased. By distributing fuel-cell plants close to loads, not only peak loads can be supplied but transmission costs and losses can be brought down. For electric cars, liquid hydrogen and oxygen tanks are used instead of a gasoline tank. Fuel:.ng is as easy as gasoline-powered cars. In remote hilly areas where micro-hydel stations are used, much of the generated power can be used for electrolysis of water to supply $H_2$ and $O_2$ to cities. Thus, generation of $H_2$ and $O_2$ is not as big a problem for fuel cells as it appears to involve. (The author was involved in such work, not only to generate $H_2$ and $O_2$ from an isolated hydro-electric station in a remote hilly area in northern British Columbia in Canada, but also develop an electric vehicle to use this fuel).

A schematic of a fuel-cell system for power generation is sketched in Fig. 10.18.

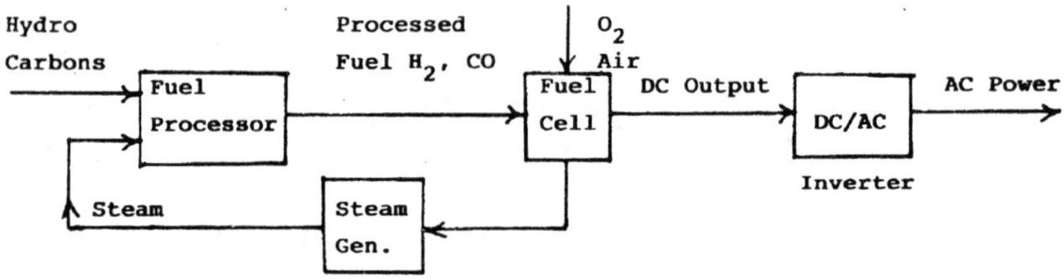


**Fig. 10.18** Block diagram of practical fuel-cell power-generation scheme

## 10.9 Summary of Technical Details of Fuel Cells

(1) *Phosphoric Acid Fuel Cells (PAFC)*

Electrolyte — $HPO_3$

Fuels — Light distillates, LPG, NG, etc. or coal gas

Power — 7.5 to 10 MW AC

The only fuel that can be directly used is $H_2$

Anode catalyst — Ni

Voltage — 0.9 V for an alkaline cell, 0.7 V for acid cell

Current density — 1 A/cm$^2$

Cost — \$3000/kW

(2) *Molten Carbonate Fuel Cell (MCFC)*

Temperature — 650°C

Voltage — 0.85 V per cell. Current density — 160 mA/cm$^2$

Electrolyte — Alkali-carbonate mixture and is a liquid at 650°C.

Liquid electrolyte is suspended in porous, insulating and chemically inert ceramic $LiAlO_2$ matrix. Consists of either 62 mole % $Li_2CO_3$, 38 mole % $K_2CO_3$, or 50 mole % each of $Li_2CO_3$ and $K_2CO_3$ in the liquid electrolyte.

Anode: Ni-Cr alloys; Cathode: Ni

(3) *High Temperature Solid-Oxide Fuel Cells (HTSOFC)*

All solid-state power system. Temperature — 1000°C.

Catalysts may not be needed. $\Delta G = 43.3$ kcal/mole at 1200°C.

Electrolyte — 8 to 10 mole % $Y_2O_3$ in dense $ZrO_2$ at 1000°C.

Pure $ZrO_2$ is an insulator. But when mixed with yittria, some bonds are vacated and $O^{=}$ moves in the electrolyte.

## 10.10 Description of Batteries: Primary, Secondary, Reserve and Advanced Battery Systems

### *10.10.1 Introduction*

Batteries are the silent work horses for energy storage and retrieval, serving human needs for electric power in safe, reliant and quick ways, if they are given proper care in design, maintenance and safety procedures. A battery converts chemical energy directly into electrical energy by means of electrochemical oxidation and reduction reaction called redox. This is done by converting the active materials which store energy in chemical form and can be retrieved suitably. There are three active parts involved:

(1) The anode which is the negative electrode. This is also called the reducing or fuel electrode and gives up electrons to the external circuit, as described earlier. It is oxidized during an electrochemical reaction.

(2) The cathode or the positive electrode or the oxidizing electrode which accepts electrons from the external circuit. It is reduced during an electrochemical reaction.

(3) The electrolyte which conducts the ions formed by the transfer of electrons between the anode and the cathode. It can be a conducting liquid such as water with dissolved salts, acids or alkalis, or solids which are ionic conductors.

Batteries can be classified into four categories as follows:

1. *Primary* These are generally incapable of being charged once they have discharged their energy. They have to be discarded after use.
2. *Secondary* These are rechargeable after discharge and brought to their original charged condition. They are also known as storage batteries or

accumulators. Most of the development in batteries has been devoted to this type of battery.

3. *Reserve* This type is capable of long-term storage. The components are isolated and assembled when called for, especially the electrolyte, which deteriorates in storage as well as self-discharge. Other systems function only when heat is applied to make the solid electrolyte conductive.
4. *Advanced* battery systems are used for heavy-duty applications such as electric vehicles, utility energy storage and renewable energy storage applications such as solar PV power, wind generation systems, ocean energy systems, etc., although these purposes can be equally well served by secondary and reserve battery systems.

### *10.10.2 Types of Batteries*

We now give an overall nomenclature of different types of batteries based on the active materials used for the three components in a battery. (There may be more components in special cases).

| A. Primary batteries | B. Secondary batteries | C. Reserve | D. Advanced |
|---|---|---|---|
| *Nomenclature* | | | |
| 1. Zinc-Carbon Cells Leclanche and Zinc Chloride cell systems | 1. Lead-Acid batteries | 1. Magnesium Water-activated batteries | 1. Lithium |
| 2. Magnesium and Aluminium cells | 2. Sealed Lead-Acid | 2. Zinc/Silver Oxide reserve batteries | 2. Zinc-Bromine batteries |
| 3. Alkaline-Manganese Dioxide cells | 3. Industrial Nickel-Cadmium batteries | 3. Ammonia batteries | 3. Metal-Air batteries Zn - Air Al - Air Mg - Air Li - Air |
| 4. Mercuric Oxide cells | 4. Sintered-plate Nickel-Cadmium batteries | 4. Li-Anode ambient temperature batteries | 4. Li - Iron Sulfide batteries |
| 5. Silver Oxide cells | 5. Sealed Ni - Cd batteries | 5. Thermal batteries | 5. Sodium Beta batteries |
| 6. Zn/Air cells | 6. Ni - Zn batteries | | |
| 7. Lithium cells | 7. Iron electrode batteries | | |
| 8. Solid electrolyte cells | 8. Silver oxide batteries | | |
| | 9. Ni - $H_2$ batteries | | |
| | 10. Ni - Metal Hydride Sealed batteries | | |
| | 11. Zn - Alkaline Manganese Dioxide cells | | |

### *10.10.3 Characteristics of Battery Systems*

The following details give the battery systems, anode and cathode material for several secondary batteries:

| | | Anode | Cathode | Voltage | Electrolyte |
|---|---|---|---|---|---|
| 1. | Lead - Acid (Plante) | Pb | $PbO_2$ | 2.0 | $H_2SO_4$ |
| 2. | Edison | Fe | NiOOH | 1.2 | KOH |

| | | Anode | Cathode | Voltage | Electrolyte |
|---|---|---|---|---|---|
| 3. | Nickel - Cadmium | Cd | NiOOH | 1.2 | KOH |
| 4. | Ni - Metal Hydride | MH | Ni Oxide | 1.2 | KOH |
| 5. | Silver - Zinc | Zn | AgO | 1.5 | KOH |
| 6. | Nickel - Zinc | Zn | NiOOH | 1.6 | KOH |
| 7. | Nickel - Hydrogen | $H_2$ | NiOOH | 1.2 | KOH |
| 8. | Silver - Cadmium | Cd | AgO | 1.1 | |
| 9. | Zinc - Air | Zn | $O_2$ (Air) | 1.5 | $H_2O$ |
| 10. | Zinc - Bromine | Zn | $Br_2$ | 1.6 | |
| 11. | Lithium - Ion | C | $LiCoO_2$ | 4.0 | Organic solvent |
| 12. | Lithium - Organic | Li | $MnO_2$ | 3.0 | $LiClO_4$ |
| 13. | Lithium - Polymer | Li | $V_6O_{13}$ | 3.0 | $LiAlCl_4$<br>$LiPF_6$<br>$LiMn_2O_4$ |
| 14. | High temperature | Li or Al | $FeS_2$ | 1.7 | |
| 15. | High temperature | Na | S | 2.0 | |

Section 10.7 has described the chemical reactions, internal Gibbs free energies and generated emf's of several important cell types.

## 10.11 Battery Applications for Large Powers

With direct energy conversion becoming so widespread and important, the power industry has to utilize intermittent power generation systems. These include wind power, ocean power, solar PV power and others. All these require storage of the power generated during some part of the day and retrieve it during idle hours. Also, with pollution problems on the increase, clean pollution-free systems are needed and welcome. Thus, storage batteries are required for every level of power from the smallest to the largest. In this section, we will only consider heavy-duty battery systems and not for electronic devices and computer applications, small appliances, etc., although UPS systems (Uninterrupted Power Supplies) use large capacity storage batteries. But in this book we are concerned with energy conversion in large magnitudes and we will restrict our description to these. Battery selection and application is a two-way process in that the proper selection of a type of battery depends upon the application by the engineer, while the application of a battery in its turn depends upon the capability or the characteristics of the battery system.

Large size primary batteries are used in the military, for navigational aids, and in rural areas as well as for standby power. But once its life is finished, a primary battery has to be discarded for ever. We will not consider primary batteries any further.

Secondary batteries find the largest application and it is superfluous to enumerate the thousands of places where they are used. We will only list some of the more common areas of its utilization here. These are:

(a) SLI — Starting, lighting and ignition in automotive areas.

(b) Standby energy demands and local levelling in energy conversion systems, including meeting peak loads in electrical power systems.

(c) Electric vehicles of all types.

(d) Solar photo voltaic systems.

(e) Ocean energy conversion systems.

(f) Wind power generation systems.

By battery type, the following gives an overall summary of some applications:

1. *Lead-Acid*: Automobiles, trucks, other traction applications, aircraft, marine, emergency power utilities, load levelling, UPS, general energy storage, electric vehicles such as tractors, material handling vehicles, submarines, standby power in power stations.

2. *Edison (Nickel-Iron)*: Due to its rugged construction and long life, the Edison battery is used for materials handling, mining operations, railroad cars, electric vehicles and other heavy-duty applications.

3. *Nickel-Cadmium*: Aircraft, industrial and emergency power, communication equipment, standby power, consumer electronics and other portable uses.

4. *Nickel-Zinc*: Electric vehicles, energy storage, emergency power, etc. The battery is still in the development stage.

5. *Silver-Zinc*: Because of the high cost but having low volume for the energy it provides (highest specific energy W/kg or W/L), it is used in military application such as submarines, torpedo propulsion, etc.

6. *Advanced Systems*: Electric vehicles and energy storage greater than 40 MW-h for 4 hours at maximum discharge rate depending on the use. These are for example: load levelling up to 10 MW for 4 hours, spinning reserve for 60 MW for up to 1 hour, frequency regulation for 20 MW up to 0.5 hours.

   In renewable energy applications such as solar, wind, wave, etc., with intermittent energy sources, advanced battery systems are most favoured. Advanced re-chargeable batteries can include the following types:

   Nickel-Zinc, Nickel-Metal Hydride, Zinc-Air ($O_2$), Aluminium-Air, Zinc-Bromine, Sodium-Sulphur, Sodium-Metal Chloride, Lithium-Iron Sulfide.

7. *High Temperature Systems*: These operate between 150 to 500°C and are much better than conventional ambient-temperature battery systems. The electrolyte is usually molten salt or other solid materials which liquify at the high temperature. They have names like Sodium Beta systems using Sodium-Sulphur or sodium-metal chlorides (nickel chloride), lithium-iron sulphide, etc. These are used in electric vehicles and stationary energy storage application. They have three times the specific energy of other systems (W/kg). The sodium-sulphur system has been used for 1 MW 8 MW-h load-levelling application at 6.6 kV ac and 1000 A with an inverter for 1 kV dc.

Some aspects of practical use of storage batteries are described in Sec. 11.3.3 in the next chapter.

## OBJECTIVE TYPE QUESTIONS

1. Gasification of coal and using the gas for generating electricity results in: (a) Removal of sulphur; (b) Using it in a gas turbine topping plant; (c) Less quantity of harmful effluents; (d) All three.
2. Coal liquifaction and subsequent use of the liquid fuel for generating electricity and transportation results in: (a) Removal of sulphur; (b) Lowering of atmospheric pollution; (c) Beats all oil embargoes; (d) All three.
3. Hydrocarbon fuels in gaseous state include: (a) Hydrogen; (b) Methane; (c) Natural gas; (d) All three.
4. Liquid hydrocarbon fuels are: (a) Methane; (b) Methanol; (c) Hydrogen; (d) Both (b) and (c).
5. Coal gasification processes include: (a) Fischer-Tropsch process, (b) Sasol process; (c) Lurgi process; (d) None of the three.
6. The Lurgi process uses: (a) Sub-bituminous coal; (b) Steam; (c) Air or Oxygen; (d) Fluidized bed of char; (e) All four.
7. Biomass includes: (a) Municipal waste; (b) Animal refuse; (c) Wood; (d) All three and many more.
8. Biomass fuels have a calorific value in the range: (a) 8,000 - 10,000 kcal/kg; (b) 3,000 - 5,000 kcal/kg; (c) 10,000 - 20,000 kcal/kg; (d) None of the three.
9. The abbreviation MSW stands for: (a) Metals suspended in water; (b) Mobile sewage works; (c) Miscellaneous solid wastes; (d) Municipal solid wastes.

10. Match the quantities indicated by letters with explanations given by numbers on the right:

| | |
|---|---|
| (a) Aerobic conversion | (i) Conversion to glucose |
| (b) Pyrolysis | (ii) Out of contact with air |
| (c) Thermo-chemical conversion | (iii) Composting |
| (d) Anaerobic digestion | (iv) Thermal process |
| (e) Enzymatic fermentation | (v) Gasification |

11. In anaerobic digestion, the end product(s) is (are): (a) Methane; (b) CO; (c) Alcohol; (d) None of the three.

12. In composting, the final product(s) is (are): (a) Methane; (b) CO; (c) Fertilizer; (d) None of the three.

13. Thermo-chemical gasification yields: (a) CO; (b) $CH_4$ (methane); (c) $H_2$; (d) All three.

14. Liquid fuels produced from sugarcane can be: (a) Ethanol; (b) Methanol ($CH_3OH$); (c) Whiskey; (d) All three.

15. Geothermal geysers are generally located in volcanic and earthquake-prone areas. (a) True; (b) False.

16. Geothermal power-generation systems can be: (a) Dry-steam plants; (b) Flash plants; (c) Binary plants; (d) Any or all three.

17. Geothermal plants are pollution-free: (a) True or (b) False.

18. Hydrogen is used as fuel in: (a) Fuel cells; (b) Automobiles; (c) Gas turbines; (d) All three.

19. The calorific value of hydrogen as fuel is of the order of: (a) 10,000 kcal/kg; (b) 20,000 kcal/kg; (c) 30,000 kcal/kg; (d) None of the three.

20. Hydrogen can be stored as: (a) Gas; (b) Liquified state; (c) Hydrides; (d) All three.

21. The Gibbs free-energy in hydrogen production using KOH as electrolyte is $\Delta G$ = 57 kcal/mole. The corresponding emf is: (a) 2.5 V; (b) 1.23 V; (c) 0.615 V; (d) None of the three.

22. When heat is applied to the junction of two dissimilar metals and an emf is generated across the cold ends, the effect is known as: (a) Peltier effect; (b) Thomson effect; (c) Seebeck effect; (d) All three.

23. When heat can be pumped from a cold junction to a hotter environment by applying a voltage, the effect is known as: (a) Peltier effect; (b) Thomson effect; (c) Seebeck effect; (d) None of the three.

24. The quantity [(Seebeck coefficient)$^2$ × thermal resistivity × electrical conductivity] is known as: (a) Thermal efficiency; (b) Figure of merit; (c) Coefficient of merit; (d) None of the three.

25. Match the names of hydrocarbons and nitrogenous gases and liquids with the chemical symbols for use in fuel cells:

| | | | | | |
|---|---|---|---|---|---|
| (a) | Methane | (i) | $NH_3$ | (a) | x |
| (b) | Acetylene | (ii) | $C_6H_6$ | (b) | vi |
| (c) | Ethylene | (iii) | $C_4H_{10}$ | (c) | ix |
| (d) | Propane | (iv) | $C_5H_{12}$ | (d) | v |
| (e) | Butane | (v) | $C_3H_8$ | (e) | iii |
| (f) | Pentane | (vi) | $C_2H_2$ | (f) | iv |
| (g) | Benzene | (vii) | $N_2H_4$ | (g) | ii |
| (h) | Octane | (viii) | $C_8H_{18}$ | (h) | viii |
| (i) | Methanol | (ix) | $C_2H_4$ | (i) | xi |
| (j) | Ammonia | (x) | $CH_4$ | (j) | i |
| (k) | Hydrazine | (xi) | $CH_3OH$ | (k) | vii |
| (l) | Decane | (xii) | $C_{10}H_{22}$ | (l) | xii |

26. When hydrocarbons are cracked with steam, the products are: (a) CO; (b) $CO_2$; (c) $H_2$; (d) All three.

27. The fuel used in a cell is usually: (a) CO; (b) $CO_2$; (c) $H_2$; (d) All three.

28. At the cathode in a fuel cell, which reaction takes place?
(a) $H_2 \rightarrow 2\,H^+ + 2\,e^-$; (b) $O + 2\,e^- + H_2O \rightarrow 2\,OH^-$; (c) $KOH + OH \rightarrow K^+ + O^- + H_2O$; (d) None of the three.

29. The electrodes in a fuel cell must be: (a) good conductors; (b) highly resistant to corrosive environment; (c) must be able to separate charges; (d) be catalytic and not take part in chemical reactions; (e) must be all four.

30. Current flow into an external load connected to a fuel cell is caused by: (a) electrons of the electrolyte; (b) electrons separated in $H_2$ at the cathode; (c) electrons separated in oxygen at the cathode; (d) electrons separated catalytically from $H_2$ at the anode.

31. 1 Faraday is the charge of how many electrons?
(a) $1.6 \times 10^{19}$; (b) $6.022 \times 10^{12}$; (c) $6.022 \times 10^{23}$; (d) $1.6022 \times 10^{23}$.

32. If 1 kcal is spent by a charge of 1 Faraday, the resulting quantity is: (a) 96,500 coul; (b) 4,186 J; (c) 1/23.06 V; (d) None are true.

33. For hydrogen-oxygen fuel cell, the Gibbs free energy change is $\Delta G = 56.7$ kcal/mole. 2 electrons are released at the anode. The emf of the cell is: (a) 0.43365 V; (b) 0.21682 V; (c) 2.46 V; (d) 1.23 V.

34. Fuel cells are used for: (a) Electric power generation; (b) Electrical vehicles; (c) Space electrical systems; (d) In all three.

[**Answers**: 1. (d); 2. (d); 3. (d); 4. (d); 5. (c); 6. (e); 7. (d); 8. (b); 9. (d); 10. (a) - (iii); (b) - (iv); (c) - (v); (d) - (ii); (e) - (i); 11. (a); 12. (c); 13. (d); 14. (d); 15. (a); 16. (d); 17. (b); 18. (d); 19. (c); 20. (d); 21. (b); 22. (c); 23. (a); 24. (b); 26. (d); 27. (c); 28. (d); 29. (e); 30. (d); 31. (b); 32. (d); 33. (d); 34. (d)].

## REVIEW QUESTIONS AND PROBLEMS

1. Enumerate the sources of sulphur and nitrogen-oxides into the atmosphere. How can these effluents be eliminated from a combustion process or minimized in generating stations or in industrial establishments?
2. Describe the Lurgi coal-gasification process. What is fluidized-bed system?
3. Describe the Fischer-Tropsch process for coal liquifaction.
4. Describe the reactions by which coal gas yields methanol liquid fuel, and how methanol can be converted back to methane gas.
5. A Lurgi process uses sub-bituminous coal with heating value of 10,000 Btu/lb (5,555 kcal/kg). The amount of coal used is 1000 tonne/hr. It produces SNG (substitute natural gas) having a total heating value $12 \times 10^9$ Btu/hr. The gas has a heating value of 20,000 Btu/lb (11,111 kcal/kg). Calculate:
   (a) Weight of gas produced per tonne of coal; (0.2724 t)
   (b) The efficiency of the process based on heating values; (54.5%)
   (c) MW power in input coal; (6460 MW)
   (d) What are the byproducts of this process?
6. Compare the C, H, O, N, S contents of wood, rice hull, and bituminous coal, as well as their heating values.
7. Enumerate the requirements of an efficient wood-burning stove.
8. List five types of conversion processes of biomass into useable gaseous and liquid fuels. Briefly describe these processes.
9. Draw the schematic diagram of anaerobic digestion system showing input materials and effluents.
10. Describe a geothermal power plant using single-flash system.
11. (a) Compare the properties of geothermal hot water and steam with fossil fuel for power generation in terms of temperature, pressure and efficiencies.

(b) A fossil-fuel plant requires 2100 kcal/kW-h, while geothermal plant requires 5500 kcal/kW-h. Compare their efficiencies (41%, 15.64%)

12. Describe the uses of geothermal energy for domestic and industrial purposes.

13. Describe why hydrogen is called a perennial source of energy for the world. Describe the reasons why hydrogen is called an energy carrier.

14. Describe at least three different processes for generating hydrogen and three systems for storing it.

15. Briefly describe: (a) Seebeck Effect; (b) Peltier Effect; (c) Thomson Effect. Draw schematic diagrams and show the heat and current flows.

16. A junction of *p*- and *n*-type materials have the following details:
Lengths: $L_n = L_p = 6.25$ cm; Areas: $A_n = 2$ cm$^2$, $A_p = 1$ cm$^2$;
Hot and cold junction temperatures: $T_h = 400°C$, $T_c = 25°C$;
Seebeck coefficients: $S_p = 300\ \mu V/°C$, $S_n = -300\ \mu V/°C$;
Specific resistances: $\rho_n = \rho_p = 10^{-5}$ ohm-m.
Calculate: (a) Total electrical resistance of the two materials in series; (b) The Seebeck open-circuit voltage of the thermo-electric generator; (c) Maximum power output; (d) Current at maximum power output.
[(a) $r_t = 9.375$ mohm; (b) 0.225 V; (c) 1.35 W; (d) $I = 12$ A].

17. The thermal conductivities in Q. 16 are $k_n = k_p = 20$ mW/cm-°C. Calculate: (a) Total thermal conductivity of the *p*- and *n*-type materials in parallel; (b) The figure of merit *Z*; (c) The coefficient of merit at maximum thermal efficiency; (d) Current at maximum thermal efficiency as a percentage of current at maximum power; (e) Power output at maximum efficiency as a percentage of maximum power output; (f) The maximum thermal efficiency.
[(a) $K = 9.6 \times 10^{-3}$ W/°C; (b) $Z = 4 \times 10^{-3}$ /°C; (c) $M = 0.02512$;
(d) $I_{maxP} = 12$ A, $I_{max\eta} = 9.42$ A $= 78.5\%\ I_{maxP}$;
(e) $P_{max\eta} = 0.934$ W $= 69.2\%\ P_{max}$; $\eta_{tm} = 29.18\%$].

18. Derive Eqs. (10.26) and (10.27).

19. Describe the mechanism of a solid-state refrigerator using Peltier cooling.

20. The following details apply for a Peltier cooling system:
Seebeck coefficients: $|S_n| = |S_p| = 300\ \mu V/°C$;
Electrical resistivities: $\rho_n = \rho_p = 2 \times 10^{-3}$ ohm-cm;
Thermal conductivities: $k_n = k_p = 15 \times 10^{-3}$ W/cm-deg;
Temperatures: 30°C and –5°C;
Dimensions of couple: $A_n = 2$ cm$^2$, $A_p = 1$ cm$^2$; $L_n = 2$ cm; $L_p = 1.5$ cm
At maximum cooling condition, calculate:

(a) Current required; (b) Electrical power input; (c) Heat removed; (d) Coefficient of performance.
[(a) $I_m = 32.16$ A; (b) $P_m = 5.8467$ W; (c) $Q_m = 1.71$ W; (d) $\phi = 29.25\%$]

21. List five types of fuel cells developed in industry. Give all materials used for cathode, anode, and the electrolyte.

22. In a lithium reaction, the Gibbs free energy change is $\Delta G = 70.22$ kcal/mole. Show from first principles how this cell can generate an emf of 3.05 V.

23. Describe the role of hydrocarbons in fuel-cell operation. If methane gas is produced in a coal-gasification process, how is this used eventually in a fuel cell as fuel?

24. (a) Prove that 1 Faraday is equal to a charge of 96,485 C;

 (b) Show that 1 kcal/Faraday = 1/23.06 V;

 (c) In a reaction involving copper, $Cu \rightarrow Cu^{++} + 2\ e^{-}$, $\Delta G = 15.53$ kcal/mole. What is the potential of the electrode with respect to the electrolyte? (0.3367 V)

25. (a) In an oxygen-hydrogen cell, describe the reactions taking place at the anode and cathode, and the voltage generated.

 (b) What are the materials for anode, cathode and possible electrolytes for the cell?

 (c) Can this type of cell offer possibilities for cogeneration? Suggest any other type of generation with which the fuel cell can function as a topping plant or bottoming plant.

CHAPTER 11

# Cogeneration and Energy Storage

## 11.1 Introduction

Cogeneration is a means of improving efficiency of power plants and industrial utilization of energy. The term involves two broad types of energy generation schemes and utilization:

(a) A power plant uses one or more types of prime movers, with one of them utilizing the exhaust heat from the other, which otherwise would have been discharged into the atmosphere and hence wasted. An example is a gas turbine whose exhaust heat is used in a heat exchanger to generate steam. Both types of turbine — the gas and steam — drive separate electrical generators to give added power. This is known as 'combined cycle'. The gas turbine usually has an efficiency of about 33% but the combined gas-steam cycle can raise the overall efficiency close to 50% by better utilization of the heat input to the gas turbine. A conventional steam plant has an efficiency of about 40% or less: Additional coal-fired boilers are also used for larger power, to increase the combined-cycle output higher than in the gas at the input to the gas turbine.

(b) An industrial system uses several types of energy obtainable from the same fuel input. An example is process steam required for a process which can also drive a steam turbine to generate electrical power for the industrial plant or sell the excess. Here is a case of both thermal and electrical powers obtained from the same source of steam.

These two ideas and power plants based on them are gaining vast popularity. We will discuss other examples involving other types of energy conversion systems later on. One very important novel system is involving generation of MHD power from the hot liquid sodium from an LMFBR nuclear reactor.

Energy storage also improves efficiency of power plants and acts as an intermediary to match generation with load characteristics better, called 'load levelling'.

These storage systems can take many forms, in addition to storage batteries which we discussed in Chap. 10, the most important ones being as follows:

(a) Pumped-storage hydro-electric power, which can be considered as mechanical form.

(b) Secondary or storage batteries, termed electro-chemical energy storage.

(c) Thermal energy storage in a variety of materials as sensible heat and latent heat as well as phase changes such as water, ice, etc.

(d) Compressed air which can in turn run gas turbines when mixed with fuel in a combustor.

(e) Flywheels.

(f) Hydrogen as an energy carrier.

(g) Superconducting magnets, the system being known as magnetic energy storage. This involves keeping a direct current circulating in a large coil made from superconducting material and discharging it into the ac system through inverters.

## 11.2 Combined Cycle Cogeneration

Gas turbines use atmospheric air usually at temperatures not exceeding 40°C (104°F) at atmospheric pressure of 0.1033 MPa (14.7 lb/in$^2$) and exhaust at 538°C (1000°F) or close to this value. The heat in the exhaust may amount to 50% of the energy in the gas and fuel at the combustor output and turbine input. The thermal efficiency is nearly 33%, since some power is necessary to run the compressor and station auxiliaries. Consider an example of a 135 MW gas turbine operating at a compression ratio of 13.5/1 in a closed cycle, where the exhaust is taken to a steam generator. The exhaust gas temperature is 600°C. By using a bottoming steam plant with efficiency of 40%, the overall efficiency is increased to 50%. Figure 11.1 shows the combined cycle or cogeneration scheme. In an open cycle, a gas turbine has a maximum compression ratio of 10/1. For other examples, see Chap. 7.

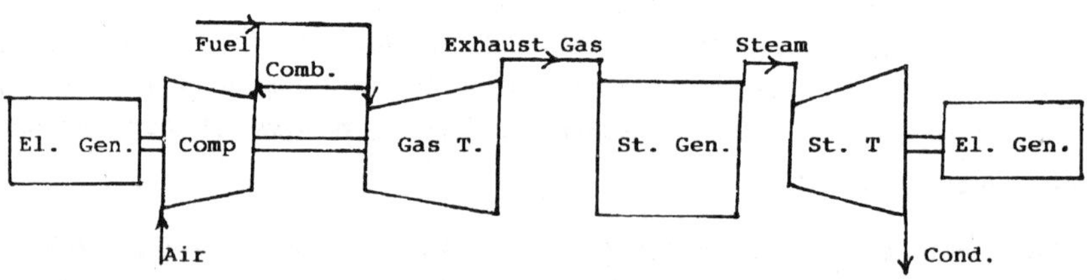


**Fig. 11.1** Block diagram of combined cycle cogeneration utilizing gas-turbine topping station and steam-turbine bottoming cycle

In other improved systems, a coal gasification plant is added to provide more power for the steam generator used above. In such a scheme, the heat required reduces as given by the following example:

Simple cycle gas turbine: 3080 kcal/kW-h

Natural gas combined cycle: 2000 kcal/kW-h

Coal gasification combined cycle: 2100 kcal/kW-h

***Example 11.1***: In the above three cases, calculate the efficiencies.

***Solution***: 1 kW-h = 3600 kJ = 860 kcal (1 kcal = 4.186 kJ)

Therefore 3080 kcal/kW-h: = $100 \times 860/3080 = 28\%$

2000 kcal/kW-h: = $100 \times 860/2000 = 43\%$

2100 kcal/kW-h: = $100 \times 860/2100 = 41\%$

Figure 11.2 shows the schematic of the combined cycle.

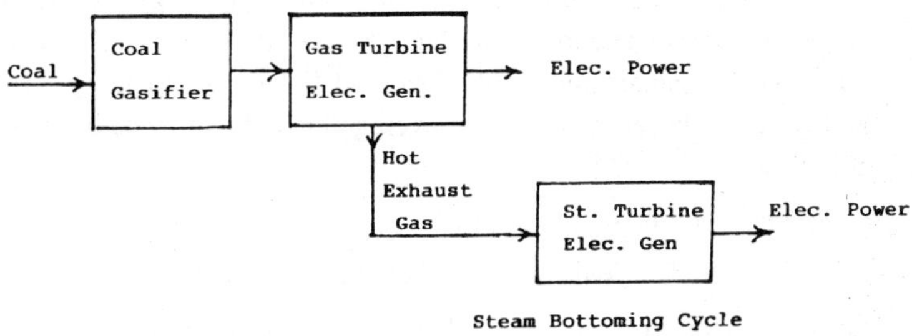


**Fig. 11.2** Combined gas and steam turbine cycles using coal gasification

In another form of cogeneration using a gas-turbine steam-turbine combined cycle, the exhaust gas from the gas turbine containing oxygen can be utilized as combustion gas for the boiler. An example of a practical scheme has a gas turbine of 120 MW and a steam turbine of 650 MW utilizing natural gas and coal. Gas turbine exhaust is nearly 420°C (788°F) and contains about 16% $O_2$. Efficiency is 41% for the combined cycle as compared to 33% for gas-turbine generation only. Additional energy to the boiler is provided by coal.

Table 11.1 shows possible components in cogeneration schemes.

**Table 11.1: Components of Cogeneration Schemes**

| Thermal Machine | Size, MWe | Efficiency range | Temp. of recoverable heat |
|---|---|---|---|
| (1) Steam turbine | 30 - 300 | 25 - 30% | 90 - 320°C |
| (2) Combustion gas turbine | 3 - 150 | 25 - 30% | 538 - 650°C |
| (3) Diesel or gasoline engines | 0.05 - 25 | 35 - 40% | 90 - 150°C |

An example of three types of energy forming a cogeneration scheme is sketched in Fig. 11.3.

By the year 2000, in the USA, about 60,000 MW of cogeneration systems are expected to be in service.

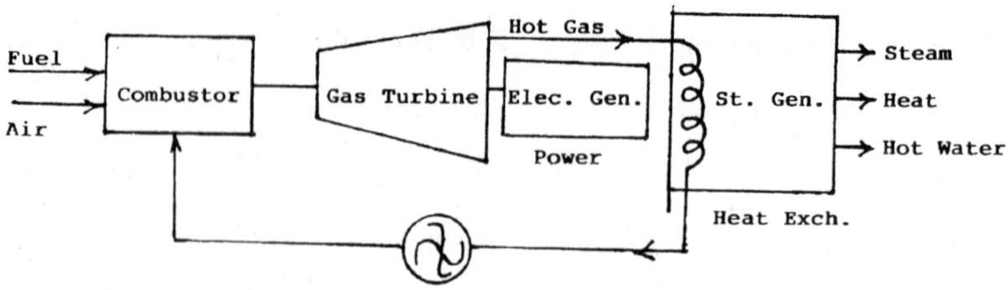


Fig. 11.3 Multiple energy output from cogeneration plant

## 11.3 Energy Storage

Energy storage has assumed a great deal of importance in recent years due to advances made in these devices and utilization of alternative sources of energy such as wind, photovoltaic cells, pumped hydro, ocean energy and others. It is estimated that in the USA by the year 2010, 8.5 Quads of energy will be stored a year for further utilization and load levelling. [Kilo = $10^3$, Mega = $10^6$, Giga = $10^9$, Terra = $10^{12}$, Quad = Quadrillion = $10^{15}$, Exa = $10^{18}$. 1 Quad of energy = $10^{15}$ Btu = $252.2 \times 10^9$ kcal]. In recent years, the average breakdown by categories in the USA is as follows:

Total = 76 Quads (annual consumption)

Oil: 43%, Gas: 22.5%, Coal: 23.7%, Other: 10.8%

Utilization: Transportation: 28%; Residential and commercial: 20%; Industrial: 22.5%; Lost: 25%.

If 10% of transportation needs utilize electric vehicles, it is anticipated that oil up to $3 \times 10^8$ barrels per year can be saved and pollution and noise will be reduced. This also reduces the $CO_2$ production by $2 \times 10^8$ tons. As will be discussed in the next chapter, $CO_2$ effluence has a 'greenhouse effect' on the climate of this globe. The $CO_2$ emission from the USA amounts to about 40% of that in the world. The energy for the vehicles is stored in storage batteries or $H_2$-$O_2$ cylinders and used as fuel cell, as has been discussed in Chap. 10.

*Energy Storage Schemes*

As mentioned earlier, energy-storage schemes can be of several types, which are: (a) Chemical form; (b) Thermal form; (c) Mechanical form; (d) Magnetic form. A comparison of several schemes is shown in Table 11.2.

**Table 11.2: Comparison of Storage Methods**

| Type | Efficiency | Upper limit |
|---|---|---|
| Pumped hydro | 75% | 2000 MW |
| Compressed air | 50% | 250 MW |
| Battery | 70% | 10 MW |
| Superconductivity | 91% | 1000 MW |

We will now discuss these schemes in details.

### *11.3.1 Pumped Hydro Schemes*

In Chap. 8, a discussion was presented of pumped-hydro plants. In practice, water is pumped from the reservoir at the exit of a power station back to the reservoir from where the power station got its water at a higher elevation. These are not restricted to low heads, but pumps have been designed for heads as high as 1500 m. The scheme is of maximum utility when there exists a cascade of power stations, each station discharging into a reservoir which forms the forebay for the next one at a lower level. The water at low-load times is pumped to the highest reservoir and utilized in all power stations at high-load periods. This helps to level the load and even supply peak-load requirements. The water turbine-generator can be designed to work as pump-motor combination, or else the two functions can be separated by installing a pump-motor unit separate from a turbine-generator unit, using the same or a different power house.

### *11.3.2 Compressed Air Energy Storage (CAES)*

The off-peak energy from steam stations, such as coal-fired or nuclear can be utilized to run air compressors. These present no environmental problems. The compressed air can be used in gas turbine in a combustor along with other fuel, such as natural gas or oil. The compressed air is stored in underground reservoirs which are usually discarded rock mines or salt mines or water-filled reservoirs called aquifers. Gas companies also use such subterranian reservoirs. Figure 11.4 shows a block diagram of the scheme. The compressor is run by operating the electrical machine as a motor through a clutch. This fills the underground air reservoirs. When required, the compressor is decoupled and the gas turbine coupled to the electrical machine through a second clutch to make it function as a generator and deliver power. The Alabama Electric Co. in the USA has a 50 MW, 26-hour storage unit with a cavern volume of $11.1 \times 10^6$ cu. ft. $= 0.31456 \times 10^6$ m$^3$.

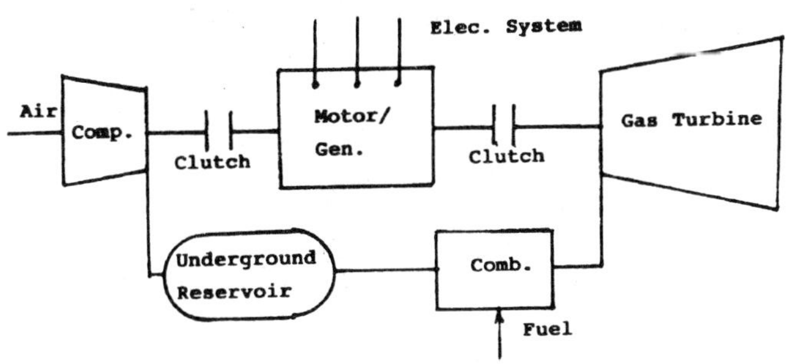


**Fig. 11.4** Compressed air energy storage system using motor/generator and compressor/gas-turbine

### *11.3.3 Storage Batteries*

In the previous chapter and sections 10.10 and 10.11, a description has been given of many types of battery systems. Here, we describe some practical aspects of the use and maintenance of large storage battery systems. The largest unit for energy storage in a power system used for load levelling is the 10 MW 40 MW-h job in California at the Chino Facility of the SC Edison Co. It works at an efficiency of 72% and has 8256 cells to yield a voltage of 12.5 kV, ac, through an inverter. In addition to load levelling, i.e. supplying the load demand properly, large storage battery units can help in taking up peak loads, cutting down on expensive spinning reserve, namely rotating machines at steam- and hydro-stations which are idling most of the day, in order to supply heavy load for a few hours when called upon to do so thereby wasting valuable fuel. The battery unit improves the efficiency of the overall system.

The most widely used application of storage batteries is still in transportation. Batteries can be classified broadly as follows: (1) normal temperature batteries using acids or alkalis as electrolytes, and (2) those that work at high temperatures using molten-salt electrolytes. These are listed below:

*I. Normal Temperature Batteries:*

(a) Lead-Acid; (b) Nickel-Iron; (c) Zinc Halide; (d) Redox; and (e) Several others (see Ch. 10).

*II. High Temperature Batteries:*

(a) Lithium-Iron Sulphide; (b) Sodium-Sulphur. These batteries work at a temperature range of 300-400°C.

We will describe these briefly.

*Lead-Acid Batteries*

These have long life although the power density in W-h/kg or kW-h/kg is lower than other types of batteries. However, these others have lower power. The reaction in the lead-acid cell is as follows:

*Overall:* $$\mathrm{Pb + PbO_2 + 2\ H_2SO_4 \underset{\text{chg}}{\overset{\text{dis}}{\rightleftarrows}} 2\ PbSO_4 + 2H_2O}$$

*Anode:* $$\mathrm{Pb + HSO_4^- \underset{\text{chg}}{\overset{\text{dis}}{\rightleftarrows}} PbSO_4 + H^+ + 2\ } e^-$$

*Cathode:* $$\mathrm{PbO_2 + 3\ H^+ + HSO_4^- + 2\ } e^- \underset{\text{chg}}{\overset{\text{dis}}{\rightleftarrows}} \mathrm{PbSO_4 + 2H_2O}$$

The above are based on considering the cell as two halves with different reactions occurring at the anode and the cathode. At the anode, $H^+$ ions and two electrons are generated, which are absorbed in the cathode, in a manner similar to Fig. 10.15 in Chap. 10.

The free Gibbs energy change Δ G = –14 kcal/mole for the reaction at the anode, and –75 kcal/mole at the cathode. These correspond to emf's of (14/2 × 23.06 = 0.303 V) and (75/2 × 23.06 = 1.627 V) giving a total open-circuit emf of 1.93 V.

The lead-dioxide plate at the cathode (negative plate) is the weakest component, since it is in paste form and embedded in meshes from which it loosens due to impact of sulphide crystals and forms a sludge. This in turn degrades the quality of the electrolyte in due course of time. When the cell is inactive, at the anode the process of self-discharge exists. This is prevented to a large extent by using antimony in the grid, where lead is packed.

When used in electric vehicles, normal-size batteries have a 100-km range per charge with 80 km/hr top speed. The vehicle can reach 0 to 50 km/hr in 30 *s*, giving an acceleration of 100 km/min. Figure 11.5 shows a battery energy storage plant to store off-peak energy from hydro, coal or nuclear base-load plants by converting power-line ac to dc and charging the battery. The battery charger can work with GTO thyristor and function as an inverter for load-levelling purposes in the electrical system.

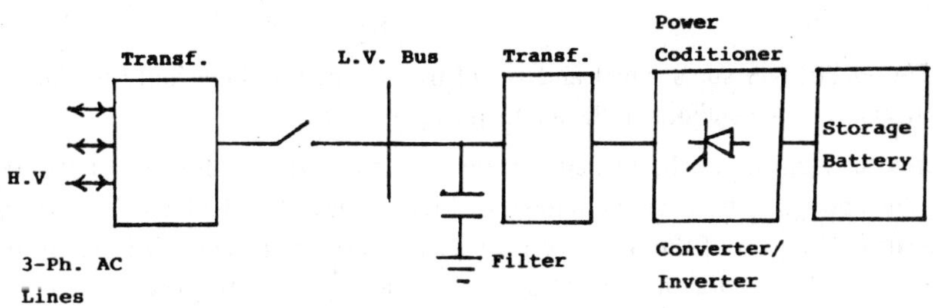


**Fig. 11.5** Block diagram of a 40 MW-h, 40 MW, 10 hr battery storage system

Lead-acid cells have a normal charge-discharge cycle life of 600 operations and 5 to 10 years of life depending on maintenance. Heavy-duty storage batteries specially manufactured for large power systems for load-levelling have a charge-discharge cycle life of nearly 2000. These cells operate at least once a day, so that there will be 365 cycles in a year.

During discharge, the specific gravity of the electrolyte falls linearly according to the equation

$$\text{Specific gravity} \quad SG = \text{Volts} - 0.84,\ SG > 1 \tag{11.1}$$

The specific gravity is therefore an indication of the charge. At full charge of 2.1 V, it is 1.26. The higher SG is due to the higher concentration of the $H_2SO_4$ acid.

***Example 11.2***: An automobile battery at a temperature of 25°C has a final voltage of 1.85 V and a full-charge SG of 1.25. Find: (a) the SG at final voltage, and (b) the full-charge voltage.

***Solution***: Using Eq. (11.1) and plugging given values

(a) $SG_d = 1.85 - 0.84 = 1.01$

(b) $V_F = \text{SG} + 0.84 = 1.25 + 0.84 = 2.09$ V

The re-chargeable lead-acid battery is known as Planté battery also, after its first inventor.

*Alkaline Battery*

This is referred to as Nickel/Iron or Nickel/Cadmium batteries. The former is also known as the Edison cell. The electrolyte is KOH. The positive plate consists of nickel peroxide, while the negative plate is iron. The reactions are as follows:

*Overall*:
$$6\ NiO_2 + 3\ Fe \underset{\text{chg}}{\overset{\text{dis}}{\rightleftarrows}} Fe_3O_4 + 2\ Ni_3O_4$$

*Actual*:
$$6\ NiO_2 + 3\ Fe + 8\ KOH \underset{\text{chg}}{\overset{\text{dis}}{\rightleftarrows}} Fe_3O_4 + 2\ Ni_3O_4 + 8\ KOH$$

The electrolyte stays intact and is not transformed, helping only to transfer electrons from the cathode to the anode through itself.

In a fully-charged cell, the active material is nickel oxy hydrate (NiOOH) and metallic sponge iron. A small amount of LiOH is added to the KOH-electrolyte, and Hg in the iron of the negative plate to increase the reactions of Fe. In the fully-charged condition the cell voltage is 1.4 V and the specific gravity of electrolyte is SG = 1.21. At full discharge it falls to 1.16.

In the Ni-Cd battery the overall reaction is

$$2\ Ni(OH)_3 + Cd \underset{\text{chg}}{\overset{\text{dis}}{\rightleftarrows}} 2\ Ni(OH)_2 + Cd(OH)_2$$

The electrolyte is still KOH with normal SG of 1.16–1.19. The oxidized nickel hydrate forms the positive plate, while the cathode is metallic cadmium sponge. The normal voltage of the cell is 1.2 V, while the open-circuit voltage may go as high as 1.4 V.

*Redox Battery*

This uses $CrCl_3$ as positive plate and $FeCl_2$ as negative plate with HCl as electrolyte.

### 11.3.4 Superconducting Magnetic Energy Storage (SMES)

In this system, energy is stored in a magnetic field. Magnets fabricated from superconducting materials are used for the following applications:

(a) Accelerators and High Energy Physics in Bubble Chambers

(b) Nuclear fusion reactors

(c) Energy storage in power systems

(d) Magneto Hydro Dynamics and Rotating Machines

(e) Reactive power compensation to damp oscillations in combined ac-dc high-voltage transmission systems with very long lines

(f) Other industrial and transportation uses such as magnetic levitation of super-fast trains.

We will describe only large energy-storage systems which compete with pumped-hydro and other systems. As an example, a coil with an inductance of 300 *H* at 5000 *A* current can store an energy of $W_s = 0.5 \text{ L I}^2 = 0.5 \times 300 \times 25 \times 10^6 \text{ J} = 3.75 \times 10^9 \text{ J}$, which is nearly 1 MW-h, since 1 MW-h = $3.6 \times 10^9$ J.

If this amount of energy is to be stored in ordinary metallic coils such as copper, the current has to be continually supplied from an external source through an ac/dc converter. When required, the ac/dc power conditioner can be made to function as a dc/ac inverter and the stored energy can be fed back to the system. But the resistance of the coil will involve a time delay. In the case of the superconducting coil, resistance is absent, so that there entails no time delay in abstracting the stored energy.

However, the most important and interesting property of the superconductor is that, once a current is sent through the coil, it keeps up the current in it without requiring an external source of voltage. It is estimated that this current can persist for up to $10^{10}$ years! The only requirement is that the conductor be maintained in the superconducting state by cooling with superfluid liquid helium at about 4° Absolute until today. High-temperature superconducting materials (nearly 1000 of them to date) are in experimental stages. Pressure also has a large influence on the superconducting property.

In 1911, K. Onnes-Kamerling liquified helium and immediately worked on the resistance of Hg, Pb, Sn, V, and Ti. This was followed by a hot pace of research activity. When a metal exhibiting a superconducting state is cooled below a critical temperature, two phenomena occur:

(1) No voltage is necessary for driving the current, which can keep circulating in the coil even after the original source of voltage is disconnected.

(2) The material rejects magnetic flux to flow in the space occupied by the material. This is the Meissner-Ochsenfeld effect.

To counteract these it was soon realized that if a magnetic field were applied on the material, the property of superconductivity vanished abruptly at a certain critical value of the H-field. This is also observed when the temperature reaches a critical value for that material. Thus, the property of superconductivity is balanced precariously on the magnetic field and the temperature. When the material loses its superconducting stage, it is followed by explosive forces, so that the coil must be braced suitably. The magnetic coil is also subject to high magnetic forces, as it carries very large currents.

In the SMES, shown schematically in Fig. 11.6, the coil is 'charged' by pumping direct current and immersing in a cryogenic fluid like liquid helium. The current then keeps circulating and there results a high magnetic field surrounding the coil. This gives rise to two types of magnetic forces: (a) a radial expansion, and (b) an axial compression. In the turns of the coil, adjacent layers in a pan-cake sandwich winding have an attractive force because the currents flow in the same direction, and hence the turns tend to come together giving rise to axial compression. Therefore, the coils must be separated by spacers not only for insulation but also for restraining the axial compression forces. However, the more powerful force is the radial expansion, whereby the coil swells which must be constrained. It is therefore usual to embed the coil in a tunnel bored from underground bedrock. The force from the coil is transmitted to the rock by suitable structural members. These forces occur with a periodicity when the coil is charged and discharged, as well as due to normal seismic activity in the region.

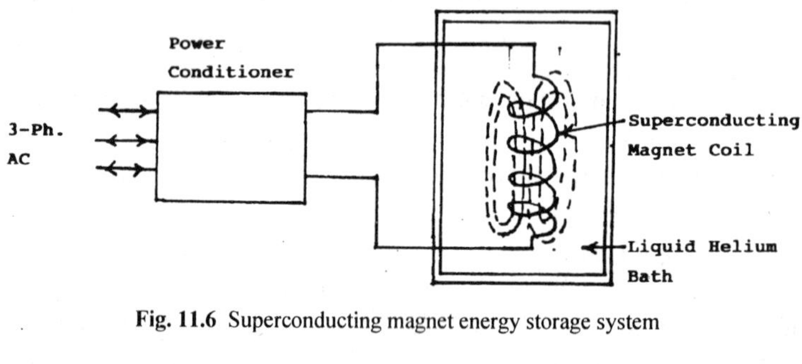


**Fig. 11.6** Superconducting magnet energy storage system

One very interesting SMES used by the Bonneville Power Administration in the USA has the following details:

| | |
|---|---|
| Maximum power capability | 10 MW |
| Maximum stored energy | 30 MJ = 8.33 kW-h |
| Coil current at full charge | 4.9 kA |

| | |
|---|---|
| Maximum coil terminal voltage | 2.18 kV |
| Coil operating temperature | 4.5 K |
| Magnetic field strength | 2.8 Tesla at 8.2 kA |

The coil is restrained from deforming axially by winding pre-stressed stainless steel strips at 12,000 psi (816 atm, 8.437 kg/mm$^2$). However, the most important aspect of the design and purpose in using this SMES is that, the unit has to charge and discharge at a frequency of 0.35 Hz continuously all year round, to stabilize an ac/dc transmission system by providing reactive power. This rapid vibration at 21 cycles per minute is transmitted to the foundation on which the coil is supported. The area is also prone to earthquakes, being in the Pacific region of the USA.

A very large SMES contemplated and designed by Bechtel Corp. stores up to 5000 MW-h with a power availability of 1000 MW at 200 kA coil current in 556 turns. The inductance of the coil is $L = 2 \times 5000 \times 3.6 \times 10^9/(2 \times 10^5)^2 = 900$ H. This will correspond to a pumped hydro storage capacity.

The major portion if not all power has to be supplied to keep the refrigeration system working constantly.

Magnets required for MHD power generation in ducts require fields up to 10 T and the energy stored is $10^9$ to $10^{10}$ J. But SMES require about 4 to 5 Tesla and up to 10,000 MW-h ($3.6 \times 10^{13}$ J).

Until today, superconducting magnets use an alloy of niobium and titanium, and temperatures of less than 4.5 K. But with the existing prospects of higher temperature superconductors using oxides of yittrium and other elements, the industry has already envisaged not only SMES application for these but predicting use in overhead transmission lines and cables. The prospects of using superconducting materials are very far reaching if these new materials can be fabricated suitably in wire form or other shapes.

## REVIEW QUESTIONS AND PROBLEMS

1. Describe cogeneration systems using: (a) A topping cycle and a bottoming cycle; (b) Providing several types of energy from the same source.
2. List at least six types of energy-storage systems used in conjunction with energy-conversion systems.
3. A gas turbine with a compression ratio of 8/1 operates at maximum cycle temperature of $T_3$ = 700°C. Air is sucked into the compressor at 25°C at the rate of 20 kg/s. Take $C_p$ = 1.005 kJ/kg-K and $\gamma = C_p/C_v = 1.4$ for compression and expansion. Calculate: (a) temperature of exhaust; (b) the heat rejected in the exhaust in kW; and (c) Brayton efficiency of the turbine.

   ($T_4$ = 537 K = 264°C; (b) 3790 kW; (c) 56.47%)

4. The heat from the exhaust in Q. 3 is taken to a heat exchanger to raise steam. The steam-turbine bottoming cycle has an efficiency of 35%. Find the total power developed by the combined cycle.
   [GT = 4917 kW, ST = 1326.5 kW; Total = 6243.5 kW]

5. Describe how the following energy-storage schemes work:
   (a) Pumped hydro schemes; (b) Compressed air; (c) Magnetic energy storage scheme.

6. A superconducting magnet coil has an inductance of 500 H and carries a current of 4000 A. Calculate the stored energy in the magnetic field in MW-h. ($0.5 \times 500 \times 4000^2$ J = 8/7.2 MW-h = 1.111 MW-h)

7. Discuss the properties of a superconducting magnetic energy storage system and what precautions have to be taken to make it operate satisfactorily.

8. Describe the construction and reactions taking place in a lead-acid storage battery during charge and discharge.
   The emf developed at the anode-electrolyte interface is 0.3 V. What is the change in Gibb's free energy here? Give magnitude and sign.
   (+ 14 kcal/mole)

9. An automobile battery at room temperature has a final voltage at discharge of 1.84 V, and initial specific gravity for the electrolyte of 1.28 at full charge. Calculate the specific gravity at final voltage and the voltage at full charge. (1.0; 2.12 V)

CHAPTER 12

# Global Energy Position and Environmental Effects

## 12.1 Introduction

The global energy position, namely the potential reserves and their rate of depletion annually, is a very vast topic of which only a part can be described and discussed in a few pages. These reserves are subject to change as old estimates are revised and new explorations, both by terrestrial and satellite methods, are carried on vigorously. Countries on the globe in so far as energy is concerned, may be divided into two broad categories: (a) Developed countries, and (b) Developing and undeveloped countries. Both these terms are difficult of definition, since some so-called developing countries have been developing their industrial economy for over five decades, since the end of the World War II in 1945, and still have not shown self-sufficiency. Indeed no country can remain stagnant and is developing the standards of living of its people. Broadly speaking, it appears that a developing country or an underdeveloped country denotes one which depends on more affluent countries for help in scientific know-how, financial and resource matters for their industrial development. Since the developed countries consume over 90% of energy used on the globe and have an equal percentage of fuel reserves, except for oil, when data are presented they pertain to these few countries. The omission of many countries is unintentional but only indicates how much energy they require to reach or even approach close to the economic standards of affluent countries, and become equal partners in trade without being the receiver for decades upon decades.

Similarly, environmental effects of energy usage are also very deep subjects and only the surface can be scratched here. However, this will give an indication of the vastness of the problem and the socio-economic implications, to use an oft-repeated general idea without being specific. To state only a few examples, the problem of disposal of nuclear wastes, the seriousness of acid rain, etc., affect present and future uses of electricity as well as on transportation. In other words the day-to-day life is affected by the pollution caused by energy-conversion systems to the environment. We conclude this book with a description and discussion of these two topics.

## 12.2 Energy Units

Since we are dealing with very vast magnitudes of energy and different types of fuels required for generation and use of energy, we will first enumerate the most useful units of measurements and conversions. The chief sources of large amounts of energy are: (a) oil, (b) coal; (c) natural gas; (d) nuclear; and (e) hydro-electric. Other primary sources are wind, wave, tide, OTEC, biomass, MHD, fuel cell, etc. Because of the difficulty involved in dealing with reserves and consumption of so many types of energy, it has become a world-wide practice to compare them in terms of oil equivalents. There is no standard for oil, but in this discussion refined oil with a calorific value of 10,000 kcal/kg (18,000 Btu/lb) will be taken. Coal with calorific value of 7,000 kcal/kg (12,600 Btu/lb) will be assumed. Natural gas of 10,000 kcal/$m^3$ (18,000 Btu/$m^3$ or about 1000 Btu/$ft^3$) will be taken in this discussion.*

Other quantities used are as follows:

1 Btu = 454/1.8 = 252.2 cal = 1055 J = 1.055 kJ. (1 cal = 4.186 J)

1 kcal = 1/0.2522 = 3.965 Btu

1 metric tonne = 1000 kg = 2205 lb. 1 Long ton = 2240 lb

1 Quad of energy = $10^{15}$ Btu = $1.055 \times 10^{15}$ kJ

1 kW-h = $3.6 \times 10^6$ J = $0.86 \times 10^3$ kcal (1 yr = $8.76 \times 10^3$ hr)

1 Exajoule = $10^{18}$ J = $0.278 \times 10^{12}$ kW-h = $278 \times 10^6$ MW-h = 278 TW-h

1 Exajoule = $31.71 \times 10^3$ MW-yr

1 US gallon = (5/6) Imperial or British gallon

1 US gallon of water weighs 8.33 lb. 1 Imp. gal. = 10 lb = 4.536 kg

Specific gravity of oil = 0.9

1 MBOE = 1 million barrels of oil equivalent

1 MBDOE = 1 million barrels per day oil equivalent

= 365 million barrels per year oil equivalent

***Example 12.1***: Calculate the energy content in 1 barrel of oil of 42 US gals with a calorific value of 10,000 kcal/kg or $1.8 \times 10^4$ Btu/lb.

***Solution***: Weight of 1 barrel of oil = $42 \times 8.33 \times 0.9$ = 315 lb = 142.9 kg. Therefore, energy = $142.9 \times 10^4$ kcal = $5.666 \times 10^6$ Btu = 1.662 kW-h. Also,

* All conversions of energy equivalents between different types of fuels depend upon initial assumptions. Therefore, there will be minor variations between different authors.

1 barrel = $1.429 \times 10^9$ cal = $1.429 \times 4.186 \times 10^9$ J = $5.9818 \times 10^9$ J (Therefore, 1 Exajoule = $10^{18}$ J = $0.167 \times 10^9$ barrels = 167 million barrels).

***Example 12.2***: Calculate the energy in kW-h, kcal, kJ, Exajoules, Btu, and Quads in 1 MBDOE per year.

***Solution***: 1 MBDOE = $365 \times 10^6$ barrel per year.
Therefore, energy content = $365 \times 10^6 \times 1.429 \times 10^6$ kcal.
1 kW-h = 860 kcal. 1 kcal = $1.1628 \times 10^{-3}$ kW-h = 1.1628 W-h

Therefore, 1 MBDOE contains $365 \times 10^{12} \times 1.429 \times 10^{-3} \times 1.168$ kW-h

$$= 0.6065 \times 10^{12} \text{ kW-h (per year)} = 0.5216 \times 10^{15} \text{ kcal}$$
$$= 2.1834 \times 10^{15} \text{ kJ} \approx 2.2 \text{ Exajoules} = 2.07 \times 10^{15} \text{ Btu} = 2.0 \text{ Quads}$$

1 Quad = 1.055 Exajoules, 1 Exajoule = 0.968 Quad

***Example 12.3***: Calculate the energy in 1 tonne oil equivalent.

***Solution***: 1 barrel of oil weighs 315 lb = 142.9 kg. 1 tonne = 2205 lb
Therefore, energy in 1 tonne of oil at $10^4$ kcal/kg = $1.429 \times 10^6$ kcal

and energy in 1 tonne of oil = $1.429 \times 10^6 \times 1000/142.9 = 10^7$ kcal

$$= 3.965 \times 10^7 \text{ Btu} = 1.1628 \times 10^5 \text{ kW-h} = 4.186 \times 10^{10} \text{ J}$$

1 million tonnes of oil equivalent = $4.186 \times 10^{16}$ J = 0.04186 Exajoule
1 TOE = 1000/142.9 BOE = 7 BOE

Also, calorific value of oil = $10^4$ kcal/kg, and 1 tonne = $10^3$ kg.

Therefore, energy in 1 tonne of oil = $10^7$ kcal

***Example 12.4***: Calculate the tonnes oil equivalent in MBDOE.

***Solution***: 1 MBDOE has an energy of $0.5216 \times 10^{15}$ kcal from Example 12.2.

1 tonne of oil equivalent has an energy of $10^7$ kcal.

Therefore, tonnes of oil equivalent = $0.5216 \times 10^8 \approx 52$ MTOE

Also, $365 \times 10^6$ barrels = $365 \times 10^6 \times 142.9/1000$ tonne = $0.5216 \times 10^8$ tonne

$$= 52.16 \times 10^6 \text{ tonne}$$

or, 1 barrel day equivalent ≈ 52 tonne.

Thus, 1 MBDOE is equivalent to $0.5216 \times 10^{15}/10^7 = 0.5216 \times 10^8$ tonne OE.

***Example 12.5***: Calculate the metric tonnes of coal equivalent for 1 barrel a day oil. Calorific value of coal = 7000 kcal/kg.

***Solution***: 1 BDOE = $0.5216 \times 10^9$ kcal. Calorific value of coal = $7 \times 10^6$ kcal/tonne. Therefore, coal equivalent = $0.5216 \times 10^9/7 \times 10^6$ = 74.5 tonne.

***Example 12.6***: A set of power stations with a load factor of 0.7 uses 1 MBDOE. Find the total installed capacity of the stations in kW, MW, and GW.

***Solution***: 1 MBDOE = $0.6065 \times 10^{12}$ kW-h per year (see Ex. 12.2).

Therefore, (KW) × 365 × 24 × 0.7 = $0.6065 \times 10^{12}$, giving

$$kW = 0.6065 \times 10^{12}/0.7 \times 8.76 \times 10^{3} = 0.099 \times 10^{9} \text{ kW}$$

$$\approx 10^{8} \text{ kW} = 100{,}000 \text{ MW} = 100 \text{ GW}$$

***Example 12.7***: Calculate cubic metres of natural gas equivalent of 1 MBDOE. 1 $m^3$ of gas has a calorific value of $10^4$ kcal.

***Solution***: 1 MBDOE = $0.52 \times 10^{15}$ kcal (see Ex. 12.2).

Therefore, volume of natural gas = $0.52 \times 10^{15}/10^{4} = 52 \times 10^{9}\ m^{3} = 52\ km^{3}$.

***Example 12.8***: Calculate the energy equivalent of 1 TW-yr in

(a) kW-h; (b) Exajoules; (c) Quads; (d) MBDOE.

***Solution***: 1 Terra Watt = $10^{12}$ W = $10^{9}$ kW = $10^{6}$ MW = $10^{3}$ GW.

1 year = 60 × 60 × 24 × 365 *s* = $31.536 \times 10^{6}$ s = 8760 hr

(a) Therefore, 1 TW-yr = $31.536 \times 10^{18}$ W-s or Joule = 31.536 Exajoule.

$$= 8.76 \times 10^{15} \text{ W-h} = 8.76 \times 10^{12} \text{ kW-h}.$$

(b) 1 TW-yr = 31.536 Exajoule

(c) 1 Exajoule = 0.948 Quad. Therefore, 31.536 Exajoule = 29.9 Quad = $29.9 \times 10^{15}$ Btu.

(d) 1 MBDOE = $0.6065 \times 10^{12}$ kW-h, and 1 TW-yr = $8.76 \times 10^{12}$ kW-h.

Therefore, 1 TW-yr = 8.76/0.6065 = 14.44 MBDOE ≈ 14.5 MBDOE

[Note that in Example 12.6, for a station with 1000 MW output, energy equivalent is $10^{-2}$ MBDOE per year. With an efficiency of 33%, fuel required is $3 \times 10^{-2}$ MBDOE per year = $3 \times 10^{4}$ BDOE per year].

From the results of the above eight examples, we can summarize the findings as follows:

$$\begin{aligned} 1 \text{ BDOE} &= 0.52 \times 10^{9} \text{ kcal} \\ &= 52 \text{ tonne of oil equivalent per year} \\ &= 74.5 \text{ metric tonne of coal equivalent per year} \\ &= 365 \text{ barrel of oil per year}. \end{aligned}$$

$$\begin{aligned} 1 \text{ MBDOE} &= 0.5 \times 10^{15} \text{ kcal} \\ &= 2.18 \text{ Exajoules } (2.18 \times 10^{18} \text{ J}) \\ &\approx 2 \text{ Quad } (2 \times 10^{15} \text{ Btu}) \\ &= 0.6065 \times 10^{12} \text{ kW–h} \end{aligned}$$

## 12.3 Global Energy Position

Energy demand of the world in TW-yr (15 MBDOE) from 1980 through 2080 is estimated to be as follows per year:

| | 1980 | 2000 | 2020 | 2040 | 2060 | 2080 | |
|---|---|---|---|---|---|---|---|
| Total | 10 | 17 | 27 | 42 | 54 | 60 | TW-yr |
| All Fossil Fuels | 9 | 11.4 | 13.8 | 16.2 | 18.6 | 21 | TW-yr |
| Oil/Gas only | 6 | 8 | 10 | 6 | 4 | 2 | TW-yr |

1 TW-yr = $8.76 \times 10^{12}$ kW-h = 31.536 Exajoule ≈ 30 Quad.

Fossil fuel includes coal, oil, and natural gas sources. The difference between fossil-fuel demand and total energy demand per year is made up from hydro-electric, nuclear and other sources. We also observe the decline of oil/gas demand after the year 2020; in one century oil will be depleted and no more will be available. (Oil-rich countries cannot take comfort and will become less affluent). However, the demand for energy is increasing from 10 to 60 TW-yr annually in the next 100 years or so, out of which fossil fuels provide from 90% in 1980 to 35% in 2080 of the total demand. This clearly indicates that alternative sources of energy must be developed. How it is done and in what form raises questions, for which rational answers must be forthcoming. It is this aspect, namely to pose problems and think of answers that is the main purpose of providing these figures, for which no accuracy is claimed at the time of writing this book, since these are subject to changes in as long a period as one century.

The general trend shows that the % increase per year in energy demand has been, is, and will be as follows:

1950 to 1975 : 5% per year

Present, 1995 : 3% per year

Future : 2% per year

Such statistics have little relevance when we consider that these growth figures show wide-spread values when we consider individual countries. Therefore, the figures are only an indication of the manner in which highly industrialized countries are planning, in view of fast depletion of natural resources, chiefly coal, oil, and natural gas.

The energy consumption per capita per year in some countries and important areas in the world is listed in Table 12.1. Between 1975 and 1985, there has been an annual increase of 3% in energy consumption globally. Between 1985 and 2000, assume a 2% annual rise in energy consumption. This yields the following ratios:

**Table 12.1: Energy Consumption per capita per year**

| Country | Tonnes Oil Equiv. (1 TOE = 7 barrels) | | | MW-h (per year) (1 TOE = 11,628 MW-h) | | | Barrels Oil Equiv. (1 b = 1662 kW-h) | | |
|---|---|---|---|---|---|---|---|---|---|
| | 1975 | 1985 | 2000 | 1975 | 1985 | 2000 | 1975 | 1985 | 2000 |
| Canada | 9 | 12.1 | 16.3 | 105 | 141 | 190 | 63 | 85 | 114 |
| USA | 8.5 | 11.4 | 15.3 | 99 | 133 | 179 | 60 | 80 | 107 |
| Latin America | 1 | 1.34 | 1.8 | 11.6 | 15.6 | 21 | 7 | 9.4 | 12.6 |
| W. Europe | 3.5 | 4.7 | 6.3 | 41 | 55 | 74 | 25 | 33 | 44 |
| E. Europe | 4 | 5.4 | 7.2 | 47 | 62.5 | 84 | 28 | 38 | 51 |
| USSR (old) | 4.2 | 5.7 | 7.6 | 49 | 65.6 | 88 | 29 | 40 | 53.4 |
| Africa | 0.44 | 0.59 | 0.8 | 5.1 | 6.9 | 9.2 | 3.1 | 4.13 | 5.6 |
| Mid East | 1 | 1.34 | 1.8 | 11.6 | 15.6 | 21. | 7 | 9.38 | 12.6 |
| China | 0.5 | 0.67 | 0.9 | 5.8 | 7.8 | 10.5 | 3.5 | 4.7 | 6.3 |
| Japan | 3.2 | 4.3 | 5.8 | 37.2 | 50 | 67.3 | 22.4 | 30 | 40.6 |
| Australia | 3.6 | 4.9 | 6.5 | 42 | 56.4 | 76 | 25.2 | 34 | 46 |
| S./S.E. Asia | 0.2 | 0.27 | 0.36 | 2.3 | 3.1 | 4.2 | 1.4 | 1.9 | 2.5 |

consumption in 1985/consumption in 1975 = $1.03^{10}$ = 1.344

and consumption in 2000/consumption in 1985 = $1.02^{15}$ = 1.346

The energy consumption in relation to population has the following values for 1985 and 2000, under the above 2% rise per year.

**Table 12.2: Population and Energy Consumption**

| Country | Population, Million | | Energy Consumption in MTOE (1 MTOE = 11.628 TW-h = 7 M bar) | |
|---|---|---|---|---|
| | 1985 | 2000 | 1985 | 2000 |
| Canada | 28 | 38 | 238 | 320 |
| USA | 260 | 350 | 2,105 | 2,833 |
| L. America | 395 | 532 | 365 | 490 |
| W. Europe | 450 | 600 | 1,460 | 1,970 |
| E. Europe | 129 | 174 | 490 | 660 |
| USSR | 310 | 420 | 1,250 | 1,680 |
| Africa | 360 | 480 | 150 | 197 |
| China | 1,020 | 1,380 | 475 | 640 |
| Japan | 135 | 180 | 415 | 560 |
| Australia* | 26 | 35 | 90 | 120 |
| S./S.E. Asia | 1,590 | 2,150 | 320 | 425 |
| Mid East | 130 | 180 | 120 | 160 |
| World | 4,840 | 6,510 | 7,460 | 10,050 |

* Australian figures include New Zealand.

### *12.3.1 Hydro-Electric Power Generation*

With the reliance on oil, coal and natural gas (fossil fuels) and the development of nuclear power, the development of hydro-electric power is lagging behind other types in rate at which annual increase of installed capacity is occurring. Table 12.3 shows the installed capacity in GW (= $10^9$ W = $10^6$ kW = $10^3$ MW) in certain areas of the world. The total world figure is approximately 480 GW for 1985. The % annual rate of increase is difficult to predict, ranging from zero to 5% in different countries.

**Table 12.3: Installed Capacity of Hydro-Electric Power (1985)**

| Country | GW | Country | GW | Country | GW |
|---|---|---|---|---|---|
| Canada | 56 | E. Europe | 10.5 | Japan | 34 |
| USA | 85 | USSR | 60 | S./S.E. Asia | 20 |
| L. America | 42 | Africa | 12 | Australia | 13 |
| W. Europe | 152 | China | 27 | Mid East | 4 |

The following Table 12.4 shows the installed capacity of different types of power stations in some developed countries as of 1985.

**Table 12.4: Installed Generating Capacity in 1985 in MW**

| Country | Thermal | Nuclear | Hydro-Electric | Total |
|---|---|---|---|---|
| Canada | 31,000 | 10,000 | 56,000 | 97,000 |
| USA | 520,000 | 80,000 | 85,000 | 685,000 |
| France | 28,000 | 37,000 | 22,000 | 87,000 |
| U.K. | 53,000 | 7,000 | 4,000 | 64,000 |
| USSR | 215,000 | 29,000 | 60,000 | 304,000 |
| China | 58,000 | 0 | 27,000 | 85,000 |
| Japan | 100,000 | 20,000 | 34,000 | 154,000 |
| W. Germany | 75,000 | 17,000 | 6,000 | 98,000 |
| Total | 1,080,000 | 200,000 | 295,000 | 1,575,000 |
| % of Total | 68.6% | 12.7% | 18.7% | 100% |

### *12.3.2 Global Energy Reserves*

Reserves of fossil fuels are given in Table 12.5 below in MTOE.

1 MTOE = $10^6$ tonne oil equivalent = 11.628 TW-h = 0.04186 Exajoules

**Table 12.5: World Fossil-Fuel Reserves in MTOE**

| Country | Coal | Oil | Nat. Gas | Total |
|---|---|---|---|---|
| Canada | 6,000 | 1,000 | 1,375 | 8,375 |
| USA | 243,000 | 4,800 | 5,250 | 253,650 |
| L. America | 6,100 | 4,700 | 2,240 | 13,040 |
| W. Europe<br>E. Europe | 200,000 | 5,000 | 5,000 | 210,000 |
| USSR | 183,000 | 11,000 | 22,500 | 216,500 |
| Africa | 18,000 | 8,000 | 5,000 | 31,000 |
| Mid East | 5,000 | 50,000 | 13,000 | 68,000 |
| China | 134,300 | 2,700 | 600 | 137,600 |
| Japan | 5,800 | — | — | 5,800 |
| S./S.E. Asia/<br>Australia | 15,800<br>50,000 | 2,600 | 2,100<br>900 | 71,400 |
| World | 870,000 | 88,000 | 57,000 | 1,015,000 |

### *12.3.3 Discussion of World Energy Position*

From the tables of data provided above, certain far-reaching conclusions can be drawn, which are best illustrated by worked examples as shown below.

***Example 12.9*:** Taking Canada as an example, the total reserves of fossil fuel is 8,375 MTOE. From Table 12.2, the energy consumption in 1985 was 238 MTOE. Neglect nuclear and other types of power potentials. Assume an annual increase of 2% in consumption. Estimate the number of years the fossil-fuel reserves can last.

***Solution*:** Let N = number of years of life of fossil fuels, F = total reserves, C = initial consumption in 1985, and $r$ = rate of annual increase.

$$\text{Then, } F = C[1 + (1 + r) + (1 + r)^2 + \ldots + (1 + r)^{N-1}]$$

$$= C\frac{(1 + r)^N - 1}{r}, \quad \text{giving } N = \frac{\text{Log}\,[1 + r \cdot (F/C)]}{\text{Log}\,(1 + r)}$$

With $r = 0.02$, $F = 8{,}375$, $C = 238$, we obtain (8,375/238 = 35.2)

$$N = \text{Log}\,(1 + 0.02 \times 35.2)/\text{Log}\,1.02 = 0.23147/0.0086$$

$$= 116.3 \times 0.23147 = 27 \text{ year}$$

The following Table 12.6 gives similar data for other countries or regions of the world.

**Table 12.6: Estimated Life of Fossil-Fuel Reserves of the World**

| Country or Region | Life, years | Country or Region | Life, years |
|---|---|---|---|
| Canada | 27 | Africa | 81 |
| USA | 62 | China | 97 |
| L. America | 27 | Japan | 12.5 |
| W. Europe<br>E. Europe | 58 | Australia<br>S./S.E. Asia/ | 76 |
| USSR | 76 | Mid East | 127.6 |
| World : 66 years | | | |

The above figures do not include nuclear, hydro-electric and other resources, and has also omitted the imports and exports of fossil fuels between different countries or regions. The most dramatic export is oil from the Middle East, and the largest importer is Japan of coal and petroleum. Also, individual countries in any region will show different life span for their reserves. For example, in the UK, the coal reserves are estimated to last for 300 years instead of 58 as shown by grouping it with other West European countries. However, the point is clear: fossil-fuel reserves will not last long at the rate energy is consumed in the world. Alternative sources of energy must be used for running civilized life.

## 12.4 Environmental Effects of Energy Conversion Systems

Every type of energy conversion system poses its own detrimental effect on the environment, while yielding beneficial returns for the economic well-being of society. Sometimes the development of energy systems can be halted or post-poned on account of harm done by the effluents from power stations, industries, urban developments and mining of the fuel, such as coal for the generation of power and transportation of oil by sea. Problems of pollution exist at all levels of civilization, namely local, regional, provincial, national and international. Each type of energy conversion system has its own characteristic type of pollution with some overlapping. Table 12.7 shows broad outlines of various types of energy systems and the resulting type of pollution.

**Table 12.7: Energy Systems and Pollution Types**

| Pollution | Source | Medium |
|---|---|---|
| Smoke and Dust | Coal- and oil-fired power plant with high ash content. Oil engines, used chiefly in transportation. Coal handling. Biomass | Air |
| $H_2S$ and $SO_x$ | Coal- and oil-fired power plant using high sulphur-content fuel. Geothermal plants | Air and water |
| $N_xO$ (NO and $N_2O$) | Fossil-fuel power plant with fuel burnt at high temperature. Petroleum refineries | Air |
| CO and $CO_2$ | Fossil-fuel power plants and transportation | Air |
| Lead, Pb | Internal combustion engines, biomass and industries | Air and water |
| Radiation (Radioactive nuclides) | Nuclear wastes and fuel processing | Air, water and human contact |
| Thermal | Fossil-fuel and nuclear power stations | Air and water |
| Acid Rain | Fossil-fuel power stations emitting $SO_x$ and $N_xO$. Smelters and steel plants | Rain and air |
| Acids | Fossil-fuel station and industrial effluents | Water |

Both air and water pollution cause harm to human and animal life as well as to agricultural crops and forests. A very critical examination of individual cases of pollution enables taking precautionary measures, which is the most important phase of planning energy-conversion schemes. Storing and subsequent disposal of industrial and nuclear wastes poses very severe problems at all levels of social and political organizations, and for all life forms, both animal and vegetable. There are many cases where industrial nations spend a lot of money to encourage poorer nations to accept wastes which has fuelled international tensions. Typical examples in recent years have been African nations becoming dumping grounds for European and North-american countries. It is unnecessary to cite such examples, except to point out that waste disposal is big business anywhere, in addition to posing danger to ecological systems. Moon shots may be used for nuclear-waste disposal!

We now discuss the generation of pollutants from energy systems, and preventive measures to be adopted to reduce their adverse effects, if not completely eliminate them. The causes of air pollution are numerous while water pollution is caused by coal mining, oil production from off-shore wells, oil spills during transportation in inland waters and oceans, and nuclear power stations. Thermal pollution is also a form of pollution of water as well as air.

## 12.5 Pollution from Coal and Preventive Measures

Coal-fired power stations were the first to be used in the 1800's and with it commenced man's desire to industrialize in a big way, thereby modifying the earth's atmosphere. The important effluents are $CO_2$, $SO_2$, NO, and $N_2O$. $CO_2$ will cause general warming of the earth at all latitudes, the most severely affected areas being the polar regions. This in turn will influence the climate of the rest of the world by creating changes in wind patterns, rainfall and life in coastal areas. It is also feared that due to general increase in temperatures, Pacific Islands will experience a lot of submerging.

The earth is a source of infra-red radiation which escapes out of the atmosphere. However, $CO_2$ and other tri-atomic molecular gases are absorbers of radiation at infra-red wavelengths, so that any increase in their content in the atmosphere will raise the temperature of the earth's surface. Since heat flows from a hot place to a colder place, the atmosphere-ocean system acting like a heat engine will transport the heat from equatorial and sub-tropical regions to the poles.

During the past 100 years, the estimated increase in $CO_2$ in the atmosphere has been about 15%, and will be 50% in the next century at an annual increase of 0.4%, $(1.004)^{100} = 1.49$. For an increase of 0.5% per year, the $CO_2$ content will rise to $(1.005)^{100} = 1.65$ or a 65% increase. $CO_2$ is chemically inert and stays in the atmosphere as it is, except that at very high altitudes (in the stratosphere) the rarified condition makes it combine with oxygen to yield CO and $O_3$, ozone. However, $CO_2$ is soluble in water, so that it dissolves in the oceans. The increase in temperature by 2000 A.D. is expected to be 1°C on the average over the surface of the earth from its 1980 value, and 2-3°C by the year 2050. Temperature changes at the polar regions will be 10°C by 2050. Some people in the opposite camp point out that between 1950 and 1965, there was indeed a decrease in temperature by 0.5°C globally even though $CO_2$ emission was present. However, the general concensus is that $CO_2$ warms the earth's surface by trapping the infra-red radiation. This gives rise to the "Green House Effect", which is considered to be local effects on the environment but very serious.

Coal gasification and liquification and their use as fuels in steam generators (boilers) reduces $CO_2$ emission considerably as will be described later on.

Coal-fired stations yield aerosols containing carbon particles, which will reflect sunlight back from the upper layers of the atmosphere like a black body. But being heavier than $CO_2$, they remain localized, whereas $CO_2$ scatters in the wind.

Table 12.8 gives a comparison of reduction in air emission obtained by gasification and liquification of coal using the fuels for firing boilers to raise steam instead of using coal directly.

**Table 12.8: Environmental Pollutants from Coal, Coal Gas and Liquid Hydrocarbon Fuels**

| Air Emission | Coal Electricity | Coal Gas | Coal Liquids |
|---|---|---|---|
| Aerosols | 100% | 11% | 20% |
| $SO_2$ | 100% | 13.3% | 42% |
| $N_xO$ | 100% | 8% | 21% |
| $CO_2$ | 100% | 80% | 95% |
| CO | 100% | 7.5% | 28% |
| HC | 100% | 6.25% | 31% |
| Solid Wastes | 100% | 27% | 40% |

The reduction of pollutants by gasification and liquification of coal are evident. Furthermore, oil and natural gas wells require $CO_2$ for their operations, which can be partly obtained from the gasification process and liquefaction.

Sulphur oxides are very obnoxious and are emitted when coal containing large sulphur content (3%) is burnt. We will discuss the phenomenon of acid rain later on. The modern practice for eliminating $SO_x$ emissions is to use the process of fluidized bed combustion (FBC). There are two types of FBC: (a) atmospheric pressure FBC called AFBC, and (b) pressurized FBC or PFBC. In both these processes, the coal is mixed with limestone or dolomite ($CaCO_3$, $CaMg(CO_3)_2$ or (CaOH) containing calcium. The coal/ealcium ratio used is nearly 2.5/1. With water they form a slurry or fluid on the grate in the furnace of the boiler on which the coal burns. PFBC is operated at 6 to 16 atmospheres and the calcium picks up sulphur up to 65% of its weight, i.e. the Ca/S ratio is 1.5 as $CaSO_4$. It operates at the high temperature of 870°C (1600°F), so that the exhaust air can be taken to a gas turbine to yield additional power by cogeneration. Coal usually contains 3% *S* so that use of coal with lower *S* content reduces $SO_x$ emission in the flue gas. This can be done by crushing coal and centrifuging it to remove iron pyrite $FeS_2$ or $Fe_2S_5$ containing most of thc sulphur.

Nitrogen oxides emitted are NO and $N_2O$ which are collectively represented as $N_xO$ or $NO_x$. This amounts to 50% of $SO_x$ emissions from coal stations and oil in vehicles and oil-fired power stations. However, natural sources and man-made sources of $NO_x$ such as fertilizers for agriculture are equally responsible. As given in Table 12.7, $NO_x$ emission from coal-fired power stations is caused by the high temperature of combustion. Therefore, efforts are made to burn coal at lower temperatures. In this respect, AFBC is preferred over PFBC.

Aerosols or solid particulates are removed by using electrostatic precipitators at the inlet to the chimney, whose height has reached 200 *m*. The $SO_2$ in the exhaust gases, if any, is also made to react with limestone and dolomite slurry and removed as $CaSO_4$ in "scrubbers" where FBC is not used. This removes up to 90% of sulphur.

## 12.6 Steam Stations and Pollution

All the pollution described in the previous section applies to steam stations fired by coal. In addition, there are other types of pollution created by steam stations, chiefly water pollution. We will deal with nuclear thermal stations in a later section. Thermal stations of all types require very large quantities of non-saline water for cooling, in addition to feed water to the boiler for raising steam. These power stations are located on river banks and on lakes. There are some stations on sea shores which use de-salinated water or, at considerable expense, sea water itself. But by far the majority of stations are situated on rivers and lakes. The major difference between the two is that, river water flows while water in lakes is stationary. In general, rivers are closer to cities than lakes are, but not necessarily so. These two factors affect pollution control laws for licencing.

In Chap. 7 it was mentioned that about 50% heat content in the exhaust from the last L.P. stage of the steam turbine is lost in the condenser, where a vacuum of 25 to 75 mm-Hg is maintained. The steam is condensed to form feed water to the boiler in a closed cycle. This condensation is carried out by the heat exchange process, which in turn requires large amounts of cooling water. A 1000 MW station may need up to 20 million $m^3$ of water annually. In order to cut down on land area required for the cooling process, cooling towers are used which are vertical. Cold water from the river or lake is pumped to the top of the tall structure and made to fall by gravity over the tubes containing the condensate, which is a mixture of steam and water. In this process the temperature of cooling water is raised and this hot water is discharged into the river or lake. In the vicinity of the power station, it is clear that in a flowing river the hotter exhaust water does not stay stagnant as it does in a lake. Therefore, thermal pollution affecting fish, eels and other acquatic life is more severe in lakes than in rivers. It has indeed been the experience in the UK that the warmer-flowing water on the downstream side of the power station encourages the growth of several kinds of fish population. Ponds are specially built to attract anglers. However, in lakes the picture is different. With constant inflow of hot water from the cooling towers, animal life is affected. In some areas legislation requires that the warm water be discharged at a depth of not less than 6 *m* below the surface and at a distance of 30 *m* from the shore. Periodic inspections of any danger to fish life are also mandatory.

At the input end of coal-handling area, a lot of coal dust is raised. Combined with the effluent gaseous products from the chimney, they pose a lot of hazard to cities located closeby. One of the most severe examples is the London smog of 1965 caused by the heavy humid atmosphere trapping solid pollutants soaked in acid created by $SO_x$ and $NH_3$. This causes breathing problems and asphyxiation.

## 12.7 Acid Rain

Effluents such as $SO_2$, NO and $NO_2$ are acidic in nature which combine with hydrogen of water in the atmosphere to form $H_2SO_4$ and $HNO_3$, the sulphuric and nitric acids, as shown by the following reaction:

$$SO_2 + H_2O + ½\,O_2 \longrightarrow 2\,H^+ + SO_4^= \longrightarrow H_2SO_4$$

where + denotes equivalent of acidity and = denotes two equivalents of negative charge. Hydroxyl radicals also contribute, as

$$SO_2 + OH \longrightarrow 2\,HSO_3\,,\ 2\,HSO_3 + 2\,OH \longrightarrow 2\,H_2SO_4$$

In addition to $H_2O$ and OH radical, ozone ($O_3$) and hydrogen peroxide ($H_2O_2$) in the atmosphere also oxidize $SO_2$ into $H_2SO_4$. The reaction of $SO_2$ to form $H_2SO_4$ is intense in the presence of sunlight and increases in summer.

On the other hand, nitric acid is generated from NO and $NO_2$ even in dark hours of the night through the reaction

$$NO + NO_2 + O_2 + H_2O \longrightarrow 2\,H^+ + 2\,NO_3^- \longrightarrow 2\,HNO_3\,.$$

Geothermal steam contains stinking $H_2S$ and forms a potential source of acid pollution in the atmosphere.

When it rains, it brings down the acids on to the ground level which affects agricultural crops, forest, and animal life. In addition, heavy metals in the effluents such as Hg, Cu, Pb, Cd, etc., which are soluble in acids can affect drinking water drawn from lakes and rivers. Metallic pipes are also corroded. Airborne acid from one region can affect another, and where smelters and power stations are located close to international boundaries, the acid rain fallout from one country on another can cause international tensions. This is called an "Acid War"

In order to prevent acid rain and its consequences, lime in the form of $CaCO_3$ or CaOH is added to small bodies of water such as ponds and lakes from which drinking water is drawn as well as for protecting acquatic life. Some other remedies for reducing sulphur content described earlier reduce danger of acid rain at the source. These are (a) switching from 3% to 1% sulphur-containing fuel, (b) coal cleaning by crushing and centrifuging to remove heavy iron pyrite containing almost 50% S, (c) by scrubbers, and (d) by using FBC. Coal liquefaction and gasification yield very low *S* in the fuel. Furthermore, such processes also yield sulphur as a by-product and can be sold. $N_xO$ is also removed in FBC.

## 12.8 Pollution-Free Energy Systems

Many direct-energy conversion systems described in earlier chapters are relatively free of pollution, posing threat to life and the environment. Such systems are MHD, photovoltaic conversion, fuel cells, wind energy conversion systems (WECS), tidal, wave, OTEC, and hydrogen. There will always be some form of minor pollution and changes to environment in every system if we include noise and vast areas of land converted to the power development, such as for wind-turbine farms, etc. Hydro-electric power development submerges lot of agricultural land in the reservoir. Tidal power development changes life patterns for fish and other acquatic life, such as lobsters in bays and river estuaries, but does not pollute the atmosphere or water with chemical effluents.

## 12.9 Hydro-Electric Power Development

A hydroelectric power station is very clean and causes no pollution of the river. However, the major concern is the dam and reservoir for storing the water required for the year. Life patterns are drastically affected for humans and animals living in the area eventually submerged by the reservoir. Vegetation is also affected. There are cases where dams that are half executed have been halted because environmental groups have brought strong arguments against completion of the rest of the structure. One potent argument is that the environmental studies prior to commencement of the dam were improperly carried out or in some cases not at all. As mentioned in Chap. 8, earthquakes may be generated by water from the reservoir leaking downwards through porous rocks and reaching hot magma below, generating steam which cracks the rocks.

Collection of silt at the dam can change the topography when a reservoir can no more serve the purpose of storing water. This can take place 50 to 100 years after building the dam. Thus, no hydro-electric power development can be considered perennial. It has a limited life span, during which the damage has been done irrevocably.

There are no remedies for such consequences other than dredging the water, move the people and animals to safer places, and compensate the residents displaced by the development for the loss of their property and start a new way of life elsewhere. On the positive side, the reservoir offers recreational facilities, while new forms of acquatic life can be cultivated and can thrive where there were none before, not to mention the benefits accrued by the development of the electrical power. Most dams and reservoirs are multi-purpose projects which improve irrigation, water transportation and control of severe floods.

## 12.10 Nuclear Power Stations and Pollution

Generation, containment and disposal of radio-active material in the form of fuel and waste products is the hottest topic of the times and will be so in the future as long as human society demands electric power for its well-being. The following types of disposal of radioactive wastes are adopted and are envisaged, which show the magnitude of the problem.

(a) The spent fuel from the reactor at the time of re-fuelling contains unused uranium and other fission ingredients. Some of them are: plutonium, (239-242), elements of the actinide series of the Periodic Table, americium, curium, neptunium, and a lot of fission products which include krypton, strontium, cerium, iodine and caesium. In addition, the radioactive waste is very hot. These wastes have to be kept intact in stainless steel containers immersed in large volumes of water to cool down. Once cool enough to be handled by remote-controlled equipment, as is the case at every stage of handling radioactive and hot materials, the waste is transferred to drums with their own cooling systems. These are then transported to fuel-processing plants, where many isotopes are separated for medical or further fuel-recovery uses. This transportation by rail cars or truck trailers has resulted in accidents, contaminating the townspeople where rail cars have derailed or trucks have met with damage and caused radioactive spills.

(b) The re-processed fuel after recovery of *Pu* or *U* or other useful isotopes is still radioactive and must be disposed off properly, since their half-lives may range from thousands to tens of thousands of years. They are mixed with water in stainless steel tanks and sealed in steel-lined concrete buildings until taken to places where they do not contaminate the environment, such as by space-ships to the moon or into outer space, burying in the earth at the bottom of oceans or in the Antarctic, deep salt mines, etc. With increase in nuclear power generation taking place year to year, the magnitude of waste disposal will increase and not decrease.

(c) At the processing plants before the reactor is fuelled, several types of precautions have to be taken for handling the fuel. This is particularly severe in uranium-enrichment plants and weapons-grade plutonium-producing plants. These products are chemically toxic in addition to their radioactivity. Thus, they are buried underground in stainless steel tanks until ready for use.

(d) In gas-cooled reactors, the radioactive gas may leak into the atmosphere. In modern reactors water is used for raising steam or cooling, which becomes radioactive and any discharge of this into rivers or the sea will contaminate water and affect marine and fresh-water life. It will also affect drinking water for everyone. It also applies to liquid sodium used in LMFBR.

(e) One proposal is to mould the cooled radioactive waste mixed with glass into vitrified bricks and store them in containers inside deep mines, in stable geological areas free from earthquakes or under the oceans.

In all cases, as far as it is within man's control, every effort has to be made to see that nuclear fuel and its waste products from nuclear reactors do not come into contact with the environment, namely the atmosphere, water, forests, animals and human beings as well as agricultural lands. There is no such thing as a half-dangerous radioactive material. However, the most serious concern to environmental pollution is by way of accidents to nuclear power plants. It is this aspect that is of utmost concern, and we will now describe some effects of such accidents which have posed a great threat to the well-being, if not survival of mankind and animal and vegetation. We shall not consider the effects of nuclear war, although the consequences are very similar.

As discussed in Chap. 2, the important nuclear decay process in fission reactions are as follows:

$$^{235}_{92}U + n \longrightarrow {}^{140}_{56}Ba + {}^{96}_{36}Kr$$

$$^{140}Ba \xrightarrow{\beta} {}^{140}_{57}La \xrightarrow{\beta} {}^{140}_{58}Ce \text{ (stable)} ; \quad {}^{96}Kr \longrightarrow {}^{94}_{36}Kr + 2\,n$$

$$^{94}Kr \xrightarrow{\beta} {}^{94}_{37}Rb \xrightarrow{\beta} {}^{94}_{38}Sr \xrightarrow{\beta} {}^{94}_{39}Y \xrightarrow{\beta} {}^{94}_{40}Zr \text{ (stable)}$$

$$^{235}_{92}U \longrightarrow {}^{231}_{90}Th + {}^{4}_{2}\alpha ; \quad {}^{131}_{53}I \xrightarrow{\beta} {}^{131}_{54}Xe \text{ (poison)}$$

We observe that the decay reactions involve $\alpha$ and $\beta$ emissions, which are followed frequently by high-energy $\gamma$-emissions. These three types of radiations affect the metabolism of all living cells. Radiation measures and limits for doses have been detailed in Sec. 2.9. The release of radiation into the atmosphere and the resulting fall-out from accidents need not be over-emphasized for their danger. While every study is made and precaution is incorporated in safety measures to prevent accidents from occurring, they do happen. This is like opening the Pandora's box and the concerned reader can spend a lifetime in studying this topic. We will only describe briefly the most talked-about accident of recent years which took place, which is termed a disaster than an accident, on the midnight of April 25-26, 1986, at Chernobyl, 80 km north of Kiev in the Ukraine. In terms of the magnitude of the fallout, it has been estimated that the explosion of this graphite-moderated water-cooled uranium-fuelled reactor was the equivalent of the explosion of a large nuclear bomb of about 20 Megatons. We shall keep away from the reasons for this accident, which are reserved for experts but which are caused by design deficiencies, very slow-acting controls and human errors, as with all accidents, whether nuclear reactor or other energy-conversion systems or any other type, including automobile, aircraft, industrial, domestic, etc.

The core of the problem appears to be the lack of a containment vessel covering the upper portion of the reactor. It is believed that such severe fallouts will not occur in reactors with full containment vessel. The explosion was so severe that even the steel roof over the reactor blew upwards and fell down but not in a position to cover the reactor and prevent the escape of the radioactive material. The presence of a "positive void coefficient" was the contributing factor for the initial explosion and melt-down of the core of the reactor and other parts. All reactors are designed with a negative void coefficient which means that as the temperature of the moderator increases, the rate of reaction decreases. The negative void coefficient prevents uncontrolled heat generation. But in the reactor at Chernobyl which blew up there was instability caused by incompatibility between power output at the generator terminals and the heat generated in the reactor core. The void coefficient refers to transformation of water into steam, which also controls the flux of neutrons moderated by the water in addition to the graphite which is used as moderator. In a positive void coefficient, the water lost as steam increases the rate of fission by lower rate of moderation of neutrons and increasing the flux of slow neutrons, if the control rods are inserted with less than the required safe speed. This happens when the control systems act slowly or not at all. In a reactor designed with negative void coefficient, the lowering of water quantity used for moderation reduces the flux of slow neutrons and thereby decreases the rate of chain reaction and heat production. The presence of graphite increased fire hazard, which is not present in reactors using water for moderation entirely, such as LWR, PWR, BWR, HWR, etc. which are standard designs in North America and elsewhere. Also, any contact of steam with graphite releases hydrogen under very high pressure to pose a potential explosion threat.

The explosion at Chernobyl damaged all pressure tubes and tore a 1000-ton cover plate off its position, discharging hot radioactive fuel to heights of 7.5 km, in addition to starting numerous fires. The radioactive nuclides released were Cs, Sr with half-lives of about 30 years and longer-lived Pu (half-life of 24,000 years). Dispersion of radioactive nuclides covered a very vast area of the Soviet Union, Europe and as far away as Japan, with Austria as the worst affected country. Other very badly affected countries were Bulgaria, Germany, Greece, Hungary, Italy, Norway and Sweden. Thus the incident assumed international magnitudes. The threat posed by contamination was not only to human population but also to agricultural crops and animals, which form the main food in these regions. As many as 31 human lives were lost at the reactor site due to burns by radiation and fires, including fire fighters who were exposed to the heat and the radiation at very close quarters.

Other forms of health hazards included fatal cancer, mental retardation in children born of mothers affected by radiation and genetic disorders. Calves were born to cows with half their face missing. While these are long-term effects, other short-term consequences include nausea, skin burns and blood disorders. It is estimated that there will eventually be 28,000 cancer fatalities.

There have been accidents at other nuclear establishments, the worst in North America being at the Three Mile Island plant in Pennsylvania in 1979, where no fatalities occurred and the radiation level was estimated to have been $4 \times 10^{-7}$ times that released from the Chernobyl plant. However, military testing of nuclear arsenal in the atmosphere generates radiation levels a few orders of magnitude higher than at Chernobyl. Such tests are being carried out in the Pacific Islands and elsewhere in desert areas, etc.

Some other environmental problems that have affected licencing or operation are that, lack of proper study of the possibility of evacuating people from the region of a nuclear plant in the event of an accident has prohibited these from commencing operation even after full completion of the nuclear establishment. This occurred in Long Island in New York State in the USA outside New York city. The entire multi-million or billion dollar enterprise has been mothballed. Licences for plants in one state or province have been cancelled because of interstate quarrels regarding potential radiation hazards to residents living in the border areas. In nuclear plants already operating under valid licences, cases of sabotage have occurred as well as mistakingly drinking heavy-water-polluted light water contaminated by traces of radioactivity. The lesson is that, in spite of all precautions taken to eliminate potential radiation hazards, much remains to be studied and there still exists possibility of exposure to radiation of different levels or degrees of severity.

## OBJECTIVE TYPE QUESTIONS

1. A country which depends for its economic advancement and technical know-how on other countries is called: (a) Developed country; (b) Developing country; (c) Underdeveloped country; (d) Both (b) and (c).

2. 1 Quad of energy equals: (a) $10^{15}$ Btu; (b) $1.055 \times 10^{15}$ kJ; (c) $0.252 \times 10^{15}$ kcal; (d) $0.3032 \times 10^{12}$ kW-h; (e) All four are true.

3. 1 Exajoule of energy equals: (a) $10^{15}$ Btu; (b) $10^{15}$ kJ; (c) $0.276 \times 10^{12}$ kW-h; (d) Both (b) and (c) are true.

4. A barrel of 42 US gallons of oil of weight 142.9 kg has a calorific value of $10^4$ kcal/kg. The energy content is: (a) 1662 kW-h; (b) $1.429 \times 10^6$ kcal; (c) $5.666 \times 10^6$ Btu; (d) All three are true.

5. 1 MBDOE is equivalent to: (a) Millions of barrels of oil per day equivalent; (b) 2 Quads of energy; (c) $365 \times 10^6$ barrels of oil per year; (d) All three are true.

6. 1 MBDOE over one year contains: (a) $0.52 \times 10^{15}$ kcal; (b) 2.2 Exajoules; (c) 606.5 TW-h; (d) All three are true.

7. The calorific value of 1 $m^3$ of natural gas is 10,000 kcal. The volume of gas equivalent of 1 MBDOE is nearly: (a) $52 \times 10^9$ $m^3$; (b) 100 $km^3$; (c) 500 $km^3$.

8. An energy of 1 TW-yr is equivalent to: (a) $8.76 \times 10^{12}$ kW-h; (b) 31.536 Exajoules; (c) 14.5 MBDOE; (d) All three are true.

9. 1 tonne oil equivalent (TOE) amounts to: (a) 7 barrels; (b) 11,628 kW-h; (c) $10^7$ kcal; (d) All three are true.

10. A country has an annual average energy consumption of 10 TOE per capita. This is equal to: (a) 116.28 MW-h; (b) 13.274 kW load per head; (c) 116,280 units of energy consumed per head per year; (d) All three are true.

11. The reserve of fossil fuels in a country is 5000 MTOE. The energy equivalent is: (a) 2093 Exajoules; (b) $581.4 \times 10^3$ TW-h; (c) 66.37 TW-yr; (d) All three are true.

12. A country uses 2000 MTOE this year and the annual increase is 3%. The total reserves now amount to 250,000 MTOE. The life of the reserves will be: (a) 63.25 yr; (b) 52.7 yr; (c) 100 yr; (d) None of the three.

13. Acid rain contains: (a) $H_2SO_4$; (b) $HNO_3$; (c) $HCO_3$; (d) All three.

14. Danger in nuclear-reactor wastes comes from: (a) Long half-life of products; (b) Radioactivity in products; (c) Closeness to human inhabitants; (d) All three reasons.

15. The danger from $CO_2$ in the atmosphere arises due to: (a) Absorption of sun's heat and warming of the atmosphere; (b) Dissolving in oceans and causing imbalance of $CO_2$ content in the atmosphere; (c) Absorption of infra-red radiation from the earth's surface; (d) None of the three.

16. Effluents obtained from burning coal and hydrocarbon fuels in power stations are: (a) Aerosols; (b) $SO_2$; (c) $N_2O$; (d) $CO_2$; (e) All four.

17. Sulphur emission can be reduced by: (a) Electrostatic precipitators; (b) Fluidized-bed combustion; (c) Removal of iron pyrite ($Fe_2S_5$) from coal fed to the boiler; (d) All three processes.

18. Aerosols are removed by: (a) Electrostatic precipitators; (b) FBC; (c) Centrifuging and removal of iron pyrite; (d) All three processes.

19. $N_2O$ emission is removed by: (a) Electrostatic precipitators; (b) FBC; (c) Removal of iron pyrites; (d) All three processes.

20. Harmful nuclear radiations include: (a) Alpha particles; (b) Beta particles; (c) Gamma rays; (d) All three.

21. When U-235 is bombarded with a neutron, the resulting products are Ba-140 and Kr-96. These are called: (a) Poisons; (b) Daughter nuclei; (c) Neutron absorbers; (d) None of the three.

22. From experience of dangers to date, reactors using water (light and heavy) are more dangerous than using graphite. (a) True, or, (b) False.

23. Nuclear reactors need lot of water for: (a) Moderator; (b) Cooling; (c) Shielding; (d) None of the three.

24. Which type(s) of pollution has (have) become international issue(s)? (a) Acid rain; (b) Nuclear reactor accidents; (c) Water pollution; (d) All three.

25. Licences for installing and operating nuclear power stations can be revoked or not granted for which reason(s)? (a) Causing harm to marine life; (b) Lack of adequate and quick evacuation facilities or routes in case of fall-out; (c) Located on the border of two states or provinces; (d) Any or all three.

[***Answers***: 1. (d); 2. (e); 3. (d); 4. (d); 5. (d); 6. (d); 7. (a); 8. (d); 9. (d); 10. (d); 11. (d); 12. (b); 13. (d); 14. (d); 15. (c); 16. (e); 17. (c); 18. (a); 19. (b); 20. (d); 21. (b); 22. (b); 23. (d); 24. (d); 25. (d).]

## REVIEW QUESTIONS AND PROBLEMS

1. The calorific values of oil, coal and natural gas in British units are 20,000 Btu/lb, 13,000 Btu/lb, and 1,200 Btu/ft$^3$, respectively. Convert these to kcal/kg and kcal/m$^3$.

   (11,111; 7,222; 12,000).

2. (a) The specific gravity of oil is 0.9, and 1 US gallon of water weighs 8.33 lb. Find the weight of 1 MBDOE consumed over one year. Give the answer in MTOE.
   (b) Calculate the energy in Exajoules and Quads in 1 MBDOE consumed over one year. Take 1 barrel to have 42 gallons and heating value of oil as $10^4$ kcal/kg.
   [(a) 52.143 MTOE; (b) 2.185 Exajoule = 2.07 Quad].

3. Describe the energy position of your country.

4. The energy consumption per capita in a country is 4 TOE per year (46.5 MW-h per year). The population is 450 million. The % increase in energy consumption is 3% per year and the fossil-fuel reserves now are 200,000 MTOE. Calculate the life of the fuel reserves. (49.6 yr).

5. It is clearly evident that the fossil-fuel reserves in the world will deplete sooner or later. Suggest how the energy requirements of the industrial world will be met after that period.

6. List at least five types of atmospheric pollutants, and five types of water pollutants. Give their sources.

7. How can the following types of pollution be eliminated or minimized from fossil-fuel plants? (a) Smoke and dust, (b) $CO_2$, (c) $SO_2$, (d) NO, and (e) Thermal.

8. Give the origin of acid rain and what measures can be taken to minimise this hazard.
9. What is meant by "green-house effect"? What is the cause of this and what are its harmful effects on global climate? How is this controlled? What measures do you suggest for eliminating the green-house effect?
10. Describe the pollutants removed from coal by gasification and liquifaction.
11. What are the beneficial and harmful effects on the environment and ecology posed by a hydro-electric power development? If a dam were to be built across a river to develop 1000 MWe in your area, give your opinion with pertinent reasons whether you would approve or disapprove the construction of the scheme. Have in mind that you have to convince environmentalists about the various objections they will have.
12. Following the material in Sec. 12.10, give a summary of the radioactive waste products that have to be disposed off which result from nuclear reactors. What are the methods adopted in current practice to make the environment safe from the dangers of radioactive waste products?
13. Give five reasons which environmentalists advance against the establishment of a nuclear power plant.
14. Describe the main reasons for nuclear power-station accidents, based on the experience at Chernobyl and other places.

# Bibliography

## General


1. *Energy*, (Pergamon Press).
2. *Energy World*, (Magazine of the Institute of Energy).
3. *Energy Policy*, (Butterworth Scientific Ltd.).
4. *Energy*, (McMaster Univ., Hamilton, Ontario, Canada).
5. *Energy Engineering*, (Journal of Assn. of Energy Engineers).
6. *Energy Conversion and Management*, (Pergamon Press).
7. *Electric Vehicle Developments*, (Butterworths).
8. *I.E.E.E. Spectrum* (345 E. 47th St., New York, N.Y.).
9. *Power Engineering Review*, I.E.E.E.
10. *IEEE Transactions on Energy Conversion.*
11. *IEE Proceedings*. Part B, (London).
12. *Electric Machines and Power Systems* (Dept. of EE, Kentucky).
13. *Electric Power System Research* (Elsevier Science Pub. Ltd.).
14. *Annual Review of Energy*, Vols. 1 to 22, 1976 to 1997. (Annual Reviews Inc., Palo Alto CA).
15. *Energy Information Abstracts Annual.*
16. L.C. Wilbur (Ed.): *Handbook of Energy Systems Engineering*, (John Wiley and Sons), 1985.
17. D.M. Considine (Ed.): *Energy Technology Handbook* (McGraw-Hill), 1977.
18. J.P. Hartnett (Ed.): *Alternative Energy Sources* (Academic Press), 1976.
19. D.N. Lapedes (Ed.): *Encyclopaedia of Energy* (McGraw-Hill), 1976.

20. R.L. Loftness (Ed.): *Energy Handbook* (Van Nostrand) 1978.

21. *Solar Energy and Wind Power: A Bibliography with Abstracts*. (National Technical Information Service, NTI Search, US Dept. of Commerce). 1974.

22. *Sun Power: A Bibliography* (US Govt. Documents).

23. *Wind Energy: A Bibliography* (Windworks, Mukwonago, Wis.).

24. *Energy Information Guide:* R. David Weber. Vol I: *General and Alternative Energy Sources;* Vol. II: *Nuclear and Electric Power*; Vol. III: *Fossil Fuels*. (LA Harbor College).

25. *Nuclear Fusion: A Bibliography with Abstracts*. D.W. Grooms, NTIS.

26. *Diesel and Gas Turbine World Wide Catalog* (Diesel and Gas Turbine Publications, Brookfield WI).

27. *Energy Progress*: Amer. Inst. of Chem. Engrs.

28. M. Ali Kettani: *Direct Energy Conversion* (Addison-Wesley), 1970.

29. S.L. Soo: *Direct Energy Conversion* (Prentice-Hall), 1968.

30. K.H. Spring (Ed.): *Direct Generation of Electricity* (Academic Press).

31. G.W. Sutton (Ed.): *Direct Energy Conversion* (McGraw-Hill), 1966.

32. S.W. Angrist: *Direct Energy Conversion* (Allyn and Bacon), 1971.

33. *Energy Information Abstracts Annual*, EIC Intelligence Inc., N.Y.

34. *Environment Abstracts Annual,* EIC Intelligence Inc., New York.

35. *Environment Index*, EIC Intelligence Inc., New York, N.Y.

36. *Asia Energy Vision 2020: Sustainable Energy Supply.* World Energy Council. Sponsored by The Institution of Engineers (India), New Delhi, 1996. (Published by Concept Publishing Co., New Delhi, India, 110 059)

**Chapter 1: Atomic Physics**

1. H.E. White: *Introduction to Atomic Spectra* (McGraw-Hill, and Dover).

2. G. Herzberg: *Atomic Spectra and Atomic Structure* (Dover), 1944.

3. K.S. Krane: *Introductory Nuclear Physics* (John Wiley and Sons), 1988.

4. S. Brandt and H.D. Dahmen: *The Picture Book of Quantum Mechanics* (John Wiley and Sons), 1985.

5. See any books on *"Introductory Quantum Mechanics"*, for example, Schiff

**Chapter 2: Nuclear Physics and Nuclear Reactors (Fission)**

1. K.S. Krane: *Introductory Nuclear Physics* (John Wiley and Sons), 1988.

2. Sybil P. Parker (Ed.): *Nuclear and Particle Physics Source Book* (McGraw-Hill), 1988.
3. H.W. Buschman: *Experimental Breeder Reactor - II: 20 Years of Operating Experience. Nuclear Safety*, 1985, vol. 26, No. 4, 1985, pp. 493-502.
4. G. Vendryes: The French LMFBR Program. *Annual Review of Energy*, 1984 pp. 263-280.
5. S.S. Penner (Ed.): *Energy*, Vol. III - *Nuclear Energy* (Addison-Wesley), 1976.
6. S.E. Hunt: *Nuclear Physics for Engineers and Scientists* (Ellis Harwood, Chichester), 1987.
7. I.R. Cameron: *Nuclear Fission Reactors*, 1982.
8. R.F. Post: *Nuclear and Particle Physics Source Book*, Sybil P. Parker (Ed.), 1988.
9. D.J. Bennett: *The Elements of Nuclear Power* (Longmans), 1981.
10. S. Glasstone and A. Sesonske: *Nuclear Reactor Engineering* (Van Nostrand), 1981.
11. C.E. Iliffe: *An Introduction to Nuclear Reactor Theory* (Manchester Univ. Press), 1984.
12. A.V. Nero, Jr.: *A Guidebook to Nuclear Reactors* (Univ. of California Press). 1979.
13. A.M. Judd: *Fast Breeder Reactors* (Pergamon Press), 1981.
14. W. Reynolds: *Fast Breeder Reactors* (Pergamon Press), 1981.
15. B.R.T. Frost: *Nuclear Fuel Elements* (Pergamon Press), 1982.
16. E.J. Henley and J. Lewins (Eds.): *Advances in Nuclear Science and Technology* (Academic Press), Vols. 1, 1969 to date.
17. *Nuclear Canada Yearbooks* by Canadian Nuclear Assn.
18. McLaren Atlantic Ltd.: *Comparative Environmental Study of Three Nuclear Generating Stations in New Brunswick, Canada*, 1974.
19. A.E. Waltar and A.B. Reynolds: *Fast Breeder Reactors* (Pergamon), 1981.

**Chapter 3: Solid State Physics and Photovoltaic Power Generation**

1. H.T. Stokes: *Solid State Physics* (Allyn and Bacon), 1987.
2. J.R. Christman: *Fundamentals of Solid State Physics* (John Wiley and Sons), 1988.

3. N.W. Ashcroft and N.D. Mermin: *Solid State Physics* (Holt, Reinhart Winston), 1976.

4. C. Kittel: *Introduction to Solid State Physics* (John Wiley), 1986.

5. F.H. Morse and M.K. Simmons: Solar Energy in *Annual Review of Energy*, vol. 1, 1976, pp. 131-158.

6. Amorphous Silicon Alloys for Solar Cells: *Annual Review of Energy*, vol. 10, 1985, pp. 1-34.

7. R.C. Neville: *The Solar Cell* (Elsevier), 1980. Has 400 references.

8. J.A. Merrigan: *Sunlight to Electricity* (MIT Press), 1975.

9. K.W. Mitchell: *CdS/CdTe Heterojunction Solar Cell* (Garland Pub. Co.) 1979.

10. W.D. Johnston, Jr.: *Solar Voltaic Cells* (Marcel Dekker), 1980.

11. K.K. Jurgen: *Impact 2000, A Place in the Sun: IEEE Spectrum*, May 1985, vol. 22, no. 5, p. 64.

12. K.W. Mitchell and K.J. Touryan: Amorphous Silicon Alloys for Cells. *Annual Review of Energy*, 1985, vol. 10, pp. 1-34.

13. G.J. Shushnar: Balance of System Costs for a 5 MW Photovoltaic Generating System. *IEEE Trans.*, PA-S, Aug. 1985, pp. 2006-2011.

14. G.T. Chinery and J.M. Wood: TVA's P.V. Activities. *IEEE Trans. PA-S*, Aug. 1985, pp.1998-2004.

15. D.L. Pulfrey: *Photovoltaic Power Generation* (Van Nostrand Reinhold), 1978. Contains 300 references up to 1978.

16. *Solar Census: Photovoltaic Edition*. AATEC Publications, P.O. Box 711G Ann Arbor, Mich., 48107. 1984. (Lists 640 organizations).

17. *VIth European Communities P.V. Solar Energy Conference*, London, 1985. (D. Reidel Pub. Co.).

18. H.S. Rauschenbach: *Solar Cell Array Design Handbook* (Van Nostrand Reinhold), 1980.

19. K.S. Tam, P. Kumar and M. Foreman: Enhancing PV Power Generation by Superconductive Magnet Energy Storage. *IEEE Trans. on Energy Conversion*, 1989, pp. 314-321.

20. J. Applebaum: Operation of Loads Powered by Separate Sources or by a Common Source of Solar Cells. *IEEE Trans. on Energy Conversion*, 1989, pp. 351-357.

21. K.L. Chopra and S.R. Das: *Thin Film Solar Cells* (Plenum Press), 1983.

22. Hass, Reinhard, *et al.*: Socio-Economic Aspects of the Austrian 200 kWp Photovoltaic Roof-top Programme. *Solar Energy,* vol. 66, No. 3, 1999, pp. 183-191.

23. Ashari, M. and Nayar, C.V.: An Optimum Dispatch Strategy Using Set Points for a PV-Diesel-Battery Hybrid Power System. *Solar Energy,* vol. 66, No. 1, 1999, pp. 1-9.

24. Peterson, Art J. Jr., *et al.*: Operational Experience of a Residential Photovoltaic Hybrid System. *Solar Energy,* vol. 65, No. 4, 1999, pp. 227-235.

25. Carlson, D.E.: Photovoltaic Technologies for Commercial Power Generation. *Annual Review of Energy,* vol. 15, 1990, pp. 85-98.

26. Dracker, R. and DeLanquil, P.: Solar Photovoltaic Power. *Annual Review of Energy,* Ch. 5, pp. 382-401, vol. 21, 1996.

27. Goosens, Dirk, *et al.*: Aeolian Dust Deposition on PV Solar Cells: The Effects of Wind Velocity and Airborne Dust Concentration on Cell Performance. *Solar Energy,* vol. 66, no. 4, 1999, pp. 277-289.

28. *Energy for Rural Island Communities,* vols. 1-18, 1985-1999.

29. Slesser, Malcolm: *Dictionary of Energy.* Schocken Books, New York. 1983. (Macmillan Press, 1982).

30. *CANMET.* Canada Centre for Mineral and Energy Technology. A Transportable Photovoltaic Array for Temporary Field Camps, 1990.

31. Takahashi, K. and Konagai, M.: Amorphous Silicon Solar Cells. *North Oxford Academic Publishers,* London, 1986.

32. Materials and New Processing Technologies for Photovoltaics. (The Electrochemical Society, Pennington, N.J., 08534-2896). Proceedings of Symposia, 1980-1999.

33. Adler, David. (Ed.): Photovoltaics for Commercial Solar Power Applications. Proceedings of the International Society for Optical Engineering, 1986.

34. Adler, David (Ed.): Photovoltaics for Solar Energy Applications II, *ibid*, 1983.

35. Deb, Satyen K. (Ed.): Physical Limitations to Photovoltaic Energy Conversion, *ibid*, 1990.

36. Luque, A. and Araujo, G.L. (Eds.): Physical Limitations to Photovoltaic Energy Conversion, *ibid*, 1990.

37. Aoki, M.: Photovoltaic Science and Engineering Conference in Japan, vol. 1 - , 1980 -. Tokyo. Japanese Journal of Applied Physics.

38. Deb, Satyendra K. (Ed.): Role of Electro-Optics in Photovoltaic Energy Conversion, 1980. Proceedings of the Society of Photo-Optical Instrumentation Engineers, Bellingham, WA, 98227, USA.

39. Seraphin, B.O. (Ed.): Solar Energy Conversion, vol. 31, 1979. *Topics in Applied Physics.* Springer-Verlag, Berlin, Heidelberg, New York.

40. Starr, Michael R. and Palz, W.: Photovoltaic Power in Europe. 1983. Solar Energy R and D in the European Community. D. Reidel Pub. Co., Dordrecht, Holland.

41. IEEE Photovoltaic Specialists Conference, vol. 1- , 1972 - . Institute of Electrical and Electronics Engineers, New York.

42. Neville, Richard C.: *Solar Energy Conversion — The Solar Cell.* Elsevier, Amsterdam, 1995.

43. Schneider, Thomas R.: Energy Applications of Superconductivity. Annual Review of Energy and Environment, vol. 16, 1991, pp. 533-555.

44. Narlikar, Anant. (Ed.): *Studies of High Temperature Superconductors.* Vols 1 - 28, 1984-1999. Nova Science Publishers, Commack, N.Y.

45. Robins, Dr. Don: Introduction to Superconductivity, IBC Technical Services Ltd., Bath House, 56 Holborn Viaduct, London ECIA 2EX, 1989.

46. IBC Technical Services Ltd., London: Superconductivity: The Opportunities, Implications and Applications, 1988.

47. Mayo, Jonathan L.: Superconductivity — The Threshold of a New Technology. TAB Books Inc., Blue Ridge Summit, PA, 1988.

48. Wolf, Stuart A. and Kresin, Vladimir Z.: *Novel Superconductivity.* Plenum Press, New York and London, 1987.

49. Maple, M.B. and Fischer, Ø.: *Superconductivity and Magnetism* in book Superconductivity in Ternary Compounds, vol. II. Springer-Verlag, Berlin Heidelberg New York. 1982.

50. *Superconducting Science and Technology*: Special Issue — Invited Papers by Leading Japanese Researchers in Superconductivity, vol. 13, no.1, January 2000. Institute of Physics, Dirac House, Temple Back, Bristol, BS1 6BE, UK.

**Chapter 4: Plasma Physics, Nuclear Fusion Power and Magnetohydrodynamics**

1. F.F. Chen: *Plasma Physics and Controlled Fusion* (Plenum Press), 1984.

2. T.J.M. Boyd and J.J. Sanderson: *Plasma Dynamics* (Thomas Nelson), 1969.

3. A.B. Cambel: *Plasma Physics and MFD* (McGraw-Hill), 1963.

4. M.O. Hegler and M. Kristiansen: *An Introduction to Controlled Thermonuclear Fusion* (Lexington Books), 1977.

5. H. Motz: *The Physics of Laser Fusion* (Academic Press), 1979.

6. *Annual Review of Energy*: Progress and Directions in Magnetic Fusion Energy, vol. 9, 1984, pp. 281-319.

7. T.A. Heppenheimer: *The Man-Made Sun: The Quest for Fusion Power* (Omni Reo), 1984.

8. R.A. Gross: *Fusion Energy* (John Wiley), 1984.

9. W.M. Stacey and M. Roberts: International Cooperation in Magnetic Fusion. *Annual Review of Energy*, 1985, vol. 10, pp. 79-107.

10. R.J. Rosa: *M.H.D. Energy Conversion* (McGraw-Hill), 1968.

11. R.F. Grundy (Ed.): *M.H.D. Energy for Electric Power Generation* (Noyes Data Corp.), 1978.

**Chapter 5: Wind Energy Conversion**

1. V. Daniel Hunt: *Windpower - A Handbook on Wind Energy Conversion Systems (WECS)* (Van Nostrand Reinhold), 1981.

2. G.L. Johnson: *Wind Energy Systems* (Prentice-Hall), 1985.

3. D.M. Simmons: *Wind Power* (Noyes Data Corp.), 1975.

4. British Wind Energy Assn.: *Wind Energy for the Eighties* (Peter Peregrinus), 1982.

5. D. Le Gourieres: *Wind Power Plants - Theory and Design* (Pergamon Press), 1982.

6. D.J. De Renzo (Ed.): *Wind Power - Recent Developments* (Noyes Data Corp.), 1979.

7. J. Park: *The Wind Power Book* (Cheshire Books), 1981.

8. A.D. Garrad (Ed.): *Wind Energy Conversion* (Mech. Eng. Pub., London), 1985.

9. BHRA: *Wind Energy Systems*, 1980.

10. D. McGuigan: *Small Scale Wind Power* (Prism Press), 1978.

11. W. Palz (Ed.): *European Wind Energy Conference*, 1984. (H.S. Stephens Assoc., Bedford, UK).

12. A J. Wortman: *Wind Turbine Engineering* (Butterworth), 1983.

13. F.P. DeMello and L.N. Hannett: Large Scale Induction Generators for Power Systems. *IEEE Trans. on PA-S*, May 1981, pp. 2610-18.

14. H.J. Allison, R. Ramakumar and W.L. Hughes: A Field-Modulated Frequency Down Conversion Power System. *IEEE Trans. Industry and Applications*, vol. I-A 9, no. 2, 1973, pp. 220-226.

15. L.R. Herman: *The Roesel Generator - Constant Frequency with Variable Speed.* Paper A 76-035-6, IEEE Winter P.E.S. Meeting, New York, Jan. 25-30, 1976.

16. E.L. Houghton and N.R. Carruthers: *Aerodynamics for Engineering Students* (Edward Arnold), 1982.

17. D.R. Smith: The Wind Farms of Almont Pass Area. *Annual Review of Energy*, 1987, vol. 12, pp. 145-184.

**Chapter 6: Ocean Energy Conversion**

1. T.J. Gray and O.K. Gashus: *Tidal Power* (Plenum Press), 1972.

2. *Severn Barrage: Proceedings of Symposium*. Inst. of Civil Engrs, London, October 1981.

3. New Brunswick Electric Power Corporation: *Feasibility of Tidal Power Development in the Bay of Fundy*. 1969.

4. A. Merlin: La Rance Tidal Power Plant in France. *IEEE Trans.* PA-S, Feb. 1982, pp. 290-294.

5. H. Andre: Bulb Units - Operating Experience. *IEEE Trans. PA-S*, 1976, pp. 1038-1044.

6. A.N. Karas: Bay of Fundy Project - Planning. *IEEE Trans. PA-S*, 1978, pp. 1600-1606.

7. S.T.Y. Lee: Bay of Fundy Project - Economic Evaluation. *IEEE Trans. PA-S*, 1978, pp. 1769-1778.

8. S.M. Seoni: Bay of Fundy Project - Generating Equipment, Electrical Transmission. *IEEE Trans. PA-S*, 1979, pp. 1750-1760.

9. G.B. Furst: Raw Tidal Energy Absorption Capability of Power Systems. *IEEE Trans. PA-S*, 1978, pp. 1910-1917.

10. R.L. Loftness: *Energy Handbook* (Van Nostrand), 1978. p. 109.

11. P.D. Dunn: *Renewable Energies* (Peter Peregrinus and IEE London), 1987.

12. D.M. Considine: *Energy Technology Handbook* (McGraw-Hill), 1977.

13. E.M. Wilson, *et al.*: *Tidal Energy Computation and Turbine Specifications* Severn Barrage Symposium, Inst. of Civil Eng., 1981.

14. G.E. Gardner and W.B. Jervis: Generator Design and Coupling to the Grid. *Severn Barrage Symposium*, Inst. of Civil Eng., London, 1981.

15. B. Count (Ed.): *Power from Sea Waves* (Academic Press), 1980.

16. R. Shaw: *Wave Energy - A Design Challenege* (Ellis Harwood, John Wiley), 1982.

17. D. Ross: *Energy from the Waves* (Pergamon Press), 1979.

18. *BHRA Fluid Engineering: Wave and Tidal Energy*, IInd Int'l Symposium, Cambridge, 1981.

19. L.C. Wilbur: *Handbook of Energy Systems Engineering* (John Wiley and Sons), 1985, p. 1300.

20. M. Kayton: Steady State and Dynamic Performance of OTEC Plant, *IEEE Trans. PA-S*, 1981, pp. 1148-1153.

21. T. Mitsui, et al.: Outline of the 100 kW OTEC Pilot Plant in the Republic of NAURU, *IEEE Trans. PA-S* 1983, pp. 3167-3171.

22. *Ocean Thermal Energy Conversion Workshops*. 1973-1975.

23. M.F. Merriam: Wind, Waves and Tides. *Annual Review of Energy*, 1978, vol. 3, pp. 29-56.

24. *OTEC*. Special Number of *Energy*, 1980, vol. 5, no. 6, 469-570.

**Chapter 7: Fossil Fuel Power Generation**

1. F.S. Aschner: *Planning Fundamentals of Thermal Power Plants* (John Wiley and Sons), 1978.

2. E.B. Woodruff, H.B. and T.F. Lammers: *Steam Plant Operation* (McGraw-Hill), 1984.

3. Inst. of Mech. Engrs., London: Modern Steam Plant Practice, 1971.

4. P. Basu (Ed.): *Fluidized Bed Boilers* (Pergamon Press), 1984.

5. R.C. Eliot (Ed.): *Boiler Fuel Additives for Pollution Reduction and Energy Saving* (Noyes Data Corp.), 1978.

6. J.W. Sawyer: *Gas Turbine Engineering Handbook* (Gas Turbine Pub. Inc., Stamford, CT), 1985.

7. A.H. Lefebvre: *Gas Turbine Combustion* (McGraw-Hill), 1983

8. R.T.C. Harman: *Gas Turbine Engineering* (John Wiley), 1981.

9. M.P. Boyce: *Gas Turbine Engineering Handbook* (Gulf Pub. Co.), 1982.

10. E. Logan, Jr.: *Turbomachinery* (Marcel Dekker), 1981.

11. J.S. Doolittle and F.J. Hale: *Thermodynamics for Engineers* (John Wiley), 1984.

12. T.D. Eastop and N.M. McConkey: *Applied Thermodynamics* (Longmans), 1982.

13. J.J. Jackson: *Steam Boiler Operation* (Prentice-Hall), 1987.

**Chapter 8: Hydro-Electric Power Generation**

1. C. Simeons: Hydro Power (including Wave, Tide, Hydrogen and Hydro-Electric), (Pergamon Press), 1980.
2. M. Le Nir, L. Monition and J. Roux: *Micro Hydro-Electric Power Stations* Translated by Joan McMullan (from the French). (John Wiley), 1984.
3. F. Schweiger and J. Gregori: Developments in the Design of Water Turbines. *International Water Power and Dam Construction*, May 1989, pp. 23-26.
4. F. Schweiger and J. Gregori: Developments in Pump Turbines. *Int'l. Water Power and Dam Construction*, October, 1982.
5. F. Schweiger and J. Gregori: Developments in Francis Turbines. *Int'l. Water Power and Dam Construction*, August 1985.
6. F. Schweiger and J. Gregori: Developments in Design of Kaplan Turbines *Int'l. Water Power and Dam Construction*, November 1987.
7. F. Schweiger and J. Gregori: Developments in Design of Bulb Turbines. *Int'l. Water Power and Dam Construction*, September 1988.

**Chapter 9: Electrical Equipment for Energy Conversion**

1. S. Linke and R.E. Schuler: Electrical Energy Transmission Technolgy. *Annual Review of Energy*, 1988, vol. 13, pp. 23-45.
2. *AC and DC Power Transmission*. Institution of Elec. Engrs. (London), Conf. Pub. No. 255, 1985.
3. R.D. Begamudre: *Electromechanical Energy Conversion with Dynamics of Machines* (Wiley Eastern, New Delhi), 1988 and (New Age Int'l), 1997.
4. K.R. Padiyar: *HVDC Power Transmission Systems- Technology and System Interactions* (Wiley Eastern and New Age Int'l.), 1992.

**Chapter 10: Miscellaneous Energy Conversion Systems**

1. D.D. Whitehurst, et al.: *Coal Liquifaction* (Academic Press), 1980.
2. S.B. Alpert and M.J. Glukman: Coal Gasification System for Power Generation. *Annual Rev. of Energy*, 1986, vol. 11, pp. 315-356.
3. M.E. Day and H.B. de W. Erasmus: Update of the Sasol Synfuel Process. *Annual Review of Energy*, 1987, vol. 12, pp 1-22.
4. G.C. Taylor, *et al.*: *Synthetic Liquid Fuel from Coal* (Univ. of Colorado, Mineral and Energy Resources), July 1985, pp. 4-10.
5. S. Shelton: Synfuels. What Kind and When? *Journal of Coal Quality*, May 1985, pp. 12-17.

6. D.K. Rider: *Energy - Hydrocarbon Fuels and Chemical Resources* (John Wiley), 1981.

7. L.C. Wilbur: *Handbook of Energy Systems Engineering*, (John Wiley), 1985.

8. J.A. Lacey: Gasification - A Key to Clean Use of Coal. *Energy World*, Feb/Mar, 1988.

9. I. Wender: Synthesis Gas as a Source of Fuels and Chemicals. *Annual Review of Energy*, 1986, vol. 11, pp. 295-314.

10. S.S. Marsden, Jr.: Methanol as a Viable Energy Source in Today's World. *Annual Review of Energy*, 1983, vol. 8, pp. 333-354.

11. H.R. Bungay: *Energy - The Biomass Option* (John Wiley), 1981.

12. L.J. Goodman and R.N. Love (Eds.): *Biomass Energy Projects* (Pergamon Press), 1981.

13. S.S. Sofer and O.R. Zaborsky: (Eds.): *Biomass Conversion Processes for Energy and Fuel* (Plenum Press), 1981.

14. H. Alter and J.J. Dunn: *Solid Waste Conversion to Energy* (Marcel Dekker), 1980.

15. F.A. Domino: *Energy from Solid Waste* (Noyes Data Corp.), 1979.

16. C. Parker and T. Roberts (Eds.): *Energy from Waste* (Elsevier), 1985.

17. W. Palz and G. Grassi (Eds.): *Energy from Biomass* (Reidel), 1982.

18. Inst. of Gas Technology: *Energy from Biomass and Waste*, 1984.

19. D.A. Tilman and E.C. Jahn (Eds.): *Progress in Biomass Conversion*, vols. 1-5, 1980-1984.

20. R.L. Loftness: *Energy Handbook* (Van Nostrand), 1978.

21. F.R. Manibog: Improved Cooking Stoves in Developing Countries. *Annual Review of Energy*, 1984, vol. 9, pp. 199 - 228.

22. H.S. Geller: Ethanol Fuel from Sugar Cane in Brazil. *Annual Review of Energy*, 1985, vol . 10, pp . 135-164.

23. E.P. Gyftapoulos and T.F. Widner: Cost-Effective Waste Energy Utilization. *Annual Review of Energy*, 1982, vol. 7, pp. 293-328.

24. P. Kruger and C. Otte (Eds.): *Geothermal Energy* (Stanford Univ. Press), 1973.

25. L.M. Edwards, *et al.* (Eds.): Handbook of Geothermal Energy (Gulf Pub. Co., Houston), 1982.

26. J. Kestin (Ed.): *Sourcebook on the Production of Electricity from Geothermal Energy* (US Dept. of Energy), 1980.

27. M. Collie (Ed.): *Geothermal Energy* (Noyes Data Corp.), 1978.

28. P. Kruger: Geothermal Energy. *Annual Review of Energy,* 1976, vol. 1, pp. 159-182.

29. Y. Osumi: Hydrogen Energy. *Chemical Economy and Engineering Review*, June 1985, vol. 17, no. 6, pp. 5-20.

30. Institute of Gas Tech.: *Hydrogen for Energy Distribution,* 1978.

31. P. Hoffman: *The Forever Fuel - The Story of Hydrogen* (Westview Press, Boulder), 1981.

32. L.O. Williams: *Hydrogen Power* (Pergamon Press), 1980.

33. D.P. Gregory and J.B. Pangborn: Hydrogen Energy. *Annual Review of Energy* , 1976, vol. 1, pp. 279-310.

34. J.B. Cadoff and E. Miller (Eds.): *Thermoelectric Materials and Devices* (Reinhold), 1960.

35. J. Kaye and J.A. Welsh: *Direct Conversion of Heat to Electricity*. (John Wiley and Sons), 1960.

36. W.J. Goldsmid: *Applications of Thermoelectricity* (Methuen), 1960.

37. J.S. Doolittle and F.J. Hale: *Thermodynamics for Engineers* (John Wiley and Sons), 1984.

38. S.W. Angrist: *Direct Energy Conversion* (Allyn and Bacon), 1971.

39. D. Linden: *Handbook of Batteries* 2nd Ed., (McGraw-Hill), 1995.

40. C.D.S. Tuck: *Modern Battery Technology* (Ellis Harwood), 1991.

41. C. Berger: *Handbook of Fuel Cell Technology* (Prentice-Hall), 1968.

42. R. Noyes: *Fuel Cells for Public Utility and Industrial Power* (Noyes Data Corp.), 1977.

43. *Energy* - An International Journal: Assessment of Research Needs for Advanced Fuel Cells. vol. 11, 1986, nos. 1/2, Jan/Feb.

44. A.J. Appleby: Advanced Fuel Cells and Their Future Market. *Annual Review of Energy* 1988, vol. 13, pp. 276-316.

**Chapter 11: Cogeneration and Energy Storage**

1. G. Polimeos: *Energy Cogeneration Handbook* (Industrial Press Inc., N.Y.), 1981.

2. L.O. Tomlinson, *et al.*: GE MS7001F Stag Combined-Cycle Power Plant. *American Power Conference Proc.*, 1987, p. 129.

3. G. Rodriguez, et al.: *10 MW 4-hr Lead Acid Battery Storage Plant. Amer. Power Conf. Proc.* 1987, p. 200.

4. Gas and Coal-Fired Combined Cycle Plant. *Amer. Power Conf. Proc.*, 1986.

5. C.A. Luongo: Superconducting Magnetic Energy for Load Levelling. *Amer. Power Conf. Proc.*, 1987, p. 207.

6. Compressed Air Energy Storage (CAES). *Amer. Power Conf. Proc.*, 1985, p. 281.

7. E.L. Clark: Cogeneration - Efficient Energy Source. *Annual Review of Energy*, 1986, vol. 11, pp. 275-294.

8. D. Lambrecht: Status of Development of Superconducting AC Generators. *IEEE Trans. on Magnetics*, September 1981, vol. Mag-17, No. 5, Special Issue. (VII-th Int'l. Conf. on Magnet Technology, pp. 1528-2365), pp. 1551-1559.

9. R.I. Schermer, H.J. Boenig and J. Dean: 30 MJ Superconducting Magnetic Energy Storage for BPA Transmission Line Stabilizer. *IEEE Trans. on Magnetics*, September 1981, pp. 1950-1953.

10. Y.M. Eyssa and M.A. Hilal: Force and Magnetic Field Calculations for Rippled Energy Storage Magnets. *IEEE Trans. on Magnetics*, Sept. 1981, pp. 1954-1957.

11. Design of Energy Storage Magnets. *J. of Physics, Part D: Applied Physics*, vol. 13, 1980, p. 719.

12. R.H. Williams: Industrial Cogeneration. *Annual Review of Energy*, 1978, vol. 3, pp. 313-356.

13. J.Jensen: *Energy Storage* (Newnes-Butterworths), 1980.

14. BHRA Int'l. Conference: *Energy Storage*, 1983.

15. INFORM Report: *Energy Storage*, 1983.

16. G. Beghi (Ed.): *Energy Storage and Transportation* (D. Reidel Pub. Co.), 1981.

17. K.V. Kordesch (Ed.): *Batteries* - Vol. 2: *Lead-Acid* (Marcel Dekker), 1977.

18. D.L. Douglas and J.R. Birk: Secondary Batteries for Energy Storage. *Annual Review of Energy*, 1980, vol. 5, pp. 61-88.

19. F.R. Kalhammer and T.R. Schneider: Energy Storage. *Annual Review of Energy*, 1976, vol. 1, pp. 311-343.

20. B. Sørensen: Energy Storage. *Annual Review of Energy*, 1984, vol. 9, pp. 1-29.

21. F.R. McLarnon and E.J. Cairns: Energy Storage. *Annual Review of Energy*, 1989, vol. 14, pp. 241-271.

**Chapter 12: Global Energy Position and Environmental Effects**


1. H. Brown: Energy in Our Future. *Annual Review of Energy*, 1976, vol. 1, pp. 1-36.
2. M. Grenon: Global Energy Resources. *Annual Rev. of Energy*, 1977, vol. 2, pp. 67-94.
3. M. Sathaye, et al.: Energy Demand in Developing Countries. *Annual Review of Energy*, 1987, vol. 12, pp. 253-282.
4. R. Schmidt and G.R. Hill: Coal - Energy Keystone. *Annual Rev. of Energy*, 1976, vol. 1, pp. 37-63.
5. D.P. Harris: World Uranium Resources. *Annual Rev. of Energy*, 1979, vol. 4, pp. 403-432.
6. T. Gold: The Origin of Natural Gas and Petroleum. *Annual Rev. of Energy* 1985, vol. 10, pp. 53-78.
7. H.H. Rogner: Natural Gas as the Fuel for the Future. *Annual Rev. of Energy*, 1989, vol. 14, pp. 47-73.
8. *World Energy Resources 1985-2020*. Wcrld energy Conference. (IPC Science and Technology Press), 1978.
9. *Yearbook of World Energy Statistics*. United Nations Publications.
10. WAES: *Workshop on Alternative Energy Strategies* (MIT Press), 1977.
11. "OTEC": Special Number. *Energy*, 1980, pp. 469-570.
12. A.M. Perry, et al.: Energy Supply and Demand - Implications of $CO_2$. *Energy*, 1982, vol. 7, no. 12, pp. 991-1004.
13. C.C. Ingram, et al.: Coal Gasification and the Natural and Economic Environment. *Energy for our World*, 11th World Energy Conference, 1980, p. 184.
14. World Meteorological Organization (WMO): Influence of Potential Climatic Change on Energy Strategy. *Energy for our World*, 11th World Energy Conference, 1980, p.213.
15. P.F. Chester, et al.: The Effect on the Environment of Producing Electricity from Coal. *Energy for our World*, 11th World Energy Conf., 1980, p. 347.
16. L.N. Overrein: Acid Precipitation - Impact on Natural Environment. *Energy for our World*, 11th World Energy Conf., p. 570.
17. J.P. Holdren, et al.: Environment Aspect of Renewable Energy Sources. *Annual Review of Energy*, 1980, vol. 5, pp. 241-291.

18. C.G. Golneke and P.H. McGauhey: Waste Materials. *Annual Rev. of Energy*, 1976, vol. 1, pp. 257-277.

19. K.E. Yeager: Coal Clean-Up Technology. *Annual Review of Energy*, 1980, vol. 5, pp. 357-387.

20. K.E. Yeager and S.B. Baruch: Environmental Issues Affecting Coal Technology. *Annual Rev. of Energy*, 1987, vol. 12, pp. 471-502.

21. C.L. Comar and L.A. Sagan: Health Effects of Energy Production and Conversion. *Annual Rev. of Energy*, 1976, vol. 1, pp. 581-600.

22. D.R. Smith: The Wind Farms of Almont Park area. *Annual Review of Energy*, 1987, vol 12, pp. 145-184.

23. I. Spiewak and A.M Weinberg: Inherently Safe Reactors. *Annual Rev. of Energy*, 1985, vol. 10, pp. 431-462.

24. R.S. Denning: The Three-Mile Island (TMI) Unit 2 Core: Post-Mortem Examination. *Annual Rev. of Energy*, 1985, vol. 10, pp. 35-52.

25. J.M. Hendrie: Safety of Nuclear Power. *Annual Rev. of Energy*, 1976, vol. 1, pp. 663-683.

26. D. Okrent and D.W. Moeller: Implications of Reactor Safety of the Accident at TMI. *Annual Rev. of Energy*, 1981, vol. 6, pp. 43-88.

27. J.T.A. Roberts, et al.: Decommissioning of Commercial Nuclear Power Plants. *Annual Rev. of Energy*, 1985, vol. 10, pp. 251-284.

28. B. Ramberg: Military Sabotage of Nuclear Facilities. *Annual Rev. of Energy*, 1985, vol. 10, pp. 495-514.

29. M. Albright and H.A. Feiveson: Plutonium Recycling. *Annual Rev. of Energy*, 1988, vol. 13, pp. 239-265.

30. C. Hohenemser: The Accident at Chernobyl. *Annual Rev. of Energy*, 1988, pp. 385-428.

31. E.W. Colglazier, Jr., and R.B. Langum: Process for Siting Nuclear Waste Repositories. *Annual Rev. of Energy*, 1988, vol. 13, pp. 315-357.

32. R.R. Gould: Energy and Acid Rain. *Annual Rev. of Energy*, 1984, vol. 9, pp. 529-559.

33. B. Keepin: Review of Global Energy and $CO_2$ Projections. *Annual Rev. of Energy*, 1986, vol. 11, pp. 357-392.

34. R.C. Kavanagh: Global Warming and Least Cost Energy Planning. *Annual Review of Energy*, 1989, vol. 14, pp. 353-373.

35. C.A.S. Hall, et al.: Impact of Production and Use of Energy on the Global Climate. *Annual Rev. of Energy*, 1978, vol. 3, pp. 395-475.

36. S. H. Schneider and B.S. Chen: $CO_2$ Warming and Coast Line Flooding, Climatic Impact. *Annual Rev. of Energy*, 1980, vol. 5, pp. 107-140.

37. S. F. Singer: The Price of World Oil. *Annual Rev. of Energy*, 1983, vol. 8, pp. 451-508.

38. D. Crabbe and R. McBride: *The World Energy Book* (Nichols Pub. Co., N.Y.), 1978.

39. Jonathan Weiner: *The Next One Hundred Years*. (Bantam Books), 1990.

40. Elizabeth Kay Berner and Robert A. Berner: *The Global Water Cycle*. (Prentice-Hall), 1987.

41. L.S. Tong: Principles of Design Improvement for Light Water Reactor. (Hemisphere Pub. Corp. and Springer-Verlag), 1988.

42. Grigori Medvedev: *The Truth About Chernobyl*. (Translated from the Russian by Evelyn Rossiter). (Basic Books), 1991.

43. Chris C. Park: *CHERNOBYL: The Long Shadow*. (Routledge), 1989.

44. Zhores A. Medvedev: *The Legacy of Chernobyl*. (Basil Blackwell), 1990.

45. Piers Paul Read: *ABLAZE: The Story of Chernobyl*. (Mandarin), 1994.

# Index

## A



## B



## C

## O



## P

## T

## X



## Z